Los Cabos

Prospective for a Natural and Tourism Paradise

Edited by

Paul Ganster
Oscar Arizpe C.
Antonina Ivanova

San Diego State University Press
Institute for Regional Studies of the Californias
2012

Support for this project was provided by the Universidad Autónoma de Baja California Sur, the Institute for Regional Studies of the Californias, and the Southwest Consortium for Environmental Research and Policy.

Cataloging-in-Publication Data
Los Cabos : prospective of a natural and tourism paradise / edited by Paul Ganster, Oscar Arizpe C., and Antonina Ivanova – San Diego, CA : San Diego State University Press: Institute for the Regional Studies of the Californias, 2012.

p. : ill., maps ; cm.

Includes bibliographic references and index.

ISBN 978-1-938537-00-4 (pbk. : English)
ISBN 978-1-938537-01-1 (pbk. : Spanish)

1. Los Cabos (Baja California Sur, Mexico) – History. 2. Los Cabos (Baja California Sur, Mexico) – Economic Conditions. 3. Los Cabos (Baja California Sur, Mexico) – Natural Resouces. 4. Los Cabos (Baja California Sur, Mexico) – Social Conditions. I. Ganster, Paul. II. Arizpe Covarrubias, Oscar. III. Ivanova, Antonina. IV. San Diego State University Press. V. San Diego State University. Institute for Regional Studies of the Californias. VI. Title: Los Cabos : Prospective of a Natural and Tourism Paradise.

© 2012
by
Institute for Regional Studies of the Californias

Published by
San Diego State University Press
and
Institute for Regional Studies of the Californias
San Diego, CA 92182

ALL RIGHTS RESERVED

Printed in the United States of America
ISBN 978-1-938537-00-4

from the local and rural perspectives that tourism development has brought to the municipality is analyzed.

Part V, first analyzes the challenges and opportunities of Los Cabos as an economic growth pole, especially from the perspective of more inclusive and sustainable development. Next, the impacts of the tourism-led development are reviewed in light of effects on income distribution, human development, and perceptions of well-being in Los Cabos. The last chapter of this section examines the principles of sustainable development and their application in the Los Cabos region.

Many individuals were responsible for the publication of *Los Cabos*. The authors from Baja California Sur and California were generous in sharing their knowledge and helpful in meeting deadlines and in responding to requests for revisions. The anonymous peer reviewers enhanced the quality of the essays. Harry Johnson, of SDSU's Geography Department, readied a number of the maps and graphics for publication. Bertha Hernández, administrator and associate editor for IRSC, carefully supervised the editing and production of this volume. She also translated the essays from Spanish to English and from English to Spanish as needed. Her attention to detail measurably improved the quality of the essays. Without her significant effort, it would not have been possible to have completed this work. Elizabeth Flesh, IRSC Graduate Assistant, assisted in the editorial tasks and completed the typesetting for the book. Elizabeth Eklund, IRSC Graduate Assistant, created the index and finalized the typesetting of the volume.

REFERENCES

Hall, C. Michael. 2007. "North-South Perspectives on Tourism, Regional Development and Peripheral Areas." Pp. 19–28 in T*ourism in Peripheries: Perspectives from the Far North and South*, Dieter K. Müller and Bruno Jansson, eds. Oxfordshire, UK: CABI.

World Commission on Environment and Development (WCED). 1987. *Our Common Future*. Oxford: Oxford University Press.

Contents

Foreword and Acknowledgements / iii

I. Natural Resources and Environment

Chapter 1. Geology and the Environment
Javier Gaitán and Oscar Arizpe C. 3

Chapter 2. Hydrogeological Conditions in the Municipality of Los Cabos
Jobst Wurl and Alva R. Valdez Aragón 23

Chapter 3. Terrestrial Flora and Fauna
Aurora Breceda, Patricia Galina, and Marco A. González 39

Chapter 4. Marine and Coastal Flora and Fauna
Oscar Arizpe C., Rafael Riosmena R., and Cynthia Valdez N. 61

Chapter 5. Living on the Edge: Sea Turtles in the Waters off Los Cabos, Baja California Sur
Melania C. López-Castro, Fabiola Villegas-Nava, María Elizabeth González Payán, Katherine Comer Santos, and Wallace J. Nichols 79

Chapter 6. Cetaceans of the Gulf of California's Southwest Coast
Jorge Urbán Ramírez, Gustavo Cárdenas Hinojosa, and Alejandro Gómez-Gallardo Unzueta 101

Chapter 7. Prospective of Natural Protected Areas in Los Cabos
Oscar Arizpe C. and Benito Bermúdez 125

Chapter 8. Los Cabos in the Face of Climate Change
G. Bazzino-Ferreri and S. Lluch-Cota 155

II. History, Society, and Culture

Chapter 9. Sea Turtles: Ancestral Heritage of the Los Cabos Region
Graciela Tiburcio Pintos and Raquel Briseño Dueñas 171

Chapter 10. Prehistory and Indigenous Cultures
Harumi Fujita 191

Chapter 11. Los Cabos: A Historical Account
Alba E. Gámez 203

Chapter 12. Education and Development of Human Resources
Bärbel Singer..221

Chapter 13. The Cultural Pavilion of the Republic: Cultural Diversity
and Biodiversity in Los Cabos
Alexandra Sauvage and Frederick Conway..235

III. The Tourism Dilemma

Chapter 14. Traditional Tourism in Los Cabos: Opportunities and
Limitations of Economic Growth
Alba E. Gámez and Paul Ganster..249

Chapter 15. Alternative Tourism and Touristic Suitability in the
Municipality of Los Cabos
Oscar Arizpe C., Alba E. Gámez, and Eduardo Juárez........................271

Chapter 16. The Paradise of Sportfishing in Los Cabos, Baja
California Sur
Ivonne Dalila Gómez Cabrera..287

Chapter 17. Tourism as a Sector of Opportunity for Agriculture and
Nearshore Fishing
Antonina Ivanova, Ivonne Dalila Gómez Cabrera,
and Alberto Torres 295

IV. Government and Quality of Life

Chapter 18. Public Administration and Government in the
Municipality of Los Cabos
J. Antonio Martínez de la Torre and Lizzeth Aguirre Osuna 315

Chapter 19. Energy Demand and Renewable Energy in Los Cabos
Heidi Romero-Schmidt, Elio Lagunes-Díaz, Alan Sweedler,
and Alfredo Ortega-Rubio..341

Chapter 20. Local Development and Design of Social Assistance
Strategies in the Municipality of Los Cabos
Angélica Montaño Armendáriz, Juan Carlos Pérez Concha,
and Carolina Castro Corazón..363

Chapter 21. The Ecological Land Use Plan of the Municipality of
Los Cabos
Oscar Arizpe C., J. L. Fermán, and Raúl Rodríguez 381

Chapter 22. Tourism, Rurality, and Urbanization in the Municipality of
Los Cabos: A Challenge for Local Development
Lorella Castorena Davis 401

V. Economy and Regional Development

Chapter 23. The Consolidation of Los Cabos as a Growth Pole:
Challenges and Opportunities
Antonina Ivanova, Reyna Ibáñez, and James Gerber 423

Chapter 24. Growth, Human Development, and Perception of Well-
Being in Los Cabos
Manuel Ángeles, Alba E. Gámez, and Paul Ganster 443

Chapter 25. The Prospect, Principles, and Practice of Sustainable
Development in Los Cabos
David Carruthers 469

VI. Conclusions

Chapter 26. Conclusions
Oscar Arizpe C. and Paul Ganster 487

Index / 493

Part I.
Natural Resources and Environment

1

Geology and Environment

Javier Gaitán and Oscar Arizpe C.

THE ORIGIN OF THE PENINSULA OF BAJA CALIFORNIA AND THE GULF OF CALIFORNIA

The geological history of the Los Cabos region is completely linked to the origins of the peninsula, dating back to the Mesozoic era, between 225 and 135 millions of years ago. After the ascent and cooling of magma during this era, different types of rocks were generated, such as intrusive igneous, granite (Gr), and metamorphic rocks, as well as other rocky material that would shape the foundation of the peninsula (Flores 1998; Flores Pérez 2005). The detachment of the peninsula led to the formation of faulted and sloped blocks that constitute the main ranges of the peninsula's southern portion. The southern end of the peninsula is formed by a granitic batholith in the shape of a mountainous complex, which is the Sierra La Laguna. This group of mountains, the southernmost in the state of Baja California Sur, is an intrusive block with a north-south direction. Its foundation is most likely a volcanic-plutonic strip (Flores 1998) with outcrops of pre-batholitic rocks composed of schist, slates, and gneisses of sedimentary origin (SARH 1991).

The most representative geological groups are:
- The intrusive igneous rocks of the Mesozoic, such as granites K (Gr) and tonalite granodiorite K (Gd tn), as well as T Cenozoic granites (Gr). The intrusive igneous rock is not very permeable and not very porous, so it does not provide many possibilities for water storage. Also, rain is more abundant here

than in the rest of the peninsula. Furthermore, the aquifers of the west coast are fed by volcanic mountains with extrusive igneous materials. Thus, in the lower parts of the mountains, there are plains formed by sedimentary soils that absorb water easily.

- Sedimentary rocks of the Cenozoic Quaternary (Q) that represent conglomerates form pluvial fans as deposits of little compaction. They have medium to high permeability. This conglomerated mantle is mainly located in part of the Santa Anita mesa and north of Cabo San Lucas.
- Geological soils, including alluvial deposits of gravel, pebbles, sand, and clay are found in waterways and river channels. In the shape of alluvial fans or terraces, they might be of igneous or metamorphic origin and they are highly permeable deposits. They are located in most of the Santa Anita mesa and all along the San José riverbed, to areas along the San José estuary.
- The coastal deposits of fine sand are mostly located on beaches. A wind mantle, which is of the smallest proportion, is located in the southwestern part of the study area.

Since 1970, following the acceptance of the theory of plate tectonics, studies intensified in the region of the peninsula of Baja California and Gulf of California. It was acknowledged globally that the origin of the Gulf of California, like the Red Sea, was associated with ongoing processes of fracturing and continental drift.

First Ideas and Observations on the Separation of the Baja California Peninsula from the Mexican Continental Massif

The chronicles of early California written by the missionaries of the Society of Jesus—who were in the peninsula of Baja California between 1697 and 1767—contain valuable information about the natural history of the region. In particular, the observations regarding the configuration of the Gulf of California made by Father Johann Jakob Baegert, who lived at the Mission San Luis Gonzaga from 1751 to 1768, constitute some of the first scientific descriptions of this Mediterranean sea. Baegert's observations were published in 1771. These refer to the gulf's numerous islands of various sizes. Due to such traits, he assumed that the peninsula had been wider than it is now known or that it had very possibly been attached to the continental massif, forming a single land mass. He also compared the Gulf of California to the Red Sea from the Old World and reflected on the idea that the Californian peninsula must have once been attached to the state of Sonora.

In 1915, Alfred Wegener, German meteorologist and author of the now classic hypothesis of continental drift (precursor idea of the theory of plate tectonics), presented several examples to show that the continents moved. These were part of his scientific argument to support his hypothesis. Examples included the Gulf of California and the peninsula of Baja California, places where he observed in detail the configuration of the coastline. As a result, he proposed that the Baja California peninsula had slid northwest in relation to the mainland, which moved to the southeast. He further stressed, based on bathymetric information between the southern tip of the peninsula and the coastal region belonging to the continental massif, that the southern peninsular part was once attached to the continental massif, precisely where the state of Jalisco is located today.

The Origin and Development of the Process of Separation of the Peninsula and the Consequent Formation of the Marine Basin Occupied by the Gulf of California

Several researchers agree that the geological history of the separation of the peninsula and the opening of the marine basin that the gulf now occupies began approximately 12 million years ago. Before this time, both physiographic features did not exist, and the land that the peninsula now occupies was attached to the continental massif. However, in some peninsular regions, rocks whose ages are older than 12 million years can be found. This indicates that the land now occupied by the Baja California peninsula shares the broad geological history of northwest Mexico, history that goes beyond the time previously indicated.

More than 12 million years ago the boundary between the Pacific and North American plates was a convergent type and subduction also developed along the western margin of Mexico's northwest. As an event associated with subduction, during this time there was intense volcanic activity on the site where the western margin of the Gulf of California is now located.

Tectonic grabens (depressed blocks) began to form, caused by the fracturing and opening of the lithosphere, which were filled with continental sediments. At this stage, a proto-Gulf was developed toward the northern part and its seawater inlet was possibly oriented west-east and was probably located at the site of the present-day town of San Ignacio. This physiographic feature subsequently evolved to form the Gulf of California. Contemporarily, river, alluvial, and volcanic sediments associated with the tectonic regime related to normal faulting and fracturing of the continent were also deposited to the south. At the end of the Miocene, normal faulting and volcanism continued their intense activity on the continent, in the region now occupied by the gulf. Likewise, the continental separation began, which later caused the gradual detachment of the land that currently makes up the region of Los Cabos. Seawater flooded the lowlands and the Gulf had a shallow depth during this period.

Evidently, about 5 million years ago in the late Miocene period and early Pliocene, the area now occupied by the region of Los Cabos was still attached to the continental massif. This region gradually detached from the continent, causing the subsequent flooding in some areas. Finally, the mouth of the gulf opened 3 million years ago; the mainland began to separate; and the detached land drifted and became annexed to the rest of the peninsular strip. The peninsula of Baja California, already separated from the continental massif, adhered to the Pacific plate, while the mainland remained part of the North America plate. During this time, a new boundary was defined between both plates of diverging types, giving rise to the creation of a center for expansion in the seabed. At present, this feature is located along the axis of the gulf.

The Peninsula of Baja California and the Gulf of California: Recent Geological and Geomorphological Features in the Geologic Timescale

The current configuration of the region occupied by the Gulf of California and the peninsula of Baja California was developed at the end of the Pliocene, 1.8 million years ago, and during the Quaternary period. This configuration was progressively shaped in the wake of divergent movements and tangential displacements along submarine faults. These dynamic processes were associated with dispersal centers that are currently located at the bottom of the gulf and throughout its axis, from its mouth in the south, to the Colorado River delta in the north.

Today, the dispersal centers mentioned and the associated transform faults make up the divergent boundary between the Pacific and North American plates. The peninsula of Baja California is part of the Pacific plate, while the countercoast and the rest of the country belong to the North American plate. This divergent boundary is the cause of the currently active efforts that continue to widen the marine basin and, consequently, to separate the peninsula at an average rate of six centimeters per year.

THE GEOLOGICAL NATURE OF THE PENINSULA OF BAJA CALIFORNIA AND THE STATE OF BAJA CALIFORNIA SUR

The different types of rocks, structures, and physiographic features of the terrestrial relief in the peninsular region and adjacent islands are the reflection of a long and complex geological past intimately linked to the evolution of plate tectonics. Regionally, both the Baja California peninsula and the Gulf of California are considered relevant features for understanding the geological history of northwestern Mexico and part of North America.

The ages of the rocks that crop out across the length and width of the peninsula include the interval between the Paleozoic and Cenozoic. The outcrops of Paleozoic rocks are very isolated and only occur in the northeastern part of the peninsula. The rocks are represented by sedimentary units of marine and continental origin; subduction complexes; and intrusive igneous and metamorphic rocks. The Mesozoic record has a greater spatial distribution and, therefore, a wide distribution of outcroppings. The rocks are represented by intrusive and extrusive igneous units, marine and continental sedimentary, and volcanic-sedimentary complexes.

The Cenozoic rocks and deposits include large volumes made up of volcanic rocks; volcanic-sedimentary rocks; and marine and continental sedimentary rocks (mostly corresponding to the Tertiary period); as well as sedimentary deposits, consolidated and unconsolidated, of the Quaternary period. This period is of prime importance because it represents the interval in which extraordinary global climate changes occurred and much of the evolution and distribution of hominids took place. As to the geological nature of the state of Baja California Sur, its territory is divided into six main regions according to the relief forms and geological characteristics. These regions are the following:

Plains of Vizcaíno and Purísima-Iray-Magdalena Region. This region is formed by broad coastal and alluvial plains that stretch from the foothills of the Sierra La Giganta eastward to the Pacific Ocean in the west. Geologically, the plains are located on two large marine paleobasins where thick sediments have been drilled and measured, on average exceeding, 4,500 meters.

Isolated Coastal Mountains and Western Isles Region. This region includes the Vizcaíno peninsula and the islands of Santa Margarita, Santa Magdalena, and Cabo San Lázaro, located in the Pacific Ocean coast. These locations stand out topographically because of their elevations that contrast abruptly with the adjacent lowlands, such as the plains of Vizcaíno and Purísima-Iray-Magdalena.

Central Volcanic Mountain Region. This region covers a considerable area of the state's eastern territory and forms the most extensive mountain range known as Sierra La Giganta. It runs longitudinally across the entire state and is part of the peninsular range. Geologically, it consists of an imposing sequence of volcanic rocks that, together, reach a thickness of up to 1,200 meters. It is, therefore, the unavoidable testimony of the intense volcanic activity of the geological past, approximately between the last 24 million and 280,000 years ago before the present.

East Tectonic Blocks and Grabens Region. This region includes areas with topography that reflects the most recent geological and structural history related to the opening of the Gulf of California and the separation of the peninsula of Baja California. Geologically, it is characterized by a series of faults that have elevated and collapsed parts of the earth's crust, and formed grabens, or depressions, and mountain blocks. An example of this is seen south of the state where the Sierra La Victoria (which includes the La Laguna, San Lázaro, and San Lorenzo mountains) and the Sierra La Trinidad make up the flanks of the Santiago-San José del Cabo basin.

Main Gulf Escarpment Region. The region includes a major part of the gulf's coastal region from north of La Paz to the south of Santa Rosalía, although the main escarpment feature again continues north of the state line. The escarpment, characterized by an abrupt relief between the mountains and the coast is clearly seen in some sections of the transpeninsular highway at Ligüí, Tabor, Loreto, and San Juan Londó. In these places, the mountain rises abruptly from the plain or adjacent coastal area. Physiographically, it forms the boundary between the highlands made up of the Central Volcanic Mountain Region and the Gulf of California depression. Geologically, it is characterized by a series of grabens and elevations separated by faults; some examples include the valley of San Juan Londó and Bahía Concepción, which are located between Loreto and Mulegé.

GEOLOGY AND GEOMORPHOLOGY OF THE REGION, INCLUDING THE MUNICIPALITY OF LOS CABOS

The geological nature of the Los Cabos region is intimately linked to the interaction of tectonic plates. Its foundation is made up of intrusive igneous rocks (like granite and granodiorites) and metamorphic rocks of Mesozoic age (98.4 to 54.1 million years). This foundation is the remnant of the tectonic activity that occurred when the peninsula and the gulf had not yet initiated their respective processes of separation and opening.

Different types of younger sedimentary rocks of Cenozoic age rest on this foundation, deposited in continental and marine environments. These deposits document the previous and contemporary geological history of the continental fracturing and movement of plates that caused the separation of the Los Cabos region from the continent. The deposits reflect a variety of environments and different tectonic conditions associated with them.

Geomorphology, Physiography, and Geology of the Municipality

The municipality of Los Cabos is geographically located between 23°40' and 22°52' north latitude, and 109°24' and 110°07' west longitude (Fig. 1) and covers an area of 3,754 km^2. It borders on the north with the municipality of La Paz and the Gulf of California, south with the Pacific Ocean, west with the municipality of La Paz and the Pacific Ocean, and east with the Gulf of California and the Pacific Ocean (INEGI 2001). It represents 5% of the area of the state of Baja California Sur (INEGI 2000). Geomorphologically and physiographically, the region, which includes the municipality of Los Cabos, is characterized by a range of mountains and a broad intermontane basin. In general, its physical landscape is characterized by mountainous areas with deep canyons with steep walls, erosive remnants that form steep peaks, large spherical blocks, and deep pools in the canyons. Wide alluvial fans that fill the basin stretch out at the foot of the mountains.

In this southern region of the state, the mountain system known as La Victoria, which occupies the central part, stands out. The La Laguna, San Lázaro, and San Lorenzo sierras make up this system. To the east of the mountain range lies the Sierra La Trinidad. Flanked by these mountains is the Santiago-San José del Cabo basin. Geologically, the mountain elevations border the basin with geological faults whose surface traces are reflected as borders of rectilinear contact. It is possible to observe this trait along the mountain range of La Victoria, looking west from the La Paz-San José del Cabo highway near the towns of Santiago, Miraflores, and Caduaño or the detour to Los Naranjos. This rectilinear boundary also stands out remarkably in aerial photographs or satellite imagery of the Los Cabos region.

Structurally, these main physiographic features pertain to two blocks and one tectonic graben. The first corresponds to the elevations of La Victoria and La Trinidad and the second to the Santiago-San José del Cabo basin. The latter elevation is considered a geological structure called half graben whose development is associated with the opening of the Gulf of California. The basin is filled with sediments that correspond to the Tertiary and Quaternary periods. The ages of the rocks vary within the interval of the middle Miocene to Pleistocene periods and record different depositional environments that range from continental to marine.

Several researchers have mapped the different geological units and have described them in reports and graphically represented them in maps. These units document various stages of faulting, deposition, subsidence, and uplifting of the crust that modified, intermittently, the conditions of the physical and biological environment within the reservoir basin.

Geology and Environment

Figure 1. Geographic Location and Adjacent Areas of the Municipality of Los Cabos

Source: INEGI 2000. 1:50,000 and POEL, Los Cabos.

Table 1. Types of Rocks Representative of the Los Cabos Region

Location	Geological Unit and Age	Main Rock Type
Sierra La Victoria	Basal crystalline complex Late Cretaceous (99.6 million years [m.y.])	Granite, granodiorite, tonalite, gneiss, schist, and mafic dikes
Sierra La Trinidad	Basal crystalline complex Late Cretaceous-early Tertiary (99.6 to 33.9 m.y.)	Granite, granodiorite, and rhyolite
Arroyo La Calera	La Calera formation Middle-late Miocene (13.6 to 11.6 m.y.)	Continental conglomerate and sandstone of reddish color
Rancho La Trinidad	Trinidad formation Late Miocene thru early Pliocene (11.6 to 3.6 m.y.)	Marine sandstone of fine to medium grain of gray-greenish color, shale, mudstone, and diatomite
Ranchos El Refugio and El Refugito	Refugio formation Early Pliocene (3.6 m.y.)	Sandstone of medium to coarse grain of gray-white color interspersed with limestone and shale
Los Barriles	Los Barriles formation Late Pliocene-early Pleistocene (3.6 to 0.78 m.y.)	Sandstone of medium to coarse grain and conglomerates with fragments ranging in size from pebbles to large blocks
Rancho El Chorro	El Chorro formation Late Pleistocene-early Holocene (0.126 to 0.0115 m.y.)	Sandstone of coarse grain and conglomerate

Source: Martínez-Gutiérrez and Sethi 1997.

Table 2. Rocks that Contain Fossils

Geological Unit	Type of Fossils
Trinidad formation	Of shallow marine and brackish environments: *Cerithea sp., Anadara, Strombus, Melongena, Murex, Conus, Oliva* Of shelf marine environments: microfossils (*Globorotalia lenguaensi* and *Globorotalia mayeri*) and diatoms and *Carcharodon megalodon* giant sharks Of shallow and high-energy marine environments: shell fragments Of terrestrial environment (horse jaw): *Merychippus-Pliohippus*
Refugio formation	Of marine and shallow environment (Gastropods, pelecypods, arthropods, and marine vertebrates): *Turritela abrupta fredea, Pecten aletes* and *Strombus obliteratus* *Carcharodon megalodon* giant sharks

Source: Martínez-Gutiérrez and Sethi 1997.

Main Geological Faults in the Region of Los Cabos

The main geological faults in the region of Los Cabos are those of San José del Cabo and La Trinidad. Both structures are of the normal type and exert a strong regional geomorphological control. The first constitutes the boundary of the Sierra La Victoria with the Santiago-San José del Cabo basin on the west side; the second separates the Sierra La Trinidad from the same basin on the east side. The La Trinidad fault was probably active during the middle-late Miocene (13.6-11.6 m.y.) and reactivated during the late Pliocene (3.6 m.y.). The San José del Cabo fault was probably active during the late Pliocene (3.6 m.y.) and is still active today.

The San José del Cabo fault is possibly the most obvious structure since it controls a prominent topographic escarpment that reaches nearly 1,000 meters of relief. Moreover, its surface trace can be followed along approximately 80 kilometers and clearly observed through aerial photographs, satellite imagery, and from some locations on land. It is considered one of the major faults known in the gulf's extensional province.

As a result of active tectonic periods and reactivation of both faults, La Victoria and La Trinidad mountains have gained height gradually and intermittently. In response to this uplifting of the land, there have been intermittent erosive pulses that have supplied significant volumes of sediments toward the basin. The geological units pertaining to the formation of Los Barriles and El Chorro are examples of these effects; for the first formation, the recorded measurement of accumulated sediment thickness reaches approximately 1,650 meters.

Further evidence of Quaternary activity of the San José del Cabo fault is clearly observed in several locations at the foot of the Sierra La Victoria. This evidence consists of the displacement of some alluvial deposits that have been raised or sunk several meters as a result of relative motion along the slip plane of the fault.

Climate in the Region

Due to its geographical location, the area of Los Cabos is under the climatic influence of various regimes, without any one predominating (Valdés 2006). However, the characteristic climates of the municipality of Los Cabos are hot-dry, north of San José del Cabo, and temperate-dry on the highest part of the La Laguna and San Lázaro mountains. In general, the climatic classification of Köppen, modified by García (1964) for Mexico, corresponds to a very dry, type BW (h') climate, warm with a regime of summer rainfall. The average annual temperature is 23.7°C. The minimum temperature recorded is 13°C, January being the coldest month of the year. Average annual rainfall is 262 mm, and the month of September is the rainiest. There are meteorological phenomena from August to November, such as hurricanes, that affect this area. During these events there are torrential rains (GEBCS 1992) (Table 3).

Tropical Cyclones

The hurricane season in the northeast Pacific usually starts in the second half of May and ends in the second half of October, except during periods of El Niño/Southern Oscillation (ENSO), which is an atmospheric oceanic phenomenon that originates in the southern hemisphere. It affects both the ocean's surface temperatures and the atmospheric pressure and, thus, climate conditions in the coastal areas of the eastern Pacific Ocean. The hurricane season starts early or ends late, and cyclones are observed in January, March, November, and December (Romero-Vadillo et al. 2007).

Table 3. Most Notable Characteristics of the Climate

Physical Parameters	Value
Average annual temperature	23.7°C
Extreme minimum temperature	8.0°C
Average minimum temperature	13.0°C
Extreme maximum temperature	38.0°C
Average maximum temperature	32.0°C
Average annual rainfall	262.7 mm
Dominant winds	NW (50%)
Average humidity	48-68%
Comfort	Adequate

Source: INEGI 1994.

Baja California Sur is the region of the northeast Pacific most vulnerable to tropical cyclones. It receives, on average, one tropical cyclone every two years. In the past 43 years (1966–2009), 35 tropical cyclones have made landfall in Baja California Sur; eight have reached the municipality of Los Cabos (Table 4). Nonetheless, many more hurricanes have made their effects felt in the municipality. Even when they have not touched Baja California Sur land, they have passed very close to its shores, generating abundant rainfall. September is the month with the highest incidence of cyclone activity in Baja California Sur.

The passage of a tropical cyclone has major effects on coastal areas. These effects may be reflected in the loss of human lives and economic losses. Similarly, some marine and coastal ecosystems suffer damages. Heavy rainfall, sea level variations, waves, and currents have great potential to cause flooding in coastal towns, which can be devastating for docks, boats, houses, and other structures along the coast. The impact of these phenomena in communities depends on many factors, ranging from the geographical conditions of the region—such as altitude, the presence of rivers or streams, soil type, and geomorphology of the area—to the type and location of housing, as well as the intensity of the cyclone (Romero-Vadillo 2003).

Table 4. Tropical Cyclones that have Made Landfall in the Municipality of Los Cabos, 1981–2009

Year	Name	Duration (days)	Maximum Category	Impact Category
1981	Irwin	5	TT	DT
1982	Paul	13	C2	C2
1989	Kiko	5	C3	C3
1990	Rachel	7	TT	TT
1995	Henriette	8	C2	C2
1998	Isis	3	C1	C1
1999	Greg	5	C1	TT
2000	Miriam	3	TT	TT
2003	Marty	9	C2	C2
2007	Henriette	5	H1	H1
2008	Julio	4	TT	TT
2008	Lowell	6	TT	DT
2008	Norbert	9	H4	H2
2009	Jimena	7	H5	H2

Source: CONAGUA 2006, 2009.

In the region of Los Cabos, the storm surge—which is an abnormal increase in sea level due to low pressure and winds from a cyclone—is usually not of great magnitude. It causes flooding only in low-lying coastal regions due to the morphological characteristics of the region. As the tip of a narrow peninsula, water that might be driven ashore by wind action can also circulate, entering the Gulf of California or moving toward the northwest in the Pacific Ocean. The areas affected by the storm surge in the municipality are east of Buenavista to Punta Arenas; south of Punta Colorada to Punta Palmilla; the mouth of the Tule Creek; Santa María Bay; Punta Los Anegados; Punta Cabeza de Ball; and the coast of Cabo San Lucas.

In the southwestern part of the municipality, the affected areas are the coastal dunes of the Pacific Ocean and specific areas such as Boca del Barranco, Migriño stream, and Punta Los Arcos. However, the magnitude and duration of the storm surge depend on the storm's trajectory and movement speed (Romero-Vadillo 2003). In addition, it is important to mention that tropical cyclones also have beneficial effects for Baja California Sur, as they bring abundant rainfall that allows for the recharge of aquifers.

Figure 2. Monthly Average Northeast Pacific Hurricanes and Monthly Average of Hurricanes that make Landfall in Baja California Sur

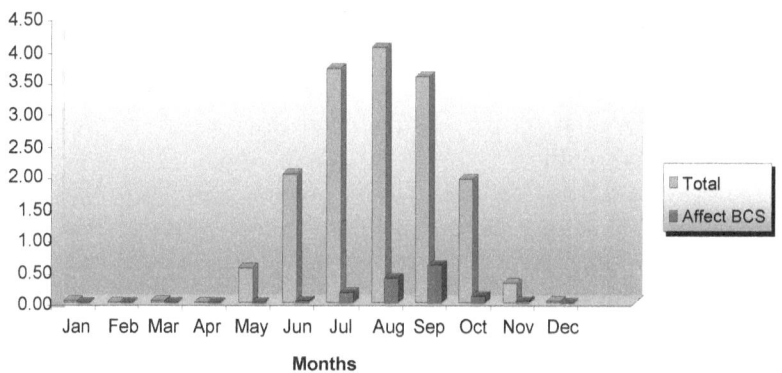

Source: CONAGUA 2009.

TOPOGRAPHY OF THE MUNICIPALITY

The orography, or the study of the physical geography of mountains and mountain ranges, of the municipality of Los Cabos has three characteristic forms of relief: hilly areas that are located in the La Laguna and San Lázaro mountains; the semiflat hilly areas located between the coast and the mountains; and the flat areas that are located on the coasts (GEBCS 1992; Flores 1998).

The La Laguna range joins two branches to the north, with the west side being more developed. In its northern portion, the range is formed by a north-south oriented mountainous region located north of La Paz and that extends toward the Bay of La Paz (GEBCS 1992, Flores 1998). It continues with the Sierra San Lorenzo, where it reaches an elevation of 1,830 meters and ends in an abrupt and steep manner in the peak of San Lázaro at more than 1,000 m (Martínez 1980).

The Sierra La Laguna shows fragmentation in various parts caused by long streams that run parallel to fractures in an approximate northeast-southwest direction. These streams produced a series of canyons that, in turn, resulted in huge blocks that define the valleys of Santiago and San José, between the La Laguna range and another mountainous region called Sierra La Trinidad. This mountain is characterized by its elongated shape with a maximum height of 890 meters, and by its streams that emanate from a point with a radial shape (Flores 1998).

In the municipality, the relief has different ranges of slopes:
- Slopes from 0 to 8% are located along most of the coastline, along the valley of the San José River and the Santa Anita mesa, as well as in the floodplains of the tourist corridor and the coastal plain
- Slopes from 9 to 15% characterize ravines, plains, and some hills
- Slopes from 16 to 32% correspond basically to hills and mountains

SOILS

The municipality of Los Cabos mainly has soils that are in the order of the *Azonal*, which are very recent soils (due to their geological origin) and typical of any climatic region. The *Regosol* are the major group of *Azonal* soils predominant in the municipality, which cover the eastern part of the region of Los Cabos. These are well-developed soils of drained deposits; they are dry sands that contain little clay, humus, and soluble salts; and they are found on abrupt or rocky slopes and in alluvial deposits. Associations of this type of soil that exist on site are the *eutric Regosol*, which predominates toward the southeast, and the *calcaric Regosol*, which predominates in the northeast. These types of soils also show secondary soils such as the associations *calcic Xerosol*, *haplic Xerosol*, and *haplic Yermosol*. Both *calcic Xerosol* and *haplic Yermosol* are soils from arid regions with highly variable amounts of organic matter (Ortiz-Villanueva 1977; INEGI 1985, 1998a; FAO 2006).

Another major group of *Azonal* in the municipality is the *Lithosol*. This type of soil is widely distributed in all climates. They constitute a mass that is perfectly weathered or rock fragments that are found mainly in the mountains (INEGI 1998a). In the region of Los Cabos, the *Lithosol* associated with the *Regosol* predominate in the west, from north to south from Sierra La Laguna and Sierra San Lorenzo, to the hills further south of Picacho San Lázaro. They are also present in the area of Cabo Pulmo, Los Frailes, Cerro Los Tesos, Cerritos Domingo, Cerro Garambillo, and in the area of Agua Escondida (INEGI 1985).

The *Fluvisol* represent recent deposits of rivers little changed, with coarse texture and are confined to river deltas or floodplains (Ortiz-Villanueva 1977; FAO 2006). In the municipality, the association of *eutric Fluvisol* soil is present in streams in the region of Los Cabos, San Dionisio, La Trinidad, San José, El Tule, Salto Seco, and Migriño (INEGI 1985).

Another order of secondary soils in the municipality of Los Cabos is the *Intrazonal*. These are halomorphic soils (saline and sodic) and hydromorphic (soils of swamps, marshes, drain areas, and plains) (INEGI 1998a). The *Solonchak* soil, representative of this order, is characterized by its high salt content. It is a soil of arid and semi-arid areas, as well as of coastal regions in all climates. The vegetation that grows in this soil type, such as mangroves and wetlands, supports a high level of salts (Ortiz-Villanueva 1977; INEGI 1998a; FAO 2006). This type of soil is found as *orthic Solonchak* association and is present in the Estero San José (INEGI 1985).

Another group of soils, the *Phaeozem*, is found in any type of slopes. These are soils rich in organic matter and can sustain any type of vegetation. Associations of this type of soil are *calcaric Phaeozem* and *haplic Phaeozem* (Ortiz-Villanueva 1977), and are located in the ravines west of the Sierra La Trinidad (INEGI 1985).

REFERENCES

Comisión Nacional del Agua (CONAGUA). 2006. Estadísticas del Agua en México. Ciclones Tropicales que impactaron directamente a México durante el periodo de 1970 a 2006. Electronic document provided by CONAGUA. http://smn.cna.gob.mx/ciclones/historia/historia70-06.pdf.

Comisión Nacional del Agua (CONAGUA). 2009. Temporada de Ciclones Tropicales 2001. http://smn.cna.gob.mx/ciclones/tempo2001/ pacifico/henriette/henriette.html.

Flores, E. 1998. *Geosudcalifornia. Geografía, agua y ciclones*. La Paz, BCS: Universidad Autónoma de Baja California Sur.

Flores Pérez, S. 2005. "Análisis de los rasgos geomorfológicos del borde oriental del bloque de Los Cabos, en el sector San Jorge-El Portezuelo y su relación con el sistema de fallas de San José del Cabo." Bachelor's thesis, Universidad Autónoma de Baja California Sur, La Paz, Baja California Sur, México.

Food and Agriculture Organization of the United Nations (FAO). 2006. *World reference base for soil resources.* Rome: FAO.

García, E. 1964. *Modificaciones al Sistema de Clasificación Climática de Köeppen (para adaptarlo a las condiciones de la República Mexicana).* México, DF: Instituto de Geografía, UNAM.

Gobierno del Estado de Baja California Sur (GEBCS). 1992. *Municipio de Los Cabos: Situación económica y sus perspectivas.* La Paz, BCS: Gobierno del Estado de BCS, Secretaría General de Gobierno, Subsecretaría de Asuntos y Coordinación de Desarrollo Municipal.

Instituto Nacional de Estadística, Geografía e Informática (INEGI). 1985. Carta Edafológica. Municipio de Los Cabos, escala 1:250 000. México, DF: INEGI.

Instituto Nacional de Estadística, Geografía e Informática (INEGI). 1994. Anuario Estadístico. Baja California Sur. INEGI-Gobierno de Baja California Sur. México, DF: INEGI.

Instituto Nacional de Estadística, Geografía e Informática (INEGI). 1998. Base de datos geográficos. Diccionario de datos edafológicos, escala 1:1000 000 (vectorial). México, DF: INEGI.

Instituto Nacional de Estadística, Geografía e Informática (INEGI). 2000. Anuario Estadístico. Baja California Sur. INEGI-Gobierno de Baja California Sur. México, DF: INEGI.

Instituto Nacional de Estadística, Geografía e Informática (INEGI). 2001. Cuaderno Estadístico Municipal de Los Cabos, Baja California Sur 2000. México, DF: INEGI.

Martínez B., A. 1980. *La ganadería en Baja California Sur.* La Paz, BCS: Gobierno del Estado de Baja California Sur, a través del Patronato del Estudiante Sudcaliforniano.

Martínez-Gutiérrez, G. and P. S. Sethi. 1997. "Miocene-Pleistocene Sediments Within the San José del Cabo Basin, Baja California, Mexico," in Johnson, M. E. and J. Ledesma-Vázquez, eds., *Pliocene Carbonates and Related Facies Flanking the Gulf of California, Baja California, Mexico.* Boulder, Colorado: Geological Society of America Special Paper 318.

Ortíz Villanueva, B. 1977. Edafología. Patena. México, DF.
Romero-Vadillo, E. 2003. "Modelación Numérica de Ondas de Tormenta en la Bahía de La Paz y Cabo San Lucas, Baja California Sur." Doctoral thesis, Centro Interdisciplinario de Ciencias Marinas, Instituto Politécnico Nacional (CICIMAR-IPN), La Paz, Baja California Sur, México.
Romero-Vadillo, E., O. Zaytsev, and R. Morales-Pérez. 2007. "Tropical Cyclone Statistics in the Northeastern Pacific." *Atmosfera* 20 (2): 197–213.
Secretaría de Agricultura y Recursos Hidráulicos (SARH). 1991. *Sinopsis Geohidrológica del Estado de Baja California Sur*. México, DF: Sistemas Gráficos, S.A. de C.V.
Valdés, A. A. 2006. "Diagnóstico, Servicios Ambientales y Valoración Económica del Agua en el Corredor Turístico-Urbano de los Cabos, B.C.S." Master's thesis, Universidad Autónoma de Baja California Sur, La Paz, Baja California Sur, México.

2

Hydrogeological Conditions in the Municipality of Los Cabos

Jobst Wurl and Alva R. Valdez Aragón

INTRODUCTION

The municipality of Los Cabos is an area of great natural and economic importance. It has become the region of greatest national urban growth rate due to the development of tourism activities. The average annual growth rate in the 1990–2000 decade amounted to 9.2%, contrasting with the state's rate of 2.9% and the nation's rate of only 1.8%. Accompanying the population growth is an increase in the demand for water resources, which, because of desert conditions in the region, come mainly from aquifers. Strong demand for water and its minimal availability limit the growth and development in the municipality. For this reason, a desalination plant was built in Los Cabos in 2006, with an annual production of 5.7 million cubic meters (mm3), equivalent to 24.6% of total annual production of potable water for urban public use in Los Cabos (CONAGUA 2009b).

CLIMATE

Climates of the municipality of Los Cabos are warm-dry north of San José del Cabo, and mild-dry in the highest part of the La Laguna and San Lázaro mountains. January is the coldest month of the year and the average annual temperature is 24°C. Los Cabos has a summer pattern of rainfall, and September has the most rainfall.

Tropical Storms

The northeast Pacific hurricane season typically starts in the second half of May and ends in the second half of October. The season is longer only during periods of the "El Niño" phenomenon (Romero-Vadillo et al. 2007). Baja California Sur (BCS) is the Mexican state most affected by tropical cyclones; over the 1966–2006 period, 31 tropical cyclones made landfall in BCS, of which eight were recorded in the municipality of Los Cabos. The passage of a tropical cyclone has great effects on coastal areas that may be reflected in the loss of human lives and economic losses, as well as damages suffered by some marine and coastal ecosystems. Tropical cyclones can produce a great amount of rainfall and are, therefore, a very important factor for aquifer recharge. According to Wurl and Martínez (2006), nearly 50% of the total annual precipitation in the area comes directly from hurricanes, and significant recharge is produced by extreme rainfall. In the municipality of Los Cabos, most extreme rainfall is generated by tropical cyclones, although on rare occasions there are heavy monsoon rains (Wurl and Martínez 2006). The effect of extreme rainfall in the total recharge of the aquifer depends on the initial condition of the watershed with respect to air humidity, water level in the main stream, soil water saturation, and intensity and duration of extreme rainfall (Wurl 2006).

Figure 1 shows the maximum precipitation isohyets within 24 hours (mm) for a return period, or recurrence interval, of 10 years. During the 2005 and the 2006 hurricane seasons, a water table rise of 3.5 meters was observed in the main stream of the hydrological basin of Santiago (near the Las Cuevas bridge). It was a result of infiltration caused by tropical storm John, which produced precipitation of 200 mm on September 1, 2006, as observed at the Las Cuevas station (see Fig. 2).

HYDROGEOLOGICAL CONDITIONS

The eastern and western slopes of the southern part of the peninsula are defined by the Sierra La Laguna, which is the division of runoff to the Pacific Ocean and to the Gulf of California. The sierra consists of an elongated ridge in a north-south direction, with elevations from 800 to 2,080 meters above sea level (Padilla et al. 1988).

Figure 1. Isohyets of Maximum Height within 24 hours (mm) for Tropical Storm John, 2006

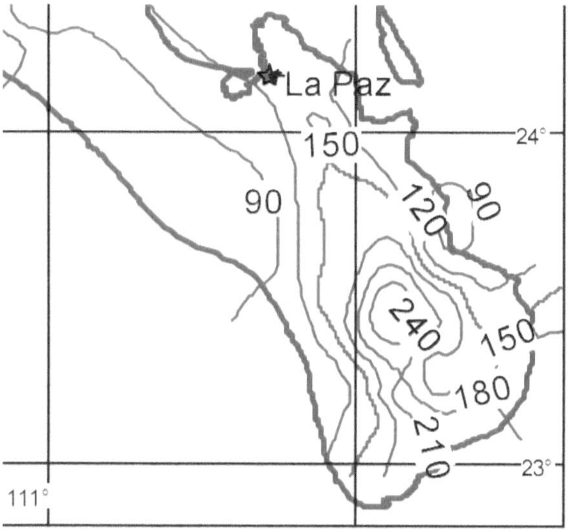

Source: Servicio Meteorológico Nacional (SMN) 2009.

Figure 2. Variation of the Water Table (meters below the rim) in the Las Cuevas Arroyo (photo of observation well) caused by High Intensity Rains during the 2006 Hurricane Season

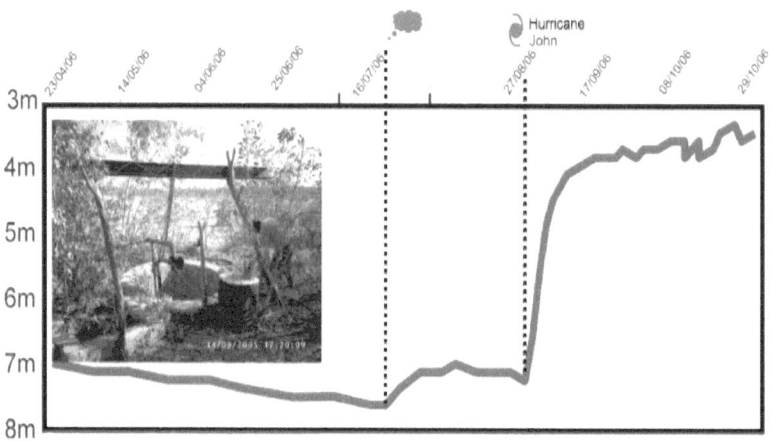

Two main hydrological basins are found on the slope of the Gulf of California, and they give origin to the arroyos of San José and Santiago. The hydrological basins of Santiago and San José del Cabo are located between two mountain ranges: Sierra La Laguna to the west and Sierra La Trinidad to the east. Between the two ridges, composed of crystalline rocks and metamorphic rocks, is a basin—a graben—that is limited by the San José del Cabo and La Trinidad faults. The contrast between the mountainous system of the Los Cabos block, segmented into smaller blocks and limited by regional fractures with an east-west general orientation and the sedimentary basin, is notable in the elevation model (Fig. 3).

Figure 3. Elevation Model of the Municipality of Los Cabos

Hydrological Aspects

In the municipality of Los Cabos there are no permanent surface water flows; the flows in the streams occur only after rain events. The main streams (Fig. 4) contribute significant volumes of water only in the rainy season. These volumes drain quickly and a great amount seeps from streams into the ground in areas where the material changes from rocky to sedimentary granular. The streams are the areas with the greatest recharge in the watershed. Colonel Aranzubia and others (1982) recorded in the San Lázaro stream, after Hurricane Paul, a runoff equivalent to 26% of total rainfall caused by this hurricane. After its infiltration, water flows underground. From the geohydrological perspective, the alluvion region of sediments is the most important area for the recharge of the Santiago and San José del Cabo aquifers. Conductivity is high, both on the surface and at greater depth in the sediments, which means a relatively high infiltration rate. Since the porosity is high (15% or more), these are unconstrained aquifers with great potential for water storage.

Figure 4. Main Drainage Networks in the Municipality's Five Aquifers: Migriño (1), Cabo San Lucas (2), San José del Cabo (3), Cabo Pulmo (4), Santiago (5). The La Pintada arroyo (6) that CONAGUA defines within the San Bartolo aquifer is part of the Santiago hydrological basin

Hydrogeological Units

In the municipality of Los Cabos, CONAGUA defines five hydrogeological units called aquifers: Cabo Pulmo, Cabo San Lucas, Migriño, Santiago, and San José del Cabo, of which only the last two show highly favorable conditions for the capture of water (Fig. 5). These two, located on the east side of Sierra La Laguna, flow into the Gulf of California. With a total area of 2,011 km² (as defined by CONAGUA), both represent around 54% of the municipality's total area (Fig. 6). Due to the favorable conditions for the capture and retention of water in these two watersheds, they recharge 93.1% of the total water supply of the municipality.

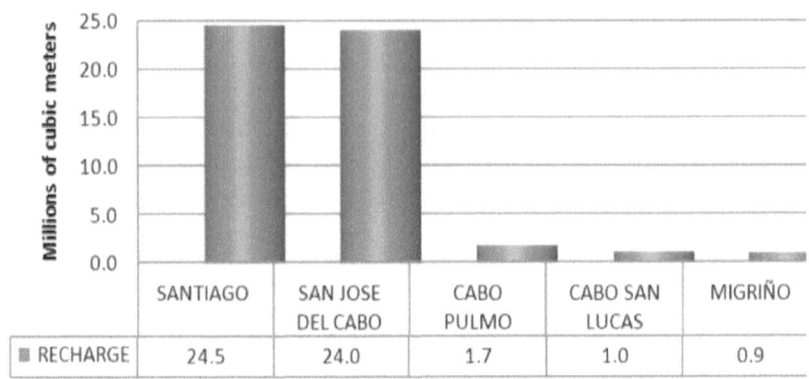

Figure 5. Annual Recharge (Mm³/Year) of the Aquifers in the Municipality of Los Cabos, 2008

Source: CONAGUA 2009a.

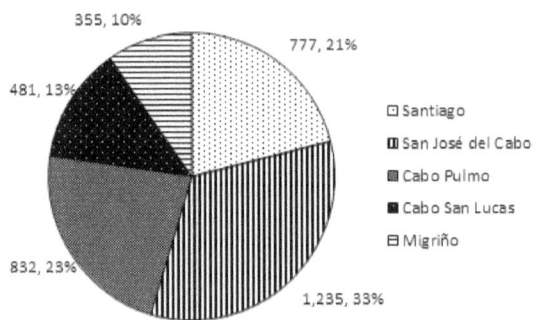

Figure 6. Area of the Aquifers in the Municipality of Los Cabos (km²)

The recharge areas of the aquifers in the municipality are determined by the presence of gravel, sand, and silts that all have high porosity and permeability. These materials represent geohydrological units of unconsolidated material with high (gravel and sand) and medium (fine sand and silt) potential for infiltration.

Availability and Demand

Water Availability

The municipality of Los Cabos is home to 32% of the state's population and only contributes 10% of the water that recharges its aquifers. Of the total volume that recharges the municipality's five aquifers (52.1 Mm^3), 8.47 Mm^3 are reserved for the conservation of the watershed ecosystems and 48.23 Mm^3 correspond to water that has been under concession for various uses. According to CONAGUA (2009a), the San José del Cabo, Cabo San Lucas, and Migriño aquifers have no additional availability of water and aquifers in Cabo Pulmo and Santiago have yearly availabilities of 4.153 and 0.888 Mm^3 (Table 1).

The concentration of the demand for water in the two main tourism locations (Cabo San Lucas and San José del Cabo, including the tourism corridor) poses serious problems of overconcession for the Cabo San Lucas and San José del Cabo watersheds.

Table 1. Contribution Volume, Concessions, and Availability (Mm^3/Year) of the Aquifers in the Municipality of Los Cabos, 2008

Aquifer	Recharge	Conservation*	Concessions	Availability	Deficit
Santiago	24.5	4.60	15.747	4.153	0.000
San José del Cabo	24.0	3.00	27.408	0.000	-6.408
Cabo Pulmo	1.7	0.17	0.642	0.888	0.000
Cabo San Lucas	1.0	0.10	4.101	0.000	-3.201
Migriño	0.9	0.60	0.333	0.000	-0.033
TOTAL	52.1	8.47	48.231	5.041	-9.642

Availability = Recharge - Conservation - Concessions
*Committed natural discharge (this volume is left for the conservation of ecosystems; it is not for concessions).
Source: CONAGUA 2009a.

However, the San José del Cabo aquifer has the greatest pressure on it, since it provides water to both tourism centers, showing an annual deficit of 6.408 Mm^3, which amounts to 26.7% of its recharge. Although at the municipal level there are 5.041 Mm^3 available, the total balance shows a 4.6 Mm^3 deficit. Since the Santiago aquifer is the only one in the region with significant additional availability, Wurl (2007) estimated the time until this aquifer reaches a balance between extraction and available recharge. Based on historical data of extractions for the Santiago aquifer, from 1968 through 2006 (Fig. 7), extraction increased considerably, and the latter years show the greatest increase in groundwater extraction. The median recharge of the Santiago aquifer, is 24.5 Mm^3, of which 4.6 Mm^3 are the committed natural discharge and 15.09 Mm^3 is the groundwater volume under concession (Diario Oficial de la Federación dated January 31, 2003). Thus, a median availability of 4.8 Mm^3 remains. Due to the constant increase of extraction in recent years (2001–2006), the extraction for the future was extrapolated until reaching an equal volume of extraction and available recharge (total annual median recharge less committed natural discharge). It is estimated that this balance was reached in 2010, according to a pessimistic scenario, or will be reached in 2015, according to an optimistic scenario.

Figure 7. Extraction Volume in m³ of Water in the Santiago Aquifer between 1968 and 2006 and Estimate of Its Increase according to Two Scenarios

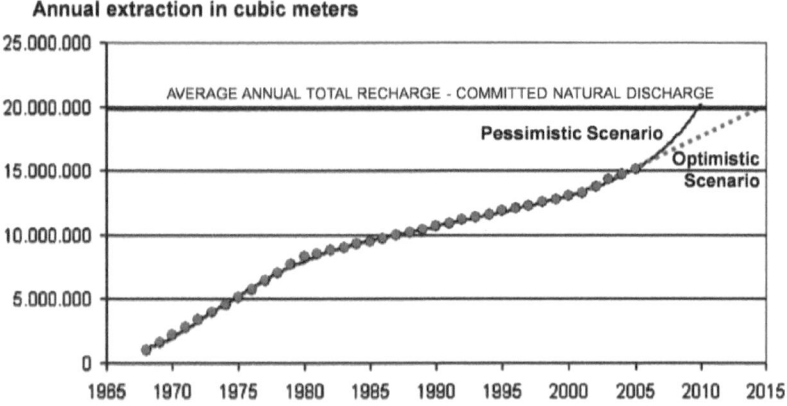

Hydrogeological Conditions in the Municipality of Los Cabos

Water Supply and Demand

Surface Water

The major source of surface water in the municipality is the San Lázaro dam, with a total capacity of 5,700,000 Mm^3; the production of surface water was 1.63 Mm^3 in 2008. There are also four additional small dams that have only limited capacity to store water.

Groundwater Concessions

Groundwater under concession in the municipality's five aquifers comprised an annual volume of 48.23 Mm^3 in 2008, and it was allocated for public-urban, agricultural, livestock-domestic, and services-industrial (including hotels) uses. Nationally in Mexico, 70% of water goes to agricultural use. However in Los Cabos, agricultural use is 35.8% of the total, the public-urban use is 40.4%, and the service-industrial sector is 21.4% (see Fig. 8).

Figure 8. Groundwater Concessions by Type of Use in Los Cabos, 2008

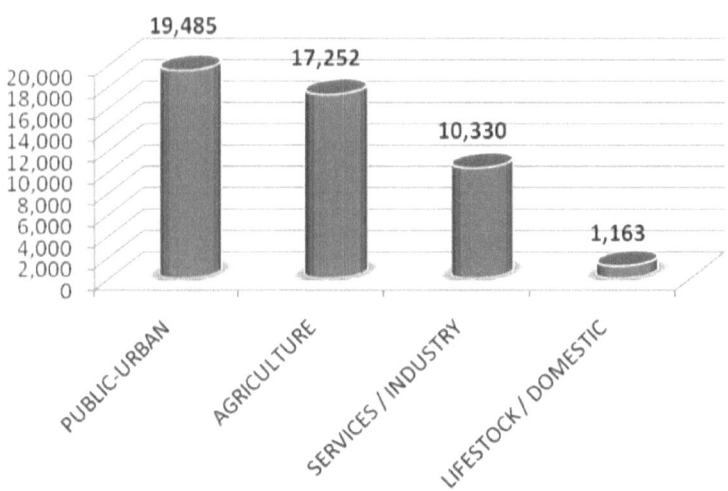

Source: CONAGUA 2009a

Public-Urban Use

The Municipal Operating Agency of the Potable Water, Sewerage, and Treatment System of Los Cabos (Organismo Operador Municipal del Sistema de Agua Potable, Alcantarillado y Saneamiento–OOMSAPAS Los Cabos) is responsible for the extraction, treatment, delivery, and distribution of potable water to urban, semiurban, and rural localities. It provides water to domestic, commercial, industrial (including hotels), and residential sectors. The volume of water used for public-urban use increased by 82.8% in the 2000–2008 period, going from 12.6 to 23.174 Mm^3. The domestic sector shows the strongest growth in demand for water, going from 7.6 to 13.4 Mm^3, which represents an increase of 76.9%, according to reports of billed water by OOMSAPAS Los Cabos (Fig. 9).

Figure 9. Growth in the Volume of Water Billed by Sector, 2000–2008 Period (Figures in Mm^3)

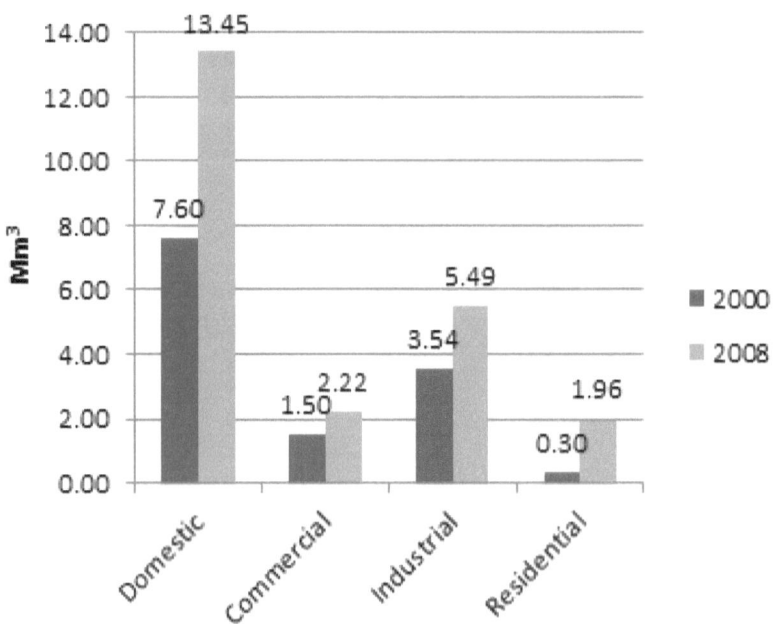

Source: Data for 2000 from Valdéz Aragón 2006 and data for 2008 from OOMSAPAS Los Cabos reports, provided by CONAGUA 2009a.

The industrial sector grew 54.9% and the commercial sector grew 47.8%, during the 2000–2008 period. The residential sector, which is included beginning in 2001, grew significantly since in 2008 it used 1.96 Mm^3, a figure very close to the commercial sector (2.2 Mm^3). It is expected that soon this sector will use more water than the commercial sector.

In 2008, according to OMSAPAS Los Cabos, the coverage of potable water for the domestic sector was 92.6%, when potable water service was provided to 49,803 households and 209,173 inhabitants. Slightly more than 4,000 homes were without service, which represent 7.4% of the municipality's total (CONAGUA 2009b).

As noted in Figure 9, the amount billed in 2008 was more than the volume under concession for public-urban use, as demand surpassed the availability of water from aquifers in the main tourism centers. As a result, alternative sources had to be used.

Diversification of Water Sources

Given that growth in water demand has accelerated in the municipality of Los Cabos due to population expansion and economic activities especially in the tourism sector, it has been necessary to reduce the supply for the two main tourist destinations of Cabo San Lucas and San José del Cabo, including the tourist corridor. Different sectors have taken steps to make better use of water, and alternative technologies have been adopted. In addition to the two natural sources made up of groundwater and surface water, three alternative sources are currently used: treated wastewater, brackish water desalinated by private plants, and seawater desalinated by the public plant established in Cabo San Lucas in 2006, with a capacity of 200 liters per second (lps) (Table 2).

Groundwater constitutes the most important source, which represents 51.4% of the total, followed by treated water with 27.15%. According to official reports of water produced by the public desalination plant for the year 2008, this source places third with a production of 5.8 Mm^3, equivalent to 12.4% of the total (Table 2).

Given the lack of availability of water from aquifers, some hotels have their own desalination plants (using brackish water wells as a supply source) and wastewater treatment plants. The desalination plants allow them to expand availability and ensure water supply in times of shortage or when there are contingencies.

Table 2. Water Sources Used to Supply the Public-Urban Sector, Mm^3, 2008

Source	Volume	%
Groundwater*	24.05	51.41
Surface water*	1.63	3.48
Public desalination plant	5.80	12.40
Private desalination plant**	2.60	5.56
Public treated water*	8.40	17.96
Private treated water***	4.30	9.19
TOTAL	46.80	100.00

*2008 data.
**2005 data from Pombo et al. 2008.
***2005 data from Valdéz Aragón 2006.
Source: Potable water production report, CONAGUA 2009c.

Also, treated water is increasingly used for irrigation of green areas and golf courses (Pombo et al. 2006). Furthermore, in the agricultural sector, in which the cultivation of organic vegetables and aromatic herbs currently dominates, the irrigation systems have been modernized in order to make efficient use of water.

Future Water Demand

Estimates of future water demand in the region of Los Cabos are based on population projections that Valdez Aragón (2006) presented in three scenarios projected through 2030, using per capita potable water allocation recommended for climates such as that of the region. The recommended amount is 250 liters/inhabitant/day (SAPALC 1996). In these projections, only the demand for the domestic sector was considered and the inefficiency of the potable water infrastructure—which amounts to an average loss of 30%—was not included (Fig. 10). Among the results that the estimates show, is that in the pessimistic and alternative scenarios by 2010, water requirements only for domestic use will exceed the current total volume of water allocated for public-urban use (19,485 Mm^3), since it is expected that the demand increases to 21,289 Mm^3. This scenario, according to CONAPO projections, is very conservative and estimates are lower than real growth. In an alternative scenario, a more moderate growth is expected in the second half of the period, estimating for 2030 a demand for 50,044 Mm^3. In the pessimistic scenario, which considers the development of the East Cape, the demand figure amounts to 124,317 Mm^3 by 2030.

Figure 10. Three Scenarios of Water Consumption for Domestic Use Projected to 2030

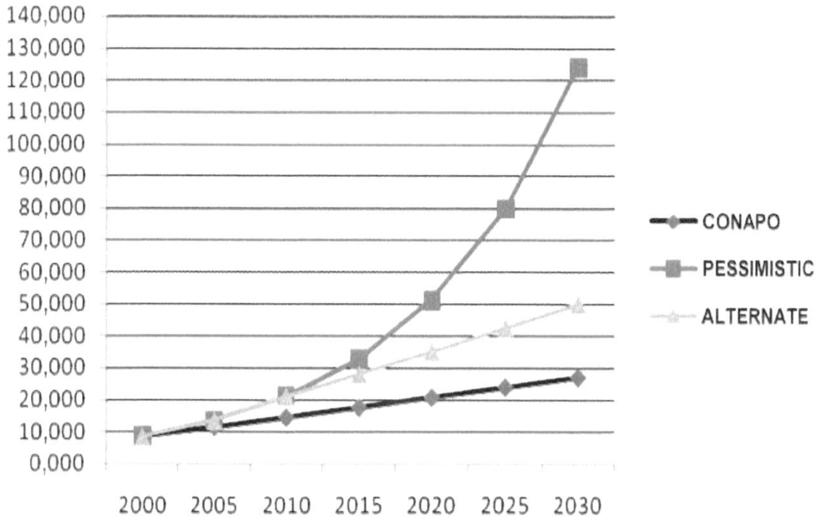

Source: Valdéz Aragón 2006.

Conclusions

The recharge from surface runoff in arid areas results from single events that are infrequent but can have an important role in the renewal of groundwater supply. Recharge in the Santiago and San José del Cabo watersheds depends to a great degree on extreme rainfall from tropical storms. In addition, the water balance indicates that the part of the runoff that reaches the sea and does not recharge the basins can be a source of induced recharge for the future.

The location of pumping wells of OOMSAPAS Los Cabos in the main stream is adequate, since filtration is increased after floods.

It is necessary to install a network of monitoring wells in strategic locations like the main stream in order to monitor the interaction between recharge and extraction.

Due to the lack of water availability in the main resorts of Los Cabos, and to the rapid growth in demand that is expected to continue in the coming years, decision makers have opted for the desalination of seawater. Desalination is seen as the alternative for all new tourism projects, and even for providing water to the community. However, although seawater can be considered an infinite resource, it is important to highlight that at present there is little information on the dispersion of hypersaline discharges from desalination plants and their effects on the marine ecosystem. Thus, it is recommended that the precautionary principle be used and desalination not be seen as a panacea. More research is needed on the capture of surface water and the reuse of treated wastewater as well as alternatives aimed at making more efficient use of resources that are now available.

REFERENCES

Comisión Nacional del Agua (CONAGUA). 2009a. Balance de los acuíferos del municipio de Los Cabos, 2008, Dirección Estatal, BCS. Unpublished data.

Comisión Nacional del Agua (CONAGUA). 2009b. Reporte Anual de Volumen Facturado en 2008, por OOMSAPAS Los Cabos; información proporcionada por CONAGUA, Dirección Estatal, BCS. Unpublished data.

Comisión Nacional del Agua (CONAGUA). 2009c. Reporte de producción de agua potable, OMSAPAS Los Cabos, 2008; información proporcionada por CONAGUA, Dirección Estatal, BCS. Unpublished data.

Coronel-Aranzubia, J. M., J. Beukena Pietersen, and R. D. Mendoza Calderón. 1982. *Análisis Hidrológico de la zona sur del estado de Baja California Sur*, 2nd research. La Paz, BCS: SARH.

Padilla, A. G., S. Pedrín Avilés, and E. Díaz Rivera. 1988. "Historia geológica y paleoecología." In *La Sierra La Laguna de Baja California Sur*, L. Arriaga and A. Ortega, comps. Centro de Investigaciones Biológicas de Baja California Sur.

Pombo, A., A. Breceda, and A. Valdez. 2008. "Desalinization and Wastewater Reuse as Technological Alternatives in an Arid Tourism Booming Region of Mexico." *Frontera Norte* 39 (20).

Romero-Vadillo, E., O. Zaytsev, and R. Morales-Pérez. 2007. "Tropical Cyclone Statistics in the Northeastern Pacific." *Atmosfera* 20 (2): 197–213.

Servicio Meteorológico Nacional (SMN). 2009. http://smn.cna.gob.mx.

Sistema del Agua Potable y Alcantarillado de Los Cabos (SAPALC). 1996. *Estudio integral de factibilidad técnica, económica y financiera para el mejoramiento de los servicios de agua potable y alcantarillado de Los Cabos*. San José del Cabo, BCS: SAPALC.

Valdéz Aragón, Alva. 2006. "Diagnóstico, Servicios Ambientales y Valoración Económica del Agua en el Corredor Turístico-Urbano de Los Cabos, BCS." Master's thesis, Autonomous University of Baja California Sur, La Paz BCS, Mexico.

Wurl, Jobst. 2006. "Investigación de los escurrimientos, provocados por lluvias extremas de ciclones tropicales en el sur de la península de Baja California Sur, México." Paper presented at "III Simposio Internacional en Ingeniería y Ciencias para la Sustentabilidad Ambiental y Semana del Ambiente 2006," 5–6 June, México, DF.

Wurl, Jobst, and Genaro Martínez Gutiérrez. 2006. "El efecto de ciclones tropicales sobre el clima en la cuenca de Santiago, BCS, México." Paper presented at "III Simposio Internacional en Ingeniería y Ciencias para la Sustentabilidad Ambiental y Semana del Ambiente 2006," 5–6 June, México, DF.

3

Terrestrial Flora and Fauna

Aurora Breceda, Patricia Galina, and Marco A. González

INTRODUCTION

The municipality of Los Cabos is located at the southern end of one of the longest peninsulas in the world. It is part of the biogeographic area known as the Los Cabos region, which stretches from south of La Paz to Los Cabos. The region's geological history is characterized by a marked geographical isolation since the mid-Miocene era (about 14 million years ago), when it became detached from the west coast of the continental massif (Durham and Allison 1960; Mina 1956; Padilla, Pedrín, and Díaz 1988; Flores 1998). Several authors have debated the accuracy of the time when the Los Cabos region was first attached to the peninsula; but most agree that there were temporary Cabo-peninsula connections, and that it was not until the Pleistocene (approximately 1.8 million years ago) that the Los Cabos region became attached to the rest of the peninsula (Durham and Allison 1960; Mina 1956). This long geological history of the Los Cabos region, marked by a profound geographical isolation, has influenced the evolution of species, which is reflected in the existence of numerous endemic species that are exclusive to this region. Thus, current flora and fauna in Los Cabos are the result of geological and evolutionary processes over time and, most recently, of the effects of human actions.

Climatic variations of the last geological period have also contributed to profound changes in the biota, punctuated by extinctions and migrations of species. The trend toward greater aridity has enabled many arid species to expand their range. Also, species of tropical and temperate affinities have found refuge in the less arid parts of the Los Cabos region, mainly in the highlands of the mountain massifs.

In addition to the geological and climatic aspects, there are processes of a shorter time scale where human action has been a determining factor in the transformation of the regional biota. From the first incursions of human groups in this territory, activities such as hunting and gathering of fruit and flowers slowly and extensively transformed nature. Later, with the arrival of the Spaniards to the peninsula, there was a profound transformation in the natural landscape with the introduction of agriculture, raising of livestock, mining, and, in general, human settlements. However, more drastic changes in the landscape and biota of this region have taken place in recent decades.

Los Cabos is undoubtedly Baja California Sur's most economically dynamic municipality of the last decades. As a result, a rapid population growth and an increase in real estate development have been generated. Similarly, there has been an increase in tourism activities that go beyond the beaches, as is the case of cross-country motor vehicle trips to arroyos and other locations.

The growth of tourism in Los Cabos has been accompanied by an increase in hotels and restaurants and, more recently, the growth in real estate sales of second homes. The latter are developments that occupy extensive areas for real estate development, mainly in the coastal zone. This phenomenon has caused the change in land use of vast areas, which was facilitated by the amendment of Article 27 of Mexico's Constitution in 1992, and the creation of the Program for the Certification of Ejido Rights and Titling of Urban Plots, whose aims are to certify and register property rights of *ejidatarios* (communal land holders). This has led to the conversion of *ejido* lands to private lands, which facilitates and promotes the sale of land for tourism purposes. This is the way that human activities as a whole have transformed and constantly transform the natural landscape and the biota of this municipality. Not only has the landscape been transformed, but the biodiversity has also been impacted.

This chapter provides a brief overview of the main characteristics of the flora and fauna of the municipality of Los Cabos, of their main uses, and the conservation issues most relevant to the local wildlife.

FLORA AND VEGETATION

Several botanists and naturalists have studied the flora of the Los Cabos region. Among the earliest records are those of Brandegee (1891, 1892nd, 1892b), who registered slightly more than 750 taxa, or groups of organisms. During the first half of the twentieth century, researchers from California universities undertook several botanical expeditions to the region. Among the most salient findings of these expeditions is the work of Shreve and Wiggins (1964) on the vegetation and flora of the Sonora Desert. Some years later, Ira Wiggins (1980) published a study of the flora of Baja California. In 1992, Lenz published a catalog of the Los Cabos region flora; a total of 1,053 taxa is reported. More recently, León de la Luz and collaborators (1999) presented their work on the flora of the Cape Region. In this effort, they registered 1,120 plant species and infraspecies, of which 153 are endemic to the region.

Of all plant species, 63% are herbs, 17% are shrubs, 6% are climbing plants, and just over 5% are trees. The rest of the species are epiphytes, parasitics, succulents, and saprophytics. All these forms of growth contribute few species to the floristic list of the Los Cabos region. The plant families with the greatest number of species are the grasses, composites, and legumes.

Gramineous plants or Poaceae are a family of plants that includes grasses. Most species are herbaceous and have pods in their leaves and cylindrical stems that are usually hollow. Their inflorescence is spike shaped and their fruits tend to be grains. Among the gramineous species in the municipality of Los Cabos are the sixweeks threeawn *(Aristida adsencionis)* and spidergrass *(Aristida ternipes)*, which are used as forage; saltgrasses and reeds also belong to this family.

Composites or Asteraceae are a very broad family of plants, both for the number of species it contains, as well as for its distribution in the world. Most species in this family are herbaceous and are distinguished by the type of star-shaped composite flowers, such as daisies or sunflowers. There have been 117 species and infraspecies of composites registered in the Los Cabos region. Among the most common are the ragweed *(Ambrosia ambrosioides)*, the seep willow *(Baccharis glutinosa)*, the singlewhorl burrobrush *(Hymenoclea monogyra)*, the goldeneye *(Viguiera deltoidea)*, and many more.

The leguminous plants are a family of trees, shrubs, and herbs that are characterized by their fruit in the shape of a legume or pods. This family's leaves are composed or formed by several leaflets, such as the mesquite or beans. Leguminous plants are abundant in the Los Cabos region. These include the peninsular acacia *(Acacia peninsularis)*, the albizzia palo escopeta *(Albizia occidentalis)*, and the palo verde *(Cercidium floridum)*.

Most plant species registered in the Los Cabos region are found in the municipality of Los Cabos. These are part of the floristic list of eight types of vegetation that are characterized by their physiognomy or appearance, and by the growth form of the most abundant species.

In a narrow strip along the coast of the municipality is the coastal vegetation, which consists of four subtypes: dunes, saltpeter deposits, rocky cliffs, and mangroves (Pérez-Navarro 1995). In the case of the municipality of Los Cabos, coastal vegetation is found mainly in the dunes and to a lesser extent in small rocky cliffs and saltpeter deposits, while mangroves are absent.

Dune vegetation has the greatest diversity within the different types of coastal vegetation of the Los Cabos region (Pérez-Navarro 1995). It is characterized by its high specialization when facing the restrictions of this coastal environment (e.g., substrate mobility, high radiation, and seawater influence). The vegetation that manages to establish itself under these conditions is very scarce. The most abundant species in the foredune—that is, the side facing the sea—are creeping or prostrate perennial herbs, and are subject to the strong action of winds and tides. The most frequent species in the vegetation of the foredunes in the municipality include the bayhops *(Ipomoea pes-caprae)*, spurges *(Euphorbia leucophylla)*, and grasses such as *Jouvea pilosa* and *Distichlis spicata* var. *stolonifera*. In the semistabilized dunes, regularly located on the crests of the dunes or at the beginning of their back side, the shrubs begin to appear along with the creeping species. Among the most common shrubs are the *guayparín (Maba intricata)*, bitter snakewood *(Condalia globosa)*, and Florida mayten *(Maytenus phyllanthoides)*. Finally, in the stabilized dunes, the dune species intermingle with those of the shrubs, such as elephant trees and ashy jatropha.

To a lesser extent, but significantly, there are rocky cliffs in the municipality that are poorly covered by vegetation that contains elements of sarcocaulescent scrub and coastal vegetation (Pérez-Navarro

1995). These plants are able to establish themselves in very restricted sites where soil accumulates, such as in crevices. Among the most prominent species are two varieties of *Hoffmeisteria fasciculata*, endemic and exclusive to this type of environment. Small saltpeter deposits and marshes that are formed by the occasional sea water or surface water floods and subsequent evaporation, are covered primarily by grasses and small shrubs—such as *Batis maritima, Salicornia subterminalis, Allenrolfea occidentalis*, among others—which are tolerant to high concentrations of salts.

In general, coastal vegetation is of great ecological importance since it provides protection and stabilization to the coastline. However, due to its proximity to the sea, it is one of the types of vegetation that has undergone the most important transformations in recent decades. This is because tourism and real estate developments are built on coastal plots at an increasingly rapid pace. In addition to the strong pressure for change in land use, coastal vegetation is extremely fragile, since it shows little resistance to the physical changes of its environment. As a result, this type of vegetation is severely threatened within the boundaries of the municipality.

Inland, behind the coastal strip, there is shrub-like vegetation. The most abundant shrubs have stems that are fleshy, thick, sometimes twisted, and some with papyraceous bark (texture similar to paper). Usually, the plant cover of tree and shrub species is relatively open. It forms a mosaic in which patches of vegetation and areas of bare soils are interspersed. Due to its physiognomy, this type of vegetation is called sarcocaulescent scrub, which refers to fleshy stem shrubs. Most of the scrub's shrubs and trees can reach 3 to 4 m in height; some cardon cacti and sweet pitahayas can reach heights of slightly more than 5 m, becoming perches for the birds.

The sarcocaulescent scrub forms one of the most widespread plant communities and occupies 38% of the municipality's area. It is located mainly in areas of low elevation—no more than 350 m in elevation—on alluvial plains and low hills. Its development occurs in very hot, warm, and semiwarm climates, with rainfall from 100 to 300 mm annually. They are generally found in shallow soils with little organic matter. Some shrub and tree species that characterize this community are also found in the lowland deciduous forest. Standing out among these are the ashy jatropha *(Jatropha cinerea)*, limberbush *(Jatropha cuneata)*, littleleaf elephant tree *(Bursera microphylla)*, and the organpipe cactus *(Stenocereus thurberi)*. Other species that are very abundant and characteristic of this type of scrub include the cardon *(Pachycereus pringlei)*, sour pitahaya *(Stenocereus gummosus)*, Brazil wood *(Haematoxylon brassiletto)*, wild plum *(Cyrtocarpa edulis)*, and Adam's tree *(Fouquieria diguetii)*. In some small areas, especially in the Pacific Ocean slope, this shrub vegetation is dominated by columnar cacti, such as the cardon and sweet pitahaya, which give the vegetation a particular look. This variation of the xerophilous scrub is called sarcocrassicaulescent scrub, whose name evokes precisely the greater abundance of columnar cacti.

The sarcocaulescent and sarcocrassicaulescent scrubs are of great importance in the municipality because, along with the coastal strip, they sustain the largest number of people. The main cities and 99% of the municipal population are located on this area. In addition to the pressures due to the growth of human settlements, the main agricultural activities are developed in the scrub. Irrigated agriculture currently takes up 4% of the scrub's range, particularly in the vicinity of San José del Cabo and the La Ribera-Santiago corridor. Extensive livestock raising, mostly cattle, is a traditional activity among the inhabitants of this area of the municipality. During almost 300 years of grazing, the livestock have caused important changes in the structure of vegetation and soil. Grazing has also favored the abundance of species that are not palatable to livestock, such as cholla and ashy jatropha. The constant trampling by livestock has caused, on the one hand, soil compaction and, on the other, the acceleration of erosion processes due to the constant consumption of herbs that protect the soil from wind and rain. Besides the livestock impact in this area, there are also forestry activities that include the collection of firewood and pruning of trees, especially the flor de San José *(Senna atomaria)* used in construction (Vázquez 2006).

Various human activities have caused a significant loss of primary vegetation in this area of the municipality. Consequently, 20% of the area occupied by the sarcocaulescent scrub is in processes of erosion or soil loss. Added to the impact generated by livestock and forestry activities is that of invasive exotic species that were introduced by human intervention in a geographical area different from their natural range. Many of these have adapted in such a way to new environments that they threaten the survival of native species. This is the case of the buffelgrass *(Pennisetum ciliare)*, a native of Africa. In recent decades, it was introduced into human-created grasslands; however, it has now escaped the grasslands, invading large areas of the municipality's sarcocaulescent scrub. Therefore, the physiognomy and structure of the vegetation have changed radically.

All these activities have significantly impacted the municipality's sarcocaulescent scrub. Most new tourism development projects in the zone are planned in the area that currently covers the coastal strip and the sarcocaulescent scrub. It should also be noted that this type of environment is not represented in any protection scheme within the municipality. Thus, it is important to consider areas that protect this type of vegetation, which is unique to the Sonoran Desert and the most diverse in the different types of xerophilous scrub.

Continuing in an ascending altitudinal gradient, a vegetation of tropical affinity is encountered, which is known as lowland deciduous forest. It develops mainly on the hillsides of the Sierra La Laguna and, to a lesser extent, in the Sierra La Trinidad, in an altitudinal gradient spanning from 400 to 1,000 m. This vegetation is the most widespread, since it covers just over 45% of the municipality's area. The lowland deciduous forest is characterized by the dominance of trees and shrubs with deciduous leaves, that is, they usually lose their leaves in the drought season. They recover their greenness with the first summer rains, when trees and shrubs develop leaves, flowers, and fruits. It is also when the climbers—such as the coral vine *(Antigonon leptopus)*, the coyote melon *(Ibervillea sonorae)*, or yellow morning glory *(Merremia aurea)*—are interwoven into the tree tops and show their bright colors. Thus, they print a stamp of exuberance and impenetrability to this forest. Most trees measure between 4 and 10 m in height and eventually may reach up to 15 m.

The lowland forest of the Sierra La Laguna represents the northwestern limit of the distribution of the lowland deciduous forest in America. It is the only vegetation of its kind in the entire peninsula and is characterized by its geographical and ecological isolation (Arriaga and León de la Luz 1989.) It also represents one of the driest communities of its type (Breceda 2005). Among the most abundant shrub species are the ashy jatropha *(Jatropha cinerea)*, jatropha *(J. vernicose)*, and yellow trumpetbush *(Tecoma stans)*. The most important tree species include the palo escopeta *(Albizia occidentalis)*, *quebracho (Lysiloma divaricatum)*, palo blanco *(L. candida)*, and *jacalosúchil (templetree) (Plumeria rubra* var. *acutifolia)*. The density of these species varies with the type of geological formation and the slope.

One of the most outstanding landscape elements of this ecosystem is the presence of ranches, located mostly in the margins of streams. There are 133 ranches and ranch settlements in this vegetation area that concentrate less than 1% of the municipality's population. The ranch settlements constitute a relevant cultural and historical element. They are the only regional ancestral nexus of the *sudcalifornianos*. The ranches represent a way of life that is isolated, dispersed, and scarce. Their origin dates back to migration flows of people who came to this territory during the colonial period; they are also representatives of a particular mode of socioterritorial appropriation (Castorena and Breceda 2009).

The main economic activity of ranchers is extensive livestock raising, particularly cattle. There are usually small fruit orchards around the ranches for consumption or making sweets. Most of the ranches are built with local materials such as posts made of flor de San José, palo de arco arbors, and palm thatch roofs.

The presence of ranch settlements and, above all, the long tradition of extensive livestock raising, have left their mark on the current nature of this forest. They have caused the *amatorramiento* of the forest; that is, the reduction of herbaceous species cover and greater abundance of shrubs that cattle do not consume. Livestock browsing also prevents many trees, such as the mauto, from fully developing, so they take on a bonsai character (Ortiz-Avila 1999). Despite the impact of livestock raising in this plant community, the lowland deciduous forest is the richest and most diverse vegetation in the south of the state. Species of tropical and arid affinity come together in this forest, which stamp a unique landscape in the peninsular territory.

The municipality's highest parts are located in the mountainous area of Sierra La Laguna, with a maximum height of 1,900 m. The oak forest develops in these areas above 1,000 m altitude and with an area equivalent to 6.5% of the municipal area. This forest is comprised of numerous individuals of *Quercus tuberculata*, locally known as oak. It is located in rugged slope sites with an annual total rainfall between 500 and 600 mm and an annual average temperature of about 20°C. The soil type is of medium depth, sandy texture, slightly acidic, with low organic matter content, and yellowish or reddish color (Morelos

1988). Structurally, this community has an arboreal stratum of 10 to 20 m tall dominated by *Q. tuberculata*. With less height, there are also dense masses of hopbush *(Dodonaea viscosa)* and *celosas (Mimosa xantii)*, accompanied by a few individuals of black oak *(Quercus devia)* and isolated individuals of *madroños (Arbutus peninsularis)*.

There are also some patches of pine-oak forest in the highest parts of the sierra with abundant black oak trees and pine trees *(Pinus lagunae)*. This pine is the only one of its kind in Baja California Sur. The pine-oak forest of the Sierra La Laguna is of great biological importance, since the nearest conifer forests are hundreds of kilometers away in the mountainous region in the north of the peninsula or in the forests of the continental massif. This geographical and ecological isolation has caused the development of multiple species unique to this region of the world. The pine-oak forest is the community with the greatest number of endemic species in the municipality of Los Cabos. Therefore, its protection and conservation is of utmost importance. Currently, all of this forest is protected within the core area of the Sierra La Laguna Biosphere Reserve.

Another type of vegetation in the municipality of Los Cabos is that formed in the streambeds. This vegetation is highly varied; it changes its composition and physiognomy depending on its location. Thus, in the bottom of the ravines of the Sierra La Laguna, there are strips of riparian vegetation that are formed mainly by palms *(palma de taco [Erythea Brandegee]* and Washington fan palm *[Washingtonia robusta])*, which may reach over 15 m in height, and by enormous cottonwood trees *(Populus brandegeei)*, which sometimes are up to 30 m in height. Occasionally, there are also willow trees *(Salix lasiolepis)*. In the plateaus and slopes, a vegetation that is almost always green is distinguishable, which in the dry season contrasts with the surrounding vegetation. It is comprised of dense patches of mesquite and palo verde that are established in the vicinity of streams. The vegetation of streams and the mesquite trees are very important for the functioning of the ecosystem. They tend to be havens for plants and animals in times of drought and food shortages. They are also corridors for wild fauna. In addition, they retain significant amounts of sediments during runoff and serve as a receptor layer of water that contributes significantly to the recharge of aquifers.

Finally, the San José estuary should be noted as one of the most outstanding environments of the Los Cabos municipality, both for its extension and its ecological and cultural importance. The San José del Cabo estuary is the largest of the Los Cabos region. It is a refuge area for migratory birds and has a great diversity of fauna, besides having a high recreation value for the local population. The San José estuary is located in the heart of this population. It is a coastal lagoon that receives freshwater from the San José creek. The vegetation that characterizes this stream consists of cattails that surround the body of water, reeds, and palm trees. Due to its importance, this estuary was declared a natural protected area under state jurisdiction on October 8, 1993. However, the strong development pressures on this area threaten the ecological stability of the system. The main threats are tourism and urban growth in its area of influence, as well as the pollution of the water body and overexploitation of the aquifer.

FAUNA

The fauna of the municipality of Los Cabos is also a reflection of the evolutionary processes of the Los Cabos region. The geographical and ecological isolation has been important in the evolution of the fauna, producing a large number of endemic or unique species. Currently, there are around 300 species of native vertebrates in the municipality that include amphibians, reptiles, birds, and mammals (Breceda et al., in press), with the group of birds being the most diverse. There are also some introduced species of amphibians and reptiles, as well as mammals that can become a problem for the rest of the species in the region. In the case of mammals, introduced species are domestic species (cats, dogs, cows, goats, donkeys, and pigs) that roam freely. In some cases, they have become feral animals and can compete for food and space with native species and cause habitat alterations.

Native amphibians that can be observed belong to three species, of which two are small toads (80–90 mm in length) and the third is a small frog (44 mm in length). The toads are found throughout the peninsula. The red-spotted toad *(Bufo punctatus*, also called *Anaxyurus punctatus)* has very characteristic red spots on the body for which it is named. The Couch's Spadefoot *(Scaphiopus couchi)*, reported for the eastern part of the peninsula, has a black spur on the hind legs that helps it dig in order to hide underground and stay hidden in the dry period. The other amphibian is the small frog *Pseudacris hypochondriaca* (formerly *Hyla regilla)*, that is green or brown with a black line on the tip of the mouth to the sides of the eyes that runs to the front legs. It is commonly found in permanent water bodies that exist in some canyons, such as the Cañón de la Zorra, and in the oases of the region (and the peninsula), such as that of Santiago. However, the bullfrog *(Rana catesbeiana)* has been introduced into the Santiago oasis. It is a large and aggressive amphibian whose presence endangers not only native amphibian species, but other reptiles like water snakes and other vertebrates since it feeds on them.

Generally, on hot and humid summer and autumn nights during the rainy season, frogs and toads are heard croaking. They take advantage of the puddles they need to reproduce. Their young in larval stages are able to develop in these water bodies. Their activity decreases in winter and spring due to the drought and cold, and they become more difficult to observe.

The reptile group is very diverse and very particular, since there is a high number of species unique to the peninsula and the Los Cabos region. Of the nearly 38 species (one amphisbaenid, one freshwater turtle, 17 lizards, and 19 snakes) (Grismer 2002), 45% are endemic. No reptiles are dangerous, except rattlesnakes if they are disturbed. The Mexican mole lizard *(Bipes biporus)* belongs to the Bipedidae family Amphisbaenia suborder; it has adapted to an exclusively underground life. It has lost its hind limbs, keeping its front ones. Of pink coloring and very small eyes, it resembles a worm, which makes it repulsive although it is completely harmless. It is only distributed in the peninsula in areas with loose and sandy soils in the scrub, along the western middle portion to the southwestern tip of Baja California.

The small river turtle, *Trachemys nebula*, is exclusive to the municipality (Grismer 2002) and reaches a carapace length of 370 mm. It is restricted to permanent freshwater areas in the Los Cabos region and the peninsula, such as oases and some streams.

With regard to lizards, there are herbivorous ones like the *Ctenosaura hemilopha* iguana and the desert iguana *(Dipsosaurus dorsalis)*. The first is a gray lizard with dark stripes whose offspring are bright green. It reaches a size of almost 300 mm. It can be seen on trees, in holes, and on shrubs and cardon cacti. The desert iguana is distinguished by its rounded head, which it keeps upright when walking. The rest of the lizards, like snakes, are carnivorous; they feed on spiders, insects, and termites. Snakes also eat other reptiles, small mammals, and birds, thus varying their diets. Some lizards also have a varied diet, such as the whiptail *(Aspidoscelis maxima)*, which is a medium-sized lizard (137 mm long) endemic to the Los Cabos region. Other species show a more selective feeding, such as the orange-throated whiptail *Aspidoscelis hyperythra (*formerly *Cnemidophorus hyperythrus)*, which feeds mainly on termites, and the chameleon *(Phrynosoma coronatum)*, with pointed scales on the head forming a crown, which feeds almost exclusively on ants.

Snakes are also very diverse. There are those that are very small and thin, like the western blind snake *(Leptotyphlops humilis)*, which can measure from 2 to 5 mm wide and up to 389 mm long. There are also the black-headed snake *(Tantilla planiceps)* and the sandsnake *(Chilomeniscus stramineus)*. The latter has orange and black rings on its body so it is called coral snake, but it is harmless and lives buried in sandy soils. Other larger snakes are the desert boa or snake with two heads *(Chairin trivirgata,* formerly known as *Lichanura trivirgata)*, with cream and dark stripes along its body; the coachwhip *(Masticophis fuliginosus,* formerly *Masticophis flagellum)*, of variable color (yellow, brown, or black), which is possible to see climbing trees and shrubs; the kingsnake *(Lampropeltis Gaetulian)*, with black and white strips; and the false coral snake or gopher snake *(Pituophis vertebralis)*, of combined yellow-orange color, black, and white. All these are the most common and all are harmless. In addition, three of the four rattlesnakes that exist in Baja California Sur can be found in the region: *Crotalus ruber, Crotalus mitchellii,* and *Crotalus enyo* (endemic to the peninsula). These are the only poisonous reptiles in the state, but very important in the food chains as predators.

Four species of sea turtles nest on the shores of the Los Cabos region, especially in the municipality: the leatherback, the black sea turtle, the Ridley, and, to a lesser extent, the loggerhead. All are endangered. Measures to protect their nests and facilitate egg incubation and release of hatchlings to prevent their disappearance are indispensable and of utmost importance. Similarly, it is necessary to control and regulate activities of motor vehicles and horses on the beaches as they can destroy nests that have not been protected and affect other species that also inhabit streams and scrubland where these recreational activities take place.

With regard to birds, it is estimated that some 218 species exist in the municipality (Breceda et al., in press). Some are restricted to coastal areas and freshwater bodies (oasis) and others are widely distributed. Most are residents, 43% are seasonal (winter), and 13% are rare or migratory. Of all birds, nearly 74 (34%) are aquatic. As a result of this diversity of birds, the San José estuary and the Sierra La Laguna are recognized internationally as Areas of Importance for the Conservation of Birds (Áreas de Importancia para la Conservación de las Aves–AICAS) (CONABIO 2004). Many species, despite being small, are very attractive, such as the verdin *(Auriparus flaviceps)*, cardinal *(Cardinalis cardinalis)*, California gnatcatcher *(Polioptila califórnica)*, the mockingbird *(Mimus poliglottos)*, and the Xantus' hummingbird *(Hylocharis xantusii)*, to name a few. Birds of prey are diverse, important, and majestic, such as the golden eagle *(Aquila chrysaetos)*, the osprey *(Pandion haliaetus)*, and the crested caracara *(Caracara cheriway)*.

There is a distribution of 45 mammal species in the municipality. The small ones are represented by a shrew, about 21 species of bats, 11 species of mice and rats, two species of rabbits *(Sylvilagus auduboni* and *Sylvilagus bachmani)*, and one hare *(Lepus californicus)*. Among the medium-sized mammals are the gray fox *(Urocyon cinereoargenteus)* and the skunk *(Spilogale gracilis)*, which are common carnivores that feed on hares, rodents, lizards, snakes, birds, and insects, as well as some fruits. Other medium-size mammals are raccoons *(Procyon lotor)* and ringtails *(Bassariscus astutus)*, with long ringed tails. The ringtails are characteristic of rocky areas, while raccoons are characteristic of areas with water bodies (streams, oases, and areas near the coast). The mule deer *(Odocoileus hemionus)* inhabits a wide altitudinal gradient, since it is possible to find it from the lower parts (a few meters above sea level) in the xerophilous scrub to the upper parts in the pine-oak forest of the Sierra La Laguna. This deer is an eye-catching species because of its size and antlers, whose tips bifurcate, unlike other deer species in Mexico. It is highly valued for its meat and as a hunting trophy.

Most animal species are of wide distribution, such as the gray fox, coyote, bobcat, hawks, owls, and the vast majority of small birds. They are found indistinctly in any type of vegetation: sarcocaulescent scrub, lowland deciduous forest, and oak-pine forest. However, there are species that are restricted to a particular type of vegetation. For example, the small iguana or desert iguana *(Dipsosaurus dorsalis)*, the desert squirrel or white-tailed antelope squirrel *(Ammospermophilus leucurus)*, and the kangaroo rat *(Dipodomys merriami)* are characteristic of the sarcocaulescent scrub and are occasionally seen in the lowland deciduous forest. Some other species prefer certain features of the environment, regardless of the type of vegetation, such as large rocks and rocky cliffs in canyons and streams. These are excellent places to observe species like the iguana; the rock lizard or crocodile *(Petrosaurus thalassinus)* of blue-green colors and metallic yellow that contrast with black stripes; and the lizards *(Sceloporus hunsakeri* and *Sceloporus liki)* of iridescent colors. These three species are endemic to the Los Cabos region as is the iguana. It is also possible to observe ringtails *(Bassariscus astutus)* at these sites.

Some reptile species are restricted to environments with higher humidity, fallen leaves, and the presence of water, such as those found in the oases and humid areas of the pine-oak forest and tropical deciduous forest. These reptiles include the gecko *(Eumeces lagunensis)* with red or blue tail and body covered with smooth scales, dark color with light-colored stripes along the same; the scorpion or San Lucan alligator lizard *Elgaria paucicarinata (*formerly *Gerrhonotus paucicarinatus)* of reddish brown color, smooth scales, endemic to the Los Cabos region; and the nocturnal lizard *Xantusia vigilis vigilis* (subspecies endemic to Sierra La Laguna), small of dark reddish brown color. These species can be found under stones or in fallen leaves.

With regard to birds, some are restricted to aquatic environments (coastal areas, oases, or estuaries). These include various species of ducks and gulls, the brown pelican *(Pelecanus occidentalis)*, the American coot *(Fulica americana)*, the frigate *(Fregata magnificens)*, the common tern or least tern *(Sterna hirundo, Sterna antillarum)*, sandpipers *(Calidris alba, C. mauri, C. minutilla)*, and cormorants *(Phalacrocorax auritus)*.

Wetlands, such as the oasis of Boca de la Sierra, Santiago, and San José estuary, allow the presence of a wide array of birds, including migratory (Rodríguez-Estrella, Rubio, and Pineda 1997; Guzmán Poo 2004; CONABIO 2004). The wetlands also allow the existence of other groups such as frogs and toads, and various endemic species of reptiles and mammals. These species subsist not only because of the presence of water, but because of the type of vegetation that develops there (palms, mesquites, and other large trees). Therefore, their conservation and proper management is important.

Mexican Official Norm 059 (NOM-059-SEMARNAT-2001) lists the species of plants and animals considered threatened, endangered, and under special protection. This list identifies some 56 species, including birds, mammals, amphibians, and reptiles. The fauna of the municipality and the Los Cabos region in general is very important because of its peculiarity (numerous endemic species and their great diversity) and the need for its protection.

Table 1 shows the fauna species in the municipality of Los Cabos under some protection category according to the Mexican Official Norm 059-SEMARNAT-2010. The threatened species include the sand lizard *(Callisaurus draconoides)*, the golden eagle *(Aquila chrysaetos)*, and the badger *(Taxidea taxus)*. The official norm also includes all species of sea turtles that nest on these shores: the loggerhead *(Caretta caretta)*, the black sea turtle *(Chelonia agassizii)*, the olive ridley sea turtle *(Lepidochelys olivacea)*, and the leatherback *(Dermochelys coriacea)*. The last two are the most common. All are under the endangered category because their populations have severely declined due to accidental or intentional hunting, illegal consumption of eggs, nest destruction, and alteration of beaches. However, a coordinated effort by the Program for the Protection of Sea Turtles and tourism enterprises has promoted the conservation of these species on the shores of Los Cabos. This has protected the nests and release of offspring, especially the olive ridley turtle, the black sea turtle, and the leatherback sea turtle. Table 1 shows the endemic species of the municipality, where 17 reptile species, 23 bird species, and one mammal species have been registered. Among the endemic species, several that are unique to the Los Cabos region stand out, such as the Cabo lizard and the Hunsaker spiny lizard, both with husky bodies and spiny scales (keeled); the Cabo whipsnake *(Masticophis aurigulus)*; and the black water garter snake *(Thamnophis valida,* formerly called *Nerodia valida)*. Similarly, 24 species and subspecies of birds are distinctive and found mainly in the Sierra La Laguna.

Despite the importance of endemic species, as of now, these do not receive special protection. Indeed, some are not even listed in the official norm. So, biodiversity is threatened since the rapid tourism and urban development in this area can, in short, place these species in a dangerous situation.

Table 1. Endemic Species and/or Included in NOM-059-SEMARNAT-2001

Endemism: BCP = Baja California Peninsula; CR = Cabo Region; CR (SL) = Subspecies unique to Sierra La Laguna; BCS = Baja California Sur. Conservation **Status** according to the NOM: P = Subject to special protection; T = Threatened; E = Endangered

Species	Common Name	Endemism	Status
REPTILES			
Bipes biporus	Mexican mole lizard (five-toed worm lizard)	BCP	P
Sceloporus licki	Cabo spiny lizard	CR	P
Sceloporus hunsakeri	Hunsaker spiny lizard	CR	P
Sceloporus zosteromus	San Lucas spiny lizard	BCP	P
Callisaurus draconoides	Zebra-tailed lizard or sand lizard		T
Coleonyx variegatus	Western banded gecko		P
Urosaurus nigricaudus	Black-tailed brush lizard	BCP	T
Ctenosaura hemilopha	Spiny iguana	BCS	P
Elgaria paucicarinata	Scorpion or San Lucas alligator lizard	CR	P
Eumeces lagunensis	San Lucas skink	BCS	T
Phyllodactylus unctus	San Lucas leaf-toed gecko	CR	P
Petrosaurus thalassinus	Baja California rock lizard	CR	P
Cnemidophorus maximus[1]	Cabo whiptail lizard	CR	P
Chilomeniscus stramineus	Variable or spotted sandsnake	BCP	P
Masticophis aurigulus	Baja California striped whipsnake	CR	T
Masticophis flagellum[2]	Coachwhip		T
Lichanura trivirgata[3]	Rosy boa		T
Hypsiglena torquata	Nightsnake		P
Thamnophis valida[4]	Water garter snake	CR	
Lampropeltis getula	Common kingsnake		T
Crotalus enyo	Baja California rattlesnake	BCP	P

Terrestrial Flora and Fauna

Table 1. *(continued)*

Species	Common Name	Endemism	Status
Crotalus ruber	Red diamond rattlesnake		P
Crotalus mitchellii	Speckled rattlesnake		P
Trachemys nebulosa	Baja California slider	BCS	
Chelonia agassizii	Black sea turtle		E
Caretta caretta	Loggerhead turtle		E
Lepidochelys olivacea	Olive ridley sea turtle		E
Dermochelys coriacea	Leatherback turtle		E
BIRDS			
Aquila chrysaetos	Golden eagle		T
Accipiter striatus	Sharp-shinned hawk		P
Accipiter cooperi	Cooper's hawk		P
Parabuteo unicinctus	Harris' hawk		P
Buteo swainsoni	Swainson's hawk		P
Glaucidium gnoma	Pygmy owl	CR	P
Falco peregrinus	Peregrine falcon		P
Falco mexicanus	Prairie falcon		T
Micrathene whitneyi	Elf owl	CR	
Chordeiles acutipennis	Lesser nighthawk	CR	
Otus kennicottii xantusi[5]	Xantus' screech owl	CR	
Asio flammeus	Short-eared owl		P
Columba fasciata vioscae	Viosca's pigeon	CR (SL)	P
Zenaida asiatica	White-winged dove	CR	
Charadrius montanus	Mountain plover		T
Hylocharis xantusii	Xantus' hummingbird	CR	
Melanerpes formicivorus	Acorn woodpecker	CR (SL)	P
Picoides scalaris	Ladder-backed woodpecker	CR	
Sitta carolinensis lagunae	San Lucas white-breasted nuthatch	CR (SL)	P
Contopus sordidulus peninsulae	Large-billed wood pewee	CR (SL)	P

Table 1. (continued)

Species	Common Name	Endemism	Status
Empidonax difficilis cineritus	San Lucas flycatcher	CR (SL)	P
Myiarchus cinerascens	Ash-throated flycatcher	CR	
Aphelocoma coerulescens	Florida scrub jay	CR	
Parus inorantus	Plain titmouse	CR	
Psaltriparus minimus grandae	Grinda's bushtit	CR (SL)	P
Vireo solitarius luscasanus	San Lucas solitary vireo	CR	P
Vireo huttoni cognatus	Hutton's vireo	CR (SL)	P
Vireo gilvus victoriae	Warbling vireo	CR (SL)	P
Geothlypis beldingi	Belding's yellowthroat	BCS	E
Polioptila californica	California gnatcatcher		T
Pipilo erythrophthalmus magnirostris	Large-billed towhee	CR (SL)	P
Piplo fuscus	Brown towhee	CR	
Turdus migratorius confinis	San Lucas robin	CR	P
Junco phaeonotus bairdi	Baird's yellow-eyed junco	CR	P
Tachybaptus dominicus	Least grebe		P
Botaurus lentiginosus	American bittern		T
Larus heermanni	Heermann's gull		P
Larus livens	Yellow-footed gull		P
Sterna antillarum	Least tern		P
Sterna elegans	Elegant tern		P
MAMMALS			
Chaetodipus dalquesti	Dalquest's pocket mouse	CR	P
Taxidea taxus	American badger		T

Taxonimic synonym or also called: [1]*Aspidoscelis maxima*; [2]*Masticophis. fuliginosus*; [3]*Chairina trivirgata*; [4]*Nerodia valida*; [5]*Megascops kennicottii*.

Use and Threats

The species that are used for sports hunting in the area include the mule deer; the black-tailed jackrabbit *(Lepus californicus)*; the desert cottontail *(Sylvilagus auduboni)*; the California quail *(Callipepla californica)*; and the white-winged mourning dove *(Zenaida macroura)*. Other species—such as the bobcat, coyote, and raccoon—are also registered for hunting.

Another way of benefiting from the fauna is through the Management Units for the management of wildlife (Unidades de Manejo–UMAS), which in the region make good use of reptiles, deer, hares, and birds. The introduction and use of exotic species such as the ostrich, wild pig, and red deer, have been proposed in some of the region's UMAS. However, the use of fauna is mainly of introduced domestic species such as cattle, goats, pigs, and horses. The horses are used for cargo and transportation.

The main threats to the region's species are the alteration and degradation of the environment or habitat due to urban and tourism development—which has had a rapid increase in recent years—as well as the change in land use for agriculture or extensive cattle raising. The introduction of invasive exotic species also threatens the region's biodiversity since it is a major cause of the disappearance of native species (Lowe et al. 2004). In the municipality of Los Cabos, two species of introduced amphibians have been registered so far: the bullfrog *(Rana catesbeiana)*, which is an extremely aggressive species and preys on other amphibians, reptiles' offspring, and even bats; and the *Smilisca Baudin* frog, whose effect on native fauna is still unknown. With regard to reptiles, there is the relatively recent introduction of the nocturnal lizard, gecko, or common house gecko *(Hemidactylus frenatus)*. It is native to the Asian Pacific Islands and is closely associated with residential dwellings. Their number has increased considerably in recent years as well as its distribution area in the municipality. However, there is no research yet that demonstrates a negative effect on the native fauna. In addition, domestic species such as cats, cows, goats, donkeys, and pigs tend to escape from domestic care, becoming feral animals that negatively impact the native flora and fauna.

The current challenge is to prevent the disappearance of the wealth of species. Measures include urban planning and careful modification of habitats that somehow allow maintaining areas of natural vegetation and intact rocky conglomerates between housing developments and not building on dunes. Also important is planned and sustainable development and adequate stewardship of resources and activities related to tourism. In addition, the control of introduced species is critical. Finally, it is necessary to make people aware of the value of the region's natural resources of the region and the importance of their conservation through the establishment of environmental education programs at all levels.

References

Arriaga, L., and J. L. León de la Luz. 1989. "The Mexican Tropical Deciduous Forest of Baja California Sur: A Floristic and Structural Approach." *Vegetatio* 84 (1): 45–52.

Brandegee, T. S. 1891. "Flora of the Cape Region of Baja California." *Proceedings of the California Academy of Sciences* 3: 218–27.

Brandegee, T. S. 1892a. "Additions to the Flora of the Cape Region of Baja California." *Proceedings of the California Academy of Sciences* 3: 218–27.

Brandegee, T. S.1892b. "The Distribution of the Flora of the Cape Region of Baja California." *Zoe* 3: 223–31.

Breceda, A. 2005. "El mosaico de vegetación de una selva baja caducifolia." Ph.D. dissertation, School of Sciences, National Autonomous University of Mexico, Mexico, DF.

Breceda, A., R. Vázquez-Miranda, Y. Echeverría, and P. Galina. In press. "Características biológicas." *La Cuenca de San José del Cabo, B.C.S., México*, A. Breceda, ed.

Castorena, L., and A. Breceda. 2009. *Remontando el Cañón de la Zorra: Ranchos y rancheros de la Sierra La Laguna*. La Paz, BCS: Instituto Sudcaliforniano de Cultura del Gobierno del Estado de Baja California Sur.

Comisión Nacional para el Conocimiento y Uso de la Biodiversidad (CONABIO). 2004. *Áreas de Importancia para la Conservación de las Aves* (AICAS) (Accessed 10 March 2009) http://conabioweb.conabio.gob.mx/aicas/doctos/aicas.html.

Durham, J. W., and E. C. Allison. 1960. "The Geologic History of Baja California and Its Marine Faunas." *Systematic Zoology* 9 (2): 47–91.

Flores, E. 1998. *Geosudcalifornia: Geografía, agua y ciclones*. La Paz, BCS: Universidad Autonóma de Baja California Sur.

Grismer, L. L. 2002. *Amphibians and Reptiles of Baja California, including Its Pacific Islands, and the Islands in the Sea of Cortés*. Berkeley: University of California Press.

Guzmán Poo, Juan. 2004. "Aves del Estero San José, San José del Cabo, B.C.S." Pp. 17–51 en *Reunión de Análisis de los Oasis de Baja California Sur: Importancia y Conservación*. R. Rodríguez E., M. Cariño O., and C. Aceves G. eds. La Paz, BCS: Centro de Investigaciones Biológicas del Noroeste (CIBNOR).

Lenz, L. W. 1992. *An Annotated Catalogue of the Plants of the Cape Region, Baja California Sur, Mexico*. Claremont, CA: The Cape Press.

León de La Luz, J. L., J. J. Pérez Navarro, M. Domínguez, and R. Domínguez. 1999. *Listados florísticos de México XVIII: Flora de la Región del Cabo de Baja California Sur*. México, DF: Instituto de Biología, Universidad Nacional Autónoma de México.

Lowe, S., M. Browne, S. Boudielas, and M. De Poorter. 2004. *100 de las especies exóticas más dañinas del mundo. Una selección del Global Invasive Species Database*. Grupo Especialista de Especies Invasoras (GEEI), Comisión de la supervivencia de Especies (CSE) y Unión Mundial para la Naturaleza (UICN) (Accessed 15 March 2009) http://www.issg.org/spanish.pdf.

Mina, F. 1956. "Bosquejo geológico de la parte sur de la Península de Baja California." Pp. 11–80 in *Congreso Geológico Internacional A-7. Vigésima sesión*, M. Maldonado Koerdell, ed. México, DF.

Morelos, S. 1988. "La vegetación: Una aproximación a través de la fotointerpretación." Pp. 69–82 in *La Sierra de la Laguna de Baja California Sur*, L. Arriaga and A. Ortega, eds. La Paz, BCS: Centro de Investigaciones Biológicas de Baja California Sur, A.C.

Ortiz-Ávila, V. 1999. "Efecto del pastoreo sobre el establecimiento de juveniles en la selva baja caducifolia de la Reserva de la Biosfera Sierra de la Laguna, B.C.S. México." Bachelor's thesis, Autonomous University of Puebla, Puebla, Mexico.

Padilla, G., S. Pedrín, and E. Díaz. 1988. "Historia geológica y paleoecológica." Pp. 27–37 in *La Sierra de la Laguna de Baja California Sur*, L. Arriaga and A. Ortega, eds. La Paz, BCS: Centro de Investigaciones Biológicas de Baja California Sur, A.C.

Pérez Navarro, J. J. 1995. "La vegetación de ambientes costeros de la Región del Cabo, Baja California Sur: Aspectos florísticos y ecológicos." Bachelor's thesis, National Autonomous University of Mexico-Iztacala, Mexico.

Rodríguez-Estrella, R., L. Rubio, and E. Pineda. 1997. "Los oasis como parches atractivos para las aves terrestres residentes e invernantes." Pp. 157–86 in *Los Oasis de la Península de Baja California*, L. Arriaga and R. Rodríguez-Estrella, eds. La Paz, BCS: Centro de Investigaciones Biológicas del Noroeste.

Shreve, F., and I. Wiggins. 1964. *Vegetation and flora of the Sonoran Desert*. 2 Vols. Stanford, CA: Stanford University Press.

Vázquez, R. 2006. "Evaluación de la deforestación por extracción de especies maderables en la Cuenca de San José del Cabo, BCS." Master's thesis, Northwest Center for Biological Research, La Paz, Baja California Sur, México.

Wiggins, J. L. 1980. *Flora of Baja California*. Stanford, CA: Stanford University Press.

4

Marine and Coastal Flora and Fauna

*Oscar Arizpe C., Rafael Riosmena R.,
and Cynthia Valdez N.*

INTRODUCTION

The state of Baja California Sur has exceptional environmental conditions, both in the terrestrial portion and especially in marine and coastal areas, which makes it the Mexican Republic's state with the greatest marine-coastal biodiversity. It has almost one-fourth of the nation's entire coastal extension, with one part in the Pacific Ocean and another in the Gulf of California. In addition, it has a high complexity of ecological and evolutionary processes in the Los Cabos region's terrestrial and aquatic environments. It also has a high endemism of flora and fauna due to its geographical isolation created by its separation from the continental massif in the Middle Miocene.

However, this wealth of flora and fauna is threatened by an accelerated population growth, and strong pressure for coastal development of the municipality of Los Cabos and its real estate sector, as well as tourism activities that go beyond the beaches. All this makes it necessary to have an in-depth knowledge of the flora and fauna and thus to implement measures that mitigate damage to them. Therefore, by maintaining the stability and health of the region's ecosystems, the flora and fauna can be admired and enjoyed.

FLORA

Historical Analyses of Marine Botanical Research in the Los Cabos Area

Dawson (1944) mentions that the first collection of a specimen for the Gulf of California was carried out in 1880, and it was done in Isla del Carmen. The specimen was identified as *Wurdemannia miniata* and was deposited in the Herbarium of the University of California at Berkeley. Subsequently, there were additional collections through expeditions by both the California Academy of Sciences and the Paris Museum of Natural History (León Diguet), as well as collections by individuals (among the most famous, E. Marchant).

In the case of the Paris Natural History Museum, these collections were developed by Diguet. The first visit took place between 1889 and 1892, but due to the great interest generated by the material collected, the museum expanded its visits to Mexico to conduct expeditions both in the peninsula and in continental Mexico between 1893 and 1913 (Lamy and Woelkerling 1998). The collections of microalgae specimens were carried out between the Espíritu Santo and San José islands. Hariot (1895) reviewed and identified three species from this material. The specimens were initially deposited in the Paris Museum of Natural History, but duplicates were later sent to different collections and reinterpretations were made with these (reviewed by Riosmena-Rodríguez et al. 1999). After 1913, no further efforts were undertaken due to political instability in Europe. However, the influence of the development of pearl oyster farming near the Espíritu Santo Island stimulated the development of a list of floristic species that were collected in the surrounding areas (Howe 1911). This expanded the knowledge of the flora and recognized Baja California Sur as a relevant area to explore the marine flora.

The effort to learn about the flora of Baja California was stimulated by the voyages of the California Academy of Sciences (CAS), which began in the late nineteenth century and continued to before World War II. As part of CAS' third expedition, collections were made in the area between Los Cabos and La Paz in 1890 by T. S. Brandengee and W. E. Bryant. During these expeditions, macroalgae specimens were identified in different locations in the eastern Pacific, but particularly by the expedition of 1921 concentrated in the Gulf of California (Setchell and Gardner 1924). As part of this expedition, 625 specimens were collected from 180 species in 40 localities, which are now deposited in the Herbarium of the University of California at Berkeley. These represent the first real catalogue of the region, since it takes into account the collections of several expeditions and the records of other works in the area (Hariot 1895; Howe 1911). However, for the Los Cabos region, there are only anecdotal collections from the port of San Lucas.

Subsequently, Dawson (1944, 1949, 1950, 1954, 1959, 1961) and Hollenberg and Norris reported around 71 species of green and brown macroalgae for the Los Cabos region, with collections in the area of the lighthouse, Punta Palmilla, Bajo de la Gorda, Los Frailes, and Cabo Pulmo (Fig. 1). Their work with the red macroalgae is the best known, but there are numerous records of their participation in voyages by different foundations in California (ORCA; Hancock; Boudette). The specimens they collected are the obligatory reference for research in the region. However, the next specific study for the Los Cabos area was conducted as part of the characterization of the Cabo Pulmo coral reef by Brusca and Thomson (1975), where a general survey was made of the biota associated with the reef. Only the most conspicuous macroalgae species were registered in this study. Between 1988 and1994, nonsystematic, comprehensive studies were carried out between the coral reef sandbars by the Marine Botany Research Program. An extensive compilation of literature for the Cabo Pulmo coral reef was obtained, and it was determined that 61 species might be represented in the flora. Subsequently, 33 species were presented by Mateo-Cid et al. (2000) for the area of Cabo Pulmo. So far, however, a summary of the knowledge of the flora for the municipality of Los Cabos has not been presented.

The Los Cabos area is characterized by a geographical gradient from the Pacific to the Gulf of California. Consistently, areas can be found in the intertidal zone where macroalgae develop, depending on their ecological and physiological characteristics. In some parts of these zones that continue to deeper parts to 60 m, a flora exists that to date has not been properly characterized. Changes in depth and hydrodynamics must be playing a key role in the organization of these communities.

Figure 1. Places Marine Life Most Studied Historically within the Municipality of Los Cabos

Source: Riosmena et al. 2005.

Within the Gulf of California area in the Cabo Pulmo reef, a rather dynamic flora develops that is under intense pressure due to grazing, contrary to what was observed on the Pacific side where physical aspects may be more important. In the corridor between San José and Cabo San Lucas, areas can be seen where urchins are dominant elements in the rocky area. Little is known about the interaction or the diet of these organisms in this region.

Baynes (1999) has described the trophic relationships of reef fish for the area of Cabo Pulmo and recognizes the great importance of the filamentous macroalgae species. At present, an intensive monitoring program is being carried out by the Reef Check organization (http://www.reefcheck.org/news/news_detail.php?id=84), in coordination with Community and Biodiversity (Comunidad y Biodiversidad–COBI) (www.cobi.org). Riosmena-Rodríguez et al. (2005) made the first attempt to characterize the macroalgea assemblages north of Cabo Pulmo, in a town known as El Rincón, which has a very dynamic flora due to its constant replacement and great pressure from grazing organisms.

Floristic and Community Structure

There have been 88 macroalgae species found in the region, which can be considered the flora known for the area of Los Cabos (Appendix 1). Anaya and Riosmena (1996) found that 61 species had been previously reported for Cabo Pulmo, which have been confirmed and increased in recent studies (Mateo Cid et al. 2000). In the systematic arrangement, it is noticeable that the better represented orders are *Caulerpales*, *Dictyotales*, and *Ceramiales*. This is uncommon for the gulf (Mateo Cid et al. 1993), because this makes them spatially dominant over incrustive organisms (Baynes 1993). In the case of the El Rincón-La Rivera area, Riosmena-Rodríguez et al. (2005) reported a total of 72 species as potential flora, of which 45 correspond to modern collections. Of all the records, 47 species belong to the *Rhodophyta* division, while algae of the *Chlorophyta* and *Phaeophyta* divisions showed very similar percentages, with 18 and 19%, respectively (Fig. 2). There are fairly common algae throughout the area, such as *Sargassum* sp., *Caulerpa* sp., and *Rodhymenia* sp., as well as coralline algae that generate a lot of pressure from competition.

The affinities of potential flora species show a very marked differential behavior among divisions. This is clearly seen in the brown algae, where most of the elements are of tropical/endemic nature, while the temperate/cosmopolitan are a minimum proportion. Something inverse is seen in red algae, where the temperate/cosmopolitan algae have a higher proportion than the tropical/endemic algae. In the case of green algae, it can be seen that the species are distributed in the same proportion (~20%) among the four types of affinities.

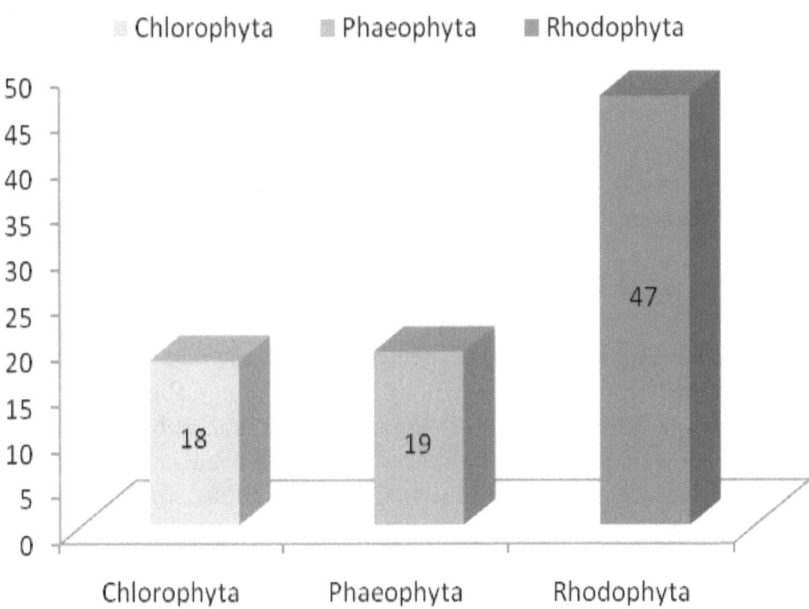

Figure 2. Number of Total Species by Division in the Municipality of Los Cabos

Source: Riosmena et al. 2005.

From the aforementioned aspects of Cabo Pulmo's coastal and marine flora, some important characterizations can be made. The specific richness is similar to other areas of the Los Cabos region (Anaya-Reyna and Riosmena-Rodríguez 1996; Baynes 1999), but a consistent reduction in richness is evident relative to other areas (Mateo-Cid et al.1993; Paul-Chávez and Riosmena-Rodríguez 2000). This is very likely associated with the increase in the diversity of fish and herbivore invertebrates (Montgomery 1980a, 1980b, 1980c, 1980d; Baynes 1999). The variation in the number of species per site and the degree of affinity to the area suggests that there is a great relationship and exchange between sites, with the exception of the subtidal area of Tachuelas in the East Cape region, which most likely is receiving a major influence of the Cabo-Pulmo reef area. The proportion of species by division shows a greater percentage of green algae rather than brown; this had not been recorded in other localities in the region (Riosmena-Rodríguez and Paul-Chávez 1997;

Paul-Chávez and Riosmena-Rodríguez 2000). Another interesting aspect is the presence of a majority of annual species rather than sporadic ones (Paul-Chávez and Riosmena-Rodríguez 2000), which suggests greater temporal stability.

With regard to assessments of coverage, it can be determined that there is a vertical structure of populations, with a very marked belt of *Gelidium-Jania* in the intertidal zone. In the case of the subtidal area, the belt establishes it as *Padina-Dictyota*. The fact that these were affected by the site shows that there are marked differences in recruitment in the area, affecting the abundance of other species (such as corallines or *Caulerpa* sp.). This structural form had not been described for the southern region, since there are few quantitative studies in the area. The possible seasonal variations will be governed by the temperature patterns in the area (Bolton and Anderson 1990) and local sedimentation events. The dominance of annual phenological groups shows that there is no major difference in community structure over the course of the year. The vertical differences are due more to a strategy of the species: more sporadic or annual in the intertidal extremity and annuals or perennials in the subtidal zone. Appendix 1 shows the algae species found.

FAUNA

Animals in the marine environment are usually grouped according to whether they float or swim in the water (called pelagic) and those that live at the bottom (benthic). The zooplankton is found within the first and the nekton within those that swim.

Zooplankton: These organisms are very important because, after phytoplankton, they are the base of the food chain. Most zooplankton species in the region of Los Cabos are tropical; the predominating groups are protozoans, jellyfish, chaetognaths, mollusks, echinoderms, abundant copepods, amphipods, euphausiids, and decapods (shrimp and crabs in egg and larval stages).

Ichthyoplankton: In general, this group of organisms is composed of eggs and larvae of fish that spend part of their life floating and drifting in ocean currents, to later integrate into the benthos or swim freely as part of the nekton. Most commercially important organisms in their first stage of life are found here, both for sportfishing and artisanal and industrial fishing, within which some authors cite (Moser et al. 1974) the eggs and larvae of sardines *(Harengula thrissina)*, thread herrings *(Opisthonema libertate)*, and round herrings *(Etrumeus teres)*, as well as those of the mackerel *(Scomber japonicus)* and carangid fish *(Chloroscombrus orqueta, Selene peruvianus,* and *Caranx caballus).*

Benthic macroinvertebrates: The main groups of the so-called zoobenthos are comprised of coelenterates, polychaetes, and a great number of mollusk and crustacean species, as well as echinoderms. Within the first group, also known as cnidarians, are species of soft and hard corals that form reefs and are highly relevant for the region. These stand out in the municipality of Los Cabos because of the presence of the northernmost reef from Alaska to Patagonia (the Cabo Pulmo coralline reef), which is a hot spot for national and international tourism attraction and research.

In the case of species with commercial importance, there are the mollusks that, although not as abundant as in other areas of Baja California Sur, are exploited in small amounts in some parts of the municipality. Included are those known as scallops *(Pinna rugosa, Atrina tuberculosa,* and *Atrina maura)*; rock oysters *(Crassostrea fisheri* and *Crassostrea iridescens)*; ark clams *(Anadara tuberculosa* and *Anadara multicostata)*; venus clams *(Chione spp.)*; red chocolate clams *(Megapitaria aurantiaca* and *Megapitaria squalida)*; sea snails *(Hexaplex brassica* and *Hexaplex nigritus)*; and giant conchs or *caracoles burros (Strombus galeatus* and *Strombus gracilior)*. In the specific case of the octopus *(Octopus spp.)*, it is commonly found in both of the region's coasts. Occasionally, there are also various crustaceans in some areas, such as lobsters of the so-called bighead blue spiny type *(Panulirus inflatus)* and several species of crabs and penaeid shrimps.

Specifically in Cabo Pulmo and Los Frailes, or in the northeastern part of the region, other invertebrates are frequently encountered that, rather than being of great extractive commercial importance, generate foreign currency as an attraction for underwater tourism. It is particularly significant to mention that in the last century, this was one of the most important regions at the national level because of the presence of mother-of-pearl *(Pinctada mazatlanica)*, which was about to disappear due to its high extraction. To date, it is subject to a special protection category in the last NOM-059-SEMARNAT (see Appendix 2).

Fish: In this group of organisms, there are both free swimmers, also called nektons, as well as benthic fish of high ornamental value. Alvarez and Reyes (2005), referring to Cabo Pulmo as a very important area from the ichthyofaunistic point of view, reported 258 species, 155 genera, and 60 fish families. In the region's rocky and coralline areas, it is common to observe different types of groupers *(Epinephelus labriformis, Epinephelus panamensis,* and *Mycteroperca rosacea)*; snappers *(Lutjanus argentiventris)*; grunts *(Haemulon sexfasciatum)*, bluechin parrotfish *(Scarus ghobban)*; and several species of stingrays *(Myliobatis californica, Zapteryx exasperata, Urolophus concentricus,* and *Dasyatis brevis)*.

In the case of nektons, species of great economic importance are notable on the municipality's coasts, such as the shark (genus *Sphyrna, Mustelus, Alopias, Carcharhinus,* and *Squatia)*, which is becoming scarce due to excessive capture. Closer to the so-called mouth of the Gulf of California, tuna are caught, also called bonito *(Sarda chilensis* and *Sarda orientalis)*, yellowfin tuna *(Thunnus albacares)*, and skipjack tuna *(Euthynnus lineatus* and *Katsuwonus pelamis)*. Finally, fish that are of great importance because of the foreign currency they generate from tourism in the region, are those subject to recreational sportfishing, such as dolphinfish *(Coryphaena hippurus)*, sailfish *(Istiophorus platypterus)*, striped marlin *(Tetrapturus audax)*, blue marlin *(Makaira Mazara)*, black marlin *(Makaira indica)*, and swordfish *(Xiphias gladius)*.

Reptiles: Turtles are the most significant marine reptiles in Los Cabos and, since they will be described in the next chapter, it will only be mentioned that their importance is substantial because they are under permanent ban and listed in the endangered category in the NOM -059-ECOL-1994. The species found in the marine part of the region are the turtles called loggerhead *(Caretta caretta)*, black sea turtle *(Chelonia agassizi)*, green turtle *(Chelonia mydas)*, leatherback *(Dermochelys coriacea)*, hawksbill *(Eretmochelys imbricata)*, and the olive ridley *(Lepidochelys olivacea)*. Those that nest on the shores of the municipality are the leatherback, the black sea turtle, the olive ridley and, to a lesser extent, the loggerhead.

Birds: It has been estimated that the bird occurrence in Los Cabos is about 218 species, from the purely coastal and restricted to freshwater bodies to the widely distributed ones (see Chapter 3, Aurora

Breceda, Patricia Galina, and Marco A. González). Due to this diversity of birds, the San José estuary and Sierra La Laguna are internationally renowned as Areas of Importance for the Conservation of Birds (Áreas de Importancia para la Conservación de las Aves–AICAS) (CONABIO 2004). Breceda (Breceda et al.) notes that some birds are restricted to aquatic environments, such as various species of ducks and gulls, the brown pelican *(Pelecanus occidentalis)*, the coot *(Fulica americana)*, the frigatebird *(Fregata magnificens)*, the common or least tern *(Sterna hirundo, Sterna antillarum)*, sandpipers *(Calidris alba, Calidris mauri, Calidris minutilla)*, and the cormorant *(Phalacrocorax auritus)*.

Marine mammals: Cetaceans make up the group of most distinctive and important marine mammals on both coasts of the municipality, some of them residents and others migratory. Besides the humpback whale *(Megaptera novaeangliae)*, gray whale *(Eschrichtius robustus)*, sperm whale *(Physeter macrocephalus)*, and orca *(Orcinus orca)*, which are commonly observed in the winter, the blue whale *(Balaenoptera musculus)*, sei and Eden's whales *(Balaenoptera borealis* and *Balaenoptera edeni)* can occasionally be found. Several species of these cetaceans, which are described in a following chapter, are under some protection category in the NOM-059-ECOL-1994. The bottlenose dolphin *(Tursiops truncatus)* is frequently seen during all seasons. All these cetaceans are of great importance as tourist attractions.

Lastly, although not in the group of cetaceans but classified as a marine mammal, it is common to find the sea lion *(Zalophus californianus)* throughout the year. It can be seen at various points in the coastal areas of the municipality, most notably in the sea lion colonies of the bays of Cabo San Lucas and Los Frailes-Cabo Pulmo. These colonies, although not for breeding, are important for tourism.

REFERENCES

Álvarez-Filip, L., and H. Reye-Bonilla. 2005. "Comparison of Community Structure and Functional Diversity of Fishes at Cabo Pulmo Coral Ref., Eastern Mexico between 1987 and 2003." Proceeding of the 10th ICRS, Okinawa 2: 265–275

Anaya-Reyna, G., and R. Riosmena-Rodríguez. 1996. "Macroalgas marinas del arrecife coralino de Cabo Pulmo-Los Frailes, B.C.S., México." *Rev. Biol. Trop.* 44: 861–864.

Baynes, W. T. 1999. "Factors Structuring a Subtidal Encrusting Community in the Southern Gulf of California." *Bull. Mar. Sci.* 64 (3): 419–450.

Bolton, J. J., and R. J. Anderson. 1990. "Correlation between Intertidal Seaweed Community Composition and Sea Water Temperature Patterns on a Geographical Scale." *Botanica Marina* 33: 447–457.

Breceda, A., P. Galina, and M. A. González. 2012. "Terrestrial Flora and Fauna." *Los Cabos: The Future of a Natural and Tourism Paradise.* San Diego: San Diego State University Press.

Brusca, R. C., and D. B. Thomson. 1975. "Pulmo Reef: The Only 'Coral Reef' in the Gulf of California." *Ciencias Marinas* 1: 37:53.

Comisión Nacional para el Conocimiento y Uso de la Biodiversidad (CONABIO). 2004. Áreas de Importancia para la Conservación de las Aves (AICAS). http://conabioweb.conabio.gob.mx/aicas/doctos/aicas.html.

Dawson, E. Y. 1944. "The Marine Algae of the Gulf of California." Allan Hancock Pacific Expeditions 3: 189–453.

Dawson, E. Y. 1949. "Resultados preliminares de un reconocimiento de las algas marinas de la costa pacífica de México." *Revista de la Sociedad Mexicana de Historia Natural* 9: 215–255.

Dawson, E. Y. 1950. "Notes on Some Pacific Mexican Dictyotaceae." *Bulletin of the Torrey Botanical Club* 77: 83–93

Dawson, E. Y. 1954. "Resumen de las investigaciones recientes sobre algas marinas de la costa Pacífica de México, con una sinopsis de la literatura, sinonimia y distribución de las especies descritas." *Revista de la Sociedad Mexicana de Historia Natural* 13: 97–197.

Dawson, E. Y. 1959. "Marine Algae from the 1958 Cruise of the Stella Polaris in the Gulf of California." Los Angeles County Museum Contributions to Science 27: 1–37.

Dawson, E. Y. 1961. "A Guide to Literature and Distributions of Pacific Benthic Algae from Alaska to the Galapagos Isles." *Pacific Science* 15: 370–461.

Hariot, P. 1895. "Algues du Golfe de California recueillies par M. Diguet." *Journal of Botany* 9: 167–170.

Hollenberg, G. J., and J. N. Norris 1977. "The Red Alga Polysiphonia (Rhodomelaceae) in the Northern Gulf of California." Smithsonian Contributions to the Marine Sciences 1: 1–21.

Howe, M. A. 1911 "Phycological Studies V. Some Marine Algae of Lower California, Mexico." *Bulletin of the Torrey Botanical Club* 38: 489–514, pls. 27–34.

Lamy, D. y W. J. Woelkerling. 1998. "The Muséum National d'Histoire Naturelle y coralline systematics." Pp. 15–242 (addendum: 685–686) in *Non-geniculate Coralline Red Algae y the Paris Muséum: Systematics y Scientific History*, W. J. Woelkerling and D. Lamy, eds. Paris: Publications Scientifique du Muséum/ADAC.

Mateo-Cid, L. E., A. C. Mendoza-González, and C. Galicia-García. 2000. "Contribución al estudio de las algas marinas bentónicas de Punta Arena y Cabo Pulmo, Baja California Sur, México." *Acta Botánica Mexicana* 52: 55–73

Mateo-Cid, L. E., I. Sánchez-Rodríguez, E. Rodríguez-Montesinos, and M. M. Casas-Valdez. 1993. "Estudio florístico de las algas marinas bentónicas de Bahía Concepción, B.C.S., México." *Ciencias Marinas* 19: 41–60.

Montgomery, W. L. 1980a. "Comparative Feeding Ecology of Two Herbivorous Damselfishes (Pomacentridae: Teleostei) from the Gulf of California, Mexico." *Journal of Experimental Marine Biology and Ecology* 47: 9–24.

Montgomery, W. L. 1980b. "Effects of Grazing by the Yellowtail Surgeonfish, Prionurus punctatus, in the Gulf of California, Mexico." *Bulletin of Marine Science* 30 (4): 901–902.

Montgomery, W. L. 1980c. "The Impact of Non-selective Grazing by the Giant Blue Damselfish, Microspathodon dorsalis, on Algal Communities in the Gulf of California, Mexico." *Bulletin of Marine Science* 30: 290–303.

Montgomery, W. L. 1980d. "Marine Macroalgae as Foods for Fishes: An Evaluation of Potential Food Quality." *Env. Biol. Fish.* 5 (2): 143–153.

Moser, H. G., E. Ahlstrom, D. Kramer, and E. G. Stevens. 1974. "Distribution and Abundance of Fish Eggs and Larvae in the Gulf of California." CalCOFI Rep.

Paul-Chávez, L., and R. Riosmena-Rodríguez 2000. "Floristic and Biogeographical Trends in Seaweed Assemblages from a Subtropical Insular Island Complex in the Gulf of California." *Pacific Science* 54: 137–147.

Riosmena-Rodríguez, R., and L. Paul-Chávez. 1997. "Sistemática y biogeografía de las macroalgas de Bahía de La Paz, B.C.S." Pp. 59–82 in *La Bahía de La Paz. Conservación e Investigación*, J. Urban-Ramírez and M. Ramírez, eds. La Paz, BCS: Universidad Autónoma de Baja California Sur-CICIMAR-SCRIPPS.

Riosmena-Rodríguez, R., G. Hinojosa-Arango, J. M. López-Vivas, K. León-Cisneros, and E. Holguin-Acosta. 2005. "Caracterización espacial y biogeográfica de las asociaciones de macroalgas de Bahía del Rincón." *Revista de Biología Tropical* 43: 23–45.

Riosmena-Rodríguez, R., Wm. J. Woelkerling, and M. S. Foster. 1999. "Taxonomic Reassessment of Rhodolith-forming Species of Lithophyllum (Corallinales: Rhodophyta) in the Gulf of California, Mexico." *Phycologia* 38: 401–417.

Setchell, W. A., and N. L. Gardner. 1924. "Expedition of the California Academy Sciences to the Gulf of California in 1921." *The Marine Algae. Proc. Calif. Acad.* 4: 605

Appendix 1

General list of macroalgae species in Los Cabos: (1) Cabo San Lucas Bay; (2) Punta Palmilla; (3) Santa María y Cabeza de Ballena Bay; (4) San José del Cabo Bay; (5) Punta la Gorda; (6) Los Frailes; (7) Cabo Pulmo; (8) El Rincón

Species	Location
Acetabularia calyculus Quoy & Gainard	7,8
Achrochaetium scinaiae Dawson	7,8
Acrosorium uncinatum (Turner) Kylin	5
Amphiroa beauvoisii Lamouroux	7
Amphiroa misakiensis Yendo	7
Amphiroa valonioides Yendo	7
Antithamnionella elegans (Berthold) Price & John	7
Callithamnion paschale Borgesen	7
Caluerpa sertularioides (Gmelin) Howe	7
Caulerpa racemosa (Forsskål) J. Agardh	2
Caulerpa racemosa var. *peltata* (Lamouroux) Eubank	2
Centroceras clavulatum (C. Agardh) Montagne	7,8
Ceramium affine Setchell & Gardner	7,8
Ceramium fimbriatum Setchell & Gardner	7
Ceramium flaccidum (Kützing) Ardissone	7,8
Chaetomorpha antennina (Bory de Saint-Vincent) Kützing	3
Chaetomorpha apiculata	2
Chaetomorpha linum (Muller) Kützing	8
Champia parvula (C. Agardh) Harvey	7,8
Chondria californica (Collins) Kylin	7,8
Cladophora albida (Nees) Kützing	1
Cladophora columbiana Collins	2,7
Cladophora graminea Collins	3,5
Cladophora microcladioides Collins	2,3,7,8
Cladophoropsis gracillima Dawson	2

Appendix 1 (continued)

Species	Location
Codium setchelli Gardner	3
Codium simulans Setchell & Gardner	8
Colpomenia sinuosa f. *tuberculata* (Saund.) Setchell & Gardner	4
Dasya sinicola (Setchel and Gardner) Dawson	7,8
Derbesia marina (Lyngbye) Solier	3
Dictyiopteris delicatula Lamoroux, 1809	1,3,4
Dictyiopteris zonaroides Farlow, 1899	4
Dictyota crenulata J. Agardh, 1847	2,3,4,6,7
Dictyota dichotoma (Hudson) Lamouroux	3
Dictyota divaricata Lamouroux	1,2,4,6,7
Dictyota flabellata (Collins) Setchell & Gardner	1
Dictyota friabilis Sigee	7
Dictyota vivesii Howe	3,5,8
Dictyota volubilis (Kützing) sensu Vickers	7
Enteromorpha intestinalis (Linnaeus)	5
Ernodesmis verticillata (Kützing) Børgesen	2
Erythrotrichia carnea (Dillwyn) J. Argardh	7,8
Galaxaura arborea Kjelmann	2
Galaxaura marginata (Ellis & Solander) Lamouroux	4
Galaxaura arborea	1,3
Gelidiella acerosa (Forskssål) J. Feldmann & G. Hamel	2,3,4
Gelidiella ligulata Dawson	7
Gelidium sclerophyllum Taylor	7
Griffisthia multiramosa	5
Halimeda discoidea Decaisne	2,4
Herposiphonia secunda f. *tenella* (C. Ag.) Ambron	3,7,8
Herposiphonia spinosa Dawson	7,8
Heterosiphonia sinicola	5
Hydrolithon decipiens (Heydrich) Foslie	7,8
Hydrolithon onkodes	7

Appendix 1 *(continued)*

Species	Location
Hypnea cervicornis J. Agardh	3,7
Jania adhaerens Lamouroux	7
Jania tenella (Kutz) Grunow	7
Laurencia pacifica Kylin	7
Liagora californica Zenh	7,8
Lithophyllum imitans Foslie	7,8
Lithophyllum margaritae (Harriot) Heydrich	7,8
Lyngbya confervoides	5
Neogoniolithon setchelli (Foslie) Adey	7
Padina concrescens Thivy	7
Padina mexicana Dawson	7
Polysiphonia johnstonii Setchell & Gardner	7
Polysiphonia pacifica Hollenberg	7
Polysiphonia simplex Hollenberg	7
Pterocladiella capillacea (Bornet & Thuret) Hommersan & Santelices	7
Ralfsia hancokii	3,4
Sarcodiotheca linearis	5
Sargassum horridum Setchell & Gardner	3
Sargassum liebmanii	2
Sargassum sinicola Setchell & Gardner	7,8
Scinaia latifrons Howe	1,6
Sphacelaria furcigera Kützing	3,7
Sphacelaria hancockii Dawson	2,3,4
Sphacelaria californica (Suvers) Setchell & Gardner	7,8
Spyridia filamentosa (Wulfen) Harvey	7,8
Ulva dactylifera Setchell & Gardner	2
Ulva lactuca Linnaeus	1,3,4
Veleroa subulata Dawson	7

Marine and Coastal Flora and Fauna

Appendix 2

Threatened, protected, or rare species in Los Cabos, according to NOM-059-SEMARNAT-2001

Group	Species	Protection category as per NOM-059-SEMARNAT-2001
INVERTEBRATES	*Isostichopus fuscus*	Endangered
INVERTEBRATES	*Pinctada mazatlanica*	Subject to special protection
INVERTEBRATES	*Spondylus calcifer*	Subject to special protection
REPTILES	*Bipes biporus*	Rare
REPTILES	*Callisaurus draconides*	Threatened
REPTILES	*Caretta caretta*	Endangered
REPTILES	*Cnemidophorus hyperythrus*	Threatened
REPTILES	*Cnemidophorus maximus*	Rare
REPTILES	*Coleonyx variegatus peninsularis*	Rare
REPTILES	*Crotalus enyo*	Threatened
REPTILES	*Crotalus mitchelli*	Subject to special protection
REPTILES	*Crotalus ruber*	Subject to special protection
REPTILES	*Ctenosaura hemilopha hemilopha*	Subject to special protection
REPTILES	*Chelonia agassizi*	Endangered
REPTILES	*Chilomeniscus stramineus*	Rare
REPTILES	*Dermochelys coriaceae*	Endangered
REPTILES	*Eretmochelys imbricata*	Endangered
REPTILES	*Eridiphas slevini*	Threatened
REPTILES	*Eumeces lagunensis*	Threatened
REPTILES	*Hypsiglena torquata*	Rare
REPTILES	*Lampropeltis getula*	Threatened
REPTILES	*Lepidochelys olivacea*	Endangered
REPTILES	*Lichanura trivirgata*	Threatened
REPTILES	*Masticophis aurigulus*	Threatened
REPTILES	*Petrosaurus thalassinus*	Rare
REPTILES	*Phyllodactylus unctus*	Rare
REPTILES	*Phyllodactylus xanti xanti*	Rare
REPTILES	*Sauromalus australis*	Threatened
REPTILES	*Trimorphodon biscutatus*	Rare

Group	Species	Protection category as per NOM-059-SEMARNAT-2001
REPTILES	*Urosaurus nigricaudus*	Threatened
BIRDS	*Buteo jamaicensis*	Subject to special protection
BIRDS	*Falco peregrinus*	Threatened
BIRDS	*Icterus cucullatus*	Threatened
BIRDS	*Icterus wagleri*	Threatened
MAMMALS	*Lepus californicus*	Rare
MAMMALS	*Odocoileis hemionus*	Threatened
MAMMALS	*Zalophus californianus*	Subject to special protection

5

Living on the Edge: Sea Turtles in the Waters off Los Cabos, Baja California Sur

Melania C. López-Castro, Fabiola Villegas-Nava, María Elizabeth González Payán, Katherine Comer Santos, and Wallace J. Nichols

INTRODUCTION

Sea turtles are important animals culturally, ecologically, and economically for the Los Cabos municipality. Known as charismatic species, sea turtles bring communities together to fight for their conservation and, in turn, for the conservation of marine habitats, nesting beaches, and for the implementation of fishing gear restrictions that protect many other species. Turtles are heavy foragers in Los Cabos coastal waters, consuming corals, fish, shellfish, mollusks, sponges, seagrass, algae, and jellyfish. If they were to disappear from the Los Cabos waters, the ocean habitat could change considerably, generating negative ecological and economic consequences. For all these reasons, sea turtles are one of the best ocean conservation ambassadors in the region of Los Cabos.

This chapter focuses on the importance of sea turtle populations and their foraging grounds, mating grounds, and migratory routes. Some of the threats to these areas and to the turtle populations using them will be discussed and recommendations for conservation and research will be provided.

Background

Sea turtles are plentiful in the waters off Los Cabos; while some reside year round in the area, others migrate to forage in nearby and distant waters, shuttling to southern nesting beaches in Mexico and Central and South America to mate, and/or arriving to nest on Los Cabos beaches. Four of the seven species of sea turtles can be found around the coast of Los Cabos: the leatherback or *laúd* (*Dermochelys coriacea*), the green or *verde/negra/prieta* (*Chelonia mydas*), the hawksbill or *carey* (*Eretmochelys imbricata*), and the olive ridley or *golfina* (*Lepidochelys olivacea*). Historical records in the area and recent records in neighboring municipalities suggest that smaller numbers of loggerheads or *caguamas/amarillas/pericas* (*Caretta caretta*) also use this area either for feeding or as a migratory pathway. All of these species are listed as vulnerable, endangered, or critically endangered (IUCN Redlist 2009) and are protected by Mexican law (SEMARNAT 2002). Nichols (2003) mentions that the lack of enforcement has resulted in an annual decline of sea turtle populations (estimated at 35,000 animals) due to illegal hunting, bycatching, and nest poaching. Other threats include habitat degradation, boat collisions, and water pollution.

To date (2009), almost all conservation efforts in Los Cabos have focused on the primary nesting grounds in Cabo Pulmo, San José del Cabo, and San Cristobal. This is partly because it is easier and cheaper to protect turtles on land than in the water, and surviving hatchlings will add to the population. However, if hatchlings do not survive long enough in the water to mate and produce viable offspring, their contribution to the population is negligible, whereas protection of large subadult and adult turtles is critical (Wallace et al. 2008). Female turtles only leave the water for a few hours of their lives to nest, and males almost never leave the water. Despite receiving far less research and conservation attention, protecting turtles in the sea is equally as important as protecting those on nesting grounds for the restoration of sea turtle populations and to have them fulfill their ecological role (Bjorndal and Jackson 2003).

IN-WATER THREATS

Specific and detailed studies on the threats to swimming populations of Los Cabos turtles have not yet been performed. However, the general threats to swimming turtles elsewhere and in areas around the Baja California peninsula include the following:

1. Bycatching. Turtles are caught primarily by trawl, pelagic longline, and coastal gillnet fisheries (Lewison et al. 2004).

2. Hunting. A strong tradition of eating turtle meat (mostly green and olive ridley turtles) still exists in the region, and meat and shells (particularly of hawksbills) are available on the black market. Lack of staff from the Attorney General of Environmental Protection (Procuraduría Federal de Protección al Ambiente–PROFEPA) and resources for enforcement against poaching remain a problem.

3. Foraging habitat destruction. Degradation of the foraging grounds reduces the amount of preferred food that, in turn, reduces the prey selectivity (turtles cannot eat their preferred food and they have to rely on other items of less quality) and forces greater migrations within these foraging grounds (Moran and Bjorndal 2005), causing stress and sometimes starvation. Invasive seagrass species such as *Gracilaria vermicullphyla* and *Acantophora spicifera* are invading areas of *Zostera marina* and *Halophila/Halodule*, which are seagrasses preferred by sea turtles (Riosmena 2010).

4. Boat collisions. Boat strikes are common threats to basking and mating turtles, because turtles congregate on the surface for long periods of time. The severity of the injuries varies but can be lethal.

5. Ocean pollution. Some anthropogenic factors that directly impact sea turtles are ingestion of plastic (Wabnitz and Nichols 2010), entanglement in fishing nets, ingestion of fishing hooks, and contact with pesticides and heavy metals. Although these contaminants can be introduced into the environment through fertilizers and pesticides used in agricultural activities, the municipality of Los Cabos is characterized by organic agricultural activities that would not produce runoff of contaminants into the ocean. This means that intense tourism activities that are typical of the region generate the

pollution in the municipality's bodies of water. These tourism activities include those related to high-rise hotels, many golf courses, the arrival of more than 250 cruise ships each year (reported in 2003; CEI 2006), and the presence of thousands of other watercraft in the region (Nájera-Hernández 2007). Poorly planned rapid urbanization with inadequate wastewater collection and treatment infrastructure, unpaved urban streets, and inadequate collection and control of solid and hazardous wastes are also factors in producing pollution that affects the local waters.

CURRENT KNOWLEDGE OF SEA TURTLES IN THE AREA

The next section highlights the sea turtle populations and their habitats in Los Cabos.

Foraging Habitat

The area of Los Cabos provides foraging or feeding areas for at least three of the five sea turtle species found in the Baja California peninsula. However, very little is known about the current status of these foraging areas. Identifying these sites could be key in developing proposals for the conservation of these species.

The ecological importance of sea turtles is related to their diets and feeding habitats. Within their foraging habitats, the turtle makes small migrations that favor positive interactions between the turtle population and the populations of the organisms on which it feeds (Hemminga and Duarte 2000). The green turtle, for instance, is well-known for depending on seagrasses and macroalgae for sustenance and the hawksbill feeds on certain sponge species in reefs (Márquez 2002). The case of the olive ridley is a little more complex. Ridleys historically have fed in coastal waters on a variety of species including fish, crustaceans, jellyfish, and mollusks (Márquez 2002).

Gardner and collaborators (2006) assessed specific heavy metals (Pb, Fe, Se, Cd, Ni, Cu, Zn, and Mn) in different tissues of green, olive ridley, loggerhead, and hawkbill turtles in the Baja California peninsula, including Cabo San Lucas, with a total of 23 turtles analyzed. They found high concentrations of cadmium (Cd), which can be extremely detrimental to the digestive system epithelium and contiguous glands. They also reported high concentrations of manganese

(Mn), which can cause anemia and problems with the nervous system through chronic exposure, and iron (Fe), which is associated with hepatic diseases in some organisms (Talavera-Sáenz 2006).

Research is recommended to record the biotic and abiotic characteristics of the region; to locate as precisely as possible with geographic information systems (GIS) the foraging areas; and to detect the species foraging in them as well as their abundance. Through gastric lavages, or stomach pumping, it is possible to analyze the stomach contents of the turtles to determine diet preferences and, to some degree, the state of their health.

Mating Turtles

During mating seasons for olive ridleys and leatherbacks (from June to February), adult turtles migrate to their reproductive areas searching for a mate and, in the case of females, also for a suitable beach to lay their eggs (Morreale et al. 2007). The distance between the coast and the nesting beach in which this mating area is located is still unknown. But, in general, mating occurs near the nesting beaches about two weeks before nesting starts (Plotkin 2003). The duration of the mating period can vary depending on the species.

Hot spots for mating activity should be identified via methods described later in this chapter. These areas need to be protected and to have proper regulations in order to prevent boats from colliding with turtles as well as other negative effects on turtles from direct and indirect fishing.

Population Numbers and Health

Scientists and decision makers need to estimate population abundances for all species in order to calculate the risk of extinction and/or the success of conservation efforts. In the Los Cabos municipality, population numbers have been tracked through nest counts, which is a widely accepted method to estimate sea turtle population numbers. However, there are some limitations in relying on this one method. The nesting beach method assumes that the nesting sample is an index of abundance in the larger population and that there is a one-to-one sex ratio in the population (Gerrodette and Tayor 1999). This means that there is a chance of over or underestimating the population size by not knowing the male component in the population. While this method could be useful in estimating the population size of the two species nesting regularly in Los Cabos, the foraging and migrating populations of the other three species are not tracked. In addition, other methods need to be developed in order to estimate the abundance of nonnesting turtles.

Another recommendation is for the municipality of Los Cabos to join the population monitoring program of the Sea Turtle Network of the Californias (Grupo Tortuguero de las Californias; grupotortuguero.com), a community-based nonprofit organization of around 500 persons from more than 30 communities dedicated to sea turtle conservation. On the rest of the Baja California peninsula, and throughout northwest Mexico, over 12 community-based teams from the Sea Turtle Network are actively tracking populations through an in-water program conducted by the nonprofit. The method used is "catch per unit effort" and follows protocol described by Ehrhart and Ogren (1999). Permitted fishers and others deploy nets 100 m long with 20-cm mesh at predetermined locations once a month during neap tides. The nets are monitored continuously for 24 hours to ensure that turtles caught do not drown. Data recorded for turtles captured include straight carapace length and width, curved carapace length and width, weight, overall health, and results of eye examinations to check for sickness or viruses. The turtles are marked with a metal tag on each front flipper (National Band and Tag Company, Newport, Kentucky) and released as soon as possible. The data are stored centrally in La Paz and analyzed on regional and local scales to determine if the number of turtles captured per 100 m of nets per hour is changing over time, and whether the animals that are being recaptured are growing (López-Castro et al. 2010).

Only Cabo Pulmo has participated in the regional peninsula-wide in-water monitoring effort coordinated by the Sea Turtle Network. However, because it is a marine park, the data collection method—using nets—is not permitted. Because of this, some scuba monitoring of the sea turtles has been conducted in the national marine park. In 2003, three turtles were identified through 11 dives between February and September, averaging nine hours to "catch" a turtle (Grupo Tortuguero 2003).

Local fishers are very knowledgeable about turtle locations and behavior in the water. In the summer of 2009, a survey was administered by the authors to 13 fishers, all males, the majority of whom were not originally from Cabo San Lucas, but from other parts of Mexico. When asked where they had seen turtles, most replied on the Pacific side of the municipality and mentioned sites near beaches where nesting areas are protected. These included Faro Viejo, San Cristóbal, Los Arcos, Las Margaritas, Migriño, Pescadero, and Cerros de Arena, although they also mentioned some beaches on the Gulf of California. It is recommended that the survey be repeated at the marina of La Playita, located east of the estuary at San José del Cabo. The fishers of the *panga* fleet there should be able to identify hot spots of in-water activity of sea turtles around the tip of the peninsula and toward Cabo Pulmo.

Migrations

Almost all species of sea turtles migrate long distances between their nesting, mating, and foraging grounds. Understanding the way in which the different developmental and reproductive areas are connected and how changes in the environment affect the movements of sea turtles is essential for the conservation of sea turtles (Webster et al. 2002; DiBacco et al. 2006; Marra et al. 2006).

The first long-distance migration occurs after the hatchlings emerge from the nest and enter the sea. They use ocean current systems to reach the open ocean and it is assumed that these turtles spend most of their time in fronts or convergence areas, where two different water masses accumulate large amounts of food available for turtles and other organisms (Luschi et al. 2003). After a few years, the juveniles typically migrate from their oceanic foraging grounds to shallow foraging grounds (Bolten 2003) where they stay until they reach sexual maturity (depending on the species, from nine to 25 years) and then return to their nesting grounds to reproduce.

Research has shown that Baja California Sur's Eastern Pacific green turtles travel from their shallow foraging grounds in the Pacific and the Gulf of California coasts of the peninsula to one of the species' main nesting beaches in Michoacán, Mexico (Nichols 2003; Esquivel-Bobadilla 2007). Records of green turtles in Cabo Pulmo (Grupo Tortuguero 2003) suggest that either green turtles feeding in the northern Gulf of California stop at this area on their way to the nesting beaches in Michoacán, or that Cabo Pulmo is also used as a foraging ground. A well-established monitoring and tagging program is needed to resolve these questions.

According to the Association for the Protection of the Environment and the Marine Turtle in Southern Baja (ASUPMATOMA) and data from the Municipal Program for the Protection of Sea Turtles in Cabo San Lucas, occasional nesting of green (black) turtles in Los Cabos occurs (Soares et al. 2009), which suggests that some foraging areas of these turtles are also connected to Baja California Sur; whether these are within the municipality of Los Cabos or another region is still unknown.

Besides reports of underwater sightings of loggerheads in the Cabo Pulmo area (Grupo Tortuguero 2003), nothing is known of their migratory pathways between Los Cabos and their nesting and foraging grounds. However, these grounds are likely located in Japan (Nichols et al. 2000).

Leatherback turtles nest on the sandy beaches of Los Cabos on both Pacific and Gulf of California coasts (González et al. 2001; Sarti 2004; Heredia et al. 2006). The route that hatchlings follow after they emerge from their nests is still unknown. Nonetheless, due to satellite telemetry tags of nesting females, it is known that immediately after laying their eggs, females migrate south to the coasts of Chile to foraging grounds (Morreale et al. 1996; Eckert and Sarti 1997). Bycatch data of fisheries in Chile and Mexico suggest that turtles usually travel south and north in a band that is between 30 and 150 km off the coast. Consequently, international efforts are being directed toward reducing the number of vessels in this band to prevent collisions and eliminating fishing gear along this corridor to avoid the capture of these endangered species (Sarti 2004).

As for the olive ridley turtle, genetic analyses of the nesting colony of Baja California indicate that there is a connection between the nesting colony in Los Cabos and Sinaloa (López-Castro et al. 2005). However, the location of foraging grounds of young olive ridleys is still unknown. More studies are necessary to determine the migratory pathways of hatchlings born in Los Cabos and of those born in other places but that come to nest in Los Cabos region. According to the representative from ASUPMATOMA, a few records of young olive ridleys (<25 cm) stranded in Los Cabos and on the coast of Sinaloa (Zavala-Norzagaray et al. 2005) suggest the presence of at least two foraging grounds—one close to the coast of Los Cabos in the Pacific and the other near the coast of Guasave in the Gulf of California.

Nichols (2003) describes a foraging area of immature and mature olive ridley turtles off Bahía Magdalena that is rich with pelagic red crabs *(Pleuroncodes planipes)*. The migratory pathways that these young turtles follow are still a mystery. This underlines the need for long-term monitoring of sea turtles and identification of foraging grounds in the area of Los Cabos.

Ecotourism

This study recommends that as an immediate step, officials take advantage of the existing tourism professionals in the Los Cabos municipality to collect in-water data on sea turtle sightings. These professionals include diving and snorkeling operators, sportfishers, sailboat companies, and whale watching tours. They could be trained to gather data on the number and location of turtles sighted and also report on tagged animals. This would be possible during routine sportfishing trips, for example. Sailfish, marlin, dorado, tuna, snook, and wahoo fishing seasons are between the months of June and November. Striped marlin, jacks and pompano, sierra, yellowtail, cabrilla, and snapper sportfishing is during the spring season, starting around February and lasting until July (http://www.mexfish.com/ [accessed 2009]). Thus, sportfishing takes place throughout the year. Reports from the combination of whale watching, sportfishing, and turtle monitoring could encourage more ecofriendly practices, and also encourage participation in the long-term monitoring programs. It will be important to promote this idea as a complement and not a conflict with sportfishing practices because the sportfishing industry already creates nearly 25,000 jobs and represents US$1.125 billion in total economic activity for Los Cabos (Southwick Associates et al. 2008).

To understand the fishers' willingness to participate in monitoring activities, 13 individuals were interviewed in the summer of 2009. It was apparent that educational programs in Los Cabos by the nonprofit ASUPMATOMA and the Municipal Program for the Protection of Sea Turtles in Cabo San Lucas are working. Several fishers mentioned they had learned from their children the value of turtles or have been to a turtle camp themselves. Of the 13 interviewed, 92% said they could recognize the different species, and named an average of 2.3 species (out of five in the waters off Los Cabos) that they could identify. Only one of the subjects indicated that he could not identify the turtle species from the boat and that he had not seen turtles while engaged in trips with tourists. When asked if they would help monitor turtles through a catch-and-release program, 88% replied yes. When asked how much they would charge to participate, two fishers responded US$20/day or just expenses, but 54% responded they would do so as volunteers.

The answers indicate a great potential for low-cost collaboration between fishers and monitoring programs. Local nonprofits could train selected fishers and place them under a permit from the Ministry of Environment and Natural Resources (Secretaría de Medio Ambiente y Recursos Naturales–SEMARNAT), so that during routine trips and perhaps during off-season whale watching and sportfishing, the captains could take tourists out for fees to search the waters for turtles, net them, photograph them, and record the location, tag number, and species.

Another long-term solution is to promote new turtle ecotourism in Los Cabos. Interest in turtles is evident as tourists already participate in the release of hatchlings on the beaches in Los Cabos (see Chapter 9 by Graciela Tiburcio Pintos and Raquel Briseño Dueñas). Successful tourist turtle camps exist all over Mexico (see Comunidad Ecológica Campesina of El Mazunte and Parque Nacional Lagunas de Chacagua on the coast of Oaxaca; the Parque Ecoarqueológico of Xcaret and Xcacel beach in Quintana Roo; Maruata, Colola, and Mexiquillo beaches in Michoacán; and Mayan Palace Hotels in Acapulco, Guerrero, and Cancún, Quintana Roo, along the hotel zone, among others) (Nieva 2009). Whale watching accounted for 7.5% of the ecotourism revenue in a Mexico-wide survey of ecobusinesses (Secretaría de Turismo 2001).

The 13 interviewed fishers were asked about the potential to start sea turtle tourism in Los Cabos. All of the subjects are fishing guides for tourists or involved in other tourism activities, such as whale watching tours. Some engage in other activities in their free time, including fishing for their own consumption, mechanic work, or diving instruction. All fishers work 12 months of the year. The average cost for whale watching tours was $39 per person for two hours: of this, the captain's share was about 66%. With respect to turtle watching as a tourism activity, 85% indicated that they would like to offer turtle viewing since they already provide whale watching. Although one commented that there is no guarantee of seeing turtles, another said that he sees up to 20 in a day. When asked how much they would charge for a tour that included snorkeling with turtles, because it was a novel idea, answers ranged from $30 to $100 per person and averaged $54. Other comments included "you cannot do it," "I am against it," and "no answer."

A conclusion of this research is that turtle watching via kayak and *panga* combined with snorkeling is an opportunity for a new niche market in Los Cabos. During these trips, tourists could help gather data on turtles, including photographs, number of individuals, locations, species, behaviors, percent that are tagged, and what the turtles were observed eating. Explicitly and directly connecting turtle tourism with conservation activities and best practices is fundamentally important for long-term protection of the species (www.seeturtles.org [accessed 2009]).

Future Research

In other areas, several methods have been used to estimate population numbers and to identify migratory pathways of adult and sub-adult sea turtles. Possibilities for Los Cabos include genetic marking (Bowen and Karl 1997; Encalada et al. 1998; Lahanas et al. 1998; Dutton et al. 1999), and satellite telemetry (Balazs 1993; Nichols et al. 2000; Polovina et al. 2000; Bentivegna 2002; Peckam et. al 2007). Potential methods for aerial surveys, mark and recapture, and scuba/snorkel transects are discussed in detail below.

Aerial transects are a fast but costly way to obtain a quick population estimate during a fixed period of time (Buckland et al. 1993). Aerial surveys have already been performed off the Pacific Coast of the Baja California peninsula north of Los Cabos as part of a binational effort to survey nearly 7,000 km of coastline with offshore extents to 170 km in 2005. Of the more than 400 turtles recorded, loggerheads were the most prevalent (77% of all sightings), followed by the olive ridleys (12%), green (7%), and leatherback (<1 %) turtles. Approximately 4% of all recorded turtles were not identified (Seminoff et al. 2007).

In-water mark-and-recapture methods are also commonly used to estimate turtle populations. First, individuals of a turtle population are captured and tagged with metal tags during one time period. Then, turtles are captured randomly during a second period. The numbers captured during both periods permit estimation of the population size (Gerrodette and Tayler 1999).

Scuba and snorkeling transects require a marked area (usually with stakes or ropes) and can provide more information than other methods. Researchers can identify the species, sex, size, and behavior of the turtles (Roos et al. 2005). This method, however, does not cover large areas.

Protection

Data collected on zones of foraging, mating, and migrations could lead to the identification of hot spots of turtle activity. Once these areas have been documented, they can be legally declared refuges and be further protected from illegal fishing, poaching, or habitat damage. Mixed uses with sportfishing operators are possible using speed control, seasonal closures, and regulating fishing gear in the refuges versus a complete fishing moratorium. Mexico already has laws to facilitate the creation of refuges. The General Wildlife Law (SEMARNAT 2008), the General Law of Ecological Equilibrium and Environmental Protection (SEMARNAP 1988), the Fisheries Law (Secretaría de Pesca 2001), and the Federal Law of the Sea (1986) allow for the creation of "safe zones" for foraging habitats.

Recommendations

As detailed throughout this chapter, major threats to migrant sea turtles in the region of Los Cabos include bycatch; direct fishing for consumption; foraging habitat destruction; boat collisions; and contamination that is part of the anthropogenic factors that directly impact turtles and include plastic ingestion, entanglement in fishing nets, hook ingestion, and contact with pesticides and heavy metals that accumulate in their tissues. To combat these threats and to understand the state of the population of sea turtles in the municipality, following is a summary of the conservation and research recommendations presented in the body of this chapter:
- Bycatch and direct fishing. Education for fishers is of critical importance to reduce poaching. Citizens such as fishing cooperative leaders can be deputized by PROFEPA to help enforce

existing laws and promote adoption of more responsible fishing techniques.
- Boat collisions. Implement no-fishing zones in the most important areas during the peak months of the olive ridley and leatherback nesting/mating season (August through approximately February) as well as marine vessel speed regulations.
- Foraging habitat destruction and contamination. Foraging sites need to be mapped and characterized. The spread of invasive seagrass and algal species needs to be controlled, trash cans should be placed on beaches, and locals and tourists need to be educated on keeping trash out of the water. Regulations and practices on the use of nonorganic agricultural products in the region should be continued.
- Monitoring. The municipality should begin a formal in-water population monitoring program using the protocol of the Sea Turtle Network of the Californias. More casual monitoring can be achieved by training sportfishers, whale watchers, and scuba operators to report on sea turtles sighted during their routine trips.
- Sea turtle ecotourism. Efforts to create new turtle ecotourism sectors should be promoted by the municipality, including training locals to identify turtles, record data, and provide natural history background on the different species.
- Research. New research should focus on determining migratory routes. Methods for this research can include use of genetic markers, biotelemetry, aerial surveys, mark and recapture, and scuba/snorkel transects. Routine boat trips by sportfishing, whale watching, and scuba/snorkeling operators can be utilized to gather data on numbers, sizes, species, and locations of turtles in the water. Data collection should be centralized and summaries shared regularly.
- Protection. Data collected could lead to the identification of hot spots of turtle activity. Once these areas have been documented, they can be legally declared refuges and be further protected from illegal fishing, poaching, or habitat damage. Mixed uses with sportfishing operators are possible using speed control, seasonal closures, and regulating fishing gear in the refuges versus a complete fishing moratorium.

Conclusions

Sea turtles live on the edge of extinction, spend a lot of time at the edge of land and sea, and, in the case of the Los Cabos nesting turtles, occupy the northernmost edge of the nesting grounds for their species (Fritts et al. 1982). Climate change may directly affect sea turtles by changing sea surface temperatures, eroding beaches, and pushing nesting grounds to warmer or cooler latitudes (Hawkes et al. 2007). Therefore, it is very important to monitor these populations over the next few years. If conservation is to be effective in Los Cabos, not only must the nesting beaches be monitored and protected, but also the migrating, foraging, and mating animals. A major effort using local knowledge and cooperation would be needed to fill in the data gaps and effectively protect the turtles in the municipality's waters.

References

Balazs, G. H. 1994. "Homeward bound: satellite tracking of Hawaiian green turtles from nesting beaches to foraging pastures." Proceedings of the Thirteenth Annual Symposium on Sea Turtle Biology and Conservation. U.S. Dep. Commer., *NOAA Tech. Memo. NOAA-TM-NMFS-SEFSC-341*, p. 205-208.

Bentivegna, F. 2002. "Intra-Mediterranean Migrations of Loggerhead Sea Turtles *(Caretta Caretta)* Monitored by Satellite Telemetry." *Marine Biology.* 141, no. 4: 795-800.

Bjorndal, K.A. 1997. "Foraging Ecology and Nutrition of Sea Turtles." Pp. 199–231 in *The Biology of Sea Turtles*, P. L. Lutz and J. A. Musick, eds. Boca Raton, FL: CRC Press.

Bjorndal, K. A., and A. B. Bolten. 2008. "Annual Variation in Source Contributions to a Mixed Stock: Implications for Quantifying Connectivity." *Molecular Ecology* 17: 2185–2193.

Bjorndal, K. A., and J. B. C. Jackson. 2003. "Roles of Sea Turtles in Marine Ecosystems: Reconstructing the Past." Pp. 259–273 in *The Biology of Sea Turtles, Volume II*, P. L. Lutz, J. A. Musick, and J. Wyneken, eds. Boca Raton, FL: CRC Press.

Bolker, B. M., T. Okuyama, K. A. Bjorndal, and A. B. Bolten. 2007. "Incorporating Multiple Mixed Stocks in Mixed Stock Analysis: 'Many to Many' Analysis." *Molecular Ecology* 16: 685–695.

Bolten, A. B. 2003. "Variation in Sea Turtle Life Patterns: Shallow vs. Oceanic Developmental Stages." Pp. 243–257 in *The Biology of Sea Turtles, Volume II*, P. L. Lutz, J. A. Musick, and J. Wyneken, eds. Boca Raton, FL: CRC Press.

Bowen, B.W., and Karl, S. A. 1997. "Population genetics, phylogeography, and molecular evolution" in P.L. Lutz and J.A. Musick eds. *The Biology of Sea Turtles*. CRC Marine Science Series, CRC Press, Inc., Boca Raton, FL.

Buckland, S, ed. 1993. *Distance Sampling: Estimating Abundance of Biological Populations*. London: Chapman & Hall.

Centro Estatal de Información (CEI). 2006. "Municipios de Baja California Sur." *Cuaderno de Datos Básicos*. La Paz, BCS: Centro Estatal de Información.

Diario Oficial de la Federación. 1990. *Acuerdo que establece veda para todas las especies y subespecies de tortugas marinas en aguas de jurisdicción nacional de los litorales del océano Pacífico, Golfo de México y Mar Caribe*. (31 May): 21–22. Mexico, DF: Diario Oficial de la Federación.

DiBacco, C., L. A. Levin, and E. Sala. 2006. "Connectivity in Marine Ecosystems: The Importance of Larval and Spore Dispersal." Pp 184–212 in *Conservation Biology 14. Connectivity Conservation*, K. R. Crooks and M. Sanjayan, eds. New York: Cambridge University Press.

Dutton, P. H., Bowen, B. W., Owens, D. W., Barragan, A., and Davis, S. K. 1999. "Global Phylogeography of the Leatherback Turtle *(Dermochelys Coriacea)*." *Journal of Zoology*. 248, no. 3: 397-409.

Eckert, K. L., and F. A. Abreu Grobois. 2001. *Conservación de tortugas marinas en la región del Gran Caribe – Un diálogo para el manejo regional efectivo*. WIDECAST, UICN/CSE Grupo Especialista en Tortugas Marinas (MTSG), WWF and Programa Ambiental del Caribe del PNUMA.

Eckert, R. 1990. *Fisiología animal: Mecanismos y adaptaciones*. Spain: McGraw Hill International.

Eckert, S. A., and M. L. Sarti. 1997. "Distant Fisheries Implicated in the Loss of the World's Largest Leatherback Nesting Population." *Mar. Tur. News*. 78: 2–7.

Ehrhart, L. M., and L. H. Ogren. 1999. "Studies in Foraging Habitats: Capturing and Handling Turtles." Pp. 61–64 in *Research and Management Techniques for Conservation of Sea Turtles*, K. L. Eckert, K. A. Bjorndal, F. A. Abreu-Grobois, and M. Donnelly, eds. IUCN/SSC Marine Turtle Specialist Group Publication No. 4.

Encalada, S. E., Lahanas, P. N., Bjorndal, K. A., Bolten, A. B., Miyamoto, M. M., and Bowen, B. W. 1996. "Phylogeography and population structure of the Atlantic and Mediterranean green turtle Chelonia mydas: a mitochondrial DNA control region sequence assessment." *Molecular Ecology* 5:473-483.

Esquivel-Escobilla, S. 2007. "Identificación de las poblaciones de origen de las tortugas prietas muestreadas en Bahía Magdalena, B.C.S., México (1995–2005)." Bachelor's thesis in sciences, Universidad Autónoma de Baja California Sur.

Frick, M., A. Panagopoulou, A. F. Rees, and K. Williams, compilers. 2006. *Book of Abstracts. Twenty-Sixth Annual Symposium on Sea Turtle Biology and Conservation. International Sea Turtle Society, Athens, Greece.* http://www.nmfs.noaa.gov/pr/pdfs/species/turtlesymposium2006_abstracts.pdf.

Fritts T.H., M. L. Stinson, and R. Marquez. 1982. "Status of Sea Turtle Nesting in Southern Baja California, Mexico." *Bull. South Calif. Acad. Sci.* 81:51–60.

Gardner, S. C., S. L. Fitzgerald, B.Acosta-Vargas, and L. Méndez-Rodríguez. 2006. "Heavy Metal Accumulation in Four Species of Sea Turtles from the Baja California Peninsula, Mexico." *Biometals* 19 (1): 91–99.

Gerrodette, T., and B. Taylor. 1999. "Estimating Population Size." Pp. 61–64 in *Research and Management Techniques for Conservation of Sea Turtles*, K. L. Eckert, K. A. Bjorndal, F. A. Abreu-Grobois, and M. Donnelly, eds. IUCN/SSC Marine Turtle Specialist Group Publication No. 4.

González, E., R. Pinal, D. Pérez, and S. Mirish. 2001. Informe del programa de investigación y protección de la tortuga marina, y educación ambiental en el estado de Baja California Sur. Temporada 2000–2001. ASUPMATOMA, A.C. p 29. In: Grupo Tortuguero de las Californias (2003) Monitoreo a largo plazo de la población de las tortugas marinas a lo largo de la Península de Baja California. Resultados del primer y segundo año. www.grupotortuguero.org/files/file/ 160Resultados.pdf.

Hawkes, L. A., A. C. Broderick, M. H. Godfrey, and B. J. Godley. 2007. "Investigating the Potential Impacts of Climate Change on a Marine Turtle Population." *Global Change Biology* 13: 1–10.

Hemminga, M., and C. M. Duarte. 2000. *Seagrass Ecology*. New York: Cambridge University Press.

Heredia, A., A. Leal, E. González, and R. Pinal. 2006. Informe final del programa de investigación y protección de tortugas marinas, y educación ambiental en el Estado de Baja California Sur. Temporada 2005–2006. Cabo San Lucas, BCS: ASUPMATOMA, A.C.

International Union for Conservation of Nature (IUCN). 2009. IUCN Red List of Threatened Species. Version 2009.1. (Accessed 21 July 2009), www.iucnredlist.org.

Lahanas, P. N., Bjorndal, K. A., Bolten, A. B., Encalada, S. E., Miyamoto, M. M., Valverde, R. A., and Bowen, B. W. 1998. "Genetic composition of a green turtle feeding ground population: evidence for multiple origins." *Mar. Biol.* 130:345-352.

Lewison, R. L., L. B. Crowder, A. J. Read, and S. A. Freeman. 2004. "Understanding Impacts of Fisheries Bycatch on Marine Megafauna." *Tree* 19: 598–604.

López-Castro, M. C., and A. Rocha-Olivares. 2005. "The Panmixia Paradigm of Eastern Pacific Olive Ridley Turtles Revised: Consequences for Their Conservation and Evolutionary Biology." *Molecular Ecology* 14: 3325–3334.

López-Castro, M. C., V. Koch, A. Mariscal-Loza, and W. J. Nichols. 2010. "Long-term Monitoring of Black Turtles Chelonia Mydas at Coastal Foraging Areas Off the Baja California Peninsula." *Endangered Species Research* 11: 35–45.

López-Mendilaharsu, M., S. C. Gardner, R. Riosmena-Rodríguez, and J. A. Seminoff. 2005. "Identifying Critical Foraging Habitats of the Green Turtle (*Chelonia mydas*) along the Pacific Coast of the Baja California Peninsula, Mexico." *Aquatic Conservation: Marine and Freshwater Ecosystems* 15 (3): 259–269.

Luschi, P., Hays, G. C., and Papi, F. 2003. "A review of long-distance movements by marine turtles, and the possible role of ocean currents." *Oikos* 103, no. 2: 293-302.

Márquez, R. 2002. *Las tortugas marinas y nuestro tiempo. La ciencia para todos*. México, DF: Fondo de Cultura Económica.

Marra, P. P., D. R. Norris, S. M. Haig, M. Webster, and J. A. Royle. 2006. "Migratory Connectivity." Pp. 157–183 in *Conservation Biology 14. Connectivity Conservation*, K. R. Crooks and M. Sanjayan, eds. Cambridge University Press.

McDermid, K. J., B. Stuercke, and G. H. Balazs. 2007. "Nutritional Composition of Marine Plants in Diet of the Green Sea Turtle (*Chelonia mydas*) in the Hawaiian Islands." *Bull. Mar. Sci.* 81(1): 55–71.

Miller, J. D. 1997. "Reproduction in Sea Turtles." Pp. 137–163 in *The Biology of Sea Turtles*, P. L. Lutz and J. A. Musick, eds. Boca Raton, FL: CRC Press.

Milton, S. L., and P. L. Lutz. 1998. "Low Extracellular Dopamine Levels are Maintained in the Anoxic Turtle Brain." *J. Cereb. Blood Flow Metab.* 18: 803–807.

Moran, K., and K. Bjorndal. 2005. "Simulated Green Turtle Grazing Affects Structure and Productivity of Seagrass Pastures." *Marine Ecology Progress Series* 305: 235–247.

Morreale, S. J., E. A. Standora, J. R. Spotila, and F. V. Paladino. 1996. "Migration Corridor for Sea Turtles." *Nat.* 384: 319–320.

Morreale, S. J., P. T. Plotkin, D. J. Shaver, and H. J. Kalb. 2007. "Adult Migration and Habitat Utilization: Ridley Turtles in Their Element." Pp. 213–229 in *Biology and Conservation of Ridley Sea Turtles*, P. T. Plotkin, ed. Baltimore, MD: The Johns Hopkins University Press.

Musick, J. A., and C. J. Limpus. 1997. "Habitat Utilization and Migration in Juvenile Sea Turtles." Pp. 51–81 in *The Biology of Sea Turtles*, P. L. Lutz and J. A. Musick, eds. Boca Raton, FL: CRC Press.

Nieva, A. 2009. *Potencial del ecoturismo en campamentos tortugueros de México*. Sea Turtle Resource Guide. (Accessed 6 August 2009), http://www.planeta.com/planeta/99/0999tortugas.html.

Nájera-Hernández, H. A. 2007. "Diagnóstico ambiental de la región costera de Cabo del Este, Municipio de Los Cabos, B. C. S., México." Thesis, Universidad Autónoma de Baja California Sur, La Paz, BCS.

Nichols, W. J. 2003. "Biology and Conservation of the Sea Turtles of the Baja California Peninsula, Mexico." Ph.D. dissertation, Dept. of Wildlife and Fisheries Science, University of Arizona, Tuscon, AZ, USA.

Nichols, W. J., A. Resendiz, J. A. Seminoff, and B. Resendiz. 2000. "Transpacific Migration of a Loggerhead Turtle Monitored by Satellite Telemetry." *Bulletin of Marine Science* 67: 937–947.

Peckham S. H., D. M. Diaz, A. Walli, G. Ruiz, and L. B. Crowder. 2007. "Small-scale Fisheries Bycatch Jeopardizes Endangered Pacific Loggerhead Turtles." *PLoS ONE* 2 (10): e1041. doi:10.1371/journal.pone.0001041

Perés, I. F. R. 1997. *Bioquímica de los microorganismos.* México: Editorial Reverté.

Plotkin, P. 2003. "Adult Migrations and Habitat Use." Pp. 225–241 in *The Biology of Sea Turtles, Volume II*, P. L. Lutz, J. A. Musick, and J. Wyneken, eds. Boca Raton, FL: CRC Press.

Polovina, J. J., Kobayashi, D. R., Parker, D. M., Seki, M. P., and Balazs, G. H. 2000. "Turtles on the Edge: Movement of Loggerhead Turtles *(Caretta Caretta)* Along Oceanic Fronts, Spanning Longline Fishing Grounds in the Central North Pacific, 1997–1998." *Fisheries Oceanography.* 9, no. 1: 71-82.

Riosmena-Rodríguez, R. 2009. Personal communication with the authors. Programa de Investigación en Botánica Marina, Departamento de Biología Marina, Universidad Autónoma de Baja California Sur, La Paz BCS.

Rincon-Díaz, M. P., and C. J. Rodríguez-Zárate. 2004. "Caracterización de las playas de anidación y zonas de alimentación de tortugas marinas en el Archipiélago de San Bernardo, Caribe Colombiano." *Bol. Invest. Mar. Cost* 33: 137–158.

Roos, D., A. D. Pelletier, S. Ciccione, M. Taquet, and G. Hughes. 2005. "Aerial and Snorkeling Census Techniques for Estimating Green Turtle Abundance on Foraging Areas: A Pilot Study in Mayotte Island (Indian Ocean)." *Aquat. Living Resour.* 18: 193–198.

Sarti, L. 2004. *Situación actual de la tortuga laúd* (Dermochelys coriacea) *en el Pacífico Mexicano y medidas para su recuperación y conservación.* México, DF: SEMARNAT.

Secretaría de Medio Ambiente, Recursos Naturales y Pesca (SEMARNAP). 1988. Ley General del Equilibrio Ecológico y la Protección al Ambiente. (28 January). México, DF: Diario Oficial de la Federación.

Secretaría de Medio Ambiente y Recursos Naturales (SEMARNAT). 1991. Reglamento para el uso y aprovechamiento del mar territorial, vías navegables, playas, zona federal marítima terrestre y terrenos ganados al mar. (21 August). México, DF: Diario Oficial de la Federación.

Secretaría de Medio Ambiente y Recursos Naturales (SEMARNAT). 2002. Protección ambiental-Especies nativas de México de flora y fauna silvestres. NOM-059-ECOL-2001. (6 March). México, DF: Diario Oficial de la Federación.

Secretaría de Medio Ambiente y Recursos Naturales (SEMARNAT). 2008. Ley General de Vida Silvestre. (3 July). México, DF: Diario Oficial de la Federación.

Secretaría de Pesca. 2001. Ley de Pesca. (25 July). México, DF: Diario Oficial de la Federación.

Secretaría de Turismo (SECTUR). 2001. *Ecotourism in Mexico: Strategic Feasibility Study of the Ecotourism Segment in Mexico.* (Accessed 29 July 2009), http://www.sectur.gob.mx/work/sites/securing/resources/LocalContent/ 8980/2/Ecoturismo.pdf.

Seminoff J. A., S. H. Peckham, T. Eguchi, A. L. Sarti-Martinez, R. Rangel, K. Forney, W. J. Nichols, E. Ocampo-Olvera, and P. H. Dutton. 2007. "Loggerhead Turtle Density and Abundance along the Pacific Coast of the Baja California Peninsula, Mexico Determined Through Aerial Surveys: A Preliminary Assessment." Pp. 23–28 in *North Pacific Loggerhead Sea Turtle Expert Workshop Report.* Honolulu, HW: Western Pacific Regional Fishery Management Council.

Soares, D., G. Tiburcio Pintos, E. Acevedo Ruiz, V. Castillo Leggs, P. Marquez Almanza, J. C. Marron Fiol, R. Marron Fiol, S. Maxey, and K. Comer Santos. 2009. "Predicted Sea Level Rise Impacts on the Nesting Beaches of Olive Ridley Turtles in Los Cabos, Mexico." Report of the 11th Annual Meeting of the Grupo Tortuguero de las Californias, A.C., 30 January-1 February, Loreto, BCS, México.

Southwick, Rob, Russell Nelson, and José Antonio Arean Martínez. 2008. *The Economic Contributions of Anglers to the Los Cabos Economy*. Commissioned by the Billfish Foundation. Southwick Associates, Inc., Fernandina Beach, FL; Nelson Resources Consulting, Inc., Oakland Park, FL; and FIRMUS Consulting, Mexico City. (Accessed 29 July 2009), http://www.billfish.org/images/uploads/TBF%20Cabo%20Economics%20Report-%20English.pdf.

Talavera-Saenz A. L. 2006. "Metales pesados en macroalgas, pastos marinos y órganos selectos de la tortuga prieta Chelonia mydas agassizzi, en el Estero Banderitas, B.C.S., México." Thesis, Universidad Autónoma de Baja California Sur, Mexico.

Villegas-Nava, F. E. 2006. "Análisis nutricional de macroalgas y pastos asociados a la alimentación de tortuga prieta *Chelonia mydas agassizii* (Bocourt 1968), en Bahía Magdalena, B.C.S., México." Thesis, Universidad Autónoma de Baja California Sur, Mexico.

Villegas-Nava, F. E. 2009. "Principios sobre la fisiología alimenticia de la tortuga verde *Chelonia mydas*." Master's thesis, Universidad Autónoma de Baja California Sur, Mexico.

Wabnitz, C., and W. J. Nichols. 2010. "Plastic Pollution: An Ocean Emergency." *Marine Turtle Newsletter* 129: 1–4

Wallace, B. P., S. S. Heppell, R. L. Lewison, S. Kelez, and L. B. Crowder. 2008. "Reproductive Values of Loggerhead Turtles in Fisheries Bycatch Worldwide." *Journal of Applied Ecology* 45: 1076–1085.

Webster, M. S., P. P. Marra, S. M. Haig, S. Bensch, and R. T. Holmes. 2002. "Links between Worlds: Unraveling Migratory Connectivity." *Trends Ecol. Evol.* 17: 76–83.

Zavala-Norzagaray, A., R. Briseño-Dueñas, M. Ramos-Salazar, J. L. Contreras, I. Miranda, R. Ayon-Romo, and A. Garibaldi. 2005. "Primer registro de juveniles de tortuga golfina (*Lepidochelys olivacea*) en el municipio de Guasave, Sinaloa, Golfo de California, México." Book of Abstracts of the 9th Annual Meeting of Grupo Tortuguero de Las Californias. http://www.grupotortuguero.org/files/file/555GT9Abstracts.pdf.

6

Cetaceans of the Gulf of California's Southwest Coast

Jorge Urbán Ramírez, Gustavo Cárdenas Hinojosa, and Alejandro Gómez-Gallardo Unzueta

INTRODUCTION

Whales, dolphins, and porpoises, that is, cetaceans (order Cetacea), are subdivided into two suborders: cetaceans with whalebone or baleen (baleen whales) (mysticetes), comprising four families and 12 species; and cetaceans with teeth, or toothed whales (odontocetes), represented in the world by nine families and 69 species (Rice 1998; International Whaling Commission 2001a). The southwest coast of the Gulf of California (between Espíritu Santo Island and Cabo San Lucas) is the richest region of Mexico's coasts in cetacean species, and one of the richest in the world. It has three families (75% of the world) and seven species (58%) of mysticetes, and four families (44%) and 19 species (27%) of odontocetes. This great diversity is due to their different environments, with tropical waters in the summer, temperate waters in the winter, a narrow continental shelf that allows major depths near the coast, and high biomass productivity generated by the influence of winds, currents, and the continental slope. The specific richness in numbers and species of these cetaceans makes this area one of the regions with the greatest diversity of cetaceans in the world (Urbán et al. 2005; Urbán 2010) (Table 1).

Some of these species are very rare and have only been recorded sporadically. These include the North Pacific right whale *(Eubalaena japonica)*, the minke whale *(Balaenoptera acutorostrata)*, and Longman's

Table 1. Recorded Cetaceans in the Gulf of California's Southwest Coast and Their Conservation Status

The taxonomic order is according to Rice (1998) and the International Whaling Commission (2001). **IUCN: CR** = Critically Endangered, **EN** = Endangered, **VU** = Vulnerable, **LC** = Least Concern, **DD** = Data Deficient; **CITES: I** = Appendix I (most endangered species in the CITES list), **II** = Appendix II (species not necessarily in current danger but could be at risk if their trade is strictly regularized); **NOM-59-ECOL-2001: IDE** = Endangered, **SP** = Under Special Protection

Scientific Name[1]	Common Name[1]	Conservation Status		
		IUCN[2]	CITES[3]	NOM-59[4]
Balaenidae Family				
Eubalaena japonica	North Pacific right whale	EN	I	IDE
Eschrichtiidae Family				
Eschrichtius robustus	gray whale	LC	I	SP
Balaenopteridae Family				
Balaenoptera musculus	blue whale	EN	I	SP
Balaenoptera physalus	common fin whale	EN	I	SP
Balaenoptera edeni	Eden's whale	DD	I	SP
Physeteridae Family				
Physeter macrocephalus	sperm whale	VU	I	SP
Kogiidae Family				
Kogia breviceps	pygmy sperm whale	DD	II	SP
Kogia sima	dwarf sperm whale	DD	II	SP
Ziphiidae Family				
Ziphius cavirostris	Cuvier's beaked whale	DD	II	SP
Berardius bairdii	Baird's beaked whale	LC	I	SP
Indopacetus pacificus	Longman's beaked whale	LC/-[6]	I	SP
Mesoplodon peruvianus	pygmy beaked whale	DD	II	SP
Mesoplodon sp. A[5]	mesoplodont sp A	DD	II	SP
Delphinidae Family				
Steno bredanensis	rough-toothed dolphin	DD	II	SP
Tursiops truncatus	bottlenose dolphin	DD	II	SP
Stenella attenuata	pantropical spotted dolphin	LC	II	SP

Table 1. *(continued)*

Scientific Name[1]	Common Name[1]	Conservation Status		
		IUCN[2]	CITES[3]	NOM-59[4]
Delphinidae Family *(continued)*				
Stenella longirostris	spinner dolphin	LC	II	SP
Delphinus delphis	Short-beaked common dolphin	DD	II	SP
Delphinus capensis	Long-beaked common dolphin	DD	II	SP
Lagenorhynchus obliquidens	Pacific white-sided dolphin	DD	II	SP
Grampus griseus	Risso's dolphin	DD	II	SP
Pseudorca crassidens	false orca	DD	II	SP
Orcinus orca	orca	LC	II	SP
Globicephala macrorhynchus	short-finned pilot whale	LC	II	SP

[1] Scientific names according to Rice (1998) and the International Whaling Commission (2001).
[2] IUCN, 2008.
[3] From CITES 2009.
[4] From NOM-59-ECOL-2001 (DOF 2002).
[5] Unidentified species, possibly new species.

beaked whale *(Indopacetus pacificus)*. For others, like the blue whale, the region is important for their reproduction and feeding. The humpback whale is a special case because it is the most common cetacean in the area, especially from December to April, and this region is one of the most important in the Pacific Ocean for its breeding activities (Urbán et al. 2000; Urbán 2001; González-Peral 2006).

Current knowledge on the population status of these species in the Gulf of California is highly variable. Recently, some research has been initiated to learn more about the diversity, abundance, and community structure of cetaceans in the area (Cárdenas 2008; Salvadeo 2008; Troy 2008). There are practically no studies on the conservation status of cetacean populations in this region that identify and assess current and potential impacts of human activities such as fishing, tourism, maritime traffic, and pollution of ports.

All large whale species are under some protection category within the International Union for Conservation of Nature (IUCN), the Convention on International Trade in Endangered Species of Wild Fauna and Flora (CITES), the Mexican Official Norm NOM-059-SEMARNAT-2001, and the Endangered Species List (DOF 2002) (Table 1).

FIELD OBSERVATIONS

As part of various field explorations by the Marine Mammal Research Program of the Autonomous University of Baja California Sur, between January 2004 and March 2007, there were 1,042 sightings recorded of five species of mysticetes and nine of odontocetes in the area between the San Lorenzo Canal, northeast of the Bay of La Paz, and Cabo San Lucas. The humpback whale was the most common species, with 837 sightings. For odontocetes, the most common species was the dwarf sperm whale *(Kogia sima)*, with 45 sightings, followed by the sperm whale *(Physeter macrocephalus)*, with 28 (Tables 2 and 3).

Table 2. Number and Proportion of Sightings of Mysticetes

Species	Common Name	No.	Prop.
M. novaeangliae	Humpback whale	837	92%
Balaenopterido	Rorqual	25	3%
B. musculus	Blue whale	24	3%
B. edeni	Eden's whale	11	1%
E. robustus	Gray whale	8	1%
B. Physalus	Common fin whale	6	1%
	Total:	911	

Note: Sightings between January 2004 and March 2007.
Source: Authors.

Table 3. Number and Proportion of Sightings of Odontocetes

Species	Common Name	No.	Prop.
K. sima	Dwarf sperm whale	45	34%
P. macrocephalus	Sperm whale	28	21%
Z. cavirostris	Cuvier's beaked whale	20	15%
K. sp.	Unidentified Kogia	8	6%
G. griseus	Risso's dolphin	7	5%
G. macrorhynchus	Short-finned pilot whale	6	5%
O. orca	Orca	6	5%
K. breviceps	Pygmy sperm whale	6	5%
M. peruvianus	Pygmy mesoplodont	3	2%
P. crassidens	False orca	1	1%
Zifido n. i.	Unidentified beaked whale	1	1%
	Total:	**131**	

Note: Sightings between January 2004 and March 2007.
Source: Authors.

HABITAT

Upon analysis of the habitat preferred by the species sighted, the humpback and gray whales showed preference for cooler waters, unlike Eden's whale *(Balaenoptera edeni)* and the common fin whale *(B. physalus)*, which preferred warmer waters. As to the depth of the sighting areas, the gray whale preferred shallower waters, whereas the tropical and common whales preferred deeper waters (Table 4). With regard to odontocetes, the false killer whale *(Pseudorca crassidens)* showed greater inclination toward higher temperatures, while the sperm whales generally preferred less warm and deeper waters, as did the pygmy beaked whale *(Mesoplodon peruvianus)* (Table 5).

Table 4. Habitat Preferences (Surface Temperature and Depth) of Mysticetes
(μ = mean; sd = standard deviation)

Species	No.	Temp. (°C)		Depth (m)	
		μ	sd	μ	sd
M. novaeangliae	837	21.8	1	400.8	438.5
B. musculus	24	23.1	2.3	654.9	490.8
B. edeni	11	24.09	3.8	865.2	677.6
E. robustus	8	21.1	1.1	331	414.4
B. physalus	6	27.1	3	747.3	765.9

Note: Sightings between January 2004 and March 2007.
Source: Authors.

Table 5. Habitat Preferences (Surface Temperature and Depth) of Odontocetes
(μ = mean; sd = standard deviation)

Species	No.	Temp. (°C)		Depth (m)	
		μ	sd	μ	sd
K. sima	45	25.9	3.1	806.0	418.0
P. macrocephalus	28	24.7	2.6	1,822.4	848.1
Z. cavirostris	20	25.9	2.9	1,071.2	590.7
G. griseus	7	27.7	3.8	1,252.5	404.1
K. breviceps	6	25.8	2.9	1,058.3	334.3
O. orca	6	27.1	1.6	1,174.5	840.8
G. macrorhynchus	6	27.0	4.6	799.0	495.4
M. peruvianus	3	27.3	1.1	1,410.0	697.5
P. crassidens	1	31.0		1,150.0	

Source: Authors.

DISTRIBUTION IN SPACE AND TIME

2004

During the period of December 2003 to May 2004, the sightings of mysticetes were dominated by the humpback whale, as this is one of its winter aggregation areas. There were also some blue whales recorded. The sightings of odontocetes, in general, were scarce, but the greatest registration was for Cuvier's beaked whale *(Ziphius cavirostris)* and the sperm whale, in addition to several records of dwarf sperm whales. The distribution of cetaceans was near the coast and oriented toward the southern tip of the peninsula, from Cabo Pulmo to Cabo San Lucas, located mainly in not very deep waters and preferring not very warm waters (Table 6, Fig. 1).

Table 6. Cetacean Species Recorded in San Lorenzo Canal–Los Cabos, December 2003-May 2004 (Specifies Total Number of Recorded Individuals, Surface Temperature, and Average Depth)

Species	No. Ind.	T (°C)	Depth (m)
M. novaeangliae	531	21.5	378.1
Balaenopterido	6	21.3	701.3
Z. cavirostris	5	21.7	912.5
P. macrocephalus	4	20.9	925.0
B. musculus	3	20.6	854.0
K. sima	3	21.3	825.0
K. sp	1	21.2	1,050.0
K. breviceps	1	20.5	1,350.0

Source: Authors.

Figure 1. Sightings of Cetaceans, December 2003-May 2004

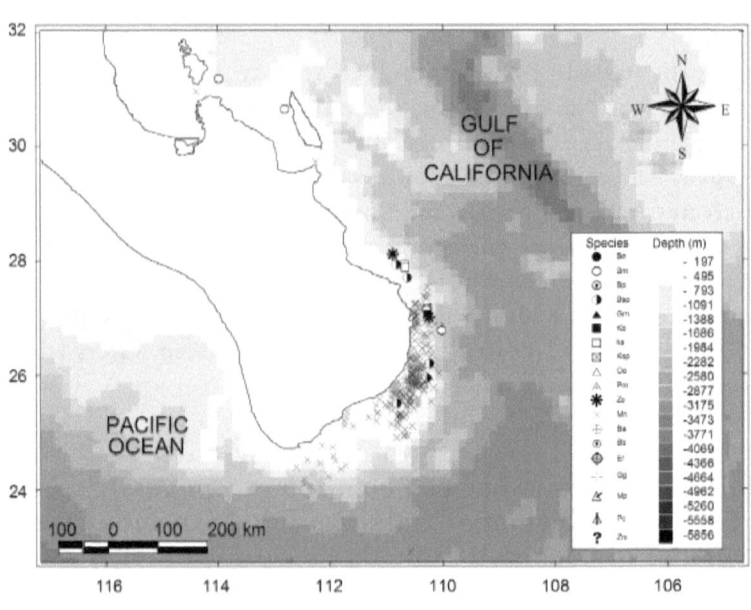

Source: Authors.

2005

During the period of December 2004 to May 2005, the diversity of mysticetes was poor, with the humpback whale most frequent. Odontocetes, however, showed high richness of species, among which are the Cuvier's beaked whale and the pygmy mesoplodont, although the pilot whale and sperm whale were sighted most frequently (Table 7, Fig. 2).

During the period of June to November 2005 from the San Lorenzo Canal to Los Cabos, there were few sightings of cetaceans. The few species of mysticetes present are those known as residents, while those of odontocetes are of warm waters (Table 8, Fig. 3).

Table 7. Cetacean Species Recorded, December 2004–May 2005 (Specifies Total Number of Recorded Individuals, Surface Temperature, and Average Depth)

Species	No. Ind.	T (°C)	Depth (m)
M. novaeangliae	477	22.4	402.8
Balaenopterido	8	24.0	983.3
G. macrorhynchus	57	25.5	940.5
P. macrocephalus	49	26.4	2,106.1
Z. cavirostris	22	26.6	1,175.0
O. orca	11	26.3	1,264.5
K. sima	8	25.8	675.6
K. breviceps	10	26.1	907.0
B. musculus	7	25.3	654.1
M. peruvianus	7	27.4	1,410.0
G. griseus	5	26.5	1,650.0
Kogia sp.	5	26.5	1,328.3
B. physalus	3	26.2	1,161.3
B. edeni	2	26.8	1,150.0
E. robustus	1	22.5	20.0
Zífido no ident.	1	25.0	237.0

Source: Authors.

Table 8. Cetacean Species Recorded, June-November 2005 (Specifies Total Number of Recorded Individuals, Surface Temperature, and Average Depth)

Species	No. Ind.	T (°C)	Depth (m)
G. macrorhynchus	77	31.0	741.5
B. physalus	4	30.5	487.5
K. sima	4	30.7	1,002.6
B. edeni	1	31.0	150.0
Kogia sp.	1	31.0	1,050.0

Source: Authors.

Figure 2. Sightings of Cetaceans, December 2004-May 2005

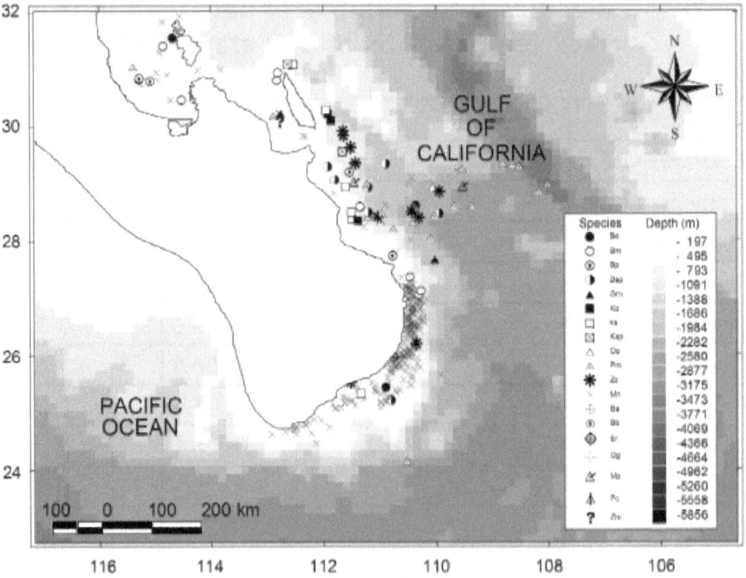

Source: Authors.

Figure 3. Sightings of Mysticetes and Odontocetes with respect to Depth, June-November 2005

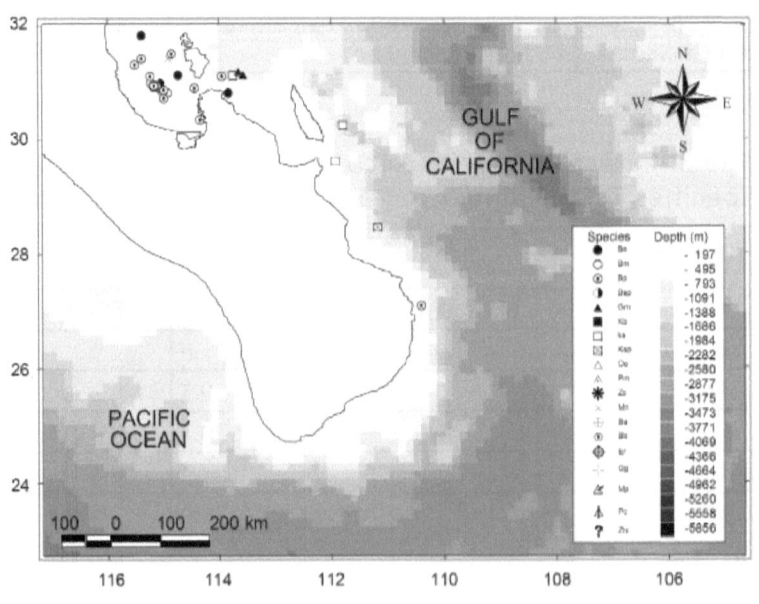

Source: Authors.

2006

During the period from December 2005 to May 2006, the records of humpback whales in the area were again very abundant, but other species of mysticetes were also found. Odontocetes were also diverse, though not very abundant. When the geographical distribution of cetaceans is considered, humpback whales were not distributed that far south, although this also had to do with a smaller sampling in the area compared to other years. Species characteristic of the zone are found again, such as the dwarf sperm whale and Cuvier's beaked whale (Table 9, Fig. 4).

During the period of June to November 2006, there were records of six whales, two tropical fin whales, and four unidentified species. Moreover, the presence of odontocetes during this period was very important in terms of abundance and diversity. Risso's dolphin *(Grampus griseus)* had a very frequent presence, followed by short-finned pilot whales *(Globicephala macrorhynchus)*, pygmy sperm whales, and killer whales *(Orcinus orca)*. The distribution of odontocetes was farther away from the coast and in deep waters, which may be related to their most common prey: mesopelagic squid and fish that prefer this type of environment (Table 10, Fig. 5).

Table 9. Cetacean Species Recorded, December 2005-May 2006 (Specifies Total Number of Recorded Individuals, Surface Temperature, and Average Depth)

Species	No. Ind.	T (°C)	Depth (m)
M. novaeangliae	328	21.5	373.0
K. sima	24	23.6	826.0
O. orca	13	26.6	1,264.3
G. griseus	10	20.0	1,400.0
B. edeni	9	21.7	778.1
E. robustus	9	20.6	414.6
B. musculus	8	22.8	803.7
Balaenopterido	8	22.2	1,125.5
Z. cavirostris	4	23.0	762.5
Kogia sp.	3	28.5	1,066.0
B. physalus	1	23.0	25.0

Source: Authors.

Figure 4. Sightings of Mysticetes and Odontocetes with respect to Depth, December 2005-May 2006

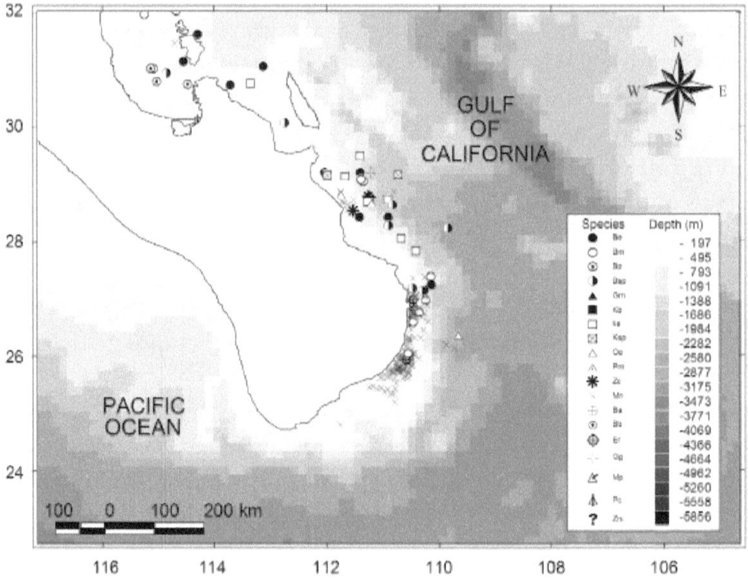

Source: Authors.

Table 10. Cetacean Species Recorded, June-November 2006 (Specifies Total Number of Recorded Individuals, Surface Temperature, and Average Depth)

Species	No. Ind.	T (°C)	Depth (m)
G. griseus	737	29.5	1,143
G. macrorhynchus	100	30.0	1,100
K. sima	30	28.0	870
P. crassidens	25	31.0	1,150
O. orca	12	30.5	725
Z. cavirostris	10	28.3	1,115
Balaenopterido	4	27.8	665
K. breviceps	3	28.0	1,139
B. edeni	2	28.0	1,621
Kogia sp.	1	30.0	667

Source: Authors.

Figure 5. Sightings of Mysticetes (top left) and Odontocetes (top right) with respect to Depth (bottom left), June-November 2006

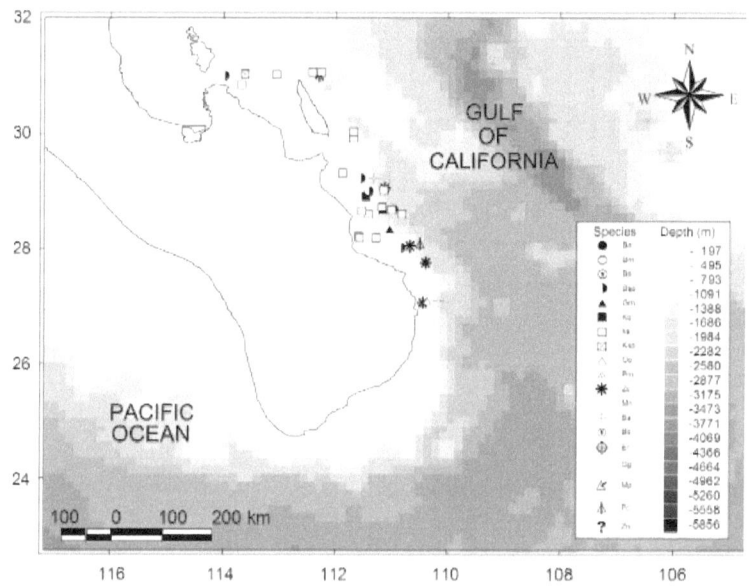

2007

During the period from January to March 2007, the humpback whale dominated sightings in this area in the winter season. However, a significant presence of the blue whale should also be noted. Among the odontocetes, the pilot whales and dwarf sperm whales were seen more frequently (it should be pointed out that there were records of two Cuvier's beaked whales). Again, the distribution of sightings of humpback whales was limited to the south, concentrating in not very deep regions between Cabo Pulmo and the lower parts of Punta Gorda, although there were some records in greater depths (Table 11, Fig. 6).

Table 11. Cetacean Species Recorded in the San Lorenzo Canal to Los Cabos, January-March 2007 (Specifies Total Number of Recorded Individuals, Surface Temperature, and Average Depth)

Species	No. Ind.	T (°C)	Depth (m)
M. novaeangliae	341	21.8	460.0
G. macrorhynchus	40	19.0	330.0
B. musculus	11	21.9	450.6
K. sima	11	22.6	649.2
P. macrocephalus	5	20.8	1,033.3
Z. cavirostris	2	22.0	750.0
E. robustus	1	22.0	140.0

Source: Authors.

Figure 6. Sightings of Mysticetes (top left) and Odontocetes (top right) with respect to Depth (bottom), January-March 2007

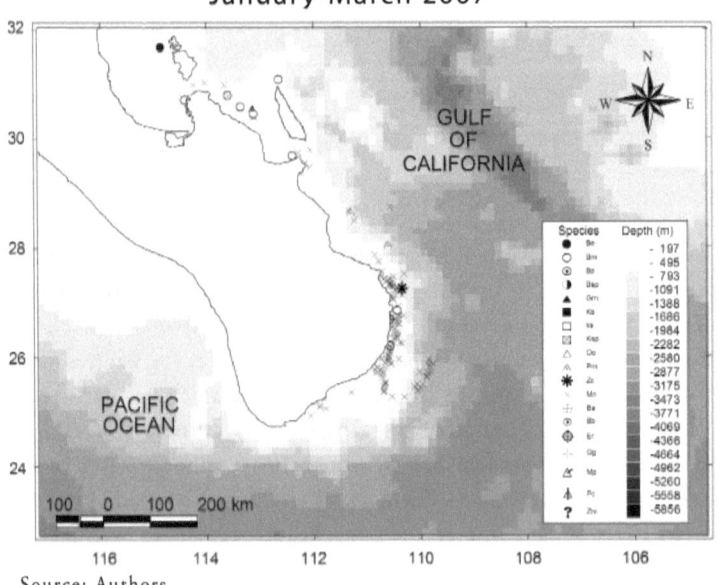

Source: Authors.

Seasonal Distribution

Winter

In order to understand the seasonal patterns of cetacean distribution in the study area, the records of sightings of each study area were grouped by season for the entire study period (2004–2007). The distribution of sightings of each species during winter clearly shows the predominance of the humpback whale, especially toward the southern end of this area, usually near the coast, in not very deep waters (Fig. 7).

Figure 7. Distribution of Winter Sightings for the San Lorenzo Canal-Los Cabos Area, 2004–2007

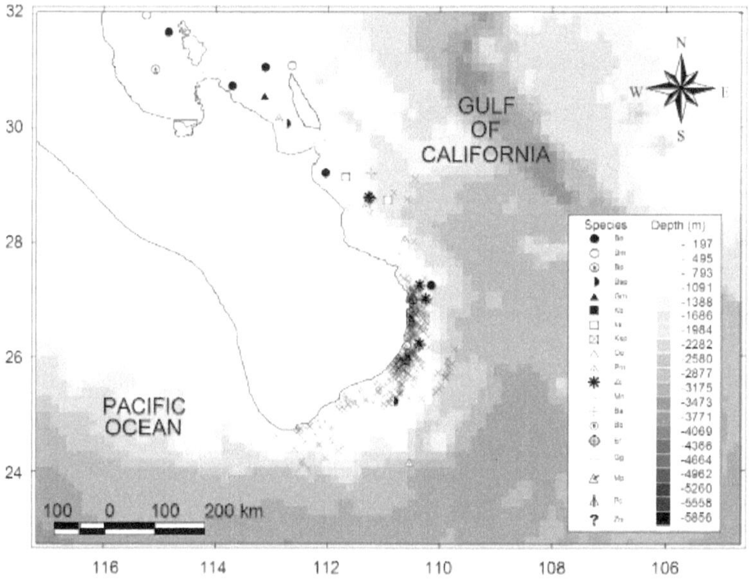

Source: Authors.

Spring

A large number of whales are recorded and humpback whales still predominate. However, north of Cabo Pulmo, a great diversity of species is seen, including sperm whales, dwarf sperm whales, orcas, pilot whales, beaked whales, and some blue whales north of the area (Fig. 8).

Figure 8. Distribution of Spring Sightings for the San Lorenzo Canal-Los Cabos Area, 2004–2007

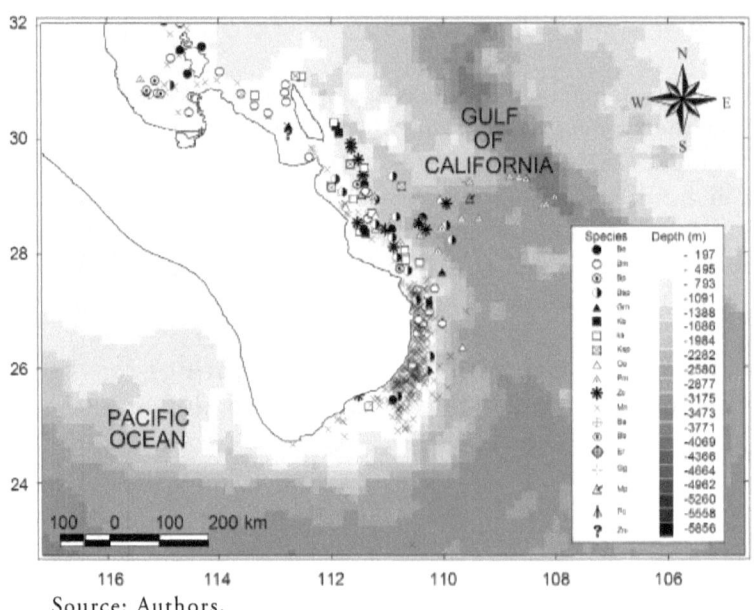

Source: Authors.

Summer

By summer, the decrease of the cetacean sightings is very noticeable. Odontocetes are found almost exclusively, particularly the dwarf sperm whale and Cuvier's beaked whale, in addition to having a more northern distribution (Fig. 9).

Fall

During the fall, the limited presence of large cetaceans is very noticeable. In this season, only sightings of dwarf sperm whales, the beaked whales, and pilot whales are noted (Fig. 10).

MAIN THREATS

Throughout the North Pacific, the major threats to cetaceans include entanglement in nets, collisions with boats, disturbance by boats (including those for whale-watching tourism), noise/acoustic injuries, impacts on their habitats and prey, and pollution in general,

Cetaceans of the Gulf of California's Southwest Coast

Figure 9. Distribution of Summer Sightings for the San Lorenzo Canal-Los Cabos Area, 2004–2007

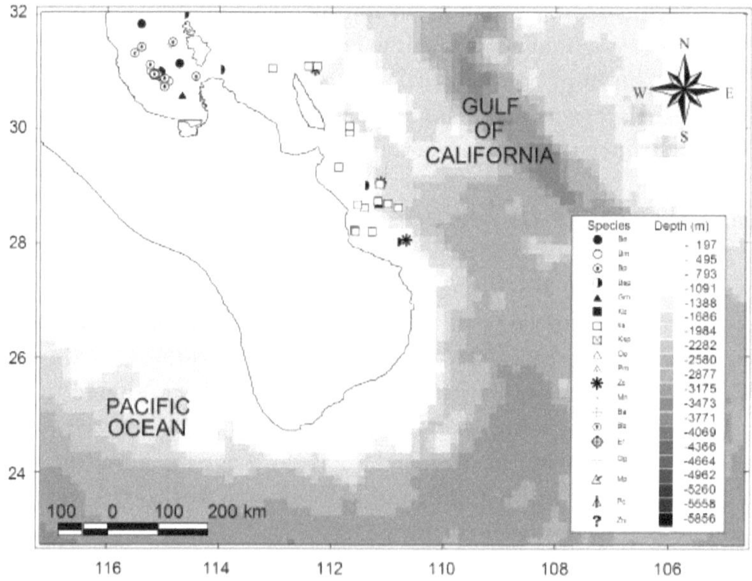

Source: Authors.

Figure 10. Distribution of Fall Sightings for the San Lorenzo Canal-Los Cabos Area, 2004–2007

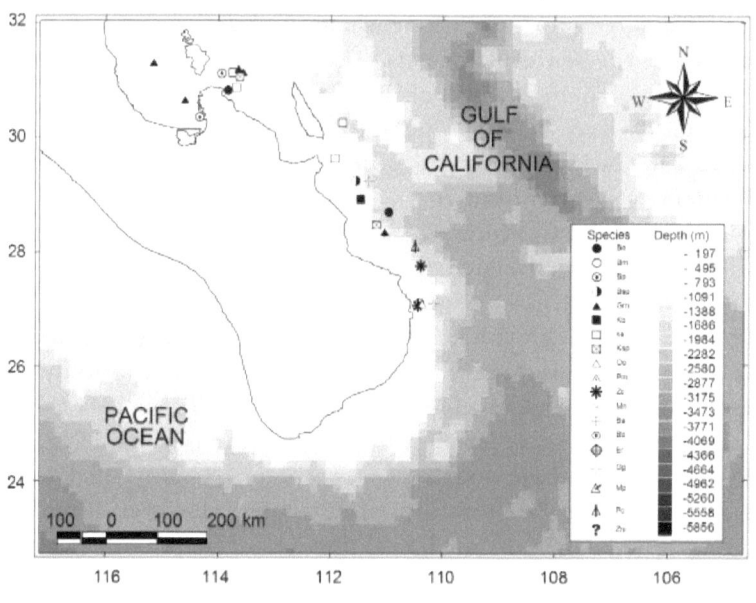

Source: Authors.

(Commission for Environmental Cooperation 2005). In Mexico, the main threats include entanglement in fishing gear, whale-watching tourism, acoustic disturbance, other forms of pursuit, and habitat degradation by chemical pollution and urban development. In this section, the humpback whale, which is the most common species in the area, will serve as an example. It has records of interactions with fishing and tourist attraction activities.

Entanglements in Fishing Gear

Between 2002 and 2007, there were 14 entanglements recorded on the coast between the Bay of La Paz and Cabo San Lucas (Table 12). In particular, two cases were documented in 2007. On March 7, 2007, in the area inside Banco Gorda, an adult was entangled in a gill net. The second sighting was on March 17 of the same year, in the San Lorenzo Canal in the Bay of La Paz. It was also an adult specimen entangled in a gill net. The animal was very weak, with very slow movements, and labored breathing.

Whale-Watching Tourism

In Mexico, cetaceans are recognized as important ecotourism components. At present, whale watching in the natural environment primarily involves three species: the gray whale *(Eschrichtius robustus)* in the west coast of the peninsula of Baja California (Ojo de Liebre Lagoon, San Ignacio Lagoon, Magdalena Bay Lagoon Complex in BCS, and Todos Santos Bay, BC); the humpback whale *(Megaptera novaeangliae)* in the Gulf of California (region of Los Cabos, BCS, and Bay of Banderas, Nayarit); and the blue whale *(Balaenoptera musculus)*, also in the Gulf of California (coasts between the Bay of La Paz and Loreto, BCS). The estimated total annual revenue from this activity is US$9. 08 million (Hoyt and Íñiguez 2008).

The accelerated growth of whale-watching tourism has brought some management problems, which has led to the need to analyze the socioeconomic, legal, and educational aspects of this activity and also to determine the impact on the whale populations (IFAW 1995; IWC 1995). Whale-watching tourism is considered a non-lethal benefit that does not jeopardize the survival of whales. However, if not done properly, it may affect the quality of the lives of the whales, becoming a possible threat.

Table 12. Records of Humpback Whales Entangled in the Rest of the Gulf of California, 2002–2007

(D = dead; F = free with no net remnants; R = free with net remnants still stuck)

Year	Date	Gender	Age	Place	Situation
2002	April		Adult	La Paz Bay	D
	April 15				F
	April 4		Young		F
	April 4	Male			D
	March				D
					F
2003	Nov. 21			Cabo Pulmo	D
2004	Jan. 10	Female		Cabo San Lucas	?
	Feb. 27		Adult	Las Ventanas Bay	F
	Feb. 27			Cabo San Lucas	R
2005	February	Female		Cabo San Lucas	R
	March		Young	La Paz Bay	R
2007	March 7		Adult	Punta Gorda	R
	March 17		Adult	San Lorenzo Canal	R

Sources: Instituto Nacional de Ecología and mass media.

Some guidelines have been developed for whale watching, thus attempting to ensure their welfare, and are primarily for operators of vessels. The guidelines stipulate the way in which to approach the animals, the number of boats allowed, and the allowable distance between the boats and the whales. They also recommend reducing the speed of the vessel in the presence of whales and avoiding sudden changes in noise levels, among other precautions (IWC 2002). Should there be some type of negative impact on whale populations due to the development of whale watching, it would not be visible in the short term. Therefore, it is necessary to continue conducting research on the populations subject to tourist observations, as well as monitoring and analyzing the regulations established to determine whether they remain appropriate or require changes (Hoyt 2002). In addition, whale watching can also serve as a platform to monitor changes in the short and long term that this activity may produce on the whales (IWC 2001b). In this context, the Mexican Official Norm

NOM-131-SEMARNAT-1998, which sets guidelines and specifications for the development of whale-watching activities related to their protection and habitat conservation, emerged in 1998 and was published on January 10, 2000.

According to Hoyt and Íñiguez (2008), while most of the watching of high-quality cetaceans in Mexico is reported and regulated, there is a considerable amount of this activity that is occasional and not reported outside the main ports of the country. There are no naturalists or guides aboard the boats, so there are fewer incentives to follow the rules and regulations that govern the activity and there is less effort to provide tours to watch high-quality cetaceans. Even charging one-fourth of the price set for official boats, there is no doubt that income from these trips can be beneficial to local communities, to the fishers during the off season, and others, but they do not capture the maximum potential of the value of cetacean watching.

Natural Protected Areas

The NPAs contribute to the conservation and sustainable management of humpback whales in Mexico, to varying degrees and depending on the region concerned. For humpback whales in the Baja California peninsula, the two NPAs that are in the area where humpbacks are concentrated are the Cabo San Lucas Arco (Arch) Natural Monument and Cabo Pulmo National Park. Due to the small dimensions of these NPAs, their contribution to the conservation of the humpback whale is limited. So, this contribution should be extended until, ideally, these two areas connect (CONANP 2009).

REFERENCES

Cárdenas H., G. 2008. "Distribución y hábitat de zífidos en la costa sudoccidental del Golfo de California (Cetacea: Ziphidae)." Master's thesis in Marine and Coastal Sciences, Universidad Autónoma de Baja California Sur.

Comisión Nacional de Áreas Naturales Protegidas (CONANP). 2009. http://www.conanp.gob.mx (December 2009).

Comisión para la Cooperación Ambiental (CCA). 2005. *Plan de acción de América del Norte para la conservación: ballena jorobada.* Montreal: CCA.

Convención sobre el Comercio Internacional de Especies Amenazadas de Fauna y Flora Silvestre (CITES). 2009. http://www.cites.org/eng/app/appendices.shtml (Mayo 2009).

Diario Oficial de la Federación (DOF). 2000. Norma Oficial Mexicana NOM-131-SEMARNAT-1998, que establece lineamientos y especificaciones para el desarrollo de actividades de observación de ballenas, relativas a su protección y la conservación de su hábitat, DOF. 10 enero 2000, antes NOM-131-ECOL-1998.

Diario Oficial de la Federación (DOF). 2002. Norma Oficial Mexicana NOM-059-ECOL-2001, Protección ambiental-Especies nativas de México de flora y fauna silvestres-Categorías de riesgo y especificaciones para su inclusión, exclusión o cambio en la lista de especies en riesgo, protección, México, D.F., 6 marzo 2002.

González-Peral, U. A. 2006. "Identidad poblacional de las ballenas jorobadas (Megaptera novaeangliae) que se congregan en Baja California Sur." Master's thesis in Marine and Coastal Sciences, Universidad Autónoma de Baja California Sur.

Hoyt, E. 2002. "Whale Watching." Pp. 1305–1310 in *Encyclopedia of Marine Mammals*, W. F. Perrin, B. Wursig, and J. G. M. Thewissen, eds. San Diego, CA: Academic Press.

Hoyt, E., and M. Íñiguez. 2008. *Estado del avistamiento de cetáceos en América Latina*. WDCS, Chippenham, UK: WDCS; East Falmouth, EEUU: IFAW; and London: *Global Ocean*.

International Fund for Animal Welfare, Tethys Research Institute, and Europe Conservation Workshop on the Scientific Aspects of Managing Whale Watching. 1995. *Report of the Workshop on the Scientific Aspects of Managing Whale Watching*. Italy: Montecastello di Vibio.

International Union for Conservation of Nature (IUCN). 2008. "Cetacean Update of the 2008 IUCN Red List of Threatened Species." (August 2008), http://cmsdata.iucn.org/downloads/cetacean_table_for_website.pdf.

International Whaling Commission (IWC). 1995. *International Convention for the Regulation of Whaling*, 1946: Schedule. Report of the International Whaling Commission 47: 1–27.

International Whaling Commission (IWC). 2001a. "Appendix 3, Classification of the Order Cetacea (whales, dolphins and porpoises)." *J. Cetacean Res. Manage* 3: v–xii.

International Whaling Commission (IWC). 2001b. "Report of the Scientific Committee, Annex N. Report of the Workshop on Assessing the Long-term Effects of Whalewatching on Cetaceans." *J. Cetacean Res, Manage* (Suppl.) 3: 308–315.

International Whaling Commission (IWC). 2002. "Report of the Scientific Committee, Annex L. Appendix 5. Report of the Sub-Committee on Whale Watching." *J. Cetacean Res. Manage* (Suppl.) 4: 339–360.

Rice D. W. 1998. *Marine Mammals of the World. Systematics and Distribution.* Lawrence, KS: Society for Marine Mammlogy.

Salvadeo, C. J. 2008. "Análisis de la comunidad de odontocetos y la relación con su ambiente, en el extremo sur occidental del Golfo de California, México (2003–2006)." Master's thesis in Sciences, Centro Interdisciplinario de Ciencias Marinas, Instituto Politécnico Nacional, La Paz, Baja California Sur.

Troyo V., B. 2008. "Estructura comunitaria de los cetáceos en el extremo suroccidental del Golfo de California durante 2005." Master's thesis in Marine and Coastal Sciences, Universidad Autónoma de Baja California Sur.

Urbán R., J. 2000a. "Familia Eschrichtidae" [sic, Eschrichtiidae]. Pp. 655–659 en *Mamíferos del Noroeste de México II*, S. T. Álvarez-Castañeda and J. L. Patton, eds. La Paz, BCS: Centro de Investigaciones Biológicas del Noroeste, S.C.

Urbán R., J. 2000b. "Familia Balaenopteridae." Pp. 661–683 en *Mamíferos del Noroeste de México II*, S. T. Álvarez-Castañeda and J. L. Patton, eds. La Paz, BCS: Centro de Investigaciones Biológicas del Noroeste, S.C.

Urbán R., J. 2001. "Estructura poblacional, abundancia y destinos migratorios de las ballenas jorobadas que inviernan en el Pacífico mexicano." Ph.D. dissertation, School of Sciences, Universidad Nacional Autónoma de México.

Urbán R., J. 2010. "Marine Mammals of the Gulf of California: An Overview of Diversity and Conservation Status." In *The Gulf of California: Biodiversity and Conservation*, R. C. Brusca, ed. Tucson, AZ: University of Arizona Press and Arizona-Sonora Desert Museum.

Urbán R., J., A. Jaramillo L., A. Aguayo et al. 2000. "Migratory Destinations of Humpback Whales Wintering in the Mexican Pacific." *Journal of Ceatcean Research and Management* 2 (2): 101–110.

Urbán R., J., L. Rojas-Bracho, M. Guerrero-Ruiz, A. Jaramillo-Legorreta, and L. T. Findley. 2005. "Cetacean Diversity and Conservation in the Gulf of California." In *Biodiversity, Ecosystems, and Conservation in Northern Mexico*, J. E. Cartron, G. Ceballos, and R. S. Felger, eds. New York: Oxford University Press.

7

Prospective of Natural Protected Areas in Los Cabos

Oscar Arizpe C. and Benito Bermúdez

INTRODUCTION

Natural resources constitute a fundamental strategic reserve for Mexico's national sovereignty and integral development; that is why the issue was raised regarding the formation of the National System of Natural Protected Areas, as well as the implementation of programs for the conservation, management, and administration of resources in such areas (CONANP 2007). These Natural Protected Areas (NPAs) become a source that generates multiple cultural and socioeconomic benefits, and allows fostering the conservation of habitats and diversity of species occupying this land.

The importance of NPAs has currently grown in an unusual manner due to the alarming environmental deterioration that human beings are causing on the planet. The strategy of NPA creation, consolidation, and management has become a key element in the conservation of the environment.

Although Article 105 of Mexico's Constitution provides for the autonomy of municipalities, in the case of NPAs at the national level, the policy for their establishment, management, and administration is the responsibility of the National Commission of Natural Protected Areas (Comisión Nacional de Áreas Naturales Protegidas–CONANP).

CONANP functions according to its Sectorial Development Plan that is renewed every six-year presidential term. For 2006–2012, the plan set the following as strategic objectives (CONANP 2007):

- Maintain the country's most representative ecosystems and their biodiversity with the joint participation of all sectors
- Develop, promote, direct, manage, and supervise programs and projects in protected areas related to protection and management, including their sustainable use as well as their restoration for conservation
- Promote the implementation of the Conservation Strategy for Development in order to improve the quality of life of local inhabitants, and induce sustainable practices that mitigate negative impacts on ecosystems and their biodiversity
- Promote tourism in protected areas as a tool for sustainable development and for enhancing sensitivity and culture for the conservation of ecosystems and their biodiversity through the Program on Tourism in Protected Areas, 2007–2012
- Consolidate national cooperation and financing, and maintain an international leadership in conservation
- Achieve the conservation of species that are at risk based on national priorities through the implementation of the Program on the Conservation of Endangered Species, 2007–2012

In the previous Sectorial Development Plan (2001) that CONANP published, it was guided by a new concept of conservation, which regulated the philosophy and conservation actions at a national and global level. From this perspective, it states that without human beings, the NPA policy makes no sense. Therefore, even when the conservation mandate and imperative focus on addressing the problems with ecosystems and their biodiversity, conditions for a dignified life and opportunities for present and future generations are to be maintained. Conservation also involves community organization and strengthening. This plan, in turn, sets "conservation as responsible for providing the sustainable character to development, and to understand and effectively implement the modern concept of conservation is that we should disaggregate and organize it according to its components, in order that conservation can be achieved through direct actions on ecosystems and their biodiversity, as well as indirect actions that influence society's behaviors and decisions" (CONANP 2007).

For the 2006–2012 period, it was determined that in order for CONANP's operation to continue under the premise of this new approach to conservation and its components, the following are the mission and vision (CONANP 2007):

Mission: To conserve the natural heritage of Mexico through protected areas and other forms of conservation, fostering a culture of conservation and sustainable development of communities settled in their surroundings.

Vision: In six years, the National Commission of Natural Protected Areas, CONANP, will have led the articulation and consolidation of a national system of protected areas and of various forms of conservation of terrestrial, aquatic, marine, coastal, and island ecosystems and their biodiversity. The system will be representative, systemic, functional, participatory, supportive, subsidiary, and effective, and will involve the three levels of government, civil society, and rural and indigenous communities.

In the late 1990s, Mexico had only 12 to 16 directors of protected areas in place and an institution with a lot of mystique and enthusiasm, but weak in resources of all kinds to take care of these areas. While these first protected areas still represent some of the nation's most important ones and with a better level of development and implementation of conservation policies, the institution has grown to more than 60 offices and today serves more than 80 protected areas. Starting in 2002, and especially from 2004, CONANP began to operate under a regionalized model that allowed making decisions that were closer to the problems in order to provide administrative support. It also provided support in negotiations and with political ties as well as with local actors through regional directors and their workgroups. Furthermore, it strengthened capacity building and institutional learning with protected areas focusing on direct conservation efforts (protection, management and use, and restoration) and regional offices on indirect conservation efforts (knowledge, culture, and management).

Baja California Sur is the state with the longest coastal extension and greatest diversity of marine resources in Mexico, with the municipality of Los Cabos standing out due to its diversity of landforms. The state has been a model of modern conservation policies in Mexico. It has great natural riches and important economic activities at the national and international level: tourism, fisheries, aquaculture, and recreational and business activities. This has provided the ideal setting to create Natural Protected Areas with successful management plans, protecting natural resources, but at the same time respecting, instructing, and supporting the socioeconomic activities of local communities. In recent years, there has been an atmosphere of trust among the residents of Baja California Sur, encouraging them to participate and to learn even more about their own environment. Baja California Sur is a leader in protecting its land because more than 40% of it is in some mode of NPA. These include the Islands of the Gulf of California Flora and Fauna Protection Area, Ojo de Liebre Lagoon System, Sierra La Laguna Biosphere Reserve, El Vizcaíno Biosphere Reserve, Loreto Bay National Park, Cabo Pulmo National Park, and the Flora and Fauna Submarine Refuge and the Ecological Conditions of the Sea Bottom of Cabo San Lucas (1973), which is now the Cabo San Lucas Flora and Fauna Protection Area (2000). There are also protected areas that are of state jurisdiction, such as the San José Estuary, and municipal areas, such as the recently created Balandra in La Paz.

The Cabo Region is considered a biogeographical unit different from the rest of Mexico and the Baja California peninsula. The unique characteristics of this region derive from its geological and natural history, which has enabled the convergence of elements of arid, tropical, and temperate ecosystems in this region. According to the criteria developed by the panel of experts from CONABIO, the Cabo Region is considered one of the country's 19 Biogeographical Provinces (CONABIO 1997) with the same name: Provincia del Cabo. In addition, in the biogeographical regionalization of the Atlas of Mexico of the National Autonomous University of Mexico's (UNAM's) Institute of Geography (Ferrusquía-Villafranca 1992), the Cabo Region is considered one of the country's 20 Biotic Provinces, characterized as a transition zone between different biogeographical domains. There are five NPAs for the protection and conservation of natural resources in the municipality of Los Cabos:

- Cabo San Lucas Flora and fauna protection area, decreed an NPA on November 29, 1973, and reclassified on June 7, 2000, with an area of 3,996 hectares (ha). This area does not have a conservation and management program (CONANP 2007)

- Sierra La Laguna: Biosphere reserve decreed June 6, 1994, with an area of 112,437 ha. This reserve has a conservation and management plan (CONANP 2007)
- Cabo Pulmo: National park incorporated into the system of Natural Protected Areas on June 6, 1995; it covers an area of 7,111 ha. This area does not have a published conservation and management plan
- San José Estuary: State ecological reserve decreed on January 10, 1994, with an area of 11,956.09 ha (CONANP 2007). The conservation plan is currently being developed by Pronatura Noroeste A. C
- Cabo San Lucas Arch Natural Monument-Cerro del Vigía: the proposal submitted in the Justificatory Technical Study is being analyzed

It is important to bear in mind that the municipality of Los Cabos has one of the world's highest human population growth rates. The demographic expansion creates great development pressure, which creates unique social, economic, and environmental problems for the region's NPAs. These problems are to be seen in the challenges faced by each NPA of Los Cabos municipality.

CABO SAN LUCAS FLORA AND FAUNA PROTECTION AREA

This area was established by a presidential decree, which was published on November 29, 1973. It was bestowed with a category according to the legislation in force through the secretarial agreement of June 7, 2000. The Cabo San Lucas Flora and Fauna Protection Area (Área de Protección de Flora y Fauna de Cabo San Lucas–APFFCSL) is an exceptional site because of its geographical position. Its habitat needs to be preserved for ecological balance and protection of wild species of flora and fauna. This NPA also addresses the phenomena of terrestrial and submarine erosion that is found along the Baja California peninsula. The signature area within the APFFCSL is located at the peninsula's *finisterre*, or tip, and is crowned by the famous rock formation that is an icon of the region and the state of Baja California Sur: the Cabo San Lucas Arch.

The APFFCSL is formed by an exact rectangular polygon, with an area of 3,996 ha; it is located between coordinates 22°50'50" and 22°54'00" North and between 109°50'00" and 109°54'00" West, off the coast of the municipality of Los Cabos. Approximately 5% is land and the remaining 95% is marine. The submarine formation is particularly important; it is characterized by the presence of submarine canyons that reach great depths at a distance very close to the coast. Although it has a small total area, it is representative of the peninsular geological formations and phenomena. It is also characterized by marine ecological processes that are typical of the cold and rich waters of the California current, which travels from north to south, and the warm waters of the Ecuador current. Together, both currents form an extensive area of mixture that, coupled with the upwelling of nutrient-rich deep waters, occur along the Baja California peninsula and end within the polygon of the protected area in its final portion.

Ocean conditions that occur at the south end of the peninsula create one of the most important regions of the eastern Pacific. Preserving this natural wealth turns out to be a huge undertaking that requires the necessary planning and regulatory instruments in order to realize the objectives of the creation of the APFFCSL. These objectives also need to be adapted to a reality that is very different from that envisaged in 1973 when the establishing decree was issued. Thus, the Conservation and Management Program (CMP) that is being developed for the area has the mission to protect the biological diversity and physical conditions of the area, maintain the natural gene pool, and promote the sustainable development of renewable resources present in the APFFCSL, additionally allowing the enjoyment by society of its environmental and recreational services.

The general objective established in the developing CMP is to conserve the APFFCSL's ecosystems and biodiversity. This includes ecological processes, natural changes, and ecosystem services that allow the continuity and evolution of life, as well as the welfare and progress of human society through a set of policies and protective measures, management (including sustainable use), and restoration. Society and government as a whole—particularly rural, fishing, and indigenous communities within the protected area and its area of influence—will become involved through processes of knowledge, culture, and management.

The CMP notes that the area is home to more than 1,000 species of marine and terrestrial flora and fauna and many of these are listed in NOM-059-SEMARNAT-2004. The listing includes species that are threatened, subject to special protection, or endangered, such as the gray and humpback whales, sea turtles, and sea lions, among other marine mammals. Also included are fish, such as the Clarion angelfish, starfish, seahorse, and black coral. In the realm of sea birds, one can find, for example, the elegant tern, frigates or *tijeretas*, gulls, and brown pelicans; in the winter season, white pelicans and sea hawks, among others, are to be found. This represents an opportunity to integrate an analysis platform and the generation of knowledge about the processes of connectivity of the ocean portions of the Mexican Pacific from the Guadalupe Island Biosphere Reserve to the Revillagigedo Archipelago Biosphere Reserve, since this is the confluence zone of the Indo-Pacific region and has species of the two different regions.

The main problems described in the APFFCSL and its area of influence begin with the anthropogenic pressure from the great growth of tourism activities and the associated increase in nautical activities, which have sparked substantial growth in the number of small and large boats that offer rides and tours in the protected area and its vicinity. Because Cabo San Lucas is one of the main destinations and nautical stopovers for international cruise ships, entertainment activities have increased in the last 10 years. To date, there is a fleet of commercial vessels dedicated to tourism services, with more than one thousand service units with a passenger transport capacity of more than 5,000 people per day. The main activities are rides and tours to the arch area, Playa del Amor (Lover's Beach), and tours of the bay, an activity that brings together an estimated 400 *panga*-type units (small boats) with outboard motor and an average capacity of 10 passengers per trip.

Another problem in the area is the operation of jet skis, approximately 350 in number. In addition, snorkeling and scuba diving activities have shown significant growth, increasing pressure on the diving sites in the submarine canyon. Added to this, the traffic of boats that circulate through the protected area, mainly conducting sport/recreational fishing in the APFFCSL's area of influence, is estimated at a daily average of 200 boats. It is not known what effect this increase in nautical-recreational activities has on marine populations in the area and within the APFFCSL. Also, precise data are not available on the conditions of the submarine canyon or conditions from modifications that could have occurred since 1973, when the creation decree was issued.

With respect to the land portion and its area of influence, it is evident that growth and development of the urban sprawl in the last 20 years have caused a rupture or split in the continuity of the ecosystem. All these pressures make actions to conserve the coastal ecosystems of this area necessary. At the same time, specific efforts are needed in tourism development that conforms to a model of objective and concrete sustainability. This will be of enormous ecological and socioeconomic benefit for the surrounding communities, which could benefit from the sustainable use of the natural resources in the APFFCSL, allowing the sustainable development of the region.

SIERRA LA LAGUNA

The area known as Sierra La Laguna is located in the municipalities of La Paz and Los Cabos, with an extension of 112,437 ha. It was declared a biosphere reserve on June 6, 1994. The Sierra La Laguna can be considered an "island" of vegetation in the arid environment of the Baja California peninsula. It is a product of a geological separation process from the continental massif and subsequent embedding in the peninsula that was a determining factor on climatic, geographical, and biological conditions of the ecosystems prevailing in the area. As a direct result of its isolation, the region has important endemisms and is even considered as a center of recent biological evolution. Its importance is due not only to its unique ecosystems, but also because of its value as a recharge area for aquifers.

In 1984, under the administration of the Secretariat of Urban Development and Ecology (Secretaría de Desarrollo Urbano y Ecología–SEDUE), activities began that moved toward establishing the Sierra La Laguna as a natural protected area. In 1994, under the administration of the Secretariat of Social Development (Secretaría de Desarrollo Social–SEDESOL), the proposal was revived and the Presidential Decree was issued on June 6, 1994. The following are among the reasons that served as bases for the declaration:

- Historical-cultural relevance. The presence throughout the area of rock/cave art that depicts fauna species such as whales, turtles, and rays , although not as monumental as the mural art of the Sierra La Giganta, are undoubtedly elements of great cultural value
- Ecological and scientific relevance. The complex geohistory of the region, characterized by its detachment from the continental massif during the Miocene and its geographical position, raise interesting questions about the current distribution of biota and its relationship to other regions
- Educational and recreational relevance. The reserve, due to its proximity to the most populous urban centers in the state, represents great potential for the development of educational activities of an environmental sort, because it forms a natural area suitable for the development of outdoor teaching activities, which contributes to the formation of an environmental culture

These elements constituted the basis for the establishment of Sierra La Laguna as an NPA, and the development and implementation of its management program (SLMP). In this SLMP (CONANP 2003), a principle is to provide communities that inhabit the reserve alternatives for economic development, training, and organization to carry out better management and conservation of their own resources. Emphasis is also placed on facilitating the management for assessing and monitoring natural resources, oversight, administration, application of appropriate and non-impacting technologies, search for fair markets for producers, and protection of biodiversity through sustainable utilization of species. The overall objective proposed is to define and establish standards, guidelines, strategies, programs, and actions to achieve conservation and sustainable use of the reserve's natural resources, with the participation of communities and agencies involved in the area.

Its demarcation is between parallels 23°42' and 23°20' and meridians 109°46' and 110°11'. The reserve has a core zone with an area of 32,519 ha between parallels 23°39' and 23°24' North latitude and meridians 109°47' and 110°03' West longitude, comprising areas of the municipalities of La Paz and Los Cabos.

The soils of the sierra are generally little developed. In the steepest parts of the reserve, lithosols dominate along with eutric regosols, that is, thin soils limited by rocks. Hydrologically, from north to south and along some 59 km, the reserve shapes the drainage divide that separates the two hydraulic basins, or watersheds, of Arroyo Caracol-Arroyo Candelaria and of La Paz-Cabo San Lucas. This means that the reserve constitutes the middle division between runoff that drains into the Pacific Ocean and into the Gulf of California. The estimated average annual rainfall in the Cabo Region ranges from 200 mm on the coast, to over 600 mm in the highlands.

These environmental factors favor the development of different types of vegetation along an altitudinal gradient characterized by: (1) scrub (sarcocaulescent and sarcocrassicaulescent), located from sea level to 500 m in elevation, which also includes mesquite; (2) lowland deciduous and subdeciduous forest, which is distributed from 350 to 800 m and covers an approximate area of 58,701 ha; (3) oak forest, located between 800 and 1,200 m, which has many tropical elements in the strata below the upper forest canopy; (4) pine-oak forest, which is set in the higher portions of the sierra; on the Pacific slope, it appears at 1,400 m, while for the Gulf of California, it is located at 1,500 m and covers about 8,272 ha; (5) gallery vegetation, located in the canyons along the altitudinal gradient; and (6) natural grassland, located mainly in the area known as Valle de La Laguna.

The high biodiversity and endemism are basically due to the particular geological history, which has allowed that unique species with characteristics of insularity be found in the reserve, since many genres represented by only one species are reported. The vast majority of species are highly susceptible to introduced predators. The previous chapter of terrestrial flora and fauna of the municipality provides a detailed description of what is present in the NPA.

In a historical and cultural context, some archaeological resources are located in the reserve, ranging from simple funerary burials and cave paintings to some ruins of ancient dwellings of the natives who inhabited the area. The presence of a more recent fauna is seen in several of the many manifestations of rock art dispersed in the area. By the late prehistorical period, these artists-hunters-fishers, all Pericú, were surprised by Spanish colonizers to whose culture and diseases they succumbed by the late eighteenth century, leaving their origin and antiquity a mystery.

With regard to land tenure, the area of the reserve is comprised of communal land and 35 private plots. With respect to plots that are domestic or federal property, there are 10 such areas in the central part of the Sierra La Laguna. The reserve is already incorporated into the Public Registry of Property and Commerce in the municipality of Los Cabos, under registration No. 28, Folio 118. Vol I. Section 5, dated September 9, 1997.

The main productive activities center on work by laborers and raising livestock; both complement each other. Raising livestock is the dominant economic activity, and the hiring of laborers allows them to earn extra financial resources for their subsistence in the region. Agriculture in the reserve is virtually nonexistent as a formal activity. The closest thing to it is the planting of vegetables (mainly onions, tomatoes, and chili peppers), basically for personal consumption and surpluses are bartered or sold.

The extraction of forest timber and nontimber products constitutes economic activities that are carried out legally and illegally. Those who harvest the products make extra income that allows them to get through difficult times. Wood products (highly valued in the region) are used for repairing and building houses and *palapas* (palm-thatched structures), installing fences, or repairing and building corrals, as well as for firewood. Among the plant species that are used in a traditional way are those used for food, medicinal, and even industrial purposes. With reference to fruit growing, it is a practice that has been carried out since the first European human settlements in the region, largely for personal consumption, without the use of registered varieties or selected lines. The most common fruit species is the mango, of a Creole variety, as well as guava, papaya, avocado, and orange and other citrus fruits.

Currently, no mining exploitation is carried out within the reserve; however, there have been mining explorations and claims. According to the Ministry of Economy, 21 mining claims exist, 11 are for exploration and 10 for exploitation. The mining claims encompass a total area of 15,596 hectares.

The development of tourism activities has been growing significantly. The estimated influx of visitors during the yearly season from October to April is 5,000. For two decades, some of the ranchers who live in the reserve have offered their services as guides and also rent pack animals and equipment, which provides extra income. However, this activity is carried out in a disorganized manner and without the preparation that would enable them to conduct their activities with greater professionalism.

Other productive activities that are carried out in the Sierra La Laguna include trade, manual labor, and handicraft production, which are largely based on the alternative use of natural resources. Notable among the craft products are leather goods, ceramics, palm weaving, and items made of wood, which are sold as special orders or to tourists that occasionally pass through the area.

Problematic Issues

The cultural-historical heritage found in the area of influence and within the reserve is important and still largely unknown. For this reason, the conservation and protection of this heritage are urgent. There are several species that are traditionally used as a forest resource within the communities of gallery forests. Among the most important are the palms, oaks, and cottonwoods; however, the trees of commercial size are very scarce so it is necessary to take protection and management measures. In the raising of livestock, there are approximately three times more animals than the system can tolerate, so it is necessary to offer alternatives to economic activities to reduce the impact on the reserve.

Due to illegal hunting of wildlife, as well as pressure placed on their habitat, some species are highly endangered, including the mountain lion *(Felis concolor)*. Other species such as rattlesnakes *(Crotalus enyo, C. mitchellii* and *C. ruber)*; red-tailed hawk *(Buteo jamaicensis)* and other birds of prey; carnivores such as the coyote *(Canis latrans)*, gray fox *(Urocyon cinereoargenteus)*, and bobcat *(Lynx rufus)*; along with mule deer *(Odocoileus hemionus)* are under pressure.

As this discussion suggests, it is necessary that each component or subcomponent of the Management Program help with the solution of these problems. The program should generate solutions geared toward reducing or combating threats of negative impacts. These include the practice of extensive livestock grazing; clandestine forest timber and nontimber extractions; mining exploration and exploitation; unemployment derived from nondiversified production practices; increased sale of properties, particularly to persons not identified with the area; excessive camping in vulnerable areas; and, a key aspect, the misuse of water resources.

CABO PULMO

A unique reef area in the Gulf of California and the northernmost part of the eastern Pacific can be found in the Bay of Cabo Pulmo: the coralline reef of Cabo Pulmo. Due to its ecotone, or transitional, character resulting from the confluence of species from the Panamic, Californian, and Indo-Pacific biogeographic provinces, the biological diversity found is one of the highest in the Mexican Pacific coast (Kerstitch 1989). It was declared a Natural Protected Area under the category of National Marine Park on June 6, 1995. This category was changed to National Park through a secretarial agreement published in the *Official Journal of the Federation* on June 7, 2000, in accordance with the General Law of Ecological Equilibrium and Environmental Protection (Ley General del Equilibrio Ecológico y la Protección al Ambiente–LGEEPA).

The main reasons for this declaration were the following:

- Cabo Pulmo is the only coralline reef ecosystem in the Gulf of California and, as such, represents a special type of habitat, ecological processes, biological communities, and physiographic features, a situation that gives it not only regional importance but also great relevance worldwide
- Its biological diversity has been documented through various studies of the reef communities that contain the most extensive coralline cover and a high percentage (78%) of the hermatypic coral species reported. The ichthyofauna richness is also considerably important since, of the 875 species reported for the Gulf of California, approximately 26% are found in the reef
- The area of Cabo Pulmo is important because it has species that are considered to be under some protection category according to NOM-059-SEMARNAT-2001. Among the most prominent are five species of sea turtles *(Caretta caretta, Chelonia agassizi, Dermochelys coriaceae, Eretmochelys imbricate,* and *Lepidochelys olivacea)* that are in the endangered category

- Traditionally, artisanal fishing was conducted in areas near the reef. Fishers would catch species to sell and there were no fixed quotas. Since the official declaration of the park, this activity has been restricted to fishing for family consumption. The species caught are mainly snapper, sea bass, and grouper
- Due to the ecotone character of the geographical area in which it is located, both endemic species of the Gulf of California, as well as affinity species with the Panamic, Indo-Pacific, and Californian biogeographical provinces can be seen
- The park and its area of influence have great historical and cultural value. Both areas have archaeological records that show the importance that the region had for the Pericú, the ancient indigenous group that populated the region of Los Cabos, south of latitude 24°. They were fishers and extracted products from the sea for both food (turtles, manta rays, groupers, triggerfish, and snappers) and ornamental uses (mollusks)

Cabo Pulmo National Park is located in the municipality of Los Cabos between 23°22'30" and 23°30'00" North latitude and 109°28'03" and 109°23'00" West longitude on the Gulf of California coast. The park covers an area of 7,111 ha. The Bay of Cabo Pulmo and Bay of Los Frailes (which are actually inlets) also form alluvial valleys composed of granitic clasts and volcanic fragments. The Bay of Cabo Pulmo has a dune area, with dunes up to an approximate height of 5 m and width of 15 m. The seabed has a minimal slope and a series of basalt bars; on three of these, a coralline community and a large number of flora and fauna species are located. These bars extend outward from the coast to a maximum depth of 20 m in its northern part, and a minimum of 2 or 3 m in some of the central and southern areas. The top part of the coral colonies in portions of the bar closest to the coast are exposed at low tide.

The federal maritime-terrestrial zone, which is 20 m inland from the highest tide, represents the terrestrial part of the park. This area includes a system of bristly dune chains in an extension that stretches from Punta Cabo Pulmo to Coral de Los Frailes. Soil units found in the area of influence include eutric regosols thick in texture in the alluvial valleys, sometimes associated with haplic xerosols and others with deep lytic phase (CONANP 2007). Fresh water in the park's area of influence and surrounding areas is scarce and limited during the dry season (May-October), so it is used in a rational way. This has been one of the factors that limit the diversification of productive activities in the area. Water is provided by three wells located in Cabo Pulmo, approximately 500 m from the coastline.

Efforts to learn about the marine flora of the coralline reef are limited to a single study by Anaya and Riosmena (1996). The extraction of specimens is carried out for scientific purposes. However, there are species that have commercial value, although there are no reports of their economic use. No endemic species have been identified nor are there any under some protection category as per NOM-059-SEMARNAT-2001. Hydrocarbons and organic matter are the main pollutants that could affect marine flora, since these may cause a bioaccumulation in algae and a eutrophication in the system.

The coral reef is approximately 20,000 years old, an antiquity that if compared with other reefs places it among the oldest in the American Pacific, since those in Panama, for example, are barely 5,000 to 5,500 years old (Glynn and McIntyre 1977). In the coastal portion of the Bay of Cabo Pulmo, there is a marine terrace from the late Pleistocene dated 125 ka ± 1,000 years, based on the corals found (Reyes Bonilla 1993b). It was formed by the variation in sea level as a result of the last depositional event of the Buenavista-San José del Cabo sedimentary sequence.

The park's reef has the most extensive coralline cover in the Gulf of California and it is home to 11 of the 14 hermatypic coral species reported for the gulf. These are: *Pocillopora verrucosa, Pocillopora capitata, Pocillopora damicornis, Pocillopora meandrina, Pavona gigantea, Pavona clivosa, Porites panamensis, Psammocora stellata, Psammocora brighami, Fungia curvata,* and *Madracis pharensis* (Reyes Bonilla 1993a); all these are considered hard corals. Similarly, in the case of the ichthyological community, there are observations of 226 reef species (Villarreal et al. 2000) of the 875 species listed for the Gulf of California (Finley et al. 1996).

Another group widely represented in the reef is that of the mollusks, as described in the previous chapter on marine fauna. Some of the identified species are *Conus brunneus* and *Conus princeps,* commonly known as cones, scorpion snail *(Murex elenensis),* sea snail *(Muricanthus princeps),* snail *(Thais kiosquiformis),* and mother of pearl *(Pinctada mazatlanica).* This group of organisms is commercially important. Some command very high prices as collectibles and other species are valuable because of the by-products obtained from them, besides being present in the list of endangered species such as the case of the mother of pearl. In this regard, there are species in the area under some protection category by Mexican laws. The endangered species, according to NOM-059-SEMARNAT-2001, are turtles that periodically visit some of the park's beaches, either for spawning or feeding.

Marine mammals that swim in and near the park boundaries can also be seen on the coast, such as the bottlenose dolphin *(Tursiops truncatus)*, spinner dolphin *(Stenella longirostris)*, and rough-toothed dolphin *(Steno bredanensis)*. Similarly, the humpback whale *(Balaenoptera novaeangliae)*, fin whale *(Balaenoptera physalus)*, and Eden's whale *(Balaenoptera edeni)* frequently enter the park's boundaries during the winter.

There are many paleontological remains of reef fauna in the area of influence of the park. In the Bay of Cabo Pulmo, there is also an archaeological site registered by Massey (1955), which was tentatively identified as an area of occupation and burial site of nomadic hunter-gatherer bands belonging to the Pericú group. Massey (1955) mentions that in the zone of influence, past the mouth of the creek, a cliff forms with a dune of approximately 600 m long, where sporadic lithic and shell workshops that he had previously reported are located.

The present settlement of Cabo Pulmo has a total of 20 dwellings of various sizes, all private and with an average of 5.5 occupants per dwelling. Regarding the dwelling characteristics, 14 have floors made from materials other than dirt, three have roofs made of cardboard sheets or waste materials, only four have piped water, one has drainage, and none have electricity. Cabo Pulmo is reached by taking a detour from the road that connects La Paz to Los Cabos; most of it is paved and 10 km are unpaved and usually in poor condition. There is communication by sea, through small boats that come from adjacent communities like Los Barriles, Buena Vista, La Ribera, San José del Cabo, and Cabo San Lucas.

Tourism services include lodging, with a hotel in Los Frailes and bungalows in Cabo Pulmo, and restaurants. There are also guide and equipment rental services for scuba diving and sportfishing. In the towns near Cabo Pulmo, such as San José del Cabo and Cabo San Lucas, there is hotel infrastructure and large-scale services; sport fishers and touring groups depart from these towns to visit Cabo Pulmo and other parts of the municipality. The main economic potential of the area is recreational in nature and includes activities such as snorkeling and scuba diving, kayaking, windsurfing, and sportfishing. In fact, over the last decade, the population of Cabo Pulmo has partly shifted its economic activities from fishing toward the provision of tourism services.

Artisanal fishing, which traditionally was practiced in the area, is currently not done in the park by the community's own decision and the decree of June 6, 1995. However, the decree permits that people from the community fish with hooks for a maximum catch of 10 kg per family per day in places designated for that purpose. Sportfishing has also become a tourist attraction outside the boundaries of the NPA.

The elements proposed in the recently formalized (November 13, 2009) Management Program for Cabo Pulmo (Programa de Manejo de Cabo Pulmo–PMCP) are guided by the overall objective of preserving the only coralline reef ecosystem present in the Gulf of California, the variety of its components and associated habitats, as well as their biotic communities through the maintenance of ecological processes and support systems upon which the integrity of the coralline reef depends. Also important is the conservation of the historical value of the area's archaeological remains and the promotion of compatible uses with its conservation. Since it was declared a national marine park and encompasses exclusively federal areas, it is considered property of the nation. Therefore, there are no problems regarding land tenure issues. It should be mentioned that there are some federal maritime-terrestrial zone concessions granted by the Secretariat of Environment and Natural Resources (Secretaría del Medio Ambiente y Recursos Naturales–SEMARNAT).

Problematic Issues

The Cabo Pulmo reef has endured fishing activities for a long time, although recently, it has been kept in good environmental conditions because the traditional fishing practices have changed. Prior to the decree declaring this region a national marine park in 1995, fishing was carried out at the reef and represented a threat to the system. The PMCP mentions that the problem of extracting organisms for ornamental uses has increased since there is no assessment of the resource, and there are no regulations for controlling the catch quotas and seasons for these species. With regard to sportfishing, it can be seen that there is little control on who fishes or the amount of the catch. Given that most boats come from communities adjacent to the park, currently several service providers from the community of Cape Pulmo offer services related to sportfishing.

Due to the scientific interest in the reef, the collecting of specimens of the different *phyla* has also been practiced for research purposes. It is also urgent that this activity be regulated in order to have a record of activities that take place on the reef. It is said locally in the park that some researchers collect and manipulate reef organisms for purposes of study. However, this is not allowed because the park's creation decree prohibits the removal of any type of specimens from the park, unless there is appropriate authorization issued by the National Commission of Natural Protected Areas.

Pollution is associated with nautical traffic and involves the emission of wastes or substances into the environment, altering water quality and producing a negative effect on the organisms of the park's ecosystems. Due to the use of fuel, boats emit small amounts of oil (gasoline, diesel, kerosene) that kill corals and, occasionally, in small quantities, cause reproductive disorders and contamination (Tilmant 1987). The use of some methods that utilize chemicals such as sodium cyanide and quinaldine, for the collection of ornamental organisms, also poses serious problems for the NPA. These methods account for the death of organisms in addition to those of the catch. Moreover, due to the frequent visits and increase in tourism groups and businesses, both domestic and foreign, the problem of solid waste in the area of influence has grown and more so in the coastal and beach area.

Tourism development, as evidenced in the construction of a large number of structures both in the area of influence and in the federal maritime-terrestrial zone of the park, generates a series of problems. Requirements for the construction of tourism infrastructure entail habitat modification by: (1) clearing land; (2) constructing docks, walls, and piers; (3) constructing channels and barriers and using explosives; and (4) extracting construction materials (sand and rock). In the case of works located in the federal maritime-terrestrial zone, the removal of material in the long run causes a loss of sediment or modification of the coast causing the process of sedimentation and turbidity that directly affects the coral habitat. It should be pointed out that in the area of Las Barracas, where sea turtle nests are located, mainly of the olive ridley *(Lepidochelys olivacea)*, there are several buildings that have invaded the federal zone. Another sea turtle nesting site is near the town of Cabo Pulmo, where the Cabo Pulmo Beach Resort, owned by foreigners, is located.

Unqualified diving has generated mechanical damage in corals and disturbance of organisms. It also caused some deterioration in the reef area in the 1985 to 1995 period; a very important recovery and improvement of the natural state of the reef were seen from 1996 to 2000 (data obtained in October 2000). This is attributed to the awareness of the population and users of its importance and care following the publication of the decree. As a result of the promulgation of the decree, the local inhabitants have been changing their view regarding the care of the reef that must be taken. However, most of the activities carried out involve the movement of boats and ships, which could lead to various impacts due to anchoring and beaching. This is mainly caused by visitors who do not know the area and have no knowledge of the importance of the reef and the recommendations for its use.

With regard to the historical and archaeological aspect of the region, the archaeological sites, described previously, are within the inventory of archaeological sites that is under the responsibility of the Subdirectorate for Public Records of Monuments and Archaeological Sites under the National Institute of Anthropology and History. Unfortunately, the influx of tourism represents a potential threat because there is a lack of protective measures and mechanisms to prevent the plundering, destruction, or modification of these cultural sites.

The involvement of the people of Cabo Pulmo in the NPA proposal was important. The Autonomous University of Baja California Sur channeled the proposal to the three levels of government for approval. Local involvement was relevant because, regardless of the proposal's academic origin and the efforts of pertinent authorities, it is crucial to count on the local communities' effort and work for conservation and proper management in any management program. Particularly in Cabo Pulmo, although the management program (PMCP) was just recently published, it has been the participation of the local people that has essentially allowed the recovery of both the reef ecosystem as well as raising the quality of life of the nearly 150 inhabitants of the area.

Cabo San Lucas Arch Natural Monument

The Cabo San Lucas Arch has been a symbol of Baja California Sur, nationally and internationally. The beauty of this rocky arch, located at the tip of the Baja California peninsula, has made it an extraordinary tourist attraction. The land's end, the Cerro El Vigía, and the Cabo San Lucas Arch constitute important landscape and regional identity features. Hence, for several years their location has been proposed as a Natural Protected Area under the category of Natural Monument. In this context, the Justificatory Technical Study (JTS) has been generated to officially declare this monument within the National System of NPA (CONANP 2008). This JTS, whose bases are later described, was under public consultation in February 2010.

Natural monuments not only represent national heritage but they are also an important part of the culture, history, and identity of communities. Moreover, some regions have an added economic value due to the locality's own activities and unique scenic features. The Cabo San Lucas Arch and Cerro El Vigía are an undeniable symbol of identity in the region. The astonishing economic growth that the region is experiencing is a real and imminent threat that may negatively impact the area if there is no formal management and conservation program in place. For over 15 years, proposals have been made to provide a preservation scheme for the Cabo San Lucas Arch and Cerro El Vigía. The demand is made not only by the Baja California Sur authorities, but also by the community itself, and by SEMARNAT through CONANP. This need to preserve the area has produced some results with the decree of the Urban Development Plan for San José del Cabo-Cabo San Lucas as well as the ecological ordinances Tourist Corridor of Los Cabos and Municipality of Los Cabos, which highlight the interest and need for conservation and sustainable development of the region. The National Monument proposal will encourage, assist, and promote the culture of respect for the environment and of preserving natural resources, which will translate into a model of environmental education for future generations.

The rationale for creating the natural protected area originates because the exponential growth of tourism activities in the region, particularly economic activities related to real estate investment, has raised concern and uneasiness in the community and with Baja California Sur authorities regarding the deterioration of the Cabo

San Lucas Arch and surrounding areas. This situation has been developing for over 10 years and there are specific references of real estate deals and projects to be undertaken in these areas. Taking concrete actions to safeguard the landscape integrity of this natural and unique element in the country cannot be postponed. According to Article 52 (Title II, Chapter I, Section II) of the LGEEPA, "To declare an area as a Natural Monument, it must have the following characteristics: be a consistent natural object in a natural place with a unique or exceptional character, with scenic, historic, or scientific value; without variety of ecosystem or necessary area to be included under management category, where only activities related to the preservation, scientific research, recreation, and education can be carried out." Thus, the following is the necessary and relevant information for the analysis of the decree proposal of the "Cabo San Lucas Arch" under the category of Natural Monument:

Name of the proposed area: Cabo San Lucas Arch Natural Monument (Monumento Natural Arco de Cabo San Lucas–MNACSL). Area: Irregular-shaped polygon with an area of 36 ha. Extension: 5,398.63 km^2; 23°47'34"–22°52'12" North latitude; 110°16'48"–109°24'36" West longitude. Access routes: Marina Boulevard, paved street that borders the Cabo San Lucas dock.

Physical Characteristics

The MNACSL is bordered on its northern part by the Bay of Cabo San Lucas; on the south by the Pacific Ocean; and on the east by the Gulf of California and Pacific Ocean convergence. It has an irregular area of about 36 ha whose topography is extremely rugged in its southern part, showing a promontory all the way to the middle of the terrain where slopes are not greater than 15%. In the north, on the shore of the bay's coastline, the slopes are characterized by being greater than 30%. The rock units that emerge in the state of Baja California Sur manifest a geochronology that covers from the Mesozoic era to the Cenozoic era. They are mainly extrusive and intrusive igneous, but there are also metamorphic and sedimentary rocks. The physiographic discontinuity of the Cabo Region has mainly intrusive igneous rocks of cretaceous and metamorphic age from the Triassic-Jurassic period, which are intruded by the previous rocks.

The Cabo San Lucas Arch-Cerro El Vigía group is located in the Phytogeographic Region of Cabo. The dominant vegetation in this area is xerophilous scrub type, which is characterized by the ability to store water in its tissues (succulent plants). Specifically, the flora that can live in this area is the so-called sarcocaulescent and sarcocrassicaulescent scrub. The first is made up of trees and shrubs such as mesquite *(Prosopis sp.)*, palo verde *(Cercidium floridum)*, trumpetbush *(Tecoma stans)*, and damiana *(Turnera diffusa)*. The second group is composed of cactaceous plants such as the cardon *(Pachycereus sp.)*, cholla *(Opuntia sp.)*, hairbrush cardon *(Pachycereus pecten-aboriginum)*, and some species of pitahayas *(Machaerocereus ssp.)*.

The arguments that support the protection of the area are in accordance with Article 45 of the General Law of Ecological Equilibrium and Environmental Protection. These are to:
- Preserve natural environments representative of different biogeographical and ecological regions and most fragile ecosystems; to ensure equilibrium and continuity of the evolutionary and ecological processes
- Safeguard the genetic diversity of wildlife species that evolutionary continuity depends upon and to ensure the preservation and sustainable use of biodiversity in the country; in particular, preserve the species that are endangered, threatened, endemic, and rare or subject to special protection
- Ensure sustainable use of ecosystems and their elements
- Provide a propitious environment for scientific research and the study of ecosystems and their equilibrium
- Generate, rescue, and disseminate knowledge, practices, and technologies, traditional or new, that allow the preservation and sustainable use of the country's biodiversity
- Protect the natural surroundings of archaeological, historical, and artistic zones, monuments, and vestiges, as well as tourist zones and other areas of importance for national recreation, culture, and identity and for indigenous peoples

The region, delimited by the proposed polygon, contains natural elements such as the Cabo San Lucas Arch and Cerro El Vigía, which are natural sites of unique and exceptional character, of aesthetic importance, and of historical value. In addition, the region shows characteristics of natural monuments as stipulated in Article 52 of the LGEEPA. In general, the ecosystems in the proposed area are in their original condition with little disturbance and in a good state of preservation. This is due to the absence of intensive anthropogenic activities such as those related to agriculture, raising livestock, mining, forestry, and so on. The economic impact of the tourism industry in the area places second nationally for beachfront destinations.

The JTS lists the main points that frame the problems that the area of the NPA proposal faces:
- Modification of the environment because of increasing erosion
- Pollution from solid waste and wastewater
- Use of resources: the presence of tourism megaprojects with negative impacts on the environment, despite environmental regulations
- Conflict between sportfishing and commercial fishing
- Conservation: tourism development of the area must be planned

Although the entire region is considered a Protection Area of Flora and Fauna (Área de Protección de Flora y Fauna–APFF), this only ensures the care and conservation of the biota. A large portion of Cerro El Vigía is left outside the polygon of the Cabo San Lucas APFF. Thus, it is urgent that actions of geoconservation of the Cabo San Lucas Arch and Cerro El Vigía are taken in order to ensure an integrated management of the area and its long-term preservation.

SAN JOSÉ ESTUARY

An important protected area is the San José Estuary. The Riparian System of the San José del Cabo Watershed and Estuary, although declared in 1994 as a state reserve, is of international interest and, in 2008, was incorporated into the Ramsar Convention system of Wetlands of International Importance. The following describes this NPA, according to the Ramsar list (Breceda 2007).

It is located in the south of Baja California Sur, Mexico, below the Tropic of Cancer, belonging biogeographically to the Cabo Region and politically to the municipality of Los Cabos. The proposed site area covers 124,219 ha and is delimited by the watersheds of the La Laguna and La Trinidad sierras. This ecosystem is of great relevance for the region, from both the hydrological and biological perspectives, because it contains unique plant species and constitutes important corridors and refuges for flora and fauna. Among the species unique to the riparian system are: *Washingtonia robusta* and *Erythea brandegeei*, endemic to the peninsula of Baja California; *Populus brandegeei var glabra*, endemic to the Sierra La Laguna; *Prunus serotina* and *Ilex brandegeana* that, within the peninsular context, are exclusively distributed in the highlands of Sierra La Laguna; *Heteromeles arbutifolia* and *Salix lasiolepis*, which show a disjunctive distribution with the Sierra de San Pedro Mártir.

Physical Characteristics of the Catchment Area

The hydrological basin belongs to Hydrological Region 6 Baja California Sur-East (La Paz), considered one of the most important for its tributary area, with an extension of 1.278 km^2. It is delimited by the watersheds of the La Laguna and La Trinidad sierras that, with their intermittent surface runoff due to scarce rainfall and permeability of materials, feed the main stream that forms the San José stream. This stream flows into the estuary of the same name and is considered the most important stream in the region. The drainage network that feeds the San José stream is dendritic or radial type and subparallel, as it follows a pattern of approximately northeast–southwest fractures that originate in the Sierra La Trinidad and the Sierra La Laguna (Flores 1998; Hernández 1998). The precipitation and actual evapotranspiration in the basin were estimated at 408 mm and 318 mm annual average, respectively (Wurl et al. 2007). The recharge in the hydraulic balance resulted in 19.3 mm, representing 24 million m^3 for the San José basin. However, there is great variability in the short term, which depends greatly on the incidence of tropical cyclones in the area at a distance less than 800 km offshore (Wurl et al. 2007). Data on the hydraulic balance in the basin indicate that there is a recharge of approximately 5% of total precipitation, about 17% in runoff, and more than 75% of rainfall is lost through evapotranspiration (Wurl et al. 2007). With regard to water quality, it goes from sweet to tolerable; its use is to provide potable water to the population and tourism developments in San José del Cabo, the tourism corridor, Cabo San Lucas, and, to a lesser extent, for agricultural and livestock use (Valdez 2006). The San José aquifer is second in recharge capacity in the municipality of Los Cabos and fifth in the state. It has 24 million m^3 of water, contributing 94% of the resource to the municipality. However, the total water from the San José aquifer granted via concessions amounted in 2003 to 26.5 million m^3, causing the overexploitation of this aquifer (Valdez 2006).

In general, the basin's riparian system and, in particular, the main streambeds are essential for capturing groundwater for the aquifer, besides constituting the main areas of sediment control.

General Ecological Characteristics

The basin's vegetation is mainly lowland deciduous forest, sarcocaulescent scrub, and oak forest; to a lesser extent, sarcocrassicaulescent scrub, palm trees, mesquites, and gallery or riparian forest are also distributed. There are several plant communities in the San José Estuary: around the body of water are tule vegetation and reeds, and inland there are palm trees—in which the Mexican fan palm *(Washingtonia robusta)* species dominates—and shrub and herbaceous strata. Guamuchil and mesquite forests are located in small portions of the area; the first is dominated by abundant *Pithecellobium dulce* trees and the second by *Prosopis articulata*.

One of the most important characteristics of this protected area is the presence of the San José oasis and the estuary of the same name, because it is one of the largest epicontinental environments of the Baja California peninsula, and the only one of its kind in the Cabo Region. This estuarine system consists of a body of fresh surface water that sustains different aquatic, subaquatic, and riparian plant associations as well as farming areas in its surroundings. The source of freshwater for the estuary is the runoff from the San José hydrological basin. The runoff converges in the watercourse of the San José stream, which flows into the body of the estuary. The boundary between the estuary and the seawater of the Gulf of California consists of a thin sand bar that allows the intrusion of marine water, but in a very low proportion to the fresh water.

The characteristic vegetation of this estuary is composed of species typical of oases, such as palm trees, reeds, and aquatic species. It is the last rest stop for waterfowl and shorebirds that migrate to areas of southern Mexico, Central America, or South America. A total of 217 species have been registered, 97 of which are migratory and 19 are under some classification of risk, such as the least tern *(Sterna antillarum browni)*. Due to the importance the estuary's avifauna, it has been recognized as an Area of Importance for the Conservation of Birds (Área de Importancia para la Conservación de Aves–AICA). Moreover, there are also artificial wetlands within the basin resulting from the construction of reservoirs, such as Boca de la Sierra and Caduaño. These are very small, but of great importance for the hydrological services they provide to local communities, as well as for their important biological role as seasonal sites for migratory birds. The bird community of this protected site is of biological relevance because of its richness, high number of migratory species, and number of species under some protection status.

There are also other taxa found in some of the risk categories as per NOM-059-SEMARNAT-2001. A total of 21 species of reptiles endemic to the peninsula have been registered in the area (Grismer 2002). Species under special protection, according to NOM-059-SEMARNAT-2001, are the San Lucas alligator lizard *(Elgaria paucicarinata)*, worm lizard *(Bipes biporus)*, spotted sandsnake *(Chilomeniscus stramineus)*, night snake *(Hypsiglena torquata)*, Western banded gecko *(Coleonyx variaegatus)*, San Lucas gecko *(Phyllodactylus unctus)*, Xantus leaf-toed gecko *(Phyllodactylus xanti)*, Sonora spiny-tailed iguana *(Ctenosaura hemilopha)*, Baja California rock lizard *(Petrosaurus thalassinus)*, Cabo spiny lizard *(Sceloporus licki)*, Hunsaker's spiny lizard *(Scelopurus hunsaker)*, and two rattlesnakes *(Crotalus mitchelli* and *Crotalus ruber)*. Under the threatened status are the common kingsnake *(Lampropeltis getula)*, chuckwalla *(Sauromalus obesus)*, and zebra-tailed lizard *(Callisaurus draconoides)*, as well as endemic species including the Baja California night snake *(Eridiphas slevini)*, Baja California striped whipsnake *(Masticophis aurigulus)*, Baja California brush lizard *(Urosaurus nigricaudus)*, San Lucas skink *(Eumeces lagunensis)*, and Baja California rattlesnake *(Crotalus enyo)*.

Several mammal species are under some risk status, according to NOM-059-SEMARNAT-2001. These include the shrew *(Notiosorex crawfordi)*, which is a threatened species, as well as the badger *(Taxidea taxus)* and Mexican long-tongued bat *(Choeronycteris Mexican)*.

The socioeconomic functions of the San José basin and particularly of the riparian system, the oases, and the estuary, are varied and relevant. Most important is its role in the water cycle and aquifer recharge. This is essential for development of economic activities such as agriculture and raising livestock. Tourism activities also depend on the functionality of this watershed. In particular, the San José Estuary is a great tourist attraction because it contrasts with the arid environment of the region and is the site of activities that include bird watching, horseback riding, and boat tours, right in the center of one of the municipality's largest and most important tourist sites. The riparian system and the oasis also constitute places of great attraction for ecotourism activities. Important locations for these are Boca de la Sierra, Miraflores, El Cajón Waterfall, and San Miguelito Waterfall.

With regard to cultural historical values, the Jesuit mission of San José del Cabo, established in 1730, is prominent, as is the historic center of this city. Among other cultural values in the basin, numerous ranch settlements are formed along streams. These preserve the ancient traditions of the early Spanish settlers in the region.

The types of land tenure of the San José watershed and estuary are communal land holdings *(ejidos)*, federal lands, and private lands. The *ejido* lands occupy 34% of the area of the proposed site or an area of 42,264 ha in seven *ejidos*. The land in state reserve and private ownership is 66% of the area. The main uses surrounding the estuary are urban use and tourism. In other areas of the basin, there are land uses related to agriculture and livestock, and forestry that includes some logging for building materials.

The most important adverse factors, mentioned in the Ramsar declaration as main problems, are related to land use change and urban growth of San José del Cabo. Increased rates of erosion due to the impact of human activities such as construction of roads, extraction of forest species, and raising livestock are of concern. The San José Estuary is under great pressure because of discharge of contaminated water into it. The introduction of exotic species such as the tilapia, guppies, and the *Cryptostegia grandiflora* shrub is also an adverse factor. However, the most important threat is the development of the large-scale tourism project Puerto Los Cabos, for which a large marina has been built at a distance of 800 m from the water body.

The state government of Baja California Sur and the government of the municipality of Los Cabos have jurisdiction over the San José Estuary Ecological Reserve. The northwest region of the basin is in the area that is part of the Sierra La Laguna Biosphere Reserve and is under federal jurisdiction through the National Commission of Natural Protected Areas (Comisión Nacional de Áreas Naturales Protegidas–CONANP). Riparian zones, since they involve streams, pertain to the National Water Commission (Comisión Nacional del Agua–CONAGUA). The San José del Cabo Estuary was declared a State Ecological Reserve on January 10, 1994, under the category of

Area Subject to Ecological Conservation. The objective of the declaration was to harmonize the recovery, preservation, and socioeconomic development through proper management of natural resources, and promote research, education, and participation of the local community. The decree specifies that the execution of private or public works will not be authorized or permitted within the area defined as core zone of the State Ecological Reserve, except for those that are strictly necessary for its conditioning, cleaning, restoration, conservation, and scientific research. However, the pressures of tourism development in the area continue to increase and the management program for the area has not functioned properly. This has led to increased protection and proper management efforts of this fragile area. It is hoped that inclusion in the internationally recognized Ramsar system, along with an appropriate management program, will support the intelligent management and conservation of this relevant area.

REFERENCES

Anaya-Reyna, G., and R. Riosmena-Rodríguez. 1996. "Macroalgas marinas del arrecife coralino de Cabo Pulmo-Los Frailes, BCS, México." *Rev. Biol. Trop.* 44: 861–864.

Brusca R., C., and D. B. Thomson. 1975. "Pulmo Reef: The Only 'Coral Reef' in the Gulf of California." *Ciencias Marinas* 1, 37-53.

Comisión Nacional de Áreas Naturales Protegidas (CONANP). 1998. *Ley General del Equilibrio Ecológico y la Protección al Ambiente (LGEEPA)*. México, DF: Diario Oficial de la Federación.

Comisión Nacional de Áreas Naturales Protegidas (CONANP). 2003. *Programa de Manejo de la Sierra La Laguna*. México, DF.

Comisión Nacional de Áreas Naturales Protegidas (CONANP). 2006a. *Programa de Conservación y Manejo Parque Nacional Cabo Pulmo México*. México, DF.

Comisión Nacional de Áreas Naturales Protegidas (CONANP). 2006b. "Estudio previo justificativo para el establecimiento del Área Natural Protegida, Área de Protección de Flora y Fauna Oasis de Baja California Sur, conformada en Archipiélago." Unpublished. México, DF.

Comisión Nacional de Áreas Naturales Protegidas (CONANP). 2006c. "Estudio previo justificativo para el establecimiento del Área Natural Protegida 'Parque Nacional Espíritu Santo.'" México, DF.

Comisión Nacional de Áreas Naturales Protegidas (CONANP). 2007. *Programa Nacional de Áreas Naturales Protegidas.* México, DF: CONANP.

Comisión Nacional de Áreas Naturales Protegidas (CONANP). 2008. "Estudio previo justificativo para el establecimiento del Monumento Natural Arco de Cabo San Lucas, en el Estado de Baja California Sur." México, DF.

Comisión Nacional para el Conocimiento y Uso de la Biodiversidad (CONABIO). 1997a. "Provincias biogeográficas de México. Escala 1:4 000 000." México, DF.

Comisión Nacional para el Conocimiento y Uso de la Biodiversidad (CONABIO). 1997b. "Mapa de climas, Escala 1:1, 000,000." México, DF.

Ferrusquía-Villafranca, I. 1992. Regionalización Biogeográfica IV.8.10, Atlas Nacional de México. Vol. II. Escala 1: 4' 000, 000, Instituto de Geografía, UNAM, México.

Findley, L. T., J. Torre, J. M. Nava, A. M. van der Heiden, and P. A. Hastings. 1996. "Preliminary Ictiofaunal Analysis from a Macrofaunal Database of the Gulf of California, Mexico." Abstract 76th annual meeting of American Society Icthiologists and Herpetologists, 13–19 June, New Orleans.

Flores, E. 1998. *Geosudcalifornia. Geografía, agua y ciclones.* La Paz, BCS: Universidad Autónoma de Baja California Sur.

Glynn, P. W., and I. G. McIntyre. 1977. "Growth Rate and Age of Coral Reefs on the Pacific Coast of Panama." *Proc. 3rd Int. Symp. Coral Reefs, Miami* 2: 251–259.

Grismer, L. L. 2002. *Amphibians and Reptile of Baja California including Its Pacific Islands and the Islands in the Sea of Cortés.* Berkeley, CA: University of California Press.

Hernández, M. A. 1998. *Desarrollo, planificación y medio ambiente en Baja California Sur.* La Paz, BCS: Universidad Autónoma de Baja California Sur.

Instituto Nacional de Estadística, Geografía e Informática (INEGI). 1985. Carta topográfica de San José del Cabo, México. México, DF: INEGI.

Kerstitch, A. N. 1989. *Sea of Cortez Marine Invertebrates: A Guide for the Pacific Coast, Mexico to Ecuador.* Monterey, CA: Sea Challengers.

Massey, W. 1955. "Culture History in the Cape Region of Baja California." Ph.D. dissertation in science, University of California, Riverside.

Reyes-Bonilla, H. 1990. "Taxonomía, distribución y algunos aspectos biogeográficos de los corales hermatípicos del Golfo de California." Bachelor's thesis in biology, Universidad Autónoma de Baja California Sur, La Paz, México.

Reyes-Bonilla, H. 1993a. "Estructura de la comunidad, influencia de la depredación y biología poblacional de coral hermatípicos en el arrecife de Cabo Pulmo, Baja California Sur." Master's thesis in science, Centro Interdisciplinario y de Estudios Superiores de Ensenada, Ensenada, B.C., México.

Reyes-Bonilla, H. 1993b. "The 1987 Coral Reef Bleaching at Cabo Pulmo Reef, Gulf of California, México." *Bull. Mar. Sci.* 52: 832–837.

Tilmant, J. T. 1987. "Impacts of Recreacional Activities on Coral Reefs." Pp. 197–214 in *Human Impacts on the Coral Reefs: Facts and Recommendations,* B. Salvat, ed. French Polynesia: Antenne Museum, E.P.H.E.

Valdez, A. 2006. "Diagnóstico, servicios ambientales y valoración económica del agua en el corredor turístico-urbano de Los Cabos, BCS." Master's thesis in science, Universidad Autónoma de Baja California Sur.

Villareal, A., H. Reyes-Bonilla, B. Bermúdez, and O. Arizpe. 2000. "Los peces del arrecife de Cabo Pulmo, Golfo de California, México: Lista sistemática y aspectos de abundancia y biogeografía." *Rev. Biol. Trop.* 48 (2/3): 413–424.

Wurl, J., P. Hernández, J. Gaytán, J. Martínez, and M. Imaz. 2007. "Manejo integral de la cuenca hidrológica forestal de San José del Cabo, BCS." In Informe Técnico CONAFOR-CONACYT (CO1–5671).

8

Los Cabos in the Face of Climate Change

G. Bazzino-Ferreri and S. Lluch-Cota

INTRODUCTION

The Los Cabos region is characterized by a pleasant climate suitable for beach tourism activities during most of the year. It has conditions of low or no cloudiness around 300 days a year, with an average temperature of 27°C. In the summer, higher temperatures are reached, about 35°C, with low humidity. Rainfall is practically nil from March to June and, during the summer, it is related to extreme tropical activity (storms and cyclones). Figure 1a (top panel) shows the annual pattern of sea temperature, with minimal values in the spring and maximum in the fall, and annual range of around 6°C. Figure 1b (center panel) also shows a series of sea temperature anomalies (monthly values minus the average of the corresponding month) of a 2°x2° quadrant around Los Cabos (points), a 24-month smoothing component (moving average) to highlight interannual tendencies (continuous line) and a moving average of 240 months to highlight tendencies in the decadal scale (discontinuous line).

Two particularly interesting aspects stand out when observing Figure 1c. First is the strong interannual variability associated with the El Niño/Southern Oscillation (ENSO), as shown in the lower panel, with particular impact of the 1940 and 1958 events, and the most famous and intense of the last century in other parts of the world, those of 1982–83 and 1997–98. The second is the series of sea temperature anomalies (center panel) that shows strong natural variations that impede the detection of any indication of sustained warming in the series, at least before the 1970s.

Figure 1a. Annual pattern of sea surface temperature in the region of Los Cabos (geographic quadrant of 2°x2° - database: ERSST and NOAA,1885–1999 period)

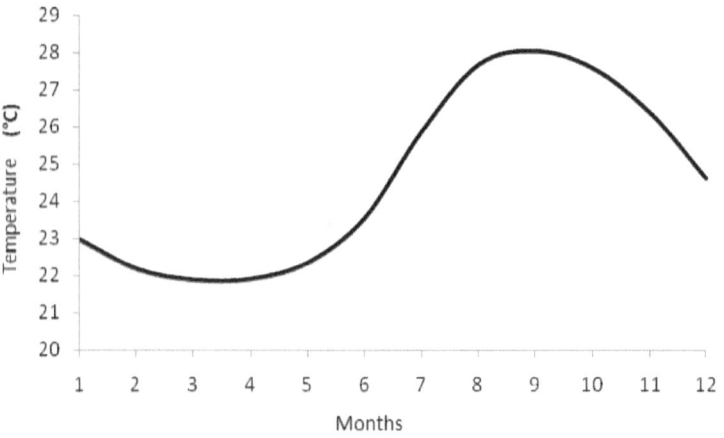

Figure 1b. A series of sea temperature anomalies (dots), 24-month smoothing component (moving average) (solid line), and a moving average of 240 months (dashed line) in the region of Los Cabos (geographic quadrant of 2°x2° - database: ERSST and NOAA, 1885–999 period)

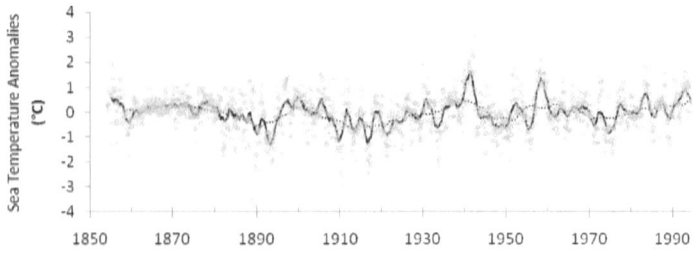

Figure 1c. Smoothed series (24-month moving average) of the Southern Oscillation Index (SOI)

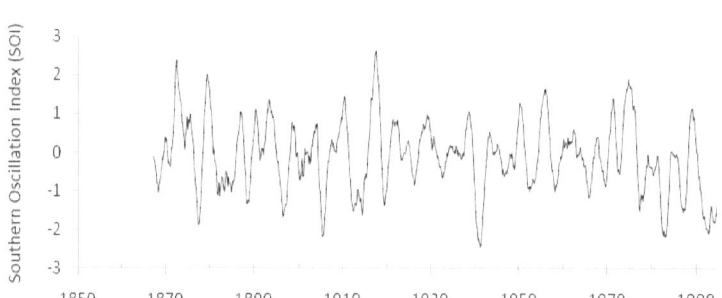

The El Niño events constitute the strongest interannual indication of climate variability in the Gulf of California (Herrera-Cervantes et al. 2007; Lluch-Cota et al. 2007) and in the eastern Pacific Ocean. This phenomenon becomes more significant if one takes into account that some of the possible future scenarios of climate change consider a probable increase in the amplitude and frequency of El Niño events (Meehl et al. 2007).

In addition to the high-frequency climate variability (interannual), there are other forms of climate variability in a temporal scale on the order of decades, whose impacts on the climate of northwestern Mexico are beginning to be identified and, at times, are confused with the climate change tendencies. The Pacific Decadal Oscillation (PDO) is a form of climate variability of the Pacific Ocean, where there are phase changes in its thermal structure in interdecadal periods, usually between 20 and 30 years. The PDO is identified by warm and cold anomalies in the Pacific Ocean, north of 20°N. During its positive or warm phase, the western Pacific becomes cooler than normal, while the eastern part tends to warm up above normal. The opposite condition occurs during the cold phase of the PDO. The presence of the PDO has been reconstructed through dendrochronologies of trees from the region of Baja California.

DETECTION AND ATTRIBUTION

In general, disasters of a hydrometeorological origin that occur in the world tend to be associated with climate change. However, such disasters are not only the result of extreme events, but largely reflect the high vulnerability of human beings. In response, the world community has dedicated great efforts and resources to scientific research. Given the latent risk of climate change, public policy design and communication of the problem with the aim of reducing potential negative impacts are ongoing challenges. To manage and reduce risks in the face of climate change, it is necessary, on the one hand, to decrease the magnitude of the threat through mitigation, that is, by reducing emissions of so-called greenhouse gases. On the other hand, it is necessary to reduce the vulnerability of economic sectors, social groups, and regions given the possible future climate scenarios, through a process of adaptation.

Two critical questions regarding climate change that are relevant to Los Cabos are:
1. Are there signs of change in the climate intense enough to affirm that climate change is real?
2. What measures can be taken before it is too late?

The answers to these questions require the establishment of the characteristics of climate change at a regional level, working on the detection of tendencies, as well as on the attribution, that is, on separating the climate's natural variability from those changes attributable to human activity. At present, it is known that the planet's global warming is happening, given that the land and ocean surface temperatures have been continuously increasing. This has led to, among other things, the decrease of the ice and snow cover, thereby causing the sea level to rise. Temperature fluctuations, both oceanic and terrestrial, are part of the various forms of the climate's natural variability, which are related to changes in solar activity, ocean-atmosphere-biosphere feedback processes, or volcanic activity. Nonetheless, it has been suggested that the phenomenon of global warming can only be explained if one considers the change in the atmosphere's composition associated with increases in carbon dioxide, methane, nitrous oxide, and other greenhouse gases.

In order to analyze the processes of climate change at a local level, it is necessary to understand the causes of climate change. For example, it is very difficult to say that an extreme meteorological event (e.g., intense hurricane) is a consequence of global climate change, as climate is characterized by atmospheric statistics in periods of months and years, and not by atmospheric instabilities of a particular day that corresponds to the weather.

In the particular case of Mexico, there are few studies of detection and attribution of climate change. However, some examples have been identified that show that the country's climate is changing. For example, the average annual temperature in Mexico has increased approximately 0.5°C in the last one hundred years, and the annual cumulative precipitation has increased by about 5%. Temperature variations in practically the entire country are consistent with temperature variations in the northern hemisphere and globally, which is to be expected since they are not exempt from the warming process.

It is difficult to entirely attribute the tendency of more or less rain at the regional level to global climate change, since there is an infrequent variation in Mexico's rainfall over periods of 30 years or more. Apparently, this is related to the Pacific Decadal Oscillation and the Atlantic Multidecadal Oscillation that, under a tendency to more precipitation in the north, tend to make it rain less in the south and vice versa.

In most of Mexico, there are clear signs of a tendency of rain events to be increasingly more intense, that is, very heavy downpours of more than 20 mm/day. The increment in the magnitude of severe storms has been a continuous process, as expected in face of a current scenario of climate change.

Another phenomenon related to climate change that has been occurring on the Mexican coast refers to the increase in sea level, thus exposing coastal areas to serious problems. It is not yet clear how other meteorological parameters, like wind and air humidity, have changed in the country as a result of climate change. Nonetheless, there have certainly been alterations that have affected the socioeconomic activities. Much remains to be done in terms of detection and attribution of climate change before starting a process of adaptation, at a regional and local level, that makes people less vulnerable to the effects of a different climate.

Issues of Interest

Studies have been carried out in recent years to detect threats and analyze the vulnerability of the state of Baja California Sur to potential climate change scenarios and, thus, propose actions to mitigate negative impacts. Among the climatic threats that have been identified for Baja California Sur, hurricanes and extreme precipitation events are prominent. According to records in recent years, cyclones, tropical storms, and hurricanes have caused economic (loss of crops and livestock), social (floods), and even fatal (loss of human life) impacts. Another potential threat detected in the region refers to areas at risk of flooding due to the rise of the sea level (1–2 meters), which are located both on the side of the Pacific Ocean and the Gulf of California.

Extreme Climate

Extreme hydrometeorological events and abnormal weather conditions often have negative impacts on Mexico and can become a disaster, depending on the magnitude of the event and the vulnerability of the sector, region, or social group. In fact, Mexico is among the countries most affected by hurricanes or tropical cyclones. In the Caribbean, Gulf of Mexico, or the Pacific Ocean (including the Gulf of California), these systems produce heavy rains on the continent. However, there is also the possibility that the convergence of moisture from a tropical cyclone, far from the Mexican coast, tends to "dry up" the continental portion and thus contribute to a decrease in rainfall over the land.

With regard to forecasting the weather or generating climate change scenarios, it is of utmost importance for Mexico to consider tropical cyclones and their influence on summer rains. However, it is still unclear how to include its effect on low-spatial resolution models and even in those of high resolution, since theories on tropical cyclogenesis do not yet allow the prediction of the formation of these phenomena. There are some strategies that would permit estimating the effect of such systems on the climate. Beyond predicting the number of storms or hurricanes, as is done currently, it is important to generate probability predictions of a greater or lesser number of hurricanes, strong or weak, far or near the coasts.

According to research conducted by the Intergovernmental Panel on Climate Change (IPCC), there is a high probability for an increase in extreme meteorological events such as heat waves and higher minimum temperatures. Also, an increase is expected in the frequency of occurrence of hurricanes (tropical cyclones), although it is unknown what could happen with their intensity.

It should be noted that the state of Baja California Sur, where the region of Los Cabos is located, is particularly vulnerable to impacts of extreme hydrometeorological phenomena such as cyclones and tropical storms originating in the Pacific Ocean, as well as the effects of El Niño or La Niña phenomena. The most frequent local impacts include loss of biodiversity, the occurrence of floods or droughts, and economic losses in agriculture, livestock raising, and tourism.

The high population growth rate seen in coastal areas, particularly at focal points of economic development (e.g., Los Cabos and La Paz), causes immigrants who settle in the periphery of these points to take increasingly greater risks. They do so without the necessary safety conditions to face eventual meteorological and environmental contingencies such as floods and hurricanes.

Mean Sea Level (MSL)

As a result of the global warming phenomenon, it is expected that the mean sea level (MSL) will increase due to the thermal expansion of waters, as well as to the melting of glaciers and polar ice caps. The magnitude of the increase and its impact can vary from place to place, depending on various factors such as the change in other climate aspects, coastal morphology, and human modifications.

The implications of this phenomenon can be of several types: (1) geophysical (erosion determines the regression and modification of the coastline); (2) biological (ecological impact due to the replacement of the original habitat); and (3) socioeconomic (since a major part of the world's population concentrates in coastal areas).

According to the different climate scenarios established by the IPCC (2001), it is expected that the MSL at a global level will have risen between 0.09 and 0.88 m between 1990 and 2010, mainly due to the thermal expansion and mass loss of glaciers and polar ice caps. However, the change in the MSL is not spatially uniform, since the rate of increase in some regions may be even higher than the world average, while in others there may be a decrease. In the case of some seas of limited size in the Pacific Ocean, which are partially isolated from the adjacent ocean, it has been seen that they can respond quickly to changes forced by climate variability (IPCC 2007).

Moreover, it is important to note that a considerable percentage of the world population lives on or very near coastlines (Forbes and Livermann 1996). In Mexico, coastal cities have grown rapidly over the last 10 years (León 2004), a trend that will continue in the coming decades. Therefore, it is likely that, as the population settled in vulnerable areas increases, the negative effects of an increment in the MSL will multiply, since material losses as well as those of human lives would increase.

In the particular case of the Gulf of California, the most vulnerable regions to an increase in the MSL would be the Upper Gulf, Mazatlán, and Los Cabos. Specific assessments were conducted in these three sites to delimit the areas that could be affected by the advancement of the MSL (between 1 and 3 meters). The Upper Gulf proved to be the most vulnerable region because it had the highest values in almost all the variables analyzed, whereas in the case of Mazatlán and Los Cabos, the most influential factor was the intense tourism present in these regions.

Los Cabos is a region with steep slopes, so the area that is located below 10 meters above the MSL is limited. However, the activities that enrich this tourist center are located in the first meters of the coast. So, an increase in the MSL would significantly affect this region. It is expected that the results generated by this type of study allow for recommendations to be taken into account in the corresponding development plans.

Ocean Acidification

According to climate models used by the IPCC, toward the end of the twenty-first century (Meehl et al. 2007), CO_2 emissions will cause a drop in the ocean surface pH of up to 0.3 units. This process, known as ocean acidification (Caldeira and Wickett 2003), causes an increase in the concentration of $H+$ ions and a reduction in the concentration of carbonate ions (CO^{2-}_3), which mainly affect marine organisms with calcium carbonate skeletons (C_aCO_3), such as corals and some plankton species (Orr et al. 2005; Kleypas et al. 2006). According to this future climate scenario, global warming and ocean acidification will negatively impact the accumulation of carbonate, causing a reduction of coral species in reef ecosystems (lower diversity and greater instability of the carbonate structures) (Höegh-Guldberg et al. 2007).

To date, there are no reports of a clear tendency of acidification in the Gulf of California. However, it is an aspect that could prove key in the region of Los Cabos and Cabo Pulmo, since coral reefs are one of the main tourist attractions for those who practice underwater activities. In addition, these regions are located on the boundary of the saturation levels in seawater of aragonite, which limits the survival of coral reefs (Kleypas et al. 2001). In fact, most coral reefs in the Gulf of California live in marginal environmental conditions (Kleypas et al. 1999), near limiting levels of temperature, phosphate, light penetration, and aragonite saturation.

According to future scenarios of acidification reported by Höegh-Guldberg et al. (2007), the Gulf of California region would be located outside the habitat suitable for coral reefs. Furthermore, there could be a synergy with other phenomena related to climate change, such as global warming of the oceans (Bindoff et al. 2007) and the associated expansion of the Oxygen Minimum Zone (Stramma et al. 2008), which would increase the sensitivity and vulnerability of coral reef communities.

Potential Effects on the Tourism Sector

Recreational Sportfishing

Recreational sportfishing is one of the most important economic activities in the region of Los Cabos and also in other tourist destinations in the Gulf of California. According to 2007 data, an estimated 354,013 persons engaged in activities related to sportfishing in Los Cabos, with an average cost of $1,785 for the payment of fishing boat rental, gasoline, transportation, and other expenses. In addition, sportfishing in Los Cabos generates about 24,426 direct jobs and just over $245 million annually (Southwick et al. 2008).

According to the 2001–2006 National Program for Tourism, sportfishing constitutes a very important option for diversification of tourism services and for adding value to tourist destinations. In this context, it is essential to assess possible interactions between this activity and the environmental variability associated with climate change. For example, it is necessary to evaluate the impact that a change in the habitat of species reserved for sportfishing would represent. In fact, a significant increase in ocean temperature could cause these species to move their distribution areas northward and, consequently, tourist destinations for sportfishing, such as Los Cabos, Los Barriles, and La Paz, would experience a decrease in their economic potential, which depends largely on this activity (Zepeda-Domínguez 2008).

Real Estate

The real estate market, associated with the tourism industry, could also suffer the consequences of climate change. It should be noted that a significant proportion of tourist visitors or residents (temporary or year-round) are elderly people who acquire properties in search of a more beneficial climate than in their countries of origin (U.S. and Canada, primarily). In this case, a rise in the global temperature could, hypothetically, modify the current extension of the temperate, tropical, and subtropical regions. Thus, some areas that previously were unpropitious for tourism for adults could acquire new climatic attributes that would affect the real estate market in a way that, to date, is unknown (Zepeda-Domínguez 2008).

Tourism occupancy in the region of Los Cabos could be affected in two ways: On the one hand, with the decline in hotel occupancy in the aftermath of extreme climatic events (hurricanes, waterspouts, etc.) and, on the other hand, with the loss of economic value of timeshares and properties associated with its greater environmental vulnerability. The two aforementioned occurrences would be the beginning of a chain that would bring the slowdown of economic activities in the state.

PERSPECTIVES

State Plan on Climate Change

From the global climate change scenarios, various sources or mechanisms have been identified with regard to climatic pressure with potential impacts on the exploitation of natural resources and productive activity. These would also impact the social and economic dynamics of the region, which complicates the adoption of sustainable strategies for development. A need has been identified for establishing climate change programs that provide authorities and different sectors of society with a tool for planning and decision making. Nationally, there is already a proposal for a National Program on Climate Change that addresses some of the general problems of the country; however, the acknowledgement of regional differences requires the establishment of regional and state level programs. To that end, a proposal has been developed that includes an action program on climate change for the state of Baja California Sur, which recognizes the extreme vulnerability of this administrative unit, derived from its geographic location and specific conditions.

Monitoring (Marine Observatory)

It is increasingly evident that the ability for predicting and early detecting anomalous conditions and, therefore, for proper planning of mitigation and adaptation measures, depends on the quality and longevity of monitoring systems for the environment, organisms, or processes in the natural environment. Mexico faces a particularly dramatic situation because of the lack of an adequate and complete network for monitoring oceans. For example, the mareographic network that operated some decades ago has been disappearing as the stations become obsolete or are simply abandoned. It is also clear when the number of observatories and fixed platforms with equipment that exist along the extensive coastline can be counted on one's fingers.

Fortunately, it is increasingly clear to the scientific community that it is a priority and it is foreseeable that in the coming years a major effort will be directed to improve and increase the marine observation facilities. One of the initiatives currently being generated is the development of marine observatories (one in La Paz, within the Gulf of California, and one in Mérida, in the Atlantic). These observatories work initially as research networks, bringing together staff interested in attacking this serious lack of information, and the goal becomes to raise funds and broaden participation to install equipment and begin the urgent task of producing time series data.

REFERENCES

Bindoff, N. L., J. Willebrand, V. Artale, A. Cazenave, J. Gregory, S. Gulev, K. Hanawa, C. Le Quéré, S. Levitus, Y. Nojiri, C. K. Shum, L. D. Talley, and A. Unnikrishnan. 2007. "Observations: Oceanic Climate Change and Sea Level." In *Climate Change 2007: The Physical Science Basis. Contribution of Working Group I to the Fourth Assessment Report of the Intergovernmental Panel on Climate Change*, S. Solomon, D. Qin, M. Manning, Z. Chen, M. Marquis, K. B. Averyt, M. Tignor, and H. L. Miller, eds. Cambridge, UK, and New York: Cambridge University Press.

Caldeira, K., and M. E. Wickett. 2003. "Anthropogenic Carbon and Ocean pH." *Nature* 425: 365.

Forbes, D., and D. Liverman. 1996. "Geological Indicators in the Coastal Zone." Pp. 175–192 in *Geoindicators: Assessing Rapid Environmental Changes in Earth System*, A. Berger and W. Iams, eds. Rotterdam; Brookfield, VT : Balkema.

Herrera-Cervantes, H., D. B. Lluch-Cota, S. E. Lluch-Cota, and G. Gutiérrez de Velasco. 2007. "The ENSO Signature in Sea-Surface Temperature in the Gulf of California." *Journal of Marine Research* 65: 589–605.

Höegh-Guldberg, O., P. J. Mumby, A. J. Hooten, R. S. Steneck, P. Greenfield, E. Gomez, C. D. Harvell, P. F. Sale, A. J. Edwards, K. Caldeira, N. Knowlton, C. M. Eakin, R. Iglesias-Prieto, N. Muthiga, R. H. Bradbury, A. Dubi, and M. E. Hatziolos. 2007. "Coral Reefs under Rapid Climate Change and Ocean Acidification." *Science* 318: 1737–1742.

Intergovernmental Panel on Climate Change (IPCC). 2001. *Climate Change 2001: The Scientific Basis. Contribution of Working Group I to the Third Assessment Report of the Intergovernmental Panel on Climate Change*, J. T. Houghton, Y. Ding, D. J. Griggs, M. Noguer, P. J. van der Linden, X. Dai, K. Maskell, and C. A. Johnson, eds. Cambridge University Press, Cambridge, United Kingdom and New York, NY, USA.

Intergovernmental Panel on Climate Change (IPCC). 2007. *Climate Change 2007: The Physical Science Basis. Contribution of Working Group I to the Fourth Assessment Report of the Intergovernmental Panel on Climate Change*, S. Solomon, D. Qin, M. Manning, Z.

Chen, M. Marquis, K. B. Averyt, M. Tignor, and H. L. Miller, eds. Cambridge University Press, Cambridge United Kingdom and New York, NY, USA.

Kleypas, J. A., J. W. McManus, and L. A. B. Meñe. 1999. "Environmental Limits to Coral Reef Development: Where Do We Draw the Line?" *Am. Zool.* 39: 146–159.

Kleypas, J. A., R. A. Feely, V. J. Fabry, C. Langdon, C. L. Sabine, and L. L. Robbins. 2006. *Impacts of Ocean Acidification on Coral Reefs and Other Marine Calcifiers. A Guide for Future Research.* Proceedings of workshop, 18–20 April 2005, St. Petersburg, FL, sponsored by NSF, NOAA, and U.S. Geological Survey.

Kleypas, J. A., R. W. Buddemeier, and J. P. Gattuso. 2001. "The Future of Coral Reefs in an Age of Global Change." *Int. J. Earth Sci.* 90: 426–437.

León, C. 2004. "Piezas de un rompecabezas: Dimensión socioeconómica de las costas de México." In *El manejo costero en México*, F. R. May, ed. Campeche, México: EPOMEX.

Lluch-Cota, S. E., E. A. Aragón-Noriega, F. Arreguín-Sánchez, D. Aurioles-Gamboa, J. J. Bautista-Romero, R. C. Brusca, R. Cervantes-Duarte, R. Cortés-Altamirano, P. Del-Monte-Luna, A. Esquivel-Herrera, G. Fernández, M. E. Hendrickx, S. Hernández-Vázquez, H. Herrera-Cervantes, M. Kahru, M. Lavín, D. Lluch-Belda, D. B. Lluch-Cota, J. López-Martínez, S. G. Marinote, M. O. Nevárez-Martínez, S. Ortega-García, E. Palacios-Castro, A. Parés-Sierra, G. Ponce-Díaz, M. Ramírez-Rodríguez, C. A. Salinas-Zavala, R. A. Schwartzlose, and A. P. Sierra-Beltrán. 2007. "The Gulf of California: Review of Ecosystem Status and Sustainability Challenges." *Progress in Oceanography* 73: 1–26.

Meehl, G. A., T. F. Stocker, W. D. Collins, P. Friedlingstein, A. T. Gaye, J. M. Gregory, A. Kitoh, R. Knutti, J. M. Murphy, A. Noda, S. C. B. Raper, I. G. Watterson, A. J. Weaver, and Z.C. Zhao. 2007. "Global Climate Projections." Pp. 747–845 in *Climate Change 2007: The Physical Science Basis. Contribution of Working Group I to the Fourth Assessment Report of the Intergovernmental Panel on Climate Change*, S. Solomon et al. eds. Cambridge, UK: Cambridge University Press.

Orr, J. C., V. J. Fabry, O. Aumont, L. Bopp, S. C. Doney, R. A. Feely, A. Gnanadesikan, N. Gruber, A. Ishida, F. Joos, R. M. Key,

K. Lindsay, E. Maier-Reimer, R. Matear, P. Monfray, A. Mouchet, R. G. Najjar, G. Kasper Plattner, K. B. Rodgers, C. L. Sabine, J. L. Sarmiento, R. Schlitzer, R. D. Slater, I. J. Totterdell, M. Weirig, Y. Yamanaka, and A. Yool. 2005. "Anthropogenic Ocean Acidification over the Twenty-First Century and Its Impact on Calcifying Organisms." *Nature* 437: 681–686.

Southwick, R., R. Nelson, and J. A. Arean Martinez. 2008. *The Economic Contributions of Anglers to the Los Cabos Economy*. Southwick Associates, Inc.; Nelson Resources Consulting, Inc.; FIRMUS Consulting. http://www.southwickassociates.com/free-reports#reports.

Stramma, L., G. C. Johnson, J. Sprintall, and V. Mohrholz. 2008. "Expanding Oxygen-minimum Zones in the Tropical Oceans." *Science* 320, 655.

Zepeda-Domínguez, J. A. 2008. Informe técnico sobre la percepción de la variabilidad ambiental y la afectación de ésta sobre los recursos naturales y la economía de las comunidades adyacentes al Golfo de California. Informe Técnico del proyecto CONACYT-SEMARNAT 2002-CO1-0278: Variabilidad y adaptación del Golfo de California ante la variabilidad y el cambio climático de California. Informe Técnico interno CIBNOR.

Part II.
History, Society, and Culture

9

Sea Turtles: Ancestral Heritage of the Los Cabos Region

Graciela Tiburcio Pintos and Raquel Briseño Dueñas

INTRODUCTION

Five of the seven species of sea turtles that exist in the world are found in the Los Cabos region of Baja California Sur (BCS). These are the olive ridley *(Lepidochelys olivacea)*, Hawksbill *(Eretmochelys imbricata)*, leatherback *(Dermochelys coriacea)*, loggerhead *(Caretta caretta)*, and the black sea turtle *(Chelonia mydas* or *Chelonia agassizii)*. The last scientific name is recognized by some taxonomists that catalogue it as a different species from *C. mydas*. All of these species are endangered (NOM-059-ECOL-2001). The olive ridley, leatherback, and black sea turtles have records of nesting in the peninsula of Baja California. The beaches of the Los Cabos region are recognized as important for nesting since the first surveys carried out in the mid-1960s (Vargas-Molinar 1973).

The marine area is used as a migratory corridor, juvenile development habitat, and feeding grounds for adults that are between 10 and 15 years of age (Chaloupka and Musick 1997). Once mature, the turtles migrate from the feeding grounds to nesting beaches where they hatched to reproduce. These migrations can be to areas close to their feeding sites or several hundreds or even thousands of kilometers distant (Seminoff et al. 2008). During the periods when they are not breeding, the adults live in coastal feeding areas, which often coincide with the habitats in which juvenile turtles develop (Seminoff et al. 2008).

Relationship of Sea Turtles and Human Groups of the Los Cabos Region

Pre-Columbian Period

The Cabo biogeographic region concurs with the demarcation of the territory recognized for the Pericú ethnic group, which ranges from Cabo San Lucas to Cabo Pulmo and includes the large islands of the south of the Gulf of California (Cerralvo, Espíritu Santo, Partida, and San José). The archaeological record of the Pericú territory is identified from the early Holocene—about ten thousand years ago—to the late Pleistocene (Fujita 2006). According to Fujita (2006), around the year 1000 of the current era, there were four great centers of socioeconomic and ceremonial importance at the sites now occupied by Cabo San Lucas, Cabo Pulmo, *Airapí* (now La Paz), and the Espíritu Santo Island. *Añuití* and *Yenecamú* are the toponyms of the Pericú ethnic group for San José del Cabo and Cabo San Lucas, the main population centers of the municipality of Los Cabos.

In cryptic codices, the inhabitants of the different areas of the region shared a legacy of life stories drawn or incised on cave walls and rocks in the open. These identify the goods provided by the desert and the sea. Of the latter, whales, manta rays, and turtles stand out as ethnohistorical evidence of fauna abundance and diversity. These graphic representations also demonstrate knowledge and beneficial use of the species by primitive human groups that colonized the coastal areas of the region (Fujita 2006, 2009). Some of the paintings and engravings that show sea turtles have been interpreted as signs of death-transmigration of spirits-reincarnation-life and of origin-creation-primeval waters (Viñas et al. 2005).

A conspicuous testimony in the Los Cabos region of the man-nature relationship between the Pericú and sea turtles is the El Médano site, where numerous remains of turtles were found with evidence of having been burnt and used as food (Poyatos de Paz and Fujita 1998). The researchers also indicate that the use of turtles is reflected not only in economic activities or strategies of appropriation and exploitation of environmental resources, but turtles also appear in funerary activities.

The nesting areas of the black sea turtles in the region of Los Cabos provided easy access for the Pericú to eggs and sea turtle meat. Moreover, the anticipated knowledge of the arrival of turtles to the beaches as well as the expected and received benefits, were translated into metaphors of abundance and longevity within their cosmogonies or belief systems.

Archaeological studies do not reflect the magnitude of human impacts and their effect on nesting sea turtles in the Los Cabos region at that stage. Exploitation of sea turtles there has been called symbiosis and beneficial use. However, there is information for other regions to the north in the peninsula of Baja California that documents that the hunting strategies of hunter-gatherer societies that included intensive use did impact other vulnerable marine and coastal species (Poyatos de Paz and Fujita 1998).

The Period of the First European Occupation

Encounters of the Pericú with explorers, missionaries, and sailors of the Manila galleons (1565–1815) and pearl seekers occurred between the sixteenth and late eighteenth centuries. The only historical basis related to sea turtles in that period for the Los Cabos region comes from the travel logs and chronicles that the Europeans kept during their stay in those places. Missionary testimonials about the abundance of sea turtles in both seas are noted by Aschmann in 1966 (cited in Nichols 2003). Furthermore, stories about pirates that ravaged these shores in the seventeenth century mention that turtles were abundant everywhere and were used as food during their journeys. Other chronicles indicate that sailors on their trips to Baja California stocked up on turtles at the beach, presumably from the nesting areas or from those that were kept on land after their capture in water. It is also indicated that turtles were caught at sea during mating or when they remained afloat while resting (O'Donnell 1974, cited in Nichols 2003). In October 1793, during his navigation in the proximity of Cabo San Lucas, Captain James Colnett reported that, "The sea, at the time, was almost covered with turtles and other tropical fish" (Colnett 1798 in Seminoff et al. 2008). These anecdotal reports, few and very imprecise, are only qualitative indicators that do not shed light on the numerical size of the species and catch levels that occurred during the years between 1600 and 1700.

Recolonization Period (Nineteenth and Twentieth Centuries)

The uses of turtles and eggs from nesting beaches and the marine area of the Los Cabos region during the nineteenth and early twentieth centuries, can be considered as the beginning of the exploitation and trade phase by human groups that came to this region, attracted by the abundance of commercial species of fish, lobster, oysters, snails, and, particularly, mother of pearl.

The bays and coastal lagoons of the northern zone of BCS, location of the most important feeding areas of the eastern Pacific for several species of sea turtles, were exploited by fishers of whales and seals who first started catching turtles as food source. When the whale and seal fisheries collapsed, they focused the capture on sea turtles, although they had been capturing them for decades. Thus, turtles caught in the early twentieth century until the close of the market in 1925, were transported to San Diego and San Francisco for processing as canned food or to sell in restaurants (Nichols 2003).

Commercial fishing of sea turtles in Mexico was formally recorded in the 1940s. In the period from 1965 to 1982, Mexico produced about 50% of the total world production of sea turtles. Baja California Sur accounted for more than half of the domestic capture (Márquez et al. 1982).

The fishery for black sea turtles was followed by that of the olive ridley turtles for use by the fur industry. The exploitation of the other three species was not of the same magnitude. For example, the leatherback sea turtle was caught in the region of Los Cabos for the purpose of extracting its fat and selling it in Ensenada. The meat was consumed locally, although it was not as favored as that of the black sea turtle.

Pedro Márquez Almanza, a descendant of the settlers of the coastal zone and one of the precursors of community participation in the Los Cabos region, recalled stories about the uses of sea turtles, stressing their complete use. The egg was consumed as food and was also attributed with aphrodisiac properties. The meat, flippers, and entrails were used as food. The blood was drunk as a tonic to combat anemia and weakness, and the fat was melted to be administered in sips to minimize respiratory problems from coughs or asthma. The carapace or plastron of the turtle was used to make needles to knit nets. The remaining boney material was stored in rustic containers until ready to be ground and the dust used as fertilizer.

The shell was used as a carrier and container of various products. Pulled by ropes that were attached to the turtle's carapace, it was used for waste disposal. Once empty, the small children enjoyed it as a sled and also to slide down the dunes at full speed.

Although the mortality of different species of sea turtles caught in the waters of Baja California during intensive commercial fishing could have represented a direct impact on breeding colonies of the Los Cabos region, this cannot be assessed for several reasons. First, a baseline is not available on the density of the nests during the period due to the isolation of the beaches until relatively recently. Second, to date, a connection has not been established between the breeding colonies of this area and the populations that are added to the feeding areas.

Figure 1. In the foreground, Juan Zumaya Adargas (El Pirulí), renowned fisher of turtles in San José del Cabo in the 1970s; behind him, a recently caught leatherback sea turtle

Source: Isabel Zumaya.

From Depredation to Conservation of Sea Turtles in the Region of Los Cabos

The first published works related to sea turtles and their nesting beaches on both coasts of Baja California Sur include Caldwell (1962) and Parsons (1962). In these, data on the location of the beaches are imprecise and provide no information on number of nests. Márquez et al. (1976), from interviews with the locals, identified as nesting sites for the olive ridley the segment of coastline located between Punta Conejo and Todos Santos on the Pacific coast. During August and September 1978, terrestrial and aerial surveys were conducted between Punta Marqués (on the Pacific side) and La Paz (on the coast of the Gulf of California) to locate nesting beaches. This research indicated that the nests were those of the olive ridley and leatherback turtles (Fritts et al. 1982). The difficult access to nesting areas and that Baja California Sur became a state only in 1974 were the probable causes that it was not until the early 1990s that the first works began on the survey and evaluation of nesting beaches through local initiatives and federal agencies located in the municipality of Los Cabos.

In 1991, the Secretariat of Urban Development and Ecology (Secretaría de Desarrollo Urbano y Ecología–SEDUE) implemented protection programs for olive ridley and leatherback turtle nests in BCS. The first turtle camp was settled in Punta San Cristóbal beach, Los Cabos, with support of two enthusiastic citizens: René Pinal and Don Manuel Orantes Murillo. Nest censuses were also conducted from the town of Todos Santos to San José del Cabo (Ramírez et al. 1996).

In 1994, Pinal and Orantes Murillo formed a nongovernmental organization (NGO) called Association for the Protection of the Environment and the Marine Turtle in Southern Baja California (Asociación Sudcaliforniana de Protección al Medio Ambiente y la Tortuga Marina–ASUPMATOMA). As a follow up to the work of the SEDUE, in the area of San Cristóbal and the beaches of El Faro to Suspiro, it confirmed leatherback turtle nests in Los Cabos. (Tiburcio et al. 1999).

On the initiative of Orantes, in response to the frequent sightings of leatherback turtle tracks, in 2000, the Sea Turtle Protection Program was started, as was the installation of the San José Estuary Turtle Camp, where 12 km of beaches were monitored. This program is managed under the auspices of the Directorate of Ecology and

Sea Turtles: Ancestral Heritage of the Los Cabos Region

Environment of the City Council of Los Cabos. After the death in 2002 of "The Grandpa of the Little Turtles," as Orantes was known, the Municipal Turtle Camp took his name. Thus, Manuel Orantes Murillo is recognized as one of the pioneers in the conservation of sea turtles in Baja California Sur and as founder of the first two and most important turtle camps in the Los Cabos region.

In 2003, the City Council of Los Cabos proposed the formation of the "Network for the Protection of Sea Turtles in the Municipality of Los Cabos." It promotes the involvement of the community and private sector to mitigate problems derived from the major process of transformation of the municipality's coastline due to the increasing boom of tourism developments. An indicator of the attention to nesting turtles in the area, after seven years of constant work, is the participation of 50 companies in the tourism industry that have been trained in the management and conservation of sea turtles.

This initiative's action plan includes the protection of nests, females, and offspring. Also, attention is given to injured turtles through veterinarians. In 2006, the establishment of the first Participatory Environmental Oversight Committee in the Field of Marine Resources took place, under the heading of "Network for the Protection of Sea Turtles." This committee has a membership of 120 persons accredited by the Attorney General of Environmental Protection (Procuraduría Federal de Protección al Ambiente–PROFEPA) and works under the coordination of the City Council of Los Cabos, the Secretariat of Environment and Natural Resources (Secretaría de Medio Ambiente y Recursos Naturales–SEMARNAT), Mexico's Navy, the National Commission of Natural Protected Areas (Comisión Nacional de Áreas Naturales Protegidas–CONANP), and with the support of civic associations such as Wildcoast, Defenders of Wildlife, and World Wildlife Fund (WWF) (Tiburcio et al. 2006b; Red 2009).

As a result of active local participation, a group has been formed in the tourism sector that employs national and international standards in the management and conservation of sea turtles. The municipal government has promoted the policy of involving the private sector and society as indispensable agents in the conservation of their natural heritage, reinforcing their identity with the resource and achieving sustainable conservation.

In 2002, the group Friends for the Conservation of Cabo Pulmo, A.C., emerged in the East Cape region. It initiated conservation actions in the area of the Cabo Pulmo National Park Natural Protected Area. In 2009, the coordination of conservation activities was transferred to the CONANP, with support from the municipal government and the community.

LOS CABOS AS AREA OF REPRODUCTION-NESTING AND PRODUCTION OF SEA TURTLE HATCHLINGS

The municipality of Los Cabos has 180 km of beaches (Gobierno Municipal de Los Cabos 2008). By 2009, there were conservation programs in the municipality for approximately 103.2 km of beaches. Thus, 57.3% of beaches were protected.

BCS beaches are located at the northern boundary of the nesting grounds of sea turtles, whose main spawning areas are found in the central and southern Pacific coast. From the first reports to date, the region of Los Cabos has most of the nests of the state (Johnson et al. 1982; Olguín 1990; Nichols 1999; Tiburcio 2006). Practically all of the municipality's beaches are favorable for nesting, which takes place year-round by three different species: the olive ridley *(Lepidochelys olivacea)*, leatherback *(Dermochelys coriacea)*, and black sea *(Chelonia mydas* or *Chelonia agassizii)* turtles. In the time series data of 10 years of monitoring, some beaches are prominent because of the number of nests and favorable characteristics for certain species. The following paragraphs detail the different species and their nesting sites, in order of the most numerous.

Olive Ridley Turtle

The olive ridley turtle is the most abundant in the area and it nests practically all year, although the months from August to November are the most active. At present, the beaches located on the Pacific (El Suspiro, Bay of Cabo San Lucas) and the Gulf of California (El Cardoncito, San José del Cabo hotel zone, El Estero, and Piedras Bolas) are important because of the placement of 100 to 200 nests per season per beach. The beaches that stand out are El Faro, with 0.6 km in length and a density of 68.3 nests/km, and El Cardoncito, with a 2.55-km beach and a density of 50.2 nests/km. It is noticeable that beaches like El Cardón and Piedras Bolas, with undeveloped coastline, have a number of nesting sites similar to beaches with development, such as the hotel zone in San José del Cabo and Bay of Cabo San Lucas, which are characterized as being highly impacted (Tiburcio 2006).

Among the nesting beaches with between 50 and 100 nests, those that stand out are in the area of East Cape (Cabo Pulmo, Las Vinoramas, La Fortuna, El Faro, and Cardoncito) and in the area of San José del Cabo (Punta Gorda and La Laguna). Also prominent is San Cristóbal on the Pacific, which, in addition to reporting between 50 and 100 nests, to date is the beach with the most years of monitoring and protection in Los Cabos (López-Castro 2002; Monroy 2005; Tiburcio 2006).

Unprotected beaches, but with anecdotal reports of the presence of nests, are El Tule Beach in the tourist corridor; Punta Colorada and Punta Arenas in the East Cape; and Migriño Beach on the Pacific, with estimates between 100 and 200 nests per season (Briseño and Grobois 2004).

The results of the Municipal Program for the Protection of Sea Turtles, "Don Manuel Orantes Turtle Camp," show an increase in the number of protected olive ridley turtle nests (Fig. 2). This behavior is also observed on the beaches of arrival and solitary nesting elsewhere in Mexico.

An important element of the olive ridley populations that nest in BCS is their probable genetic uniformity, as reported by López-Castro et al. (2005).

Furthermore, the results of the protection of sea turtles also show an increase in the protection effort both in beach extension and participating staff and, thus, the number of nests reported (Fig. 3).

Leatherback Sea Turtle

In Mexico, since 1995, the number of leatherback turtle nestings is monitored by aerial censuses through systematic and standardized oversight. The beaches of Agua Blanca in the municipality of La Paz, and the Punta Gorda and San Luis beaches, in the municipality of Los Cabos, are rated as of secondary importance. That is, they are beaches with important nesting density, but are not outstanding (Sarti 2004). Most populations in various parts of the world have shown a decline of over 80% in less than 20 years as well as erratic behavior. In recent years, for example, turtles have laid their eggs in places not known

Figure 2. Protected Olive Ridley Turtle Nests by the Program for the Protection of Sea Turtles of the City Council of Los Cabos, BCS, of the "Don Manuel Orantes Camp" in 35 km of the Costa Azul-Destiladeras Beaches

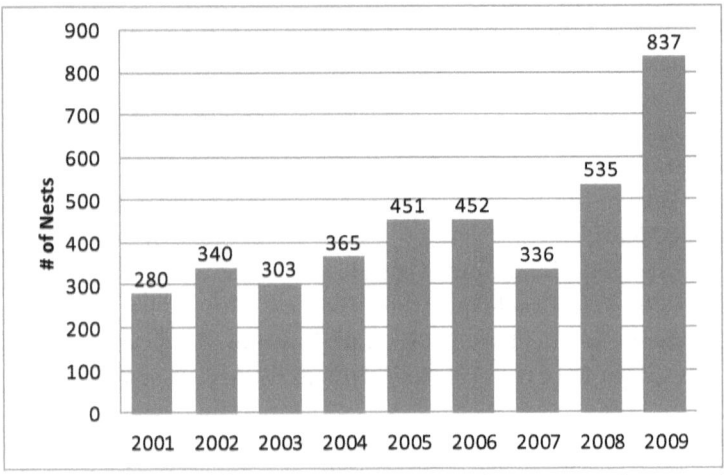

Source: Coordinación del Programa para Protección, Conservación e Investigación de la Tortuga Marina del H. X Ayuntamiento de Los Cabos, BCS.

Figure 3. Protection Efforts by the Sea Turtle Protection Network (Reported and Protected Nests)

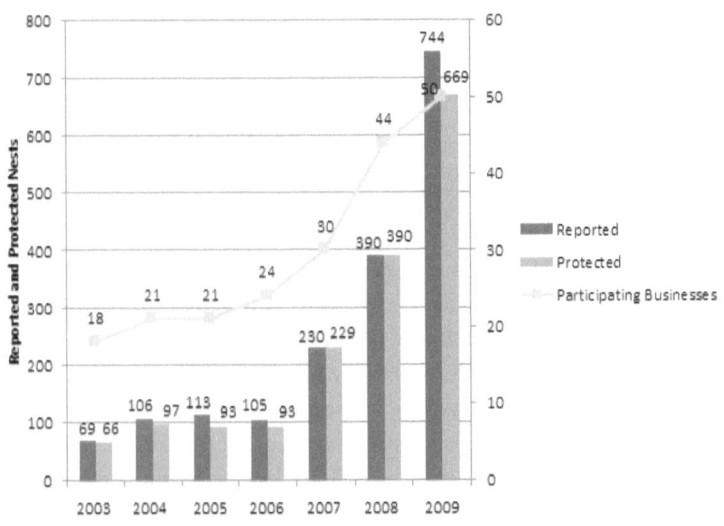

Source: Coordinación del Programa para Protección, Conservación e Investigación de la Tortuga Marina del H. X Ayuntamiento de Los Cabos, BCS.

Figure 4. Protected Leatherback Turtle Nests by the Program for the Protection of Sea Turtles of the City Council of Los Cabos, BCS, "Don Manuel Orantes Camp," in 35 km of the Costa Azul-Destiladeras Beaches

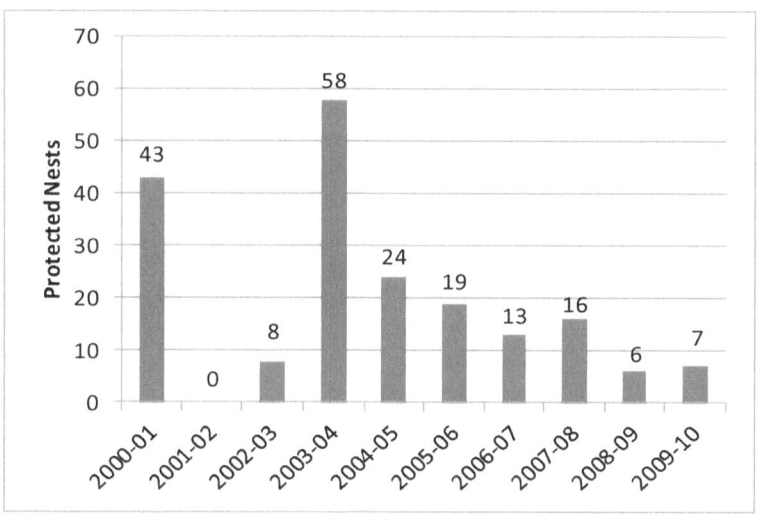

Source: Coordinación del Programa para Protección, Conservación e Investigación de la Tortuga Marina del H. X Ayuntamiento de Los Cabos, BCS.

as spawning areas for leatherbacks, while priority beaches show little nesting. A similar pattern is seen in the Los Cabos region. Nesting sites are decreasing, since in the 2000–2001 season there were more than 88 nests recorded in approximately 12 km.

Punta Gorda was the beach with the largest number of nestings (30 nests in its 1.4-km extension), and a density of 20 nests/km (Tiburcio 2006). Moreover, in the 2009–2010 season, only 19 nests were recorded along 100 km, without recording nestings in Punta Gorda. La Laguna Beach and El Médano in Cabo San Lucas had seven nestings, while El Suspiro Beach on the Pacific had five nests (Fig. 4). The leatherback turtle nests in Los Cabos from October to April, with the largest number of nestings in January.

The nesting of leatherback turtles in the state of BCS concentrates primarily in the municipalities of Los Cabos and La Paz. Its status as a critically endangered species requires that each of the nests be handled with special care, since low temperatures in natural nests reduce the hatching success in this region.

Black Sea Turtle

As an abundant species in feeding areas, Dawson (1944) and Carr (1961) reported the potential nesting of black sea turtles on the peninsula of Baja California, based on the large number of additional feeding habitats. However, not until 2002 was there a first report of the hatching of black turtles in the municipality of Los Cabos. From that time, the nesting reports for black sea turtles are more common, with those from August through October the most frequent. In addition, there have been reports of black turtle nestings on beaches in the municipality of La Paz (El Sargento Beach and Todos Santos), but it is the East Cape area that has the greatest concentration of nests (from nine to 11 per season) (Tiburcio et al. 2010).

MAIN THREATS

Each year, thousands of hatchlings emerge from their eggs along the Los Cabos coast; unfortunately, few survive. It is estimated that perhaps only one of 1,000 hatchlings reaches adulthood. For the Los Cabos region, 11 main threats have been identified (Tiburcio 2006), whether caused by humankind or nature (Table 1).

CONSERVATION STRATEGIES FOR NESTING AREAS IN LOS CABOS

The long-term protection of sea turtles means looking for solutions that reduce the risks that limit their survival. In Los Cabos, important conservation programs have been carried out, which are based on developing actions that will address the main identified threats that affect sea turtles. Many of these actions are linked or overlap; this feature is considered appropriate to promote a comprehensive and unified approach in the conservation and management of sea turtles.

The management efforts of sea turtle protection programs are outstanding through the protection of nests and hatchling releases throughout the year. Between 2000 and 2009, the Municipal Government Program for Protection of the Sea Turtle released 371,089 hatchlings of olive ridleys; 1,243 of black sea turtles; and 4,116 of leatherbacks.

Table 1. Threats in the Municipality of Los Cabos that Affect Sea Turtles

Type of Factor	Factor
Human threats	Human looting (turtles and eggs)
	Vehicular, pedestrians, and livestock traffic
	Incidental fishing
	Coastal development
	Lighting
	Injury by boats
	Pollution
	Depredation by dogs
Natural threats	Depredation by coyotes, crabs, crows, vultures, foxes and seabirds
	Meteorological impacts
	Destroyed by the tide

Source: Authors.

In a parallel fashion, important educational strategies are carried out with the intention of raising awareness, educating, guiding, informing, and motivating the community to promote principles and values that entail actions and activities for environmental protection and restoration, as well as sustainable use of natural resources. Such is the case of the "Adopt a Sea Turtle" Program by ASUPMATOMA (Pinal et al. 2001), and the educational program called "One in a Thousand" of the municipal government (Tiburcio et al. 2006b). Likewise, the government of Los Cabos, in coordination with El Grupo Tortuguero, Propenínsula, and Promotora Estrella Azul are organizing the Annual Meeting of El Grupo Tortuguero Youth, with the participation of children and young people from the entire state of BCS (Tiburcio et al. 2006a). In addition, the dissemination of scientific and traditional knowledge through materials such as videos, stickers, posters, T-shirts, sea turtle identification guides, comics, and stories for free distribution are promoted.

With regard to the generation of knowledge of sea turtles and their nesting beaches, a number of activities are carried out in the Los Cabos region. These include tracking of population tendencies of nesting turtles; sampling for genetic analysis; temperature recording and monitoring as a management tool in hatcheries; tracking thermal variations in beaches; and applying satellite telemetry and tagging for tracking migratory routes of sea turtles.

Besides the protection of nests and sea turtles, strategies are being adopted for conserving nesting grounds that include the reduction of artificial lighting; protection of areas with significant numbers of nestings; and protection of dunes. In addition, proper codes of conduct for these areas are being promoted, respecting the reproductive cycle of sea turtles (Tiburcio et al. 2004, 2006a).

Actions for the conservation of marine turtles and their habitats in the Los Cabos region conducted by the government of the municipality of Los Cabos have been recognized by several institutions. In 2007, the Municipality of Los Cabos was awarded a special mention as a finalist in the AENOR-México (Spanish Association for Standardization and Certification [Asociación Española de Normalización y Certificación]) award for the best implementation practice of Quality and Management Systems and Environmental Management.

SEA TURTLES, LEGACY OF THE PAST FOR THE FUTURE: CONCLUDING REMARKS

Every action for sea turtle conservation implicitly carries survival of the species as a long-term goal. This means a duality between saving the decimated populations and conserving critical habitats, actions that involve the human populations that interact with the sea turtles.

The elaboration of appropriate management plans for sea turtles is a difficult task, mainly due to their biological characteristics, such as long periods of maturation, migratory habits, and high mortality rate in their early stages of development. However, the conservation experience gained so far allows the design of conservation proposals that aim to restore sea turtle populations in such a way that they can again be used by inhabitants under a sustainable management.

Protection strategies of important habitats for sea turtles should be fully incorporated into integral management initiatives of the coastal zone at the local, national, regional, and international levels. The management of sea turtles should be incorporated into municipal development plans. Coastal management plans should be developed, recommending the protection of nesting areas and adjacent areas to ensure the maintenance of habitat quality and the functional structure of ecosystems. Areas with the highest number of nestings should receive maximum protection and activities that have negative impacts should be prohibited. However, to achieve these objectives, the actions must be integrated and coordinated within their total area of geographical distribution, so that activities are not conducted only in a portion of their distribution and thus undermine the management and conservation in other areas.

Within sustainable management, there is the possibility of carrying out tourism projects for conservation that focus on sea turtle sightings. However, the initiatives regarding the management of turtles as an attraction, from the perspective of conservation associated with productive use, are still in a take-off stage (Cariño and Monteforte 2008). Sea turtles can represent an important tourist attraction and a productive alternative for communities that participate in conservation of different species of sea turtles in the Los Cabos region.

To speak of Los Cabos and its natural resources and not mention sea turtles is simply not recognizing an ecologically, historically, and culturally important part of destiny. There is an intimate relationship between the community and turtles that goes beyond simple consumption.

References

Aschmann, H. 1966. *The Natural and Human History of Baja California*. Los Angeles, CA: Dawson's Book Shop.

Briseño, D. R., and F. A. Grobois. 2004. *Las tortugas y sus playas de anidación en México*. Universidad Nacional Autónoma de México, Instituto de Ciencias del Mar y Limnología Estación Mazatlán, Informe final del Proyecto P066.

Caldwell, D. K. 1962. "Sea Turtles in Baja California Waters (with Special Reference to those of the Gulf of California) and the Description of a New Subspecies of Northeastern Pacific Green Turtle, Chelonia Mydas Carrinegra," *Los Angeles County Mus. Contr. Sci.* 61: 3–31.

Cariño Micheline, and Mario Monteforte. 2008. *Del saqueo a la conservación: Historia ambiental contemporánea de BCS, 1940–2003*. Mexico, DF: SEMARNAT-INE, CONACYT, and UABCS.

Carr, A. F. 1961. "Pacific Turtle Problem." *Nat. Hist.* 76 (8): 64–71.

Chaloupka, M. Y., and J. A. Musick. 1997. "Age, Growth, and Population Dynamics." Pp. 233–276 in *The Biology of Sea Turtles*, P. L. Lutz and J. A. Musick, eds. Boca Raton, FL: CRC Press.

Dawson, E. Y. 1944. "Some Ethnobotanical Notes on the Seri Indians." *Desert Plant Life* 16 (9): 133–138.

Fritts, T. H., M. L. Stinson, and R. Márquez. 1982. "Status of Sea Turtle Nesting in Southern Baja California, México." *Bull. Southern California Acad. Sci.* 81 (2): 51–60.

Fujita, Harumi. 2006. "The Cape Region." Pp. 82–98 in *The Prehistory of Baja California: Advances in the Archaeology of the Forgotten Peninsula,* Don Laylander and Jerry D. Moore, eds. Gainesville, FL: University Press of Florida.

Fujita, Harumi. 2009. Informe final del proyecto "El poblamiento de América visto desde la isla Espíritu Santo, B.C.S." Mexico, DF: INAH Technical Archives.

Gobierno Municipal del H. X Ayuntamiento de Los Cabos, BCS. 2008. *Programa de Ordenamiento Ecológico Local del Municipio de Los Cabos BCS (POEL-MLC).*

López-Castro, M. C. 2002. "Densidad y características de anidación de la tortuga Golfina *(Lepidochelys olivacea)*, en Cabo Pulmo, B.C.S. (2000)." Bachelor's thesis, Universidad Autónoma de Baja California Sur.

López-Castro, M. C., and A. Rocha-Olivares. 2005. "The Panmixia Paradigm of Easten Pacific Olive Ridley Turtles Revised: Consequences for Their Conservation and Evolutionary Biology." *Molecular Ecology* 14 (11): 3325 –3334 (Fact. Impacto 2004: 4.375).

Márquez, M. R., A. Villanueva, and C. Peñaflores. 1976. "Sinopsis de datos biológicos sobre la tortuga Golfina *(Lepidochelys olivácea)* (Eschscholtz, 1829), FAO-INP." *Sinopsis sobre la pesca* (2): 1–67.

Márquez, M. R., A. Villanueva, C. Peñaflores, and D. Ríos. 1982. "Situación actual y recomendaciones para el manejo de las tortugas marinas en la costa occidental mexicana, en especial la tortuga golfina *(Lepidochelys olivacea)*." *Ciencia Pesquera* (3): 83–91.

Monroy, G. Y. 2005. "Determinación de zonas de importancia para la anidación de la tortuga marina *(Lepidochelys olivacea)*, en la región de San José del Cabo, B.C.S." Bachelor's thesis, Universidad Autónoma Metropolitana.

Nichols, W. J. 1999. "Biology and Conservation of Baja California Sea Turtles." Ph.D. dissertation, Wildlife and Fisheries Science, University of Arizona, Tucson.

Nichols, Wallace J. 2003. "Biology and Conservation of the Sea Turtles of the Baja California Peninsula, Mexico." Thesis, Dept. of Wildlife and Fisheries.

Norma Oficial Mexicana NOM-059-ECOL-2002. Determina las especies y subespecies de flora y fauna silvestre, terrestre y acuática en peligro de extinción, amenazada, raras y las sujetas a protección especial, y que establece especificaciones para su protección. Tomo CDLXXXVIII, Núm. 10. México, DF, 6 de marzo de 2002.

Olguín-Mena, M. 1990. "Las tortugas marinas en la costa oriental de Baja California y costa occidental de Baja California Sur, México." Bachelor's thesis, Universidad Autónoma de Baja California Sur.

Parsons, J. J. 1962. *The Green Turtle and Man.* Gainsville, FL: University Press of Florida.

Pinal, R., M. Orantes, D. Pérez, R. M. Escobar, E. González, and L. de la Rosa. 2001. "Adopt a Sea Turtle." Environmental Education Program for the Protection of the Sea Turtle of Los Cabos, Baja California Sur, México. Abstracts XX Annual Symposium on Sea Turtle Biology and Conservation, Orlando, Florida.

Poyatos de Paz, Gema, and Harumi Fujita. 1998. "Equilibrio entre el hombre y la naturaleza: Los indígenas costeros de El Médano, Baja California Sur, México." *Revista Española de Antropología Americana* 28:11–38.

Ramírez, J. C., A. Vellanoweth, and M. Orantes. 1996. Informe del Programa de Protección de Tortuga Golfina y Laúd en Punta San Cristóbal, B.C.S., Asociación Sudcaliforniana para la Protección al Medio Ambiente y la Tortuga Marina, A.C. (ASUPMATOMA), Cabo San Lucas, B.C.S.-México.

Red para la Protección de la Tortuga Marina. 2009. (Accessed 5 August 2009) http://cabotortugas.org/.

Sarti, L. 2004. *Situación actual de la tortuga laúd (Dermochelys coriacea) en el Pacífico mexicano y medidas para su recuperación y conservación*. Secretaría del Medio Ambiente y Recursos Naturales. Publication sponsored by World Wildlife Fund (WWF).

Seminoff, Jeffrey A., Antonio Reséndiz-Hidalgo, Beatriz Jiménez de Reséndiz, Wallace J. Nichols, and T. Todd-Jones. 2008. "Tortugas Marinas." In *Bahía de Los Ángeles: Recursos naturales y comunidad*, Línea base 2007, Gustavo D. Danemann and Exequiel Ezcurra, eds. Pronatura Noroeste AC, Secretaría de Medio Ambiente y Recursos Naturales, Instituto Nacional de Ecología, and San Diego Natural History Museum.

Tiburcio, P. G. 2006. "Anidación de tortugas marina en el municipio de Los Cabos, Baja California Sur, México y propuesta para su conservación." Master's thesis, Ciencias Marinas y Costeras con Orientación a Manejo Sustentable de Zonas Costeras, Universidad Autónoma de Baja California Sur.

Tiburcio, P. G., A. Cruz M., S. García R., K. Dean, Y. García M., and M. Bañagas O. 2006a. "Meeting of the Youth of the Californias for the Conservation of Marine Turtles, Baja California Sur, Mexico." Book of Abstracts, XXVI Annual Symposium on Sea Turtle Biology and Conservation, Crete, Greece.

Tiburcio, P. G., D. García G., R. Briseño D., P. Márquez A., V. Castillo L., E. Acevedo R. S. Burgoín M., and Y. García M. 2006b. "Creating a Network for the Protection of Sea Turtles in the Tourist Corridor of the Municipal of Los Cabos, Baja California Sur, Mexico." Book of Abstracts, XXVI Annual Symposium on Sea Turtle Biology and Conservation, Crete, Greece.

Tiburcio, P. G., J. E. García, and L. Villarías. 2006c. "'Una Entre Mil' (One in a Thousand): A Look at the Sea Turtles of Mexico – Environmental Education Program in Los Cabos, Baja California Sur." Book of Abstracts, XXVI Annual Symposium on Sea Turtle Biology and Conservation, Crete, Greece.

Tiburcio P. G., P. Márquez A, E. Acevedo R., R. Marrón F., J. Marrón F., M. Bañaga C., J. González V., F. Camacho R., E. Nery R., J. N. Pinto V., K. Oceguera C., and C. Villalobos M. 2010. "Reportes de anidación de tortuga prieta *(Chelonia agassizii)* en Baja California Sur, México." Proceedings of the XII Meeting of Grupo Tortuguero de las Californias, Loreto, BCS.

Tiburcio, P. G., P. Márquez A., J. M. Sández C., and J. R. Guzmán. 2004a. "First Nesting Report of Black Sea Turtles *(Chelonia mydas agassizii)* in Baja California Sur, Mexico." Abstracts, XXIV Annual Symposium on Sea Turtle Biology and Conservation, San José de Costa Rica.

Tiburcio, P. G., P. Márquez A., J. M. Sández C., M. R. Duarte, and M. F. Calderón C. 2004b. "Red para la protección de la tortuga marina en el corredor turístico del municipio de Los Cabos, BCS, México." Abstracts, XXIV Annual Symposium on Sea Turtle Biology and Conservation, San José de Costa Rica.

Tiburcio, P. G., R. Pinal, and M. Orantes. 1999. "Programa de protección y conservación de tortugas marinas en la península de Baja California Sur, mediante el Centro de Investigación y Protección de la Tortuga Marina San Cristóbal, Análisis Preliminar de 4 Temporadas." Proceedings of the XVI Encuentro Nacional Interuniversitario para la Conservación de Tortugas Marinas, Mazatlán, Sin., 1999.

Vargas-Molinar, T. P. E. 1973. *Resultados preliminares de marcado de tortugas marinas en aguas mexicanas (1966-1970)*. Instituto Nacional de la Pesca, series inf. INP/SI.

Viñas, R., A. Rubio, and V. del Castillo. 2005. "La Cueva del Porcelano: Hipótesis interpretativas y consideraciones sobre las fases del gran mural." In *Arte rupestre en México. Ensayos 1990-2004*, M. P. Casado (ed.) and L. Mirambell (coord.). México, DF: INAH.

10

Prehistory and Indigenous Cultures

Harumi Fujita

INTRODUCTION

Archaeological research carried out in the municipality of Los Cabos by the National Institute of Anthropology and History (Instituto Nacional de Antropología e Historia–INAH) reveals the existence of 111 sites, mostly in the coastal zone. The most common site type is made up of shell middens, with the presence of mollusk remains as a result of pre-Hispanic collection and consumption. Several prehistoric sites were also located in the area of San Dionisio, inland from the coast. There are also pictographic sites, funerary caves, quarries, and lithic workshops in both the coastal zone and in the mountainous area. Through various archaeological salvage efforts, conducted by INAH and funded by tourism development companies in Los Cabos, it was possible to estimate the type of prehistoric life based on archaeological materials and flora and fauna remains recovered, which date from approximately 7,000 years ago. This chapter will only address the general aspects of the salvage archaeology conducted in El Médano in Cabo San Lucas.

Various historical sources provide information about the indigenous people in this southern region at the time of European contact. Mention is made of their physical appearance and their clothes, ornaments, tools, housing, daily and ceremonial activities, customs, and sociopolitical organization, as well as the local natural landscape. The natives of the area of Cabo San Lucas, at the time of contact, were the Pericú.

Archaeological Research

The first archaeological find was a human burial associated with offerings, deposited in a cave located in El Zorrillo in the southern part of the Sierra La Laguna. It was described by L. Belding, accompanying Ten Kate, in the late nineteenth century. After exploring the cave, a burial with two skeletons was found. One was an adult male, wrapped in palm bark and tied with twine. The other was apparently a girl about 12 years old who had two mother-of-pearl polished shells with finely serrated edges and a hole at the top, so they assumed it was a pectoral decoration. They proposed that these skeletons represented the last two remains of the Pericú group (Belding 1885). The exploration of funerary caves and other prehistoric sites was carried out by William Massey (1955), in the 1940s, defining the culture of Las Palmas. In the 1980s, archaeologists Fermín Reygadas and Guillermo Velásquez (1983) focused on the relationship between archaeological sites and the ecological context, travelling from the eastern slope of the Sierra La Laguna to the coast, by La Capilla. INAH archaeologists Jesús Mora and Baudelina García-Uranga (1980, 1981) conducted an archaeological survey in the region and registered several sites. Kelly Carmean (1994) conducted a road trip in the area of San Dionisio, locating 92 sites in 1991.

During several seasons of fieldwork for the project "Identifying and Cataloging Archaeological Sites in the Area of Cabo, BCS," the author of this chapter registered 111 sites between 1991 and 2007 in the municipality of Los Cabos (Fujita 1991, 1994, 1996, 2000). The following section details the sites classified as shell middens, funerary cave, quarry and lithic workshop, and pictographic site.

Shell Middens

Shell middens show mollusk remains as a result of pre-Hispanic collection and consumption. Most of them are temporary campgrounds of ancient hunters-gatherers-fishermen, with evidence of campfires, tools, and daily and ceremonial objects, as well as palaeodiet remains. Human burials were discovered in three shell middens. Two prehistoric areas were identified that cover both daily and ceremonial life: El Médano, in Cabo San Lucas (Fig. 1), and the Cabo Pulmo complex.

Figure 1. Excavation in Unit No. 7 at the El Médano Site in Cabo San Lucas

Source: Author.

Funerary Caves

Seven funerary caves were registered in this municipality. The caves are exclusively for funeral use and have several secondary burials painted in red ocher and offerings of both everyday and ceremonial objects. They are known as an exclusive place that manifests the funeral customs of Las Palmas. These customs spread throughout the entire Los Cabos region, including from the Espíritu Santo and Cerralvo islands in the northeastern part of La Paz to Cabo San Lucas, in the later period between 1000 and 1700 AD. Among the offerings associated with some burials are wooden boards and atlatl (dart throwers), mother-of-pearl pectorals, sea snail beads of the *Olivella* genus, deer bone awls and spatulas, pelican bone whistles, baskets, trays made of sewn palm leaves, and so forth (Carmean and Molto 1991; Fujita 2003, 2006; Massey 1955; Tyson 1977).

Pictographic Sites

Four sites with rock paintings were found. In the Los Cabos region, the color used for this task is red, with several shades. The motifs of the paintings are both abstract and naturalistic. Since these places are isolated and without association with daily activities, they can be considered ceremonial sites.

The paintings at the Cerro Los Chavalos #1 site were done on a huge integrated block. There are four concentrations of paintings with abstract figures that consist of several sets of vertical and diagonal lines in parallel form, and five circles or ovals with vertical lines that might be considered to be the symbol of the vulva (Fujita 1994). The Palo Escopeta site consists of large granite rocks that form a roof and a nearly vertical wall similar to a cave (where the paintings were done) and two rocks that form a floor (Photograph 2). Numerous straight and wavy lines are represented in a vertical direction on the wall, as well as straight horizontal lines on the right side of the roof. There is a radial figure of nine lines with a filled circle in the center on the left side of the roof. Another uncommon figure is the circle (Fujita 1995).

The Palo Verde site is located on the south slope of Picacho de San Lázaro where there is a very large rock on which the shapes of 25 painted human hands and over 40 straight vertical lines in parallel form and some in horizontal form can be observed (Fujita 1991). On the south side of a whitish granite block, called La Vinorama, there is a shelter-type formation where some paintings were made; these consist of four fish in vertical form. The head of the largest fish faces upward and it has an arrow running through the top and middle of the body. Due to the characteristics of the body, as well as the shape of the head and tail, it looks like a rooster fish. Also, a fish harpoon with three points is represented, as well as a very simple anthropomorphic feature on the right side. The end of the harpoon corresponds to the height of the arm of this man; thus, a relationship can be established between man, the working tool (i.e., the harpoon, and the object of work (i.e., the fish), which implies the fishing technique in the pre-Hispanic period (Fujita 1994). This information coincides with the ethnohistorical sources about the most popular fishing instrument (spear, harpoon, and dart) observed in the Los Cabos region, and provided by travelers and Jesuit missionaries in the seventeenth and eighteenth centuries.

Figure 2. Composite Photograph of Rock Painting at the Palo Escopeta Site

Source: Author.

Francisco Esteban Carbonel describes the fishing process carried out by the indigenous people in San Bernabé Bay (present-day Cabo San Lucas Bay) in the summer of 1632, as follows: "Taking 5 or 6 darts for spearing, they would head out in their rafts. They would spear the fish, and if they did not die with one dart, they would throw the rest at them. And, because wood is light, they did not let the fish sink to the bottom" (Mathes 1970: document 37). Some Woodes Rogers sailors observed in Cabo San Lucas (1709–1710) that two natives dived with a dart and, while they were under water, raised their dart with a fish in the tip, which was taken by another native watching from a raft (Mathes 1980). Subsequently, George Shelvocke describes about fishing with harpoons, observed in the same place in August 1721, that: "The natives went to sea with their harpoons in rafts rowing with double paddles and would fish the largest albacore" (Mathes 1980). Moreover, summarizing the task of fishing among the natives of the southern region of the Baja California peninsula, Miguel del Barco (1982) mentions that the natives departed on rafts and traveled a league or more, depending on the fish they found, which were caught with a spear or harpoon. The speared fish also provide data on other fishing techniques, as this indicates that the fish were caught using some long, pointy tool, probably a spear, harpoon, dart, or bow and arrow.

Quarries and Lithic Workshops

Four sites were catalogued as quarries and lithic workshops of andesite and porphyry, both igneous rocks (Fujita 1994, 2000). Evidence is present of extraction of large flakes from cores, which is the first phase of production to later manufacture implements of stone. In the majority of cases, the plain flakes with an edge were used for cutting. In other occasions, the Indians fabricated more elaborate tools using percussion and pressure flaking techniques. The tools included knives, projectile points, scrapers, raspers, and so forth.

CABO PULMO COMPLEX

The northern boundary of the Cabo Pulmo complex is the pictographic site and funerary cave on the Los Chiles creek and its southern boundary is the coastal site of Coral de los Frailes, where a total of 13 sites were recorded. In this complex, there are sites of daily coastal life classified as shell middens, places where stone tools were manufactured and known as quarries and lithic workshops, and ceremonial sites. In addition, there is a pictographic site and three funerary caves, one of which was explored by William Massey (1955) and cataloged as Cerro Cuevoso and dated as 75 BC.

There is a spring on the hillside north of Cabo Pulmo and this complex had the source of potable water throughout the year. In the shell middens in the Cabo Pulmo site there are remains of shells, especially mother-of-pearl, and some lithic tools to process seeds, such as *metates* (concave-shaped stone for grinding) and *manos* (handheld stone for grinding with a metate). Numerous porphyry and andesite chips were scattered in the shell midden, as well as a large amount of ash and burnt stones. Although cultural materials and faunal remains that indicate terrestrial hunting were scarce, the presence of four wooden atlatls in the funerary cave in Cerro Cuevoso shows that hunting was also a means of survival (Fujita 1994; Massey 1955).

Cabo Pulmo is famous for its reefs that spread among several rows of rocky banks, inhabited by a variety of fish, crustaceans, mollusks, and sea urchins. These banks also reduce wave energy, and enable the people of Cabo Pulmo to enter the sea for food. In all funerary caves belonging to the Las Palmas culture, one can imagine that the funeral ceremony was well organized. In such societies there was a leader who coordinated subsistence activities and a shaman who conducted religious activities. Honored individuals could have been relatives of the leaders or shamans, since the total number of burials is not as high.

El Médano

El Médano is located in the northeast part of the present town of Cabo San Lucas on the beach of the same name. This pre-Hispanic settlement includes an area of 59,000 m^2 on a marine terrace covered with coarse sand, with a maximum altitude of 17 m, associated with the mouth of the creek. The site was identified by the remains of charcoal and ash that reflect the use of fire, lithic materials such as fragments of metates and manos; indicators of the collection, preparation and consumption of seeds; and mollusk remains that reflect the exploitation of marine resources (Fujita 1991). According to historical sources, El Médano was located on a high hill, beside a freshwater lagoon and also a saltwater lagoon; it was near the creek and several natives lived there (Mathes 1980). After several negotiations between the INAH and the Caboland (S.A. de C.V.) company, which intended to build a hotel on the archaeological site, the company accepted the obligations stipulated in the Federal Law on Monuments and Archaeological Areas, covering all the requirements to carry out archaeological salvage work. The work was conducted in 1992, coordinated by the INAH Center in Baja California Sur (Fujita et al. 1996).

Through the extensive and intensive excavations, abundant evidence was found of pre-Hispanic life dating about 5,000 years ago. Among the important findings, were 10 poorly preserved human burials, five of them with offerings or related objects. Burial #7 contained the most abundant offering. It consisted of five mother-of-pearl pectorals with biconical perforations and incisions as decoration (the edges of the shells were cut to give a semicircular and semirectangular shape), four awls manufactured of deer bone, a projectile point blank, a mano for grinding with yellow pigment, and several clods of red and yellow pigment. Burial #2 had a necklace formed by more than 150 sea snails in five rows to the top of the neck. Burial #3 had four fish vertebrae as offerings and different shell species. Burial #5 was deposited on black grayish sand with traces of coal and ash; in it were the remains of sea turtle, shells, and a large stone chip. Burial # 6 contained several piles of mussels *(Modiolus capax)* arranged from largest to smallest. Thirteen shark teeth were found in and around this accumulation. A broken projectile point was next to the shells. Burial #8 contained a few shell remnants (Beltrán 1994).

Other important findings are stone tools. In addition to stone flakes and stones with traces of use, several more elaborate tools (projectile points, knives, drills, scrapers, raspers, sharpeners, and chopping knives) were recovered. Also found were 41 projectile points of different sizes and types. Among the raw materials used for the points were rhyolite, quartz, microcrystalline quartz, chalcedony, basalt, a quartz/glass crystal, and a majolica ceramic pot. There are different forms for the points, although the leaf-shape predominates. Three points have a diamond shape and others have fins and a peduncle or stem. Most are points used for darts. A few are for the spear and measured more than 10 cm long. No arrowheads were found. No site in the Los Cabos region has as much variety of raw materials and types of projectile points as does this site.

As far as grinding stones, 530 metates and 1,749 manos and pestles/hammers were recovered. Several of them have red pigment. The raw material most used for worked rock is porphyry, and for grinding stones it is granite and granodiorite, which are local materials. For the manufacture of projectile points, other rocks were used and the majority is foreign material. A concentration of six projectile points was found at 3.50 m deep, as well as a place with an accumulation of stones, and five manos over and around a metate. In another location, a pile of ground red pigment was found. This type of place is known as a "cache" (Tsutsumi 2000), a common characteristic for seminomadic or semisedentary groups returning to the site regularly, and who did not take with them heavy objects to other camps for short stays.

Other unusual findings at this site are probably ceremonial objects, such as several (chile) snails with intentional holes in the internal lip; abalone fragments that are rare in this part of the peninsula; and two stone artifacts shaped in a spindle form, similar in shape to a U.S. football.

The composition and quantity of lithic tools and flora and fauna remains suggest that the main subsistence activity was the collection, preparation, and consumption of plant resources, complemented by the exploitation of marine resources. The human groups that inhabited El Médano built provisional shelters, gathered plants, prepared seeds with metates and manos, fished, gathered mollusks and sea urchins, and hunted marine and terrestrial fauna. One of the customs of the natives was painting their bodies with red, black, and yellow pigment (Mathes 1980). Some individuals were buried at this site, probably after a ceremony. In some cases, objects were left by way of offerings (Fujita et al. 1996; Poyatos and Fujita 1998).

The earliest human occupation in El Médano began about 5,000 years ago, according to radiocarbon dating using a shell sample of 5641 ± 112 BP, calibrated from 3650 to 3360 BC and continued until after the time of contact. Between 3000 BC and 1000 AD, the duration of occupation in this place may have been short. In the latter part of the pre-Hispanic period, this site became more stable and developed as a socioeconomic and ideological center, as evidenced by the great variety and quantity of archaeological material of both daily life and ceremonial events, human burials with offerings, and palaeodiet remains (Fujita 2004, 2006). The relationship between natives and early Europeans is evidenced at this site through some ceramic pots, including majolica and glass types that were used as raw material to manufacture projectile points. Therefore, the Pericú of Cabo San Lucas continued their way of survival maintaining their autonomy, even with European contact, since, for example, instead of using ceramic, glass, or clothing, they considered these as a raw material for manufacturing tools such as projectile points, or they shredded the clothes that they received as gifts to carry their crops like mesh bags (Fujita and Poyatos 1997; Mathes 1980).

Conclusions

Archaeological research carried out in the southern region of the peninsula of Baja California, reveals the prehistory of at least 7,000 years (Piña et al. 2009). The natives of this region were hunters-gatherers-fishermen and understood the nature of the sea and land, which they made the most of according to the seasons. Their lifestyle was nomadic and seminomadic at first, and in the later period some coastal sites were more stable with more population and a stronger social organization that was reflected in the increase of archaeological material and palaeodiet remains. The appearance of places and ceremonial objects such as burials with offerings in the shell middens and funerary caves belonging to the funeral custom of Las Palmas were also characteristics of this period. They also had storage areas, in order to return to the same place regularly. El Médano in Cabo San Lucas is considered an important socioeconomic and religious center in the later period. In addition, there is evidence of trade in certain objects and shells, such as the mother-of-pearl, (chile) snail, and abalone. The Cabo Pulmo complex consists of several settlements and ceremonial sites, indicating that there was a strong social organization of the group. The remaining sites in this region were occupied for a shorter duration.

REFERENCES

Belding, L. 1885. "The Pericue Indians." *West American Scientist* 1 (4): 21–22.

Beltrán Medina, José Carlos. 1994. *Informe sobre las actividades desarrolladas durante el salvamento arqueológico del Médano, Baja California Sur*. México, DF: Archivo técnico del INAH.

Carmean, Kelly. 1994. "Archaeological Investigations in the Cape Region's Cañón de San Dionisio." *Pacific Coast Archaeological Society Quarterly* 30 (1): 24–51.

Carmean, K., and E. Molto. 1991. "The Las Palmas Burial Tradition of the Cape Region, Baja California Sur." *Pacific Coast Archaeological Society Quarterly* 27 (4): 23–38.

Del Barco, Miguel. 1982. *Historia natural y crónica de la Antigua California*. Preliminary study, notes and appendices by M. León-Portilla, México, DF: UNAM.

Fujita, Harumi. 1991. *Informe de los trabajos realizados en el proyecto Identificación y Catalogación de los Sitios Arqueológicos del Área del Cabo, BCS*. México, DF: Archivo técnico del INAH.

Fujita, Harumi. 1994. *Informe de la tercera temporada de campo del proyecto Identificación y Catalogación de los Sitios Arqueológicos del Área del Cabo, BCS*. México, DF: Archivo técnico del INAH.

Fujita, Harumi. 1995. "Manifestación rupestre en la región austral de BCS." *Revista COBACH* 10: 25–29.

Fujita, Harumi. 1996. *Informe de la sexta temporada de campo del proyecto Identificación y Catalogación de los Sitios Arqueológicos del Área del Cabo, BCS.* México, DF: Archivo técnico del INAH.

Fujita, Harumi. 2000. *Informe del recorrido de superficie realizado en la localidad denominada "El Rincón" en el municipio de Los Cabos, La Paz, BCS.* México, DF: Archivo del Centro INAH BCS.

Fujita, Harumi. 2003. "Enterramientos en concheros y cuevas de Baja California Sur." *Revista Arqueología Mexicana* 11 (62): 40–43.

Fujita, Harumi. 2004. "El desierto rodeado del mar: Condiciones favorables para la supervivencia de los indígenas de Baja California Sur." Pp. 203–224 in *Desierto y fronteras: El norte de México y otros contextos culturales, V Coloquio*, Paul Kirchhoff, ed. México, DF: UNAM.

Fujita, Harumi. 2006. "The Cape Region." Pp. 82–98 in *The Prehistory of Baja California: Advances in the Archaeology of the Forgotten Peninsula.* Gainesville: University Press of Florida.

Fujita, Harumi. 2008. "Investigaciones arqueológicas en la Isla Cerralvo, BCS: Análisis comparativo de patrón de asentamiento con la isla Espíritu Santo." Paper presented and the 2nd Encuentro de Historia y Antropología de BCS, La Paz, BCS.

Fujita, Harumi, Alfonso Rosales, and Ma. de la Luz Gutiérrez. 1996. "Una puerta en el tiempo: El Médano: Un conchero en Cabo San Lucas." *Revista Noroccidente* 35–52.

Fujita, Harumi, Aline Lara, Iziar Martínez Rojo, Raúl Aguilera, and Armando Franco Pérez. 2007. *Informe del salvamento arqueológico "Vista Serena", Municipio de Los Cabos, BCS.* México, DF: Archivo técnico del INAH.

Fujita, Harumi, and Gema Poyatos de Paz. 1997. "Continuidad del modo de subsistencia reflejado en el sitio arqueológico en El Médano de Cabo San Lucas." *Memoria del IV Simposio de Baja California Indígena,* Ensenada, BC, Cultura Nativa de Baja California.

García-Uranga, Baudelina, and Jesús Mora. 1980. *Informe sobre los trabajos correspondientes a la primera temporada de campo en la península de Baja California, México.* México DF: Archivo técnico del INAH.

García-Uranga, Baudelina, and Jesús Mora. 1981. *Informe sobre los trabajos correspondientes a la segunda temporada de campo en la península de Baja California, México.* México DF: Archivo técnico del INAH.

Massey, William. 1955. "Culture History in the Cape Region of Baja California." Ph.D. dissertation, Department of Anthropology, University of California at Berkeley.

Mathes, Michael. 1970. Document 37 in *Californiana II: Documentos para la historia de la explotación comercial de California, 1611–1679.* José Porrúa Turanzas: Madrid.

Mathes, Michael. 1980. "Antecedentes Históricos." Pp. 23–80 in *Importancia de Cabo San Lucas.* La Paz, BCS: FONAPAS.

Piña Villalobos, Luisa, Harumi Fujita, and Karim Bulhusen. 2009. *Informe del salvamento arqueológico en el predio "La Capilla" en la Bahía Las Palmas, Municipio de Los Cabos, BCS.* México DF: Archivo técnico del INAH.

Poyatos de Paz, Gema, and Harumi Fujita. 1998. "Equilibrio entre el hombre y la naturaleza: Los indígenas costeros de El Médano, Baja California Sur, México." *Revista Española de Antropología Americana* 28: 11–38.

Reygadas, Fermín, and Guillermo Velásquez. 1983. *El grupo Pericú de Baja California.* La Paz, BCS: FONAPAS.

Tsutsumi, Takashi. 2000. "Environmental Adaptations by the Analysis of End-scrapers in the Upper Paleolithic Japan." *Kokogaku Kenkyu (Quarterly of Archaeological Studies)* 47 (186): 66–84.

Tyson, Rose. 1977. "Human Skeletal Material from the Cape Region of Baja California, Mexico: The American Collections." *Journal de la Société des Américanistes* 64: 167–181.

11

Los Cabos: A Historical Account

Alba E. Gámez

INTRODUCTION

This chapter presents a review of the ancient and recent history of Los Cabos, a region located on the southernmost part of the Baja California peninsula, the long strip that enters into the Pacific Ocean in northwest Mexico. With regard to this land, a contention that is still common even among the Baja California Sur population that settled years ago in the region, is that the state of Baja California Sur (BCS) lacks a culture of its own, and even that its history has little relevance. Several elements may help explain this situation. These include the absence, unlike in the rest of the country, of impressive physical archaeological remains, such as pyramids or other standing structures; the annihilation of indigenous groups and the denial of their descendents through the process of the Spanish and missionary conquest; the arid and rugged environment itself that for centuries, and only until a few decades ago, inhibited the establishment of permanent and large population settlements; and a distorted notion of history and the construction of Mexicanness from the central government that disdained Baja California Sur because of its remoteness and apparent lack of inputs favored by the postrevolutionary Mexican nationalism.

Moreover, another reason likely is the lack of interest on the part of the local political class, with some exceptions, throughout the political formation of the territory to carry out and disseminate an alternative understanding of the regional histories and cultures.[1] This could be explained because the population that Baja California Sur inherited was largely white and tended to identify with the lure of the Porfirian brilliance and the link with exterior elites. As Preciado Llamas (2003) says: "The local political class was eminently *porfirista* [pro-Porfirio Díaz]." Currently, although miscegenation processes based on migration have transformed the state's demography, the lack of an economic, political, and cultural project beyond a six-year period of the election cycles that strengthens regional development, shows that the tendencies of the political class remain essentially the same.

It was not until the late 1960s, and for reasons of personal interest, that historian León Portilla (1995) promoted and made possible (with resources from the Institute of Historical Research of the National Autonomous University of Mexico) the creation of a State Historical Archive, which opened in May 1969. Unfortunately (one need only ask young people, including of college level), the process of compiling records has not run parallel with the dissemination of their contents or their use as part of a broader political vision that disseminates a sense of identity and belonging to the population and promotes regional development.

Nonetheless, the antecedents of Baja California Sur and in general of the Mexican California, as referred to by León Portilla himself, are long standing. On the economic and strategic side, history goes back to the invasions in the sixteenth century carried out by Hernán Cortés and English pirates and, in the seventeenth century, by the Spanish Crown. Also, in the nineteenth century, British, Japanese, Russian, and, of course, U.S. companies exploited mining, forestry, fishery, and salt resources through obtaining concessions from the federal government or simply operated through the lack of oversight. Hence, it can be sustained that Baja California Sur has been globalized but in an enclave mode, both in time and space. That is, historically, localized regions of the BCS territory have been integrated dynamically into the international market as suppliers of raw materials or primary

---

1. León Portilla (1995) notes the lack of interest in organizing the depleted historical records of half the peninsula by the authorities of the then southern territory, and highlights the exceptions of Luis del Castillo Negrete (1837–1842), Rafael Espinosa (1849), Adrian Valadés in the late nineteenth century, and Amado Aguirre (1927–1929). Aguirre also published a compilation of documents in 1928.

products. The influence of an economic pattern linked to outside the local productive organization has been very relevant, because its enclave nature and lack of government planning led to an economic and social disarticulation in the region, not only in relation to the land itself, but to the continental massif. This disarticulation takes place even in modern times.

On the academic side, Mexican and U.S. researchers have made efforts to learn about the Californian past. As León Portilla (1995) recounts, Joaquin Díaz Mercado published in 1937 in Mexico a bibliography on topics related to the peninsula and, in 1957, on the U.S. side, Ellen Katherine Barrett identified 5,000 titles regarding these lands. Since then, the number of publications on both sides of the U.S.-Mexican border has increased. Nonetheless, in Baja California Sur there is no information or collection system that integrates these publications. When they are done by foreigners, including through field studies, only rarely does a record of them remain in Baja California Sur institutions. In case they are registered, there are no transfer mechanisms of their results to the general population.

This chapter aims to provide an overview of the Los Cabos history that contributes to disseminating an understanding of the Baja California Sur transformation from a critical perspective, which draws from the past in order to build a better present and future. The text is organized into three sections. The first section presents the background of the indigenous settlers in the middle portion of the peninsula; the second relates to the globalized but enclave nature of the Los Cabos economy of the late nineteenth and early twentieth centuries; and, lastly, a brief comment is provided regarding the emergence of Los Cabos as an integrated tourism center, considering that specific chapters on this topic are included in this book.

PRE-HISPANIC INDIGENOUS SETTLERS IN THE PENINSULA

Before the first Europeans settled in what is today the peninsula of Baja California, it was inhabited by descendants of the first humans to reach America. Their legacy is found in archaeological sites and cave paintings that are extraordinary, not only for their aesthetic character, but for their uniqueness. The antiquity of their settlements is disputed, although it is recognized to be between 6,000 and 40,000 years old (Ponce Aguilar 2002; Inner Explorations n.d.).

The origins and reasons for the extinction of these groups of people are unknown, but narratives of the missionaries claim that they were different from the indigenous population of the sixteenth century (the Cochimi were located in the middle of the half peninsula, the Guaycura at its center, and the Pericú in the south). Even with regard to these three groups, ethnic differentiation was great, since the Pericú were dissimilar to others (León Portilla 1995). It is understood, therefore, that the indigenous people encountered by missionaries and Spaniards came in human waves, pushed by other populations from the north of the continent.

The settlement of the region now known as Los Cabos, the southernmost border of the peninsula of Baja California, had—as a particular stimulus—the benefit of a permanent and abundant water source that comes from the Sierra La Laguna and is very near the coast. This condition also configured the diversity and interrelationship of the pre-Hispanic settlers and a higher density in the occupation of space that is still observed. The Sierra La Laguna, which in turn feeds the hydrological basins of the Gulf, Pacific, and valley of La Paz, forms the largest freshwater reservoir of the peninsula: the San José Estuary. It is nominally a natural protected area at the state level, but is now in danger of disappearing because of housing development within its boundaries.

Two indigenous groups inhabited this vast area marked by the availability of water sources: the Guaycura and Pericú. Written records concerning this region are unclear because of the low value placed on the local cultures by the Europeans who had first contact with them. Nonetheless, it is understood that the Pericú dominated the southern part and the Guaycura the northern part, albeit with a moving boundary. The Pericú could reach the Guaycura northern regions such as Bahía de Las Cruces and the nearshore islands via the Gulf of California. They occupied an area by the Pacific Ocean further north than present-day Todos Santos. The division between these groups, however, is a matter of discussion, since it is based on the testimony of religious missionaries from the seventeenth and eighteenth centuries, and has been doubted by some specialists who no longer even use the ethnic names.

Los Cabos: A Historical Account

Before the introduction of the western style of life, indigenous groups had a nomadic culture, with extensive utilization of natural resources as hunters-gatherers. The information from archaeological discoveries point out to their similarities to the aboriginal peoples of Australia and the bushmen of Africa in terms of technology use (Rodríguez Tompa 2002). However, like these groups, their knowledge of the environment allowed them to live well, in a region classified as semiarid, until the arrival of diseases and war technology of the first Europeans.

During the first two centuries (sixteenth and seventeenth) of colonization, the peninsula, particularly the southern region—for its good ports and safe waters—received special interest from the Spanish empire. Several exploratory expeditions mapped the coast and establishments of settlers were attempted, but all failed. The colonization model of these centuries was the same one used in the conquest of central Mexico: the subjugation of indigenous groups, although by the Jesuit missionaries, and then the Dominicans and Franciscans.

Thus, the Westernization of the southern half of the peninsula, which began with the establishment of the mission of Loreto in 1697, was consolidated toward the south with the construction in 1730 of the Mission San José del Cabo Añuití by missionary Father Nicolás Tamaral and Father Visitor José de Echeverría. However, the penetration of the missionary lifestyle faced Pericú resistance, which was notable compared to other peninsular groups because of its scope and manifestations. During 1733 and 1734, attacks by indigenous groups on the four missions located in the southern part of the peninsula were frequent. These reached a peak with the deaths of missionaries Nicolás Tamaral, in San José del Cabo, and Lorenzo Carranco in Santiago in October 1734 (Ponce Aguilar 2002). Years after the uprising, indigenous discontent turned into demands for land ownership and the right to trade and travel, but these were rejected both by missionaries and the Spanish Crown.[2] In the second half of the century, the removal and death of almost all indigenous people of the Los Cabos area was a fact. In 1755, the surviving Pericú had been

---

2. As Ponce Aguilar (2002) states, years after the 1733–1734 rebellion, 20 natives stole the Mission Santiago's boat, reaching Ahome, Sinaloa; but after six months imprisonment in the mission there, they were returned in a boat that Loreto's captain governor sent, without their requests favorably resolved. Shortly thereafter, a second boat theft occurred with similar results.

taken first to the Mission Todos Santos and then to Mission Santiago; in 1782, there were only 28 Indians in Mission San José and not even the transfer of neophytes from Todos Santos in 1794 restored a population in which not one birth had been recorded for years (Rodríguez Tomp 2004).

Without underestimating the goodwill of the Jesuit work, records of missionary life in the California peninsula have allowed historians and researchers to uncover the style, transformation, and destruction of local indigenous life. Journals and missionary documents reflect an interesting variety of perspectives that ranged from the most frank disgust for the region and its inhabitants, such as that of Father Juan Jacobo Baegert (see Lemmon 1979), to those that best sought to endow the indigenous people with "reason." Anyway, such records are relevant because they provide information nearest to Antigua California.

Regardless of the lens through which missionary action is now perceived, two of its findings stand out and are of major significance in the evolution of the peninsula and, especially, of Baja California Sur. On the one hand, the irreparable destruction of the indigenous peoples stands out and, on the other hand, the emergence of a cultural system different from the one that had prevailed in the region for centuries. With regard to the latter, two issues should be taken into consideration: (1) that it is undeniable that the missions are an essential part of history and the (skimpy) architectural heritage of Baja California Sur citizens, and (2) that it was in the vicinity of the missions that a peculiar ranch culture was developed, survived, and still lives in Baja California Sur's rural environment, although it is endangered.

On that last vein, it should be pointed out that authors such as Cariño Olvera (2004) have indicated the integration (and hence survival) of indigenous elements into the ranch culture in an indigenous and Western cultural fusion, which would have allowed Europeans to establish sedentary settlements in such a rugged environment. Even though Rodríguez Tomp (2004) mentions a mestizo population that cared for the land and livestock, and also exploited minerals since Jesuit times, oddly enough little has been said about the conditions of miscegenation. Nonetheless, this might be explained because missionary or subsequent censuses divided the population only between Indians and whites (see Trejo 2004). As they became diluted through subsequent *mestizaje*, they blended into the group called *gente de razón* or non-indigenous, or perhaps because no one cared. A genetic analysis of indigenous remains and their comparison with descendants of old families in Baja California Sur, to include the surviving ranch population, could help clarify this.

THE WESTERNIZATION OF PENINSULAR LIFE

The decline of the indigenous population due to the change in lifestyle and diseases, the distance from the continental massif, the geographical characteristics, and the dryness of the peninsula complicated its settlement. Of 50,000 persons who lived in the peninsula at the end of the sixteenth century, only 8,000 remained by the decade of the 1760s. By 1847, the number of inhabitants had decreased to 7,500, even when considering the Mexicans and foreigners who had migrated to the region. It was not until the late nineteenth century that the population levels of 200 years earlier were recovered, with 40,000 people (León Portilla 1995). By then, European and mestizo inhabitants (the latter because of the immigration of ethnic groups from Sonora and even other countries) predominated.

With regard to the southern part of the peninsula, in 1812 the number of inhabitants was 1,690 and this increased to 6,575 in 1850, due in large part to the growth of San José, a municipality that accounted for half the population of the southern region and which benefited from the production and trade of food with foreigners (Trejo 2004). It is pertinent to note that in 1824, Upper and Lower California were integrated into a single jurisdiction and the first municipal division was created on the peninsula, with four municipalities: San José del Cabo and Loreto in the south; Santa Gertrudis and San Pedro Mártir in the north. The conformation of San José as a municipality recognized the demographic, economic, and political importance of the area.

The centralist measures of Antonio López de Santa Anna in 1838, which abolished the state governments in Mexico, meant the transformation of the Baja California province. The population of the peninsula was then 6,500 people. The municipalities of San José del Cabo and La Paz made up the Partido Sur, inhabited by 4,500 persons. Loreto, or the Partido Centro, was inhabited by 1,200 people; and the Partido de Fronteras contained only 800 inhabitants (Gámez 2004). In turn, these measures eliminated the local expenditure of taxes, which undermined the autonomy of municipal spending. However, following the U.S. invasion of 1847, new political boundaries were established and the peninsula was divided into the territories of Baja California Norte and Baja California Sur. In 1895, San José del Cabo, together with a vigorous Santiago, included about 20% of the 35,100 inhabitants of the Southern Territory, distributed in 1,000 homes inhabited by 7.3 persons on average (Borges 1999). As can be seen, San José experienced at that time a population decline compared to half a century earlier. This situation was due to the increase of migrants in the mining settlements of mid-century in San Antonio (silver and gold) and Santa Rosalía (copper), as well as the strengthening of the city and port of La Paz as capital of the territory in place of Loreto, whose decline would be irreparable.

Even so, the Los Cabos economy remained relevant, especially because of its relationship with the outside. San José was the most important export site of the Southern Territory after Santa Rosalía, where the French company El Boleo was leader in worldwide copper production. Agricultural and fisheries production, directed mainly to U.S. markets, as well as water supply for merchant ships in transit to Acapulco and other ports on the mainland coast, facilitated for Los Cabos a close linkage with immigrants who arrived in the southern half of the peninsula encouraged by pearl trade, mining, commerce, and agricultural activities. Among these were foreign residents converted to owners of livestock sites and orchards. In an 1857 report, of the 31 foreigners registered as owners of livestock sites and orchards in the Southern Territory, 30% were based in San José and San Lucas; three were French, four English, one Italian, and one Spanish (Trejo 2004). This type of presence resulted in a rural and ranch population of blue and green eyes, still commonly found in the south of the peninsula.

This situation reflected a settlement pattern different from most of Mexico, on which a Creole discourse was built and in which the destruction of local indigenous groups and their cultures was an insignificant fact. According to Torre Iglesias (1980 cited in Ibarra Rivera 2001), once the "aboriginal remains" from the eighteenth century disappeared, in the Baja California Sur of the nineteenth century, the indigenous (Yaqui), presence was "miniscule." The population consisted predominantly of flows of Spanish, French, Italians, Saxons, Arabs, Portuguese, Chinese, Filipinos, Germans, North Americans, and even Greeks. The population, stated Torre Iglesias (1980 cited in Ibarra Rivera 2001), developed as:

[...] a global race that unites within all the virtues of fellow participants, a white, refined, intelligent, hospitable race that gives a unique trait to California and gives us from the bearded rancher individual to the blue-eyed blonde child [...]

As a result of agricultural prosperity in the late nineteenth and early twentieth centuries, San José del Cabo developed an urban dimension. The municipal government's finances were in good condition, so infrastructure works were carried out, as well as spending on education (public education was the highest individual line item in municipal expenditures, representing one-fifth of the budget), health, communications, the slaughterhouse, the jail, and urban beautification (Gobernación 1823). Regardless, reports from political leaders of the Partido Sur del Distrito pointed out to deficiencies in student achievement and lack of adequate records and regulations in the municipal administration (Gobernación 1901).

The drought in the last five years of the nineteenth century caused an unprecedented livestock and agricultural crisis in the area. In Cabo San Lucas, 1,200 head of cattle died between 1895 and 1901, while the area planted was reduced from 250 hectares in 1900 to only 70 in 1901. The lack of rain, coupled with the difficulty of digging wells, caused a drop in sugar cane production, one of the main crops in the area. As a result, it was feared that the region would become depopulated given the waves of emigration in search of employment. Proof of this is that, during the second half of 1900, the mines of Santa Rosalía recruited 452 people. The food shortage in the local market was a matter of concern. Before, as in the case of sugar and corn, food was exported even to the opposite coast of Mexico, but now the high freight and passenger fares by the Curacao Steam Company, meant rising food prices and resulting protests to the District's political chief (Gámez 2004).

After the drought, and although the number of inhabitants decreased, economic recovery stopped emigration and contributed to the growth of Los Cabos' urban infrastructure. In 1910, the San José population was estimated at 4,300 persons (800 fewer individuals than 10 years before) and that of Santiago at 2,800 (almost 200 more than in 1910). Although smaller than the population of 1895, both constituted one-sixth of the 42,500 inhabitants of the Southern Territory. The agricultural production of June 1910 included 483 tons of *piloncillo*, sugar loaf, but evidenced the local shortage of corn and beans (Gobernación 1910), showing the enclave character of the Los Cabos region that, like the rest of the territory, depended on the external market as an engine of growth.

During the 1920s and 1930s of the twentieth century—the boom era of the region of Los Cabos—the most important production was *piloncillo* and tomato, the latter mainly sold to the U.S. market. In 1924, in San José del Cabo, the production of the planting and cultivation of sugar cane was processed in 41 mills and up to 690 tons of *piloncillo* were produced for export. Furthermore, 90 tons of tomatoes were harvested. On a smaller scale, mango, avocado, citrus fruits, oregano, and damiana, a native shrub used for medicinal purposes and flavoring liqueur were produced. Parallel to the agricultural prosperity, cattle herds that year totaled more than 24,000 head of cattle.

In the municipality of Santiago, agriculture was the predominant economic activity with the planting of 200 hectares of sugar cane and, on a smaller scale, grains and legumes. Livestock raising there was mainly for self-consumption. In Cabo San Lucas, the seafood company Productos Marinos de Cabo San Lucas, S.A., had been established in 1925 with the presence of the factory ship Calmex. When it sank, the plant was transferred to land from which, for five decades, tuna was packed and marketed under the brand Pando. This was owned by Elías Pando, a Spaniard who made soaps, among other products (Ochoa 2003).

Economic growth in the 1920s resulted in greater infrastructure, such as construction in 1926 of the road between San José and Cabo San Lucas. Also at this time, the collusion between economic and political powers grew stronger, as evidenced by the coincidence of the principal owners of the area on the list of mayors and delegates. The regime of a free municipality ended in 1928 and, the following year, the six municipalities that existed in Baja California Sur became delegations, although with the same names. Their representatives were appointed by the political head of the Territory. His designation by the President of the Republic would continue until 1971, when the category of free municipality was reinstated, although this time with only three municipalities: Mulegé, Comondú, and La Paz.

The Great Depression in the 1930s had disastrous effects on the Los Cabos economy. The once productive splendor was turned into a recession aggravated by depopulation due to lack of employment and infrastructure deterioration, as narrated by Steinbeck (1951), especially, regarding San Lucas in 1940. That era showed the vulnerability of the region as a production and marketing model anchored in the external market, and with little internal and interregional diversification that resulted in a gradual loss of economic importance.

RECENT HISTORY

After World War II, droughts and decreasing sugar prices caused the decline of Los Cabos agriculture and livestock raising. For populations in the ranch settlements, this was a time of hardship that caused migration to the more vigorous Santo Domingo Valley in Comondú, where agriculture for export was carried out, and then to the urban areas of San José and to an incipient Cabo San Lucas.[3] For those who remained on the ranches, working conditions and marketing of their products had not changed significantly because of the lack of technological development and intermediary actions.[4] By the 1970s, although *ejido* lands were being opened to urban development, Cabo San Lucas remained a small town.

In 1975, Baja California Sur and Quintana Roo were the last territories to join the Mexican federal pact. Relevant changes were made for such integration. With regard to Baja California Sur—which remained geographically, economically, and politically distant from continental Mexico—it had been provided with communications media and new maritime transportation routes. In June 1971, the free zone status had been extended (due to the historical request of local businesses) and the construction of Federal Highway No. 1 Benito Juárez, which traverses the peninsula; it was begun in 1929 and completed in 1973. The telephone, postal, and telegraph systems were expanded; airports and infrastructure were built for the region. Federal investments were obtained for the extraction of phosphate rock. Importantly, in 1974 Baja California Sur joined the national tourism growth through the integrally planned tourism centers of Loreto-Nopoló and San José del Cabo-Cabo San Lucas.[5]

---

3. Interview with María Isabel Agúndez Ochoa, octogenarian resident of Cabo San Lucas, BCS, March 22, 2010.
4. Interview with Fortunato Ceseña, septuagenarian resident of the San Nicolás Property, Los Cabos, BCS, March 23, 2010.
5. Gámez and Ganster, in this volume, analyze the emergence of traditional tourism in the region of Los Cabos.

With all the aforementioned, the number and composition of the population changed. In 1960 there were 81,594 inhabitants and in 1970 the southern half of the peninsula was inhabited by 128,019 people. Over a period of 10 years, the population grew slightly over 36%. The urban composition was predominant, increasing from 36% to 54% of the total population. Administratively, in 1981 the Los Cabos region was separated from La Paz, becoming the fourth municipality in the state. The subsequent population growth in Baja California Sur would be noticeable, with immigration to Los Cabos with the growth of the tourism industry and related sectors a determining factor. In 1990, the Los Cabos population was 43,920 inhabitants (14% of state total); in 2000, it was 105,469 (25%); and, in 2005, it was 164,162 people (35%). The latter figure represented an annual mean growth rate during 2000–2005, of 8.1% (INEGI 2006). Preliminary data for 2010 indicate 238,352 inhabitants for Los Cabos or 37.4% of the state total (INEGI 2011), which shows average annual growth rates of 9% over the last five years, and 12.6% per year when considering the last decade.

The composition of the Los Cabos population has changed dramatically with the population growth and economic structure that were driven by tourism. From being a small fishing town at the beginning of the twentieth century, Cabo San Lucas has displaced San José del Cabo as the region's economic center and is second in the state after the state capital. In the middle of the last decade, migration flows that arrived in Los Cabos were mainly from Sinaloa, Guerrero, and the state of Mexico (INEGI 2006). However, it is also worthwhile to note the presence of foreigners as semipermanent residents. This group, together with the large influx of visitors from other countries, has led to a social formation different from the rest of the country, which reinforces the Baja California Sur traditional trait of differentiation versus continental Mexico.

Los Cabos has been built as a recreational or second home center where there is an unequal appropriation of scarce resources and the geographical space between nationals and foreigners, between tourism and other sectors. Thus, although there is a middle-income group, large marginal areas coexist with other areas that focus on luxury consumption of goods and services (see Ángeles, Gámez, and Ganster in this volume). These groups are linked primarily through the workplace. Working relationships bind the population, and the characteristics of their relationship are expressed in a polarized social structure. If this is evident in small coastal communities linked to tourism (see Menares Parra 2008), the situation becomes exaggerated in urban places such as Cabo San Lucas, San José del Cabo, or even in Buenavista and La Ribera, where tourism and related economic activities provided the initial stimulus to their economic takeoff.

In this context, rural populations adjacent to Los Cabos, as in the rest of the state, tend to be expelled because of the lack of economic opportunities in their hometowns, and to be absorbed by urban concentrations devoted to tourism. This is a process in which matters of identity, social networking, and building a more integrated society are being left behind. Thus, the opportunity to make good use of the advantages and contributions of those who come from elsewhere outside the country, state, or Los Cabos region and those who have traditionally lived there is lost. So, while human development indicators in Los Cabos show a material bonanza, considered very good, a more detailed review of the municipal aggregate shows marked inequalities (see Ángeles, Gámez, and Ganster in this book).

FINAL REMARKS

The Mexican government, emanating from the 1910 Revolution, forged and disseminated a national identity based on the glories of indigenous peoples before the Spanish conquest.[6] Thus, without pre-Hispanic monuments and frequent population movements to the continental massif, Baja California Sur did not seem to contribute to that identity or to identify with it. This created a void that, throughout the nineteenth century, was filled by the local elite's contact with foreigners, from which derived enclave economies, the enjoyment of international fashion, and a classical education for the middle and upper classes according to North American and European standards.

The understanding of the history or histories of Baja California Sur from written records lacked at the outset the voice of the indigenous peoples. The physical eradication of Indian groups made recovery of their voice impossible, although at least some of their survival strategies in the natural world have been maintained in the mountain

---

6. The use of the Indian cultures to construct the mestizo tradition of Mexican nationality did not mean the economic, political, or social inclusion of contemporary Indian peoples. This has generated the call for a reevaluation of the relations between the Mexican state and Indian people (see Olguín Martínez 1998).

ranches. This social group is made up of the earliest settlers in the peninsula. Academia and popular culture have sought to recover the value and worth of the ranchers' existence, but the way of life inherited after the missionary colonization faces a seemingly inevitable extinction given its economic dislocation and lack of a conservation policy for this cultural heritage.

Paradoxically, because it has implied the destruction of a society-nature relationship according to the environmental conditions of the Baja California Sur territory, the adoption of tourism as a growth model in the state has stimulated the reconstruction of local history, and attention has been turned toward cave and rock paintings, oases, and ranch culture. Enrolled within this context is the relative mass production of regional sweets; relearning to make palm and ceramic handicrafts in the communities; the emergence of artisans in the cities; and the economic revaluation of the landscape by the communities themselves. This could be positive and feeds the curiosity and admiration of domestic and foreign visitors to the peninsula who, for years, have written and pushed for the recognition of local natural and social values. But a state program for authentic rescue and cultural identification does not exist, given the rush to offer something else to tourists besides just beaches and ocean views. Of course, there is also not a state program for integration of foreigners and Mexican nationals.

In that sense, it should not be surprising that when measured by criteria such as environmental and ecological quality, social and cultural integrity, condition of historic buildings and archaeological sites, aesthetic appeal, quality of tourism management, and its future prospects, Los Cabos has been rated as one of the worst tourist destinations in the world (National Geographic Traveler 2009). This observation endorses the calls to develop a less aggressive growth model regarding the exploitation of natural resources, particularly in Los Cabos, a region that contributes nearly 80% of the million and one half visitors who visit the state (Agúndez Montaño 2010). The idea is that through regulation and planning schemes, tourism does not die from success; that is, that it does not exhaust the resources (natural, social) on which this sector is based.

The history or histories, old and new, of Los Cabos, are broader and deeper than what has been expressed here and deserve to be studied and disseminated. Culture (and history) has a strategic political importance and it is distressing that Baja California Sur decision makers have not become aware of it. The relevance of Los Cabos lies in the ancient heritage it preserves and, to a large extent, its role in the (de)construction of the current Baja California Sur society. The future of Los Cabos, anchored in the investment of mass tourism, which increasingly is being extrapolated to other areas of the state, has shown a definitive character in the social, economic, political, and cultural conformation of Baja California Sur. In this context, and given the weaknesses of linking the growth of a region in the foreign market, as the Los Cabos history has shown, it is necessary to review its achievements and social costs; it is important to include the voices and experiences of its actors. Thus, if it could not ensure, at least it could start the foundations of a more prosperous, more inclusive, society.

REFERENCES

Agúndez Montaño, Narciso. 2010. "Documento socioeconómico." *V Informe de Trabajo*. La Paz, BCS. (Accessed 24 abril 2010), http://www.bcs.gob.mx/varios/5toDoctoSocioeconomico.pdf.

Ángeles, Manuel, Alba E. Gámez and Paul Ganster, "Growth, Human Development, and Perception of Well-Being in Los Cabos," in *Los Cabos: The Future of a Natural and Tourism Paradise*, Paul Ganster, Oscar Arizpe C., and Antonina Ivanova, eds. 2012. San Diego, CA: San Diego State University Press and Institute for Regional Studies of the Californias.

Archivo Histórico Pablo L. Martínez, *Producción agrícola de San José*. Fomento. 1910. Exp. 16, Vol. 563. La Paz, BCS.

Borges Conteras, José J. 1999. "Loreto en la vida económica de Baja California Sur." *Revista CSH,* serie científica 4–5.

Cariño Olvera, Micheline. 2004. "Historia ecológica de Baja California sur, 1500–1940." Pp. 451–491 in *Historia General de Baja California Sur III. Región, sociedad y cultura,* Edith González Cruz, gral. coord., and Francisco Altable, ed. La Paz, BCS: CONACYT-SEP-UABCS-XI Ayuntamiento de La Paz.

Gámez, Alba E. 2004. "Los Cabos: Economía y población." Pp. 247–278 in *Historia General de Baja California Sur III. Región, sociedad y cultura,* Edith González Cruz, gral. coord., and

Francisco Altable, ed. La Paz, BCS: CONACYT-SEP-UABCS-XI Ayuntamiento de La Paz.

Gámez, Alba E. and Paul Ganster, "Traditional Tourism in Los Cabos: Opportunities and Limitations of Economic Growth," in *Los Cabos: The Future of a Natural and Tourism Paradise,* Paul Ganster, Oscar Arizpe C., and Antonina Ivanova, eds. 2012. San Diego, CA: San Diego State University Press and Institute for Regional Studies of the Californias.

García Mascareño, Joel. 2004. "La población de Baja California Sur durante el siglo veinte." Pp. 493–506 in *Historia General de Baja California Sur III. Región, sociedad y cultura,* Edith González Cruz, gral. coord., and Francisco Altable, ed. La Paz, BCS: CONACYT-SEP-UABCS-XI Ayuntamiento de La Paz.

Gobernación. 1893. *Informe de Bonifacio Topete sobre su visita practicada al Partido Sur del Distrito.* Archivo Histórico Pablo L. Martínez, Exp. 138, Vol. 253, La Paz, BCS.

Gobernación. 1901. *Informe de la visita a la municipalidad de San José,* 6 de mayo, 1893. Archivo Histórico Pablo L. Martínez, Exp. 327, Vol. 226, La Paz, BCS.

Ibarra Rivera, Gilberto. 2001. *El habla popular en Baja California Sur.* La Paz, BCS: Gobierno del Estado de BCS-SEP-Coordinación de Programas de Bienestar Social-Instituto Sudcaliforniano de Cultura.

Inner Explorations. No Date (n.d.). *An Interview with Harumi Fujita on the Archaeology of Baja California Sur, and Possibly One of the Oldest Sites in the Americas.* (Accessed 24 March 2010), http://www.innerexplorations.com/bajatext/an.htm.

Instituto Nacional de Estadística, Geografía e Informática (INEGI). 2006. *Resultados Definitivos del II Conteo de Población y Vivienda 2005 para el Estado de Baja California Sur,* Comunicado No. 090/06, INEGI, La Paz, BCS, 24 de mayo. (Accessed 1 April 2010), http://www.inegi.org.mx/ inegi/contenidos/espanol/ prensa/Boletines/Boletin/Comunicados/Especiales/2006/Mayo/comunica7.doc.

Instituto Nacional de Estadística, Geografía e Informática (INEGI). 2011. *Censo de Población y Vivienda 2010. Resultados preliminares. Entidad Federativa. Baja California Sur.* (Accessed 5 February 2011), http://www.inegi.org.mx/sistemas/TabuladosBasicos/preliminares2010.aspx.

Lemmon, Alfred. 1979. "Preliminary Investigation: Music in the Jesuit Missions of Baja California (1698–1767)." *The Journal of San Diego History* 25 (4) (Accessed 5 abril 2010), https://www.sandiegohistory. org/journal/79fall/music.htm.

León Portilla, Miguel. 1995. *La California Mexicana. Ensayos acerca de su historia.* México, DF: UNAM-UABC.

Menares Parra, Brunilda. 2008. "Construcción y usos de espacios en la localidad de Cabo Pulmo, Baja California Sur, México." Pp. 277–292 in *Turismo y sustentabilidad en Cabo Pulmo,* Alba E. Gámez, ed. La Paz, BCS: SDSU Press-UABCS-CONACYT.

National Geographic Traveler. 2009. *133 Places Rated: The List, by Score.* (November-December). (Accessed 24 April 2010), http://traveler.nationalgeographic.com/2009/11/destinations-rated/north-america-text/13#cabo.

Ochoa, Arnulfo. 2003. *A flor de agua: La pesquería del atún en Ensenada.* México, DF: CONACULTA, Plaza y Valdés.

Olguín Martínez, Gabriela. 1998. "Estado nacional y pueblos indígenas. El caso de México." *Nueva Sociedad* 153 (January-February): 93–103. (Accessed 5 February 2011), http://www.nuso.org/upload/articulos/2655_1.pdf.

Ponce Aguilar, Antonio. 2002. *Historia de Baja California. De cueva pintada a la modernidad.* 2nd Edition. (Accessed 5 April 2010), http://loyola.tij.uia.mx/ebooks/cueva_pintada.html.

Preciado Llamas, Juan. 2003. "El Porfiriato en Baja California Sur." Pp. 381–434 in *Historia General de Baja California Sur II. Los procesos políticos,* Edith González Cruz, gral. coord., and María Eugenia Altable, ed. La Paz, BCS: CONACYT-SEP-UABCS-IIH-XI Ayuntamiento de La Paz.

Rodríguez Tomp, Rosa Elba. 2002. *Cautivos de dios: Los cazadores-recolectores de Baja California durante el período colonial.* México, DF: CIESAS.

Rodríguez Tomp, Rosa Elba. 2004. "El declive de la población indígena en la península de California." Pp. 319–346 in *Historia General de Baja California Sur III. Región, sociedad y cultura,* Edith González Cruz, gral. coord., and Francisco Altable, ed. La Paz, BCS: CONACYT-SEP-UABCS-XI Ayuntamiento de La Paz.

Steinbeck, John. 1955. *Por el Mar de Cortés.* Trans. María Teresa Gispert, Luis de Caralt, ed. (Accessed 19 April 2010), http://www.scribd.com/doc/29967644/Steinbeck-John-Por-el-Mar-de-Cortes.

Torre Iglesias, Manuel. 1980. *Sudcalifornia en la leyenda y en la historia*. México, DF: Federación Editorial Mexicana.

Trejo Barajas, Dení. 2004. "La población de Baja California, siglos XVIII y XIX. Declinación y crecimiento." Pp. 347–376 in *Historia General de Baja California Sur III. Región, sociedad y cultura,* Edith González Cruz, gral. coord., and Francisco Altable, ed. La Paz, BCS: CONACYT-SEP-UABCS-XI Ayuntamiento de La Paz.

12

Education and Development of Human Resources

Bärbel Singer

INTRODUCTION

The interrelationships of economic development, education, and formation of human resources have been studied from the most diverse perspectives—from historical, economic, sociological, psychological, educational, humanistic, and legal points of view. Since the 1980s—within the context of a growing globalization and the large-scale implementation of neoliberal economic policies in the so-called first world countries and, subsequently, in the least developed countries—the paradigm of the economy and knowledge society, a term coined by the Organisation for Economic Co-operation and Development (OECD), has become firmly imbedded in speeches and public policies around the world. The world's most important international economic and financial institutions have embraced the principles of the knowledge economy. Its theory emphasizes the value of the knowledge of a population, that is, intellectual capital, which can give the nation a competitive advantage in the global market for science, technology, inventions, patents, and knowledge generation (Rangel 2005). This human view entails a lifetime of learning.

The concept of human capital, created by Theodore Shultz (1980), Gary Becker (1964), Jacob Mincer (1958) in the late 1950s and early 1960s, focuses on training the workforce and on education for the job. Education is considered an investment. It is assumed that through the level and quality of education, productivity increases, which entails economic growth. Romer (1986) and Grossman and Helpman (1991) continued to develop the concept in the 1980s and early 1990s, emphasizing the importance of innovation, research, and development as a driving force of economic growth. For them, public investment in education represents the foundation for the formation of human capital. According to these authors, investment in quality education guarantees a job with a high salary.

Both theories—the knowledge economy and human capital—are strongly debated in various academic circles. The experiences of several economic and financial crises over the past 20 years, which affected many countries to a greater or lesser extent, served to test the performance of such theories. In an attempt to go beyond such a limited vision of humans as a mere instrument of production, Amartya Sen proposed the theory of human development in 2000, and its main postulate is the well-being and quality of life of individuals in harmony with their environment. Both the concepts of social and economic justice and human rights have a place in the theory of human development. Longevity, purchasing power, and level of knowledge are the three components that reflect the level of well-being of the population and, as a whole, determine the progress of a country. This proposal represents the latest attempt to try to understand the role of education and its function in the interaction between individual well-being and socioeconomic development.

DEMOGRAPHY AND MIGRATION

The municipality of Los Cabos, located on the southern tip of Baja California Sur (BCS), Mexico, represents a very interesting case study in terms of its demography, the educational and socioeconomic profile of its inhabitants, and the impact that these mean for its development. It should be noted that the municipality of Los Cabos is one of the most dynamic in the country. According to figures from the National Population Council (Consejo Nacional de Población–CONAPO), by 2009, the state of BCS had a total population of 565,400. The most populous municipality is La Paz—where the state capital is also located—with 230,078 inhabitants, followed by the municipality of Los Cabos, with 204,711 inhabitants. By 2012, the population of Los Cabos will have increased to 238,958, surpassing La Paz with its 236,768 inhabitants. Finally, following the projections, it is estimated that in just over 20 years the population of the municipality of Los Cabos will have doubled, and will have 443,544 inhabitants in 2030, including more than half of the state's population (CONAPO 2005).

It should be made clear that this population explosion in large part is not due to the demographics of the people of Los Cabos. The municipality of Los Cabos has become a magnet for immigration, both interstate and international. What makes the town so attractive? The Development Plan of the Tenth City Council of Los Cabos, 2008–2011, affirms, by way of explanation, that as a result of the municipality operating as a tourist center, it has a high demand for labor, both skilled and unskilled. The usual claim from different sectors, widely accepted by the Los Cabos community and the different levels of government, focuses on the lack of laborers with suitable characteristics. Just two examples need be mentioned. First, it is common knowledge that the major hotel companies, especially foreign, "import" their top management and administrative-level personnel. Second, large construction companies, to a great extent, also bring in their workers from other states of Mexico (Ayuntamiento de Los Cabos 2008).

Table 1 shows the flow of foreign tourists and Mexicans living abroad who temporarily entered national territory, arriving in BCS and Los Cabos in 2005.

Table 1. Non-Immigrant Tourists and Mexican Nationals Residing Abroad, 2005

Non-Immigrant Tourists			Mexican Nationals Residing Abroad		
Location	Arrivals	Departures	Location	Arrivals	Departures
BCS	1,059,594	1,043,516	BCS	15,050	15,060
Los Cabos	998,779	986,455	Los Cabos	12,322	13,102

Source: Instituto Nacional de Migración, Delegación Regional, Departamento de Programación, Informática y Estadística, 2005.

If a comparison is done of the arrivals and departures of foreigners who have a permit to legally stay and/or temporarily work in Mexico, as non-immigrant visitors,[1] with the arrivals and departures of Mexicans living in the country, a migratory movement three times stronger by nationals is detected (see Table 2). Thus, interstate migration acquires special importance. It should be noted that statistics do not distinguish whether a person had multiple arrivals and/or departures. In 2005, the municipality of Los Cabos received 58.7% of the 18,359 national migrants who arrived in BCS, that is, 10,771 persons. The migration flow has slowed down a bit. While in 2000, 11.3% of the national immigrants said they had come to this municipality in the last five years; in 2005, only 9.8% claimed the same. The origin of migrants is predominantly Sinaloa, Guerrero, Oaxaca, the State of Mexico, and Veracruz (Ayuntamiento de Los Cabos 2008).

Table 2. Non-Immigrant Visitors and Mexican Nationals Residing in the Country, 2005

Non-Immigrant Visitors			Mexican Nationals Residing in the Country		
Location	Arrivals	Departures	Location	Arrivals	Departures
BCS	8,242	8,132	BCS	24,545	22,410
Los Cabos	6,380	6,647	Los Cabos	18,210	16,985

Source: Instituto Nacional de Migración, Delegación Regional, Departamento de Programación, Informática y Estadística, 2005.

Foreigners who reside and work legally in Mexico can request to change their status to immigrant, generally after having resided in the country for a minimum of five years. Subsequently, if they wish to establish permanent residency, they can become a resident after another five-year stay and meeting a number of requirements (Instituto Nacional de Migración: www.inami.gob.mx). Approximately one-third of non-immigrant foreign visitors opted for this immigration status (Table 3).

---

1. According to the National Migration Institute, this category refers to investors, financiers, technicians/scientists, professionals, and advisors, among others (www.inami.gob.mx).

Education and Development of Human Resources

Table 3. Immigrants and Residents, 2005

Location	Arrivals	Departures
BCS	2,510	2,416
Los Cabos	2,203	2,140

Source: Instituto Nacional de Migración, Delegación Regional, Departamento de Programación, Informática y Estadística, 2005.

From the aforementioned, several questions arise: to what extent can workers coming from other states of the country or abroad meet the requirements of the jobs offered in the municipality of Los Cabos? How are job offers characterized? What kind of knowledge is required for these jobs? How are educational resources characterized? How is the offering of human resources characterized? What kind of education, formation, or training do people of Los Cabos have? In what ways could the people of Los Cabos be prepared to fill these job vacancies?

HUMAN DEVELOPMENT

Before delving into the analysis of job offerings, educational resources, and human resource development in the municipality of Los Cabos, some indicators that are useful for understanding the problems of Los Cabos will be reviewed. The United Nations Development Programme (UNDP) is developing annual evaluations of countries in order to measure the impact of policies used and to carry out worldwide comparisons. Based primarily on the work of Amartya Sen (2000), the intent is to analyze progress in life expectancy, quality of life, and knowledge. The topic of interest, that is, the level of knowledge, is calculated based on the combination of literacy rates and enrollment in primary, secondary, and tertiary education. The set of indicators is reflected in the Human Development Index (HDI). The rating goes from 0 to1, 1 being the highest rating (PNUD 2002).

Data from some selected indicators (see Tables 4–6) draw a picture in which, on average, more employment opportunities and better pay than at the national level can be found in the municipality of Los Cabos. The low indices of economic inactivity and working as street vendors, along with high per capita income that is twice the national average and high per capita income in the municipality of La Paz, contribute significantly to the high human development index that ranks the municipality of Los Cabos at number 38 of all municipalities in Mexico and the state of BCS in ninth place among all states.

In the area of knowledge, the very low rate of illiteracy in BCS, even below the national average, is to be noted. However, the municipality of Los Cabos shows the lowest rate in the state with only 54.1% school attendance of the age group of 6–24 years, lagging behind with a difference of almost 9 percentage points over the national and state averages and with more than 13 percentage points below the municipality of La Paz. The average education in Los Cabos is 8.1 grades, that is, the majority of the population between ages 6 and 24 years completed the six grades of primary school and two years of junior high school. The education level is still above the national average, but below the state average.

ECONOMIC ACTIVITY, EMPLOYMENT, AND INCOME

In the state of BCS, 58.7% of the population age 14 or older is economically active. Applying this percentage to the municipality of Los Cabos, 71,107 people represent the economically active population (EAP) (Ayuntamiento de Los Cabos, 2008).

Table 4. Literacy, School Attendance, Education

Country, State, Municipality	% Literate Age 15+	Literacy Rate	% Population Without Complete Primary Schooling Age 15+	% School Attendance Ages 6 to 24	Enrollment Rate	Education Rate
Mexico	90.5	0.905	26.99	62.8	0.628	0.812
BCS	95.8	0.958	20.98	63.2	0.632	0.849
La Paz	96.8	0.968	16.40	67.8	0.678	0.871
Los Cabos	96.2	0.962	20.79	54.1	0.541	0.822

Source: Calculated from the Anexo Estadístico: Índice de Desarrollo Humano por Municipio (Statistical Annex: Human Development Index by Municipality), CONAPO 2000; PNUD 2002.

Education and Development of Human Resources

Table 5. Income, Economic Activity

Country, State, Municipality	GDP Per Capita in Dollars	GDP Per Capita Index	% Population With Incomes of up to 2 Minimum Wages	% of Economic Activity	% of Population in Peddling Activities
Mexico	7,495	0.721	56.4	50.7	14.8
BCS	8,722	0.746	40.9	45.1	14.1
La Paz	7,414	0.719	40.6	46	15.2
Los Cabos	15,018	0.836	29.6	38	13.6

Source: Calculated from the Anexo Estadístico: Índice de Desarrollo Humano por Municipio (Statistical Annex: Human Development Index by Municipality), CONAPO 2000; PNUD 2002.

Table 6. Human Development Index (HDI)

Country, State, Municipality	Human Development Index	Rank	Place at the State and Municipality Levels
Mexico	0.789	Medium high	
BCS	0.818	High	9
La Paz	0.817	High	118

Source: Calculated from the Anexo Estadístico: Índice de Desarrollo Humano por Municipio (Statistical Annex: Human Development Index by Municipality), CONAPO 2000.

Table 7. Economic Distribution of the Population of BCS

Indicator	First Quarter, 2008
BCS	546,343
14 years or older	405,572
Economically active population (EAP)	262,445
Employed	255,429

Source: INEGI, ENOE 2008.

The service industry accounts for approximately 80% of the gross domestic product (GDP), with the tourism subsector being the most important (Plan Municipal de Desarrollo 2008).

Tables 8 and 9 provide selected information from the 2004 economic census (INEGI 2004). In the municipality of Los Cabos, there were 4,771 recorded businesses that provided employment to 29,621 inhabitants. Retail trade is the sector with the largest number of businesses, followed by the services sector, hotels and restaurants, transportation, and manufacturing.

Table 8. Businesses, Los Cabos

Sector* The first five in size	Businesses	Income (thousands of pesos)
Retail trade	2,270	218,162
Other services (except government activities)	584	38,556
Temporary lodging and preparation of food and beverage services	479	393,402
Transportation, postal services, and storage	325	81,881
Manufacturing industry	270	59,689

*Note: Excludes data on agricultural and forestry activities.
Source: INEGI, Censos Económicos 2004.

If businesses are grouped in order of highest to lowest income, at the top of the list as generators of higher wages are the hotel and restaurant services, retail trade, business support services and waste management, transportation, and the manufacturing industry. The total generation of income amounted to 1,243.7 million pesos.

Brenner and Aguilar (2002) and Aguilar, Graizbord, and Sánchez Crispín (1996) agree that only one-third of the jobs in the tourism sector are considered specialized. They warn that the local population might be excluded from the skilled and better paid jobs as domestic and international migrants tend to occupy these positions. In the present case, there are data that suggest that the demand for unskilled workers is met, at least in part, by temporary migrants from the inte-

Table 9. Income, Los Cabos

Sector* The first five in size	Businesses	Income (thousands of pesos)
Temporary lodging and preparation of food and beverages services	479	393,402
Retail trade	2,270	218,162
Business support services, waste management, remediation services	86	145,363
Wholesale trade	110	92,171
Transportation, postal services, and storage	325	81,881

*Note: Excludes data on agricultural and forestry activities.
Source: INEGI, Censos Económicos 2004.

rior who agree to work for a low salary instead of being unemployed or receiving lower wages in their state of origin. Either way, there are still insufficient data to fully understand the problem.

Foremost among the strategic objectives of the 2005–2011 National Development Plan is to improve levels of job organization and training in order to increase social capital, although it is not clear what concrete actions would be directed toward this purpose (Gobierno Estatal de Baja California Sur 2005).

EDUCATION

The 2005–2011 State Development Plan (Plan Estatal de Desarrollo– PED), has among its governing programmatic principles the improvement and expansion of educational offerings, as well as providing greater articulation of research and higher education centers. The government of BCS has set as one of its strategic objectives the design and operation of an educational model for equity, sustainable development, and social coexistence (Gobierno Estatal de Baja California Sur 2005). At the municipal level, through the Office of Education, the Development Plan for Los Cabos stipulates the development of a comprehensive diagnosis for an in-depth understanding of the state of education. It is also proposed to reduce the educational lag at the middle and higher middle levels in cooperation with state and federal authorities (Ayuntamiento de Los Cabos 2008).

The data for the municipality of Los Cabos, provided by the Secretariat of Public Education (Secretaría de Educación Pública–SEP) for the different educational levels in the 2006–2007 school year, shows that a significant number of students enter late into basic education; they are older than age 6 or 7 when they start first grade. Due to this late entry, this group graduates from elementary school at between 12 and 15 years of age. These students are mostly children from families with limited resources who are migrants or live in small and remote communities. It should be pointed out that the primary education subsystem consists of three categories: general, community, and migrant children (SEP BCS 2006–2007; Ayuntamiento de Los Cabos 2008).

Currently, the state education system has as its priority goal that all young people complete junior high school with satisfactory results. In the 2006–2007 school term, 9,557 students were enrolled in a junior high school in the municipality of Los Cabos. Two-thirds attended a public school and one-third a private one. The gap in age, as previously described (not all students attending the first grade of junior high school are 13 years old) makes it difficult to correlate with the total population of 13-to-15 year olds. Thus, it is hard to determine the percentage of 13-to-15 year olds in junior high school (Ayuntamiento de Los Cabos 2008; SEP BCS 2005, 2006–2007).

The level of higher secondary education, or *preparatoria*, had an enrollment of 5,052 students in 21 schools in the municipality of Los Cabos for the 2006-2007 school year, representing 46% of young people age 15 to 18 years old. Forty-three percent of these attended a high school with a general orientation, 44% were at a technology-oriented high school, and 13% studied at an open high school. Rates of failure and terminal efficiency improved during the cycle, and failures decreased from 43.7% to 38.5% and terminal efficiency increased to 54.4% at the end of the school term (Ayuntamiento de Los Cabos 2008; SEP BCS 2005, 2006–2007).

In 1998, the Catholic University and the University of Tijuana (CUT) (both private institutions) opened campuses in the municipality of Los Cabos. Since 2000, the Autonomous University of

Baja California Sur (Universidad Autónoma de Baja California Sur–UABCS) and the Technological Institute of Higher Education of Los Cabos (Instituto Tecnológico de Estudios Superiores de Los Cabos–ITESLC) have also begun operations in Los Cabos. In addition, the National Pedagogic University (Universidad Pedagógica Nacional–UPN) supports a campus in San José del Cabo and another in Cabo San Lucas. The World University (Universidad Mundial–UNIMUNDO), the University of Veracruz (UNIVER) and the University of Professional Development (Universidad del Desarrollo Profesional–UNIDEP) complete the list of higher education institutions. There are only three public institutions. The higher education subsystem consists of three levels: technical, undergraduate, and graduate. Technical higher education is not available in Los Cabos. In the 2006–2007 school year, 2,265 students enrolled in higher education and of these 42 were in a graduate program. The majority study at the undergraduate level, 63% study for a bachelor's degree, 29% a technology program, and 8% preferred to study at a school that prepares elementary school teachers (*educación normalista*) (Ayuntamiento de Los Cabos 2008; SEP BCS 2006–2007).

In order to include the greatest diversity possible, including all sectors of society, the first consultation forum on the development of the municipality of Los Cabos, was held on October 2, 2008. The following is a compilation of the proposals submitted by participants from all sectors of the community on what education and what types of educational programs, specifically higher and technical education, should be implemented in the municipality:

- New undergraduate majors: medicine, accounting, biology, psychology, arts, real estate, gastronomy
- New graduate programs: Master's in Tourism, Arts, Law, Environmental Education

In general, the audience reached consensus on the following:

- Expand educational options in coordination with international universities; have more universities and new majors at the undergraduate and postgraduate levels
- Add courses to the educational programs of higher education that strengthen and promote local culture and identity, ethics, humanism, and civility
- Increase quality of education: raise the level of education in private universities, evaluating the existing ones; improve

evaluation methods of students and teachers; certify quality of educational programs
- Create research centers
- Offer technical careers and trade schools
- Provide training: have work competency programs; offer certificate programs *(diplomados)*, tourism courses, and Chinese language courses[2]

Conclusion

Interrelationships among education, personal well-being, productivity, economic development, and work competency are complex and, as economies and productive activities become more globalized, they will become even more complex. The debate and research will continue. Perhaps the questions posed cannot yet be answered in a satisfactorily manner, but decisions can be made on what and how local life should be.

In the case of the municipality of Los Cabos, it is necessary to know the reasons why people decide not to study or continue studying. Do they study in another municipality, state, or country? Is the desired major not offered locally? Do they need to work? The comprehensive diagnosis on education that the Department of Education plans to carry out can provide valuable data on these matters. Of course, the institutions of higher education will also be able to participate in the development of a proposal for new courses of study.

In addition, the private sector will be able to articulate what human resource profile it requires and what types are its job vacancies in order to find solutions jointly with the education sector on how to prepare local people for these positions, rather than import them from elsewhere. The companies themselves, or through their chambers, could develop and offer the necessary training.

It will be essential to formalize coordination mechanisms in order to bring the private and educational sectors closer together. This would contribute to the strengthening and reactivation of existing coordinating organizations such as the State Commission for Higher Education Planning (Comisión Estatal para la Planeación

---

2. First Consultation Forum on the Development of the Municipality of Los Cabos, Minutes, October 2008.

de la Educación Superior–COEPES), whose function is to coordinate secondary and higher education in BCS, as well as the State Commission for High School Education Planning (Comisión Estatal para la Planeación de la Educación Media Superior–COEPPE).

The question is asked again: what is the role of education? What can quality education be expected to provide? Is education the magic wand that turns dreams into reality? Is education the key that opens the door to success, prosperity, and personal satisfaction? At times, in the official and media discourse, education has been blamed for the ills of society—and of the economy. Is the education system responsible that not enough jobs were created? What happens if the highly educated and specialized workforce does not find where to use this knowledge? Obviously, education is not the cure for everything. However, the path traced by the United Nations Educational Scientific and Cultural Organization (UNESCO), "Education for all as the goal of the millennium," shows the way. Education is a human right, with access to quality education for all sectors of society, not only for those who can pay.

REFERENCES

Aguilar, Adrián Guillermo, Boris Graizbord, and Álvaro Sánchez Crispín. 1996. *Las ciudades intermedias y el desarrollo de México.* México, DF: El Colegio de México.

Ayuntamiento de Los Cabos. 2008. *Plan de Desarrollo Municipal 2008–2011.* Los Cabos, BCS: X. Ayuntamiento de Los Cabos.

Becker, Gary S. 1964. *Human Capital: A Theoretical and Empirical Analysis, with Special Reference to Education.* Chicago: University of Chicago Press.

Brenner, Ludger, and Adrián Guillermo Aguilar. 2002. "State-Planned Tourism Destinations: The Case of Huatulco, Mexico." *Tourism Geographies* 7 (2): 138–164.

Congreso del Estado de Baja California Sur. *Plan Estatal de Desarrollo, 2005-2011.* www.cbcs.gob.mx.

Consejo Nacional de Población (CONAPO). 2000. *Índice de desarrollo humano por municipio.* www.conapo.gob.mx.

Consejo Nacional de Población (CONAPO). 2005. *Población total de los municipios 2005–2030.* www.conapo.gob.mx.

Ganster, Paul, Oscar Arizpe, and Antonina Ivanova, eds. 2007. *Loreto: El futuro de la primera capital de las Californias.* San Diego, CA: San Diego State University Press and Institute for Regional Studies of the Californias.

Gobierno Estatal de Baja California Sur. 2005. *Plan Estatal de Desarrollo, 2005–2011.* www.cbcs.gob.mx/

Grossman, Gene, and Elhanan Helpman. 1991. *Innovation and Growth in the Global Economy.* Cambridge: MIT Press.

Instituto Nacional de Estadística y Geografía (INEGI). 2004. *Censos Económicos 2004.* www.inegi.gob.mx

Instituto Nacional de Estadística y Geografía (INEGI) and Secretaría de Trabajo y de Previsión Social. 2008. *Encuesta Nacional de Ocupación y Empleo.*

Instituto Nacional de Migración. www.inami.gob.mx.

Mincer, Jacob. 1958. "Investment in Human Capital and Personal Income Distribution." *The Journal of Political Economy.*

Organización de las Naciones Unidas para la Educación, Ciencia y Cultura. *Educación para todos (EPT).* Portal.unesco.org/education/es.

Primer Foro de Consulta sobre Desarrollo del Municipio de Los Cabos, Relatoría, Octubre 2008.

Programa de las Naciones Unidas para el Desarrollo (PNUD). 2002. *Informe sobre desarrollo humano.* www.undp.org.mx/desarrollohumano/informefr.html.

Rangel, Ernesto. 2005. "La geografía económica del conocimiento en la era global: Una aproximación desde el foro de cooperación económica Asia-Pacífico." In *Globalización y regionalismo: Educación, equidad, justicia,* Antonina Ivanova and E. Rangel, eds. La Paz, BCS: UABCS, Universidad de Colima.

Romer, Paul. 1986. "Increasing Returns and Long-run Growth." *Journal of Political Economy* 94 (5).

Secretaría de Educación Pública (SEP). www.sepbcs.gob.mx

Sen, Amartya K. 2000. *Development as Freedom.* New York: Random House.

Shultz, Theodore W. 1980. *Invirtiendo en la gente.* Barcelona: Ed. Ariel.

13

The Cultural Pavilion of the Republic: Cultural Diversity and Biodiversity in Los Cabos

Alexandra Sauvage and Frederick Conway

INTRODUCTION

The Cultural Pavilion of the Republic (Pabellón Cultural de la República–PCR) is the main cultural project of the state of Baja California Sur to commemorate the 1810 revolution for independence and the social revolution of 1910. Since its opening was planned for September 2010, but the opening of the first stage took place only in April 2011, the Pavilion is still in draft form at the time of writing this text. Therefore, this study cannot cover the analysis of the Pavilion as a functioning institution, with its achievements and shortcomings. Rather, the analysis is on how the Pavilion pretends to achieve its objectives within its obligation to articulate them by demonstrating national identity to be emulated by society. While the finished project will be a cultural center that will consist of several activities such as concerts, theater, and radio programs, this chapter is focused on the space of the museum, whose collections will permanently transmit the values and cultural objectives of the Pavilion.

The ambitious project of the PCR in Los Cabos is surprising. This area is a famous tourism destination of a sun and beach sort. Foreigners who travel to Mexico for cultural reasons tend more to visit the pyramids of the Mayan Riviera than the Californian peninsula (SECTUR 2008b). As in the Mediterranean Riviera—where the coast is reserved for recreation, relaxation, and sports, while the cultural centers are located in the capital cities of Spain, France, Italy, Greece, and Turkey—Baja California Sur concentrates its institutions in the capital city of La Paz and recreational activities are in the municipality of Los Cabos, giving each place a distinctive character commonly perceived among Baja California Sur people. Selecting Cabo San Lucas to place an institution of this type, then, does not follow this same logic. The important presence of foreign tourists may perhaps justify the construction and maintenance of an expensive cultural complex in Los Cabos and that the area is the place of origin of the political class that is currently in state power. But its existence has yet to respond to the questions: to what culture(s) will it dedicate itself, under what perspectives, and what are the objectives?

The world of museums has experienced drastic changes in the last three decades, both in terms of financial, political, and social resources, as well as in terms of functions, whether the management of collections, the discourse of exhibitions, or the civic-cultural education that museums offer. These changes have produced tensions concerning the purpose of the cultural institution:

> Museums...are surprisingly protean organizations. They have different and often multiple mandates and complex and contradictory goals. They experience conflicting demands made on them from a range of interested parties, including funders, audiences, government officials, professional communities, collectors, and peoples who are represented in the museum displays (Karp et al. 2006).

The difficulties of the PCR in finding the purpose of its project confirm, in its particular context, these tensions at play. It must comply with the scope of the national commemoration of the centennials, with the needs for the promotion and preservation of the natural heritage, and with the defense of the local cultural identity within the framework of globalization. How can the PCR articulate all of these requirements and respond to the expectations of an increasingly demanding public? Some answers to these questions lie in the functions that have been given to cultural institutions and, in particular, to museums since their inception.

The Cultural Pavilion of the Republic

WHY A CULTURAL CENTER IN LOS CABOS?

Since its creation in the nineteenth century, the public museum is related to the development of the nation state (Bennett 1995; Hooper-Greenhill 2000). An indispensable tool for any country with pretensions of becoming a nation respected as such, the museum was always a prestigious institution. It is associated with the authority of scientific knowledge, value and rarity of the treasures under its care, and sense of belonging it offers citizens, since they can visit national collections to learn about their history and identify as a unique people.

Cultural Heritage as an Identity Vector

In Mexico, this institution began with the creation of the Mexican National Museum, on March 18, 1825. Through the museum, the state's goal was to "rescue, guard, study, and exhibit objects" considered "indispensable elements for their government programs" (Rico Mansard 2004). The state promoted Mexican culture to develop and sustain the patriotism of citizens, who could identify with the strong and positive image of the nation. This remains a fundamental role of museums; at the same time, they serve as showcases and as guardians of the culture of a community, region, or country. They also continue to have an aura of prestige, and government leaders regularly use them as national "masterpieces" under their mandates.[1]

In the present case, although the term "pavilion" has its origins in military vocabulary that is then transmitted to the architecture one, the word was chosen in reference to the pavilions of universal expositions, whose objective is to demonstrate the technological and cultural excellence within an implicit competition among the participating nations. Thus, the Pavilion of the Republic was clearly intended as a place to showcase the richness of cultural diversity in Mexico, primarily to foreign tourists who come to visit Cabo San Lucas. It is hoped that this will serve as an incentive for them to

---

[1]. France is perhaps the most famous example of the use of museums as government greatness: The Museum of Modern Art by Georges Pompidou, the Kanaka Cultural Center and the renovation of the Louvre with the pyramid under Mitterand's administration, and the recent Museum of Ethnography of Paris under Jacques Chirac.

continue traveling to other parts of Mexico. The first project documents submitted to the state government of BCS bear witness to this desire to both strengthen as well as share the peninsula's cultural sense of belonging with the rest of Mexico. Since 2006, the slogan for the PCR is "From Los Cabos, Mexico, to the World" and the project intends to follow as a guiding thread Mexico's locations classified as World Heritage Sites, since Mexico ranks first on the American continent regarding registered sites, and seventh worldwide. In addition, Baja California Sur has three of these sites. This official and universalizing recognition by UNESCO of the national cultural wealth implicitly supports the rationale for the project. Explicitly, it is considered that this project contributes "to strengthen our country's image internationally," (Vázquez Ceja 2006). In 2007, this justification was accurate in terms of its urgency, noting that "About two million foreign tourists arrive in Los Cabos who do not find an array of art, history, and culture that will bring them closer to what Mexico is about " and that with the PCR, the intent is "to strengthen the Mexicanness in a tourist destination that is constituted into a cultural border" (Vázquez Ceja 2007).

Social Role of the Cultural Institution

Besides its cultural function that is commonly distinguished, the museum also plays a vital social role in the management of the city. Therefore, governments have used the museum not only to educate its population, but also to regenerate the urban landscape of a depressed neighborhood and/or promote socioeconomic activities through cultural consumption (Hernández 2006; Greffe 1999; MacKercher and du Cros 2002). The institution thus becomes an effective tool for integrated social control, more so in times of fast and radical changes, such as those that modern nations of the nineteenth century knew, and those now known by the city of Cabo San Lucas upon experiencing the vicissitudes of globalization. In this sense, it is not surprising that when discussing the purposes of the PCR in Los Cabos, the former president of the BCS municipality, Luis Armando Díaz, referred to the main goal as:

> Through art and culture, we want to confront the growing problem of social disintegration that negatively impacts a

part of our society. We intend for the Cultural Pavilion of the Republic to become an advanced organizer of the Los Cabos society capable of reversing social problems that afflict us today. We also want it to be an excellent host of tourism in which visitors will find an important selection of local and national art and culture.[2]

The establishment of the PCR in Los Cabos is fully justified by its cultural and environmental education functions, economic impacts, and social management, but its credibility will rather depend on what it proposes to its visitors. It is the quality of its content that will justify its cost of 700 million pesos and, there, the purpose of the museum is fundamental. The greatest obstacle to its good development is that within a short time of its opening, only the architectural project has been established; the museological discourse and museographics script have not yet been determined. In other words, it is like a book project with only a cover and no story to tell. Only with solid and attractive museological discourse—or the discussion of the museum experience from the perspectives of the visitors and the institution—and museographics script will the PCR be able to comply with its management sphere of social cohesion needed in the state, and with the aspiration of becoming an icon that identifies Los Cabos to the world.

CULTURE AND BIODIVERSITY: MEXICAN IDENTITY THROUGH CULTURAL OR NATURAL HERITAGE?

The fact that the elements pointed out have not been determined yet, does not mean that there have not been proposals about what the museum should contain. Rather, a contrary explanation could proceed: neither the museological discourse nor the museographic script was defined within the priorities of the PCR creation, so none of the propositions, to date, has been imposed as definitive. The first was included in the original project; it is a representation of Mexico's cultural diversity. The second one reduced the ambition to a geographical level, concentrating on the valuation of the heritage of the Californian peninsula and its biological diversity.

---

2. http://www.bcs.gob.mx/index.php?option=com_content&task=blogcategory&id=498&Itemid=251 (28 February 2009).

The Cultural Heritage of Mexico, but which One of All?

In 2007, the project was proposed as "a monumental and emblematic creation" where it put "at the disposal of Mexican nationals a reunion with their origins, and offered to transport the international traveler to the knowledge of the historical, cultural, and artistic roots" (Vázquez Ceja 2007) of the nation. This approach has several positive impacts. The first is that it presents the cultural richness of Mexico in the south of the peninsula, a place generally perceived by Mexicans as isolated from the country, since it is more difficult for a person from BCS to visit national heritage sites of the rest of the republic than it is for a person from Guadalajara, Querétaro, or Oaxaca. The second is that the population from Los Cabos was formed by an important national migration, and valuing the national heritage offers positive recognition of the different regional identities. Several studies have confirmed a better social integration of emigrant citizens in the state when their cultural specificities were recognized by national institutions (Sandell 2002). A third point is that it reestablishes that the south of the peninsula belongs to the Mexican Republic. In a context where everyday activities are carried out in English and the usual currency is U.S. dollars for the vast majority of *cabeños*, it is essential to relocate the region within the cultural framework of the nation, both in the eyes of locals and of visitors.

That said, and knowing the cultural diversity of Mexico, what is the national cultural framework? Or, to retake the terms of the Pavilion proposal document, with which cultural "roots" is the "reunion" or discovery proposed? As analyzed by Enrique Florescano (1993), Mexican cultural origins depended on the dominant social groups at the time of establishing the Mexican nation. At the time, cultural heritage, then valued, was selected according to Eurocentric values of the settlers and their descendants. They glorified colonial history and heritage, as well as the monumental heritage of "pre-Hispanic civilizations" (a term commonly used that denote precisely the Eurocentric perspective), which allowed them to differentiate themselves from the Spaniards. This implies that they marginalized indigenous cultures of the time (which did not fall within the concept of "pre-Hispanic civilization") and other non-dominant cultural groups, like the Chinese and Africans, through their exclusion from the national identity or their definition in negative terms. These values inherited from the Western colonial order of the eighteenth, nineteenth, and twentieth centuries are now recognized as obsolete in cultural terms. The main museums of Europe, North America, and Australia, particularly those preserving an Indian heritage, are modifying the discourse of their collections to update it to the contemporary context of valorization of cultural diversity outside the colonial criteria (Sauvage 2007).

What does this worldwide transformation of museums mean for the Pavilion? First, that the simple valorization of the monumental heritage does not comply with the ambition of making the Pavilion an institution at the peak of what is done in the twenty-first century. A famous example of failure of an institution that wanted to impose itself as the most prestigious of its kind in Europe is the Quai Branly Museum, which opened its doors in Paris in 2006. Its loyalty to the colonial discourse was widely criticized, to the point that it was identified as "the museum of what museums were," despite proposing a museology with the most advanced technological materials (Jeudy 2006).

Second, to continue to value the monumental aspect of Mexican cultural heritage is to keep underestimating the indigenous cultures of BCS, which suffer from remaining in the shadow of the Aztec and Mayan pyramids. A good way to depart from the colonial criteria is to complement the BCS cultural heritage, currently valued—essentially the religious heritage, basic and essential cultural relation of the Creole settlers of the West—with recognition of the Pericú, Guaycura, and Cochimí cultures, outside the colonial criteria of "primitivism," of "progress," and a supposed hierarchy of civilizations. Mountain ranchers also created a different and unique culture closely related to the environment of the peninsula. Another aspect that could be integrated is the non-European migrations to the peninsula, for example, the acknowledgement of the contribution of Chinese migrants to the economic and cultural development of the state. This update of the discourse of cultural heritage, besides placing the Pavilion clearly in the twenty-first century, would place the BCS culture as unique and different from other regions of Mexico, enriching the nation with an additional element of cultural diversity, and thus following UNESCO's present criteria.[3]

---

3. See UNESCO's web portal on cultural diversity: http://portal.unesco.org/culture/es/ev.php-URL_ID = 35396&URL_DO=DO_TOPIC&URL_SECTION=201.html (01-March-2009).

Natural Heritage and Identity: What Relevance do They have for The Pavilion's Museum?

In 2008, an alternative museographic project on "biodiversity" was adopted. While the relationship of culture with identity previously described is not a familiar one, because the former promotes the latter through its manifestations, the relationship of biological diversity to identity seems less obvious. Its explanation lies in the fact that this relationship has been interrupted in the West for several centuries with the perception of a supposed dichotomy between "culture" and "nature." Lately, research on environmental history and cultural geography, as well as media debates on the environmental impact of mankind on its natural environment, have led to rethinking this relationship, and there is a rediscovery of the influence of nature over culture and identity.

Whereas before nature was conceived without human beings, to the extent that policies of expulsion of residents existed where it was decided to establish a natural area, the most recent developments in ecology and environmental conservation consider that humankind is part of the ecosystem. Moreover, it is recognized that the very concept of nature is a cultural construction. Therefore, it is perceived differently by different cultural groups.

This renewed man-nature relationship is reflected primarily in the concept of sustainability—which recognizes the human impact on ecosystems—and that human life depends on the health of ecosystems. In these aspects, the history of Baja California Sur can be proud of having several models of sustainable cultures, from indigenous peoples who inhabited its land, to the arrival of Spanish colonists, and to the ranching communities that remained after the abandonment of the missions. These stories of the past are being increasingly recognized as sources of inspiration for the design of current and future sustainable projects. Their presence in the museum would allow an ideal articulation between regional history and current interests in sustainable development.

At another level, since the seventies, the field of human geography has developed an in-depth study on the importance of space and the environment on identity, whose main expression is the feeling of belonging to a place (Relph 1976; Tuan 1974). To feel in "the motherland," however, is not automatic at the regional or national level or in an entity larger than the local space where the individual lives his/her direct experiences. The museum would reinforce this sense of belonging by exposing the relationship of the people of BCS and of Mexicans with their motherland. This "imagined community" (Anderson 2006) would help to forge the social cohesion that is so expected in the state. But for a place to become a space to which its inhabitants feel rooted, the place must become "visible" through symbolic events or icons (Tuan 1974).

In this regard, the PCR, foreseen as an architectural icon of Los Cabos, could completely fulfill its function. Moreover, it recognizes that biodiversity is not something that is experienced directly, but that it is learned and imagined. The BCS families that have lived in Los Cabos for several generations usually do not know more about ecological diversity in Baja California Sur than national migrants or tourists who arrive in the state. This means that all groups, however diverse they might be, are in the same position of needing to learn about the biological heritage of the peninsula. While for the national population this heritage can become a source of regional and national pride, for tourists—who generally come to Los Cabos for outdoor recreation—it can be assimilated as an attraction in the region that is worth preserving.

While a museum on biodiversity is easily justified in the state, the PCR will have to surpass the irony of developing it in a place that to date is the least sustainable of Baja California Sur. A museum on biodiversity will only be plausible if it also shows the threats that exist to the environment and the challenges for its conservation. In other words, the issue of sustainability is as essential as the sense of belonging to social cohesion.

There, the greatest obstacle to this project on biodiversity and ecology is its coherence with the chosen architectural design that is a monumental building with high maintenance costs due to its technological equipment, air conditioning, and electricity consumption. A more appropriate building would have been one that follows the perspective of the California Academy of Sciences in Los Angeles, at the forefront of sustainable technologies (Grossman 2008). It would have also been adaptable to the proposal presented in the architectural competition of the botanical garden, with constructions of adobe and medians with palm trees, guamúchil, and mesquite. The botanical garden, in addition to its natural virtues, is today one of the urban operations most valued worldwide, as confirmed by the cities of San Diego, Paris, Sydney, and London.

Conclusion

Evidently, the museum project in Los Cabos is more than relevant, and its potential for sending a clear and strong message to the world is great. However, in order to do so, it is necessary to define a museological project and its museographic script as soon as possible. As indicated by Víctor Toledo (1997), Mexico is one of the biologically richest countries of the world: its ecological diversity classifies it as "among the 10 bioculturally richest nations in the planet." If the original idea of the guiding thread to the sites registered as world heritage of humankind is retaken, the state of Baja California Sur is home to at least three sites registered in the natural heritage section. This reinforces the need to include the ecological dimension at the same level as culture, regardless of the selected museological discourse and museographic script. For its part, the cultural dimension should not simply retake the models established in the modern era, but embrace the concept of cultural diversity, as promoted by UNESCO.

A focus only on the monumental aspects of the Mexican cultural heritage runs certain risks of criticism for not valuing the non-dominant cultures in an angle that reflects the colonial order. At the same time, a celebration of biological diversity that does not mention the threats that development processes present to it, nor the need to reach a level of sustainability, risks being criticized for ignoring environmental realities of Los Cabos and other parts of the state. Including prehistoric and historic cultures of indigenous peoples and ranchers of the peninsula could constitute a bridge between the two themes of cultural and natural heritage.

A historical discourse that integrates culture with nature would be especially suitable for recognizing the unique richness of the natural and cultural heritage in the state of Baja California Sur. It would provide an additional element of cultural diversity of the national heritage and would articulate in a simple and powerful way the interests of contemporary society in placing itself in this globalized world and heading toward a sustainable management of its wealth.

REFERENCES

Anderson, Benedict. 2006. *Imagined Communities: Reflections on the Origin and Spread of Nationalism.* London: Verso.

Bellido Grant, María Luisa. 2001. *Arte, museos y nuevas tecnologías.* Gijón, Spain: Ediciones Trea.

Bennett, Tony. 1995. *The Birth of the Museum: History, Theory, Politics.* London: Routledge.

Florescano, Enrique. 1993. *El mito de Quetzalcóatl.* Mexico, DF: Fondo de Cultura Económica.

Florescano, Enrique. 2005. *Imágenes de la Patria a través de los siglos.* México, DF: Taurus.

Greffe, Xavier. 1999. *La gestion du patrimoine culturel.* Paris: Antropos.

Grossman, Rachel. 2008. "California Academy of Sciences." *Architecture Week* 405 (12 November). http://www.architectureweek.com/2008/1112/index.html.

Hernández, Francisca. 2006. *Planteamientos teóricos de museología.* Gijón, Spain: Ediciones Trea.

Hooper-Greenhill, Eileen. 2000. *Museums and the Interpretation of Visual Culture.* London: Routledge.

Jardel, Enrique, and Bruce Benz. 1997. "El conocimiento tradicional del manejo de los recursos naturales y la diversidad biológica." In *El Patrimonio Nacional de México*, vol. I, Enrique Florescano, coord. México, DF: CFE.

Jeudy, Pierre Henry. 2006. "Un sanctuaire de l'ethnologie." *Libération* (20 June).

Karp, Ivan, Corinne A. Kratz, Lynn Szwaja, and Tomás Ybarra-Frausto. 2006. *Museum Frictions. Public Cultures/Global Transformations.* Durham, NC: Duke University Press.

MacKercher, Bob, and Hilary du Cros. 2002. *Cultural Tourism. The Partnership between Tourism and Cultural Heritage Management.* Binghamton, NY: Haworth Hospitality Press.

Relph, E. C. 1976. *Place and Placelessness.* London: Pion.

Rico Mansard, Luisa Fernanda. 2004. *Exhibir para educar. Objetos, colecciones y museos de la Ciudad de México* (1790–1910). Barcelona: Pomares.

Sandell, Richard, ed. 2002. *Museums, Society, Inequality.* London: Routledge.
Sauvage, Alexandra. 2007. "Narratives of Colonization: The Musée du Quai Branly in Context." *reCollections: Journal of the National Museum of Australia* 2 (2): 135–152. http://recollections.nma.gov.au/ejournal_library/attachments/volume_2_number_2/narratives_of_colonisation/files/23958/NarrativesOfColonisation.pdf.
Secretaría de Turismo (SECTUR). 2008a. *Programa Sectorial de Turismo 2007–2012.* (Accessed 28 June 2008), http://www.sectur.gob.mx/wb/sectur/sect_programa_sectorial_de_turismo_20072012.
Secretaría de Turismo (SECTUR). 2008b. *Resumen Ejecutivo del Estudio Estratégico de Viabilidad del Turismo Cultural en México.* (Accessed 30 June 2008), http://www.sectur.gob.mx/wb/sectur/sect_Turismo_Cultural.
Toledo, Víctor. 1997. "La diversidad ecológica de México." In *El Patrimonio Nacional de México*, vol. I and II, Enrique Florescano, coord. México, DF: CFE.
Tuan, Yi-fu. 1974. *Topophilia: A Study of Environmental Perception, Attitudes, and Values.* Englewood Cliffs, NJ: Prentice-Hall.
Vázquez Ceja, José Luis. 2006. "Centro Cultural Pabellón de la República." (December). Unpublished document.
Vázquez Ceja, José Luis. 2007. "Pabellón Cultural de la Republica, México 2010." (January). Unpublished document.

Part III.
The Tourism Dilemma

14

Traditional Tourism in Los Cabos: Opportunities and Limitations of Economic Growth

Alba E. Gámez and Paul Ganster

INTRODUCTION

Tourism in Baja California Sur (BCS) exemplifies the internationalization of the services sector and the integration of relatively isolated regions into global market processes. The success of the Los Cabos corridor (between San José del Cabo and Cabo San Lucas)—one of the most dynamic tourist areas in Mexico—has been central to this trend in the state. This chapter analyzes the effects of and perspectives on tourism growth that is tightly linked to the U.S. market. This growth has changed the local demographic pattern and has increased economic and other opportunities for BCS. At the same time, the state has become more vulnerable to negative external impacts, including environmental deterioration, intraregional economic disparities, and social exclusion. The chapter is divided into three sections. The first section addresses the economic importance of tourism internationally and for Mexico. The second part highlights the most recent patterns in the sector's performance in BCS, of which Los Cabos as the state's most important tourist destination is crucial. The third part reflects on the relation between growth and development linked to tourism in the region. In conclusion, a call is made for the need to reconsider how to sustain growth and stop the development of negative tourism-related patterns—concerns that government officials, private investors, and the local community should share and act upon.

THE GLOBALIZATION OF TOURISM

Tourism has become a dynamic economic sector worldwide. In many countries, economic activities related to tourism have helped to finance the trade deficit and have been a source of job creation. This has resulted from the increase in international tourist arrivals, which from 1950 to 2005 grew at an average annual rate of 6.5%. In 1950, the movement totaled 25 million people and grew to an estimated 924 million persons in 2008, when tourism constituted 10% of the world's gross domestic product. Tourism also generated 30% of world services exports and 70% of those were in developing countries, making it one of the main sources of income for one-third of all countries. It also created 240 million jobs worldwide (UNWTO 2008, 2009). It is not surprising, then, that government policies include this sector as a programmatic priority, especially in countries that in terms of infrastructure and quality of services lag behind other destinations. Government interest has been encouraged by not only the increase of visitor numbers but also by a change in trends within the international tourism demand. Regions such as Europe and the United States dominated the international tourist flow with over 95% in 1950, 76% in 2000, and 69% in 2008; however, they now face new competitors that challenge their control of this market (UNWTO 2008, 2009).

For many developing countries, and particularly small economies that cannot benefit from large economies of scale in industrial production and trade, tourism has provided an opportunity to benefit from this global trend. The basis of their appeal to international tourists has been their natural resources such as scenic beauty and pristine beaches, the opening of their economies to foreign investment, and the low cost of transportation, among other factors. The benefits have been represented as a positive impact in terms of regional development, insofar as tourism ignites interrelated elements that include growing job opportunities, inflow of foreign investment, and creation of intersectoral linkages. The latter are mainly those directly dependent on tourism, such as construction, communications, and transportation services, as well as the entertainment and food sectors (Ángeles 2008).

On the negative side, the domination of the tourism process by international firms and national companies located outside the region, the demand for low-skilled workers, changes in the traditional patterns of production and social organization, and the "enclave" character of tourist sites and thus the dependence on foreign markets are pointed out in the literature (Pearce 1988: 43–44). Also, adverse external effects such as pollution, overpopulation, prostitution, and problems related to public health have emerged with all traditional tourism megadevelopments. These raise questions about the approach taken toward the growth of tourism. The high vulnerability associated with dependence on external markets and capital is cause for concern. This is especially the case when the number of visitors to a resort area declines because the destination has lost its appeal, has been subject to natural disasters, or has been affected by economic or political crises. Thus, vulnerability and exhaustion of economic, social, or environmental resources call attention to the danger of the overspecialization of markets and products in which regions such as Los Cabos have engaged. As Berry (2001: 84) points out:

> The effects of outside dependency and control are made worse when industries which existed in an area prior to tourism suffer 'crowding out' due to available resources being channeled into tourism, resulting in a decline in those industries [Williams 1993]. Such a situation leads to even greater dependency on tourism, with obvious economic and social consequences, if and when tourism goes into decline. The evidence so far in places like Antigua, Minorca and Baunei, has indicated that existing industries must be maintained at all costs […]. If this is not possible, then the local government must encourage the creation of new alternatives to tourism.

It should be noted that a new market segment—alternative tourism—has emerged worldwide as a distinct experience to traditional tourism. This type of tourism is more in line with environmentally friendly experiences. In some cases, the results have been mixed.[1] However, the traditional type of tourism (related to mass tourism, resort-type destinations, and limited social interaction of visitors with local people) keeps defining tourism both at the national and international levels.

Inquiries about the causes for the prosperity or decline of tourist destinations have been discussed in the context of Butler's (1980) tourism area life cycle theory. This theory posits a slow initial process of growth in tourism regions or resorts, followed by a rapid increase of visitors (and investment) for a period of time; afterward, there is a phase of stability (a peak is reached) that is followed by decline. Criticisms of Butler's theory range from it being too simplistic to the difficulty in defining boundaries between stages. It is also considered vague and imprecise in its application and policy remedies (for a thorough review see Berry 2001). Nonetheless, it has called attention to the danger faced even by successful tourist destinations, which might not remain so forever, and that the issue of destinations coming to an end should be approached. Although the reasons for failure vary, the overexploitation of the natural resources that make some tourist destinations successful also makes them decline from exhaustion of these resources. In the case of peripheral regions where tourism is used as a tool for regional development, their intrinsic fragility (Ángeles 2008) might intensify the risk for failure. Some authors (Hall 2007: 34) suggest that tourism needs to be "integrated with other potential possibilities of development if it is to make a positive contribution" to those areas. Other researchers point out that the planned tourism developments by the National Trust Fund

---

[1]. As part of the international agenda post-World War II, the environment issue received wide attention both at the international and national levels. To natural resource conservation, social and economic concerns were added so that a scheme in which these three areas combined gave way to the notion of sustainability. The tourism sector, both public and private, echoed this trend (UNWTO 2009, WTTC 2009), although criticisms exist about the effectiveness of the new discourse. Simply put, if sustainable is what persists, then polluting or socially biased tourist activities can be sustainable as long as they continue to exist (Butler 1999: 20). Also, it has been recognized that not all tourism in rural or relatively inhabited areas is alternative tourism and not all alternative tourism is sustainable tourism (Guerrero et al. 2007). What actually links them is how local actors relate to the tourism activities (Barrera and Muñoz 2003); yet, even in those cases in which local actors are indeed part of the processes of tourism management and tourism flourishes, there is the risk to "die due to success." This would result from the negative externalities associated with economic growth and the increased inflow of visitors.

for Tourism Development (Fondo Nacional de Fomento al Turismo–FONATUR) and its partners have not produced regional development and have not created high value-added jobs for people from the region (Brenner and Aguilar 2002).

BCS is certainly on the periphery due to its geographical remoteness, lack of local policymaking, dependency on the centralized government, weak internal economic linkages, and dependency on outside innovation and pristine natural resources that make the region attractive (Hall 2007). Tourism in the state is often portrayed as a means of regional development, but it has overwhelmed other economic activities.

In Los Cabos, there has been an overpowering geographical and sectoral concentration of investment, revenue, and human mobility in the tourism sector at the same time that social, environmental, and economic distortions associated with rapid economic growth are present. Los Cabos, the region that best shows the success of resort tourism growth in the state, is a clear example of this. Despite these obvious problems, Los Cabos has become the model of tourism development applied elsewhere in the state.

TOURISM IN BCS AND THE IMPORTANCE OF THE LOS CABOS REGION

Current conditions in the international economy present discouraging times for the tourism sector worldwide. The global growth rate of international visitors in 2008 was only 2%, five points lower than the preceding year. Europe suffered the most, experiencing negative rates; tourism in the Asian region declined as air travel and hotel demand slowed after a decade of impressive growth. Although international tourism organizations predict the strengthening of the sector in the long run, forecasts for 2009 suggest no immediate recovery and even anticipate negative rates of 1 to 2% (UNWTO 2009), depending on the general economy's performance. According to the World Tourism Organization, the general framework of the tourism sector will be trips that are close to home and likely to have reduced lengths of stay and expenditures. Careful selection by tourists may discriminate in favor of destinations that give value for money and that cost-saving measures by tourism-related companies are foreseeable. This gloomy scenario will undoubtedly imply job losses and a stronger competition among tourist destinations in the context of a diminishing demand. In addition, a restructuring of the sector will likely take place, especially in those regions or cases in which investment or financial flows have not been committed or have been suddenly withdrawn. If this pattern is not quickly reversed, those weaker destinations will face disadvantages when the economy recovers.

In Mexico, tourism is the third major source of income, after oil exports and remittances by Mexican workers abroad. From 2002–2006, tourism represented 9% of the gross domestic product (GDP) and a similar percentage of employment. From 19.7 million visitors received in 2002, the country hosted 22.6 million people in 2008 (INEGI 2009a). The downturn of the world economy adversely affected Mexico's position, but international agency forecasts place it among the top 10 countries in terms of employment, tourism market share, and revenues "as soon as the world economy recovers" (WTTC 2009).

Baja California Sur constitutes 3.8% of Mexico's territory, but its small economy is just 0.6% of Mexico's GDP, number of businesses, and employment (data for 2006 INEGI 2009b; Ángeles 2008). Geography and climate are relevant factors in explaining Baja California Sur's situation. Its arid climate and lack of water resources for many decades hindered population growth throughout the state. The state's nearly insular configuration was aggravated by the lack of effective transportation linkages with the country's mainland. Although chained to the process of international trade in the 1880s, for most of the following century BCS remained relatively isolated from Mexico's pattern of growth. Since attention was mainly focused on the northern part of the peninsula that bordered with the United States, BCS remained relatively uninhabited and somehow detached from international integration until the 1980s.

Key to the reversal of this pattern was the Mexican federal government's promotion in the late 1960s of a national plan to foster tourism as a means to stimulate regional development. The implementation of a scheme of "integrally planned" tourism centers (CTIP, initials in Spanish) by FONATUR included two locations in BCS: Loreto and Los Cabos (García 1992). At that time, BCS was politically divided into three municipalities: Mulegé, Comondú, and La Paz, which was also the state capital. In 1981, Los Cabos became the fourth municipality, and Loreto joined as the fifth in 1992. The plan to develop Loreto and Los Cabos accelerated in the mid-1980s with the process of economic liberalization pursued by the Mexican federal government. Tourism in BCS, though, was not a spontaneous activity but the result of a state initiative based on protectionism-related policies. Financial, legal, and institutional stimuli were profusely provided to the private sector in order to develop tourism destinations anchored on (mostly) foreign investment. Yet, such projects were disassociated from local conditions and communities and did not address environmental or social concerns. As a result, the empowerment and impact of economic and social processes associated with the sector's expansion based on local and foreign, private, and public actors greatly differed.

In contrast to Loreto and the rest of the state, tourism flows reached unprecedented levels in the Los Cabos area, both in absolute and relative terms. Although Los Cabos began as a small fishing and agricultural community, it has turned into one of Mexico's most dynamic tourism destinations, focusing on traditional tourism (sun, sand, beaches, golf, sportfishing, and entertainment). From accounting for 18% of total BCS visitors in 1976 (out of 274,456), the percentage increased to 29% in 1980 (out of 669,749 tourists) and to 34% in 1985 (out of 446,663). In 1990, Los Cabos received nearly half of the 532,700 travelers who arrived in BCS, and 56% of the 560,300 visitors the following year (Gámez 2004). That pattern continued during the 1990s, and the state has enjoyed acceptable rates of tourism growth during the last 10 years.

At present, the importance of the tourism sector in the BCS economy is clear: it includes 24% of businesses, 29% of employment, 22% of wages and salaries, and 32% of value added (Ángeles, Gámez, and Ivanova 2009a & 2009b). Table 1 shows the absolute and relative values of tourism growth, measured according to common methodology by the number of visitors registered in hotel accommodations. Data displayed merit an explanation, especially regarding years 2001 and 2005. In the first case, the extraordinary 78% increase in visitors could be explained by the September 11 events in the United States. Instead of being deterred, U.S. tourists were encouraged in their decision to travel to BCS and especially to Los Cabos. Amidst the concern that followed the terrorist attacks, BCS was still perceived as a safe destination that was close to home and far away from the international turmoil. In the second case, important methodological changes in data collection that reflect federal standards seem to be behind the sudden decrease of 38%.

Table 1. Total Visitors in Hotel Accommodations in BCS, 1998–2008

Year	Total	Annual Variation (%)
1998	776,407	0
1999	797,775	2.8
2000	869,326	1.4
2001	1,553,328	78.7
2002	1,602,702	3.2
2003	1,946,276	3.8
2004	1,996,173	2.6
2005	1,235,602	-38
2006	1,470,348	19
2007	1,507,670	2.6
2008	1,702,632	13

Sources: Gobierno del Estado de BCS 2005, 2009.

Even discarding the 2001–2004 period as exceptional in terms of the total number of visitors, new peaks were reached that were above 1.5 million tourists beginning in 2007. Despite methodological adjustments, visitors continued arriving due mostly to the performance of Los Cabos. As seen in Table 2, this region accounted for 70% of the 1.24 million tourists that arrived in BCS in 2005, 86% of all foreigners and 38% of all nationals. These proportions subsequently increased in 2008 to 91% of all foreigners and 42% of national tourists.

Table 2. Tourist Hotel Occupancy by Municipality and Origin in BCS, 2005–2008 (%)

Municipality	Total				National Tourists				Foreign Tourists			
	'05	'06	'07	'08	'05	'06	'07	'08	'05	'06	'07	'08
Los Cabos	70	72	73	73	38	41	42	42	86	88	90	91
La Paz	19	16	16	18	44	36	34	39	6	6	6	5
Loreto	11	12	11	9	18	23	23	19	8	6	4	4
%	100	100	100	100	100	100	100	100	100	100	100	100
Total BCS (millions)	1.23	1.47	1.50	1.70	.42	.5	.54	.63	.82	.96	.97	1.07

Sourcce: Gobierno del Estado de BCS 2009.

Tourism growth from 1976 to 1992 in both Comondú and Mulegé was only 13% for the period. Even now, data for those municipalities are not recorded, although their tourism infrastructure (number of hotels and hotel rooms) is included in official reports. In the case of Loreto, its minimal importance for tourism was evident in the low numbers and small state share of visitors, which was less than 11% per year even during the highest peaks of tourist inflows to BCS. La Paz, the traditionally most important destination, which had 50% of the state's tourists in the 1980s, had long ago been displaced by Los Cabos. By 2000, La Paz had only 28% of visitors (Ángeles and Gámez 2008) and this dropped to 18% in 2008. The decline of La Paz as a tourist destination is explained not only by the enormous financial resources directed to Los Cabos, but also by the trade liberalization processes that began during the Miguel de la Madrid presidency in the early 1980s and accelerated during the administration of Carlos Salinas de Gortari (1988–1994). Mexican nationals used to flock to La Paz and its tax-free zone to buy imports from the United States and elsewhere at a time when the rest of the country's economy was protected by high tariff levels. As a result, La Paz flourished as a trade and tourism mecca. However, the cost advantages of trade in imported goods were eliminated and visitor flows diminished with the implementation of the North American Free Trade Agreement beginning in 1994. Expensive airfares, distance, and inadequate transportation to and from Mexico's mainland were factors that added to this decline (Ángeles and Gámez 2008).

During the 2005–2008 period, tourist arrivals measured by hotel occupancy grew on average 12% per year. In 2007, arrivals slowed to a 3% increase as a result of the recovery of Cancún, a destination devastated by Hurricane Wilma in 2005 and whose demand was absorbed by Los Cabos. However, by 2008, the growth rate was 13% in BCS, which was indicative of a generally favorable business environment for resorts and the tourism sector. However, the current economic crisis that began in 2007 hints at difficulties, especially for smaller firms (CEMDA 2009), which lack collateral or support from parent or sister companies and cannot face lack of demand and/or increasing costs and remain in business.

It is to be noted that cruise ship tourism is on the rise in BCS, mainly because of Los Cabos, and this adds to the number of visitors to BCS. From 2005–2008, the cruise passenger growth rate was

32.4%, and the number of cruises increased by 58%. In 2008, Los Cabos received 94% of passengers and 77% of cruises that reached the state. Far from competing with Los Cabos, Loreto was even below La Paz in both indicators (Gobierno del Estado de BCS 2009). In every regard concerning intraregional competition in the tourism sector, Los Cabos towers over the rest. According to FONATUR, Los Cabos is deemed as the second most important cruise ship port in Mexico and the aim is to strengthen its golf and cruise tourism. The expected outcome is to add 4,500 new international tourists by 2012 and174 more hotel rooms that will increase annual revenue by 5.5 million dollars. Key to this process is maintaining the market segment in which the region has specialized: high income visitors from California, Arizona, Nevada, Texas, New Mexico, Washington, Colorado, and New York (FONATUR 2009). However, in 2011, the cruise ship visits to Los Cabos were threatened by the violence in parts of the mainland such as Mazatlán and Puerto Vallarta, which caused at least one major cruise line to cancel its departures to the Pacific west coast "Riviera" from U.S. ports (Aguilera 2011).

As a consequence of the dynamism of Los Cabos, a rapidly increasing number of jobs have been created, although wages in the state are below the national average (INEGI 2009b). This has been accompanied by an extremely high population growth rate—which averaged 10% annually during the last decade—as well as development of tourism, communications, and transportation infrastructure. In 2008, Los Cabos had over 13,000 hotel rooms, and its appeal to high-income foreign visitors unquestionably had an enormous economic impact. Revenues in hotel occupancy alone meant 420.4 million dollars in 2008, 5% less than the previous year, but 22% more than in 2005 (Gobierno del Estado de BCS 2009).

The growing hotel industry and promotion campaigns have reinforced the internationally oriented nature of tourism, especially in Los Cabos. As Table 2 shows, foreign tourists were 63% of total visitors in 2008 in BCS, and Los Cabos hosted 91% of them. During the 2005–2008 period, Los Cabos visitors were 80% foreign and 20% national, which continues an ongoing trend. The United States and Canada constitute the main markets, although tourists from Europe and Asia also visit the area. The state origin of U.S. visitors to the Los Cabos region in 2008 is shown in Table 3.

Table 3. Distribution of U.S. Visitors by State of Origin, 2008

State	%
Texas	5.4
California	41.7
Florida	3.9
Colorado	8.2
Washington	2.4
Oregon	5.0
Arizona	5.0
Nevada	18.0
Idaho	1.8
New Mexico	6.6
Other	1.2

Source: Montaño et al. 2009.

Another feature of tourism growth is the high income level of visitors, especially in Los Cabos, as compared to other destinations in Mexico. Average per capita income was estimated at US$77,000 (Montaño et al. 2009); depending on the season, daily expenditures average US$250–450, which is nearly twice the average in the rest of Mexico (CEMDA 2009). The type of hotel accommodations in Los Cabos matches such features.

In the early 1980s, there were approximately 30 hotels in the state. In 2004, there were 267 hotels and 13,701 rooms. By municipality, Los Cabos has most of the hotel infrastructure in BCS. Although in 2008 it had 39% of the hotels in the state, it had 77% of all rooms, most of them rated as four and five star or above (see Table 3), mainly in large international resorts. Hotel occupancy rates are at about 67% to 70% (CEMDA 2009), which has encouraged a continuous inflow of investment for hotel infrastructure. In this regard, the construction of rooms grew about 10% during the 2005–2008 period, but in 2008 it was -2% from the previous year. This was undoubtedly a result of the economic recession, especially since the last quarter of 2008.

Table 4. Number of Hotels and Rooms in BCS by Municipality, 2005-2008 (%)

Municipality	Hotels				Rooms			
	2005	2006	2007	2008	2005	2006	2007	2008
Los Cabos	37	39	34	39	71	74	77	76
La Paz	27	25	25	25	16	14	12	13
Mulegé	19	21	19	18	5	6	5	5
Loreto	8	8	11	11	5	4	3	4
Comondú	7	7	7	7	2	2	2	2
%	100	100	100	100	100	100	100	100
BCS (units)	267	290	291	294	14,005	15,384	17,253	17,299

Source: Gobierno del Estado de BCS 2009.

Other regions of BCS are lagging behind Los Cabos in hotel infrastructure. La Paz is in second place with one-fourth of hotels, but only slightly more than one-tenth of total rooms. It should be mentioned that very few hotels in La Paz, or for that matter in the rest of the state, compare to the high standards of Los Cabos. It is interesting to see that Loreto, where investment on tourism infrastructure has been comparatively higher as a CTIP, rates below Mulegé. This reflects an increase in hotel demand in Mulegé, but this has not been recorded in official statistics of visitor inflow.

Interregional differences in tourism infrastructure and number of visitors dictate the type of tourism policy orientation. Perspectives of growth for Los Cabos seem to be favorable in the midterm. The impact of the world economic crisis and that in California and the United States, which has severely hit BCS and Los Cabos, is still to be assessed. Also unclear are the effects of the H1N1 (swine) flu that greatly affected Mexico's tourism industry in early 2009. All of these events contributed to the general turmoil surrounding a sector that so heavily depends on the exterior. To date, BCS has been spared the violence that has negatively impacted foreign tourism in other areas of Mexico, particularly the northern border region. But the violence in other regions of Mexico does cause many tourists to avoid even BCS, a safe and secure region.

Enormous investments have been made and continue in the region. Most investors are foreign; 70% of direct foreign investment in BCS has been directed to La Paz and mostly to Los Cabos. The tourism subsector of hotels and lodging has absorbed most of this investment (Ángeles and Gámez 2008).

TOURISM, GROWTH, AND DEVELOPMENT

The results of tourism growth are evident in the arrival of capital and labor inflows. To Los Cabos, this has meant a complete deconstruction of its natural landscape and remaking of its urban infrastructure. However, high rates of economic and demographic growth have been accompanied by strong negative externalities and undesired by-products. These include inadequate provision of public services for an increasing population; chaotic urbanization and hazardous distribution of neighborhoods; irregularities in land appropriation; problems with present and future availability of water for human and productive uses; real estate speculation; disruption of traditional culture; environmental pollution; drug addiction; and prostitution, to mention some. A 2006 report by the International Community Foundation (ICF 2006) assessed current and future needs of Baja California Sur regarding expanding charitable giving across the state and documents many of the problems. The study shows a wide range of underserved social needs that could be improved with appropriate funding. Even if higher wages and job opportunities are available for the local population—which is constantly augmented by the incoming flow of people from Mexico's mainland—the importance of low-skilled labor in construction or tertiary activities sector means that large numbers of people are characterized by low education levels and poor quality of life. This situation has led to the state government's recognition that there has been inadequate planning of tourism growth, which has favored Los Cabos in detriment to other state regions (Gobierno del Estado de BCS 1999). It is also clear that economic activities related to tourism have had minimal benefits to most of the workers in the sector, including construction (Gerber 2007). The success of Los Cabos as an international destination has made tourism increasingly important in the state's economy. Recently, investments in tourism and residential projects have increased in

Los Cabos: Prospective for a Natural and Tourism Paradise

La Paz and Loreto, but lag behind in Los Cabos. At the same time, awareness of the importance of the real estate and construction sectors linked to tourism and the building of residential complexes have also been accompanied by concerns. These relate to the lack of linkages among productive activities, overconcentration on those sectors (Ángeles 2002), and also to the negative impacts on the environment and society.

Alternative tourism, with its low environmental and social impact, has been at the forefront of official pronouncements about public policy related to tourism in BCS. It has also been recommended by many academic studies. Yet, in practice, tourism activities have focused on the traditional megaresort model. In this respect, the ongoing or proposed construction of over 40 tourism and second-home megaprojects with multiple golf courses in an arid zone, such as BCS, seems incompatible with any true notion of sustainability. Prior to the 2000s, the rest of the state lagged in megaprojects, but investment projects and construction of resorts and second homes along other areas of the coastline show the spreading of the Los Cabos-type of tourism model.

Significant parts of the municipalities of Comondú and Mulegé (in the central and northern portions of the state), and areas adjacent to Loreto and La Paz, have become investment magnets, especially in the last five years. Federal, state, and municipal governments promote and justify such developments in the name of job and infrastructure creation. Although large condominiums seem to be out of order in Los Cabos in order to preserve the low-tourism density that makes it attractive, they have not been ruled out in other regions (CEMDA 2009). For instance, in La Paz a 6,000-room project with 2,000 in condominiums, in just its initial stage, was approved in an area known as "El Mogote," a sand barrier peninsula in the La Paz Bay facing the city. There was opposition to the project on several grounds. It was built on public property sold at a cheap price (about US$1.5 per sq. meter) to investors who, at the low end, list a two-bedroom house for US$200,000 (Paraíso del Mar 2009). The residential project represents a huge strain in terms of scarce resources such as water. With the project still under construction, the developers asked the city for 10 million liters of water, but only 260,000 could be supplied. The natural landscape was completely modified, or "Manhattanized." The project, an exclusive residential area targeted at foreigners, meant that access to land that was deemed emblematic of the area was lost to the public. This was reflected in significant social discontent (Vigna 2008).

In Cabo Cortés, closer to the Los Cabos tourist corridor, a 2.3 billion dollar U.S.-Spanish investment was authorized in 2008 to build 5,000 hotel rooms and 8,000 houses over a 12-to-15-year time span. In the seaside town of La Ribera, US$500 million will be invested in a marina, golf course, and condominiums (CEMDA 2009). In this case, environmental concerns are significant since this project is likely to adversely impact a nearby natural protected area of Cabo Pulmo that has a rare and valuable coral reef. This is a clear case where imprudent tourism development has the potential to alter or destroy the pristine natural environment that was the original attraction of the area for tourism.

Although increasing employment is clearly important, there should be a more careful screening of investment projects. This would ensure that jobs announced are actually jobs created. In addition, a follow-up should be in place regarding the creation of more permanent—and well paid—direct and indirect employment. This is a relevant point given that most jobs are generated in the low-paying subsectors of construction and services at the start of a given project and, by definition, these positions tend to be temporary. Also, workers who migrate from the mainland for these construction jobs tend to remain with their families in irregular, marginal settlements and make a living as best they can.

There is a clear division of labor in the tourism industry according to qualifications, which tend to favor non-locals. More empirical research is needed in this regard, but in a tourist destination where foreigners are the primary target and prices are well over one hundred thousand dollars for entry-level condominiums, language and interpersonal skills that identify sellers with buyers are crucial. Unfortunately, these two factors are not characteristic of most of the Mexican population arriving in Los Cabos in the quest for jobs, but they are for many foreigners themselves. More highly educated and experienced Mexicans from the mainland or other megatourism areas also have a distinct advantage over local residents in the higher paid tourism positions.

Final Remarks

Tourism in Baja California Sur, as in many other relatively isolated places, is not a new phenomenon. Since the early twentieth century, visitors have travelled to the region to enjoy the same features that are now sold at a high price: scenic beauty and a still pristine natural environment. The differences now in the early twenty-first century rest on the type of organization of the production and the speed of the consolidation of the industry from small scale, locally based service provision, to foreign-owned huge resorts and the accompanying economic, political, social, and environmental impacts surrounding that transformation. The development of BCS (or rather Los Cabos) into an international tourist destination was probably only a matter of time. In addition to its natural attributes and closeness to the United States market, government deregulation since the mid-1980s and significant federal investment support through FONATUR laid the foundations for private capital to take advantage of a promising area for business opportunity.

Yet, if the Los Cabos CTIP exemplifies the economic success of tourism, it is also proof that unregulated private interest, when combined with a weak government that is indifferent to the general good, can generate unfortunate (though predictable and preventable) distortions. A clear example of this is the fact that in Cabo San Lucas, public spaces of incalculable value for the state in general and for tourism in particular have been done away with. The clearest cases in point are the destruction of the former coast road, or *malecón* (in a sun and beach destination), or the existence of large "misery belts" of marginalized populations, side by side with some of the most expensive hotels in the world. In addition, in a state lacking a strategy for the development of human capital, the provision of services for high-income tourists (the main group of visitors) has been shown to rely on qualified foreign (or extra-regional) employees. In economic terms, tourism promotion in Los Cabos has been successful. However, as Ángeles, Gámez, and Ivanova (2009a & 2009b) point out, these same conditions should encourage the public and private sectors, as well as civil society, to develop strategies that promote well-being through diversification and endogenous growth.

At best, BCS is overly dependent on tourism, with the well-known consequences of relying on a single sector for development. At worst, its recent growth has been based on land speculation, environmental exhaustion, and labor exploitation.

Studies (Steinitz et al. 2004, 2005) have been carried out for Loreto and La Paz that encourage rational planning in order to maximize public benefit from economic growth. To this extent, they provide *alternative futures* for those regions that show disadvantages of using a model of tourism growth that has failed to achieve development. Comprehensive analyses (Ganster et al. 2006) have also highlighted the need to readdress this pattern of economic growth, as well as its social and environmental impacts. Yet, although government authorities have celebrated those projects, considering the "development" speed and extent of resort-type destinations in the state, little has been done to restructure the current model of tourism expansion.

Tourism is an extraordinary tool for economic growth. However, it has enormous impacts not only on the economy, but also on society and in the use of natural resources. It is essential that a rigorous process of medium- and long-term planning of tourism activities be established in the state and in Los Cabos.

Despite its chaotic growth, Cabo San Lucas is still a relatively small place. Much can be done to stop and reverse the negative externalities it clearly displays, as well as the pattern of regional polarization that pervades beyond its borders. This would imply a real statewide development plan in order to avoid unbalances and pressure over scarce and vulnerable natural resources in the region, water among them. Adequate planning that prevents traffic congestion such as that at the entrance of the city not only would solve the problem of urban image deterioration, but also help preserve the landscape that attracts visitors in the first place. In addition, it would improve the quality of life of local inhabitants and reduce the costs to tourism companies and visitors. As Butler (1980, 1999) said, tourist destinations—especially those mainly based on landscapes, such as Los Cabos—do not last forever. Everyone should keep this in mind and plan accordingly, particularly government officials who bear responsibility for the general good.

REFERENCES

Aguilera, Elizabeth. 2011. "Cruise Lines Continue to Nix Mexican Ports." *San Diego Union-Tribune* (27 June), www.signonsandiego.com/news/2011/jun/27.

Ángeles, Manuel. 2002. *La naturaleza de enclave de la economía sudcaliforniana con base en la matriz de insumo producto de 17 sectores*. Mimeo, Department of Economics, UABCS, La Paz, BCS.

Ángeles, Manuel. 2008. *El desarrollo de las economías pequeñas ante la actual globalización*. Working paper, Department of Economics, UABCS, La Paz, BCS.

Ángeles, Manuel, and Alba Gámez. 2008. "Globalización y desarrollo regional, el caso del sector turismo en Baja California Sur." Pp. 463–484 in *Globalización y regionalismo: Economía y sustentabilidad*, Antonina Ivanova and Arturo Guillén, coords. México, DF: Porrúa.

Ángeles, M., A. E. Gámez, and A. Ivanova. 2009a. "Consideraciones sobre turismo y economía en Baja California Sur." *Alternative de BCS* (January): 18-21.

Ángeles, M., A. E. Gámez, and A. Ivanova. 2009b. "¿Cuál es el impacto del turismo en la economía sudcaliforniana?" *Panorama*.

Barrera, Ernesto, and Roberto Muñoz. 2003. *Manual de turismo rural para micro pequeños y medianos empresarios rurales. Serie de instrumentos técnicos para la microempresa rural*. Fondo Internacional de Desarrollo Agrícola-Programa de Apoyo a la Microempresa Rural de América Latina y el Caribe.

Berry, Edward Norman. 2001. "An Application of Butler's (1980) Tourist Area Life Cycle Theory to the Cairns Region, Australia, 1876–1998." Ph.D. dissertation, School of Tropical Environmental and Geography Studies, James Cook University of North Queensland, Australia, Cairns Campus.

Brenner, Ludger, and Adrián Guillermo Aguilar. 2002. "Luxury Tourism and Regional Economic Development in Mexico." *The Professional Geographer* 54 (4): 500–520.

Butler, Richard W. 1980. "The Concept of a Tourism Area Cycle of Evolution: Implications for Management Resources." *The Canadian Geographer* 24 (1): 5–16.

Butler, Richard W. 1999. "Sustainable Tourism: A State-of-the-Art Review." *Tourism Geographies* 1 (1): 7–25.

Centro Mexicano de Derecho Ambiental (CEMDA). 2009. *Los Cabos: Paraíso amenazado.* (Accessed 14 April 2009), http://www.cemda.org.mx/artman2/publish/CEMDA_EN_LOS_MEDIOS_62/ Los_Cabos_para_so_amenazado.php.

Comisión para la Cooperación Ambiental (CCA). 1999. "Desarrollo del turismo sustentable en áreas naturales en América del Norte: Antecedentes, problemática y potencial turismo sustentable en áreas naturales." Documento de discusión preparado para el Diálogo sobre Turismo Sustentable en Áreas Naturales en América del Norte, 27–28 de mayo, Comisión para la Cooperación Ambiental, Montreal, Canadá, Quintana Roo, México.

Fondo Nacional de Fomento al Turismo (FONATUR). 2009. Centro Integralmente planeado Los Cabos. Información general. (Accessed 12 April 2009), http://www.fonatur.gob.mx/es/Des_loscabos/des-loscabos.asp.

Gámez, Alba E. 2004. "Los Cabos: Economía y población." Pp. 247–278 in *Historia General de Baja California Sur. Economía, política, sociedad y cultura*, Tomo III, Edith González, comp. La Paz, BCS: UABCS-Plaza y Valdés.

Ganster, Paul, Oscar Arizpe, and Antonina Ivanova. 2006. *Loreto: El futuro de la primera capital de las Californias.* San Diego, CA: San Diego State University Press, Institute for Regional Studies of the Californias.

García Villa, Adolfo. 1992. *La planificación de centros turísticos en México.* México, DF: Limusa.

Gerber, James. 2007. "Un análisis comparativo de dos polos de desarrollo turístico: Loreto y Los Cabos." Pp. 247–259 in *Loreto: El futuro de la primera capital de las Californias*, Paul Ganster, Oscar Arizpe, and Antonina Ivanova, eds. San Diego, CA: San Diego State University Press, Institute for Regional Studies of the Californias.

Gobierno del Estado de Baja California Sur. 1999. *Plan Estatal de Desarrollo 1999–2005.* La Paz, BCS: Secretaría de Promoción y Desarrollo Económico.

Gobierno del Estado de Baja California Sur. 2005. *Compendio Estadístico 1998–2004. Cuaderno de Datos Básicos 2005.* La Paz, BCS: Centro Estatal de Información, Secretaría de Promoción y Desarrollo Económico.

Gobierno del Estado de Baja California Sur. 2009. *IV Informe de Gobierno del Ing. Narciso Agúndez Montaño. Anexo gráfico y estadístico*. La Paz, BCS: Gobierno del Estado de BCS.

Guerrero, E., S. Sguerra, and C. Rey. 2007. *Áreas Protegidas en América Latina. De Santa Marta 1997 a Bariloche 2007*. Bogotá: Parques Nacionales Naturales de Colombia y Comité Colombiano UICN.

Hall, C. Michael. 2007. "North-South Perspectives on Tourism, Regional Development and Peripheral Areas." Pp. 19–28 in *Tourism in Peripheries: Perspectives from the Far North and South*, Dieter K. Müller and Bruno Jansson, eds. Oxfordshire, UK: CABI.

Instituto Nacional de Geografía, Estadística e Informática (INEGI). 2009a. *Estadística, Geografía, Información estadística, Temas, Economía, Sectores económicos, Turismo*. Aguascalientes, AGS: INEGI. http://www.inegi.org.mx/inegi/default. aspx?s=est&c=6447&e=&i=.

Instituto Nacional de Geografía, Estadística e Informática (INEGI). 2009b. *Baja California Sur. Actividades económicas*. Aguascalientes, AGS: INEGI. http://cuentame.inegi. gob.mx/monografias /informacion/bcs/economia/default. aspx?tema=me&e=03

International Community Foundation (ICF). 2006. *Baja California Sur Community-Based Opportunities and Needs*. San Diego, CA: ICF. http://www.icfdn.org/publications/na2006/index.htm.

Montaño, Angélica, Juan Carlos Pérez, and Diana Higuera. 2010. "Competitividad del desarrollo turístico de Los Cabos: Las oportunidades para las PyMES." In *Turismo, sustentabilidad y desarrollo regional en Sudcalifornia*, A. E. Gámez, A. Ivanova, and A. Montaño, eds. La Paz, BCS: UABCS, 2010.

Paraíso del Mar. 2009. *The Resort Neighborhoods of Paraiso del Mar*. http://www.paradiseofthesea.com/en/project_info_project_ summary.html

Pearce, Douglas. 1988. *Desarrollo turístico. Su planificación y ubicación geográficas*. México, DF: Trillas.

Scherrer, Jim. 2009. "Retirement on the Mexican Riviera." *Press Release Distribution*. (Accessed 15 February 2009), http://www. prlog.org/10182938-retirement-on-the-mexican-riviera.html.

Steinitz, Carl, Robert Faris, Juan Carlos Vargas-Moreno, Guoping Huang, Shiau-Yun Lu, Oscar Arizpe, Manuel Ángeles, Fausto Santiago, Antonina Ivanova, Alba E. Gámez, Kathryn Baird, Thomas Maddock III, Hoori Ajami, Leonardo Huato, Martha J. Haro, Michael Flaxman, Paul Ganster, Angélica Villegas, and Catalina López. 2005. *Alternative Futures for Loreto, Baja California Sur, Mexico*. Cambridge: Harvard University. www.futursalternativosloreto.org.mx.

Steinitz, Carl, Robert Faris, Michael Flaxman, Juan Carlos Vargas-Moreno, Tess Canfield, Oscar Arizpe, Manuel Ángeles, Micheline Cariño, Fausto Santiago, Tom Maddock III, Carolyn Dragoo, Kathryn Baird, and Lucio Godínez. 2004. *Alternative Futures for the Region of La Paz, Baja California Sur, Mexico*. Cambridge: Harvard University.

United Nations World Tourism Organization (UNWTO). 2005 *Making Tourism More Sustainable - A Guide for Policy Makers*. http://www.e-unwto.org/content/w715w4/?p=0ef9688179a94fb08c63036081aa68ea&pi=1.

United Nations World Tourism Organization (UNWTO). 2008. *UNWTO Barometer* 6 (2) (8 June), http://unwto.org/facts/eng/pdf/barometer/ unwto_Barom08_2_en_Excerpt.pdf.

United Nations World Tourism Organization (UNWTO). 2009. *UNWTO Barometer* 7 (1) (January): Madrid: World Tourism Organization.

Vigna, Anne. 2008. "La gran mentira del 'ecoturismo' en Centroamérica y México." *Le Monde Diplomatique Mexico* 4 (December): 1, 20–22

World Travel and Tourism Council (WTTC). 2008. *Progress and Priorities 2008/09*. (8 June), http://www.wttc.org/bin/pdf/original_pdf_file/progress_and_priorities_2008.pdf.

World Travel and Tourism Council (WTTC). 2009. *Travel and Tourism Economic Impact: Executive Summary*. (4 October), http://www.wttc.org/bin/pdf/original_pdf_file/exec_summary_2009.pdf.

15

Alternative Tourism and Touristic Suitability in the Municipality of Los Cabos

Oscar Arizpe C., Alba E. Gámez, and Eduardo Juárez

INTRODUCTION

The state of Baja California Sur has a natural vocation for tourism development. The contrasts of mountains, deserts, and beaches have formed an unrivaled scenic hallmark. The flora and fauna richness, both terrestrial and marine, is another distinctive attraction of this geography; the Gulf of California is considered the largest aquarium in the world because of its high biodiversity. All that makes Baja California Sur a place of extremely attractive resources for visitors. Within its territory, there are three places that have made tourism the state's main activity: Loreto, La Paz, and Los Cabos. The last has become one of the tourism centers with greatest growth in the country and the most important for the state of BCS.

The municipality of Los Cabos, located on the southernmost portion of Baja California Sur, has a great cultural and historical value. In addition, its natural beauty has transformed it into an eminent tourism area that generates important benefits to both the regional and national economies. There is a notable increase in the demand for services and infrastructure that has been characterized as serving high-income users and primarily focusing on the foreign market. This situation and the attractions of the area linked to its coastal position have generated a wide range of activities such as beach recreation, scuba diving, and sportfishing, among others. As a result of the economic stimulus that tourism has provided through the creation of jobs in recent years, primarily in construction and the service sector, Los Cabos has become one of the regions with greatest urban growth in the country, with annual average population growth rates of 10%.

However, the big push that was given to Los Cabos as an integrally planned tourism center[1] has inhibited the proper utilization of other areas with great tourism potential in the rest of the state of Baja California Sur and even within the same municipality of Los Cabos. A related feature is that the planning for the tourism center did not include the non-tourist population settlements. As a result, the most noticeable aspects of Cabo San Lucas to visitors are precisely the lack of urban planning (roads, housing, transportation, and communications for the local inhabitants), as well as social problems linked to health and quality of life and others of economic nature with profound social impacts.

Uncontrolled urbanization has increased because the region faces, in addition to a strong pressure from the rapid growth of human settlements in Cabo San Lucas and San José, economic depression in rural areas, and adverse environmental effects given the proliferation of various tourism projects proposed for the region that are resort type or denominated as traditional tourism. A more harmonious distribution of tourism activities that is based on the characteristics of the different localities that make up the municipality would allow mitigating the adverse impacts of tourism, thus preventing the current oversaturation. Moreover, a study of the environment, its natural and cultural attractions, infrastructure, and services available would not only facilitate ongoing distribution of resources, but also long-term planning, with resultant benefits to society, the ecosystem, and the different public and private actors. With these considerations,

---

1. In the late 1960s, the federal government developed a master plan that intended to make tourism an important generator of foreign exchange, create jobs, and ensure the emergence of external economies that would support regional development (García 1992; Urciaga 2004). To do this, it promoted the creation of five tourism centers distributed around the country that it called integrally planned (Centros Integralmente Planeados–CIPs). Among them was the Cabo San Lucas-San José del Cabo corridor, given its geographical characteristics and natural attractions. As indicated in the chapter by Gámez and Ganster in this book, the development of Los Cabos as a tourist destination, however, did not gain momentum until the late 1980s. The tourism promotion of the state has made this area the most important destination of BCS and one of the main beach centers nationally and internationally.

this chapter presents a review of tourism in the state in order to show the relevance of diversifying tourism activity in the municipality, not only sectorally, but also geographically.

CHARACTERISTICS OF LOS CABOS TOURISM

Tourism activities in Los Cabos take place mainly along the San José del Cabo-Cabo San Lucas corridor and in these two towns. Tourism growth is based on the market for visitors with high purchasing power who seek sun-beach recreation and who demand high comfort standards, which has attracted strong investment for the creation of infrastructure and services to satisfy this market (Urciaga 2004; SEMARNAT 2005). The format for this type of tourism in Los Cabos lies in the attractions offered by its beaches, landscapes, sportfishing, and related activities that imply the use of a modern infrastructure.

Reflecting the economic importance of tourism in Los Cabos, the massive number of visitors it receives overshadows the rest of the state. Thus, in 2008, continuing a trend that dates back to the late 1980s, it received 70% of the 1.7 million tourists who visited BCS (Gobierno del Estado de BCS 2009). Unlike other municipalities, as mentioned earlier, its influx is mainly composed of foreign tourism, which has generally represented 80% of the total and in 2008 reached 91%.

Concomitantly, the state's hotel availability has increased markedly. Thus, while in 1999 there were 77 hotels (CEI 2001) and 6,474 rooms, by 2005 there were 99 hotels and 9,967 rooms (CEI 2006). In 2005 and 2006 the annual growth rate was 8.6% and 9.8% with regard to the number of rooms (CEI 2006). In 2006, the municipality of Los Cabos had 11,929 rooms in 114 hotels (Table 1), representing 74.4% of the hotel infrastructure in the state. Although Los Cabos has hotels rated with 1 or 2 stars, most are high categories (3, 4, 5, and Grand Tourism), given the characteristics of the visitors received (Tables 1 and 2).

According to the latest available data (Gobierno del Estado de BCS 2009), in 2008, there were already 115 hotels in the municipality, although their concentration is evident in the San José del Cabo-Cabo San Lucas corridor. This uneven geographical distribution of hotel infrastructure in the municipality is also accompanied by different types of infrastructure according to geographic location, as follows:

Table 1. Tourism Infrastructure in the Municipality of Los Cabos

Hotel Categories	Total
3, 4, 5 stars and Grand Tourism	11,281 hotel rooms
1 and 2 stars	648 hotel rooms
Communication Routes	
Paved roads	174.75 km
Airports and airstrips	1 national airport 3 airstrips
Seaports	1 port
Services (Development of Related Activities)	Total Sites
Scuba diving	2
Sportfishing	No specific sites
Flore and fauna watching	2

Source: SECTUR 2006.

As shown in Table 2, of the 115 existing hotels in Los Cabos in 2008, 48% are located in Cabo San Lucas, 18% in the San Lucas-San José corridor, and 28% in San José. That is, only 6% of all the municipality's hotels are located elsewhere. The same tendency is evident in other service categories (CEI 2006). In 2008, 94 food stores were recorded; 91 of these were located in Cabo San Lucas and San José del Cabo. With regard to facilities for recreational vehicles (RVs), there are only two and both are in Cabo San Lucas. As to the 18 travel agencies registered in the municipality, 11 are in Cabo San Lucas and seven are in San José.

Another category considered in the infrastructure is that of tour guides, a service provided by 86 registered guides, of whom 60 are located in Cabo San Lucas and 26 in San José. Regarding the 11 diving service establishments, five are in Cabo San Lucas, three in San José, two in Cabo Pulmo, and one in Buena Vista. In the category of land-based tourist transporters, six establishments provide this service; two are in Cabo San Lucas, three in San José, and one in Buena Vista. There are 13 marine tourist transporters and all are located in Cabo San Lucas. Of the 23 ecotourism businesses registered in the municipality, 12 are located in Cabo San Lucas, eight in San José, two in Cabo Pulmo, and one in Buena Vista. With regard to the 20 establishments engaged in sportfishing, 14 are in Cabo San Lucas, two are in San José, and four are in Buena Vista. There are 17 car rental companies that are registered, with seven in Cabo San Lucas and 10 in San José. There are two marinas, the traditional facility in Cabo San Lucas and a new marina in San José. Of the eight golf courses that have been built in the municipality, six are located in the Cabo San Lucas-San José del Cabo tourism corridor and two in the town of San José. Of the 16 airlines that serve this municipality, only one has flights to Cabo San Lucas, and the remaining 15 use the San José International Airport. A service that has increased in the tourism influx in this municipality is the organization of events and conferences. For the latter purpose, there are 13 convention centers, of which six are in Cabo San Lucas, six in San José, and one in Buena Vista (SECTUR 2006).

Table 2. Hotel Infrastructure Distribution by Location in Los Cabos, 2008

Location	Grand Tourism	Special Class	5 Stars	4 Stars	3 Stars	2 Stars	1 Star	Unclassified
San José	1	-	5	6	1	3	2	11
Cabo San Lucas	3	6	12	7	11	4	3	9
Tourism corridor	7	4	8	3	2	-	-	-
Buenavista	-	1	-	2	-	-	-	-
Cabo Pulmo	-	-	-	-	1	-	-	1
Santiago	-	-	-	-	-	-	-	1
Total	11	11	25	18	15	7	5	23

Source: Gobierno del Estado de BCS 2009.

In sum, of the 15 indicators that the state Secretariat of Tourism reports to characterize the tourism infrastructure, it can be said that 56.4% of it is in Cabo San Lucas, 31.1% in San José del Cabo, 6.2% in the San Lucas-San José del Cabo corridor, 0.06% in Santiago, 2% in Cabo Pulmo, and 4.2% in Buena Vista. These data clearly show why Cabo San Lucas is the municipality's most important tourist center, followed by San José. They also make it possible to visualize how in the rest of the municipality's locations (perhaps with the exception of Buena Vista) the growth level of the tourism activity is very limited. If these data are extrapolated to the development of the area, it follows that the benefits of the activity have not permeated the local economic structure, but that the existing tourism infrastructure is more suited to an enclave economy structure than to planned and sustainable tourism development (Ángeles and Gámez 2008).

TOWARD AN ALTERNATIVE MODEL OF TOURISM

As has been observed—similar to what happens in many parts of the world—the region's growth has focused on traditional tourism, sometimes also called high-density tourism. The increasing importance of this activity, not only locally but internationally, has also been producing its diversification. Worldwide, there is an increasingly intense development of tourism destinations, essentially characterized by the search for unconventional ways and places where the effects of human presence are minimal and allow involvement with the conservation or intelligent use of ecosystems, giving origin to alternative tourism. Wearing and Neil (2000) define this type of tourism as the series of touristic modalities whose objective is to be consistent with natural, social, and community values, allowing both hosts and visitors to enjoy positive and shared experiences. In turn, Gámez (2008) details that within this type of tourism is ecotourism (recreational activities of appreciation and knowledge of nature), adventure tourism (recreational sports activities associated with challenges imposed by nature), and rural tourism (coexistence and interaction activities with the rural community in all everyday social, cultural, and productive expressions).

In the region of Los Cabos, particularly in the last decade, it has repeatedly been mentioned in various forums that the development model of high-density sun-and-beach tourism traditionally followed in the municipality cannot be maintained in the long term; thus, it is necessary to study other more sustainable alternatives for development. Concern about the concentration of tourism and the social and environmental effects derived from it led to the signing in February 2007 of a cooperative agreement between the City Council of Los Cabos and the Autonomous University of Baja California

Alternative Tourism and Touristic Suitability in Los Cabos

Sur (Universidad Autónoma de Baja California Sur–UABCS) so that actions be carried out over two years to formulate and implement the Ecological Ordinance of the Municipality. Based on sectoral workshops and questionnaires to the public and key actors, it was necessary for socioeconomic development of the municipality to be carried out in harmony with the environment, promoting rational knowledge and integration of social, economic, and environmental processes to achieve a better quality of life for all (Arizpe et al. 2008).

These actions made it possible to evaluate and propose land-use regulation and productive activities that would effectively guide the municipality's planning and sustainable development with special emphasis on analyzing the tourism activity and proposing a more appropriate and sustainable long-term tourism model. One of the first results of the Ecological Land Use Plan was clarifying that, in addition to the beaches on which most of the tourist activity concentrates, particularly in the San Lucas-San José corridor, the municipality has a wide variety of natural sites and excellent prospects for sustainable development of this activity, some of which are already subject to tourism use although at a smaller scale. Among the natural attractions of the municipality are the canyons (cañada de La Zorra), mountain ranges (La Laguna, La Trinidad, and San Lorenzo), wetlands (Estero San José), natural protected areas (Sierra La Laguna Biosphere Reserve, Cabo San Lucas Flora and Fauna Protected Area, Cabo Pulmo National Park), and flora and fauna species (endemic, migratory, species suitable for hunting, etc.). Other sites that may spark the visitors' interest are those that are archaeological, historical, and paleontological (Table 3).

Representatives and members of the tourism sector expressed as part of the Public Participation Strategy for the Ecological Land Use Plan that the following components are necessary to enable the development of the tourism activities in the municipality: potable water, beaches, tourism infrastructure, communication routes, sewage system, land-use planning, El Arco, sea views, mangroves, tourism developments, golf courses, and marinas (Arizpe et al. 2008).

From this list, the environmental attributes that were most mentioned and some considered for the development of traditional, high-density, and alternative tourism models, were the following: scenery, flora and fauna, tourism infrastructure (tourism developments, golf courses), communication routes, natural attractions (beaches, El

Arco, natural landscape, wetlands), services (water sports area, marinas), and the presence of natural protected areas on the sites of paleontological and anthropological importance. These are integrated in the following section as part of the tourism models that are described in the next section.

Table 3. Natural and Cultural Attractions and Services in the Municipality of Los Cabos

Natural Attractions	Description
Fauna	Important presence of endemic, at risk, and migratory species; species suitable for hunting
Vegetation	Important presence of endemic and at risk species; species of medicinal and ornamental use
Natural Landscape	Beaches, canyons, mountain ranges, coastal lagoons, bays, natural monuments
Natural Protected Areas	Cabo San Lucas Flora and Fauna Protected Area Cabo Pulmo National Park Sierra La Laguna Biosphere Reserve
Cultural Attractions	Totals
Archeological	25 sites: Cave/rock paintings, shell middens, burials, and caves
Paleontological	15 sites: Fossil deposits
Historical	2 sites: Missions

Source: SECTUR 2006.

SUITABILITY MODELS OF THE TOURISM SECTOR FOR THE REGION OF LOS CABOS

The initial proposal of the tourism model generated in this study regarding the Ecological Land Use Plan included the following indices, indicators, and weighting (Arizpe et al. 2008):

TI = NATA (0.11) + CULTA (0.05) + SERV (0.35) + INFRA (0.5)

The traditional Tourism Index (TI) of this model was formed by the indices of natural attractions (NATA), cultural attractions (CULTA), services (SERV), and infrastructure (INFRA); weighting placed infrastructure as the most important, then services, and with less importance were natural attractions followed by cultural attractions. The members of the tourism sector proposed in public participation workshops the modification of the values given to the model indices. The indices were constituted by the same indicators and the latter retained the same weight. The final version of the model, indices, and indicators are described as follows:

TI = NATA (0.25) + CULTA (0.15) + SERV (0.3) + INFRA (0.3)
INDEX OF NATURAL ATTRACTIONS (NATA) =
NPA (0.11) + VA (0.11) + FA (0.11) + BE (0.45) + LAG/BA (0.22)

NPA = Existence/nonexistence of natural protected areas
VA = Existence/nonexistence of natural attractions because of vegetation
FA = Existence/nonexistence of natural attractions because of fauna
BE = Number of beaches
LAG/BA = Existence/nonexistence of lagoons and bays

INDEX OF CULTURAL ATTRACTIONS (CULTA) =
ARQ (0.33) + HIST (0.33) + PAL (0.33)

ARQ = Number of archeological sites
HIST = Number of historical sites
PAL = Number of paleontological sites

INDEX OF TOURISM SERVICES (SERV) =
COAST (0.665) + TERRS (0.335)
COASTAL TOURISM SERVICES (COAST) =
PORT + NAUT + DI + SPFI + MARF + ZOSU

PORT = Number of port services
NAUT = Number of nautical services
DI = Number of diving services
SPFI = Number of sportfishing services
MARF = Number of marine fauna watching sites
ZOSU = Number of surfing sites

TERRESTRIAL TOURISM SERVICES (TERRS) = CAMP + ALTT

CAMP = Number of camping services
ALTT = Number of alternative tourism services

INDEX OF TOURISM INFRASTRUCTURE (INFRA) = ICOM (0.4) + HOTI (0.6)
INDEX OF COMMUNICATION ROUTES (ICOM) = PAV (0.3) + UNPAV (0.1) + INTA (0.3) + DOMA (0.2) + AIRS (0.1)

PAV = Kilometers of paved roads
UNPAV = Kilometers of unpaved roads
INTA = Existence/nonexistence of international airports
DOMA = Existence/nonexistence of domestic airports
AIRS = Existence/nonexistence of airstrips

INDEX OF HOTEL INFRASTUCTURE (HOTI) = HOTR3–5

HOTR3–5 = Number of hotel rooms rated 3, 4, and 5 stars.

A high-density suitability in the tourism sector was obtained with this model for the municipality of Los Cabos, as shown in Map 1. Suitability is "very high" in the Cabo San Lucas-San José del Cabo tourist corridor. A "high" suitability is for the coastal area of the municipality with some Environmental Units (EU) with medium suitability. The "very high" suitability covers only 3.1%, while the "high" suitability covers 25.7% of the municipality's area. The areas of "medium" suitability for tourism are located in the environmental units of the Sierra La Trinidad and the central part of the municipality. Suitability is low for this sector in the north part that includes the Sierra La Laguna, the Sierra La Trinidad surroundings, and the non-coastal southwest part. Finally, it was observed that for high-density tourism, 28.8% of the area of the municipality of Los Cabos has a capacity for development of the activity.

It is important to note that, at present, alternative tourism, especially the sustainable type, is in vogue and has broad prospects both worldwide and in the region studied. In this regard, the suitability model proposal was also developed for alternative tourism with the same methodological strategy. The components of the model are the

Map 1. Suitability of Traditional Tourism in the Municipality of Los Cabos

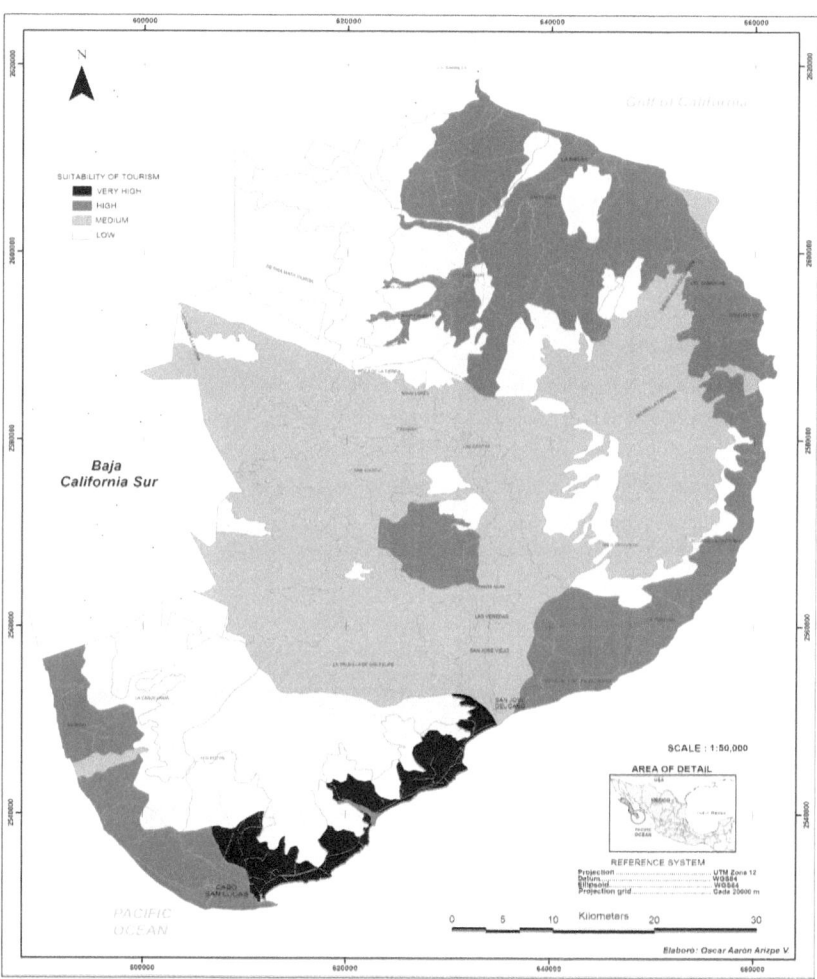

same, but the weighting is quite different from traditional tourism indices. For the alternative tourism index (ALTTI), the index for natural attractions (NATA) had the highest weighting, followed by the cultural attractions (CULTA), and, with a lower value were the indices of services (SERV) and tourist infrastructure (INFRA), that in the case of traditional tourism had the most relevant and therefore greater values.

ALTTI = NATA (4) + CULTA (2) + SERV (1) + INFRA (1)

As shown in Map 2, the results in this case indicate that there are three major regions with greater suitability or capacity for the development of alternative tourism located in the northern part of the municipality:

- East Cape region, mainly the coastal area of Cabo Pulmo National Park
- San Dionisio-La Zorra streambed area in the northeastern part of the municipality
- Sierra La Laguna Biosphere Reserve and its southern part

The last two regions were not important in the assessment results for traditional tourism.

Thus, it can be seen that it is possible to apply this methodology for characterization of all microregions in the area of interest. It is also possible to develop suitability models and their resulting maps for any type of tourism, provided that a detailed process is followed regarding their evaluation and precise weighting of the components, indicators, and indices. This can provide guidance, with objective criteria and a quantitative formal methodology, to planning and sustainable development of the tourism activity.

FINAL CONSIDERATIONS

Given the rapid growth of the tourism sector and its associated real estate sector in Baja California Sur and in the municipality of Los Cabos, a challenge has emerged to lay the foundations in order to make tourism centers sustainable development sites. This refers to those places with orderly growth, where development planning aims to preserve the long-term success of the destination, and where the population sees its standard of living increased. Unfortunately, this has not been achieved in any of the tourist destinations in the country or the state. This puts at risk the future growth of the sector itself by increasing the vulnerability of tourism centers that do not maintain the quality of services and natural resources that visitors expect.

Despite the obvious manifestations of the visual, economic, and social imbalances that impose a heavy burden on government agencies responsible for providing public services, urban planning mistakes

Map 2. Suitability for Alternative Tourism in the Municipality of Los Cabos

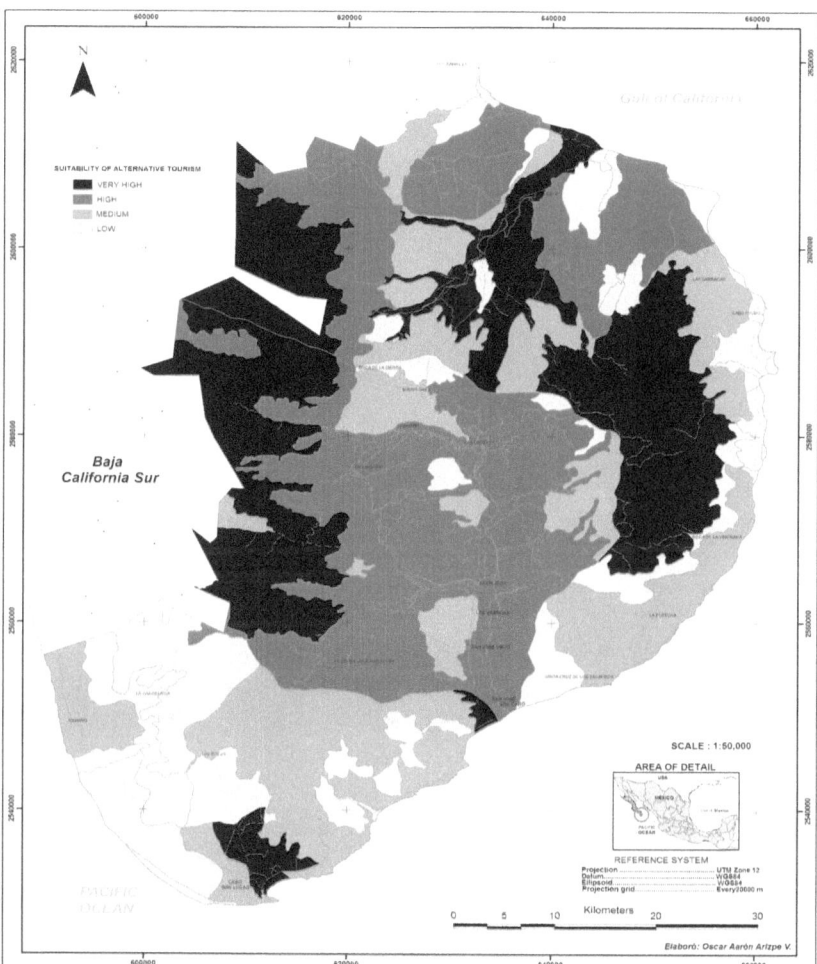

are still being made. These include allowing overbuilding. Beaches are polluted and ecosystems that once were emblems of the area are destroyed. Towns are now saturated with traffic. The overcrowding and the emergence of the pockets of misery deteriorate the urban image and generate disincentives for tourists as well as profound discomfort for the resident population.

Reversing this situation is a challenge for society, government, and the private sector. It is also a challenge to understand that the type and rate of tourism growth in Los Cabos will not continue indefinitely. It is therefore a collective responsibility to make provisions for the future of the region through effective planning. In this sense, it is necessary to promote models that consider that not all the land is suitable for the same type of tourism activities or with the same intensity. The development and application of the notion of present and future tourism suitability of the municipality's different locations (and any other part of the area) would allow having the elements of anticipation, planning, and adaptation of the sector to the vagaries of the international economy and the carrying capacity of the ecosystem.

References

Ángeles, Manuel, and Alba Gámez. 2008. "Globalización y desarrollo regional. El Caso del sector turismo en Baja California Sur." Pp. 463–484 in *Globalización y regionalismo: Economía y sustentabilidad,* Antonina Ivanova and Arturo Guillén, coords. México, DF: Porrúa.

Arizpe, Oscar, J. Fermán, R. Rivera, J, Ramírez, and R. Rodríguez. 2008. "Evaluation and Land Use Planning Process of a High Population Growth Rate Municipality: Los Cabos, Mexico." *WIT Transactions on Ecology and Environment* 5 (108): 87–95.

Centro Estatal de Información (CEI). 2001. *Compendio Estadístico 1998–2000 Municipios de Baja California Sur. Cuaderno de Datos Básicos 2001*. La Paz, BCS: Secretaría de Promoción y Desarrollo Económico, Gobierno del Estado de Baja California Sur.

Centro Estatal de Información (CEI). 2006. *Cuaderno de Datos Básicos 2006*. La Paz, BCS: Secretaría de Promoción y Desarrollo Económico, Gobierno del Estado de Baja California Sur.

Gámez, Alba E. 2008. "El crecimiento del sector turismo en Baja California Sur." Pp. 365–388 in *Del saqueo a la conservación. Historia ambiental contemporánea de Baja California Sur, 1940–2003,* Micheline Cariño and Mario Monteforte, coords. La Paz, BCS: UABCS-SEMARNAT-INE-CONACYT.

García Villa, Adolfo.1992. *La planificación de centros turísticos en México*. México, DF: Limusa.

Gobierno del Estado de Baja California Sur. 2009. *IV Informe de Gobierno del Ing. Narciso Agúndez Montaño. Anexo Gráfico y Estadístico.* La Paz, BCS: Gobierno del Estado de BCS.

Secretaría de Turismo (SECTUR) del Gobierno del Estado de BCS. 2006. *Informe final de prestadores de servicios turísticos del municipio de Los Cabos.* La Paz, BCS: Secretaría Estatal de Turismo Baja California Sur.

Secretaría de Medio Ambiente y Recursos Naturales (SEMARNAT). 2005. *Indicadores básicos del desempeño ambiental de México: 2005.* México, DF: PNUD-SEMARNAT.

Urciaga García, José. 2004. "Turismo alternativo. Una estrategia de desarrollo del espacio rural para Baja California Sur." *Prospectiva Económica* 3 (5): 177–197.

Wearing, Stephen, and John Neil. 2000. *Ecoturismo. Impacto, tendencias y posibilidades.* Madrid: Síntesis.

16

The Paradise of Sportfishing in Los Cabos, Baja California Sur

Ivonne Dalila Gómez Cabrera

INTRODUCTION

Sportfishing is practiced for purposes of entertainment or recreation, with authorized fishing gear as well as regulations and official standards that are in force. This activity is one of the primary tourist attractions in the Gulf of California and Baja California Sur, as their waters are among the richest in the world in terms of species for sport and commercial value, with more than 3,000 species (SECTUR 2010). Sportfishing, therefore, is an important source of employment and income.

One of the main places where sportfishing is practiced in the state is in Los Cabos. In fact, it is important to note that Los Cabos was born and became a tourist destination with large hotels and golf courses due to sportfishing for marlin. Through the years, Cabo San Lucas has become known as the world capital of marlin sportfishing.

The following includes a description of the primary sites for different species and of fishing and fishing tournaments. The final section will briefly address the problems that this activity faces in Los Cabos.

DESCRIPTION OF SPORTFISHING IN LOS CABOS

Due to the currents that have a high content of plankton and other nutrients from the Pacific Ocean and the Sea of Cortés, a great variety of fish can be found in the waters near Los Cabos. All types of marlin (black marlin, blue marlin, and striped marlin), dorado (mahi mahi), yellowfin tuna, wahoo, seabass, and roosterfish, among many others, are present. These are the most sought after species for sportfishing in Los Cabos.

According to the Ministry of Tourism, the municipality of Los Cabos places third in order of importance regarding sport/recreational fishing in Mexico (see Table 1).

Table 1. Fishing Sites and Main Species in the Municipality of Los Cabos

Sites	Species
Cabo Pulmo, BCS	bonito, tuna, corbina, red snapper, dorado, yellowtail, roosterfish, sailfish, marlin, wahoo, dogfish, hammerhead shark
Cabo San Lucas, BCS	bonito, tuna, red snapper, dorado, yellowtail, roosterfish, sailfish, marlin, wahoo, dogfish, hammerhead shark
San José del Cabo, BCS	bonito, tuna, red snapper, dorado, yellowtail, roosterfish, sailfish, marlin, wahoo, dogfish, hammerhead shark
Buena Vista, BCS	bonito, tuna, corbina, red snapper, dorado, yellowtail, sailfish, marlin, roosterfish, wahoo, dogfish, hammerhead shark

Source: SECTUR 2010.

According to the National Fisheries Chart, published August 19, 2000, in the Official Journal of the Federation *(Diario Oficial de la Federación)*, in terms of species reserved for sportfishing, striped marlin, blue marlin, and sailfish make up more than 99% of total sport catch of billfish in the Mexican Pacific Ocean. The areas of greatest importance are the regions of Los Cabos and Buena Vista, Baja California Sur. The annual average catch for these combined areas is estimated at 18,551 (+/-3.44) billfish (CONAPESCA 2004).

With regard to protected species, sportfishing in Mexico is regulated by the Mexican Official Standard NOM-017-PESC-1994, which specifies the use of gear and tackle, as well as the catch quota

and size by species. The sportfishing rules are summarized in the following points:
- Nine species: six called billfish (four types of marlin, sailfish, and swordfish), plus tarpon, roosterfish, and dorado, are intended exclusively for sportfishing within a range of 50 nautical miles, counting from the baseline from which the territorial sea is measured
- It is strictly prohibited to carry out any commercial fishing with a sportfishing license or to simulate sportfishing activities for the purpose of profit
- It is the duty of the sport fishers to have a sportfishing license.
- Sport fishers must respect federal regulations regarding minimum sizes, closed seasons, and can only use rods or lines with hooks, bait, or lures
- Service providers are required to submit fishing logbooks
- The catch limits are five specimens per day per fisher in continental waters and 10 in marine waters

According to the sportfishing regulations, a license issued by the Ministry of Environment and Natural Resources (Secretaría de Medio Ambiente y Recursos Naturales–SEMARNAT) is required. However, there are specialized high-quality service providers in Los Cabos that rent boats and the necessary equipment, and include the fishing license as part of the tour price.

As suggested in fishing regulations, billfish (marlin and sailfish) are protected species, so the practice of catch-and-release fishing is required. When one is caught, it is weighed, measured, and photographed and then returned to sea. If done with due care, the fish has excellent possibilities of survival. In fact, in terms of sportfishing around the world, Los Cabos is the first to give cash prizes to teams for releasing live fish once they were measured in the Annual Tournament of Sportfishing. This tournament is in 15th place of popularity in the list of fishing tournaments, and it takes place in November. This makes this tournament a leader in ecological conservation.

In October of each year, among several other tournaments, an important competition takes place in Cabo San Lucas in which many boats participate. The event is called Bisbee Black & Blue Jack Pot, and the goal is to catch blue or black marlin. The 2010 tournament had 103 boats participate and cash prizes totaled $1.9 million. There is a tournament category for catch and release, indicating growing conservation efforts (www.bisbee.com/).

Overall, summer is the best fishing season; it is when black marlin and blue marlin can be caught, especially in Cabo San Lucas, though there are also grouper, mackerel *(jurel de Castilla)*, and corbina. In winter, the type of species fished include mackerel and corbina.

Economically speaking, sportfishing is very important for Los Cabos, since the income generated by the activity produces a multiplier effect in three sectors of the economy: tourism, fisheries, and industry (SEPESCA 1991). In 2007 and 2008, the Billfish Foundation conducted a comprehensive study to estimate the amount of money, jobs, and tax revenues attributable to recreational fishers in the region of Los Cabos (Southwick et al. 2008). For the study, visitors were interviewed, both fishers and other tourists. It was estimated that 354,013 persons, the great majority international visitors, in 2007, fished in Los Cabos. While in Los Cabos, they spent approximately US$1,785 each on lodging, boat rental, food, transportation, fishing equipment, fuel, and much more. These costs, in turn, initiated a series of economic effects with impact on the local economy, including:

- US$633.6 million in retail sales, representing new revenue for Los Cabos received from the fishers
- 24,426 jobs
- US$245.5 million in revenue from local and federal taxes
- US $1,125 million in total economic activity

It is important to mention that the study provides good approximations of the economic spillover that sportfishing generates in Los Cabos. However, it does not allow the quantification of various flows and variables from an integrated macroeconomic perspective. Therefore, the actual size of the sector and its value are judged only through fragmented indicators and isolated data that do not allow the assessment of their real importance for the development of the region as a whole. The extent of their impacts is not limited in number and economic value of catch species nor in the tax revenues that the treasury receives for fishing licenses. It also includes important added values like jobs, wages, and capital investment in many industrial and commercial businesses related to sportfishing.

Another area that is special for sportfishing in the Los Cabos municipality is East Cape (Cabo del Este), located 120 kilometers south of La Paz on the Sea of Cortés. It includes the areas of Punta Pescadero, Los Barriles, Buenavista, La Ribera, Cabo Pulmo, and Los Frailes. In the course of three decades (since its beginnings in 1958), this area has turned into a paradise for sportfishing due to the abundance of species such as marlin, tuna, swordfish, snapper, dorado, and sailfish, which makes fishing in that area attractive for any type of fisher. As a result, Buenavista—from being a fishing village—has grown each year and increasingly directs its efforts toward tourism. For its part, the Los Barriles area has a fleet that includes fishing boats and fully equipped cruise vessels with experienced captains who know how to take fishers to locations where it is likely to encounter large fish. Due to its abundant natural resources and peaceful lifestyle, the region of East Cape is becoming one of the favorite attractions of Baja California Sur.

The sustainability of fisheries is related to different criteria in decision making: biological and ecological (knowledge of the dynamics of the fishery resource; effect of fisheries on the ecosystem); technical (fishing gear and equipment); economic (prices, revenue, incentives for conservation); social (employment); and fishery management (season closures, minimum catch sizes, control of fishing pressure, legal framework), among others. For this reason, a multidisciplinary approach should be employed, one that enables the use, management, and conservation of these natural resources, with a goal of long-term sustainability (Cortés Ortiz, Ponce Díaz, and Ángeles Villa 2006).

Given its characteristics, sportfishing falls well within the framework of fisheries sustainability, since it impacts the environment and the resource. However, it does it in such a way that the effect is less intense than commercial fishing, as this type of fishing is highly selective. Of the fish that are caught, many are released before being boated, and some of these survive.

The tourism industry in Mexico emphasizes that sportfishers generate more economic benefits for each billfish they catch than the value of the fish sold by commercial fishers in the market. This argument is based on economic activity induced in the tourism industry such as lodging, food, and boat rental expenses, and other services (CONAPESCA 2004).

Competition between sportfishing and commercial fishing has intensified and fisheries authorities are facing this situation without being able to provide an adequate solution to the situation of efficient allocation of stocks of fisheries resources. On the contrary, with the establishment of the NOM-029 this debate resurfaced and revived. The objective of NOM-029 is to regulate the fishing of sharks and rays. However, fishing for marlin, swordfish, and sailfish for commercial purposes is being justified and legalized by listing it as shark meat in the disembarkation records.

Concluding Remarks

Cabo San Lucas has become the world capital of marlin sportfishing, so that sportfishing is for Los Cabos, and even for the state of Baja California Sur, an economic powerhouse with an annual economic impact derived mainly from foreign visitors who come to fish and take part in fishing tournaments. Sport and recreational fishing is a category of the fishing activity that takes place within a scheme of sustainability. It is practiced for recreational purposes and it links humans with nature, particularly to fisheries resources. Thus, it is convenient to establish an appropriate regulation to promote it and encourage it in an orderly fashion. However, there are information shortcomings for the sector. Direct and indirect data sources are very limited. A comprehensive information system that describes sportfishing and its characteristics in a timely and realistic manner is lacking for the state and national levels. It is understood worldwide that the activity associated with sportfishing, both marine and freshwater, is diverse and very important. However, it is not possible for Los Cabos to establish precisely the importance of the sector.

The main problem that sportfishing faces in Los Cabos is the clash of interests between sportfishing and commercial fishing due to the major direct and indirect competition that generates considerable pressure on seaside resources of high commercial value and commercial exploitation of species destined for sportfishing. Efforts to solve these problems have been insufficient. It is necessary to characterize, estimate, and compare the economic value of sportfishing and commercial fishing in Los Cabos in order to generate a database to enable decision makers to efficiently allocate fishery resources among its alternative uses.

References

Casas Valdez, M. M., G. Ponce Díaz, A. Hernández Llamas, M. A. González Ojeda, F. Galván Magaña, E. Guzmán Vizcarra, S. Hernández Vázquez, A. Valdez Barajas, and A. Sui Qui. 1996. "Recursos pesqueros y acuícolas de Baja California Sur: Estado actual y perspectivas de aprovechamiento y desarrollo." Pp. 1–15 in *Estudio del potencial pesquero y acuícola de Baja California Sur,* Vol. I, M. Casas Valdez and G. Ponce Díaz, eds. SEMARNAP, Gobierno del Estado de Baja California Sur, FAO, Instituto Nacional de la Pesca, UABCS, CIBNOR, CICIMAR, CETMAR.

Comisión Nacional de Acuacultura y Pesca (CONAPESCA). 2004. *Plan de acción: Estrategia integral para el desarrollo de la pesca deportiva.* México, DF: SAGARPA-CONAPESCA, Unidad de enlace para el desarrollo de la pesca deportiva.

Comisión Nacional de Acuacultura y Pesca (CONAPESCA) and Secretaría de Agricultura, Ganadería, Desarrollo Rural, Pesca y Alimentación (SAGARPA). 2004. *Anuario estadístico de acuacultura y pesca 2004.* Mazatlán, SIN: CONAPESCA.

Comisión Nacional de Acuacultura y Pesca (CONAPESCA) and Secretaría de Agricultura, Ganadería, Desarrollo Rural, Pesca y Alimentación (SAGARPA). 2008. http://www.conapesca.sagarpa.gob.mx/.

Cortés Ortiz, R., G. Ponce Díaz, and M. Ángeles Villa. 2006. "El sector pesquero en Baja California Sur: Un enfoque de insumo-producto." *Región y Sociedad XVIII* (35): 107–129.

Diario Oficial de la Federación. 1995. Norma Oficial Mexicana NOM-017-pesc-1994. Para regular las Actividades de Pesca Recreativa en la Aguas de Jurisdicción Federal de los Estados Unidos Mexicanos. Tomo No. 15–19. México, DF: DOF.

Instituto Nacional de Estadística, Geografía e Informática (INEGI). 1991. Datos básicos de la geografía de México. (Accessed 23 May 2008), http://cuentame.inegi.gob.mx/monografias/informacion/BCS/Territorio/default.aspx?tema=ME&e=03.

Instituto Nacional de Estadística, Geografía e Informática (INEGI). 2005. Perspectiva estadística, Baja California Sur. (Accessed 23 May 2008), http://www.inegi.gob.mx/est/contenidos/ espanol/sistemas/perspectivas/perspectiva-bcs.pdf.

Instituto Nacional de Estadística, Geografía e Informática (INEGI). 2006. Sistema de Cuentas Nacionales de México. Producto Interno Bruto por entidad Federativa 1999–2004. (Accessed 23 May 2008), http://cuentame.inegi.gob.mx/monografias/informacion/bcs/ economia/pib.aspx?tema=me&e=03.

Secretaría de Agricultura, Ganadería, Desarrollo Rural, Pesca y Alimentación (SAGARPA). 2009. "Producción pesquera 2008." *El sudcaliforniano* (29 March).

Secretaría de Medio Ambiente y Recursos Naturales (SEMARNAT). 2005. *Ordenamiento ecológico marino del golfo de California. Recuento y estado actual.* México, DF: SEMARNAT.

Secretaría de Pesca (SEPESCA). 1991. *Fomento y modernización de la pesca deportivo-recreativa 1991–1994.* México, DF: Secretaría de Pesca.

Secretaría de Turismo (SECTUR). 2002. "Comportamiento y tendencias de la pesca deportivo-recreativa en México." México, DF: SECTUR.

Secretaría de Turismo (SECTUR). 2010. "Guía oficial de pesca deportiva y recreativa en México." México, DF: SECTUR.

Southwick, Rob, Russell Nelson, and José Antonio Arean Martínez. 2008. *The Economic Contributions of Anglers to the Los Cabos Economy.* Commissioned by the Billfish Foundation. Southwick Associates, Inc., Fernandina Beach, FL; Nelson Resources Consulting, Inc., Oakland Park, FL; and FIRMUS Consulting, Mexico City.

17

Tourism as a Sector of Opportunity for Agriculture and Nearshore Fishing

Antonina Ivanova, Ivonne Dalila Gómez Cabrera, and Alberto Torres

INTRODUCTION: THE MULTIPLIER IMPACT OF TOURISM ACTIVITIES

As indicated by the development plans of the municipality of Los Cabos, tourism has risen as a priority for development. This is of course due to the generation of revenue and creation of jobs. However, the 2008–2011 municipal development plan specifies some indicators that are positioning tourism in a broader perspective, inserting it into a general system of development. Among the basic principles that govern the system's indicators are integration of tourism into the context of planning for growth and also analysis of the benefits of tourism to the local economy.

Important objectives planned to be achieved in association with tourism development are improving quality of life of the supporting population[1] and measuring the benefits generated at the destination as a result of tourism and associate tourism activities. In this sense, it is very important to determine the economic benefits generated by tourism, which can be divided into direct, indirect, and induced. The first are those produced for companies that directly serve tourism demand. Indirect impacts are those that take place through the chain of intersectorial relationships, which originate from the direct impact (West and Gamage 2001). Finally, the origin of induced effects is in

---

[1]. For additional details on the indicators associated with the development of tourism in Los Cabos, see Ochoa Felipe y Asociados, S.C. (2004).

the spending of income that has been generated as a result of direct and indirect impacts (Hernández Martín 2004).

Direct impacts are the easiest to understand because they are the result of tourist spending in businesses that operate for this sector, generating income for employers and employees. At the same time, they produce a flow of resources toward local government in the form of taxes (Acerenza 2006). However, the economic benefits that tourism provides are not only limited to activities that are directly related to tourists. Tourism, like exports, has a multiplier effect on the locality in which it develops (Valdés et al. 2008). This is precisely the indirect impact, which means the circulation of income from the tourism sector to other sectors of the local economy.

The extent to which the local economy is able to retain revenues from tourism depends on its degree of self-sufficiency. If the locality is capable of producing goods and services purchased by tourists, then the greater the multiplier effect, the benefits to the local economy (Tyrrell and Johnston 2001), and the impact on the people's living standards. The more goods needed to be imported from outside the region, the lower the multiplier effect (Hernández Martín 2004). However, in several tourist centers, tourism development depends on imports of products from more diversified economies. As Pattullo (1996) states, tourists in the Caribbean do not consume local mangoes and bananas, but rather drink Florida orange juice and eat bananas from Colombia or canned pineapple from Hawaii. And although according to researchers, this is more typical for small island states and not for large economies like Mexico or Brazil (Wilson 2004), the state of Baja California Sur, due to its insular nature, shows the same characteristics. The municipality of Los Cabos, located on the southern tip of the peninsula, shows a strong dependence on imported products for all aspects of its development, both from external markets (U.S. placing first) and from the Mexico's mainland, thus diluting the economic benefits generated by tourism for the local economy.

Although much has been written about the ties between tourism development with trade and construction, almost nothing has been said about their impact on the primary sector. According to the 2004 economic census, a total of 4,771 businesses were registered in the municipality of Los Cabos, of which only 1.8% were for agricultural activities, livestock raising, forestry, fishing, and hunting

(Ayuntamiento de Los Cabos 2008). However, there are areas worldwide where strong tourism development has exerted a significant multiplier effect on agriculture and fishing.[2]

Therefore, it is very important to find ways to take advantage of tourism development and link it with supplies from the primary sectors of the municipality (and state). This essay discusses the evolution of the agriculture and fisheries sectors[3] in the municipality of Los Cabos and analyzes their potential to provide inputs for the tourism sector, thus promoting its development and creating the opportunity for some diversification of the economic structure of the municipality.

Agriculture in Los Cabos

Main Characteristics of Agricultural Activities in the Municipality of Los Cabos

The semidesert climate, with temperate zones, and a limited area of fertile soil make farming a moderate activity in the municipality of Los Cabos. Los Cabos ranks fourth in the state in cultivated areas, behind Mulegé, Comondú, and La Paz. Added to that, water use and the inclination of people toward the tertiary sector, especially tourism,[4] have led to a decline in agricultural activities in recent years, as shown in Figure 1.

Agriculture in the municipality of Los Cabos had a significant increase from 1999 to 2004, when the value of production grew slightly more than 417%. From 2004 to 2006, the trend was reversed, showing a decrease of almost 70%. For 2007 and 2008 (preliminary figures), a recovery of almost 9% is seen. In this regard, strengthening the idea of the previous paragraph, according to studies by the Ministry of Agriculture, Livestock, Rural Development, Fisheries and Food (Secretaría de Agricultura, Ganadería, Desarrollo Rural, Pesca y Alimentación–SAGARPA 2003):

---

2. For example, in Asturias, Spain, the multiplier effect received by the agriculture and fisheries sectors places it in an important place, after the construction, financial services, trade, and transportation sectors (Valdés et al. 2008), while the analysis by Antara (1999) shows that agriculture in Bali is positioned after the construction, transportation, and trade sectors (surpassing the financial sector).
3. This essay discusses only commercial fishing, since chapter 16 of this book is devoted to sportfishing.
4. "Tourism is in a frank consolidation process and is, without doubt, the growth engine of the entity, since it generates an important economic revenue and better paid jobs" (Ayuntamiento de Los Cabos 2008).

In the last two decades, the Agricultural/Livestock Sector in the municipality of Los Cabos has been developed in a political-economic medium that has preponderantly favored activities such as tourism and the construction industry, marginalizing the development of primary activities such as: agriculture, livestock raising, and beekeeping, which have natural potentials inadequately exploited.

Figure 1. Value of Agricultural Production in the Municipality of Los Cabos, 1999–2008

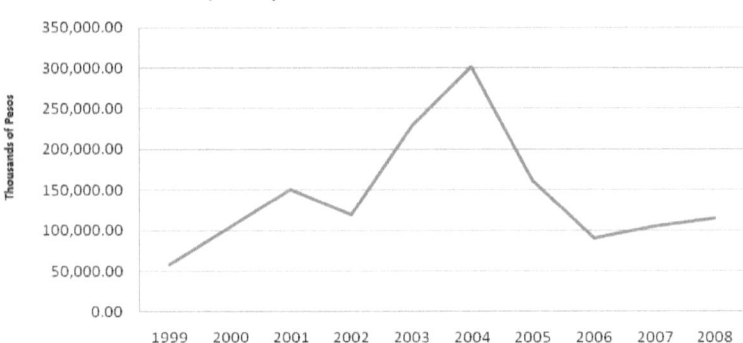

Based on the information presented in the 2008–2011 Municipal Development Plan (Plan de Desarrollo Municipal–PDM), the water allotment for agricultural activities is about 18 million m^3, from 112 deep wells, four springs, five diversion dams, and a recharge structure distributed in different areas of Santiago, Miraflores, La Ribera, and San José del Cabo (Ayuntamiento de Los Cabos 2008).

The register of agricultural producers in the municipality shows 860, of which 682 are *ejidatarios* (communal land holders) and 178 are smallholders (Ayuntamiento de Los Cabos 2008). For their productive organization, they are distributed in the following *ejidos* (communal lands): La Ribera, Las Cuevas, Santa Cruz, Santiago, San Jorge, Agua Caliente, El Zacatal, General Melitón Albáñez, Boca de la Sierra, El Ranchito, Miraflores, Las Casitas, Caduaño, Ranchería San Vicente, San José del Cabo, Ranchería La Trinidad, Migriño, La Candelaria, and Cabo San Lucas.[5] In addition, some exporting

---

[5]. Based on information from SAGARPA presented in the BCS Geographic Information System, http://www.oeidrus-bcs.gob.mx/sigbcs/ (Consulted 28 March 2009).

firms are important. These include Productores Orgánicos del Cabo S.S.S. de R.L. de C.V., Condimentos Frescos DAGO's, Ángel Salvador Ceseña Burgoin, Nuevo Mundo Orgánico, Agrícola Cabeña, Agroproductos del Cabo, and Mercado Independiente de Exportación del Cabo, among others.

Moreover, agriculture has seen development in terms of technical components that have improved cultivation, application of inputs, and harvesting work. According to SAGARPA (2003), "There have also been advances in irrigation technology, particularly with regard to infrastructure for the transportation of water to the fields, there still being a need to install pressurized irrigation systems to optimize the use of this resource, which would reduce production costs and increase capitalization."

The limited agricultural potential of Los Cabos, both in land use and type of agriculture, had the characteristics shown in Table 1 during the 2002–2005 period. As Table 1 shows, only 3% of the total area of the municipality was used for agriculture at that time. Of the land used for agriculture, 49.6% was irrigated cropland and 50.4% for cultivated pastures.

Table 1. Agricultural Land Use and Vegetation in the Municipality of Los Cabos, 2002–2005

Total Area according to Land Use and Vegetation					
Total (Hectares)	Agriculture	Pastureland	Forest	Jungle	Scrubland
370,959	11,546	1,089	11,138	170,283	152,032
Agricultural Area according to Type of Agriculture					
Total (Hectares)	Seasonal	Humid	Irrigated	Cultivated Pastureland	Cultivated Forest
11,546	915	0	5,728	5,818	0

Source: Authors' calculations based on data from INEGI. Land Use and Vegetation Map, 1:250 000. Series III.

At the end of the 2007 period, the harvested area was 2,023 hectares, showing a yield of 620 ton/ha, reflected in the production of 20,617 tons, worth an estimated $105,175,149 pesos (Table 2). The main crops were mangos, red tomatoes, forage sorghum, oranges, organic basil, corn grain, avocado, papaya, cherry tomatoes, green peppers, watermelon, and zucchini. Table 2 shows the main features in the production of conventional and organic crops in 2007.

Table 2. Crop Groups in the Municipality of Los Cabos, 2007

Group	Area (Has)		Production Volume (Ton)	Yield (Ton/Has)	ARP* ($/Ton)	Production Value (Pesos)
	Sown	Harvested				
Staples	286	229	801	4	4,940	3,957,375
Citrus	121	101	988	10	4,822	4,764,000
Forage	80	51	4,040	80	1,200	4,848,000
Fruits	926	543	7,280	13	3,536	25,740,000
Vegetables	37	37	501	14	6,152	3,083,500
Organic Vegetables	570	464	6,991	15	8,812	61,600,368
Organic Inudstrial	4	4	16	4	76,252	1,181,906

*Average rural price.
Source: Authors' calculations based on data provided by the Oficina Estatal para el Desarrollo Rural Sustentable, Secretaría de Promoción y Desarrollo Económico de BCS 2009.

Organic Crops

The organic crops in the Los Cabos agricultural sector are mainly for export. Their value is considerable in some international markets. It derives from the assurances to consumers through certification techniques, methods, processes, packaging, packing, and sanitary measures, among other things, to which the crops are subjected. In contrast to traditional agriculture, over the past 20 years the municipality of Los Cabos has taken advantage of the variety of climates, as well as its conditions of isolation and plant health for the organic certification of crops.

The land transportation and airport infrastructure has facilitated exports of these crops to the U.S. From there, the products are distributed in markets of the United States, the European Union, and Asia. Prominent in this production are organic crops, especially spices and medicinal plants, vegetables, and those considered industrial. The first group includes mint, basil, dill, marjoram, oregano, rosemary, sage, tarragon, and thyme. In the vegetable group are eggplant, zucchini, green pepper, chives, cucumber, red tomato, cilantro, green beans, and cherry tomatoes, among others. Finally, mint is recognized as industrial because of processing, marketing, and use. Figure 2 shows recent traditional and organic agriculture in Los Cabos.

As can be seen in Figure 2, the difference in value of traditional and organic production has decreased significantly in recent years, since the share of organic agriculture in the municipality's total fell from 78% to 56%. This situation is associated with the contraction of international markets due to the economic crisis accentuated in 2008. This is explained by the higher prices for organic agricultural products, which impede their efficient marketing in the domestic market, so most are placed abroad, showing a strong dependence on foreign demand.

Figure 2. Value in Pesos of Traditional and Organic Agricultural Production in the Municipality of Los Cabos, 2005–2008

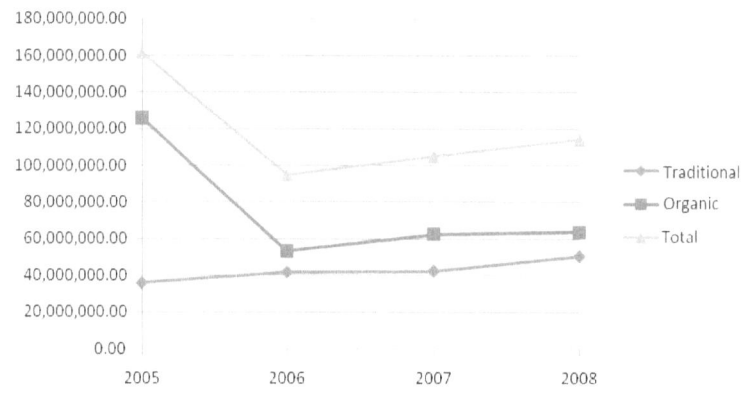

Source: Authors' calculations based on data provided by Oficina Estatal para el Desarrollo Rural Sustentable, Secretaría de Promoción y Desarrollo Económico de BCS 2009.

Notwithstanding the decline in sales of organic crops, the results of collaborative work in the face of adverse situations can be seen. One successful case that stands out is the company Productores Orgánicos del Cabo, Sociedad de Solidaridad Social, de Responsabilidad

Limitada de Capital Variable, which in 1996 received the National Exportation Award in the category of agricultural companies. It was recognized as an example of a small and medium enterprise (pequeña y mediana empresa–PyME) in the exporting business with a successful venture into international markets. A pioneer in its field in Mexico's northwest, Productores Orgánicos del Cabo is a company whose business is the export of certified organic agricultural products. This was the result of a rural development project that is based on the use and optimization of the region's natural resources.[6]

COMMERCIAL FISHING IN THE MUNICIPALITY OF LOS CABOS

In Los Cabos, commercial fishing for human consumption, in relation to the rest of the state's ports, is not a significant activity. This area has the least participation in both production volume and in absolute value. However, sportfishing has been promoted since it generates tourism and high levels of revenue. The Los Cabos area stands out for its importance in sportfishing due to its richness in species such as dorado, sailfish, and marlin, among others. This activity produces important foreign exchange inflows for the region, as it is identified as one of the major tourist attractions.

Los Cabos became a tourist destination with large hotels and golf courses due to marlin fishing. Through the years, Cabo San Lucas has become the world capital of marlin sportfishing.

Description of Nearshore Fishing in Los Cabos

Fish production in the municipality of Los Cabos reached a value of 8,989 million pesos in 2008. The main species SAGARPA reported were bait (54%), scale (37%), and oysters (8%) (see Table 3). It should be pointed out that the fishing value produced by the municipality of Los Cabos represents barely 1% of total value produced in Baja California Sur, which amounts to 754,524 million pesos.

---

6. The information presented on Productores Orgánicos del Cabo was prepared with notes from the paper "Un Caso Exitoso de Producción y Comercialización Orgánica" (A Successful Case of Organic Production and Marketing), presented on October 20, 2004, by Rosa Icela Ruiz Araiza and Denise Fabiola Cuadras Gómez at the Fifth Student Congress on Foreign Trade organized by the Foreign Trade Bachelor's Degree of the Autonomous University of Baja California Sur.

The small share of commercial fishing in the economic activities of Los Cabos is because many fish species are coveted for sportfishing and include the black, blue, and striped marlin; sailfish; swordfish; dorado; tuna; cabrilla (sea bass); mackerel; wahoo; rooster fish; and snapper. Nearshore fishing in BCS is in critical condition. The main

Table 3. Volume and Value of Fish Production in the Municipality of Los Cabos

Species	Los Cabos		
	Weight/Tons		Value
	Live	Unloaded	Thousands in Pesos
Bait	46.00	46.00	4,845.00
Scale	149.00	147.00	3,322.00
Oyster	113.00	102.00	707.00
Ray and similar	0.16	0.08	0.70
Dogfish	10.00	9.00	111.00
Tuna	0.24	0.24	4.00
Total	318.00	304.00	8,989.00

Source: SAGARPA. Published in *El Sudcaliforniano* (29 March 2009).

problems are: (1) lack of institutional coordination for the management and protection of marine resources, as well as legal loopholes that make sanctioning infractions difficult; (2) negative impact on the ecosystem by practices that downplay the importance of conservation of marine resources; (3) overexploitation of coastal resources of high commercial value and commercial exploitation of species reserved for sportfishing; and (4) high intermediation in the marketing process, which reduces the profitability of the catch (SEMARNAT 2005).

The state's fishing fleet consists of approximately 3,700 vessels, of which 98% are boats used in coastal fishing. The larger vessels show a gradual deterioration, since most were built more than 15 years ago. Financial problems have led to a lack of attention to their repair and maintenance, thus resulting in a less technical and economic efficiency (SCT 2004).

The Interrelationship of Sportfishing and Commercial Fishing in Los Cabos

There is a conflict between commercial fishing and sportfishing in the state of BCS due to aspects of resource allocation. The following section discusses the two sides of this conflict.

The sportfishers sector, strongly linked to tourism interests, argues that the results of the exploitation of billfish, whether through commercial licenses or "incidental catch," are the cause for the decrease in visitors—especially foreigners—to the main fishing areas. The tourism industry in Mexico notes that sportfishers generate more economic benefits for every billfish they capture than the value of the fish sold in the market by commercial fishers. This argument is based on the economic activity induced in the tourism industry, such as expenditures related to accommodations, food, boat rentals, and other services (CONAPESCA 2004).

For its part, commercial fishing demands changes in the Federal Fisheries Act in order to have access to marine species reserved for sportfishing. Commercial fishers argue that scientific studies have concluded that natural populations of billfish (mainly sailfish) have increased partially (Macías-Zamora et al. 1994). This is because foreign fishing fleets have been banned from within Mexico's Exclusive Economic Zone (200 nautical miles), enacted in 1976, and therefore the resource is "underutilized." They also argue, in the international framework, that restrictions that self-limit the exploitation of these fish have negative economic consequences for those who self-impose restrictions. This is especially the case when the country imposing the self-limits is a small producer, as is Mexico. Other countries benefit and Mexico competes at a serious disadvantage in the use of these resources (CONAPESCA 2004).

In addition, there is a conflict of interests among the conservation, tourism, and coastal fishing sectors because of the entanglement of sea lions and the damage they cause to the nets and catch. This derives from the spatial and temporal competition between sea lions and fishers for the same resources.

With regard to this conflict, the study by The Billfish Foundation found that 88% of international anglers who have fished in Cabo said they would be less likely to return if they knew that commercial fishing of billfish had increased. Eighty-five percent said they would be much more likely to return if commercial fishing of billfish was restricted or had been stopped completely (Southwick et al. 2008).

CONCLUDING REMARKS

Based on information from the preceding paragraphs, some considerations are presented on alternatives that tourism brings about for future development of agriculture and commercial fishing in the municipality of Los Cabos as presented. The variety of microclimates, the introduction of technical procedures for crops, and the type of soil and moisture provide an environment suitable for producing crops of high quality, flavor, and consistency in the municipality of Los Cabos. However, agricultural activity has had a downturn since 2005. Beyond the problems caused by natural disasters or water shortages for production, the decline can be associated with the contraction of foreign markets, where the main demand for organic crops is found. The inclusion of innovative alternatives for rural production, promotion of investment, and modernization of the agricultural sector, seen in the public agenda through the Municipal Development Plan, show a positive outlook for recovery in the domestic market and an improved participation in international markets. In addition, programs established at the federal level—such as SAGARPA's Programs for Promotion and Capitalization and Alliance for the Rural Sector, Bank of Mexico's Instituted Trusts in Relation to Agriculture (Fideicomisos Instituidos en Relación con la Agricultura–FIRA), and the Shared Risk Trust (Fideicomiso de Riesgo Compartido–FIRCO) and taken into account in the State Development Plan 2005–2011—appear as instruments for the support of capitalization and linkages of the agricultural sector in Los Cabos.

Finally, the adherence of producers and cooperative members to the rules and procedures established by SAGARPA regarding Good Agricultural Practices (Buenas Prácticas Agrícolas–BPAs) and Good Manufacturing Practices (Buenas Prácticas de Manufactura–BPMs), as well as the appropriate techniques on matters of agrifood safety—applied by the National Service for Agrifood Health, Safety, and Quality (Servicio Nacional de Sanidad, Inocuidad y Calidad Agroalimentaria–SENASICA)—in addition to complying with regulations issued by international entities—such as the U.S. Department of Agriculture (USDA)—are short-term tasks that will strengthen the positioning of this activity in local, national, and foreign markets.

The priority placed on tourism development, in general, has deprived the agricultural sector of critical resources (labor and capital) because of the lower return rates on invested capital in agriculture due to low prices and low productivity (Ruiz Chávez 2008). However, as tourism grows, the demand for food is increasing. Tourism is a stimulus for agricultural production and marketing, especially in fruits and vegetables, with big opportunities for organic products. Currently, most food demand generated by the tourism sector in Los Cabos is supplied through imports, both from foreign markets as well as from the Mexican mainland. This weakens the multiplier effect of tourism for the municipality. If local production does not respond to this growing demand, then the tourism industry will be accompanied by higher levels of food imports with associated negative economic effects. If direct marketing channels are established and attractive prices are offered by local producers to the major hotel chains, it will be possible to generate a secure and stable market for agricultural products. In addition to favoring the local agricultural sector, this could reduce dependence on imported products and make better use of the multiplier effect of tourism in order to boost the benefits for the local economy.

Another area of opportunity for agriculture in the municipality of Los Cabos is the growing interest on rural tourism. In this sense, the families of the nearby ranches can offer tourist services. The ranch culture has become a major tourist attraction. Rural tourism generates additional demand for agricultural products, such as traditional candy and goat cheese, among others. By generating income, creating infrastructure, and generating employment, tourism acts as a stabilizing factor for agricultural labor (Orduña Luna 2009). The multiplier effect of tourism generates other agricultural activities, such as collecting wild fruits, aromatic plants, and so forth.

Given that sportfishing has achieved great importance in the municipality of Los Cabos and that it generates a significant share of income, it does not seem wise to grant the commercial fishing sector access to the species destined for sportfishing. However, it is believed that it is possible to promote direct sales to major hotels and restaurants of some species such as scale fish and oysters. This will generate income for fishing communities without involving intermediaries. Of course, sustainable management of these resources must be promoted in order to prevent overexploitation, and a clear definition of fishing gear to be used to avoid damaging the reefs and other diving attractions must be clearly specified.

The concept of ecotourism is developing more in Los Cabos to complement the traditional activity of sun and beach. With this approach, which focuses on the use of coastal resources for the practice of water sports like swimming and diving, the economic value of fish and coral reefs acquires a new dimension. Indeed, the harvest and degradation of these resources could damage the reputation of Los Cabos as a tourist destination. Moreover, aquaculture of luxury products like pearls could be promoted for the tourism industry, an activity that is enjoying great demand and generates important revenue in most island countries (FAO 1994). The coordination of traditional fishing and tourism (including sportfishing and diving) is necessary to avoid allocation problems and conflicts among different users of coastal areas.

In conclusion, there are areas of opportunities among agriculture, fisheries, and tourism, with a potential to reduce imports, create jobs, and, thus, increase the multiplier effect of tourism. To seize opportunities, it is not possible to solely rely on market forces, but it is necessary to carry out certain support activities. In this regard, an analysis must be made of local production capabilities aimed at the main tourist seasons and of the availability of human and financial resources. In order to link producers with the hotel sector, it would be helpful to develop regional directories with information on local producers (FAO 1994), the seasonality of local production, and food quality and safety standards, as well as the representation of regional providers in fairs dedicated to sales for the hotel sector. To ensure reliable and regular supply to hotels, contractual arrangements between hotels and producers could be promoted.

The production of agriculture and commercial fishing has not been until now aimed at taking advantage of the possibilities offered by tourism demand. Appropriate policies are needed, as well as an institutional base, to promote and maintain the links among agriculture, coastal fishing, and tourism, both in the municipality of Los Cabos and throughout the state of Baja California Sur.

That tourism growth favors the sharp decline in primary sectors and even their disappearance, leading to exclusive dependency on a single economic sector, should not be regarded as something desirable nor even inevitable, but rather as an indicator of low-level planning of the development process. This may affect the sustainability of tourism in the medium or long term. Therefore, it is necessary to promote actions to maintain the operation and development of agriculture and commercial fishing by taking advantage of the multiplier impact of tourism.

REFERENCES

Antara, M. 1999. "Linkages between Tourism and Agriculture in Bali-Indonesia: A Social Accounting Matrix Approach." Paper presented at the Sustainable Tourism: The Balinese Perspective International Seminar, Denpasar-Bali, 3 August.

Acerenza, M. A. 2006. *Efectos económicos, socioculturales y ambientales del turismo.* México, DF: Trillas.

Ayuntamiento de Los Cabos. 2008. *Plan de Desarrollo Municipal 2008–2011.* (Accessed 14 March 2008), http://www.loscabos.gob.mx/wordpress/wp-content/PDF/plan_desarrollo.pdf.

Comisión Nacional de Acuacultura y Pesca (CONAPESCA). 2004. *Plan de acción: Estrategia integral para el desarrollo de la pesca deportiva.* México, DF: SAGARPA-CONAPESCA, Unidad de enlace para el desarrollo de la pesca deportiva.

Comisión Nacional de Acuacultura y Pesca (CONAPESCA) and Secretaría de Agricultura, Ganadería, Desarrollo Rural, Pesca y Alimentación (SAGARPA). 2004. *Anuario estadístico de acuacultura y pesca 2004.* Mazatlán, SIN: CONAPESCA.

Cortés Ortiz R., G. Ponce Díaz, M. Ángeles Villa. 2006. "El sector pesquero en Baja California Sur: Un enfoque de insumo-producto." *Revista Región y Sociedad XVIII* (35): 107–129.

Food and Agriculture Organization of the United Nations (FAO). 1994. "The Role of Agriculture, Forestry and Fisheries in the Sustainable Development of Small Island Developing States." Paper presented at The United Nations Global Conference on the Sustainable Development of Small Island Developing States,

Rome (Accessed 12 December 2009), http://www.fao.org/docrep/t3384e/t3384e00.htm#Contents.

Hernández Martín, R. 2004. "Impacto económico del turismo. El papel de las importaciones como fugas del modelo." *Revista ICE* 817 (Accessed 15 December 2009), http://www.revistasice.com/cmsrevistasICE/pdfs/ICE_817_23-34__B81C35A65AD11B8D459C2D981F9A6641.pdf.

Instituto Nacional de Estadística y Geografía (INEGI). 2007. "Censo agropecuario. Carta de Uso del Suelo y Vegetación. Superficie Total por Distrito de Desarrollo Rural y Municipio." (Accessed 14 March 2008), http://www.oeidrus-bcs.gob.mx/Info_dependencias/INEGI/UsodeSuelo-BCS.pdf.

Macías-Zamora, R., A. L. Vidaurri-Sotelo, and H. Santana-Hernández. 1994. "Analysis of the tendency of catch per unit effort in the Mexican Pacific sail fishery." *Ciencias Marinas* 20(3): 393-408.

Ochoa, Felipe y Asociados, S.C. 2004. "Estudios integrados sobre la evolución, situación actual y perspectivas económicas y sociales, así como para la definición de un Plan de Crecimiento Ordenado para el Municipio de los Cabos, BCS del Proyecto Los Cabos 2025." Executive version.

Oficina Estatal para el Desarrollo Rural Sustentable de la Secretaría de Promoción y Desarrollo Económico de BCS. Interview carried out in 2009.

Orduña Luna, F. 2009. "Agroturismo: Una opción innovadora en la producción pecuaria." Paper presented at III Jornada de Desarrollo Rural, Huesca, Spain.

Pattullo, Polly. 1996. *Last Resorts: The Cost of Tourism in The Caribbean*. London: Cassell.

Productores Orgánicos del Cabo, Sociedad de Solidaridad Social, de Responsabilidad Limitada de Capital Variable, San José del Cabo, Baja California Sur. Interviews carried out in 2007 and 2008.

Ruiz Chávez, O. 2008. "Turismo: Factor de desarrollo y competitividad en México." Working paper 46. México, DF: Centro de Estudios Sociales y de Opinión Pública.

Secretaría de Agricultura, Ganadería, Desarrollo Rural, Pesca y Alimentación (SAGARPA). 2003. "Distrito de Desarrollo Rural Los Cabos. Información agrícola." México: SAGARPA, Delegación Baja California Sur. (Accessed 14 March 2008), http://www.sagarpa.gob.mx/dlg/bajacaliforniasur/Informacion/Distritos/DDR04/DatosGralAgr.htm.

Secretaría de Agricultura, Ganadería, Desarrollo Rural, Pesca y Alimentación (SAGARPA). 2008. "Producción pesquera 2008." *El Sudcaliforniano* (29 March 2009).

Secretaría de Agricultura, Ganadería, Desarrollo Rural, Pesca y Alimentación (SAGARPA). 2009. "Estadísticas. Servicio de Información Agroalimentaria y Pesquera." México, OIEDRUS, Baja California Sur. (Accessed 14 March 2008), http://www.oeidrus-bcs.gob.mx/.

Secretaría de Comunicaciones y Transportes (SCT). 2004. Programa de Gran Visión de Desarrollo Litoral (PRODELI), Estado de Baja California Sur, Propuesta de PRORED, 15 December.

Secretaría de Medio Ambiente y Recursos Naturales (SEMARNAT). 2005. Ordenamiento ecológico marino del golfo de California. Recuento y estado actual.

Secretaría de Turismo (SECTUR). 2002. "Comportamiento y tendencias de la pesca deportivo-recreativa en México." México, DF: SECTUR.

Southwick, Rob, Russell Nelson, and José Antonio Arean Martínez. 2008. *The Economic Contributions of Anglers to the Los Cabos Economy.* Commissioned by the Billfish Foundation. Southwick Associates, Inc., Fernandina Beach, FL; Nelson Resources Consulting, Inc., Oakland Park, FL; and FIRMUS Consulting, Mexico City.

Tyrrell, T., and R. Johnston. 2001. "A Framework for Assessing Direct Economic Impacts of Tourism Events: Distinguishing Origins, Destinations, and Causes of Expenditures." *Journal of Travel Research* 40 (1): 94–100.

Valdés, L., R. Aza, J. Baños, E. Torres, and E. del Valle. 2008). "Evaluación del impacto económico del turismo a nivel regional. El caso de Asturias" Paper presented at the Conocimiento como valor diferencial de los destinos turísticos International Tourism Conference, Málaga, Spain, 29–31 October. (Accessed 20 December 2009), http://www.iafet.com/subidas/documentos/sesion3/sesion3_11_completo_PM.pdf.

West, G. R., and A. Gamage. 2001. "Macro Effects of Tourism in Victoria, Australia: A Nonlinear Input-Output Approach." *Journal of Travel Research* 40 (1): 101–109.

Wilson, T. D. 2004. "The Impact of Tourism in Latin America." *Latin American Perspectives* 35 (3): 3–20.

Part IV.
Government and Quality of Life

18

Public Administration and Government in the Municipality of Los Cabos

*J. Antonio Martínez de la Torre
and Lizzeth Aguirre Osuna*

THE ORIGINS OF THE MUNICIPALITY OF LOS CABOS

The site of the municipal seat, before being called San José del Cabo, was designated by the Pericú as "Anuiti." It was later named San Bernabé by Sebastián Vizcaíno who arrived there for the first time on the day of this saint on July 11, 1602. A mission was founded there in 1730 by the Jesuit Nicolás Tamaral, and named San José in honor of Don José de la Fuente Peña y Castrejón, Marquis of Villa Puente and benefactor of the colonization of the peninsula. Subsequently, the name of Los Cabos was added to differentiate it from San José de Comondú and due to the proximity to Cabo San Lucas. As for Cabo San Lucas, the Pericú called it "Yenecami" and afterward the missionaries named it Cabo San Lucas.

In 1917, the governor of the Federal District, Lacroix Rovirrosa, issued a circular that established the constitutional reform that proclaimed the municipality free and as an autonomous entity. As a result, that same year a council was established that administered the municipality of San José del Cabo, in the municipal seat of the same name. In 1928, when the current state of Baja California Sur had the status of federal territory, the Organic Law of the Federal District and Federal Territories was reformed to abolish the regime of the free municipality, replacing them with political delegations. Remaining as political delegations in the territory of Baja California Sur were

Mulegé, Comondú, La Paz, Todos Santos, Santiago, and San José del Cabo.

In 1971, the free municipalities were legally reestablished in the federal territories. In 1972, three municipalities were created in the territory of Baja California Sur: Mulegé, Comondú, and La Paz, with their municipal heads in Santa Rosalía, Ciudad Constitución, and La Paz, respectively. Three years later, Congress granted statehood to the southern territories of Baja California and to Quintana Roo so that by 1975, the first constitutional governor of the Free and Sovereign State of Baja California Sur assumed office.

In 1981, the state legislature approved the creation of the municipality of Los Cabos and, by 1982, the coat of arms that identifies it was adopted (Figure 1). It consists of four quadrants. The lower left contains the representation of the arrival of the missionaries to Baja California Sur lands inhabited by the Pericú indigenous groups and this speaks to the historical background of the founding of many towns in the region. The lower right portion portrays the economic activities of the municipality. The upper left reflects the support that has been given to the development of cultural values in the municipality. The upper right is Lieutenant José Antonio Mijares who was killed in 1847 in the battle at San José del Cabo against the U.S. invaders. At the center of the coat of arms is the famous Arch, which has brought fame and boosted tourism in the cities of Cabo San Lucas and San José del Cabo (Secretaría de Gobernación 1987).

Figure 1. Coat of Arms of the Municipality of Los Cabos

Table 1. Chronology of Historical Facts Prior to the Creation of the Current Municipality of Los Cabos

Year	Event
1730	Mission San José del Cabo was founded by visitor Father José Echeverría.
1768	California Jesuits departed Loreto on February 3 aboard a boat and 13 Franciscans arrived that same year to replace them.
1822	Fernando de la Toba declared the freedom of the territory, and Second Lieutenant José María Mata proclaimed and called for an oath to the Independence of Mexico, hoisting the Flag of the Three Guarantees.
1824	The first Constitution of independent Mexico was promulgated; it formed all of Baja California into a single territory, administered by a governor in Alta California and a Vice Governor in Loreto.
1847	In February, a group of Baja California Sur patriots led by Mauricio Castro met in Santa Anita, a town close to San José del Cabo, attacking the U.S. invaders. The organized forces in San José del Cabo were directed by José Matías Moreno, Vicente Mejía, and José Antonio Mijares, navy lieutenant who arrived in Baja California with the patriotic desire to attack the invaders and defend Mexico.
1855	In Baja California, General José María Blancarte joined the Plan de Ayala, with the recognition of civil and military authorities of the territory.
1857	The Plan of Tacubaya was proclaimed, which was contrary to liberal principles of the Constitution of 1857.
1913	The revolutionary movement began supported by Manuel González and Pedro Orozco. Felix Ortega, with the flags of the Plan of Guadalupe, summoned the inhabitants of the district to take up arms.
1915	Ildefonso Green Ceseña fought for the constitutionalists together with Urbano Angulo and José Acevedo, expelling the *Villistas* toward the northern territory.
1917	The governor of the Federal District, Lacroix Rovirrosa, had a circular delivered to the municipal presidents of the district, which established the constitutional reform that proclaimed the free municipality as an autonomous entity.
1917	According to the provisions of the constitutional reform, the municipality of San José del Cabo was administered politically by a council.
1928	The Organic Law of the Federal District and Federal Territories is amended, which provided for the abolition of the internal regime of the free municipality, replacing it with government delegations.
1929	Remaining as political delegations were: Mulegé, Comondú, La Paz, Todos Santos, Santiago, and San José del Cabo.
1971	The free municipalities were reestablished in Baja California Sur.
1972	Three municipalities were established: Mulegé, Comondú, and La Paz, with municipal seats in Santa Rosalía, Ciudad Constitución, and La Paz, respectively.

Table 1. (continued)

Year	Event
1974	Congress granted statehood to the territories of Baja California Sur and Quintana Roo.
1975	The first Constitutional Governor of the Free and Sovereign State of Baja California Sur assumed office.
1981	The state legislature decreed the creation of the fourth municipality of the state: the municipality of Los Cabos.
1981	The first municipal council started its administration on January 1.

Source: Centro Estatal de Desarrollo Municipal del Gobierno del Estado de Baja California Sur 1997.

STRUCTURE AND FUNCTIONS OF THE MUNICIPAL ADMINISTRATION

The municipality of Los Cabos is made up of the municipal seat, which is the city of San José del Cabo, and four delegations: Cabo San Lucas, Miraflores, Santiago, and La Rivera. In addition, these have 33 subdelegations, with about 100 social welfare committees. Delegates are elected by referendum every three years.

Table 2. Municipal Administration of Los Cabos

Classification	Subdelegations
Municipal subdelegations of the municipal seat	El Zacatal I, El Rosarito, La Playa, Las Ánimas, Santa Rosa, San José Viejo, Las Veredas, Palo Escopeta, Santa Catarina, San Bernabé, San Felipe, Santa Anita, and Salto de Gavarín
Subdelegations of the municipal delegation of Cabo San Lucas	El Sauzal, La Candelaria, and San Vicente
Subdelegations of the municipal delegation of Miraflores	Caduaño, El Ranchito, La Boca de la Sierra, La Calabaza, Las Casitas, and Los Frailes
Subdelegations that depend on the municipal delegation of Santiago	Agua Caliente, Buena Vista, El Zacatal II, Las Cuevas, San Dionisio, and San Jorge
Subdelegations of the municipal delegation of La Ribera	Cabo Pulmo and Santa Cruz

Source: Authors.

The administrative structure of the council of Los Cabos does not differ substantially from the structure of the rest of the councils of the state, as shown in Figure 2.

Figure 2. Organizational Chart of the Administration of the Municipality of Los Cabos

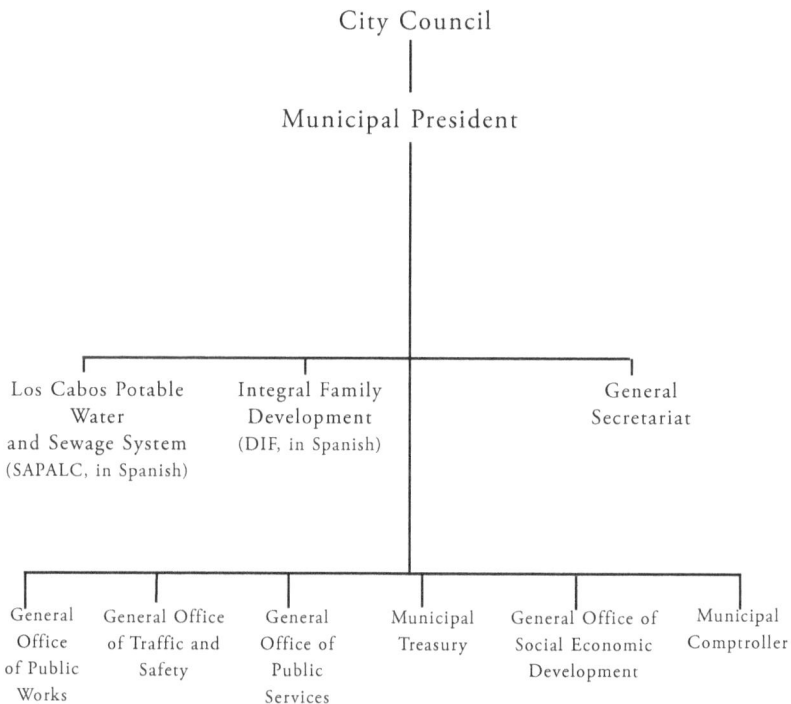

Source: Authors.

Table 3 Administration of the Municipality of Los Cabos

Main Positions	Municipal Government and City Council Commissions
Municipal president (mayor)	The municipal government comprises the municipal president (mayor), a trustee, the municipal treasurer, and 6 council members
Trustee	Governance Commission
8 Council members of relative majority	Treasury and Patrimony Commission
6 Council members of proportional representation	Human Settlements and Public Works Commission
Municipal general secretary	Public Services Commission
	Tourism Commission
Municipal treasurer	Development Commission
Municipal comptroller	Regulations Commission
Senior officer	Social Welfare Commission
4 General directors	Education and Culture Commission
	Ecology Commission
	Civil Protection Commission
	Transparency Commission

Source: H. XI Ayuntamiento de Los Cabos: www.loscabos.gob.mx.

The 10 municipal administrations from 1981 to the present were directed by the municipal presidents included in Table 4.

Table 4. Chronology of Municipal Presidents

Municipal President	Administration
Héctor Palacios Avilés	1981–1984
Francisco Palacios Ceseña	1984–1987
León Cota Collins	1987–1990
Manuel Salvador Castro Castro	1993–1996
Miguel Ángel Olachea Palacios	1996–1999
Narciso Agúndez Montaño	1999–2002
Ulises Omar Ceseña Montaño	2002–2005
Luis Armando Díaz	2005–2008
Oscar René Núñez Cosío	2008–2011
José Antonio Agúndez Montaño	2011–2014

The duties of the municipality of Los Cabos are established in the federal and state legal frameworks. Thus, the country's political Constitution states in Article 115 that "the municipalities, with the assistance of states, when necessary and as prescribed by law, will be responsible for the following public services:
- Potable water and sewage systems
- Public lighting
- Cleanup
- Markets and supply centers
- Cemeteries
- Slaughterhouses
- Streets, parks, and gardens
- Public safety and traffic
- Other that the local legislatures determine"

It is common practice for municipalities to assume other duties, in addition to those stipulated in Article 115 of the Constitution, such as in the case of Los Cabos:
- The promotion of economic activity, through the Department of Tourism, the Municipal Development Council, and the Directorate of Development
- Special attention to vulnerable groups through the Office of Rural Services and the Integral Family Development (Desarrollo Integral de la Familia–DIF) federal program for children
- Culture and sports through the Directorate of Social Welfare

These functions are legalized by Title I, Chapter Three of the Organic Law of the Municipal Public Administration of the State of Baja California Sur, in which the faculties and obligations of the city councils are set in more detail. It is important to note that Article 34 gives the municipality the authority to formulate, approve, and administer zoning and municipal urban development plans; participate in the creation and management of its land reserves; control and oversee land use in its jurisdictions; intervene in the regularization of urban land holdings; and participate in the creation and management of ecological areas and reserves. To that end, and in accordance with the objectives specified in the third paragraph of Article 27 of the political Constitution of Mexico, the city councils of the state's municipalities shall be able to issue regulations and administrative provisions as may be necessary.

As can be seen in the previous paragraph, Los Cabos, like all the country's municipalities, has authority over land use that can potentially serve as a powerful instrument to strengthen their support of economic development activities. Article 115 of the Constitution, in Section V, states that:

> The municipalities, in terms of related federal and state laws, are empowered to formulate, approve, and administer zoning and municipal urban development plans; participate in the creation and administration of their federal reserves; control and oversee land use in their territorial jurisdictions; intervene in the regularization of urban land holdings; grant building licenses and permits; and participate in the creation and management of ecological reserve areas.

However, the lack of resources and the lack of legal clarity regarding the apportionment of federal, state, and municipal competencies on land use, contribute to the municipalities not being able to fully use these powers for purposes of economic development and urban management. The fundamental public functions of the municipality of Los Cabos are now ruled by the 20 regulations that are shown in Table 5.

FINANCES OF THE MUNICIPALITY OF LOS CABOS

Vargas (2004) notes: "The viability of the municipal institution is linked to its economic strength and, frankly, this is where the municipalities of Baja California Sur have their Achilles heel. The origin of most of the problems they currently face is the weakness of municipal finances." The country's municipalities show a strong dependence on the fiscal resources they are granted by the federal government and the states. There has been progress in the legislation that grants greater autonomy to municipalities, such as the process of decentralization to the states for education, health, and public safety, as well as recent tax reforms that will allow states to appropriate a share of revenue they collect from small contributors (Borges 2004). These reforms decentralize resources from the federation to state governments that, in turn, centralize the distribution of fiscal resources to the municipalities. However, the federation still gets 97% of the total tax collected in Mexico, while the share for states and municipalities is 1.3% and 1.4%, respectively (Borges 2004).

Table 5. Municipal Regulations

Regulation	Bulletin	Date Issued
1. Regulation for municipal acquisitions	8	Mar 10, 1995
2. Regulation for carrying out non-established business and trades in public thoroughfares	1	Jan 10, 1994
3. Internal regulation for the city council	9	Mar 10, 1992
4. Regulation for the collection of the special contribution of 1.3%	15	Aug 30, 1991
5. Regulation of hygiene and cleanliness	23	Nov 10, 1990
6. Regulation for the operation of promotion and sale of condominiums and timeshare properties	38	Dec 31, 1989
7. Regulation for boxing and wrestling	28	Sept 30, 1988
8. Regulation for expert appraisals	19	Jul 20, 1986
9. Regulation for the neighborhood civic board	22	Jun 20, 1982
10. Regulation for the nomenclature commission	29	Sept 30, 1982
11. Police force and good government	27	Aug 20, 2000
12. Regulation for markets	26	Jul 20, 1981
13. Regulation for environmental protection	14	Apr 20, 1998
14. Regulation for recreation and entertainment	14	Apr 20, 1998
15. Regulation for civil security and prevention and control of fires and disasters	14	Apr 20, 1998
16. Regulation for Community Participation Committees	14	Apr 20, 1998
17. Regulation for safety standards and health measures in the construction industry	14	Apr 20, 1998
18. Regulation for urban image	55 BIS	Dec 31, 1999
19. Regulation for music workers	3	Jan 20, 2000
20. Regulation for Los Cabos Potable Water and Sewage System (Sistema de Agua Potable y Alcantarillado de Los Cabos–SAPALC)	38	Oct 10, 1996

In Los Cabos, as is common in the municipalities of the country, its own revenues depend in great measure on taxes related to the real estate activity, such as property taxes and the buying and selling of real estate. The provision of potable water and sewerage services also brings in income.

Public Revenue and Expenditures

Public revenues are regulated by the Treasury Law for the municipality of Los Cabos. This law was reformed significantly in 2007 (Congress of BCS, December 12, 2007). Among other reforms, seven articles were added, which refer mainly to surcharges and penalties for breach of municipal provisions.

Article 185 of the Treasury Law establishes tax incentives for the promotion of productive investment and job creation in the form of reductions in payments of property taxes; taxes on real estate acquisitions in relation to the taxes that are allocated exclusively for the purposes of the economic activity of the individual who will benefit; refund of fees for registration in the Public Registry, of Property, and Commerce of the constitutive deeds of corporations; and fee waivers for registration in the Public Registry of meeting minutes through which there is an agreement on increasing the social capital of partnerships, credit contracts, and statutes of foreign corporations. Reductions are also granted on payments of fees for construction permits and connection to potable water and sewer mains, and accreditation of the total property acquisition versus the fees of cooperation whose coverage would correspond to the investor for public works that the municipality carries out in those properties.

Article 186 states that the beneficiary subjects to receive tax incentives are the following: all those physical persons or corporations or economic units that have obtained favorable resolution to their request for these, in accordance with the procedure established in the Law on Economic Development of the State of Baja California Sur. So, it would be interesting to know the characteristics and amounts of tax incentives given thus far, firstly, to assess their importance in the collection and, secondly, to assess, albeit briefly, their results in terms of promoting investment and employment.

Figure 2 shows that public revenue (the same as public expenditures in accounting) for the municipality of Los Cabos grew at a slower pace than for the BCS group of municipalities. However, Figure 2 clearly shows that public revenue per capita grew faster in the municipality of Los Cabos than in the BCS group of municipalities. It is important to note that, accounting-wise, the total annual revenue must be equal to the total annual expenditures. Thus, these trends for public revenue are also applicable to public spending.

Figure 2. BCS and Los Cabos Public Revenue, 1993–2001

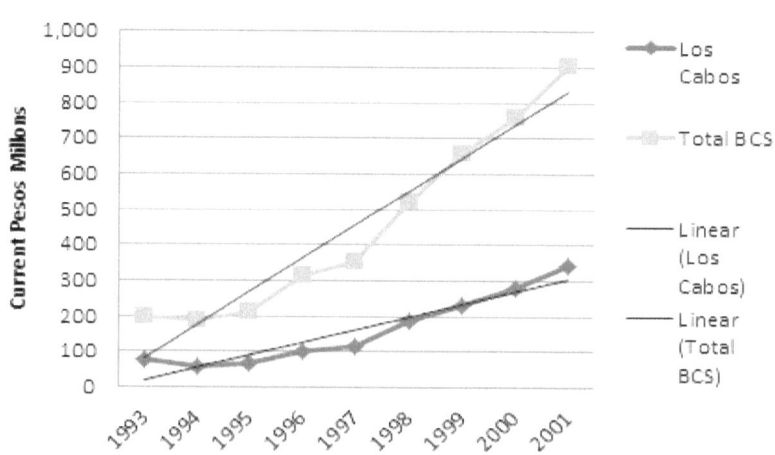

Source: Developed by authors with data from the Appendix's Table 1. INEGI, Municipal System Database, August 13, 2010.

Figure 3. BCS and Los Cabos Public Revenue Per Capita, 1995–2000

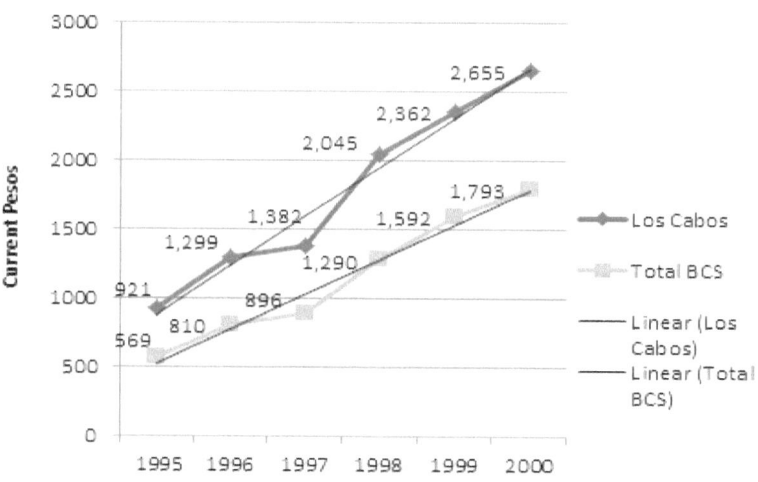

Source: Developed by authors with data from the Appendix's Table 2. INEGI, Municipal System Database, August 13, 2010, censuses for 1990, 1995, and 2000, and intercensus estimates by the authors.

The fact that Los Cabos public revenue and expenditures per capita increased at a rate notably higher than the BCS group of municipalities, only reflects the relatively greater dynamism of the economy and demographic growth of the municipality in relation to the rest of the state. During the period of nine years (1993–2001), in six of them, Los Cabos public revenue was higher than that of the municipality of La Paz, which has a 17% larger population, although not including the floating population of tourists, which is much higher in Los Cabos than in La Paz. The relative advantage of Los Cabos over the rest of the state's municipalities in the area of public revenue does not seem to be reflected in a better allocation of municipal public services.

Municipal Public Services

As part of the process of developing the 2008–2011 Municipal Development Plan, the Tenth City Council of Los Cabos conducted an exemplary program of public consultation, which is a rich source of information to learn about the condition of municipal public services and their problems, proposals from the community, and the policies of the government to improve those services. The plan indicated that the policies and actions intended to be carried out during the period of three years grouped into five guiding central themes. These are (1) social development, (2) sustainable development, (3) economic development, (4) institutional development, and (5) development within a safe surrounding. The body of the plan focused on the 10 guiding themes that were defined in the so-called Plan of 100. These themes are:
- Public safety
- Water
- Garbage and solid waste
- Infrastructure
- Tourism
- Public administration
- Land reserves
- Public transportation
- Environment
- Integral Family Development (Desarrollo Integral de la Familia–DIF), social development and sports

The municipality has experienced rapid population growth, with average annual growth rates of 9.2% during 1990–2000, and 8.1% for the 1990–2005 period. Although the growth rate has decreased in recent years, it is still higher than the national average. The municipality must not only provide public services to the more than 164,162 inhabitants recorded in 2005 (INEGI 2007), who lived in 43,473 houses; it should also consider the large floating tourist populations derived from more than 1.5 million visitors to the municipality each year.

PUBLIC SAFETY

The security personnel of the municipality of Los Cabos are comprised of 602 police officers: 458 preventive, 122 for traffic, and 22 more for businesses. Thus, it has 3.1 officers per thousand inhabitants. It also has a vehicle fleet of 90 units, seven motorcycles, and seven ATVs. The public safety system includes the division of the municipality into seven sectors (four in San José del Cabo and three in Cabo San Lucas), four headquarters, and 20 substations.

According to data from the General Office of Public Safety and Traffic, the majority of arrests are for excessive alcohol consumption and disturbing the peace, 39.8% and 13.88%, respectively, of the administrative offenses. With regard to the lower courts, various types of theft account for 35% and domestic violence for 14% of arrests. Possession of drugs is the greatest crime for the federal courts.

Citizens that were consulted through their petitions revealed two major problems in this area. One was the lack of training of the police and the other was the proliferation of small-scale drug dealing. Other problems that were identified as important by the citizens were, in order of importance:

- Greater insecurity in specific areas and neighborhoods
- Assaults on roads, robberies, graffiti, and so on
- Lack of crime prevention
- Inadequate response to the public
- Lack of prevention of road accidents (awareness, signs, etc.)
- Corruption within the municipal police
- Lack of citizen participation (campaigns, evaluation, proposals, awareness, reporting, etc.)
- Lack of municipal public safety personnel

With regard to citizen proposals, the professionalization of police agents, actions against small-scale drug dealing, and more support for safety in neighborhoods, were the most repeated proposals.

It is important to note that the *Cabeña* citizenry is aware of the need to strengthen prevention as a policy to reduce crime both in the field of administrative offenses and of the lower courts. In this sense, citizen representatives proposed that implementation of prevention programs for civic organizations, greater policing in neighborhoods, prevention campaigns in the media, and other measures should not be forgotten.

Given the lack of trust in the police authority that the municipality's citizens share with the rest of the country, the fact that the Los Cabos municipal administration (2005–2008) created the Internal Inspectorate Unit is considered a major breakthrough. Its objectives are to improve the performance of the police force, prevent abuses of authority, and avoid wrongdoings of public servants in acts that contravene the procedures or norms applicable to public safety. The Reception Department for Grievances and Complaints in the last year of the 2005–2008 government, responded to more than 200 complaints filed by citizens against members of the General Directorate of Public Safety and Municipal Transit.

Public Services

Garbage Collection

The collection of solid waste is carried out by a private company under contract to provide services for specific periods. It serves 95 neighborhoods in the four delegations, where coverage is 90%. San José del Cabo has 60% coverage. The average efficiency of the residential collection is 88.2%. Monthly, 14,232 tons of garbage and more than 3,500 tons of other solid waste are generated and collected, of which 5,400 tons are collected in San José del Cabo and 3,634 in Cabo San Lucas.

There are two controlled landfills for final disposal: Palo Escopeta, with an annual solid waste deposit of 6,000 tons, and Candelaria, with 7,500 tons, with a useful lifespan of only one and five years, respectively. The cleanup of beaches and streets is one of the most persistent demands of the *Cabeña* population.

Public perception about the quality of solid waste collection services is of interest. When asked whether vehicles and staff are sufficient to provide the service, the responses were grouped as follows: slightly more than 60.77% of citizens believe that there are not enough vehicles or equipment necessary to provide the garbage collection service, whereas 27.27% consider it is sufficient. The cleanup service is rated as bad by 43.30% of the townsfolk, 33.49% say it is good, and 11.48% indicate that it is very good. That is, 45% are satisfied with the service and 53% are dissatisfied.

The main suggestion of citizens to improve trash collection services advocates increasing cleanup campaigns in the municipality. The second most important is to raise awareness regarding care for the environment. The third recommendation is that route schedules should be established for the garbage collection vehicles. Other citizen proposals were to acquire more garbage collection trucks; place garbage cans on public thoroughfares; impose fines for throwing garbage in prohibited places; improve garbage collection teamwork; hold the city council responsible for garbage collection; and grant the collection service concession to a reasonable company.

Public Lighting

Public lighting in the municipality of Los Cabos includes 13,900 lights that cover 81% of the urban space. More than 70% of these lights are on the streets of Cabo San Lucas and San José del Cabo. Most of the population and the large tourist developments are located in these delegations. It is important to mention that there is great inequality in public lighting between the tourist areas that have good service and the neighborhoods that have poor service. This is an old problem that Los Cabos shares with the rest of the tourist towns in the country.

Municipal Slaughterhouses

The municipality has three slaughterhouses: one in San José del Cabo, one in Cabo San Lucas, and one in the delegation of Miraflores. According to the Municipal Development Plan, the three slaughterhouses meet Mexican sanitation regulations and follow standard procedures for providing meat products suitable for human consumption. However, in another section of this plan, public consultation demanded that another slaughterhouse be built. The monthly average of animals processed is 360, resulting in approximately 4,320 animals per year. Most of the animals butchered are cattle.

Public Works

There are 552.24 km of built roads in San José del Cabo and Cabo San Lucas. The enormous backlog for paving roads that existed has been largely abated, especially in the low-income neighborhoods. During the three years of the previous municipal administration, the paving of streets and avenues substantially increased, greatly improving the road network. In the previous triennium, the number of square meters paved in 2006 and 2007 increased by 114% in each of those years. A total of 98% of the projects were located in the delegations with large populations and tourism activities: San José del Cabo and Cabo San Lucas. Smaller delegations—La Ribera, Santiago, and Miraflores—have a significant backlog of roads to be paved.

The public consultation for the Municipal Development Plan identified the following as priorities: construction of alternate routes; paving of streets and roads; construction of recreational, sporting, and educational infrastructure; more bridges; more hospitals; placement of more signs and smart traffic lights; making the drainage system functional; and more wastewater treatment plants. With regard to the question on the quality of public works developed by the municipality, 62% said they considered it good and 28% judged it fair. That is, for 90% of the citizens, the quality of the infrastructure is from fair to good.

Water

The World Water Council and the Water Advisory Council indicate that there is a "water crisis" when the annual per capita availability is 2,000 to 2,500 cubic meters (m^3). There is a "chronic shortage" when availability is from 1,500 to 2,000 m^3. Moreover, the National Water Commission (Comisión Nacional del Agua–CONAGUA) recently published a list of Mexican cities that have water availability below 1,000 m^3 per inhabitant per year. Cities that stand out due to their low water availability per inhabitant are Mexico City, with 379 m^3;

La Paz, with 436 m³; and Los Cabos, with 701 m³. These cities are included in the country's 100 cities that in the next five years will experience a severe shortage of water (X Ayuntamiento de Los Cabos 2008).

As a result of its rapid population growth, Los Cabos faces an exponential increase in the demand for potable water. Currently, 54,087 persons make up the user registry of the Municipal Operating Agency of the Potable Water, Sewage, and Wastewater System of Los Cabos (Organismo Operador Municipal del Sistema de Agua Potable, Alcantarillado y Saneamiento–OOMSAPAS Los Cabos), representing a growth of approximately 50% as of May 2005: 47,414 are domestic users; 2,767 are commercial; 3,411 are multifamily residential; and 494 are industrial. Each water connection produces an average revenue of 324.51 pesos, which yields a total annual revenue of 210.3 million pesos (X Ayuntamiento de Los Cabos 2008).

The monthly production of potable water totals 24.35 million m³. Some 19.06% is lost through the distribution network, which is very low compared with national standards, so that 19.7 million m³ actually reach users. The global efficiency index is currently 72%, which in relation to national and state averages is very good. Thus, for example, in La Paz this index is only 36%. The global efficiency index is determined by the volume of water produced, invoiced, and payment collected, relating the physical efficiency (volume of water invoiced/volume of water produced) to the commercial efficiency (volume of water payment collected/volume of water invoiced). An important factor is that the water demand of hotels is considerable, but most of them are supplied potable water through municipal networks. A few hotels still have their own wells or desalination plants (X Ayuntamiento de Los Cabos 2008).

The municipality's main source of water supply is the San José del Cabo aquifer. It is the only supply source for this delegation and is also the main source for Cabo San Lucas and the tourist corridor between these two locations. Its supply capacity is 650 liters per second (lps), and the aquifer is in balance according to CONAGUA. The water extracted from the aquifer is transported to urban areas through two aqueducts nearly 50 km in length to Cabo San Lucas. Potable water and sanitary drainage networks provide 95% coverage. Further exploitation of this aquifer would endanger it. Therefore, it was decided that a desalination plant be installed in Cabo San Lucas; it produces 200 lps, or a total of 17,280 m³ per day (X Ayuntamiento de Los Cabos 2008). A Spanish company provided 30% of the cost of construction of the plant and has a 20-year concession to operate the facility. This arrangement and the cost to the municipality are a matter of public debate.

The desalination plant supplies about 115,000 inhabitants in the areas of Mesa Colorada, Las Palmas, Progreso, Tierra y Libertad, Rosa Delia, Los Cangrejos, Casa Blanca, and downtown Cabo San Lucas. In addition, private tourist developments have 25 desalination plants capable of producing over 8,000 m^3 per day (X Ayuntamiento de Los Cabos 2008).

Public perceptions about the potable water service provided by OOMSAPAS seem to be good. About 50% of citizens approve of the water service and just over 80% of citizens consider the service from fair to good (X Ayuntamiento de Los Cabos 2008).

In the state of Baja California Sur, there are nine public wastewater treatment plants that operate with activated sludge technology. Three are located in the municipality of Los Cabos; one in San José del Cabo; and two in Cabo San Lucas. Four additional plants are planned, which will be able to treat an additional 450 lps of wastewater. Furthermore, many hotels and some commercial establishments have treatment plants, which manage to clean up for reuse a total of 515 lps. Some examples of these private plants are those at BMO, Arenal, Country Club, Hotel Riu, Miramar, Cabo Real, Palmilla, Marquis, Westin Regina, Neptuno, Los Patios, Miraflores, Santiago, La Ribera, Villa Serena, El Tezal, Costco, and Home Depot, among others (X Ayuntamiento de Los Cabos 2008).

Tourism

The public consultation for the development plan convened hoteliers, service providers, entrepreneurs, representatives of civil society, and citizens in general. These participants indicated that the priorities for tourism in order of importance are the following:
1. Implement outreach campaigns in tourist areas
2. Provide greater security for tourists
3. Improve quality of tourism services
4. Ongoing training of staff that provides services to tourists (taxi drivers, hoteliers, shopkeepers, etc.)
5. Cleanup tourist areas, beaches, roads, streets, and so forth
6. Solve the problems of public transport services

7. Attention to the preservation of natural species
8. Periodic meetings with hoteliers and other merchants to reach agreements on the issue of tourism
9. Provide services to tourists with quality and warmth
10. Impart tourism-related subjects in school

These priorities suggest that the problems the municipality's tourism sector faces are essentially a reflection of the problems that public consultations generally highlighted for Los Cabos. The problem of public insecurity in the municipality stands out, which is addressed here for tourists. There is also overlap in the problems of outreach, garbage collection, and the problems and conflicts of public transport services that directly affect tourists.

Public Administration

The administrative services provided by the municipal government were well rated by the citizens during the consultation process for the development plan. The responses on the quality of service provided, either in general or by the treasury office, are shown in Table 6.

Table 6. Citizen Rating of Administrative Services

Rating Entity	Good	Fair	Bad
Municipal government	28.8%	54.2%	10.2%
Treasury	39.0%	42.0%	19.0%

Source: X Ayuntamiento de Los Cabos 2008.

With regard to the quality of services provided by the offices of Civil Registry and the Public Property Registry, the development plan does not report the evaluation of citizens but it does report the proposals to improve the services of those offices. This could be interpreted as the existence of significant problems in their services to the public. The proposals in the case of the Civil Registry office were: (1) train its staff, (2) improve delivery of services, (3) raise level of sensitivity among staff, and (4) ensure prompt attention. As for the office of the Public Registry of Property and Trade, members of the public proposed: (1) administrative modernization, (2) better delivery of services, (3) efficiency in service, and (4) training for staff.

Land Use and Holdings

The public consultation on land reserves for the drafting of the municipality's development plan shows clearly the presence of two serious problems: invasions of real estate, such as lots and residential constructions, and irregularity in land holdings. These problems are likely related and their common features are the slowness and inability of the appropriate authorities to prevent, avoid, and enforce appropriate sanctions on the invaders, especially the organizers of land invasions who repeatedly and with impunity continue to break the law.

During the second half of 2009, there were three high-profile cases of land invasion in Cabo San Lucas that ended in evictions by the police force. The first case is of the property "Las Margaritas III" invaded on August 6, 2009 (Sarabia 2009). The second land invasion was in the area called "Mesa Colorada," where 70 families were evicted on October 13 from land that they had invaded a few months earlier (Cabomil 2009). The third case is the invasion of the "Los Caracoles" housing development, where 68 houses were occupied illegally for seven months, until the invaders were evicted in mid-October.

Public Transportation

Public consultation on this issue convened transporters, entrepreneurs, leaders of organizations, and citizens in general. It is symptomatic of major problems in this area that 100% of participants agreed that public transportation should be completely modernized. When asked, "Do you think that the municipal government fulfills its duties adequately regarding public transportation?," 68% responded that it is not adequately fulfilling these duties while 32% said that it is complying properly.

Citizens also agreed to propose a comprehensive modernization program for public transportation. That program should include acquisition of new equipment; training of drivers; improving roads; properly maintaining transportation units; properly establishing routes, schedules, and stops; ending transportation monopolies; and providing greater oversight of the service.

Environment

In the consultation, representatives of organizations, entrepreneurs, groups, and associations related to environmental protection focused their proposals on two issues that they feel require priority attention in the municipality. The first issue concerns the need to promote a culture of care for the environment; the second relates to the conservation of the Estero de San José del Cabo Ecological Reserve.

With regard to the promotion of a culture of caring for the environment, campaigns were proposed with citizen participation for cleaning up garbage and against pollution from sewage. Proposals also included the formation of a civic committee as well as public awareness and recycling programs. A program for the management of the reserve is being proposed for the conservation of the Estero de San José del Cabo Ecological Reserve.

It is important to point out that the municipality has an ecological ordinance plan and is preparing a second phase at the sectorial level. Furthermore, the municipality is included within the National Clean Municipality Program for Certification (Programa Nacional de Municipio Limpio para la Certificación), both in the ecological ordinance plan and the National Clean Municipality Program (Plan Nacional de Municipio Limpio), which proved to be little known by the people consulted.

Social Development, Culture, and Sports

The persons consulted in the field of social development indicate concerns primarily for the protection of and assistance to vulnerable groups such as the elderly, single mothers, street children, and people with disabilities. One of the obvious shortcomings in the municipality is the lack of cultural activities and centers such as theaters and schools of arts. That is why many of the citizen proposals refer to the creation of theaters, expansion of the Casa de la Cultura, or the creation of classical dance groups.

As for sports, the construction of equipped sports facilities is suggested and, especially, the promotion of sports primarily among women. Sports are one of the most neglected activities in the country, and Los Cabos is no exception. Paradoxically, intensive promotion of sports should be a priority if only for being one of the main solutions to combat obesity because Baja California Sur has one of the highest obesity rates in a country that unfortunately has one of the highest obesity rates in the world. It is well known that obesity increases health problems and requires much greater national health expenditures.

CONCLUSIONS AND FINAL COMMENTS

The problems confronted by the administration of the municipality of Los Cabos are typical of Mexican tourist areas with rapid population and economic growth. Los Cabos also has as a common feature with other similar areas like Cancún and Ixtapa-Zihuatanejo, having received a great initial boost for getting under way by the National Trust Fund for Tourism Development (Fondo Nacional de Fomento al Turismo–FONATUR), in the form of construction of adequate basic infrastructure for tourism, as a fundamental activity of the program of Integrally Planned Tourism Centers of that agency.

In relation to the tourist areas of great dynamism, there is talk of a model or pattern of development of these areas in Mexico. In essence, dynamic resorts in the country, such as in Los Cabos, experience undercapitalized urban development where rapid population growth drives demand for public services beyond the capacity of local governments to meet them adequately. Thus, there is a permanent deficit in quantity and quality of paved roads, potable water, sewage services, green areas, and sports and cultural centers, among others.

The relatively high crime and the inefficiency of police and judicial administration are also characteristics of these areas. Therefore, as is the case of Los Cabos, the demand to end the high levels of public insecurity and small-scale drug dealing is reflected in opinion polls as a top priority.

Another characteristic of the development pattern of dynamic resorts in Mexico is the presence of great inequality in all aspects of social life. For example, the huge difference of the first world image of urban areas where the major hotels in Cabo San Lucas are located is dramatic, particularly when compared to the image of deteriorating low-income neighborhoods. The poverty belts of the city are particularly striking. Of course, this enormous difference in urban image also means great inequality in the provision of public services and infrastructure.

The serious problem of land invasions in Los Cabos is also a key element of the development pattern of dynamic resorts in the country. The recurrent invasions of land and housing units are the result of poverty and inequality, irregularity in land holdings, the ineffectiveness of the law, and the existence of worrying levels of public corruption. Invasions are a good example of what today is called "the crisis of governance in the management of development processes in underdeveloped countries and regions." In the discipline of economics, this translates into an uncertainty of private property ownership, which affects the amount and return on investment, without which there is no development or growth.

If regions such as the municipality of Los Cabos aspire to reach higher levels of sustainable development, then its society and government must find ways toward equity, justice, public safety, efficiency of public administration, and respect for private property and the natural environment.

REFERENCES

Borges Contreras, José. 2004. "Transformación del federalismo fiscal para fortalecer al municipio." *Panorama* 47 (January-March).

Cabomil. 2009. "Desalojan a 70 familias que pretendían invadir en Mesa Colorada." (Accessed 14 October 2009), http://www.cabomil.com.mx/esp/artman2/publish/Noticias/Desalojan_a_70_familias_que_pretend_an_invadir_en_Mesa_Colorada.php.

Centro Estatal de Desarrollo Municipal del Gobierno del Estado de Baja California Sur. 1997. "Monografía del Municipio de Los Cabos." La Paz, BCS.

Congreso de Baja California. 2004. Decreto 1445, La Paz, BCS, 12 December 2004.

Congreso del Estado de Baja California Sur. 1986. "Ley Orgánica de la Administración Pública Municipal del Estado de Baja California Sur." La Paz, BCS: Congreso del Estado de Baja California Sur.

Dirección Municipal de Comunicación Social de Los Cabos, BCS. http://websrv.loscabos.gob.mx/directorio/.

Gámez Vázquez, Sandino. 2008. "La desaladora de La Paz." http://www.scribd.com/doc/ 6451380/La-desaladora-de-La-Paz.

Instituto Nacional de Estadística, Geografía e Informática (INEGI). 2007. "Censo Económico, 2005." Aguascalientes, AGS: INEGI.

Secretaría de Gobernación, Centro Nacional de Estudios Municipales, Gobierno del Estado de Baja California Sur. 1987. "Los Municipios de Baja California Sur." *Colección: Enciclopedia de los Municipios de México*. México, DF: Talleres Gráficos de la Nación.

Sarabia, Porfirio. 2009. "Conato de invasión ¡hubo hasta balazos!" *El Sudcaliforniano* (7 August 2008), http://www.oem.com.mx/elsudcaliforniano/notas/n1275630.htm.

Vargas Aguiar, Mario. 2004. "El municipio: Su evolución en Baja California Sur." *Panorama* 47 (January-March).

X Ayuntamiento de Los Cabos. 2008. *Plan de Desarrollo Municipal, 2008–2011*. San José del Cabo, BCS: X Ayuntamiento de Los Cabos.

XI. H. Ayuntamiento de Los Cabos. Website 2011. www.loscabos.gob.mx.

APPENDIX

Table 1 [see p. 337 source Fig. 2]: BCS and Los Cabos Public Revenue, 1993–2001, in Current Pesos

Municipalities	1993	1994	1995	1996	1997	1998	2001
Comondú	33,399,000	37,892,128	38,909,269	64,792,000	46,144,000	79,491,995	111,382,873
Mulegé	23,534,000	22,735,000	26,524,000	37,060,000	45,561,000	68,126,659	104,292,111
La Paz	58,606,000	63,316,496	72,403,504	93,332,593	124,225,206	156,569,114	301,361,788
Loreto	8,081,000	11,192,496	10,369,000	16,758,000	20,245,000	29,534,142	46,277,658
Los Cabos	76,232,000	55,893,738	65,404,528	101,310,298	117,485,039	188,095,611	342,713,591
Total BCS	199,852,000	191,029,858	213,610,301	313,252,891	353,660,245	521,817,521	906,028,021

Source: INEGI, Sistema Municipal de Base de Datos (SIMBAD). August 13, 2010.

Table 2 [see p. 337 source Fig. 3]: BCS and Los Cabos Public Revenue Per Capita, 1995–2000, in Current Pesos

Municipalities	1995	1996	1997	1998	1999	2000
Comondú	589	982	710	1,232	1,422	1,497
Mulegé	577	806	990	1,481	2,033	1,854
La Paz	397	500	661	820	1,066	1,291
Loreto	1,038	1,611	1,892	2,685	3,059	3,822
Los Cabos	921	1,299	1,382	2,045	2,362	2,655
Total BCS	569	810	896	1,290	1,592	1,793

Source: Based on Chart 1, Censos de Población for the years 1990, 1995 and 2000, and census estimations.

19

Energy Demand and Renewable Energy in Los Cabos

Heidi Romero-Schmidt, Elio Lagunes-Díaz, Alan Sweedler, and Alfredo Ortega-Rubio

INTRODUCTION

Los Cabos has become the main tourism destination in the state of Baja California Sur (BCS) and one of the most attractive and exclusive in Mexico. On a national level, it is the beach destination with the greatest population growth rate. It also has the largest flow of travelers, showing a constant increase in tourism-related infrastructure and number of flights.

The importance and great potential of development for tourism, as well as the population growth, have created an explosive demand for housing and urban infrastructure. These have triggered a great pressure for urban land, public services, and electric infrastructure and energy. This chapter analyses the effects of this growth on energy demand and the alternatives and options to satisfy those requirements.

OVERVIEW

The Los Cabos area is located 220 km from La Paz, in the southernmost end of the Baja California peninsula. It has an area of 3,451.52 km^2 (1,332.64 Mile^2), with a population of 164,162 inhabitants, according to the 2005 official census (Fig. 1) (Ayuntamiento de Los Cabos 2008). The population in Los Cabos has shown an exponential increase, with annual mean growth rates of 9.2% and 8.1% for the 1996–2000 and 2001–2005 periods, respectively. These are very high numbers considering that by 2005 Mexico's annual natural population increase was less than 2% (Instituto Nacional de Estadística y Geografía–INEGI 2005). The fact that there are 47.6 inhabitants per km² makes Los Cabos the most densely populated municipality in all of Baja California Sur, since the average for the state is 7.0 inhabitants per km². These numbers are reflected more clearly in San José del Cabo and Cabo San Lucas, where population has multiplied nearly threefold in the last 10 years, adding up to 64.2% of the total population of the municipality (INEGI 2005). This growth, at an explosive and accelerated pace, has fostered a dramatic increase in demand for electricity by the industrial, commercial, residential, and tourist sectors in the state.

Figure 1. Population Growth in Los Cabos

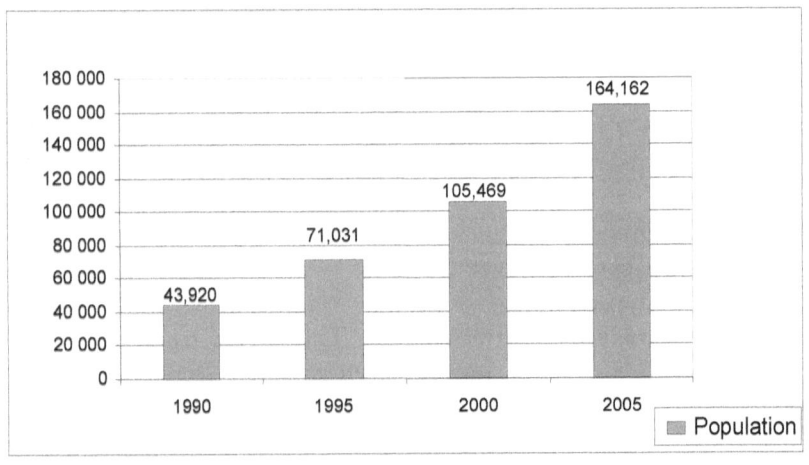

Source: INEGI, Censo de Población y Vivienda 2005.

The scarcity and depletion of groundwater resources and urban expansion in Los Cabos, La Paz, and Loreto, could make desalination—an energy intensive process—a primary source of fresh water in the near future. Of course, desalination is not the only option to obtain fresh water; other countries are now dealing with recycling and reuse of water, as well as available practices for water conservation and efficient use of fresh water.

Unfortunately, the tendency of public policies in La Paz, Loreto, and Los Cabos is to use desalination as the only future source of fresh water. So, energy supply is vital to achieve the competitive and sustainable development of the state; thus there is need for affordable prices, sufficient infrastructure, and reliability of supply (Escobar and Jiménez 2009).

Baja California Sur is not connected to the main national grid—the national electricity system. It has an isolated system with power generation based mainly on fossil fuels (Fig. 2). The state of Baja California, its northern neighbor, is also isolated from the rest of the country, and its grid is hundreds of miles away from that of BCS.

Figure 2. BCS Power Generation System

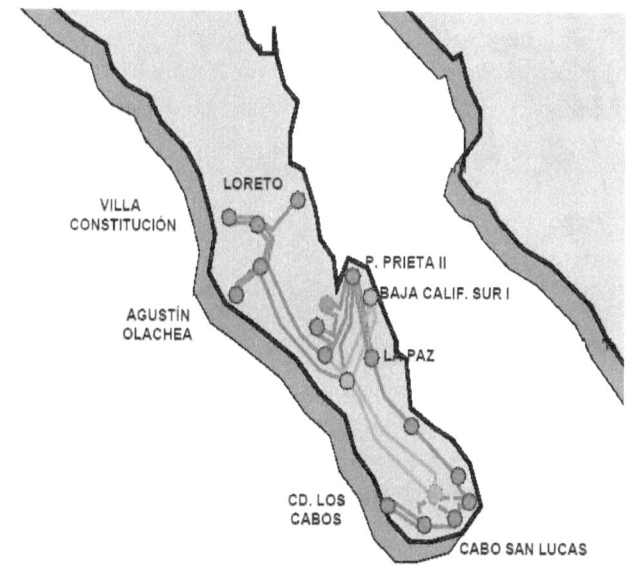

Source: CFE.

Power generation in BCS is done mainly through conventional steam power plants, which use *combustóleo* (refined heavy fuel oil). These plants generate about 45% of the power for the state. Internal combustion plants, fueled by a mixture of *combustóleo* and diesel, supply 47% of the grid demands; diesel-based turbogas technology plants contribute 7% of the power generation in BCS (Lagunes Díaz 2008).

Natural energy sources, such as petroleum, natural gas, and hydroelectric energy, are abundant in other regions of Mexico, but are not found within the state. There is no pipeline system that links BCS with the rest of Mexico, so fuels must be ferried by sea, making distribution costly.

The Federal Electricity Commission (Comisión Federal de Electricidad–CFE), Mexico's power supplier and authority, claims that 10 internal combustion and turbogas plants will be built in the next decade, replacing steam generation that uses heavy fuel oil. The CFE does not include the installation of renewable facilities in its plans.

The state has few areas with quality winds and has no perennial streams. Solar energy is mainly planed for water heating and to power rural areas. Due to the state's high dependency on fossil fuels, it is a challenge to accurately identify any options for achieving a sustainable energy system from the long-term perspective of economic development of the state. Solar energy is one of the best possibilities to address such a challenge, given that it is a large potential resource.

REGULATORY CONTEXT

According to Articles 27 and 28 of the Mexican Constitution, the CFE is the only company responsible for providing public electrical energy service in the country. However, in February 1999, reforms were enacted, granting private participation in electrical generation in the following forms: independent generation, cogeneration, small generation, self-supply, and export and import as a complement of public investment. This reform would contribute to the development of the economy and welfare of the population.

RECENT ACHIEVEMENTS IN ENERGY REGULATION IN MEXICO

The public sector has realized actions that prove its commitment to improve energy supply by modifying and creating policies of energy administration. It has:
- Created the environmental policy for the use of solar energy

- Signed the first electrical energy sales contract with a private company, which supplied the municipality of Santa Catarina, Nuevo León
- Established the following Mexican Official Standards (Normas Oficiales Mexicanas–NOMs): (1) protect the environment during the building, exploitation, and abandonment in the use of wind energy (in phase of approval); (2) determine the thermal performance and functionality of solar water heaters (in force); and (3) establish the criteria for the use of solar energy in new and remodeled facilities that require hot water for productive activities, determining that at least 30% of the energy demand for heating shall come from solar heaters (in force) (Torres and Gómez 2006)
- Issued the Law for the Sustainable Use of Energy
- Issued the Law for the Use of Renewable Energies and Financing of Energy Transition, November 2008. This law aims to govern the use of renewable energy sources (RES) and clean technologies for producing energy, as well as to establish the national strategy and instruments for financing the energy transition
- Issued the most recent NOM on June 19, 2009: the Regulation of the Law of Biofuels, published in the Official Journal of the Federation. This NOM seeks to modify the Interconnection Contract Model for self-supply with intermittent renewable energies by the Energy Regulatory Commission (Comisión Reguladora de Energía–CRE). It also aims to create a method for estimating and certifying the contribution in capacity of these sources to the energy grid

OTHER INITIATIVES

Other initiatives that have been undertaken include the following:
- Modification of the Law of Income Tax. It consists of a fiscal credit of 30% for investment in renewable generation systems to provide power for residential areas (Torres and Gómez 2006)
- Establishment of a special Law on Production and Services. It proposes to establish a special taxation of 0.5% on the disposition and import of electrical energy and to use the funds raised through this tax to encourage Renewable Energy Sources (RES) in the generation of power (Torres and Gómez 2006)

- Modification of the Federal Law of Rights. It seeks payment for the right to use fossil fuels, in function of the carbon dioxide (CO_2) emissions generated in the combustion, under the principle of "pollute and pay." There would be different rates for liquid, solid, and natural gas fuels. The funds raised would also be used to promote the (RES)
- Development of policy with support from the International Bank for Development and the German Technical Cooperation (Deutsche Gesellschaft für Technische Zusammenarbeit–GTZ); the Energy Secretariat will perform feasibility studies for bio-ethanol and biodiesel. These analyses will function as a basis for the development of a Mexican policy in the subject of biofuel use for transport (Eckermann 2008)

The RES are the more attractive options within the National Energy Matrix. With the approved reforms, there is a legal framework that favors the development of these technologies in the country, since their potential for renewable generation is outstanding.

POWER DEMAND IN BCS

Electric energy consumption in 2007 was 1,577,983 MWh, distributed among 205,894 users from all sectors. The sales value was 2.241 million pesos (Table 1)

It is noteworthy that the industrial sector is the greatest consumer of electricity, followed closely by the residential sector. The industrial activity is represented mainly by medium-sized industries, that is, small welding companies, car service agencies, and local food processors. Only two of the industrial users fall within the "great industrial" rate. The commercial sector—including hotels and stores—is third in energy consumption, since BCS has a significant tourist activity. Indeed, it generates the highest energy related CO_2 emissions per capita for this activity in the nation, ahead of Quintana Roo, where Cancún is located (Fig. 3).

The annual growth rate of energy consumption for the state is forecast at about 7%, from 2005 to 2014, the highest rate in the country; the national average is 5.3% (Fig. 4).

Table 1. Users, Amount, and Economic Value of Energy Sales by Service Type in BCS, 2007

Type of Service	Users (a)	Consumption (Megawatts/Hour) (g)	Sales (Thousands of pesos) (g)
Domestic (b)	176,478	552,469	647,209
Public lighting (c)	1,034	36,767	68,306
Water pumping (d)	251	50,905	61,006
Agricultural (e)	1,087	136,827	54,571
Industrial (f)	2,076	618,597	964,347
Commercial	24,968	182,418	445,666
Total	205,894	1,577,983	2,241,104

(a) Number of contracts for energy supply, as of December 31, 2007; (b) Rate 5A; (c) Rate 6; (d) Rates: 9, 9M, 9CU, and 9N; (e) Rates: 2, 3, 7, OM, HM, H-MC, HS, H-SL, HT, and H-TL; and temporary services; (f) Rate: ? (g) Includes temporary contracts.
Sources: CFE, Baja California Division. Gerencia Divisional; Departamento de Estudios y Estadísticas, INEGI.

Figure 3. Commercial Sector Power-Related CO_2 Emissions

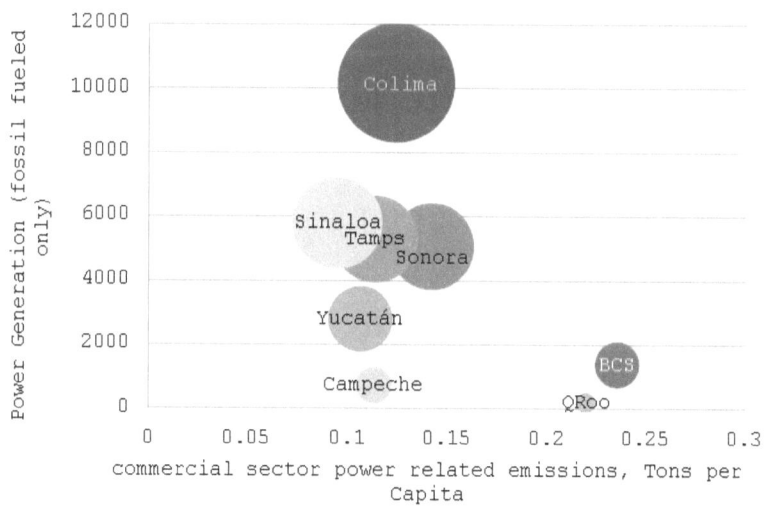

Note: size of bubble represents total emissions.

Figure 4. Expected Gross Maximum Demand Growth by Region

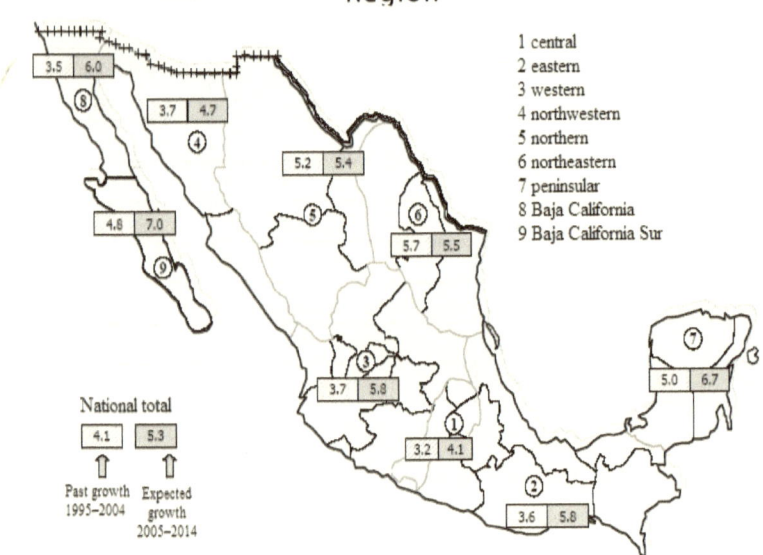

Note: Does not include self-supply and exportation.
Source: Bolívar-Villagómez 2005.

ALTERNATE RESOURCES IN THE STATE

Currently, the CFE operates a hybrid generating plant in San Juanico, BCS, integrated with 17 kW from photovoltaic cells, 100 kW from windmills, and a diesel generator with 80 kW capacity (Torres and Gómez 2006). Among renewable energies, the geothermal field Tres Vírgenes, with 10 MW capacity, has significant input to the local grid. Solar and wind energy are widely used for rural power generation. A wind generator of 0.6 MW was installed in Guerrero Negro; it supplies energy to the salt industry (Lagunes Díaz 2008).

Renewable technologies supply a small share of the total power for the state, compared to 409 MW installed capacity of hydrocarbon-based plants. Renewable sources make up only about 2.68% of the total installed capacity. This is a very small portion, suggesting there is a large opportunity for growth of renewable resources.

ENERGY DEMAND AND SUPPLY IN LOS CABOS

The municipality of Los Cabos has the highest consumption of MWh in BCS (Table 2), despite the fact that it does not have the largest number of users. For instance, the La Paz per capita usage is approximately 1.32 MW, but for los Cabos, per capita usage is approximately 4.39 MW.

Table 2. Consumption by Municipality in BCS, by Sector (MWh) as of December 2007

Municipality	Domestic (a)	Public Lighting (b)	Water and Wastewater Pumping (c)	Agriculture (d)	Industrial and Services (e)	Total
La Paz	227,276	18,261	16,880	18,577	238,992	519,986
Los Cabos	226,277	9,069	17,719	2,518	464,992	720,575
Comondú	42,021	5,319	6,707	103,273	44,445	201,765
Loreto	19,537	1,369	4,276	0	13,841	39,023
Mulegé	37,357	2,749	5,323	12,459	38,746	96,634
State Total	552,468	36,767	50,905	136,827	801,016	1,577,983

(a) Rates: 1, 1A, 1B, 1C, 1D, 1E, 1F, and DAC; (b) Rate 5A; (c) Rate 6; (d) Rates: 9, 9M, 9CU, and 9N; (e) Rates: 2, 3, 7, OM, HM, H-MC, HS, H-SL, HT, and H-TL; includes temporary contracts.
Sources: CFE, División Baja California. Gerencia Divisional; Departamento de Estudios y Estadísticas, INEGI.

The tourism sector in BCS represents 50% of the state's gross domestic product (GDP). The most active region is Los Cabos, which comprises three sites: Cabo San Lucas, San José del Cabo, and the Los Cabos Corridor (Rowe et al. 2009). Nevertheless, Buena Vista, Santiago, and East Cape are now the most promoted sites for international tourism investments.

Table 3. Electrical Service Users by Municipality, by Sector, as of December 31, 2007

Municipality	Domestic (a)	Public Lighting (b)	Water and Wastewater Pumping (c)	Agriculture (d)	Industrial and Services (e)	Total
La Paz	73,394	503	63	238	10,165	84,363
Los Cabos	65,580	268	90	68	10,182	76,188
Comondú	18,664	96	45	628	3,289	22,722
Loreto	4,650	66	13	0	880	5,609
Mulegé	14,190	101	40	153	2,528	17,012
State Total	176,478	1,034	251	1,087	27,044	205,894

(a) Rates: 1, 1A, 1B, 1C, 1D, 1E, 1F, and DA; (b) Rate 5A; (c) Rate 6; (d) Rates: 9, 9M, 9CU, and 9N; (e) Rates: 2, 3, 7, OM, HM, H-MC, HS, H-SL, HT, and H-TL; includes temporary contracts.
Sources: CFE, División Baja California. Gerencia Divisional; Departamento de Estudios y Estadísticas INEGI

ELECTRIC ENERGY CONSUMPTION

Los Cabos has a total of 90 hotels, with 12,662 available rooms. Energy consumption is directly related to the rating of the hotel, as can be seen in Table 4.

Table 4. Annual Power Consumption by Hotel Rating inLos Cabos

Rating	No. of Hotels	No. of Rooms	KWh/Year	Real Index KWh/Room/Year
★	2	24	184,896	7,704
★★	4	507	6,629,515	13,076
★★★	16	576	9,475,891	16,451
★★★★	27	2,149	71,742,225	33,384
★★★★★	41	9,406	557,666,200	59,288
Total	90	12,662	879,770,586	-

Source: Adapted from Final report V 2.0–September 2008 (Rowe et al. 2009).

THERMAL ENERGY CONSUMPTION

With reference to fuel consumption, be it diesel, LP gas, or natural gas for water heating, this is proportional to the amount of water consumed by room. Table 5 shows the average thermal energy consumption by hotel rating in Los Cabos.

Table 5. Annual Thermal Energy Consumption by Hotel Rating

Los Cabos			Thermal Energy	
Rating	No. of Hotels	No. of Rooms	KWh/Year	Real Index KWh/Room/Year
★	2	24	304,304	12,679
★★	4	507	4,928,714	9,721
★★★	16	576	2,388,077	4,146
★★★★	27	2,149	9,721,373	4,524
★★★★★	41	9,406	15,457,129	1,643
Total	90	12,662	32,799,597	-

Source: Adapted from Final report V 2.0–September 2008 (Rowe et al. 2009).

RENEWABLE ENERGY POTENTIAL

Fossil fuels are the main cause of global warming. In order to reduce dependency on them as a main energy source, other options should be explored. A good choice would be to take advantage of solar energy and its diverse secondary expressions, such as wind, hydro, and biomass energy, the so-called renewable energies.

Solar irradiance implies an enormous potential. For example, the energy that Earth receives every 10 days is equivalent to all known reserves of crude oil, carbon, and gas (Kessel 2008; Poy 2007). The solar radiation that reaches the surface of the Earth during an hour amounts to the same energy consumed by all human activities in one year.

Mexico has one of the world's greatest indices of insolation, with an average of 5 kWh/(m^2d). Despite this, the solar energy used in Mexico is far below 1% of all energy consumption, including fossil hydrocarbons (Poy 2007). Although solar energy is plentiful and widely distributed, its exploitation implies concentration of the resource. Because of this, it is more costly than other types of energy. This, however, is not the case for water heating.

The exploitation of solar energy is done by means of two technologies: (1) photovoltaic, which converts solar energy into electricity through photoelectrical cells, usually based on silicon; and (2) solar thermal, which uses solar energy to heat fluids with the aid of solar collectors that focus sunbeams, heating fluids up to 100°C (flat type) or concentrators that focus onto a main tower, reaching up to 500°C (Torres and Gómez 2006).

Photovoltaic (PV) systems are currently feasible for sites that are away from the electrical grid. They are applicable to rural electrification and telephones, water pumping, and corrosion protection, among other uses. The investment and generation costs for PV systems range from US$3,500 to US$7,000 per installed KW and US$0.25 to US$0.5 per generated KWh. The investment cost for flat collectors is US$242 per installed square meter (SENER 2006; Farell 2008; Eckermann 2008). As long as solar PV generation remains so costly, really ambitious projects of solar energy cannot be developed. In addition, as long as tidal and wave energy does not pass the experimental development phase, it will be difficult for BCS to use a significant share of renewable resources to generate energy (Lagunes Díaz 2008). This is largely a matter of state policy and subsidies. Spain has very large PV and solar thermal projects, as does Germany, because of incentives in tariffs and subsidies. Mexico could do the same, if it chose to do so.

SOLAR ENERGY

Incoming solar radiation in Los Cabos ranges between 5.81 and 6.48 kWh/(m^{2}d) (Rowe et al. 2009; SWERA n.d.), which is above twice the average in the United States and is among the greatest in the world. In Los Cabos, some hotels have solar heating systems for swimming pools and tap water for rooms. For instance, the Hotel Presidente Intercontinental in San José del Cabo has had solar heaters since 1999. Currently, there are 400 collectors for 450 double suites, with a daily capacity of 72 M^3, to an annual average temperature of 57°C. This represents 90% savings in fuels. Sixty percent of the water is for tap use and 40% is for the swimming pool. This facility saves an average of seven hours of boiler activity, which consumes 70 liters of gas per hour, saving a total of 500 gas liters at a current price of $5 pesos per liter. When the hotel is at 40% to 45% occupation rate, boilers are not required. The solar equipment is used for the swimming pool only during the six coolest months in the year. This proves that solar thermal energy for heating water is cost effective for the Los Cabos tourism industry and could be expanded. With the reforms and fiscal stimulus to come, it is expected that this type of energy will gain more interest from construction companies and the government, since it represents savings in the long term.

WIND RESOURCES

Mexico has a huge wind power potential. Its coastal regions are the main sites identified for having high quality winds, specifically in the states of Baja California, Baja California Sur, Sonora, Oaxaca, and Yucatán. However, wind energy exploitation faces technical, economical, and financial limitations. On the one hand, its natural intermittency is a disadvantage against technologies that can maintain a continuous supply of power; on the other hand, its installation poses a costly initial investment (SENER 2006; Moscarella 2008). Another important limitation in Mexico is the lack of information on the wind resource. Support for the national mapping of the resource has been provided by international organizations and educational institutes (SENER 2006).

Energy generated from wind is well-developed and is cost effective in most places, with some subsidies. It can complement PV energy, since wind is sometimes strongest at night. Baja California is developing some ambitious wind projects (Moscarella 2008).

In BCS, the wind power plant that has functioned in Guerrero Negro since 1998 has a 600-kW capacity, it operates parallel to the diesel plant that serves the zone and one sole 44 m-diameter turbine with a tower 50 m high. The operation of the wind power plant could be enhanced with newer equipment and updated technologies.

In July 2009, the state government signed an agreement to use wind power for public lighting. This agreement authorized a private company to generate wind power, thus representing a monthly savings of $280,000 pesos for the local administration (Guadarrama 2009).

With regard to independent energy generators, the Law of Public Electricity Service defines a payment for capacity and a payment for energy supply. The wind projects, given their intermittent nature, do not meet the criteria for receiving the capacity payment; hence, the only income they may receive is the supply payment (SENER 2006).

The main advantage of wind power is that it is a source of clean and perennial energy. Its operation does not emit exhaust gases. Nonetheless, negative effects include impacts on the landscape and on birds, as well as noise pollution.

The main issue that hinders renewable generation in Mexico and BCS is the availability of fossil fuels, mostly oil. As long as the government provides oil at a relatively low cost, it will be difficult for renewables to compete. It should be pointed out that oil is a "mixed blessing."

Figure 5. Potential Areas for the Installation of Up to 5,000 MW of Wind Power

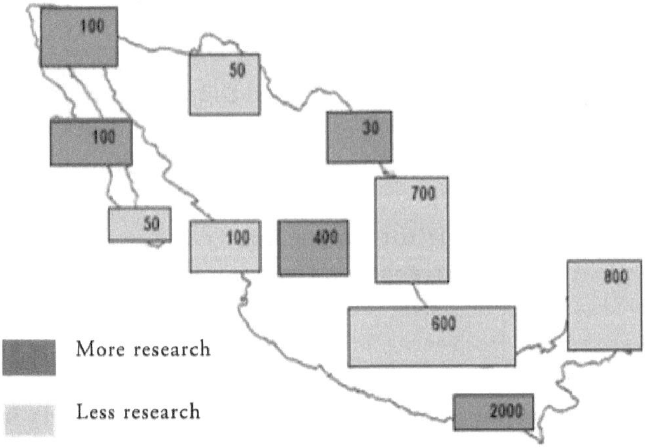

Source: Klapp et al. 2007.

OTHER RENEWABLE ENERGY SOURCES

Bioenergy

Biomass energy is used as a fuel through direct combustion or by its conversion to gaseous or liquid fuels, like biogas and biodiesel. The main biofuels are cane bagasse (used mainly for electric and thermal energy in the sugar industry) and firewood (used for heating and cooking).

Hot Water Springs

In a recent survey, researchers from the Institute of Geophysics (located a few meters away from the coast of the Baja California peninsula), detected a spring of hot water that can reach 100°C at shallow depth. Other hot springs, measuring three meters deep, have been located inland not far from the beach. Several hot springs have also been detected in the peninsular coast in Los Cabos, Santispac, Centavito, and Maneadero. The most outstanding case is in Los Cabos, where a temperature of 85°C was registered in an exploration well. There are plans for a desalination plant that will take advantage of this hot water. It is also possible that it will be used for electrical generation and, if its temperature is below 100°C, for thermal desalination.

A small binary cycle geothermal plant and 120 tons of hot water per hour could generate one MWh power. This energy would be enough for a reverse osmosis desalination plant to produce up to 5,000 m^3 of freshwater daily. A great advantage is that desalination can be continuous because it would work regardless of weather and time of day, all year round. Geothermal energy to produce freshwater does not cause the negative impacts that fossil fuels do.

City Solid Waste

The use of city solid waste as a source for electricity generation offers environmental and economic advantages. Solid waste should be considered an energy resource since, when deposited in landfills, it produces biogas that contains 50% methane. It can also be incinerated to produce steam to make electricity or gasified into a mixture that contains CO, H_2, and CH_4. Thus, the guidelines of the National Commission for Energy Conservation (Comisión Nacional para el Ahorro de Energía–CONAE) would be implemented to help reduce emissions of greenhouse gases and contribute to the sanitation of the landfill.

Bioenergía de Nuevo León, in Monterrey, is the first project in Mexico that uses biogas emitted by a landfill to generate power, with a capacity of 7 MW. The project was developed with partial aid from the Global Environment Facility (GEF), through the World Bank. The changes in regulations that are taking place in Mexico will permit projects of this nature to be carried out in more landfills. The Social Development Secretariat (Secretaría de Desarrollo

Social–SEDESOL) offers support for such projects, from the design of landfills to power generation. Currently, it has four projects in the pre-investment phase and it is collaborating in the development of six more (Torres and Gómez 2006).

ALTERNATIVES FOR ELECTRICITY GENERATION

Hybrid Systems

Mexico has limited experience with hybrid-generation systems that employ wind and solar generators. The CFE has carried out very few projects. Good incoming solar radiation and quality winds in some rural regions make projects of this nature feasible in Mexico (Duarte 2008).

Tidal Power

Mexico could have a great source of energy such as tides, ocean current, waves, thermal gradients, biomass, and others along its 11,000-km coastline. However, no systematic survey has been performed to evaluate this alternative (Huacuz Villamar 2008).

A RENEWABLE ENERGY SCENARIO FOR LOS CABOS

According to a 2008 market survey carried out in the region, most hotel managers in Los Cabos have heard about RES (Table 8). There is little knowledge, though, about the technologies required to produce energy from renewable sources and the monetary investment needed. Nevertheless, there is interest in learning more about these options. Figure 6 shows the main barriers for the implementation of RES technologies. Currently, the exploitation of these alternative sources in Los Cabos is limited to a few PV systems and solar water heaters (Rowe et al. 2009).

A potential 83.5% energy savings is calculated solely by substituting fuel with solar heating for water used in hotel rooms, laundries, kitchens, and so forth (Rowe et al. 2009). This is a very important point that needs to be stressed. A mean incoming solar radiation of 5.89 kWh/(m^{2}d), and an investment for acquisition and installation of solar water heaters of \$3,500 pesos/m^2, is a base price at the lower range, from which minimum investment in this field might be assumed (Rowe et al. 2009).

Table 6. Degree of RES Knowledge of Hotel Managers

Energy	Good	Regular	None
Photovoltaic	1	22	5
Wind	0	10	9
Solar Thermal	2	16	10
Biomass	0	5	23
Interest	6	11	0

Source: Rowe et al. 2009

Figure 6. Barriers to Implementation of RES Technologies

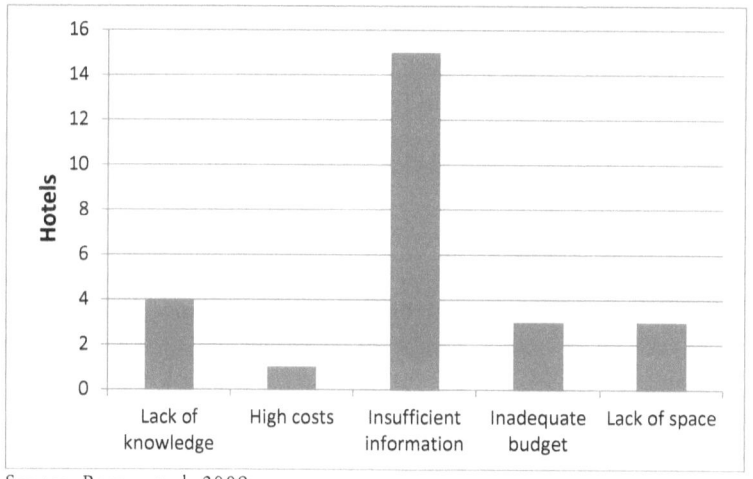

Source: Rowe, et al. 2009.

OPPORTUNITIES AND CHALLENGES: RECOMMENDATIONS

Electric Power

- Renewable energy investment represents a great business opportunity in Los Cabos, mainly in the hotel sector
- Energy consumption is proportional to hotel rating. The 3–5 star hotels have high use of thermal energy, with potential energy savings above 70%
- The energy bill represents up to 20% of operational costs for

hotels and, according to each establishment, poses the second or third highest budget expenditure in operating costs. A hotel that pays one million pesos every two months may reduce costs by 0.2 million pesos, increasing its profit and the possibility for new investments
- A great potential for energy savings lies in the improvement of the efficiency of HVAC systems, as well as in the investment in intelligent systems for the management of energy, insulation, water heating, and lighting (IPSE 2009)

Thermal and Electric Energy

- The potential for thermal and electric energy savings in the hotel industry is around 2,087 million kWh/year, which is about the annual production of two windfields, such as the CEMEX one in La Ventosa; such energy would have a value of US$1.1 million. This could be translated into energy savings of about 2,283 million pesos yearly, with an investment budget of 4,566 million pesos (ESD and IPSE n.d.)

Solar Water Heaters

- There is a great economic benefit in the use of solar water heaters (SWH). Solar energy heats the water, thus no electricity or gas is used
- Thermal energy substitution is about 2,388 million Megajoules (MJ)/year, equivalent to 416,827 oil barrels. If the solar water heating potential areas in the region were exploited, with an economic benefit of 729.1 million pesos per year, installation costs would be about 1,957.5 million pesos, with a return period of 2.7 years (ESD and IPSE n.d.)

CONCLUSION

According to the National Association of Solar Energy (Asociación Nacional de Energía Solar–ANES), for each five million square meters of installed solar water heating, in less than 10 years, the LP gas saved would amount to 15 million tons. This would prevent the emission of 30 million tons of CO_2, the main agent of the Greenhouse effect (Greenpeace 2006; Moscarella 2008).

The renewable energy sector offers a number of benefits beyond energy supply. Its massive application represents potential new sources of employment, including in the industrial process for production and installation. They also foster a cleaner environment and a more secure energy supply, among other benefits. The growth of Los Cabos means the opportunity to enact building codes for new tourism developments that include the use of renewable energy. Work is necessary in order to raise awareness; to build more capacity in public, private, and social organizations; to strengthen or create technological outreach centers; and to establish new financial schemes. In other words: a new national energy culture is needed. BCS, a place isolated from the national grid, has a geographical advantage for trying new technologies, as well as changing the way energy is delivered locally and, in the future, domestically and internationally (Abasta 2008).

REFERENCES

Abasta, Noemí. 2008. "Renewable Energy." *A-List International.* http://alist-international.com/features/index2.php?option=com_content&do_pdf=1&id=25.

Alonso, Gustavo. 2007. "Status of the Mexican Electricity Generation." Pp. 77–86 in *Towards a Cleaner Planet,* Jaime Klapp, Jorge L. Cervantes-Cota, and José Federico Chávez Alcalá, eds. New York: Springer.

Bolívar-Villagómez, Héctor. 2005. *Elementos para la evaluación de proyectos de inversión.* Mexico: UNAM.

Constitución Política de los Estados Unidos Mexicanos. http://constitucion.gob.mx.

Duarte, Esteban. 2008. "Energía Alternativa." *La voz de Michoacán.* http://www.vozdemichoacan.com.mx/columnas/duarte000024.html.

Eckermann, André. 2008. Energía Solar en México–Estado actual y perspectivas. German Renewable Energy Day, Power. Mex. 2008 Ministerio Federal Alemán de Economía. Ciudad de México, 14 de octubre del 2008. www.gtz.de/en/praxis/12538.html.

Energy for Sustainable Development (ESD) (Transénergie [France]) and Ingeniería y Proyectos de Sistemas Energéticos (IPSE [Mexico]). n.d. *Eficiencia energética y energía renovable en el sector hotelero.* Commissioned by Basel Agency for Sustainable Energy (BASE) and Comisión Nacional para el Uso Eficiente de la Energía (CONUEE), http://www.energy-base.org/fileadmin/template/BASE/Reports/Reporte_Ejecutivo.pdf.

Energy for Sustainable Development (ESD) (Transénergie [France]) and Ingeniería y Proyectos de Sistemas Energéticos (IPSE [Mexico]). 2009. *Análisis de mercado para la aplicación de tecnologías de energías renovables y eficiencia energética en hoteles en México, y mercado potencial para el sector financiero.* Commissioned by Basel Agency for Sustainable Energy (BASE) and Comisión Nacional para el Uso Eficiente de la Energía (CONUEE), http://www.energy-base.org/fileadmin/template/BASE/Reports/Estudio_de_Mercado_Mexico_-_Hoteles_y_EE.pdf.

Escobar Delgadillo, Jésica Lorena, and Jesús Salvador Jiménez Rivera. 2009. "Crisis económica, crisis energética y libre mercado." *Revista Digital Universitaria* 10 (5), http://www.revista.unam.mx/vol.10/num5/art29/int29-2.htm.

Farell, Adam. 2008. "Brief Explanation of Solar Hot Water Heaters." *Articlesbase.* http://www.articlesbase.com/online-business-articles/brief-explanation-of-solar-hot-water-heaters-315783.html.

Greenpeace México. 2006. *Calentadores solares: Energía renovable en tu hogar.* http://www.greenpeace.org/raw/content/mexico/prensa/reports/calentadores-solares-energ-a.pdf.

Guadarrama, Rafael H. 2009. "Firman convenio para acceder a fuente de energía alterna para alimentar alumbrado público en BCS." *Once Noticias.* http://noticias.arquired.com.mx/shwClipping.ared?kID=303e202c1e.

Holm, Dieter. 2005. "Un futuro para el mundo en desarrollo basada en las fuentes renovables de energía." White paper. International Solar Energy Society (ISES) Freiburg, Germany. http://whitepaper.ises.org.

Huacuz Villamar, Jorge M. 2008. "¿Qué ofrecen las energías renovables para el suministro nacional?" (April/June), http://www.iie.org.mx/boletin022008/divulga.pdf.

Instituto Nacional de Estadística y Geografía (INEGI). n.d. Estadísticas Económicas. http://www. inegi.gob.mx.

Instituto Nacional de Estadística y Geografía (INEGI). 2005. Censo de Población y Vivienda 2005. http://www.inegi.gob.mx.

Instituto Nacional para el Federalismo y el Desarrollo Municipal (INAFED). 2005. "Estado de Baja California Sur." *Enciclopedia de los Municipios de México.* Instituto Nacional para el Federalismo y el Desarrollo Municipal y Gobierno del Estado de Baja California Sur. (Cited 2009), http://www.e-local.gob.mx/wb2/ELOCAL/EMM_bajasur.

Kessel Martínez, Georgina. 2008. "Discurso de la Dra. Georgina Kessel Martínez." Thirty-second National Week of Solar Energy, 22 October, Mérida, Yucatán. http://www.conae.gob.mx/wb/CONAE/semana_nacional_de_energia_solar.

Klapp, Jaime, Jorge L. Cervantes-Cota, and José Federico Chávez Alcalá (Eds.). 2007. *Towards a Cleaner Planet: Energy for the Future.* New York: Springer.

Lagunes Díaz, Elio Guarionex. 2008. "Panorama eléctrico de Baja California Sur: Estado actual, proyecciones y optimización numérica del recurso eléctrico." Master's thesis, Centro de Investigaciones Biológicas del Noroeste, La Paz, BCS, México.

Moscarella B., John Paul. 2008. *ESCO's y proyectos de energía renovable.* Enviro-Pro, México 2008. (Cited [DATE]), http://www.conae.gob.mx/work/sites/CONAE/resources/LocalContent/6419/8/EscosECONERGY.pdf.

Poy Solano, Laura. 2007. "México llega tarde al desarrollo de energías renovables: CIE-UNAM." *La Jornada* (5 June).

Ríos Granados, Gabriela. n.d. *Incentivos fiscales por el uso de energías renovables: Caso de desalación de agua de mar y agua salobre.* http://www.bibliojuridica.org/libros/6/2524/12.pdf.

Rowe, Léonore, Hernando Romero Paredes Rubio, Arturo Romero Paredes Rubio, Bárbara Reveles González, Martina Chidiak, and Leonardo Stanley. 2009. *Análisis de mercado para la aplicación de tecnologías de energías renovables y eficiencia energética en hoteles en México, y mercado potencial para el sector financiero.* CONUEE and BASE.

Secretaría de Energía (SENER). 2006. Fuentes renovables de energía. http://www.sener.gob.mx/res/PE_y_DT/pe/FolletoERenMex-SENER-GTZ_ISBN.pdf.

Solar and Wind Energy Resource Assessment (SWERA). n.d. http://na.unep.net/swera/.

Sunway de México. La energía solar a su servicio. Hotel en los cabos. http://www.oficinaonline.com/sunwaymexico/equiporesidencial/.

Torres Roldán, Francisco, and Emmanuel Gómez Morales. 2006. Energías renovables para el desarrollo sustentable en México, Centro Mario Molina (SENER). http://www.gtz.de/de/dokumente/sp-en-energias-renovables-mexico-2006.pdf.

X Ayuntamiento de los Cabos. 2008. *Plan de Desarrollo Municipal 2008–2011*. México: Gobierno del Estado de BCS.

20

Local Development and Design of Social Assistance Strategies in the Municipality of Los Cabos

Angélica Montaño Armendáriz, Juan Carlos Pérez Concha, and Carolina Castro Corazón

INTRODUCTION

In recent years, attempts have been made to implement a "Local Development Model" in the municipalities of Baja California Sur, specifically in Los Cabos, based on a municipal strategic planning process. This process also includes the social, economic, political, and sustainability demands presented by the community, which were compiled in the Municipal Development Plan (MDP). Also considered is the inclusion of the municipality of Los Cabos in the *Agenda desde lo local*[1] (Agenda from the local perspective) since 2008.

This work is a summary of a research and outreach project developed between the Autonomous University of Baja California Sur (Universidad Autónoma de Baja California Sur–UABCS) and the

---

1. The *Agenda desde lo local* (Agenda from the local perspective) is a program and methodology developed since 2004 by Mexico's Ministry of the Interior through the National Institute for Federalism and Municipal Development (Instituto Nacional para el Federalismo y el Desarrollo Municipal–INAFED), to promote the integral development of the municipalities. The agenda highlights programs and actions of the three branches of government into areas of opportunity identified in a self-diagnosis and prioritized by the municipalities themselves according to the strategic objectives of their plans of government (Instituto Nacional para el Federalismo y el Desarrollo Municipal–INAFED 2008: 29). The agenda is composed of 39 indicators or public policy topics, broken down into 270 measurement parameters. The program was created to strengthen the management capabilities of local governments so they can carry out a strategic planning process for development.

System for Integral Family Development (Sistema para Desarrollo Integral de la Familia–SDIF) of the municipality of Los Cabos; the latter has provided the necessary information and fieldwork for the development of the research project. It should be noted that this document has as its foundation and framework the Development Plan of the System for Integral Family Development of Los Cabos, 2008–2011, as well as its organization and procedures manual. These documents also contribute to achieving the task of implementing the local municipal assistance programs through local development strategies.

The document has three parts:
1. The first part presents the theoretical, methodological, and conceptual aspects of the Local Economic Development (LED) Model, which will guide the analyses.
2. The second part includes the information gathered from fieldwork and documentary research; it specifically corresponds to the contextualization and diagnostic analyses of the municipality of Los Cabos.
3. The third stage summarizes the guidelines and strategies of the social assistance programs that have been implemented in the SDIF of the municipality of Los Cabos.

METHODOLOGICAL ELEMENTS FOR THE ARTICULATION BETWEEN LOCAL DEVELOPMENT AND LOCAL ASSISTANCE IN THE MUNICIPALITY OF LOS CABOS

General Aspects

In order to formulate the "Local Development Strategies" in the field of social development—specifically the SDIF social assistance programs in the municipality of Los Cabos—it is important to provide a brief analysis of the set of theoretical approaches related to local development issues. It is also important to analyze the most prominent methodological approaches related to the topic analyzed in this essay.

In a broad sense, the theory of local development began to take shape in the 1980s, and its application responds—basically—to the following circumstances:

Local Development and Design of Social Assistance Strategies

- The change in the training and integration of markets, nationally and internationally
- The effects of the globalization process of the world economy
- The emergence, growth, and economies of scale in new information and communications technologies
- The economic, social, cultural, technological, and environmental changes that have generated a new impetus to economic development, which are directed mainly toward the role played by local actors

In general, local development constitutes a new approach to development based and founded on the use of resources. After analyzing different authors who have studied and discussed the theme in-depth, it was found that the simplest—but precise—definition of this concept is formulated by Fernando Casanova (2004), who noted that:

> When we refer to local development, we understand a process in which a local community (or local government), maintaining its own identity and its territory, generates and strengthens its economic, social, and cultural dynamics, facilitating the articulation of each of these subsystems, achieving greater intervention and control between them.

According to Casanova (2004), to implement this model in order to improve the quality of life and welfare of the population in a given territory, the participation of actors, sectors, and forces that interact within limits of that territory is necessary, and they must have a common plan and project that combine factors such as the following:

- Generation of economic growth
- Social and cultural change
- Ecological sustainability
- Equity
- Spatial and territorial quality and balance
- Gender approach/focus

Based on Casanova's definition of local development, development is understood as a local condition within a country in which the genuine needs of the population are satisfied with the rational and sustainable use of natural resources and systems, based always on the respect for cultural aspects, social conditions, and human rights. This general definition of development includes specification that social groups have access to organizations and basic services like education, housing, health, and nutrition and that these lead to a better quality of life and social welfare (García 2004).

The analysis of the local development concept goes back to the beginning of the 1980s, when the notion of locality in the theory of development was introduced for the first time (Sanchis 1999). The development model was thus emerging from below or was a model of "Endogenous Local Development." According to the model, growth is carried out taking advantage of the set of human resources and materials from a given area. Citing Vázquez Barquero, Sanchis (1999) states that even if the model emerges as an alternative to the mentioned model (or of concentration/dissemination), both models show a high degree of compatibility, so it is necessary to incorporate both elements in the local development process. Thus, the local development model has the following characteristics (Sanchiz 1999):

- Land is an agent of social transformation and not simply a physical support for development: Land ranges from functional space to active space
- The potential development of an area depends on its own resources
- It offers a microeconomic perspective (and not macroeconomic) and of product (not sectoral), in addition to territorial (and not functional)
- It shows as relevant the prominent role and performance of public administration, especially the local one, but also the regional and central ones
- Joint action is necessary on the part of public managers and private agents through collective interaction

Local development is a development strategy that is based on and arises from the characteristics and singularities of each region and collectivity. From the aforementioned, it is presumed that it is the community (as development agent) that should determine the performance method and relevance of policies, programs, and actions to execute. Each local development model has its own style and, although it may be feasible to replicate, it must always be rebuilt depending on the characteristics of the new application site. Thus, the main objective of local development consists of promoting the achievement of a better quality of life for the population as a whole, from an economic, social, cultural, and environmental human rights perspective based strictly on governance, social capital development, and economic development (Pérez and Carrillo 2005).

According to the bibliography of different specialists in the field, there is a series of elements that characterize local development:
- Its local character: given that it circumscribes to a perfectly defined territory, especially municipal and, above all, sub-regional
- Its social dimension: since its actions are directed preferably toward the creation of jobs, giving priority to personal development
- Its institutional dimension (or administrative political dimension): by being controlled by the public administration or the government, it ensures the coordination (as well as design and management) of the various agents involved in their respective levels of operation
- Its economic dimension: since initiatives are carried out based on profitability and efficiency
- Its cooperative dimension: given the magnitude of the process, it requires the collaboration and involvement of multiple community agencies and representative of diverse types, but with a common denominator that is the development of society in a locality

In one way or another, all the elements referred to are incorporated into the 39 indicators of the *Agenda desde lo local* that is being implemented in Mexico through the INAFED and which, in turn, allows the definition of strategies for Local Economic Development (LED). The latter is a concept that applies to a variety of tools and methodological approaches that seek to strengthen the participation of local governments: the municipalities. Thus, the strategies focus on what are known as "endogenous" factors, which are (INAFED 2008):
- Local economic fabric
- Human, physical, material, and natural resources
- Local institutional framework
- Social organization, culture, and social agents

Conceptual Differences between Local Development and Traditional Development Policies

In order to better understand what characterizes local development (LD) with respect to the traditional development policies (TDPs) that have been applied in Latin America, particularly Mexico, it is useful to succinctly describe the main differences between the two concepts.

In the TDPs, the focus is through a vertical relationship from top to bottom; thus, decisions on policies and management of development programs come from above (with the federal government responsible). The difference is that in LD, projects are proposed from the territorial level (municipalities being the political-administrative body responsible for this field of action); that is, from bottom to top. This implies a decentralized and horizontal development administration among the various public and private actors. In general, the TDPs focus on sectoral aspects, giving priority to sectors that could be important in carrying forward national development plans, policies, and programs. As for LD, it promotes development beginning with the realities, needs, vocations, and advantages of a region, progressively promoting the use of economic potentials of a municipality.

The federal government manages resources, promotional programs, grants, and incentives of various kinds as mechanisms to boost economic activities. By contrast, local governments seek to generate the most ideal conditions for the development of economic activities located in, or with potential in, their region. In general, the LD approach generates the following advantages over the TDPs (Pinell 2004):

- At the social level, it strengthens society by generating or promoting social dialogue
- It contributes to transparency and accountability of public institutions (to be understood as the three levels of government in Mexico)
- At the economic level, by promoting economic activity in a territory, it allows for strategies to be adjusted and dependent upon the characteristics of each area (determination and use of the competitive advantage and resource potential)
- It creates jobs and improves their quality by actively involving the institutions that make up the social fabric in the territories (municipal)

Finally, it is worth noting that—for purposes of this work—the LD is understood as a process in which a local society, maintaining its own identity and territory, generates and strengthens its economic, social, and cultural dynamics, facilitating the articulation of each one of these subsystems. To carry out this process, it is essential to involve the community, agents, and sectors that interact within the limits of a given territory. They must have a common project that combines the generation of economic growth, equity, social change, ecological sustainability, a gender focus, spatial and land balance, with the aim of improving the quality of life and welfare of the population, which has been a guiding principle of public policy in recent years in the municipality of Los Cabos.

Diagnosis and Contextualization of the Municipality of Los Cabos

Geographical Characteristics of the State of Baja California Sur and the Municipality of Los Cabos

The state of Baja California Sur (BCS) is located in the northwestern region of the Mexican Republic. It has 2,705 km of coastline, which represent about 25% of the nation's total and constitute one of the state's major competitive advantages in terms of attracting tourists. Tourism is one of its main economic activities (INEGI 2005) due to its strategic geographic location, in particular, its relative proximity to the states of the southwestern United States. This U.S. region provides the majority of tourists visiting the state. In administrative terms, BCS is divided into five municipalities, in which 637,026 inhabitants reside (according to the 2010 census) (INEGI 2011b).

The municipality of Los Cabos is located on the southern tip of the Baja California peninsula. It has an area of 3,750 km², which represents 5.07% of the state's total area. It has a hot and dry climate, with maximum temperatures of 47°C and annual averages of 23°C. Thus, water and forest resources are limited, as is its rainfall. This results in sporadic streams that form only when there is heavy rainfall and hurricanes.

The municipality is divided into three regions: South Gulf, North of Los Cabos, and Cabo San Lucas-San José del Cabo. Basically, tourism development is concentrated in this last area, specifically in the so-called "San José del Cabo-Cabo San Lucas Tourist Corridor." Since 2008, however, the South Gulf area has begun to develop with megaprojects and marinas. An increase in tourism activities is projected in this area for the coming years, since it is estimated that the tourism corridor is close to reaching its limit regarding investments in new tourism development projects.

Demographics of the Municipality of Los Cabos

Los Cabos is the second largest municipality in terms of population, with 238,485 inhabitants, which represent 37.4% of the state's total. However, it should be noted that in 1995 Los Cabos included only 18.9% of the state population (INEGI 2011b). The density is 63.6 inhabitants per km², far more than the 8.6 inhabitants per km² that is the average for the state as a whole. It is important to note that this municipality has a high rate of population growth. According to INEGI, the number of inhabitants in Los Cabos increased by 126.1% between the 2000 and 2010 censuses (equivalent to 2.5 times the growth shown by BCS for the same period).

Population Growth

Figure 1 shows the rapid population growth between 1990 and 2010 when the number of inhabitants increased by 443% (INEGI 2011b). This high population growth is associated with the development and consolidation of the tourism development pole. This pole demands a great amount of labor (skilled and unskilled, which attracts a strong migratory flow) and services related to the demands of tourism, a situation that creates major local problems. To the resident population must be added a high (but undetermined) percentage of a floating population and transit tourism, which contributes to increased demand for public and social services. Los Cabos forms a typical tourist municipality with large marginalized urban areas that lack infrastructure.

Population by Age Groups

Demographic statistics of the National Institute of Statistics, Geography, and Information (Instituto Nacional de Estadística, Geografía e Informática—INEGI) provide the distribution of the population of Los Cabos by quinquennial age groups. This information is useful for the creation of public policies by population segment, since it allows the identification of the existing universe of children and youth populations, as well as adults of working age and groups of elderly people. In general, besides a slight predominance of

Table 1. Total Population by BCS Municipalities

Municipality	Total			Variation between 2000 and 2010	Percentage with regard to BCS
	2000	2005	2010		
Comundú	63,864	63,830	70,816	+ 10.9%	11.1%
Mulegé	45,989	52,743	59,114	+ 28.5%	9.3%
La Paz	196,907	219,596	251,871	+ 27.9%	39.5%
Los Cabos	105,469	164,162	238,487	+ 126.1%	37.4%
Loreto	11,812	11,839	16,738	+ 41.7%	2.6%
BCS	424,041	512,170	637,026	+ 50.2%	100%

Source: INEGI 2011b.

Table 2. Population Density by BCS Municipalities (Inhabitants per km^2)

Municipality	2000	2010
Comundú	3.5	3.9
Mulegé	1.4	1.8
La Paz	12.8	16.4
Los Cabos	28.1	63.6
Loreto	2.7	3.8
BCS	5.7	8.6

Source: Authors' calculations based on INEGI 2011b.

men over women, Los Cabos is inserted in a transition process of the population known as demographic dividend. It addresses the widening of the middle strata of the population pyramid (specifically in the 10-to 34-years age groups), but in Los Cabos a contraction is not seen in the early-age groups (under 9 years). This is when the portion of the population that is of working age is increasing. This phenomenon is generating growth in household formation and change in demand patterns of markets such as employment and housing, as well as in strategic sectors such as education and health.

Figure 1. Los Cabos: Demographic Growth between 1990 and 2010

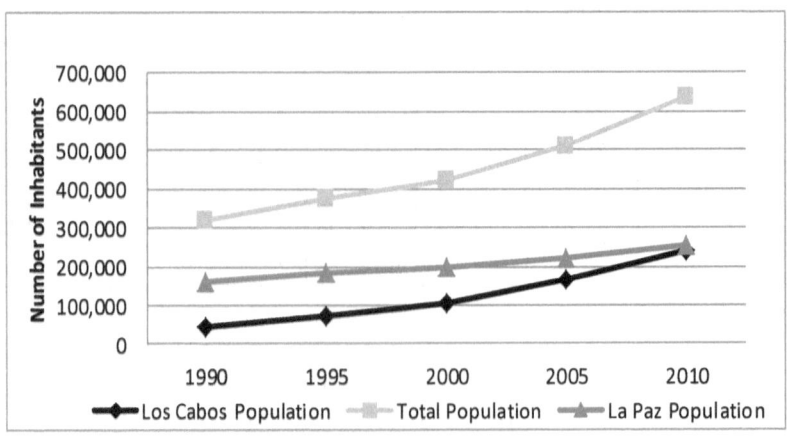

Source: Authors' calculations based on INEGI 2011b.

Table 3. Los Cabos Main Sectors and Number of Inhabitants

Location	1990	1995	2005
Cabo San Lucas centro	16,059	37,984	56,811
San José del Cabo centro	14,892	31,102	48,518
Colonia del Sol	-	10,159	27,057
Colonia Los Cangrejos	612	3,888	6,999
Colonia Las Palmas	Did not exist	3,451	Not available
Colonia San José Viejo	1,067	3,090	3,808
Colonia San Bernabé	522	1,281	2,090
La Ribera	974	1,527	1,757
Miraflores	1,187	1,325	1,389
Santiago	784	783	784
Buenavista	331	693	544

Source: X Ayuntamiento Constitucional de Los Cabos 2008.

Local Development and Design of Social Assistance Strategies

Table 4. Los Cabos: Population by Quinquennial Groups and Gender

Total Population by Age Range		Gender	
		Male	Female
Los Cabos	238,487	123,101	115,386
Age 0–4	26,146	13,189	12,957
Age 5–9	24,355	12,372	11,983
Age 10–14	21,650	11,123	10,527
Age 15–19	20,774	10,528	10,246
Age 20–24	22,903	11,707	11,196
Age 25–29	24,696	12,693	12,003
Age 30–34	23,792	12,299	11,493
Age 35–39	20,849	11,022	9,827
Age 40–44	15,089	8,156	6,933
Age 45–49	10,847	5,845	5,002
Age 50–54	7,728	4,082	3,646
Age 55–59	5,367	2,830	2,537
Age 60–64	3,740	1,963	1,777
Age 65–69	2,344	1,224	1,120
Age 70–74	1,357	686	671
Age 75–79	820	402	418
Age 80–84	446	202	244
Age 85–89	285	131	154
Age 90 and older	159	68	91
Not specified	5,140	2,579	2,561

Source: INEGI 2011b.

Social Impact of the Migratory Influx

Another characteristic of Los Cabos is the high migratory inflows attracted by the tourism sector growth and large investments in infrastructure that are being made in the area. According to the 2000 population census, 46.7% of the total population comes from other entities of the Mexican Republic; this increased to 54.3% in the 2010 census (INEGI 2011b). Thus, besides the problems of social exclusion generated by economic disparities associated with modern tourism developments, there are important social problems derived from an accelerated process of immigration of Mexican nationals whose diverse customs and habits represent a mosaic of the different regions of the nation. At the same time, this diversity creates a series of problems of family disintegration, child neglect or abuse, school dropouts, or early entry into the streets of children at risk. The last circumstance has become evident in Cabo San Lucas, the main tourist destination in Baja California Sur.

In this framework, characterized by deep and obvious social and economic contrasts, the SDIF in Los Cabos has carried out a significant administrative effort aiming to maximize and make efficient use of resources in order to provide social services with quality and professionalism. The purpose of SDIF is precisely to reduce social inequalities and support the population that finds itself in vulnerable conditions.

LOCAL DEVELOPMENT AND SOCIAL ASSISTANCE STRATEGIES IN THE MUNICIPALITY OF LOS CABOS

Administratively, the 2008–2011 Municipal Development Plan suggests that social assistance was one of the top priorities of the Los Cabos Tenth City Council Administration, hence "the municipal government, in coordination with the System for Integral Family Development, will implement actions aimed at supporting and favoring the most vulnerable population so that it obtains a better quality of life, and will promote social assistance policies that favor an integral family development" (X. Ayuntamiento Constitucional de Los Cabos 2008). In line with this objective, the Los Cabos SDIF defined two work strategies (SDIF Los Cabos 2008):

1. Social and community assistance through which the most urgent social needs of the target population are addressed.
2. Economic development of women: it is a strategy that tends to support or encourage the inclusion of women in productive activities in the area.

Overall, the Los Cabos SDIF is the public institution that serves families, groups, and people in vulnerable situations; that is, people

Local Development and Design of Social Assistance Strategies

who are at a disadvantage with respect to the rest of society and, therefore, combine several high-risk situations. Thus, the target populations of programs, projects, and services of this institution are:
- Children and teenagers in conditions of distress, risk, or vulnerability
- Women and youth in conditions of neglect, abuse, or disability
- Seniors who require care
- People with disabilities
- Victims of disasters
- Women who have aspirations and want to live better
- People who lack basic necessities for subsistence or a minimum of welfare

Social Assistance Strategic Programs

The Los Cabos SDIF, in the field of social assistance public policies, considers that: "social assistance should not be seen merely as a means of providing relief to the needs of a vulnerable population, but as an engine of development that, through training, education, and counseling, supports the population in order to maximize its self-management capabilities and incorporate it into human development" (SDIF Los Cabos 2008). Thus, the SDIF conceives social assistance as a set of actions to promote support, social integration, and healthy development of individuals, families, and population groups that are vulnerable or at risk because of their disadvantaged status, abandonment, and lack of physical, mental, legal, and social protection.

The vision of the DIF System of the Los Cabos Tenth City Council Administration is to professionalize services that are provided and to serve as the governing body of social assistance in the administrative structure of the municipality. Therefore, in this respect, its role is to regulate, manage, organize, and guarantee the provision of services with efficiency, equity, quality, and human warmth, attempting to link public and private assistance, always considering family as a strengthening nucleus of society.

The high population growth rate, coupled with steady immigration, promotes the existence of sectors and neighborhoods with important levels of marginality. This produces a wide diversity of demands for social assistance services. As a result, a strategic area was defined in the Los Cabos SDIF for the implementation of federal and state programs in the field of social assistance (SDIF Los Cabos 2008), such as:

- Nutritional care and improvement of the population in conditions of vulnerability, through the Federal Food Program Coordination
- Promotion of family and community development through the Development Centers Programs and the Social Promotion Program
- Protection and assistance to the population in distress, and to individuals and groups in vulnerable situations, which involve the Medical Social Assistance Program and the Basic Rehabilitation Unit
- Protection and advocacy of child and family, as well as care for mothers and adolescents at risk
- Creation of soup kitchens and regional meal programs, to provide food to children in schools located in neighborhoods with high levels of marginalization

Economic Development Strategies with a Gender Approach

Since women who are mothers are the axis around which the family develops, one of the SDIF strategies has been to more directly address the economic needs of women and support their incorporation into the workforce. The intent is to improve their family quality of life. Special attention is paid to women who are single mothers and/or heads of household, as this segment of the population is one of the priorities for care, given their high number in Los Cabos. Three lines of action are carried out in order to implement this strategy:

1. Coordination and management of productive investment projects and services with a gender approach. An undertaking of great relevance has been to encourage the incorporation of low-income women into economic development through the generation of their own jobs in order to contribute to improving the quality of life for their families. For this reason, an area was created in the SDIF organizational structure in Los Cabos that focused on the development and management of productive and service projects with a gender approach. Through this area, the intent is to encourage women to partake in productive projects through training courses to become "enterprising" women. The support of productive projects for women seeks to change the traditional social and political image of social

assistance. The aim is for the SDIF to become more actively involved in all activities related to the integral development of women and its effect on the family, especially for poor or more socially unprotected women. It should be noted that these projects are directed primarily at maximizing women's economic activity in the rural sector of Los Cabos, through the implementation of federal funding programs such as Productive Options; the Support Fund for the Micro, Small, and Medium Enterprises (Fondo de Apoyo para la Micro, Pequeña y Mediana Empresa–Fondo PYMES); the National Fund for Support of Solidarity Enterprises (Fondo Nacional de Apoyos para Empresas en Solidaridad–FONAES) of the Ministry of Economy; or the Women's Program in the Agrarian Sector (Programa de la Mujer en el Sector Agrario–PROMUSAG) of the Agrarian Reform Secretariat; among others. This action has contributed directly to the generation of productive jobs for women, thereby fostering improvement in their quality of life and increased self-esteem, while at the same time favoring development of the family.

2. Development and operation of child care facilities: paradoxically, in a municipality where men make up 52% of the population, women are heads of households in 16% of homes. It is the highest level in the state, based on estimates by the Los Cabos Tenth City Council's SDIF. This shows that the degree of family disintegration that exists in the Los Cabos municipality is high, as is the need for women to economically support their families while preserving the family unit, given the abandonment of men or because they are single mothers. At the same time, according to the 2000 census,[2] in Baja California Sur, 90% of total recorded households are "Family" type, but is only 85% in the municipality of Los Cabos. Also, the number of "Non Family" household types is 9% statewide and 14% in Los Cabos, where "Single Parent" households predominate and the head of household responsibility falls on women. Together with the aforementioned and also according to INEGI data, the child-woman ratio is 47% (this indicator is 40% at the state level), which contributes to increased pressure for child care facilities for children of working mothers.

Given these figures, and as a way to respond to the constant demands from working mothers and female heads of households who

---

2. Data produced by the 2000 census are used because INEGI had not published the 2010 census results at the time of concluding this essay.

lack social assistance services in other institutions, the Los Cabos SDIF has promoted and supported the installation, equipping, and operation of child care facilities in order to care for children under age six during their mothers' working hours. To this end, three actions were implemented:

- Establishing a day care center with the Los Cabos City Council own resources. The center provides this service to mothers who are self-employed or work in the private sector, with preference given to the segment of women who are heads of households and work, as well as having very low incomes
- The signing of cooperation agreements with governmental organizations and agencies in order to provide care to mothers who work in the municipality's public sector
- Negotiations with federal programs that address these types of problems. By joining the "Habitat Agenda," the municipality of Los Cabos negotiated the installation and operation of the "Community Child Care Centers," which operate in the low-income neighborhoods where this program is implemented. In this framework, two child care and development centers were built and put into operation with capacity for 100 children each. There are plans to put into operation the first SDIF child care facilities in rural areas (La Ribera and Santiago)

3. Incorporation of the Los Cabos SDIF into the "Habitat Agenda" to support development and training of women to join the labor market. In the framework of participatory planning for local development in Los Cabos, it was found that women are very interested in joining the workforce or contributing to their family income. This situation is corroborated by observing that, in the 40 job training courses offered by the SDIF and the Habitat Agenda, a total of 613 women have benefited in the first year. This is in addition to two courses for the formulation of productive projects and creation of microenterprises in order to facilitate the employment of women.

Women's economic needs are large and growing day by day in Los Cabos. As a result, the goal of the local development planning process on this issue is ambitious: to incorporate at least 600 women into the productive sector. In order to achieve this goal, it will be necessary to promote the formulation and management of projects for the creation of women's microenterprises, negotiate with federal and state agencies for resources to finance these investment projects, and promote investments in municipal infrastructure that favor the development of women and, consequently, their families. The process of incorporating low-income women into economic development is already under way, with a dynamic that no political or social process will be able to stop. From the theoretical point of view, the next step of this research process is the evaluation of social assistance strategies and, above all, measuring their impact on local development indicators measured in the *Agenda desde lo local* (Agenda from the local perspective), through which the municipality is also evaluated.

References

Casanova, F. 2004. *Desarrollo local, tejidos productivos y formación: Abordajes alternativos para la formación y el trabajo de los jóvenes.* Montevideo, Uruguay: Organización Internacional del Trabajo (Cinterfor/OIT).

Centro de Investigación y Docencia Económicas (CIDE). 2004. *Prácticas municipales exitosas.* México: CIDE, Instituto Federal de Acceso a la Información (IFAI), Universidad Autónoma de Querétaro, and Ford Foundation, Premio Gobierno y Gestión Local.

García, R. 2004. *Gestión local creativa: Experiencias innovadoras en México.* México, DF: Centro de Investigación y Docencia Económicas.

Instituto Nacional de Estadística, Geografía e Informática (INEGI). 2005. *XII censo general de población y vivienda 2000 y II conteo de población y vivienda 2005: Resultados definitivos.* (Accessed March 2009), www.inegi.org.mx.

Instituto Nacional de Estadística, Geografía e Informática (INEGI). 2011a. *México en cifras: Información nacional.* (Accessed March 2011), www.inegi.org.mx.

Instituto Nacional de Estadística, Geografía e Informática (INEGI). 2011b. *Censo de población y vivienda 2010: Tabulador del cuestionario básico.* (Accessed March 2011), www.censo2010.org.mx.

Instituto Nacional para el Federalismo y el Desarrollo Municipal (INAFED). 2008. *Agenda desde lo local: Descentralización estratégica para el desarrollo de lo local.* 4th Edition. México, DF: INAFED/Secretaría de Gobernación.

Pérez, B., and E. Carrillo. 2005. *Desarrollo local: Manual de uso.* 1st Edition. Spain: Federación Andaluza de Municipios y Provincias (FAMP) and ESIC Editorial.

Pinell, Pablo (consultant). 2004. *Perspectivas de la promoción del desarrollo local-municipal: El caso Boliviano.* Serie Documentos de Trabajo. Santa Cruz, Bolivia: Grupo Nacional de Trabajo para la Participación (GNTP) and LogoLink.

Sanchis, J. R. 1999. "Las estrategias de desarrollo local: aproximación metodológica desde una perspectiva socioeconómica e integral." *Revista de dirección, organización y administración de empresas* 21 (January): 147–160.

Secretaría de Turismo (SECTUR). 2000. "Estudio de gran visión del turismo en México: Perspectivas 2020." (Accessed March 2009), www.sectur.gob.mx/work/sites/sectur.

Sistema para el Desarrollo Integral de la Familia del X Ayuntamiento Constitucional de Los Cabos (SDIF Los Cabos). 2008. *Plan de Desarrollo y Programa Operativo del Sistema para el Desarrollo Integral de la Familia del X Ayuntamiento de Los Cabos 2008–2011.* Unedited. San José del Cabo, BCS, México.

X Ayuntamiento Constitucional de Los Cabos. 2008. *Plan de Desarrollo Municipal 2008–2011.* Unedited. San José del Cabo, BCS, México.

21

The Ecological Land Use Plan of the Municipality of Los Cabos

Oscar Arizpe C., J. L. Fermán, and Raúl Rodríguez

INTRODUCTION

Environmental land-use planning,[1] regardless of the name used in each country, for more than a decade has been considered internationally as one of the fundamental instruments in land-use planning for the development of those nations that aim to achieve sustainability. The main purpose of the environmental land-use planning is to guide development planning, for which it integrates and adapts approaches, methods, and procedures that allow the conversion of development policies into concrete actions to solve the specific problems experienced by the country.

A key part of the study of land-use planning is the incorporation of the interests of productive sectors and the impacts that their activities generate. These studies also identify intersectoral conflicts generated by the different values and perceptions that each sector has on the environment. The land use studies resolve, prevent, and minimize these environmental conflicts through interdisciplinary analysis, currently considered the basis for the regulation of productive activities in relation to land use suitability. In Mexico, according to the General Law of Ecological Equilibrium and Environmental

---

1. In Mexico, the usual term used is *ordenamiento ecológico del territorio*, which translates literally as ecological ordinance of the territory. However, the nearest equivalent term in use in English is "environmental land-use planning," which will be used in the English-language version of this essay.

Protection (LGEEPA), it is a planning process intended to assess and program land use and manage natural resources in order to achieve the proper use of resources and the preservation of nature (DOF 2003). As of January 28, 1988, with the enactment of LGEEPA, the regulation on matters of ecological planning at the local level is suggested, but it does not have a format to adhere to. Although the possibility of establishing coordination agreements among participating agencies is included, there were yet no tools for their realization. In 1989, the national development plan sets as a priority the care for the environment and the first local ecological land use plans emerged, one of the first being that of the municipality of Los Cabos, enacted in August 1995.

The advantages of this Los Cabos plan begin with its creation because, as a result, it surpasses many other municipalities in Mexico in terms of land-use planning. Its formal establishment aims to give the local government the necessary tools to develop environmental policies and management decisions in addition to contemplating in a comprehensive and analytical manner the local interests and detecting intersectoral conflicts.

Among its disadvantages is the one that refers to the environmental land use plan of the municipality of Los Cabos (Programa de Ordenamiento Ecológico Local del municipio de Los Cabos–POEL-MLC) that is in force. It was created within the ecological plan projects of regions with priority productive activities, and it turned out to be an environmental planning instrument intended for land use assessment and planning, but with a specific focus on the region's urban and tourism development (SEDESOL-INE 1995). This POEL-MLC was completed in January 1992; so, by the date of publication (1995), tourism and urban growth had already exceeded the planning capabilities and policies of this instrument. Coupled with this, various problems have emerged, such as rapid population growth, problems with land holdings, irregular settlements in the federal maritime-terrestrial area, and fragmentation of natural vegetation. The resulting impacts include deterioration of the coastline and water quality; high rates of erosion, sedimentation, and pollution; and loss of habitat for flora and fauna. These impacts not only modified the characteristics of the municipality, but also noticeably diminished the operating capacity of the POEL-MLC. Another shortcoming in this program that is still in force is that the information sources used in its development were from 1990 or before. As a result, most of these data are no longer current, both because of rapid changes in the municipality of Los Cabos and the amount of research generated since 1990.

The land use and management aspects of productive activities in the study area find themselves in a complex legal problem that hinders access among the users and the administration of the area. Therefore, the scope of the POEL-MLC, thus far, reinforces the municipality's environmental laws and serves as conceptual support, because urban growth has surpassed the plan's ability for direct control. Moreover, since 1996, there have been important reforms made in the federal legislation regarding the ecological land use plan.

In 2003, the decree of the LGEEPA regulation includes conceptual revolutions in the generation, maintenance, and updating of ecological plans and regulations. Noteworthy among these is that the local ecological plan will follow a constant updating process, according to the municipality's capacities. Additionally, for a decade, there have been powerful tools worldwide that are useful in different fields, such as Geographic Information Systems (GIS), which allow the programming and regulation of land, as well as the adaptability of developed models. This creates a platform for evaluation, management, and continuous updating for decision makers and, specifically in this case, for municipal authorities. The major limitation that the current POEL-MLC presents is the scale of work that is 1:250 000 (SEDESOL-INE 1995), since it represents a regional and not a local scale. Therefore, the existing environmental policy instrument is not very applicable in terms of programming and regulating land use in the municipality of Los Cabos.

Given the above, the rationale developed was to carry out, according to the law, the POEL-MLC's updating process with the most recent information. This information would have to consider the municipality's current problems, help identify important sectoral conflicts, and rethink land use planning and regulation. In addition, the intent would be to protect the environment and preserve, restore, and use in a sustainable manner the natural resources in the implementation of economic activities and those related to human settlements in the municipality of Los Cabos.

Ecological Land-Use Planning Program (2007–2009)

The process for preparing the most recent POEL-MLC proposal began with the formalization of the planning committee through the signing of the coordination agreement on May 29, 2006, in La Paz. This agreement establishes the commitment among the three levels of government to participate in a regional planning process that has as its main objective to promote the sustainable development of the municipality. Therefore, one of the main commitments set forth in the coordination agreement is the formation of the POEL-MLC committee, which was formally established on July 21, 2006. The committee is a representative body whose main purpose is to promote the genuine participation of all sectors involved in the region, which is why it is composed of individuals, organizations, and institutions from the public, private, and social sectors in the region. The committee has the duty to establish mechanisms for dialogue and agreements so that the POEL-MLC is legitimate and effectively addresses the environmental, economic, and social problems posed by the municipality's sustainable development, through a permanent process of democratic planning. According to the LGEEPA regulation (DOF 2003), this committee shall adapt to what the coordination agreement determines, and has the power to:

- Promote the articulation of the respective ecological land-use planning program with the overall ecological land-use planning program
- Verify that the ecological planning processes observe the provisions set forth in chapter two of the LGEEPA regulation
- Verify that the results of the ecological land-use planning process are registered in the environmental logbook when they meet the requirements established in the National Information Subsystem
- Suggest the modification of plans, programs, and sectoral actions in the study area and the signing of necessary agreements

The ecological land-use planning committee is made up of two bodies: the executive and technical. The first has representatives from the three levels of government and a representative from civil society. Its presidency is vested in the city council of the municipality of Los Cabos. The main responsibilities of the executive body are to make decisions in the process and ensure that the interests of the sectors represented on the committee are reflected in the ecological land-use planning program.

The technical body is made up of representatives of the three levels of government and representatives from the following sectors: tourism, conservation, business chambers, professional associations, academic, and communal lands *(ejidos)*. The main function of this body is to meet the technical and information needs of the executive body and thus facilitate its decision making.

In an effort to develop the study proposal for the POEL-MLC, a collaboration agreement was established in February 2007 between the city council of Los Cabos and the Autonomous University of Baja California Sur (Universidad Autónoma de Baja California Sur–UABCS). The overall objective of this study was to evaluate and propose the regulation of land use and economic activities that would effectively guide the planning and sustainable development of the municipality. The specific objectives were to:

1. Characterize the status of the natural, social, and economic components of the municipality of Los Cabos.
2. Produce a geographic information system that would assess any point in the region, considering the integration of all its factors and, therefore, serve as a basis for decision making for the region's sustainable development.
3. Prepare the analysis of the area to be planned, the land suitability models and maps, and sectoral interactions in the municipality.
4. Demarcate the areas of special attention for protection.
5. Examine the evolution of environmental conflicts from the production of behavior of natural, social, and economic variables that could influence the pattern of occupation in the municipality.
6. Propose a land use pattern that maximizes consensus among sectors, minimizes environmental conflicts, and favors the sustainable development of the municipality of Los Cabos.

For the development of the study objectives, a methodological sequence was proposed based on characterization, diagnosis, prognosis, and proposal phases (Fig. 1), which are defined in Articles 42 to 45 of the LGEEPA regulation in terms of the ecological land use plan (DOF 2003).

Figure 1. Ecological Land-Use Planning Methodology with Phases and Main Products

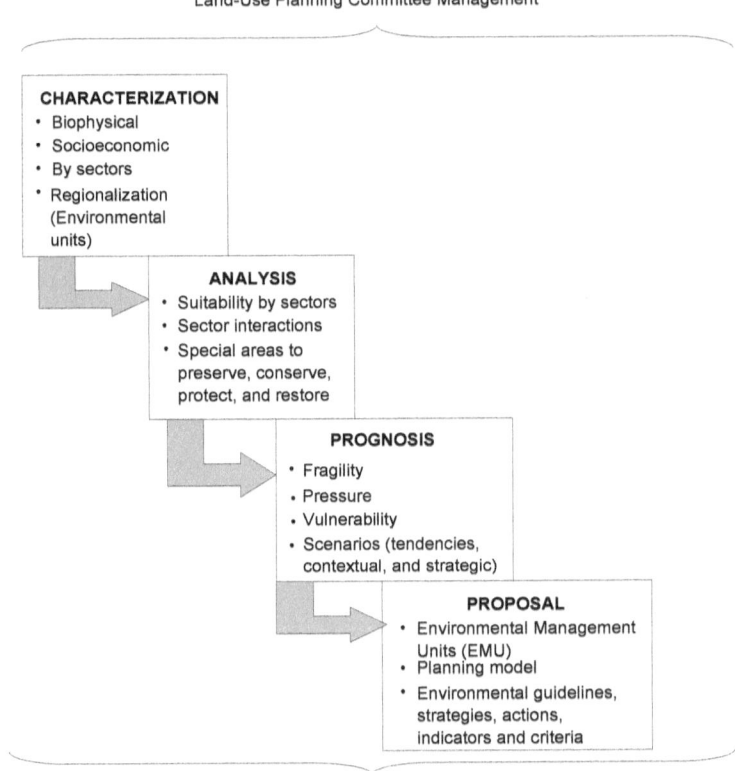

Source: SEMARNAT 2006a.

POEL-MC Phases

Characterization Phase

This section includes a description of the municipality of Los Cabos, including its physical, biological, and socioeconomic characteristics; a detailed description of the conservation, tourism, and agricultural/livestock sectors; and the regionalization of the study area. To this end, an analysis and integration of all existing data until 2007 were carried out, including biological, geological, and environmental information in general, as well as economic and social data for all areas of the municipality. The scale of analysis for this study, given in the terms of reference for local plans and specifically for the municipality of Los Cabos, is 1:50 000 for the entire municipality. However, a 1:20 000 scale is used for the region between Cabo Pulmo and Los Frailes in the East Cape area. This information also included an analysis of existing satellite imagery for the region, with special attention to land use and changes over time. Finally, surveys of georeferenced information were conducted in the field, verifying and adjusting as required due to the accuracy of the available records and other data.

Regionalization

According to existing information and its reliability, timeliness, and, above all, relevance in characterizing the municipality of Los Cabos, regionalization was the result of the characterization of the study area based on the six subbasins, five types of physiography, and three major types of vegetation in the municipality (Table 1).

Table 1. Classification System of Criteria and Codes Used for Regionalization

Level	Environment	System		Landscape		Unit	
		Surface Hydrology	Code	Physiography	Code	Vegetation	Code
Criteria	Terrestrial	1) Subbasin 3Aa	3Aa	1) Dunes	D	1) Shrub	S
		2) Subbasin 6Aa	6Aa	2) Slopes	S	2) Lowland forest	L
		3) Subbasin 6Ab	6Ab	3) Valleys	V		
		4) Subbasin 6Ac	6Ac	4) Hills	H		
		5) Subbasin 6Ad	6Ad	5) Sierras	S	3) Forest	F

Source: UABCS 2008.

The municipality was divided into 81 environmental units (EU) by integrating these elements into a geographical information system. These units have an identification code that is based on the classification system used. The resulting units were the raw material for the assessment of the suitability of the land, as well as the basis for subsequent development of environmental management units.

Diagnostic Phase

One of the key points of this phase was the development of so-called suitability (aptitude) models, which are the elements that can best represent the interests of the sectors involved in a region in relation to the use and/or conservation of natural resources. The suitability model for conservation, tourism, and agricultural/livestock sectors was established for the POEL-MLC. These three sectors were determined as the most important by the executive and technical bodies. The definition of the suitability of each sector was obtained by integrating environmental attributes. Some attributes were from the questionnaires of April 2007 to the different sectors. Others that could determine the best conditions for development of activities specific to each sector were from interviews with the sectors' key actors, published research, experts from academic institutions, and officials from the federal, state, and municipal governments. The result was a simple algorithm (direct sum of components) that structures a suitability index for each sector. The components of these indices had varying levels of importance in relation to the suitability of the sectors; thus, the model results in a weighted index, which was finally adjusted and discussed in detail in meetings with members of each sector.

Forecast Phase

The evolution of environmental conflicts was assessed in this phase starting with predicting the behavior of environmental attributes and social and economic variables that influence the land use pattern in the municipality of Los Cabos. In addition, an analysis was performed on the behavior and deterioration of the environmental attributes related to the suitability of the sectors. There are two main elements that define the behavior and deterioration of environmental attributes: the first is the population (both density as well as growth rate); the second is the transformed land use and its change with respect to natural space. Together, these two elements define the pressure tendency exerted on the environmental attributes and is the basis for the analysis of their behavior and deterioration.

The analysis of population growth was from the 2000 national census and the 2005 count, and was expressed in the degree of change and population density by environmental unit, which was a very important element for the construction of scenarios. These describe the likely evolution of environmental conflicts in the municipality. From the analysis of variables, the indices of fragility, pressure, and vulnerability; future development projects; and environmental policies were constructed.

Tendency Scenario

The tendency scenario was initially obtained based on increased societal pressure; behavior analysis in space and time of the pressure developed by productive sectors (tourism and agricultural/livestock suitability); by population (density and growth trend between 2000 and 2005); land use (density of transformed space); and the calculation of the pressure composite index (PI).

Contextual Scenario

This scenario was built by analyzing the spatial and temporal behavior of changes in the suitability of the tourism sector according to plans for future development of various projects (resorts, residential units, roads, and so forth) in the municipality. Information from these projects is presented as the pressure per project (PPP) from the proportion of projects that occupies an environmental unit. This is considered as a scenario of context, since it shows a potential pressure.

Strategic Scenario

This was based on the vulnerability analysis (relationship between pressure and the fragility of the biophysical environment) and expressed through the spatial determination of environmental policies.

The vulnerability index (VI) is integrated from the pressure (PI) and fragility (FI) indices (WRI 1995; Kaly et al. 1999; UNEP 2001; Turvey 2007) described previously. The vulnerability index spatially defines the areas where a greater demand is exerted on the most fragile natural resources.

VI = PI + FI
PI = Pressure Index
FI = Fragility Index (conservation sector suitability index)

Proposal Phase

The Ecological Land-Use Planning Program was developed during this phase. It is composed of two main elements:
- Ecological Land-Use Planning Model
- Ecological strategies

Ecological Land-Use Planning Model

The Ecological Land-Use Planning Model is the representation of the Environmental Management Units (EMU) in a geographic information system, with its respective policies, environmental guidelines, strategies, actions, indicators, and ecological criteria. An EMU is the minimum unit of the ecological ordinance area, which is assigned ecological guidelines and strategies. It also represents the strategic management unit that allows the minimization of environmental conflicts, maximizing the consensus among sectors regarding the use of land.

The following criteria were used to define the EMUs:
- Suitability by sector
- Predominant sectoral interactions (high and very high class)
- Areas of special attention for protection
- Vulnerability
- Natural Protected Areas
- Polygon of Urban Development Directing Plan (UDP) of San José del Cabo-Cabo San Lucas (Gobierno de BCS 1999)

Ecological Policies and Strategies

Description of each EMU was carried out with integrated information from the maps used for its definition and presented in tabular form with the following data:
- Suitability of sectors and level of suitability
- Sectors with high and very high interaction
- Areas of special attention for protection and their justification
- Level of fragility and pressure

Environmental policies are defined as a strategic scenario for each environmental unit, and were determined basically from the composite indexes of fragility (FI) and pressure (PI) (Table 2). The policies considered were: sustainable use, conservation, and preservation (SEMARNAT 2006a):

Table 2. Decision Matrix based on Fragility and Pressure to Assign the Environmental Policy to Each Environmental Unit

Fragility	Pressure	Environmental Policy
Very High	Very High	Preservation
Very High	High	
Very High	Medium	
Very High	High	
Very High	Low	
Very High	Low	
High	Very High	Conservation
High	High	
High	Medium	
High	Medium	
High	Low	
High	Low	
Medium	Very High	Sustainable Use
Medium	High	
Medium	Medium	
Medium	Medium	
Low	Medium	
Low	High	

Source: SEMARNAT 2006b.

- Sustainable use: environmental areas or units appropriate for the use and management of natural resources. Includes areas with current or potential use. Any use of natural resources must consider the principles of sustainability
- Conservation: is considered an intermediate environmental policy between sustainable use and preservation, so it applies to the area or environmental units in which productive activities or urban tracts of land can be developed, considering the protection of environmental services provided by natural resources
- Preservation: is assigned to areas or environmental units that maintain the relevant characteristics of the natural environment in order to ensure balance and continuity of evolutionary and ecological processes. Activities related to the protection of the biophysical components of ecosystems are promoted and productive activities or human settlements are limited

The ecological guideline that reflects the desired state of the EMU was defined taking into account the suitability, current land use, and environmental policy. For compliance with assigned ecological guidelines, ecological strategies were established for each EMU. The strategies represent the specific objectives presented to achieve the proposed ecological guidelines and are shaped by the actions that define the authorized, prohibited, or conditioned land uses. Environmental indicators, which were defined for each of the strategies, will allow the assessment of compliance with ecological guidelines and effectiveness of strategies in reducing environmental conflicts.

Finally, the ecological regulatory criteria were defined, which included general and specific aspects (for each production activity) that regulate the different land uses in the ordinance area of the municipality of Los Cabos.

Environmental Management Units and Assigned Policies

The results of EMUs, defined in the entire municipality, and the policies in each, are presented in the map within Figure 2. For each EMU, its location, extent, environmental policies, as well as ecological strategies, guidelines, and criteria, were developed and proposed in detail.

Table 3. Number of Environmental Management Units (EMU) by Environmental Policy, Area, and Percentage of Land that EMUs Occupy Overall

Environmental Policy	Number of EMUs	Area	
		Hectares	Percentage
Preservation	8	112,636.33	30
Conservation	13	178,528.69	48
Sustainable Use	12	84,268.46	22
Total	33	375,433.48	100

Source: UABCS 2008

It is important to point out that, as can be seen in the following example of EMU 1, details were provided regarding the actions that can be carried out and, where appropriate, be restricted for each of the strategies defined for each EMU. These topics were discussed at sectoral and plenary meetings the first months of 2008.

CURRENT STATUS

The results of the entire study were presented in analysis and discussion sessions to both the executive and technical bodies for the land use plan as well as to municipal officials, including members of the city council of Los Cabos, during March 2008. Additionally, the study was available for public consultation on the website of the Secretariat of Environment and Natural Resources (Secretaría de Medio Ambiente y Recursos Naturales–SEMARNAT) and in the specific environmental logbook (register) created for this purpose. Public presentations in several forums were also made. The full document—adjusted to the Ecological Land Use Model—and proposals for its implementation were submitted in compliance with the specifications of the city council, in late April 2008.

As of that date, the executive and technical bodies, together with the aforementioned authorities and members of the current city council of Los Cabos, are analyzing ways to carry out its eventual decree and implementation.

Figure 2. Ecological Land Use Model of the Municipality of Los Cabos

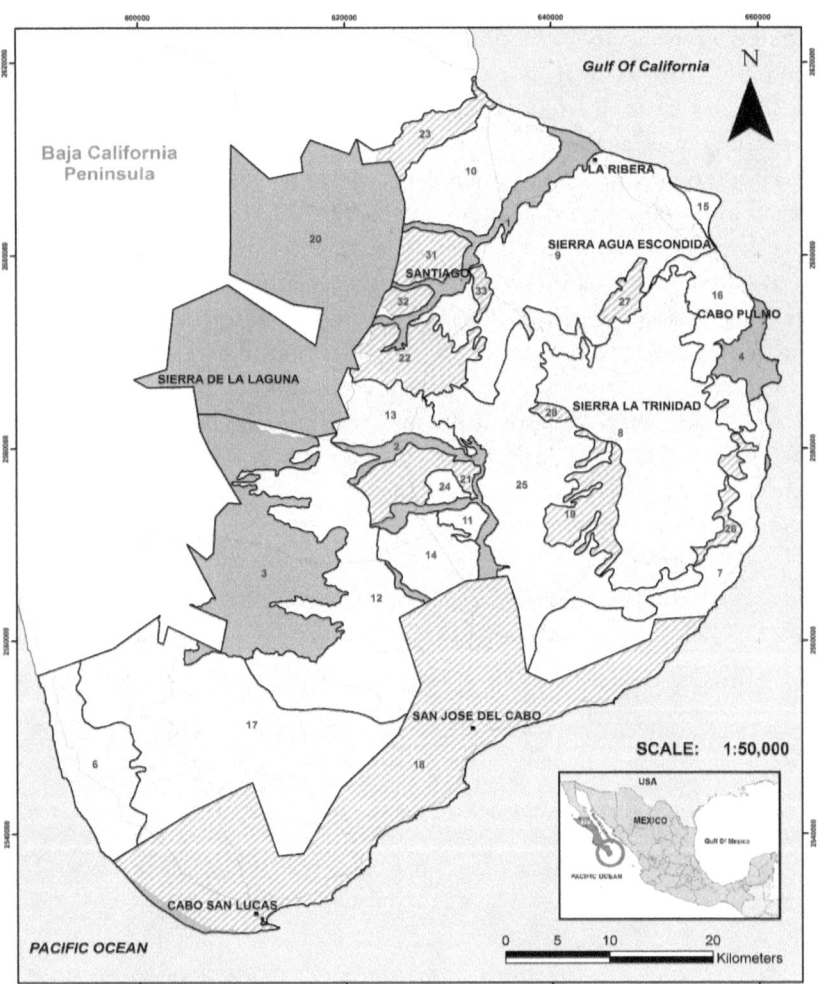

The Ecological Land Use Plan of the Municipality of Los Cabos

LEGEND

SYMBOLS

■ Settlements

| 1 | Environmental Management Units : 1, 2,...33

ENVIRONMENTAL POLICIES

▨ SUSTAINABLE USE

☐ CONSERVATION

▦ PRESERVATION

REFERENCE SYSTEM

Projection: UTM Zone 12
Datum: WGS84
Ellipsoid: WGS84
Projection grid: 20000m
Geographic grid: Grade 1

Cartography source:
Coastline: Digital thematic cartography, Scale 1:50,000 and, Vector data, Scale 1:250,000 (INEGI, 2000).
Municipal division: Municipal Geostatistical Frame 2000 (INEGI, 2000)

Created by: Oscar Arizpe Vicencio

Figure 3. Environmental Management Unit (EMU) 1

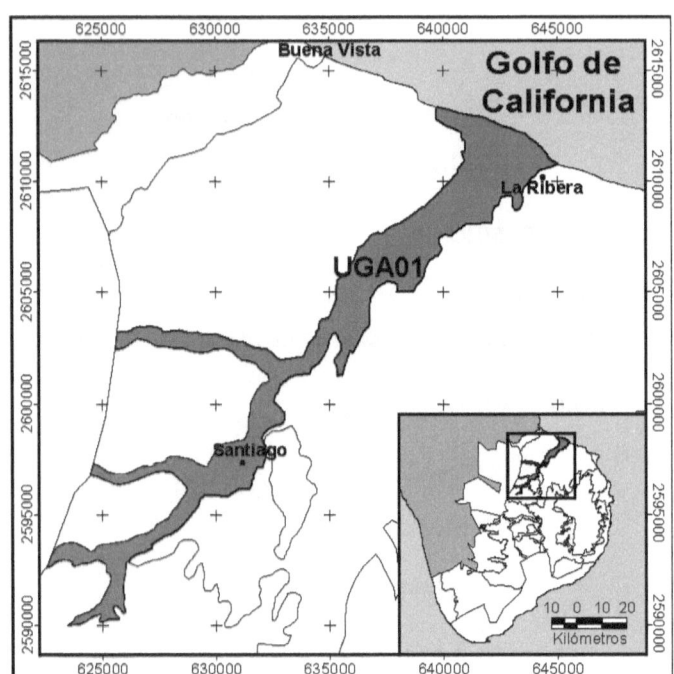

CODE FOR THE ENVIRONMENTAL MANAGEMENT UNIT: EMU 1
Name: San Dionisio-La Zorra
Location: Northeast part of the municipality; borders of the Gulf of California to the north and the Sierra La Laguna Biosphere Reserve to the west
Total Area: 58.1639 km^2
Main towns: Santiago

Detailed Actions for Each Ecological Strategy	
Sector	Sector Suitability
Conservation	Very High
Agriculture/Livestock	Very High
Tourism	Very High

Figure 3. *(continued)*

Areas of Special Attention for Protection	Justification
San Dionisio-La Zorra streambed and main tributaries	• Risk area during hurricane season and susceptible to storm surge flooding • Recharge area of Santiago aquifer

Environmental Policy

Preservation

Ecological Guideline

Preserve the conditions that allow the natural recharge of the Santiago aquifer, as well as improve and monitor economic activities and human settlements for the conservation of environmental attributes

Ecological Strategy A: maintain natural process of aquifer recharge

Action A.1: Prohibit desiccation of oases, springs, or water holes, as well as the obstruction of surface runoff due to construction of bridges, levees, roads, unpaved roads, pathways, and other works

Action A.2: Monitoring the water balance (extraction and recharge) of the Santiago aquifer
Action A.3: Regulation of groundwater extraction and water concessions
Action A.4: Regulate stream canalization works and reservoirs for use of surface water
Action A.5: Prohibit removal of rock, sand, and other materials in this stream
Action A.6: Prohibit clearing/leveling on slopes of streambeds and their tributaries

Environmental Indicators

- Rate of change in the coverage of surface water bodies
- Recharge volume/extraction volume
- Sustainable management program of the Santiago aquifer
- Vegetation cover change rate of the Santiago aquifer's basin

Figure 3. (continued)

Ecological Strategy B: restrict growth of settlements
Action B.1: Implement oversight programs in streambed zones to ensure compliance with regulations in the area Action B.2: Improve quality of public services in existing settlements according to environmental regulations Action B.3: Develop an urban land use plan to regulate human settlements and control their growth Environmental Indicators • Rate of change in the coverage of urban zones in areas adjacent to streams • Rate of change in the coverage of natural space in streambeds • Urban ordinance program for EMU settlements • Rate of change in the coastal development in the EMU coastal area
Ecological Strategy C: develop sustainable agricultural and livestock activities
Action C.1: Make agricultural irrigation systems and water supply for livestock regions more efficient Action C.2: Implement technologies to improve agricultural production and promote the conversion of livestock from extensive grazing/browsing to feedlot Action C.3: Transform traditional crops to organic crops Action C.4: Evaluate the area's livestock potential in order to control the growth of livestock activities Action C.5: Perform studies at finer scales (1:20 000–1:10 000) to determine the feasibility of establishing agricultural areas outside the flood risk area of the San Dionisio-La Zorra streambed Action C.6: Perform studies at finer scales (1: 10 000) to assess the agricultural and livestock potential of adjacent EMUs with a use policy to promote the development of agricultural activities outside this EMU Environmental Indicators • Water volume/production (agricultural or livestock) • Feedlot livestock production • Rate of change in the coverage and volume of organic crop production • Rate of change in the coverage of agricultural land use • Agricultural/livestock ordinance at a 1:10 000 scale

Figure 3. *(continued)*

Ecological Regulatory Criteria	
G1, G2, G3, G4, G5, G6, G7, G9, G10, G11, G12, G13, G14, G16	VC1, VC2, VC3, VC4, VC5, VC7
	E1, E2
A1, A3, A5, A7, A8, A10, A12, A13, A14, A17	CO2, CO3, CO7, CO8, CO10, CO12, CO13, CO14, CO15, CO16
P2, P3, P5, P6, P8, P10, P12, P13, P14, P15, P16	R1, R2, R3, R6, R8, R10
	M1, M2
IN1	LC4, LC7, LC8, LC9
AC1	FF1, FF3, FF5, FF6, FF8, FF9
T1, T2, T5, T6, T7, T21, T22, T23	AH1, AH4
HO1, HO2, HO12, HO13, HO14, HO15, HO19	

References

Diario Oficial de la Federación (DOF). 2003. *Decreto del reglamento de la Ley General del Equilibrio Ecológico y la Protección al Ambiente* (8 August).

Gobierno de Baja California Sur. 1999. *Plan Estatal de Desarrollo 1999–2005*. La Paz, BCS: Gobierno de BCS.

Kaly, U., L. Briguglio, H. MacLeod, S. Schmall, C. Platt, and R. Pal. 1999. *Environmental Vulnerability Index* (EVI). SOPAC Technical Report 275. Fiji Islands: South Pacific Applied Geoscience Commission (SOPAC).

Secretaría de Desarrollo Social e Instituto Nacional de Ecología (SEDESOL-INE). 1995. *Programa de ordenamiento ecológico de regiones geográficas con actividades productivas prioritarias. Programa de ordenamiento ecológico para el desarrollo turístico y urbano del municipio de Los Cabos, BCS*. México, DF: SEDESOL-INE.

Secretaría de Medio Ambiente y Recursos Naturales (SEMARNAT). 2006a. *Manual del proceso de ordenamiento ecológico*. México, DF: SEMARNAT.

Secretaría de Medio Ambiente y Recursos Naturales (SEMARNAT). 2006b. *Programa de Ordenamiento Ecológico Marino del Golfo de California*. México, DF: SEMARNAT.

Turvey, R. 2007. "Vulnerability Assessment of Developing Countries: The Case of Small-Island Developing States." *Development Policy Review* 25 (2): 243–264.

United Nations Environmental Programme (UNEP). 2001. *Report on Environmental and Sustainability Indicators for Latin America and the Caribbean.* Sixth Meeting of the Inter-Sessional Committee—Forum of Ministers of the Environment of Latin America and the Caribbean. UNEP/LACIG.XIII/Inf.4. UNEP, Nairobi, Kenya.

Universidad Autónoma de Baja California Sur (UABCS). 2008. *Informe final de la actualización del programa de ordenamiento ecológico del municipio de Los Cabos.* México: IX Ayuntamiento del Municipio de Los Cabos.

World Resources Institute (WRI). 1995. *Environmental Indicators: A Systematic Approach to Measuring and Reporting on Environmental Policy Performance in the Context of Sustainable Development.* Washington, DC: WRI.

22

Tourism, Rurality, and Urbanization in the Municipality of Los Cabos: A Challenge for Local Development

Lorella Castorena Davis

INTRODUCTION

The growth of the tourism industry in the municipality of Los Cabos is an outcome of a series of national policies that, since the late 1960s, have been promoted by the Bank of Mexico to strengthen tourism development in the country through the Tourism Promotion and Infrastructure Fund (Fondo de Promoción e Infraestructura Turística–INFRATUR). Toward the end of 1968, the Bank of Mexico's technicians selected seven sites as ideal for transforming into tourism developments: San José del Cabo, Cabo San Lucas, and Loreto in Baja California Sur; Ixtapa, in Guerrero; Puerto Escondido and Huatulco in Oaxaca; and Cancún, in Quintana Roo.[1]

---

1. The federal government allocated important public resources to the development of the tourism sector, which until then had occurred naturally, and whose main destination for international tourism was the port of Acapulco. The responsibility to encourage this activity, through funding of the hotel sector and the supply of infrastructure and urban-tourist equipment, fell on the then created National Fund for Tourism Development (Fondo Nacional de Fomento al Turismo–FONATUR), under the form of a federal government trust. In 1969, Cancún was begun as the first Integrally Planned Tourism Center under the concept of an urban-tourism complex with a distinctive image (the Mexican Caribbean) that considered not only the construction of infrastructure necessary for the complicated tourism support, but also the establishment of a population center, considered as a city of services, that would house, and ended up housing, its inhabitants. After the Cancún experience, tourism developments were created in Ixtapa-Zihuatanejo, on the Costa Grande of Guerrero; Los Cabos and Loreto-Nopoló, in the south of the Baja California peninsula; and

Los Cabos: Prospective for a Natural and Tourism Paradise

The location of Los Cabos as a tourist region was the result of this federal policy that was imposed in exceptional areas of the Mexican Caribbean and Pacific coasts under the model of an Integrally Planned Center (Centro Integralmente Planeado–CIP), designed by the National Trust Fund for Tourism Development (Fondo Nacional de Fomento al Turismo–FONATUR) in the late 1960s. In 1976, just two years after the constitutional transition for Baja California Sur from federal territory to state, FONATUR broke ground that boosted tourism development in Los Cabos under the CIP model. It included the then small city of San José del Cabo, the town of Cabo San Lucas, and the stretch along the coast that gave birth to the Los Cabos Tourist Corridor (Corredor Turístico Los Cabos–CTLC). Since then, the urban region of Los Cabos has become one of the most dynamic in the country. At the same time, the emergence of an extraordinarily complex and culturally diverse society is evidenced. The urban population increase can be explained from two complementary perspectives. On the one hand, there is a natural growth caused by birth-rates that are higher than death rates, resulting from greater coverage and access to health services, education, and recreation that are concentrated in urban areas. On the other hand, it comes from the complexity derived from both the migration of the rural population to urban areas, as well as the urban-urban migration.

The causes that explain this growing movement of people to urban centers are many and complex. The breakdown of traditional social structures contributes to the rural-urban migration—pushing men and women to leave their hometowns in search of diversified labor and wage opportunities—as does the attraction exerted by the growth of the tertiary sector and urban facilities/services, as well as the expectation of improving living conditions and of personal growth. Meanwhile, urban-urban migration stems from the displacement from macro cities, which has resulted in an increase and diversification of the country's urban systems.

Since 1970, Baja California Sur and, in particular, the municipalities of La Paz and Los Cabos have been immersed in an intense process of demographic growth. In both, it is the result of the concentration of population in urban areas, as well as migration.

Bahías de Huatulco, on the coast of Oaxaca, which until the 1990s was the last CIP. During the presidential administration of Vicente Fox (2000–2006), a new CIP was created on the Nayarit coast, along with the Costa Maya Integrated Tourism Plan and the Sea of Cortez megaproject (FONATUR 2006).

Between 1950 and 1960, the state's rural population still represented more than 60% of the total. By 1970, the urban population had increased to 53.9%, until reaching current conditions in which it is over 81%; this is more than 10 percentage points above the national average.

Only 17 of the 2,745 total registered population sites are urban and they have 81.3% of the total population of Baja California Sur. The municipalities of Los Cabos and La Paz have more than 53% of the total urban sites, of which only the city of La Paz exceeds 200,000 inhabitants. In Los Cabos, the urban population is settled mainly in the metropolitan areas that include the cities of San José del Cabo, Cabo San Lucas, intermediate localities between one city and the other, and their respective surroundings. The purpose of this chapter is to address the challenge that, from the local perspective, tourism development has meant to the municipality of Los Cabos.

TOWARD A MUNICIPAL REGIONALIZATION

The municipality of Los Cabos was created in 1980 and the first city council of Los Cabos took office in January 1981. The municipal seat was established in San José del Cabo. Four delegations were established in Cabo San Lucas, La Ribera, Miraflores, and Santiago.

The population density of the municipality of Los Cabos varies significantly, depending on whether locations are rural or urban. While the rural population is sparse and scattered in towns, ranch settlements, and ranches, the urban population is large and agglomerated around cities.[2] This phenomenon, which is common in all contemporary societies, has distinctive characteristics when looking at forms of land use from an almost insular space.

The municipality of Los Cabos is territorially articulated with the Baja California peninsula by the transpeninsular highway. It links the

---

2. In principle, the criterion used to distinguish the rural from the urban population is the same one used by the National Institute for Statistics and Geography (Instituto Nacional de Estadística y Geografía–INEGI): urban population lives in localities with more than 2,500 inhabitants; rural population lives in localities with less than 2,500 inhabitants. Population scales were created based on the history of Baja California Sur rural settlements in order to distinguish, towns, ranch settlements-*ejido* population centers (EPC), ranches, and fishing communities-EPC, also by number of inhabitants and other considerations to be addressed in the diagnostic section. In order to determine the scales, towns are those with more than 500 inhabitants; ranch settlements are all localities with more than fifty and up to 499 inhabitants; and ranches, all localities with fewer than 49 inhabitants.

main localities of the municipality and the municipality with the rest of the Baja California peninsula and Mexico's northern border.

In addition to communication by land, the municipality of Los Cabos is linked by air and sea. The San José del Cabo International Airport and the port of Pichilingue in La Paz are the key links. The distance separating Los Cabos from Mexico and the world is quickly and efficiently overcome through a network of air routes operated by a dozen national and international airlines. The sea crossing by way of the Gulf of California to the mainland is made by a navigation line that has a fleet of three passenger and cargo ships that covers the La Paz-Mazatlán and La Paz-Topolobampo routes. Overall, these fulfill the function of linking the municipality on a global scale without which it would be impossible to understand the depth of the changes alluded to earlier in this section.

Notwithstanding the importance of the means of communication and transportation in the process of creating an almost insular space such as that of Baja California Sur, these are insufficient to explain the complexity implied in the local-global connection. It was already mentioned that the municipal population is distributed and settled in both rural and urban areas. However, this statement by itself contributes little to the analysis of the complex set of social relations that are intertwined and operate at various levels, depending on the place to which they ascribe.

The municipal space can be divided into three regions with distinctive population characteristics. These regions involve three different forms of land use. The smallest unit is the ranch and the largest is the urban agglomerate that is observed in the Los Cabos Tourist Corridor. Each of these forms of land use has its own internal structure, determined by economic activities as well as history, customs, institutional structures, power relations, and the divisions of class, race, age, and gender. These places are understood as the intersection of a diverse set of flows and interactions that operate in a range of spatial scales that provide a series of social activities that articulate, in a different way for the different inhabitants, the local with the regional, national, and global. The following is the proposed regionalization:

1. Inland rural region: land of great extension that is located above 100 meters in altitude; sparsely populated, consisting of ranches, ranch settlements, *ejido* population centers, and towns. Its main

economic activities are livestock raising, horticulture, trade deriving from both, and an emerging rural tourism

2. Coastal rural region: vast territory stretching from the coast and up to 100 meters altitude; sparsely populated, includes small fishing communities and towns. Its main economic activities are real estate developments, tourism, and sportfishing. These communities are subjected to an intense process of socioeconomic transformation brought about by tourism, which has led them to abandon traditional activities such as nearshore fishing, livestock raising, and horticulture

3. Urban region: territory less extensive than previous two; densely populated and with heterogeneous and complex forms of social organization, typical of modern urban society. Economic activities are diverse; those related to the so-called service sector predominate and, more specifically, all those connected with tourism

Inland Rural Region

A group of small communities is located and dispersed in this territory. The population is settled in towns, ranch settlements, and ranches connected through livestock raising as their main economic activity and horticulture as a secondary economic activity. Both activities were the basis on which the old Baja California Sur rurality was built.

Altogether, the inland rural population represents about 3% of the municipality's total; this is slightly more than 4,883 people. A total of 44.5% of these are in the towns of Santiago (784) and Miraflores (1,389); 32.4% in a dozen ranch settlements (1,586); and 23% in a little over two hundred ranches (1,124). Table 1 provides data for the inland rural population, divided into men and women by region, towns, ranch settlements, and ranches. The table also includes indices of masculinity and femininity for this region.

The larger proportion of men has been a characteristic in the history of the Baja California Sur population. In general, the populations where men outnumber women are characteristic of migrant flows to the region. Historically, the Baja California Sur rural environment has shown a masculinity index greater than 100, which is largely because livestock raising, an eminently male activity, has been the main economic activity.

Los Cabos: Prospective for a Natural and Tourism Paradise

Table 1. Inland Rural Region (IRR), Total Population, Men/ Women Percentage, Masculinity and Femininity Indexes* in Towns, Ranch Settlements, and Ranches, Municipality of Los Cabos, 2005

Spatial Scope	Total	Men		Women		Masculinity Index	Femininity Index
		Total	%	Total	%		
IRR	5,042	2,622	52.00	2,420	48.00	108.35	92.30
Towns	2,173	1,152	53.01	1,021	46.99	112.83	88.63
Miraflores	1,389	757	54.50	632	45.50	119.78	83.49
Santiago	784	395	50.38	389	49.62	101.54	98.48
Ranch Settlements	1,605	845	52.65	760	47.35	111.18	89.94
Agua Caliente	166	83	50.00	83	50.00	-	-
Boca de La Sierra	147	78	53.06	69	46.94	-	-
Caduaño	283	150	53.00	133	47.00	112.78	88.67
El Chapulí	90	40	44.44	50	55.56	-	-
El Ranchito	200	111	55.50	89	44.50	-	-
El Zacatal	79	43	54.43	36	45.57	-	-
El Zorrillo	81	39	48.15	42	51.85	-	-
La Candelaria	128	74	57.81	54	42.19	-	-
Matancitas	173	90	52.02	83	47.98	-	-
Palo Escopeta	114	59	51.75	55	48.25	-	-
Panamá	78	42	53.85	36	46.15	-	-
Rancho Viejo	66	36	54.55	30	45.45	-	-
San Jorge	68	38	55.88	30	44.12	-	-
Ranches**	1,264	746	59.02	518	40.98	144.02	69.44

*The masculinity index (MI) and femininity index (FI) are demographic indices that express the ratio of men versus women and women versus men in a given territory, formulated in percentages. These are calculated using the formula *men / women * 100*. It is not possible to calculate these indices in communities with fewer than 100 inhabitants.
** The total population of IRR ranches is approximate; it is distributed in more than 200 ranches over 100 m of altitude. The population that is settled in ranches varies from one inhabitant minimum and up to 49 maximum. However, due to a numerical proximity criterion, it was decided that three ranches would be left in this category: Santa Rita (51), El Chorro (55), and Guamuchilar (53). The rest of the ranches have less than from 50 inhabitants, but most have between one and nine inhabitants on average.
Source: INEGI 2005.

Tourism, Rurality, and Urbanization in the Municipality of Los Cabos

Ranches and Ranch Settlements

These represent one of the oldest strategies of land use of the peninsula of Baja California. As a social group, ranchers and their families were the only representatives of the rural society of Baja California Sur during the nineteenth century and first half of the twentieth century. Their dominance was lost in the 1940s, with the location of the first agricultural *colonias* (settlements) and the beginning of the ejido (communal lands) distribution. The lands of agricultural settlements were granted to a more or less broad contingent of agricultural laborers from central regions of Mexico such as Jalisco and Querétaro. Meanwhile, the *ejidos* were distributed among agricultural laborers from Michoacán and Oaxaca and among some groups of ranchers, as occurred in the inland *ejidos* of Boca de La Sierra, San Jorge, Agua Caliente, Caduaño, El Ranchito, and La Candelaria.

The forms of land use made by the agricultural laborers differ from those of the ranchers. While the latter raise livestock, agricultural laborers in the agricultural settlements (and very few *ejidos*) have used their plots for agriculture.

The social and cultural organization of ranch communities is determined by the demography where few inhabitants are located in a dispersed and isolated manner. In reality, ranches are small production units whose economic structure corresponds to what some authors have identified as pastoral societies, dependent on a subsistence economy based on livestock raising. Of ancient peninsular roots, ranchers are owners (private or partnership) of production units made up of large tracts of uninhabited land, intended for the free grazing of livestock such as cattle, horses, mules, and donkeys, and historically were located close to a permanent source of water.

The predominant family structure corresponds to the patriarchal model, in which authority and power of decision rests entirely on the father or male head of household. The organization of productive work corresponds to the male head of the family who, accompanied by his male offspring and sometimes by day laborers, dedicate themselves entirely to activities pertaining to a livestock production unit. It is they who make all major decisions in the family and, while acknowledging that their lives are modest, they feel great pride in knowing themselves owners or heirs of a virile culture based on physical strength and invested in a hard corporal work that involves dealing with large and heavy animals that demand the skill of a man on horseback. Being a rancher is for them a source of pride and prestige: they value their quality of life, heritage, and being working men.

The Towns: Santiago and Miraflores

Overall, the dynamics of these towns have been strongly linked to the system of ranches and ranch settlements in the region. However, in the last two decades, and as a result of urban and tourism development, the economic and social dynamics in both towns have been modified.

Santiago was founded as a Jesuit mission in 1721. By the late eighteenth century, it had already been transformed into a nodal location for the development of ranches of the Sierra La Laguna and adjacent ranch settlements such as San Jorge and Caduaño. Since then, and throughout most of the twentieth century, Santiago was the trade center for horticultural and livestock products in the area, and supplier of the necessary basic products for ranches and ranch settlements. This led to a trade circuit of rural goods and services to which Miraflores was also joined. In both towns, there is trade with the products of horticulture and the processing of some livestock-derived products, ranging from cheese and dried meats, to tannery and furs.[3]

Even though forms of expression of the traditional rural society persist in both towns, the two are immersed in a process of social change caused by urban and tourism development in Los Cabos. Many orchards have been sold to farmers (of national or foreign origin), specialized in the production of vegetables. Some have converted the old orchards into organic production, or use them to plant grasses for golf courses.

But the phenomenon that has most impacted the lives in these towns is the mobility of its inhabitants to the tourist area of Los Cabos. This phenomenon is most evident in Miraflores, which has been transformed into a sort of bedroom town for many of the women and men of working age who travel every day to their employment in the tourist or urban sector. From some years ago, Miraflores seems like a small town inhabited only by women and elderly men, children, and youth of school age.

---

3. The trade of tanning leather or making it into coats; is also used as lining and decorations in certain clothes and for making working clothes and tools characteristic of ranchers.

Tourism, Rurality, and Urbanization in the Municipality of Los Cabos

Coastal Rural Region

The coastal rural territory of the municipality of Los Cabos is divided into two strips. The first is more extensive and populated; it stretches from north to south, facing the Gulf of California, from Buenavista to Punta Gorda. Buena Vista, La Ribera, Cabo Pulmo, and Los Frailes are locations that are linked territorially to the tourist development known as Cabo del Este (East Cape), with a predominance of small three- and four-star hotels, beach clubs specializing in sportfishing, diving, adventure tourism, and ecotourism, as well as coastal real estate developments that have led to a growing number of exclusive residential complexes that have radically transformed the small communities of Los Cabos nearshore fishers, cattle ranchers, and horticulturists.

The second coastal strip is less extensive and sparsely populated. It is located facing the Pacific Ocean. It is linked to the tourism and real estate development that stretches along the coast from Todos Santos, El Pescadero, and Cerritos in the municipality of La Paz to El Migriño and La Laguna in the municipality of Los Cabos.

Overall, coastal rural communities, considered for analysis, represent less than 2% of the total municipal population. As in the inland rural region, the masculinity index is over 100, as noted in Table 2.

Table 2. Coastal Rural Region (CRR), Total Population by Gender, and Masculinity and Femininity Indexes

Coastal Rural Region	Total Population	Men		Women		Masculinity Index	Femininity Index
		Abs.*	%	Abs.	%		
La Ribera	1,757	923	52.53	834	47.47	110.67	90.36
Buena Vista	544	289	53.13	255	46.88	113.33	88.24
Cabo Pulmo	58	31	53.45	27	46.55	-	-
Los Frailes	8	4	50.00	4	50.00	-	-
Migriño	16	7	43.75	9	56.25	-	-
CRR	2,383	1,254	51.78	1,129	48.22	111	90

*Absolute.
Source: INEGI 2005

The tourism-real estate development has brought to all these localities an undetermined number of foreign inhabitants. Although not counted as permanent residents in the area, they occupy residences during certain periods or permanently—but undefined legally—that are located the length and width of the rural coast of the municipality of Los Cabos.[4] These inhabitants and their properties require a range of goods and services that has modified the coastal rural area.

Whether private or *ejido* communities, the fact is that in the localities included in this characterization of the coastal rural region, not only have the coastal lands been sold, but the changes in the economically active population have been generated. Employment has moved out of the primary and secondary sectors of the economy toward the tertiary sector of the economy, which on average represents about 62% of the workforce.

Communities connected to the East Cape corridor have received the greatest impact from the tourism-real estate development. In Buena Vista, La Ribera, Cabo Pulmo, and Los Frailes, hotels, houses, and condominiums are being built and occupy much of the beachfront. A significant area of land and large numbers of houses with ocean front, access, or views are offered on websites specialized in selling real estate.

The small coastal towns are immersed in a complex transition process that has disrupted them. The sale of land implies the abandonment of traditional productive activities such as livestock raising and horticulture. The replacement of nearshore fishing with sportfishing means that the use, control, and benefit of fish resources remain in the hands of companies dedicated to sportfishing and not in those of the fishers. These traditional fishers also face the reductions in catch volumes from nearshore fishing to benefit sportfishing.

The loss of direct access to the use, control, and benefit of the main resources denotes the transition of an almost self-consumption or subsistence economy to a modern or market economy. In this transition, men have retained within their families and their main communities the power of decisions regarding use of the proceeds from the sale or reconversion of the land, orchards, livestock, and fisheries. However, they have been removed from making decisions with regard to modern regional development. Many of the once rich coastal resource owners face declining economic power and political management capabilities. While women have had little or no access to the control and benefit of the resources, they have not participated in

---

4. For example, according to the Second National Population and Housing Count 2005 (INEGI 2005), in the coastal rural region of the Gulf of California, permanently residing were 24 Americans (gender not specified), with 12 in La Ribera, 10 in Buenavista, and two in Cabo Pulmo.

the power to decide on the purpose of these, not within their family or their community. Women are further behind than men in making decisions about modern regional development.

If one adds that the average level of schooling in the coastal rural region for both sexes is eight years—that is, not completing basic studies—then the possibilities diminish that local men and women will benefit from jobs that require higher degrees of training or professional education. Those who run the new regional business structure and who have the best jobs are mostly migrants.

The result of this process is the inclusion of both sexes in jobs that do not require high qualifications, but some experience. This is the case of fishers who have gone from independent fishers or partners in cooperatives to providers of tourism services in sportfishing and diving. In turn, women have been fully incorporated into formal employment as shop assistants, waitresses, housekeepers, general service employees, and domestic workers. The best trained men and women work in education, health, and public services.

Although the population size of the coastal rural region is small, it has increased in La Ribera and Buena Vista since 1990 by 44.5%. However, it is foreseeable that the development caused by the construction of the Cabo Riviera resort will exert a strong influence in La Ribera and neighboring towns. Work began in October 2009 and includes the construction of four hotels, condominiums, a golf course, a marina, beachfront lots, and a shopping plaza. There will be a large number of service providers. Therefore, the nearly 1,800 town residents[5] will be greatly exceeded, and the huge demand for public services that a project of this nature will entail has not been considered.

Urban Region of the Municipality of Los Cabos

Compared with the inland rural region and the coastal rural region, the area of the urban region is significantly less; it has a higher population density and a high degree of complexity. As stated in the introduction,

---

5. As stated by the governor at the groundbreaking ceremony, the project will generate 3,000 direct jobs and approximately 4,500 indirect jobs, figures that triple the economically active population (EAP) in the case of direct jobs in the locality, and quadruple it in the case of indirect jobs. According to 2005 INEGI data, La Ribera had 1,190 people over the age of fifteen years; and from this number the economically inactive population would have to subtract the EAP (students, housewives, retirees, pensioners, and the disabled). These data indicate that the creation of jobs related to the new development will attract a significantly larger population than the current one.

since the 1980s the impact of tourism development on urbanization and municipal population growth has been significant.

Before becoming the poles that articulate the urban complex that sits on the tourist corridor, San José del Cabo and Cabo San Lucas were small towns located in one of the most beautiful landscapes of the southern peninsula. San José del Cabo was founded as a mission in 1730 by the Jesuit Nicolás Tamaral. He introduced the orchards that during the first decades of the twentieth century would make San José an important producer of sugar cane, vegetables, and citrus fruits, as well as one of the major livestock sites in the south of the peninsula. Both the production of sugarcane and tomatoes turned San José into a thriving agricultural/livestock-type town until the late 1950s, when these products lost value in the international market.

During the first decades of the twentieth century, the port of San José del Cabo was the second most important shipping port in the Baja California Sur territory after Santa Rosalía, but the loss of economic centrality of agricultural production affected maritime transport. Subsequently, as a result of the construction of the port in Cabo San Lucas, the port of San José practically ceased to function as such. When the port of Cabo San Lucas was closed to commercial shipping to become a cruise ship marina and port, the function of cargo port was assumed by the port of Pichilingue, located near the city of La Paz.

Off of Cabo San Lucas, the waters of the Gulf of California and the Pacific Ocean meet. This exceptional site was used as a port and safe haven on the Pacific sailing routes since the Vizcaíno expeditions. It was a small fishing town that could only be reached by sea or overland with animals. It remained virtually uninhabited during the nineteenth and early twentieth centuries until the 1920s when a road was built that joined it to San José del Cabo. Thus, it was linked to the rest of the peninsula since, at that time, the state's southernmost region was accessed through the road that connected San José to La Paz, via San Antonio and El Triunfo.

Due to its geographical position, which facilitated maritime communication with the mainland, as well as to its proximity to the deep cold waters of the Pacific where tuna was abundant, in 1917 a North American company began the exploitation of this species and established a floating processing plant off of Cabo San Lucas. This gave origin to what became its main economic activity during much of the twentieth century. Given the promising future of the tuna industry, the

Compañía de Productos Marinos, S.A., was founded in 1927, which soon joined the other seafood companies of Abelardo L. Rodríguez. Subsequently, it was acquired by Spanish businessman Elías Pando. Until its transfer to the port of San Carlos, the tuna packing plant was an unequivocal sign of the fishing identity of Cabo San Lucas.

The new era of San José del Cabo and Cabo San Lucas began with the construction of hotels Punta Palmilla and Chileno in the late 1950s. These hotels, which were characterized by luxury and comfort in their facilities, laid the foundations for the future development of the tourist corridor. At first, tourist access was by air and sea, either on private light or small airplanes that landed at airstrips built by the hoteliers on their own land, or by shallow-draft private yachts that sailed mainly from marinas located in the U.S. cities of Los Angeles and San Diego. The local townspeople did not have access to these channels of communication; they had to use the road that communicated them with each other, with the capital of the then territory, and also the local shipping companies that quite often navigated the La Paz–San José del Cabo–Cabo San Lucas route.

This region remained relatively isolated from the rest of the country until the 1970s, although it already had several other hotels that were built with the same intention of luxury and comfort as the first. Such is the case of the Hotel Hacienda Cabo San Lucas, the Camino Real, and Hotel Finisterra. Beginning in 1970, and as a result of infrastructure works that were promoted to support the conversion of the federal territory to a state, the foundations were established in Baja California Sur that ended its isolation.

In 1972, and as a result of pressure from the local community, the Cabo San Lucas-Puerto Vallarta ferry route was opened, for which an arrival port was built next to the tuna plant port facilities. According to López (López-López and Sánchez-Crispín 2002), the opening of the new route, in addition to the rapid transport of goods, allowed the massive arrival of domestic tourism that contravened the interests of hotel owners to turn the area into a luxury tourism site, which by 1974 had already been chosen by FONATUR to house the Integrally Planned Center. As a result of pressure from hoteliers and FONATUR itself, the ferry route to Puerto Vallarta was canceled and the port became the Cabo San Lucas Marina.

The municipality of Los Cabos was established six years after the conversion from a federal territory to a federal state as a result of organized pressures by San José del Cabo's civil society. It was unacceptable to them to be part of the municipality of La Paz, among other less important issues, because Los Cabos would lose the opportunity to manage a region whose development was already envisioned (Del Río and Altable 2000). Since then, the flow of public and private investment has radically modified the urban area's landscape of Los Cabos, to become a CIP that is dominated by high-income foreign and domestic visitors.

The small and peaceful towns of San José del Cabo and Cabo San Lucas, separated by little more than 30 kilometers, are territorially articulated to give rise to a sprawling urban agglomeration that concentrates a system of economic, political, and cultural relations that extend over their respective conurbations and connect throughout the tourist corridor. In fact, this is the axis that links the entire urban region and gives way to an agglomeration of economic functions and human settlements scattered along the coastal road, with interstitial semirural zones, uncontrolled periurban areas, and unequally distributed services through a discontinuous infrastructure.[6]

The urban region is composed of the two cities, their respective conurbations, and a series of small places that INEGI recorded as independent, but in reality are part of the urban fabric and its sociodemographic dynamics. Some are old ranches or population nuclei that have been absorbed by urban growth; others are located mainly in the corridor's intermediate sector and correspond to *colonias*, subdivisions, condominium buildings, housing developments, and hotel complexes.

According to the Second National Population and Housing Count 2005 (INEGI 2005), the Urban Region population amounted to 151,334 people, just over 92% of the municipal total. Of these, 149,972 were concentrated in eight places: Cabo San Lucas, Colonia del Sol, Colonia Los Cangrejos, San José del Cabo, San José Viejo, San Bernabé, La Playa, and Las Veredas. Together, they represent 99% of municipal growth for the 2000–2005 period; in absolute numbers, the population of the eight

---

6. This definition has been developed from the ideas put forward by Catalan city planners Manuel Castells and Jordi Borja to distinguish between urbanization and city: "Urbanization refers to the continuous or discontinuous spatial articulation, of population and activities. By contrast, the city, both in the tradition of urban sociology as well as in the awareness of citizens in the entire world, entails a specific system of social relations, culture, and, above all, political institutions of self-governance" (Borja and Castells 2000).

localities increased by 58,165 people and the municipal population by 58,693, just 528 more than in the Urban Region.[7]

One of the major problems in the urban region is the disparity between urban facilities and services for tourism and those for the lower-middle and lower class sectors of the *colonias* and housing units of the local population. While the tourist areas have electricity, potable water, drainage systems, and all the streets are paved, the efficiency and delivery of these services to the middle, low, and marginal sectors of local society decrease significantly. Here, two urban realities come face to face. One is exuberant and luxurious intended for tourism and the upper and upper-middle classes that represent the most favored sectors of local society. The other is home to a diverse mass of workers who mostly originate in other states of Mexico and are distributed among the cities and conurbations. They live with a high deficit in the provision of basic public services in locations where the urban image is far from the architectural and service standards that prevail in the sectors destined for tourism or for the most privileged classes of local society.

At this point, it should be noted that two phenomena contribute to deepening social inequality. The first is closely related to the linear conformation of the urban region. The urbanization of Los Cabos follows a linear design, a coastal route destined primarily for tourist use that links and connects the cities located on the fringes. While in the intermediate and exterior stretches of the corridor, urban growth has remained longitudinal and parallel to the main artery, it has overflowed the cities at the fringes and extends toward the conurbations. The city of San José linearly expands and widens along the road to Las Veredas. In turn, Cabo San Lucas extends northward toward Los Pozos along the Las Palmas-Los Pozos road and on the lower part of the mountain. It extends southward toward Los Médanos and toward the northwest in line with the transpeninsular highway.

Urban expansion has been primarily residential. The increase in population that took place in the last two decades has caused a great demand for housing and public services.[8] Some middle-income

---

7. The population of the eight localities increased from 91,807 people in 2000 to 149,972 in 2005. The municipal population increased during the same period from 105,469 to 164,162 (INEGI 2000, 2005).
8. Public services mean: garbage collection, street lighting, paving, potable water, drainage, sewage systems, wastewater treatment plants, urban transportation, roads, schools, health services, markets, and public safety.

subdivisions, social interest housing units, low-income neighborhoods, and irregular settlements that emerged from the invasion of national or *ejido* land are located in the conurbations.

Housing that has all services available is concentrated in the tourist locations of the corridor, in upper-and middle-class housing subdivisions and neighborhoods, in the central areas of both cities, and in some social interest housing units. In the rest of the housing units, the coverage of electricity, piped water, and drainage is heterogeneous (78% overall) and depends on the type of settlement concerned.

Sixty-four percent of urban settlements, roads, and streets are not paved. Public transportation, security, and garbage collection show deficiencies. Irregular housing located in marginal settlements or invaded areas, characterized by lack of public services, difficult maintenance conditions, and precarious legal status of occupation, tends to be the typical form of housing for the vast majority of households headed by poor or marginalized men and women.

The social and economic life of the Los Cabos Tourist Corridor is organized around this diffuse and complex agglomeration in a discontinuous way. Not all localities show the same sociodemographic patterns. As shown in Table 3, only eight of the 66 localities with available data that constitute the Los Cabos Tourist Corridor account for 65.9% of the relative growth of the municipal population, with respect to the relative growth observed by the state population, during the 2000–2005 period. Together, the eight localities represent 99% of the population growth of the municipality of Los Cabos for the same period. Some 149,972 people live in them, and 1,362 are distributed among the remaining 108 localities.

Table 3. Relative Growth of Main Localities and Municipal Growth with Respect to State Growth, 2000–2005

Locality	2000	2005	Absolute Growth	Relative Growth
Total main localities (8)	91,807	149,972	58,165	66.00
Total municipal	105,469	164,162	58,693	66.60*
Total state	424,041	512,170	88,139	100.00

* Total relative growth of eight main localities of the CTLC, with respect to municipal growth, is 99.10%.

Source: Prepared by author with data from INEGI 2000 and 2005.

Table 4 shows in detail that the locations of greatest population growth in the Los Cabos Tourist Corridor are the city of Cabo San Lucas and its Colonia del Sol and Colonia Los Cangrejos conurbations; and San José del Cabo and its conurbations in Las Veredas, San Bernabé, La Playa, and San José Viejo.

The overall average income calculated on minimum wages is that of five minimum wages per month. The level of education varies greatly among the social strata as does the distribution of goods in the homes. The vast wealth produced by the tourist activity is not reflected nor distributed in the same way for all sectors of local society. However, the Los Cabos Tourist Corridor continues to be a magnet for migrants. They find in it the possibility of an improvement

Table 4. Population Residing in Localities with More than 1,000 Inhabitants, Absolute and Relative Growth in the Municipality of Los Cabos, 2000–2005

Locality	Population			
	Total		Absolute Growth	Relative Growth (%)
	2000	2005		
Cabo San Lucas	37,984	56,811	18,827	49.57
San José del Cabo	31,102	48,518	17,416	56.00
Colonia del Sol	10,159	27,057	16,898	166.34
Las Veredas	3,888	6,999	3,111	80.02
Colonia Los Cangrejos	3,451	3,451*	000	0.00
San José Viejo	3,090	3,808	718	23.24
San Bernabé	1,281	2,090	809	63.15
La Playa	852	1,238	386	45.31
Total	91,807	149,972	58,165	63.36
Total municipal	105,469	164,162	58,693	55.65
Total state	424,041	512,170	88,139	20.79

* Colonia Los Cangrejos is part of the Cabo San Lucas conurbation; it was one of the two new localities, along with Colonia del Sol, recorded in the 2000 census. However, in the 2005 Population and Housing Count, Colonia Los Cangrejos was not counted. Thus, the same number of people is reported, even when a proportional increase is foreseeable, similar to that presented in the Colonia del Sol or the city of Cabo San Lucas.
Source: Prepared by author with data from INEGI 2000 and 2005.

in living conditions compared to what they had in their hometowns, despite the obvious precarious conditions that prevail in the middle-lower and lower social level settlements.

The challenge is as indicated in the title of this chapter: management, from the local perspective, of major and contradictory problems caused by urban growth and development of tourism activities.

REFERENCES

Borja, J., and M. Castells. 2000. *Local y global. La gestión de las ciudades en la era de la información*. Madrid: Taurus Ediciones.

Bourdieu, Pierre. 1998. *Capital cultural, escuela y espacio social*. México, DF: Siglo XXI.

Castorena, L., P. Santelices, and M. Pacheco. 2008. "Mujeres de sal: Género y turismo sustentable en Cabo Pulmo." Pp. 223–248 in *Turismo y sustentabilidad en Cabo Pulmo, B.C.S.*, Alba E. Gámez, ed. San Diego, CA: San Diego State University, Universidad Autónoma de Baja California Sur, and Consejo Nacional de Ciencia y Tecnología.

Castorena, Lorella, and Aurora Breceda. 2008. *Remontando el Cañón de la Zorra, ranchos y rancheros de la Sierra La Laguna*. México: ISC/SECTUR/UABCS.

Castorena, Lorella, and Denise Soares. 2001. *Mujeres y hombres que aran en el desierto y el mar. Diagnóstico sociambiental con perspectiva de género en la Reserva de la Biosfera El Vizcaíno*. México: AECI/SEMARNAT.

Castorena Davis, Lorella, ed. 2006. *Los afanes y los días... de las mujeres. Trabajo, empleo, socio-demografía, violencia, políticas públicas y ambiente en clave regional*. Cuadernos Universitarios. La Paz, BCS: Universidad Autónoma de Baja California Sur.

Del Río, Ignacio, and María Eugenia Altable. 2000. *Breve historia de Baja California Sur*. México: El Colegio de México, Fideicomiso Historia de las Américas, Fondo de Cultura Económica.

Instituto Nacional de Estadística, Geografía e Informática (INEGI). 2000. *XII Censo General de Población y Vivienda*. Aguascalientes, AGS: INEGI.

Instituto Nacional de Estadística, Geografía e Informática (INEGI). 2005. *II Conteo de Población y Vivienda*. Aguascalientes, AGS: INEGI.

Instituto Nacional de Estadística, Geografía e Informática (INEGI). 2006. *Cuaderno Estadístico Municipal de Los Cabos,* Edición 2006. Aguascalientes, AGS: INEGI.

Instituto Nacional de Estadística, Geografía e Informática (INEGI). 2007. *Anuario Estadístico de Baja California Sur,* Edición 2007. Aguascalientes, AGS: INEGI.

Instituto Nacional de Estadística, Geografía e Informática (INEGI). 2008. *Mujeres y Hombres 2008.* Decimosegunda edición. Aguascalientes, AGS: INEGI.

Instituto Nacional de Estadística, Geografía e Informática (INEGI) and Encuesta Nacional sobre la Dinámica de las Relaciones en los Hogares (ENDIREH). 2006a. *Panorama de la violencia contra las mujeres, Baja California Sur.* Aguascalientes, AGS: INEGI.

Instituto Nacional de Estadística, Geografía e Informática (INEGI) and Encuesta Nacional sobre la Dinámica de las Relaciones en los Hogares (ENDIREH). 2006b. *Resultados por entidad federativa: Baja California Sur.* Aguascalientes, AGS: INEGI.

López-López, Álvaro, and Álvaro Sánchez-Crispín. 2002. "Canales de articulación en el Corredor Turístico Los Cabos, Baja California Sur, México." *Cuadernos de Turismo 9* (January-June): 53–66. University of Murcia, Spain.

Part V.
Economy and Regional Development

23

The Consolidation of Los Cabos as a Growth Pole: Challenges and Opportunities

Antonina Ivanova, Reyna Ibáñez, and James Gerber

INTRODUCTION

It is often said that Los Cabos has become a development pole that is in constant growth. But, what are the implications of this statement? What benefits and/or disadvantages does that development pole generate to society, investors, and the environment itself? What are the challenges to approach a more equitable and sustainable development model? This chapter is designed to answer each of these questions, beginning with a brief reflection on the implications, origin, and evolution of Los Cabos as a tourism development pole. It is followed by an analysis of the strengths, weaknesses, opportunities, and threats in Los Cabos, which provides useful information for designing measures to face the challenges of the municipality to thereby ensure continuity of its economic dynamics and, at the same time, make it more inclusive and sustainable.

IMPLICATIONS AND CHARACTERISTICS OF A DEVELOPMENT POLE

There is no fully consensual or universally accepted theoretical definition of what in practice is a development pole. One could speak of its existence only if, as a whole, it is large enough to exert a dominant influence in its economic sphere (Hermansen 1974); it is characterized by having a driving industry that is key to regional or local growth; and it also exerts beneficial effects on the geographical area in which it is located (Paelinck 1965).

The establishment of development poles was a worldwide strategy, carried out in the late 1970s, mainly in developing countries and in areas with potential for an economic boom. Its purpose was to generate the development of different types of industries and the public sector attempted to attract such growth-inducing industries through incentives and tax benefits. In turn, these industries and new enterprises had to be able to create jobs, remove externalities, and attract other economic activities. As a result (in theory), high rates of investment and reinvestment of benefits are generated and there are a number of advantages due to the existence or creation of infrastructure and social capital and learning and imitation effects that cause an improvement in local levels of knowledge and techniques, as well as business and management capabilities.

These growth poles would then be engines of regional development[1] and economic growth (Zárate and Rubio 2005). However, the complexity of factors involved in regional development does not always allow that all these objectives be achieved in practical terms. That is because these are regularly accompanied by some degree of polarization and differentiation in some economic or social sectors. The result is an unbalanced growth since it does not spread equally to all sectors and all places. Furthermore, in reality the effect of the creation of some growth poles has been negative in terms of employment due to the impact that has occurred in the local structure of prices and wages. Therefore, many authors have begun using the term "development pole" only as a concept that includes the geographic concentration of economic activities in general (Peña 2006). Thus, in order for a growth pole to generate social and economic changes, it requires the active participation of the social and business sectors so that, through a timely regulatory framework and joint efforts, they are able to achieve a maximum extraction of the benefits of this scheme.

---

1. Regional development is the generating process of economic wealth, social welfare, and sustainability that, when manifested in equal opportunities for all people, sectors, and regions tends to be reflected in the harmony of cities and regions themselves. When development is inharmonious, it sacrifices any of these components, but preferably welfare and sustainability for the sake of economic growth (Miguel, Torres 2007).

Origin and Evolution of Los Cabos as a Tourism Growth Pole

In Baja California Sur, the rapid growth is evident within the development poles related to tourism activities. The concentration of such poles occurs within the municipality of Los Cabos, specifically within the area that makes up the tourist corridor. This municipality, along with Mexico City, Cancún, Guadalajara, Puerto Vallarta, and Acapulco, has become one of the most visited destines by international tourists in Mexico. In 1976, the agency for tourism development in Mexico, namely the National Trust Fund for Tourism Development (Fondo Nacional de Fomento al Turismo–FONATUR), selected Los Cabos as a site for large-scale tourism development. This agency also planned Cancún, Huatulco, and Ixtapa, and is currently planning additional tourism developments in order to strengthen strategies to create a faster and, potentially, broader economic growth.

In this regard, more than thirty years after its creation as a growth pole, Los Cabos has become a growing economy, the result of a mix between the injection of mainly government and foreign capital. Thus, a notable increase has been achieved in the levels of investment and employment. However, it is evident that the development of the Los Cabos region, far from providing benefits at a wider scale at the regional level, has become consolidated more like an enclave economy.[2] Moreover, it is also obvious that little benefit has been generated for the Los Cabos society, whose reality and lifestyle is almost foreign to the structure and amenities of existing hotel complexes, since there are even neighborhoods that lack basic services. Despite the imbalances, it is considered that the development pole in Los Cabos has a number of important strengths and opportunities to become a region that is conducive to sustainability and equity, as long as challenges are overcome through a timely and efficient development planning.

---

2. It refers to the presence of monopolistic capital in a much less developed economic and social environment. The notion of enclave refers to an unevenness or imbalance between the economic power of a monopolistic company (or companies) and the rest of the national or regional economy in which it (they) operates; it is a contrasting image of strong inequalities between one and another form of economic organization (Vilas 2009).

NUMBER OF VISITORS AND SIZE OF TOURISM SECTOR IN LOS CABOS

The tourism influx in the municipality of Los Cabos, in general terms, has grown, as corroborated through a series of indicators. For example, during the 2005–2008 period, the total number of passengers (in flights and cruises) grew by 25%, despite the closure of several airlines and the tropical hurricanes that pass through this area. Regarding the number of visitors registered at hotels, an important growth of almost 160% is recorded during that period.[3] Most tourists are foreigners. In 1998, from a total of 471,900 visitors, 83% were foreign tourists and 17% domestic tourists; in 2008, the percentage of foreign tourists dropped a small amount to 79% of the total, while domestic tourism amounted to 21% of the total.

Figure 1. Tourist Numbers and Origins in the Municipality of Los Cabos, 2005–2008

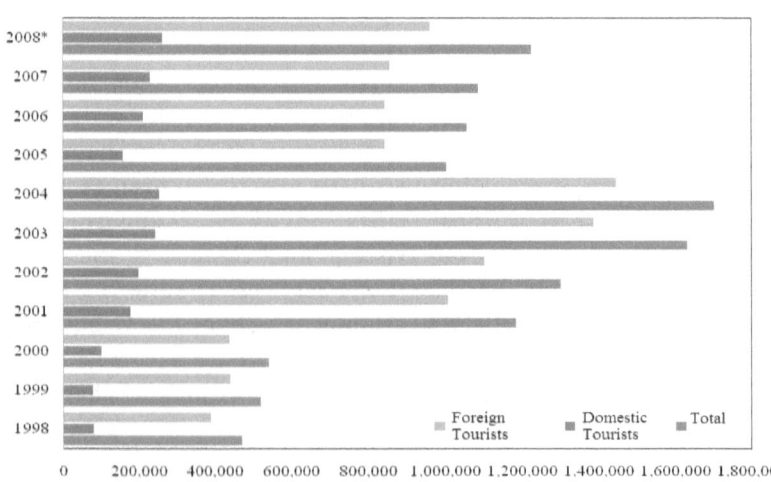

*Preliminary figures.
Sources: GOB-BCS 2009; SECTUR 2009.

---

3. In 1976, the number of visitors was 12,300 (FONATUR 2004). This means that from approximately 1976 to 2008 a growth of more than 1,000% has been generated.

A large number of studies have shown that the nationality of foreign tourists is mainly American. This is due to the proximity of Baja California Sur to the United States and the constant commercial and cultural exchange that the peninsula has maintained with San Diego, other California counties, and cities in Texas. Tourists from Canada, Asia, and Europe also visit, but in percentage terms, their numbers are lower. The domestic tourist comes mainly from the center of the country, although tourists also visit from within the state and from Baja California.

In general, the tourism influx showed an upward trend, despite events that threatened to paralyze global tourism activities. Examples of these events include the terrorist attacks of September 11, 2001, and the global economic crisis that became evident in 2008. With regard to the size and general characteristics of tourism services, according to data from 2003, Los Cabos had 98 hotels and 8,926 rooms.[4] Furthermore, the supply of tourist services in Los Cabos is by far higher than in the rest of the state's municipalities, allowing it to maintain a dominant position due to its large hotel infrastructure.

Figure 2 shows that the capacity of Los Cabos hotels is the largest in the state. The Los Cabos hotels average 91 rooms, whereas the state average is 49 rooms per hotel. Currently, the supply of tourist services in the municipality has diversified. This derives from the growing investment in hotel infrastructure, the promotion of the destination, and the new tourism development policies that have greatly favored the growth of tourism. It also stems from the importance that new forms of tourism have gained, allowing visitors to this destination to enjoy various activities and attractions. These include enjoying and contemplating the beaches and scenery; practicing sportfishing; walking interpretive trails; attending environmental education workshops; bird watching and observing other fauna (both terrestrial and marine) and flora; water sports like snorkeling and diving; riding boats, motorcycles, and horses; skydiving; and participating in different nightlife entertainment activities. Recently, the increased demand for these activities has led service providers to the design and operation of tours that include visits to rural, archeological, or high biological value sites, thus expanding the possibilities of development and income earning in rural areas.

---

4. In 1976, the number of hotels in Los Cabos was only 10 and the number of rooms was 544 (FONATUR 2004). This means that from approximately 1976 to 2003, there has been a growth of more than 5,000% in the supply of hotel rooms.

Figure 2. Comparison of Number of Hotel Rooms in Los Cabos and Other BCS Municipalities, 2001–2003

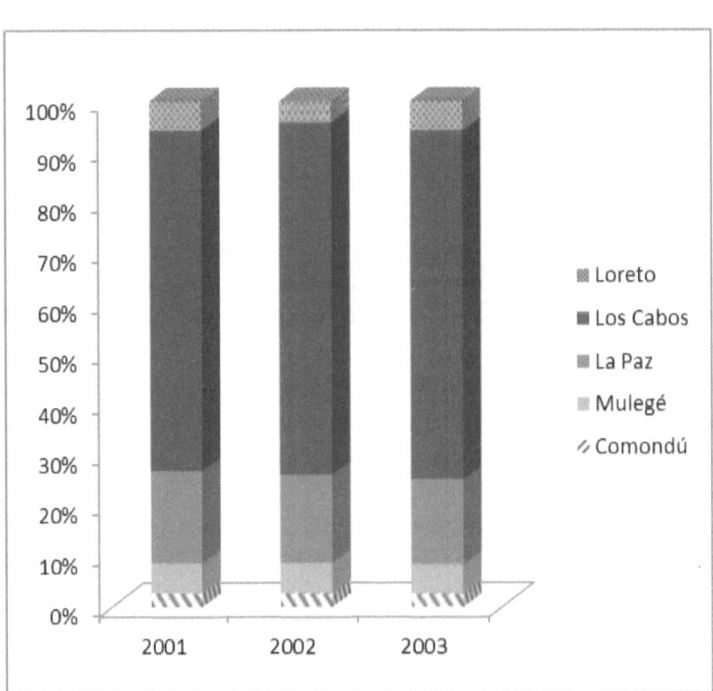

OVERVIEW OF EMPLOYMENT, OCCUPATION, AND SALARY

As shown in Figure 3, a major part of the Los Cabos workforce is employed in the hotel and restaurant sectors; in fact, one-fourth of the population is employed directly in these sectors. In addition, a portion of workers in the commerce sector depends directly or indirectly on tourism-related sales. Furthermore, the construction industry that results from tourism growth is a major source of employment.

The economic dynamics of this municipality have been reflected in employment opportunities for its population that even serve as options for the population of other municipalities and/or states. This occurs especially because of the emergence of tourism and its multiplier effects in other economic activities and regions of the country.

Figure 3. Employment by Sector

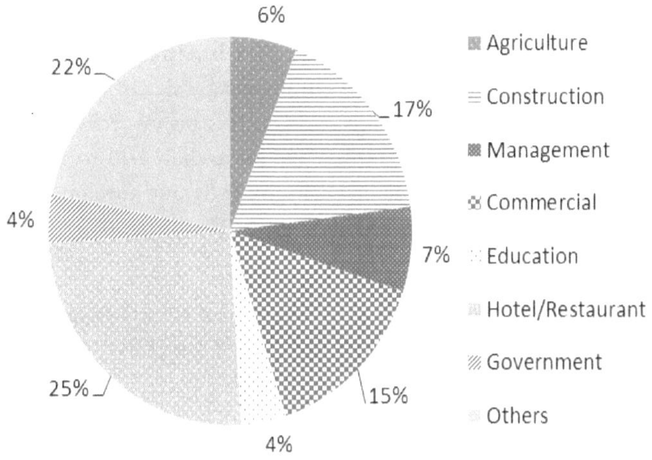

- Agriculture 6%
- Construction 17%
- Management 7%
- Commercial 15%
- Education 4%
- Hotel/Restaurant 25%
- Government 4%
- Others 22%

Source: INEGI 2001a.

Figure 4. Occupation in the Hotel and Restaurant Sectors

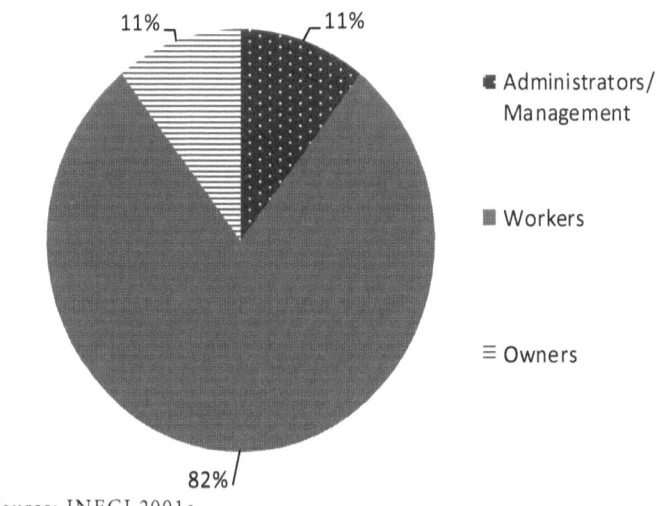

- Administrators/Management 11%
- Workers 82%
- Owners 11%

Source: INEGI 2001a.

Upon analysis of the characteristics of the hotel and restaurant sectors, it is evident that there is a small number of people who are owners or family members who work in the business. Most employees, however, are workers or managers of a business.

Figure 5 shows the distribution of employees by size of business, specifically within the hotel and restaurant sectors. It is noteworthy that approximately 50% of hotels and restaurants have more than 100 employees. This pattern reflects the large amount of both domestic and foreign investment, responsible for tourism growth in this region (Gerber 2007).

Figure 5. Business Size and Number of Employees in the Hotel and Restaurant Sectors

Number of Employees	Number of Businesses
501-1000	7.8
251-500	24.5
101-250	19.5
51-100	11.5
31-50	11
21-30	3.8
16-20	3.5
11-15	4
6-10	7.2
3-5	6.5
0-2	3.5

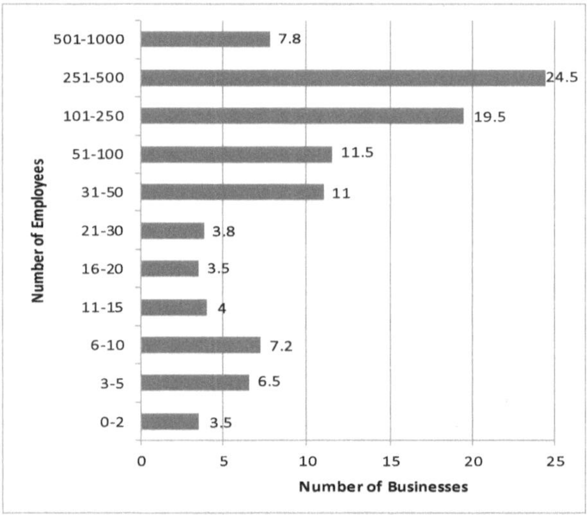

Source: INEGI 2001a.

Figure 6 shows the distribution of wages and salaries in all sectors, measured in terms of multiples of the minimum wage in force, and that, according to the National Minimum Wages Commission (CONASAMI 2004), in Baja California Sur it amounts to $45.24 pesos per day. As can be seen, more than 20% receive the equivalent of one or two minimum salaries; more than 50% receive between two and five minimum salaries; and only 4% receive more than ten minimum salaries. These data may imply that the tourism industry provides good job opportunities, at least in terms of salary, which also constitutes one of the main reasons that inhabitants from other states go to Los Cabos in search of better job opportunities.

Figure 6. Distribution of Wages per Minimum Salary (MS)

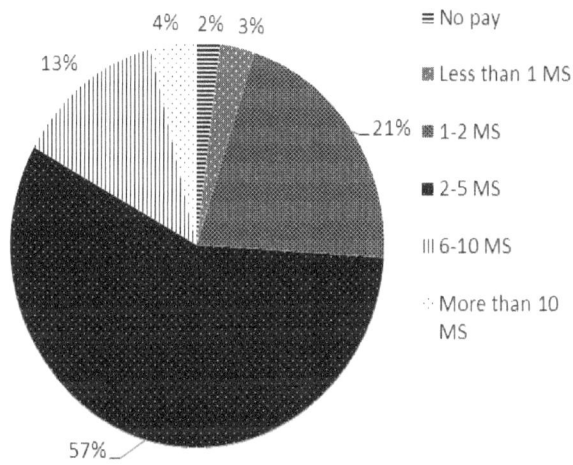

Source: INEGI 2001a.

Table 1 shows the specificity of Los Cabos regarding the high number of people born outside the municipality who create increased competition and supply workers for the labor market. This also causes a greater demand for public services, which is often not possible to provide. In general, it appears that the Los Cabos economy shows many characteristics of other regions of Latin America where relatively dynamic economies have hardly succeeded in reducing poverty and inequality (Gerber 2007). This is due in part to the lack of access of the poor to basic goods and services and, ultimately, to the implementation of economic policies that do not consider social factors (Birdsall and London 1997).

Table 1. Population Born Outside of Los Cabos and BCS, 2000

Place	Born Outside of Place (%)
Baja California Sur	32.50
Los Cabos	49.50

Source: INEGI 2001b.

THE CONSOLIDATION OF LOS CABOS AS A GROWTH POLE: CHALLENGES, STRENGTHS, WEAKNESSES, OPPORTUNITIES, AND THREATS

The development of Los Cabos has different dynamics from the rest of the state due to the intense tourism activity. The multimillion-dollar investment projects developed there require an amount of labor that has made the migration rate to San José del Cabo and Cabo San Lucas one of the highest in the country. While it is true that employment generation is one of the primary needs of the state and country in general, the hasty concentration of a significant number of people entails another problem that is not easy to solve.

This demonstrates that all economic activity directly or indirectly involves environmental- and social-type impacts. For example, the natural capital of Baja California Sur, with its incomparable biodiversity and beauty of its land and marine environment, attracts tourists to the region. New residents and tourists create a demand for food and restaurants, auto repair, construction and maintenance of houses, and other necessary services. The goods and services they require—including wastewater services to new neighborhoods, electricity, and schools for their children—even if indirect, will be additional impacts of tourism. These indirect impacts will affect both the environment and the demand for basic infrastructure and social services (Gerber 2007). Therefore, it is very necessary to update the planning and land ordinance tools.

Currently, there is no municipal program for urban development to control land occupation and urban growth. However, there are elements in the State Law for Urban Development to carry out these tasks. The municipality's Ecological Ordinance Program requires an

The Consolidation of Los Cabos as a Growth Pole

update. There are no urban development programs for the population centers in Cabo del Este, which is subject to strong development pressure in the short and medium term.

Important problems affect both tourism development and the welfare of the local population. First, there is the lack of paved roads. It is estimated that 68% of all roads in the municipality are unpaved. San José del Cabo has about 80% of its roads paved, but not so for Cabo San Lucas, where the percentage is only 30%. Dirt roads predominate in the rest of the settlements. A second problem is the lack of efficient urban transportation. Taxis are the main means of transportation in the municipality. This is because local public transportation is deficient and slow, since it is made up of a small number of buses in poor condition that exclusively service the periphery of urban areas of Cabo San Lucas and San José del Cabo. A third problem is the inadequate provision of public security services. Currently, there is one security agent for every 340 inhabitants and a public safety vehicle for every 1,894 inhabitants, figures below those for other municipalities nationwide.

All the aforementioned negatively impact the successful consolidation of Los Cabos as a development pole, since economic development is abated by the unfavorable effects on the environment and society. If all these factors, both favorable and unfavorable, are classified, four components result: strengths,[5] weaknesses,[6] opportunities,[7] and threats.[8] These are shown in Table 2:

Despite the limitation of this study, it is obvious that this tourist destination is facing broad challenges, which clearly include social, environmental, economic, and even institutional aspects. Therefore, integral solutions are needed that take into account, in a proper perspective, each of the aforementioned aspects.

---

5. Strengths refer to internal characteristics that represent advantages to achieve favorable objectives or positions. Thus, a strength can be the special capabilities or activities that develop positively and allow a business or region to respond effectively to an opportunity or threat.
6. Weaknesses are related to the inadequate management of economic activities and to the lack of resources or skills. Together, these factors cause an entity or company to have an unfavorable position when facing development challenges.
7. Opportunities are those factors that are favorable and exploitable, and should be discovered in the surroundings in which one studies. They also are situations, resources, or external characteristics that can be beneficially used.
8. Threats refer to present or future unfavorable situations; external aspects or characteristics that represent disadvantages over which there is no direct control, but that should be considered for setting objectives and designing strategies to minimize their adverse impact on development processes (Guzón 2002).

Table 2. Strengths, Weaknesses, Opportunities, and Threats on the Consolidation of Los Cabos as a Growth Pole

Strengths	Weaknesses
A) Economic • Competitive advantages in terms of geographical location and high potential for development of alternative tourism • International recognition for its world-class sporting tournaments, including golf and sportfishing • Consolidation as a tourism development pole, with an important infrastructure, megadevelopments, and investment multiplier effect • Municipality tending toward self-sufficiency, since 70% of budget is financed through own resources • Considered one of the nation's most important municipalities on matters of tax collection • Has the state's highest Human Development Index (HDI), higher than the state average, and number 38 nationally, surpassing Loreto, Cancún, and Acapulco (CONAPO 2001) • High wage level in comparison to the rest of the state • Constant demand for workforce • Installed infrastructure: shopping centers of good size and importance • Due to its geographic location, offers the possibility of establishment and development of new industries • Proximity to land communication routes and ports connecting the north and south of the state and country	**A) Economic** • Insufficient basic, urban, and tourist infrastructure • Unbalanced tourism development in microregions • Low social infrastructure growth compared to tourism infrastructure • High dependency on foreign investment • Excessive growth of informal economy, mainly from street vendors **B) Social** • Lack of cultural and recreational spaces • Insufficient training and professionalization of technical and professional workforce • Tourism culture requires improvement • High rates of drug addiction, prostitution, vagrancy, school dropouts • Problems related to loss and transformation of local culture and customs (acculturation and transculturation) • Constant arrival of immigrants that sometimes displace the local workforce • Clashes among strategic groups for the consolidation of development: environmentalists, fishers, transportation operators, investors, commercial airlines, and government • Discontentment of society due to lack of routes or the restricted access to beaches occupied by tourism developments

Table 2. *(continued)*

Strengths	Weaknesses
B) Social • Organizational capacity in public and private spheres • Hospitable and peaceful city compared to other tourist destinations and cities in the nation • Good prospects for technical and professional employment • Gastronomic culture **C) Institutional** • Existence of institutional programs such as the route of the missions; Sea of Cortez ecotourism circuit; and South Gulf special program • Educational institutions with technical studies; from high school to higher education focused on tourism • Places 15 at the national level within the Institutional Competitiveness Index (Cabrero, Orihuela, and Ziccardi 2007) **D) Environmental** • Existence of urban development and land ordinance plans • Decrees of areas intended for conservation	**C) Institutional** • Lack of promotion of historical-cultural sites and ecotourism activities • Lack of timely and reliable tourism databases and indicators • Serious conflicts on matters of land tenure • Growth in the number of irregular settlements **D) Environmental** • Lack of optimal systems for treatment of hotel waste and trash in general • Modification of coastline due to intensive and disorderly growth of urban and marine tourism infrastructure • Deterioration and pollution of coastal wetlands (marshes, mangroves) due to construction of urban developments, communication arteries, landfills, compaction, etc. • Marine pollution due to stormwater runoff carrying waste • Visual and noise pollution
Opportunities	**Threats**
A) Economic • Outstanding revenue generation • Strong public and private investment, domestic and foreign, and important revenue streams due to financial and real estate services • Existence of research that indicates that municipalities with high tourism activity have a medium to low level of marginalization • Growth in demand for activities that allow fostering local development	**A) Economic** • Urban and welfare lag, and unfairness in benefits from development • Global recession that directly affects investment and employment generation • Displacement and marginalization of primary activities

Table 2. (continued)

Opportunities	Threats
B) Social • Increasing interest from society on issues related to sustainability **C) Institutional** • Strong promotion of programs for creation of temporary jobs • Creation of standards and programs to promote quality in tourism services • Interest from federal government in immediately solving critical conflicts for tourism development **D) Environmental** • Interest from international agencies to protect areas of the municipality in conservation areas	**B) Social** • Severe problem of social marginalization, loss of values and local identity • Increasing foreign interference and influence in political and social life • Worsening of social problems propitiated by the creation of poverty belts and the growth of urban poverty **C) Institutional** • Lack of updated legal and regulatory framework and in line with current conflicts **D) Environmental** • Noncompliance with environmental regulations • Environmental impact due to rapid population growth that has exceeded the regulatory management capacity and implementation of public policies

Source: Prepared by authors based on data from documentary research by Gámez and Montaño 2003.

CONCLUSIONS: TOWARD EQUITY AND SUSTAINABILITY OF THE DEVELOPMENT POLE

The challenges to overcome in order to approach sustainability and equity in Los Cabos[9] can be divided into the following main groups:
1. Transform Los Cabos into a true development pole, with an important multiplier effect in the regional and state economy:
   • Establish for large hotels supply chains of agricultural/livestock goods produced in the state, for example, meat, fruits, and vegetables. This policy could generate a trigger effect not only for the municipality, but for other regions of the state, such as the valley of Santo Domingo

---

9. To formulate the challenges to be overcome, the opinions expressed by members of the Los Cabos community in the First Public Consultation Forum have been taken into account.

- Promote the establishment of small and medium enterprises connected directly or indirectly to tourism, such as cultural tourism, ecotourism, or adventure tourism, including the necessary support services, such as handicrafts production, and so forth
- Support creation of revenue in rural areas and ranches through tours to learn about the culture and typical ranch activities of Baja California Sur
- Establish training and financing programs for microentrepreneurs in urban and rural areas
2. Include the local population in the economic benefits generated by tourism development. This must be reflected, first, in a better quality of life of inhabitants in urban and rural areas and, second, in the participation of society in government actions through permanent communication schemes, permanent citizen complaint programs, and participation plans. The following are some specific activities in this regard:
    - Implement where none exist and improve public services, social security, and health services with broad coverage
    - Improve availability and access to education at the primary, secondary, and higher education levels
    - Improve public transportation (suburban train)
    - Promote integral housing developments, dignified housing
    - Enhance culture and recreation
    - Support vulnerable sectors through:
        - Training program for women
        - Programs for the disabled
        - Awareness toward people with disabilities
3. Establish and implement urban development policies and regulations:
    - Laws and regulations
        - Regulate building height
        - Restrict and regulate street vendors
        - Apply the Law of Condominium Regime
        - Update and enforce the regulation of urban image
        - Implement outreach programs on regulations for the population
        - Update the Urban Development Plan and the Local Ecological Urban Development Program
        - Develop ordinance for water activities on beaches

- Impose fines for violating urban sanitation regulations
- Planning
  - Define concept of urban landscape and scenic values
  - Find balance between monotony and visual chaos, harmony, aesthetic values
  - Keep downtown areas of each city with same style, design, color (e.g., San Miguel de Allende, Taxco models)
  - Build more parks and provide for their maintenance; gardens with native vegetation
  - Place bilingual street and road signs

4. Maintain competitiveness of Los Cabos as a tourist destination:
   - Avoid vulnerability related to foreign tourism
     - Complement tertiary sector with primary (agriculture, fisheries)
     - Create regional centers of handicrafts production
   - Avoid the risk of "massification" of the destination. Full positioning and successful performance experienced by the destination will continue to attract major investors seeking profitability for their businesses. This phenomenon can pressure for a rapid increase in supply at risk of losing quality and cheapening the destination. For example, the paradigm of destinations with a high concentration of "all inclusive" supply has experienced lower levels of average fares/prices and local complementary spending. Complement traditional "sun and beach" tourism activities with alternative tourism activities.

5. Destination planning:

   In order to comply with the previously mentioned points, the main challenge of the municipality is to plan the development of this destination. Proper planning should be based on precise indicators and studies. It is no longer possible to continue with an unchecked growth scheme, erroneously and invalidly planned, since future repercussions can be very costly in social, economic, and environmental terms. They may even endanger the existence and cause the loss of the growth dynamics of this municipality and possibly of the state itself. In addition, the implementation of training workshops, funding, and assistance for legal and financial planning could help considerably to overcome the legal, financial, and administrative constraints faced by small and medium enterprises. Also, these could generate a more active participation from society. These actions, together with more in-depth analyses, are particularly critical in areas where future tourism development can be linked with other economic sectors at the municipal and state levels. Finally, it is necessary to assess the impacts on the environment, which should be protected as the main potential and basis for tourism activities, in order to guarantee a long-term economic and social development on the solid foundation of sustainability and to benefit the Los Cabos society.

References

Birdsall, Nancy, and Juan Luis Londo. 1997. "Asset Inequality Does Matter: Lessons from Latin America." *American Economic Review* 87 (2) 32–37.

Cabrero Mendoza, Enrique, Isela Orihuela Jurado, and Alicia Ziccardi Contigiani. 2007. *Competitividad de las ciudades mexicanas: La nueva agenda de los municipios urbanos.* México, DF: Centro de Investigación y Docencia Económicas (CIDE) and Secretaría de Economía (SE).

Centro Estatal de Información (CEI). 2005. *Cuadernillo de datos básicos de los municipios de Baja California Sur.* La Paz, BCS: CEI.

Comisión Nacional de Población (CONAPO). 2001. *Índices de desarrollo humano, 2000.* (Accessed 4 April 2009), http://www.conapo.gob.mx/publicaciones/indicesoc/IDH2000/ desarrollo_humano.pdf.

Comisión Nacional de Salarios Mínimos (CONASAMI). 2004. *Salario mínimo.* (Accessed 4 April 2009), http:/www.inegi.gob.mx/est/contenidos/espanol/tematicos/coyontura/pubcoy/entidades/03/sm.asp?c=4199&e=03.

Fondo Nacional de Fomento al Turismo (FONATUR). 2004. *Estadísticas sobre el turismo.* (Accessed 4 April 2009), http://www.fonatur.gob.mx/index_estadisticas.html.

Gámez, Alba, and Bertha Montaño. 2003. "Diagnóstico estratégico del sector turismo en Baja California Sur." Pp. 277–312 in *Diagnóstico estratégico de Baja California Sur,* Antonina Ivanova and Ángeles Villa, eds. La Paz, BCS: Universidad Autónoma de Baja California Sur and Secretaría de Educación Pública.

Gerber, James. 2007. "Un análisis comparativo de dos polos de desarrollo turístico: Loreto y Los Cabos." Pp. 247–259 in *Loreto: El futuro de la primera capital de las Californias*, Paul Ganster, Oscar Arizpe, and Antonina Ivanova, eds. San Diego, CA: San Diego State University Press and Institute for Regional Studies of the Californias.

Gobierno del Estado de Baja California Sur (GOB-BCS). 2009. *4to. Informe de gobierno del Ing. Narciso Agúndez. Documento gráfico y estadístico*. La Paz, BCS: GOB-BCS.

Guzón, Ada. 2002. "Participación local, experiencias de trabajo comunitario en ciudad de La Habana." Unedited report. La Habana, Cuba

Hermansen, Tormod. 1974. "Polos y centros de desarrollo en el desarrollo nacional y regional. Elementos de un marco teórico para un enfoque sintético." *Eure* 4 (10): 55–93.

Instituto Nacional de Estadística, Geografía e Informática (INEGI). 2001a. *Resultados definitivos. Censos económicos 1999*. Aguascalientes, AGS: INEGI.

Instituto Nacional de Estadística, Geografía e Informática (INEGI). 2001b. *Tabulados básicos: Baja California Sur. XII censo de poblacion y de vivienda*. Aguascalientes AGS: INEGI.

López López, Álvaro. 2002. "Análisis de los flujos turísticos en el corredor Los Cabos, Baja California Sur." *Investigaciones Geográficas. Boletín del Instituto de Geografía*, UNAM 47: 131–149. (Accessed 4 April 2009), http://www.igeograf.unam.mx/web/iggweb/publicaciones/ boletin_editorial/boletin/bol47/b47art8.pdf.

Miguel, Andrés, and Julio Torres. 2007. "Las desigualdades del desarrollo regional en México." *Oaxaca Población Siglo XXI* 7 (20). (Accessed 4 April 2009), http://www.oaxaca.gob.mx/digepo/sub/Revistas/Num20/desregmex.pdf.

Paelinck, J. 1965. "La théorie du développement régional polarisé." *Cahiers de L'ISEA* 15 (March).

Peña Sánchez, A. R. 2006. "Las disparidades económicas interregionales en Andalucía." Ph.D. dissertation, University of Cádiz, Madrid, Spain. (Accessed 4 April 2009), http://www.eumed.net/tesis/2006/arps/.

Secretaría de Turismo (SECTUR). 2009. *Reporte de indicadores turísticos de Baja California Sur*. La Paz, BCS: Dirección de Planeación y Desarrollo Turístico, Departamento de Estadística.

Vilas, Carlos. 2009. "La economía de enclave en la Costa Atlántica de Nicaragua." Universidad de Nicaragua. Unpublished.

Zárate, Martín, and María Teresa Rubio Benito. 2005. *Geografía humana: Sociedad, economía y territorio.* Madrid, España: Editorial Ramón Areces. (Accessed 4 April 2009), ttp://books.google.com.mx/books?id=tirgxdwrm0MC&pg=PA120&dq=geografia+humana+zarate#PPA409,M1.

24

Growth, Human Development, and Perception of Well-Being in Los Cabos

Manuel Ángeles, Alba E. Gámez, and Paul Ganster

INTRODUCTION

The economy of Baja California Sur (BCS) has been traditionally based on the service sector and anchored in the government sector, commerce, and, especially during the last couple of decades, in tourism and related fields. The importance of tourism is evident in regions such as Los Cabos and, although the more diverse economic base of the municipality of La Paz dilutes the direct impact of visitor flows, the construction of tourism projects there is prominent as well, especially along the coast. The relevance of traditional tourism and second homes, together with the boom in real estate speculation that is linked to those activities, is such that recent estimates of gross domestic product (GDP) suggest that about 40% of the state's economy relates to them. Meanwhile, the latest economic census revealed that nearly one-third of the Baja California Sur residents are employed in tourism.

After a quick characterization of the growth model based on tourism that prevails in BCS, this chapter analyzes its impacts on income distribution and human development, and provides state- and municipal-level data. In addition, the marginalization indicators that the National Population Council (Consejo Nacional de Población–CONAPO) produces are used to conduct a comparative study of the municipality of Los Cabos and the rest of the state. In addition, these indicators are used to compare the Los Cabos communities of

San José del Cabo, Cabo San Lucas, and Colina del Sol. Finally, the results of an opinion poll recently carried out in Cabo San Lucas regarding the perception of well-being held by certain sectors of the community are discussed.

CHARACTERISTIC OF THE BAJA CALIFORNIA SUR ECONOMIC-TOURISM MODEL

Tourism in Baja California Sur developed only on a small scale until 1960, but it was strengthened in the following two decades by the growth of the import trade for resale, which attracted Mexicans from elsewhere in the country. BCS had a significant comparative advantage in this type of trade due to the free zone, while in the rest of the country there was a tariff protection. However, the economic liberalization processes that were initiated in the early 1980s, and that deepened with the signing of the North American Free Trade Agreement (NAFTA) and its implementation beginning in 1994, eliminated the comparative advantage for sales of imported goods that supported the state's trade and with it the flow of mostly Mexican visitors. The negative effects on tourism of the decline in commerce were later redressed through tourism development policies.

Through the implementation of the scheme of "integrally planned" tourism centers (centros integralmente planeados—CIPs) that was carried out by the National Fund for Tourism Development (Fondo Nacional de Fomento al Turismo–FONATUR) in Los Cabos beginning in the 1970s, tourism in BCS not only regained its previous position, but it reached unexpected dimensions. From being a small fishing and agricultural area, the region of Los Cabos has become one of Mexico's most dynamic tourist destinations. Focusing on conventional tourism (sun, sand, and surf; sportfishing; and fun), Los Cabos received 1.1 million visitors in 2008, equivalent to 73% of the state total (see Table 1 and CEI 2009). Its dynamism as a source of employment has stimulated demographic growth, as well as tourism and communications infrastructure. The municipality of Los Cabos has more than 14,000 hotel rooms (Table 2), and its ability to attract foreign visitors with high incomes makes it unquestionable that it generates enormous revenues, whose magnitude and impact have never been properly analyzed.

Table 1. BCS: Foreign and Domestic Tourists by Hotel Locality, 2007

Locality	Domestic	Foreign	Total
Cabo San Lucas	90,740	444,347	535,087
La Paz	54,265	186,167	240,432
Loreto	45,386	125,654	171,040
San José del Cabo	69,251	108,656	177,907
Los Cabos Corridor	70,613	312,591	383,204
Rest of the state	105,775	361,372	467,147
BCS	648,200	1,326,617	197,482

Source: INEGI 2007, Table 20.5.

Table 2. BCS: Hotel Rooms by Municipality, 2007

Municipality	Rooms
Los Cabos	14,053
La Paz	2,118
Loreto	579
Comondú	377
Mulegé	56
BCS	17,183

Source: INEGI 2007, Table 20.2.

Although alternative tourism in its versions of low environmental effects and low negative social impacts has been highlighted in the government discourse, in practice, tourism has focused on large investment projects with high economic, social, ecological, and environmental impacts. Accompanying this is the construction of second homes mainly for U.S. and Canadian retirees that has led to growing real estate speculation. Finally, a dynamic marina (the Nautical Ladder/Route, now Sea of Cortez project) and cruise tourism have been added. It is estimated that there are currently more than 40 real estate megaprojects under construction or awaiting approval or funding in the municipality of Los Cabos, and that each will include at least one golf course and will require a "community of support."[1]

The aforementioned growth model necessarily has strong negative consequences in terms of sustainability. If this concept is defined according to the criteria of the Brundtland Commission that are now generally accepted in order to find a balance among economic growth, environmental protection, and both social and intergenerational equity, then the performance evaluation of BCS in general and Los Cabos in particular becomes a matter of great complexity. However, this study is inevitable if the Baja California Sur population is to have a dignified future. Among the negative externalities or unwanted effects seen in Los Cabos, population growth stands out, which has averaged about 10% per year over the last decade. This obviously is much faster than the provision of housing, basic infrastructure, schools, health centers, and recreational and cultural facilities. Added to that is the deterioration of the environment, the landscape, and the aggravation of water scarcity given the inadequacy of the local aquifer to supply the needs of the local population and tourism. In addition, the construction of megaprojects with multiple golf courses, in a semiarid zone, lacks a minimal sense of sustainability.

Both mass tourism ("all inclusive") and that of greater economic exclusiveness have generated enormous conflicts in the Los Cabos region with respect to land use, possession, and benefits, especially along the coast. These conflicts have now extended eastward, beyond the limits of the municipality of Los Cabos and are entering into the municipality of La Paz. Among the most significant conflicts are those that are related to sectoral economic activities (marine vs.

---

1. In the area of the current Cabo Pulmo (National Marine Park, the only coral reef system in the Mexican Pacific), a "gigaproject" (Cabo Cortés) is being considered, which entails the appropriation of seven kilometers of beach, the construction of four golf courses, 400 nautical slips, 8,000 "exclusive homes," 60,000 square meters of commercial space, and a "typical Mexican town" with schools, etc., which will host the 20,000 "support workers" for the visiting population (UrbanFreak 2008; Multipress 2008). The investment has been projected at over 2.6 billion dollars over a 15-year period, and the region will grow from 58 inhabitants to 60,000 or more. Previously, the press (not the state government) had announced an investment in Loreto by the (now failed) Spanish company Fadesa of four billion euros, with 6,500 houses, 7,000 hotel and condominium rooms, and four golf courses; all this in a region that has only 15,000 inhabitants and a single water source that, according to the authority in charge, will be able to supply a maximum of 20,000 people. In the event these are carried out, the projects of Loreto Bay and Fadesa (or its successor) could increase the population of Loreto from 120,000 to 240,000 inhabitants (Steinitz et al. 2005). Loreto's own government in 2005 projected a growth of up to 65,000 inhabitants, more than five times the current population.

fishing); social activities (the interests of the *ejidatarios* [communal land holders] and fishers); international activities (the rights of the Baja California Sur population and tourists with second residences); and equity activities (the dignified access to satisfaction of well-being, including the enjoyment of the landscape and free transit on the beaches). A clear example of the effects of the ongoing economic model is the privatization of a long stretch of coastal road that runs from Cabo San Lucas to San José del Cabo (35 km), in exchange for support for building a new road (from which, incidently, there is no longer a view of the sea; the viewshed was privatized). Everything indicates that the scenic beauty, the wide geographic expanse, and the low population density of Baja California Sur are seen as limitless resources that represent an open invitation for the multiplication of resorts, golf courses, and residential complexes, without obligations or precautions for investors in terms of the immediate and future effects of these projects. Even in the case of projects considered environmentally friendly, there is no information on the monitoring of the ongoing impacts of these investments.

The foregoing is explained by the absence of a state development plan that promotes economic diversification and social and environmental balance. So far, government strategies and actions have defined the promotion of private investment in tourism developments or resorts as the development strategy, emphasizing job creation as a clear goal of this development. Without denying the enormous importance of a greater number of jobs, there should be a more careful and selective management of the investment policy in order to guarantee the maintenance and improvement of these places of work in the future, of their quality, and the assurance of a greater quality of life for the population.

The announcements of spectacular investments and a major generation of jobs in areas such as La Ribera, east of Los Cabos; Loreto; Colinas del Puerto; Los Cabos port; and Cabo Cortés, among many others, are not linked to social or environmental contingency plans or to a public policy framework that suggests a rational planning of resources. According to Ángeles, Gámez, and Ivanova (2009a):

> It is surprising that for an entity "with a great vocation for tourism," above all else, the government did not follow the national example or that of other tourist destinations, to provide satellite accounts for tourism. Given this

lack, *there is no way of knowing what will be the impact on the economy of any of the projects announced, nor by the revenue or by the employment.* Investment figures are mere announcements, while the effects of that investment on local revenues are not known.

The lack of accurate information that goes beyond mere advertising and gives account of the real impacts of the tourism and real estate sector is not exclusive of state-level government agencies. Other studies have already emphasized significant discrepancies between the figures that the National Institute for Statistics and Geography (Instituto Nacional de Estadística y Geografía–INEGI) reports in national accounts and those it reports in the economic censuses for the state's economy. One or the other, or both, are wrong. Thus, estimates must be made for the portion of the value added that is due to tourism. At the time of writing this paper, the GDP of BCS amounted to 10.5 billion pesos at 1993 prices (INEGI 2007). Of these, 30.1% was due to the Finance, Insurance, and Real Estate sector; 19.0% to Commerce, Restaurants, and Hotels; and 11.4% to Transportation, Storage, and Communications. It is estimated that 90% of the first sector is attributable to real estate, and assuming that one-half of the second and one-third of the third are related to tourism, then the result is that about 40% of GDP depends on tourism.

Moreover, the census reported value[2] added for the state of 11.3 billion pesos in 2003, the year of the last economic census available at the time of this writing. This was more than the GDP of the time (8.9 billion) by almost 27%, which denotes a strong inconsistency in the estimates that urgently needs to be corrected. It is noteworthy that the real estate sector in the economic census constitutes only 2.4 per cent of the census value added, although it has already been seen that in the GDP, this sector accounts for almost 30% of the total. Otherwise, the economic census seems to properly reflect the weight of the tourism sector in the state: 23.7% of establishments, 29.2% of employment, 21.8% of wages, and 32.2% of value added[3] (see Ángeles, Gámez, and Ivanova 2009a, 2009b).

---

2. It is important to bear in mind that the value added of each economic activity is equal to the income it generates, after deducting the costs of inputs. Put simply, the value added consists of remunerations and profits.
3. For lack of more detailed information in the economic censuses, this stage does not include the economic impact of investment for tourism purposes.

In addition, important information is revealed when calculating the share of wages in total income (value added) generated. For example, remunerations are 16.7% of income in the real estate sector, 53% in leisure and guest services, 42% in restaurants and hotels, and only 28% in transportation. Gains or profits exceed 50% of total income in each and every one of the activities related to tourism. For the sector as a whole, 37.7% of value added relates to salaries and the rest to other areas, mostly profits. That is, tourism has been good business for investors.

This fact is confirmed with full clarity through the use of the state's Social Accounting Matrix (SAM) (Ángeles, Sermeño, and Cortés 2006), which shows total remunerations in the tourist sectors distributed by income quintile. Recalling that a "quintile" represents 20% of all households, the results in terms of the distribution of remunerations (see Table 3) are impressive by their enormous inequality. While the higher income level (Q5) receives 85% of wages and salaries generated in real estate, the lower level (Q1) receives only 0.26%. In restaurants and hotels, the highest income quintile earns nearly half of the remunerations and the lowest quintile just slightly over 2% of them.[4]

Table 3. BCS: Contribution of Tourism Sector to Salaries and Wages by Quintile (%)

Quintile/Sector	Real Estate Sector	Restaurant and Hotels	Entertainment and Recreation
Q1	0.26	2.28	2.28
Q2	1.82	9.07	9.07
Q3	3.99	14.24	14.24
Q4	9.18	25.51	25.51
Q5	84.75	48.90	48.90

Note: the identity of proportions in restaurants and hotels, and entertainment and recreation, is in the original INEGI data. These estimates are from the state's Social Accounting Matrix (Ángeles, Sermeño, and Cortés 2006).

---

4. In entertainment and recreation, the National Survey of Household Income and Expenditures (Encuesta Nacional de Ingresos y Gastos de los Hogares–ENIGH) uses the same percentages as in restaurants and hotels. The ENIGH used in Ángeles, Sermeño, and Cortés (2006) is for 2002.

Finally, the economic enclave nature of the productive sectors of BCS that are connected outside the region but lack strong intersectoral linkages within the state, makes any impact analysis complicated because much of the revenue generated in the state is filtered to the outside (Ángeles 2008). It is therefore urgent that the state government take responsibility for building and maintaining a reliable information system that includes a satellite account (with data on the origin of production, distribution of value added, and sectoral distribution of visitor spending). This would allow real studies to be carried out that illustrate and *quantify* the impact of spending and investment in the regional economy, which should be an indispensable tool for public policy.

Human Development Index

The Human Development Index (HDI), proposed by the United Nations Development Programme (UNDP), is derived from the works of Amartya Sen (1973, 2000). The index is based on the idea that the fundamental objective of development is to expand the capacity of individuals to enjoy a healthier and more creative life, with the proper means to participate fully and productively in their social environment. A society that respects and promotes the quality of life of its members positions itself at a high level in the HDI. The HDI measures the average achievements of a country in three basic aspects of human development: longevity, knowledge, and a decent standard of living. Longevity is measured by life expectancy at birth; knowledge as a combination of adult literacy and the combined school enrollment of primary, secondary, and high school; and the standard of living is measured by the gross national income per capita. The HDI is calculated on a scale of 0 to 1.0; a score of 0.8 and above is considered high human development, while less than 0.5 indicates a low one.

The UNDP publishes an annual report on human development that compares more than 170 countries. The observed differences in the HDI cannot be explained by looking only at the investment and economic growth; it is possible that even with similar levels of growth, human development opportunities for individuals differ as a result of social, cultural, institutional, or political aspects, among others. This is particularly true in societies where the distribution of wealth and income is very uneven, as has historically been the case in Mexico and, increasingly, Baja California Sur (PNUD-Mexico 2008).

The 2007 HDI Report (PNUD-Mexico 2008) analyzes comprehensive information for Mexico, which includes its 32 states and more than 2,400 municipalities. This was the first time that all HDI elements were available for all regions of Mexico and over time, using data from 2000 and 2005. The results showed a scenario of considerable regional inequality at all levels: international, interstate, and within states at the municipal level. According to the report, in 2000, Mexico's HDI was 0.794 (compared to 0.942 for Norway, the country which then had the world's highest HDI); five years later, Mexico's HDI was placed at 0.807, number 52 in the world, below Cuba and above Bulgaria.[5]

But while in 2000 Mexico City reported a level of development of 10.2% higher than the national average, the state of Chiapas was 11.8% below the average. The explanation for these differences is found in the subindices that make up the HDI. For example, there was a 6% difference between Mexico City and Chiapas regarding the life expectancy indicator, but the difference between them grew to 24 points with respect to the education index and to an equal number with reference to income per capita. In 2005, the two continued to exemplify the extremes of development and underdevelopment, but Chiapas had reduced the gap. The HDI level in Mexico City exceeded the national average by 10.3%, while the Chiapas HDI was located 1% above the national average. The reduction of inequality of the global human development indicator is due to the advances observed in Chiapas in the fields of longevity and education. For longevity, the gap between both regions was only five points, while in education a difference of 17 points remained. In terms of per capita income, the gap continued to be an enormous 44.3%.

Baja California Sur has traditionally shown relatively high development indices as measured by the HDI, maintaining sixth

---

5. Due to the current global crisis, these figures are already outdated and surely Mexico's place in the world order of 2010 will be lower, since a fall is expected for GDP on the order of 8 to 10 percent. Given the traditionally slow paces of growth in the past nearly three decades, the country will take three to five years to recover production and income levels of 2008. Note also that the 2008 ENIGH has already reported a sharp increase in poverty (more than five million additional poor), and that was done with data prior to the financial crisis.

place nationally between 2000 and 2005 (PNUD-Mexico 2008). Throughout its history, the state has been able to take advantage of its small population, social cohesion, strong federal transfers, and the subsequent boom periods related to agricultural production (1950s and 1960s), its status as a duty-free trade center (1970–1985), and, currently, tourism and real estate speculation.

In terms of the HDI individual components, during the period reported by the UNDP, BCS remained consistently in the top six places in education and health, but showed a lag with respect to the income component, which increased only marginally from 0.75 in 2000 to 0.78 in 2005 (PNUD-Mexico 2008). In 2000, BCS per capita income, estimated by the purchasing power parity (PPP), was five points above the national average; in 2005, only 3.4%. In addition, the gap with the leading entity (the Federal District) had expanded from 6.2% to 17.6%. This took place despite the fact that in recent years the BCS GDP growth was twice the national average, reaching 7.5% in 2007. Among the various factors that may explain this phenomenon (cf. Ángeles 2008), one merits special attention in the context of this research. That is, the excessive emphasis on a growth model based almost exclusively on traditional tourism (either all inclusive or exclusive), the construction of tourism megaprojects and/or second homes with high social and environmental impact, and their effects on immigration, exclusion, marginalization, and creation of enclaves (economic, social, and cultural), without properly addressing the needs of the population.

Table 4 shows the HDI and its components for BCS, its five municipalities, and Mexico. Statewide, the figures for 2000–2005 show increases in longevity (2.25%) and knowledge (1%), but also a *decrease* of 1% in the income component, implying that in monetary terms, on average, Baja California Sur people were poorer in 2005 than five years earlier. Recalling the results presented earlier regarding income distribution in the state, it is not difficult to conclude that this average conceals strong alterations in the conditions of life of quintiles Q1 to Q3, with no evidence (to date of this writing, but subject to analysis of results of the last ENIGH) of major effects on the highest quintile. The UNDP-Mexico (2008) notes that BCS—still one of the most egalitarian states of Mexico—showed the most pronounced bias toward greater inequality of all entities of the nation. For the 2000–2005 period, the UNDP reported a 30% increase in the value of the state Gini coefficient, and a 25% increase in the coefficient of variation. The Gini coefficient is a measure of inequality, where a higher coefficient represents greater concentration at the top and reflects greater inequality. The coefficient of variation increase means that income is moving away from the mean and that the middle class is shrinking.

Development Indicators at the Municipal Level

To complement and expand the information available at federal and state levels, the UNDP-Mexico has built human development indices for the more than 2,400 municipalities in Mexico, while the National Population Council (CONAPO 2006a) has published marginalization indices for municipalities and localities. The HDI by municipality is based on indicators similar to those used for state and national HDIs. These include level of GDP per capita expressed in international dollars; the percentage of people age 15 and older who know how to read and write a simple message (and therefore are not illiterate); the percentage of people between ages six and 24 who attend school; and the infant mortality rate. The level of income per person is used to build the GDP index per capita; the education variables are the bases for the knowledge index; and infant mortality becomes the indicator of child survival, which is sometimes used as the life expectancy or longevity index (CONAPO 2006a). Table 4 shows relevant data for 2000 to 2005.

As previously mentioned, BCS has a relatively high level of human development, which in 2005 placed the state at the level of the Bahamas and the Seychelles Islands (49–50 in the UNDP global ranking). However, there are regional variations in Baja California Sur, as shown in Table 4. In 2005, La Paz stood out with the highest HDI value in the state (0.90), reaching a par with Kuwait or the Czech Republic (32 in the world); Los Cabos, with 0.88, was similar to Qatar (number 35 in the world); Loreto (0.86) was similar to Estonia and Lithuania (43 and 44); Comondú (0.84) was at the level of Cuba; and Mulegé (0.85) was getting closer to Russia (50 in the world). All BCS municipalities have what the UNDP considers a high level of development, although it differs in the HDI components.

The municipality of Los Cabos has the highest per capita income (US$20,811, according to the PPP), almost one-third more than the state average and more than double the national average. La Paz is the largest city in BCS in terms of population and has the second highest per capita income that is estimated at US$18,726, almost 11% less than that of Los Cabos.

Table 4. Human Development Indicators in Baja California Sur, Its Municipalities, and Mexico, 2000 and 2005

Human Development Index (HDI)	La Paz	Los Cabos	Loreto	Mulegé	Comondú	BCS	Mexico
HDI, 2000 position	50	72	118	201	267	6	54
HDI, 2000 value	0.84	0.83	0.82	0.80	0.79	0.83	0.79
HDI, 2005 position	17	63	108	192	233	6	52
HDI, 2005 value	0.90	0.88	0.86	0.85	0.84	0.84	0.81
Infant mortality rate, 2000	21.50	20.31	23.62	24.24	24.76	22.89	71.00
Infant mortality rate, 2005	10.46	14.48	15.78	19.48	16.12	15.26	75.60
Education rate, 2000	96.68	96.06	95.47	94.25	92.91	95.07	91.40
Education rate, 2005	97.13	95.43	96.28	93.74	93.85	95.29	91.60
School enrollment, 2000	67.58	53.17	64.41	61.20	64.19	62.11	na
School enrollment, 2005	72.01	59.86	69.80	59.80	69.95	66.28	na
Per capita income (PCI), 2000	12,074	13,252	10,626	9,567	8,284	10,761	9,023
Per capita income (PCI), 2005	18,726	20,811	13,657	16,577	9,924	15,939	10,751
Income index, 2000	0.80	0.82	0.78	0.76	0.74	0.79	0.75
Income index, 2005	0.87	0.89	0.82	0.85	0.77	0.78	0.76
Health index, 2000[b]	0.84	0.85	0.82	0.82	0.81	0.83	0.82
Health index, 2005[b]	0.94	0.90	0.89	0.86	0.89	0.84	0.83
Education index, 2000	0.87	0.82	0.85	0.83	0.83	0.85	0.82
Education index, 2005	0.89	0.84	0.87	0.82	0.86	0.89	0.84

Notes: ([a]) The positions of BCS and its municipalities are at the national level; that of Mexico refers to the international level. There are 32 states and slightly more than 2,400 municipalities in the country.
([b]) For Mexico, the health indicator is longevity rather than the infant mortality rate that is used for states and municipalities.
Source: PNUD-México 2008.

The Los Cabos region is of particular interest in this analysis since, by representing about 35% of the state's economic activity and generating by far the highest level of per capita income, the municipality has the sufficient specific weight to raise the state median income. In addition, Los Cabos represents one of the areas of greatest tourism concentration in Mexico and, in fact, a destination of great worldwide importance. It should be noted again that Los Cabos grew from a small fishers' settlement in the late 1970s to having 14,000 hotel rooms and a population growth of 10% per year that was accompanied by weaknesses in physical and social infrastructure.

In other human development indicators, BCS shows more balance, although La Paz leads in health and education. Los Cabos follows in the health index, as shown in Table 4. Importantly for its future development possibilities, Los Cabos shows a lag of five points behind La Paz and three points behind the already poor school attendance figure seen at the state level in BCS. This reflects the large immigration flows to Los Cabos; an inadequate health and education infrastructure; and the inclusion of youth in the labor market at an early age, given their different circumstances and those of their families. It should not be forgotten that while Los Cabos is an attractor of migrants due to its (until recently) high rates of employment and attractive wage levels compared to other regions of Mexico, the area is also a generator of marginalization. In fact, it can be categorically stated that this model of development *depends* on the existence of groups that, lacking other options, dedicate themselves to work related to tourism.

This hypothesis about socioeconomic conditions in Los Cabos finds further evidence in another set of development indicators: the marginalization index published by CONAPO. If the HDI looks for evidence of development (longer life, better education, more income), the marginalization index identifies and quantifies those who have been left aside from the process of growth and development. The index consists of nine indicators. The first is the population and the other eight measure shortcomings and deficiencies with respect to educational attainment, availability of basic services, housing conditions, community size (as a measure of relative isolation), and income levels. There are data for Mexico, the 32 federal entities, and its municipalities. The relevant data for this study are presented in Table 5.

Table 5. BCS: Population, Socioeconomic Indicators, and Marginalization by Municipality, 2000 and 2005

Component	La Paz	Los Cabos	Loreto	Mulegé	Comondú	BCS	Mexico
Population, 2000	196,910	105,470	11,810	45,990	63,860	424,040	97,483,412
Population, 2005	219,600	164,160	11,840	52,740	63,830	512,170	103,263,388
% illiteracy, age 15 and older, 2000	3.20	3.80	4.40	5.50	7.00	4.20	9.50
% illiteracy, age 15 and older, 2005	2.60	3.20	3.60	6.10	6.10	3.60	8.40
% incomplete elementary education, age 15 and older, 2000	16.40	20.80	25.30	28.00	30.70	21.00	28.50
% incomplete elementary education, age 15 and older, 2005	12.80	15.20	17.40	26.00	24.70		23.10
% houses without drainage or toilets, 2000	2.50	3.50	6.70	8.70	3.90	3.70	9.90
% houses without drainage or toilets, 2005	1.30	0.90	1.60	6.80	2.00	1.80	5.30
% houses without electricity, 2000	3.70	6.30	5.40	6.00	3.50	4.60	4.80
% houses without electricity, 2005	2.70	1.90	9.90	3.40	3.90	2.90	2.50
% houses without piped water, 2000	5.60	6.70	6.40	10.20	5.00	6.30	11.20
% houses without piped water, 2005	5.70	22.50	7.20	8.90	5.00	11.30	10.10
% overcrowded houses, 2000	34.30	47.20	41.40	35.90	40.00	38.80	45.90
% overcrowded houses, 2005	29.50	43.20	37.50	34.20	35.00	35.20	40.60
% houses with dirt floors, 2000	6.80	12.40	19.10	13.30	14.60	10.40	14.80
% houses with dirt floors, 2005	4.70	10.80	16.20	9.20	11.80	8.30	11.50

Table 5. (continued)

Component	La Paz	Los Cabos	Loreto	Mulegé	Comondú	BCS	Mexico
% localities with 5,000 or less inhabitants, 2000	17.20	24.90	15.30	54.70	32.30	25.40	31.00
% localities with 5,000 or less inhabitants, 2005	13.80	15.10	13.10	48.00	30.60	19.80	29.00
% under 2 MS or less, 2000	35.40	23.10	45.00	54.60	32.29	35.82	51.00
% under 2 MS or less, 2005 (*)	24.10	15.70	30.60	30.20	37.20	24.10	45.30
Marginalization index, 2000	-1.77	-1.59	-1.38	-1.23	-1.20	-0.82	
Marginalization index, 2005	-1.78	1.52	-1.34	-1.20	-1.25	-0.72	
Marginalization degree, 2000	Very low	Very low	Very low	Low	Low	Low	
Marginalization degree, 2005	Very low	Very low	Very low	Low	Very low	Low	
State rank, 2000	5	4	3	2	1		
State rank, 2005	5	4	3	1	2		
National rank, 2000 (**)	2,383	2,318	2,246	2,167	2,147	27	
National rank, 2005	2,404	2,315	2,257	2,164	2,197	24	

(*) MS, minimum salary, in 2009 about US$115 per month.
(**) Mexico has slightly more than 2,400 municipalities.
Sources: CONAPO 2006a, 2006b; PNUD-México 2008.

As can be seen, the municipality of La Paz contains 43% or, most of the state population. Los Cabos follows closely for in 2000, one-fourth of the Baja California Sur population lived there; five years later, it was one-third. Los Cabos is the richest municipality in terms of the minimum salary (MS), since 85% of the employed population earns more than two MS. This implies that only 15.1% of the employed population earns two MS or less, compared with the state average of 24.1% (see Ivanova, Ibáñez, and Gerber 2012, in this volume). Yet, Los Cabos has a higher percentage of its population without piped water (22.5%) and overcrowded (43.2% compared with 29.5% in La Paz, and surpassing the national average of 40.6%). It also has more houses with dirt floors (11% vs. 5% in La Paz).

The purpose of the marginalization index, as well as of the municipal HDI, is to establish comparisons among the localities of Mexico. The marginalization index also addresses the fact that polarization among regions of the country is extreme: four of the five municipalities of Baja California Sur (La Paz, Los Cabos, Loreto, and Comondú) are located in the ranges of "very low" marginalization, and only Mulegé is in the "low" marginalization range (Table 5). These low and very low marginalization rates occur despite the fact that nearly one-fourth of the population in Los Cabos never finished elementary school, 22.5% of households do not have running water, and it is the national leader in overcrowding. However, it is still classified as a municipality with very low marginalization.[6]

The results for Los Cabos show a rapid and anarchic growth of the population and insufficient infrastructure. In fact, three worlds coexist in Los Cabos: (1) that of tourists (mostly foreign) who can pay hotel rates that range up to one thousand dollars a night or who can buy a million-dollar home in the exclusive El Pedregal subdivision or in one of the new residential complexes; (2) the usually retired foreign resident, and a small Mexican middle class employed in commerce, government, and tourist services and others; and (3) a very large proportion of construction workers, gardeners, stewards, drivers, and employees in the tourism sector, as well as those in the informal sector.

A broader picture emerges when looking at data for the level of localities, as shown in Table 6, which was developed based on the marginalization index by locality (CONAPO 2006b). Data are presented for the main urban areas of BCS by municipality, in order to explore the impact of tourism growth on human development. The data show that La Paz has a population of about 190,000 people, followed by three adjacent localities in the municipality of Los Cabos (Cabo San Lucas, San José del Cabo, and Colonia del Sol), which had

---

6. It is interesting to recall the statements of Governor N. Agúndez regarding the arrival in the state of Hurricane Jimena, in August 2009, to the effect of the more than 15,000 families in Los Cabos living in areas at risk in irregular housing (León 2009). Taking the municipal average of 3.8 persons per household, this would mean that 57,000 people (34% of the population in 2005) lived in conditions of vulnerability. This is certainly an underestimate, since the families of lower income are likely to live in areas at risk and are larger than average.

a combined population of more than 130,000 people in 2005. The city of La Paz shows statistics of "acceptable" marginalization, taking into account the national standards. The most problematic aspects of La Paz are the degree of overcrowding (17.9%) and the proportion of the adult population without a completed primary education (10.3%). In Los Cabos—although San José and Cabo San Lucas follow the pattern of the municipality—the locality of Colonia del Sol shows the clearest official data about the degree of marginalization in this region.

Table 6. BCS: Population, Socioeconomic Indicators, and Marginalization by Urban Area, 2000 and 2005

Municipality	La Paz	Los Cabos			Loreto	Mulegé	Comondú
Localities	La Paz	Cabo San Lucas	San José del Cabo	Colonia del Sol	Loreto	Santa Rosalía	Ciudad Constitución
Population	189,178	56,811	48,518	27,057	10,823	9,768	37,221
% illiteracy, age 15 and older	1.9	2.1	3.4	4.7	2.5	1.9	5.3
% incomplete elementary education, age 15 and older	10.3	10.7	15.7	19.7	14.2	13.2	20.5
% houses without sewers or toilets	0.4	0.2	0.8	2.8	0.9	0.4	0.7
% houses without electricity	2.2	4.6	4.6	3.8	2.6	1.5	1.9
% houses without piped water	3.9	14.2	11.9	61.1	2.3	3.9	0.8
% overcrowded houses	17.9	25.1	32.8	54.7	24.4	17.9	22.8
% houses with dirt floors	2.9	3.5	9.7	23.1	9.9	3.1	6.4
% houses without refrigerator	4.4	14.1	12.7	19.1	8.1	6.2	6.9
Marginalization index	-1.70	-1.55	-1.41	0.94	-1.55	-1.67	-1.51
Marginalization degree	Very low	Very low	Very low	Average	Very low	Very low	Very low

Source: CONAPO 2006a, 2006b.

Colonia del Sol can be seen as a kind of BCS Soweto, Netzahualcóyotl, or Chalco, which has been created by tourism. Most of its 27,000 inhabitants attend to some aspect of the needs of the more than one million tourists who annually arrive in Los Cabos, but naturally they do not enjoy the luxuries of some of the most exclusive hotels in the world. Many of the workers come from Mexico's southern states like Oaxaca, Guerrero, and Chiapas. They become employed in activities that many Baja California Sur people no longer want, such as masonry and construction, gardening, and maintenance and cleaning, among others.

As shown in Table 6, more than half the residents in Colonia del Sol have not completed primary school, compared with 10.7% seen in Cabo San Lucas, or 15.7% in San José del Cabo. One-fifth of households in Colonia del Sol have no refrigerator, one-fourth have dirt floors, more than one half are overcrowded, and almost one-third have no piped water. Social and health problems are common, although—as the press points out—they do not extend to the tourism centers. Nationally, the degree of marginalization is considered "average."[7]

OBSERVATIONS ON WELL-BEING IN CABO SAN LUCAS

The HDI and the marginalization index are quantitative approaches to explaining the development of a particular geographical area at a particular moment in time; in fact, they are designed to be used in the type of comparisons that were made in earlier paragraphs. Due to their nature, these indicators necessarily show a lag—in this case of many years—between what the "hard" data say and what is lived in the society under study.

As mentioned in a previous study on the municipality of Loreto (Carrillio and Ángeles 2007), well-being is a very complex concept that incorporates a good number of social and personal dimensions. At the social level, well-being relates to the degree of organization, community integration, and security within society experienced by individuals, families, and various groups. In addition, well-being

---

[7]. It will be recalled that both Cabo San Lucas and San José del Cabo, and indeed BCS in general, received a classification of "very low" marginalization, under the national benchmark. The locality of Colinas del Sol is the only one near the area of large tourism flows in Los Cabos for which there is official information published. However, many communities in similar circumstances are known in the region, such as Tierra y Libertad.

can be a person's subjective response to his/her environment. Understanding the well-being of a person demands an understanding of both the surroundings and the individual's responses to those surroundings. The feeling of well-being refers to the general sense of a person and a balance between those factors that create a sense of vulnerability and those that provide security and protection.

To capture some of the subjective aspects of human development and well-being in the context of this chapter, in May 2009, a group of students majoring in Foreign Trade and Alternative Tourism of the Autonomous University of Baja California Sur (Universidad Autónoma de Baja California Sur–UABCS), Los Cabos campus, assisted in conducting a survey aimed at gathering opinions on quality of life, well-being, safety, and environmental conditions. At the end of the survey, the respondent was asked to indicate from a preprepared list what factors might be necessary to improve the quality of life in Cabo San Lucas and to elaborate on his/her answers. Interviews were conducted at random in the home neighborhoods of the 24 students involved (each of whom completed five surveys). The results, then, reflect the perceptions and feelings of the sector of the population to which the students belong, that is, the low- and middle-income population. Tables 7 to 11 present the results.

When considering the deep economic crisis that existed when the survey was completed, it is not surprising that survey respondents considered employment as the most important quality of life indicator, especially because they were affected by the reduction in economic activities and the rise of unemployment. In 2009, BCS was among the 10 states with the highest unemployment in the country, and that was only in the first half of the year. Thus, 11,961 formal jobs were lost, that is, workers affiliated with the Mexican Social Security Institute (Instituto Mexicano del Seguro Social–IMSS). Hotel occupancy dropped to a low of 5%, but then showed a very important recovery to 50%. Real wages fell due both to constant price increases of basic goods, as well as unfavorable labor negotiations for workers and loss of job security that results from outsourcing contracts.

The provision of more space for recreation was placed in second position among the demands of the surveyed population, followed by that of greater educational opportunities, higher salaries, and greater attention to the health needs of the people (see Table 7). When asked about their perceptions of the economic situation (Table 8), about one-third responded that it was good or average, while almost 70% said it was bad. With respect to security/safety (Table 9), only 2% of survey respondents said they felt safe in their surroundings, 49% said they felt moderately safe, and 46% felt unsafe. In general, survey respondents said they were satisfied with the region's air quality, but showed great concern over noise pollution (73%), potable water supply (98%), and garbage collection (82%), as shown in Table 10.

Table 7. CSL: Order of Quality of Life Indicators

Rank	Indicator
1	Employment
2	Recreational areas
3	Schools and universities
4	Better salaries
5	Hospitals and medical care

N = 120
Source: CSL Survey, May 2009.

Table 8. CSL: Perception of Economic Well-Being

Perception	Answers %
The economic situation is good	10.2
The economic situation is average	20.4
The economic situation is bad	69.4

Source: CSL Survey, May 2009.

Table 9. CSL: Perception of Security/Safety

Perception	Answers %
Very safe	2.04
Moderately safe	48.97
Unsafe	46.93

Note: 2.04% did not answer the question.
Source: CSL Survey, May 2009.

Table 10. CSL: Satisfaction with Environmental Conditions

Environmental Conditions	Excellent	Good	Regular	Bad
Air quality	28.57	51.02	20.40	0
Quality of beaches	12.24	44.89	20.40	22.44
Noise	6.12	20.40	51.02	22.44
Availability and quality of potable water	2.04	30.61	51.02	16.32
Parks and green areas	2.04	32.65	26.53	38.77
Solid waste collection and disposal	0	18.36	40.81	40.81

Source: CSL Survey, May 2009.

Table 11. Factors that would Improve Quality of Life in Cabo San Lucas

There is need for more...	Yes (%)	No (%)	No Answer
Hospitals and medical care	79.59	20.41	
Shopping centers	46.93	53.07	
Employment	95.91	4.09	
Recreational areas	91.83	8.17	
Infrastructure Investment	89.79	10.21	
Industry	75.51	20.4	
Public transportation	69.38	30.62	2.08
Schools and universities	89.79	10.21	
Movie theaters	42.85	57.15	
Higher wages	81.63	18.37	
Other	53.06	42.85	4.08

Source: CSL Survey, May 2009.

Additionally, respondents were asked to comment on their answers, providing the interviewer a brief explanation. These can be summarized as follows:
- Economy: overdependence on tourism, little or no sectoral diversification in productive activities or employment
- Security/Safety: feeling of vulnerability and lack of safety/security

- Health: ongoing need to transfer patients to La Paz or other locations for treatment and surgery not available in Los Cabos
- Recreation: very few accessible places and with poor maintenance
- Beaches: most are privatized; the number of public beaches is approaching zero; they lack maintenance
- Water: highly chlorinated and subject to constant supply interruptions
- Entertainment (movie theaters): sufficient for the current population, but too expensive and thus not accessible from the economic point of view
- Education: public schools (including universities) provide quality education and certain educational opportunities, but with very limited availability. Private schools are expensive and lack academic credibility

At a minimum, addressing these types of problems should be the core of an action plan by authorities at all levels of government.

Concluding Remarks

The importance of tourism is undeniable in the economic growth of the municipality of Los Cabos and of BCS. Several factors made tourism practically the only source of growth for large areas of the state, including: (1) the dissapearance of agricultural subsidies that BCS received from 1930 on and that created the agricultural boom of the 1940s and 1950s; (2) the elimination of comparative trade advantages that the state had by virtue of its free zone status; and (3) Mexico joining the General Agreement on Tariffs and Trade (GATT) and the North American Free Trade Agreement (NAFTA).

In a span of two decades, the population of Los Cabos increased from 10,000 inhabitants in 1970 to almost 170,000 in 2005 (Table 5; INEGI 2007). From being a group of small agricultural, livestock, and fishing settlements, the municipality has come to have more than 14,000 hotel rooms, golf courses, and exclusive resorts that are visited by more than one million tourists a year. Los Cabos has become the most dynamic population center in the state and second nationally, only behind Cancún.

However, problems abound in this tourism center. Much of the municipality's coastline has been privatized, especially the 33-km stretch of the tourist corridor between San José and Cabo San Lucas. Thus, of the 42 officially recognized beaches, only one remains public; the local population does not have access to the rest of them. In addition, tourism has brought wealth to Los Cabos, but it has also been a source of marginalization given that population growth—which, in turn, is based on the needs of tourism—has exceeded by far the municipality's ability to provide basic goods and services.

In general, socioeconomic and demographic indices and statistics show that BCS is one of the most prosperous states in Mexico, and Los Cabos a region that is richer than the large majority of municipalities.[8] However, both the municipality and the state show signs of decline. For nearly 15 years, BCS has moved downward from the highest levels of per capita income and from the average national per capita income; in fact, it did so at 1% in absolute terms during the 2000–2005 period. In addition, the municipality of Los Cabos has shown an increase in inequality in the provision of key public and human services, such as education and health, not to mention a noticeable increase in the inequality of income distribution. Along with the image of elegant hotels and second home complexes, there has been a substantial increase in what have euphemistically been called "support communities" (León and Aguilera 2008), like Colonia del Sol. Clearly, rapid tourism growth has exceeded the response capacity of municipalities so that the context in which families function affects their reality and perceptions of their well-being and quality of life.

The availability of the HDI and the marginalization index by localities allows the identification of a phenomenon that, although visible in Los Cabos, is hidden in the state's general indicators. Based on that information, it is not only pertinent but necessary to promote strategies that prevent the social and economic polarization linked to tourism that is experienced in the state, especially in destinations such as Los Cabos. The aforementioned is particularly relevant because the tourism development model practiced in Los Cabos is currently being promoted in other areas of the state without addressing its consequences on the environment, society, and even economies of local communities or of newly established settlements. The absence of a rational regulation of the use of natural resources (like water) is having negative impacts that, in the long run, will be devastating for the tourism sector itself and for populations that have made of it, or of associated economic activities, their way of life.

---

8. According to the PNUD-México (2008), of the 2,400 municipalities in Mexico, Los Cabos places number 70 in terms of HDI. La Paz is number 50, and first place is held by Mexico City's Benito Juárez Delegation.

In view of the foregoing, it is necessary that in BCS—particularly in Los Cabos—a reform process be initiated of the traditional tourism model of growth applied up to now, which tends to benefit the few, generates a rising inequality, and damages the environment. Moreover, the global economic crisis highlights the vulnerability of those regions that rely exclusively on a single resource or market as a development strategy. The degree of dependence—that in good times is celebrated as the consumers' preference—should be taken as a warning of what it can represent in times of recession or far-reaching crises.

REFERENCES

Ángeles, M. 2008. "Especificidades del desarrollo en economías pequeñas: Los casos de Hawai y Baja California Sur y una propuesta de análisis para las economías insulares del Pacífico del Sur, 1970–2002." Mimeo. La Paz, BCS: UABCS, Departamento de Economía.

Ángeles, M., A. E. Gámez, and A. Ivanova. 2009a. "Consideraciones sobre turismo y economía en Baja California Sur." *Alternativa de BCS* (enero): 18–21.

Ángeles, M., A. Gámez, and A. Ivanova. 2009b. "¿Cuál es el impacto del turismo en la economía sudcaliforniana?" *Panorama*.

Ángeles, M., J. Sermeño, and R. Cortés. 2006. *La matriz de contabilidad social de Baja California Sur*. La Paz, BCS: UABCS.

Carrilio, T. 2001. "Family Support Program Development–Integrating Research, Practice and Policy." *Journal of Family Social Work* 6 (3): 53–78.

Carrilio, T., and M. Ángeles. 2007. "Human and Social Development in Loreto." Pp. 267–282 in *Loreto: the Future of the First Capital of the Californias,* Paul Ganster, Oscar Arizpe, and Antonina Ivanova, eds. San Diego: San Diego State University Press and Institute for Regional Studies of the Californias.

Carrilio, T., and P. Ganster. 2007. "The Quality of Life in Loreto: Challenges and Opportunities." Pp. 283–300 in *Loreto: the Future of the First Capital of the Californias,* Paul Ganster, Oscar Arizpe, and Antonina Ivanova, eds. San Diego: San Diego State University Press and Institute for Regional Studies of the Californias.

Centro Estatal de Información (CEI). 2009. *Documento de trabajo.* La Paz, BCS: Centro Estatal de Información, Secretaría de Promoción y Desarrollo Económico, Gobierno del Estado de Baja California Sur.
Consejo Nacional de Población (CONAPO). 2006a. *Índices de marginación por Municipio,* 2005. http://www.conapo.gob.mx.
Consejo Nacional de Población (CONAPO). 2006b. *Índices de marginación por Localidad,* 2005. http://www.conapo.gob.mx.
Instituto Nacional de Estadística, Geografía e Informática (INEGI). 2007. *Anuario estadístico del estado de Baja California Sur.* Aguascalientes, AGS.: INEGI.
Instituto Nacional de Estadística, Geografía e Informática (INEGI). 2008. *Censos económicos 2004.* http://www.inegi.gob.mx/inegi/default.aspx?s=est&c=10357.
Ivanova, A., R. Ibáñez, and J. Gerber. 2012. "La consolidación de Los Cabos como un polo de crecimiento: Retos y oportunidades." *Los Cabos: The Future of a Natural and Tourism Paradise.* San Diego: San Diego State University Press.
León, R., and A. Aguilera. 2008. "La firma española Hansa confirma plan para erigir *comunidad turística* en BCS." *La Jornada* (4 November), http://www.jornada.unam.mx/2008/11/04/index.php?section=politica&article=007n1pol.
López, J. A. 2009. "España, segundo inversionista en el sector turístico: Fonatur." *Milenio* (16 November), http://impreso.milenio.com/node/7067428.
Multipress. 2008. *Turismo: Los Cabos.* www.multipress.com.mx/articulos.php.
Programa de las Naciones Unidas para el Desarrollo (PNUD-México). 2008. *Índices de desarrollo humano por municipio, 2000–2005.* PNUD-México.
Sen, A. K. 1973. *On Economic Inequality.* London: Oxford University Press.
Sen, A. K. 2000. *Development as Freedom.* New York: Random House.
Steinitz, C., R. Faris, J. C. Vargas-Moreno, G. Huang, S-Y. Lu, O. Arizpe, M. Ángeles, F. Santiago, A. Ivanova, A. E. Gámez, K. Baird, T. Maddock III, H. Ajami, L. Huato, M. J. Haro, M. Flaxman, P. Ganster, A. Villegas, and C. López. 2005. *Alternative Futures for Loreto, Baja California Sur, Mexico.* Cambridge: Harvard University. www.futursalternativosloreto.org.mx.

Steinitz, C., R. Faris, M. Flaxman, J. C. Vargas-Moreno, T. Canfield, O. Arizpe, M. Ángeles, M. Cariño, F. Santiago, T. Maddock III, C. Dragoo, K. Baird, and L. Godínez. 2004. *Alternative Futures for the Region of La Paz, Baja California Sur, Mexico*. Cambridge: Harvard University.

UrbanFreak. 2008. *Proyecto Cabo Cortés en BCS*. www.urbanfreak.net/showthread.php.

25

The Prospect, Principles, and Practice of Sustainable Development in Los Cabos

David Carruthers

INTRODUCTION

In the late 1980s and early 1990s, sustainable development emerged as the dominant international discourse for interpreting and managing relationships between development and the environment. It remains an immensely attractive concept today because it promises to satisfy demands for environmental protection, economic growth, and social equity, both North and South. It has prompted so many business, government, scholarly, and non-governmental gatherings that one observer once called it "the mantra that launched a thousand conferences" (Dowie 1995). Nearly everyone favors sustainability, including national and local governments, private firms, international institutions, non-governmental organizations, activists, and academics.

Mexico was one of 182 signatory states to enshrine a commitment to sustainable development at the 1992 United Nations Conference on Environment and Development (UNCED) in Rio de Janeiro (Earth Summit). For nearly two decades, officials in Mexico's executive, legislative, and judicial branches have sought to institutionalize that policy commitment. By today, the nation's environmental, land-use planning, wildlife, and natural resource management laws, norms, and institutions widely reflect and attempt to explicate the discourse, principles, and goals of sustainability (Díez 2006; SEMARNAT 2006; Urciaga et al. 2008). This is true at not only the national level, but also at the state and local levels, including Baja California Sur (BCS) and the municipality of Los Cabos.

In spite of its popularity, the precise meaning of sustainable development has always been essentially contested and controversial (Sachs 1993). The concept is at once highly ambitious and fundamentally ambiguous (Dryzek 1997). The most widely cited definition comes from the 1987 report of the Brundtland Commission, *Our Common Future:* "Humanity has the ability to make development sustainable to ensure that it meets the needs of the present without compromising the ability of future generations to meet their own needs" (World Commission on Environment and Development - WCED 1987). This definition highlights an obligation to provide for intergenerational and distributive equity. Beyond that, the concept is highly malleable, multidimensional, and subject to myriad interpretations, depending upon one's theoretical perspectives, political leanings, or practical aims (Torgerson 1995; Carruthers 2005). Therefore, it has proven difficult to measure, implement, or operationalize, both in scholarship and in public policy (Daly 1996).

Attentive to these conceptual challenges, this chapter offers an overview of the prospect, principles, and practice of sustainable development in Los Cabos. After a brief note on research methodology, the first section presents a general conceptual discussion that guides the analysis to follow. The next three sections explore the environmental, economic, and social dimensions of sustainability, respectively, across selected issues that emerged from this research. The chapter concludes with a short reflection on the prospects for sustainable development in Los Cabos.

METHODOLOGY AND CONCEPTUALIZATION

This study is based on the results of fieldwork conducted in La Paz and Los Cabos in January 2009. An inductive, quasi-ethnographic methodology was employed; 17 semistructured, interviews were conducted and recorded with a variety of active participants, stakeholders, observers, and experts on the environment-development nexus in the cape region of Baja California Sur. Interviewees included scholarly experts in economics, environmental history, biology, wildlife conservation, and natural resource management; officials representing several of the most important federal, state, and local government agencies; directors and members of both local and national environmentally oriented non-governmental organizations (NGOs); representatives of *ejidos* (communities sharing a communal form of land tenure associated with Mexico's revolutionary agrarian reform); and businesspersons in the fields of agriculture, tourism, and real estate. A few site visits were also carried out to an organic farm, a farmer's market, and a one-day workshop in the *ejido* community of Santiago with a team from the municipal environmental agency (Dirección Municipal de Ecología y Medio Ambiente). This workshop was designed to solicit *ejidal* participation in the drafting of the municipal Ecological Land Use Plan (Plan de Ordenamiento Ecológico).

Given the broad range of possible interpretations of sustainability, no particular conceptualization was imposed during these interviews. Rather, respondents were invited to share their thoughts regarding the meaning, scope, or application of sustainable development in the context of Los Cabos. Some chose to organize their responses around various substantive environmental and/or developmental issues, and shared their assessments about the region's prospects in terms of those. Others emphasized conceptual themes, or practical and legal matters involved in the implementation of sustainability in policy practice.

These different actors have adopted, criticized, or promoted the language of sustainability variously as a noble proposition, a trendy slogan, a utopian ideal, an abstraction, a lifestyle philosophy, a concrete principle, a marketing tool, a decision-making guide, an analytical heuristic, or a framework for public policy. Despite the diversity of these responses, however, the majority of interviews revealed a consistent grounding in the mainstream thinking about sustainable development as shaped by the United Nations, that is, in the general terms outlined by the Brundtland Commission or the Agenda 21 formulation from the Earth Summit (Sitarz 1993).

This "three pillars" tradition envisages sustainable development as an effort to seek balance along three key dimensions of sustainability: environmental, economic, and social. A similarly familiar reference is to the "three Es" of sustainability: Environmental integrity, Economic efficiency, and social Equity (President's Council on Sustainable Development 1999; Wheeler 2004). Many writers employ metaphors such as a three-legged stool that cannot stand unless all three dimensions are achieved and maintained in equilibrium, or a Venn diagram in which the area of intersection among the three circles represents a mutually enhancing domain of sustainability (Faucheux et al. 1996). In the most general sense, sustainability represents this quest for synergy that satisfies the ecological, economic, and social needs of today, without undercutting that same prospect for future generations.

This triad provides the structure for this chapter, with a caveat: these categories are neither discrete nor mutually exclusive. The topics that emerged from these conversations are indeed multidimensional, cutting across the three. For example, the goal of ecological integrity produces controversy, because scientific knowledge presents a degree of uncertainty about where the thresholds might lie for the healthy continuance of a species or ecosystem. In the economic realm, some economists assert that sustainable development requires sustained economic growth (Schmidheiny 1992), while others charge that open-ended economic growth is fundamentally incompatible with sustainability (Daly 1990; Czech 2000). The social dimension likewise invites debates about intergenerational equity, distributive equity (which might conflict with an economic growth imperative), democratic opening, social justice, political recognition, community capabilities, and so on. Moreover, balance is elusive in practice. The effort to reconcile all three dimensions encounters trade-offs, sacrifices, or prioritization of one dimension over another. In spite of these conceptual and practical challenges, sustainability is Mexico's dominant environmental policy framework, providing a useful lens through which to view the environment-development problematic in Los Cabos.

Sustainability: Environmental Dimensions

Modern natural resource management is premised on the idea that scientific knowledge can guide utilization of resources in a sustainable fashion, for instance, by identifying a maximum renewable timber or fisheries harvest. Several respondents spoke of sustainability in terms of recognizing and respecting ecosystem limits, and enforcing them through policy. However, ecological systems are complex, even the best available scientific knowledge is incomplete and uncertain, and policy solutions are often contentious or manipulated. Although interviewees voiced a broad range of environmental concerns, freshwater scarcity, energy dependence, the health of marine resources, and the environmental impacts of rapid urbanization received the most attention.

While habitability of the peninsula is limited by extreme aridity, BCS benefits from the Sierra La Laguna, which captures significant seasonal monsoonal moisture, recharging freshwater aquifers and feeding the streams and rivers of the coastal lowlands. However, natural scientists as well as spokespersons from NGOs, government agencies, and the private tourism sector all expressed grave concern about overexploitation of the aquifers that support Los Cabos. All agreed that rapid population growth and high-water-intensity tourism have led to an unsustainable drawdown of freshwater aquifers, as well as saline intrusion.

Identifying a path to sustainable freshwater use is controversial. Several interviewees—including state government officials, scholars, and businesspersons—opined that desalination is a suitable technology, which, in combination with water-conservation measures, should provide a sustainable supply into the future. One state official asserted that all of the estimated 28 small, private desalination plants currently in use "are in full compliance with all environmental laws," as is the large municipal facility for Cabo San Lucas. In contrast, a federal environmental official and several other interviewees rejected desalination as an unsustainable technology, prohibitively energy inefficient, with potentially deleterious impacts on marine habitat, such as hypersaline and chemical discharges, and aquatic larval and juvenile kill. Without desalination, sustainable water use becomes more challenging, relying upon better stewardship of the highlands, much greater dedication to water conservation and recycling, and, perhaps, ultimately, significant changes in the resort model of tourism.

In an oil-rich country, energy dependence might lack the urgency of water scarcity, but public officials and others noted that the region's isolation from the national grid and its reliance on liquid-fueled power plants would be difficult to defend by most criteria of sustainability. Several interviewees were frustrated by the lack of promotion of energy conservation measures, solar technologies, wave or wind technologies, and other sustainable and renewable forms of energy. Proper price incentives, government subsidies, and support programs are needed to encourage conservation and adoption of sustainable energy alternatives for the longer run.

Los Cabos: Prospective for a Natural and Tourism Paradise

Every interviewee spoke of the vital importance of healthy marine resources for the future of Los Cabos. Given the prominence of sportfishing in the region's identity, fisheries depletion is an obvious threat. An official from the Secretariat of Environment and Natural Resources (Secretaría de Medio Ambiente y Recursos Naturales–SEMARNAT) noted a clash between the sportfishing industry and the commercial fishing industry (based largely on the mainland). Commercial overharvest nearly depleted several key fisheries; however, he claims that the 1995 establishment of the Cabo Pulmo Marine Reserve has helped replenish stocks. He and others are optimistic about a new cultural preference toward catch and release among sportfishers, though it is not clear that these achievements alone can reverse the long-term decline of fisheries in the Sea of Cortez and the Pacific.

Other marine discussions centered on the health of coral reefs and threats to the sea turtle population. One critic of desalination argued that proposed developments for Cabo Pulmo would endanger the health of the reefs. Another expert on the sea turtle restoration project defined them as a keystone species in the health of the coastal ecosystem as a whole, asserting that any further decline in turtle populations would threaten the health of the marlin, dorado (mahi mahi), and other popular sport fisheries.

For most environmental issues in Los Cabos, the question of sustainability ultimately comes back to rapid population growth. If sustainability requires respect for the "carrying capacity" of local ecological systems, most observers agree that three decades of uncontrolled urbanization has had significant negative impacts on delicate coastal and desert ecologies. As the tourism boom fostered by the National Trust Fund for Tourism Development (Fondo Nacional de Fomento al Turismo–FONATUR) unfolded, it created an employment magnet with a national reach. Even public officials and developers concur that the staggering pace of population growth proceeded with very little planning, zoning, or code enforcement. One real estate developer admitted that his profession paid no attention to sustainability; he was concerned chiefly with the bottom line: "density, number of rooms per hectare, profitability." Interviewees raised the associated challenges of inadequate urban infrastructure and housing. One hotel industry spokesperson pointed to a major sewage spill into the marine environment on the day of the interview as emblematic: "this is the opposite of sustainable, of development that won't compromise the needs of future generations."

A point of concern shared by many interviewees was the seemingly inevitable prospect that the model of tourism and urban development that has characterized the transformation of the tourist corridor over the past 35 years will continue eastward around the cape, eventually transforming Cabo Pulmo, La Ribera, and other relatively undeveloped regions in an equally problematic way. Conservationists worry about reproducing the corridor's negative impacts on habitats and native species. One economist described a planned development for Cabo Pulmo, for instance, as "fundamentally incompatible with sustainability."

SUSTAINABILITY: ECONOMIC DIMENSIONS

According to the state secretary of social development, the main economic challenge is one of "reconversion," which he defines as a coordinated effort to reorient the way the economy functions, in order to bring it closer to the indices of sustainability. He believes this process is well under way in the principal economic sectors of the region, including tourism, fisheries, agriculture, and mining.

There was a clear consensus that tourism is, in one observer's words, "the natural vocation of Baja California Sur." Officials, residents, and businesses take obvious pride in the region's scenery. They understand intimately that the economic survival of Los Cabos ultimately depends on careful stewardship. One said: "If we destroy the natural beauty of this place, we lose everything." Another said: "We don't have industry. We don't have oil. What we have is fishing and beautiful landscapes." Surprisingly, there was also wide agreement that the *sol y playa* model of resort tourism has largely not operated within the parameters of sustainability, however defined. By today, most public officials, and even many private businesses, regularly invoke the language of sustainability. Several activists and scholars said that they are skeptical of this trend, viewing the green language as empty, faddish, or cynical. Others, however, believe that Los Cabos, the state, and indeed the country are in the midst of a cultural transformation toward greater environmental consciousness.

The prospects for an authentically sustainable tourist economy are difficult to gauge, with contrary trends in play. The dominant model of tourism development has tremendous inertia, guided by a short-term economic logic that has historically undervalued sustainability, not just in Los Cabos, but also in previous FONATUR poles of development, from Acapulco to Cancún. Conservationists are alarmed by proposed East Cape developments that appear to presume an ongoing expansion of the unsustainable tourist corridor of today.

However, there are encouraging signs of an emerging sustainability ethic, such as a cultural consensus valuing natural and marine protected areas, from the sierra, to the coastline, to the coral reef (CEMDA 2006; Gámez 2008). One SEMARNAT official estimates that about 40 percent of BCS is now under some form of protection. In his view, *Bajacalifornianos* once had a difficult time imagining sustainable alternatives. By today, though, they have witnessed the recovery of fish stocks in Cabo Pulmo made possible by the marine protections. In addition, they associate Mexico's 1998 protection of whales (Mexican Official Norm [NOM] 131) with demonstrably sustainable economic success in whale-watching tourism in San Ignacio and Puerto San Carlos.

According to one hotelier, sustainability in his industry will require learning from the mistakes of the past, as well as taking the positive lessons from successful developments elsewhere. He points to parts of Spain or the Canary Islands for examples of tourism that have proven profitable without undermining their ecological futures (Acerenza 2007). One lesson is the importance of effective land-use planning. Public and private actors must collaborate to ensure that viable housing for workers keeps a parallel pace with the development of rooms for tourists. It is true that the corridor now has in place strict regulations that govern water use and protect the San José estuary. However, the lack of infrastructure to support the workforce ultimately blights the surrounding landscape with irregular settlements and informal housing, which he fears will eventually drive tourists away. This pattern, often repeated in Mexico's tourism history, is ultimately environmentally and economically unsustainable.

Two additional indicators of change are the rising interest in green hotel certification and hotel participation in sea turtle restoration. The Hotel Pueblo Bonito, for example, is Green Globe benchmarked (www.greenglobe.org), and other resorts are looking into various internationally recognized environmental certification programs. The coordinator of the Los Cabos municipal sea turtle protection program likewise gives high marks to the Hotel Network for Sea Turtle

Conservation (Red Hotelera para la Conservación de la Tortuga Marina). The municipal program began in 2000, with only three government employees who could not possibly monitor the municipality's 183 kilometers of coastline. Efficacy leaped dramatically with the formation of the hotel network in 2003. It enlisted the participation of hotel staff and security who regularly stroll the beaches and can readily locate nests, eggs, and juveniles. The municipal program provided training and, by today, 44 businesses are active in the network (which has since dropped the word "hotel"). Nearly one thousand employees have been trained in sea turtle protection, enabling routine coverage of over 100 kilometers of coastline and earning the program several national awards.

Another important prospect is the emergence of ecotourism, geotourism, and agrotourism that might distribute economic benefits inland. Public, private, and non-profit actors share the view that tremendous, scarcely tapped potential exists for low-impact tourism alternatives, including environmental hikes and rustic cabins in the sierra, *alta cocina* (Mexican *haute cuisine*) cooking schools on organic farms, mountain biking tours, overnight stays in *ejidal* ranching or farming communities, birdwatching or wildlife tours, artisanal fisheries, and the like. One *ejido* representative suggested that, with the proper vision and leadership, FONATUR could promote more sustainable tourism by helping *ejidatarios* with credit and training, so that they could hold on to their properties rather than sell them. This way, they would be able to develop small- and medium-sized enterprises to benefit the small communities left behind by the coastal boom.

The fishing and mining economies are likewise showing signs of reconversion. By the state secretary's estimate, nearly 95% of sportfishing is now catch and release. He also points to new policies to promote less polluting motors on boats, new permitting systems that enable professional fishers to serve as guides, increased monitoring and enforcement of catch quotas, and state policies designed to support a promising aquaculture sector. In mining, new techniques have been developed at San Antonio to derive value from old tailings. Miners are working inside a protected area, restoring the site, promoting conservation, and turning a profit.

Finally, the agricultural economy of Los Cabos also demonstrates economic reconversion. Since Productores Orgánicos del Cabo was formed in 1985, production in the municipality has gradually shifted predominantly into intensive, organic cultivation. Today, the del Cabo company alone supports nearly 400 small farm and *ejido* families. They mostly work plots under four hectares, using intensive cultivation techniques and water-saving drip irrigation and cistern-capture systems. Thus, these families help produce high-value-added, counter-seasonal crops destined for the U.S. export market, as well as, increasingly, for high-end restaurants in Los Cabos (Riedy 2010). For rural communities that had been losing their youth to the tourist jobs in the corridor, this agricultural recovery supports viable rural livelihoods. It also helps to rescue the ecological knowledge that comes from 250 years of sustainable, self-sufficient living in the ranchos.

SUSTAINABILITY: SOCIAL AND POLITICAL DIMENSIONS

The state secretary of social development views enhanced social well-being as both cause and effect of sustainability. Economic growth is not an end in itself; rather, it is a means toward a better life for citizens today and in the future. Many interviewees gave Los Cabos comparatively low marks on the dimension of social equity. The regional pattern of growth evinces a major gap in income and opportunity, with entrenched socioeconomic marginalization and social injustice. The glamorous hotels, luxury condominiums, villas, spas, and golf resorts that service their elite clienteles stand in stark contrast with rural poverty and land abandonment in surrounding areas. Here, informal settlements crowd the urban arroyos where workers and families struggle to maintain a dignified life with limited access to such basics as housing, electricity, sewage, health care, education, and security.

Conversely, social participation is essential to the realization of economically viable and ecologically sustainable initiatives. According to the director of the Friends of Cabo Pulmo Conservation (Amigos para la Conservación de Cabo Pulmo), multiple studies have demonstrated a clear correlation between the involvement of citizens and the health of the environment. Sustainability and conservation initiatives are most successful when they integrate the surrounding community. To realize sustainability, a community must share a common vision, which must develop from within; it cannot be imposed by governments or other interests. Citizens must learn to value what they have, and recognize their responsibility to participate in its preservation. A hotelier agrees: "sustainability must involve everyone:

citizens, businesses, government agencies, students, and workers." Likewise, from the director of the sea turtle restoration program: "most conservation programs fail because they don't get the community involved." While recognizing that a "charismatic species" greatly facilitated their task, she attributes the program's success to the spirited participation not just of the hotel network, but also of students, families, and the larger community.

In a fast-growing region with enormous socioeconomic cleavages and a population base representing recent migrants from all corners of the republic, it can be enormously difficult to build or sustain a community vision and participatory spirit. Several observers remarked that, compared to Cabo San Lucas, San José del Cabo has historically maintained a stronger sense of community, with a more coherent connection to place. Nonetheless, some in the tourism industry hope to promote a stronger community identity among recent migrants to Cabo San Lucas. Hotels and community organizations are attempting to strengthen bonds and deepen local ties to Mexico's rich cultural heritage (Pueblo Bonito n.d.).

Mexico's political landscape is also changing in ways that work for and against sustainability. As national-level democratization of the 1990s and 2000s has trickled down to subnational levels, municipal and state governments have acquired more power and generated new political space for civic participation. According to the municipal director of ecology and environment, Los Cabos was one of the first municipalities in the republic to draft an Ecological Zoning Plan in 1995, followed by a municipal Urban Development Plan in 1999. At the time of this research, both plans were being updated. Representatives of all the sectors who were interviewed confirmed a shared conviction that the current revision of the ecological plan is unprecedented. First, by inviting broad public participation, including activists, NGOs, hoteliers, businesses and firms, *ejido* communities, attorneys, university scientists, and conservationists, it has become a laboratory for democratic learning, in contrast with the top-down paternalism of the past (CEMDA 2007). Second, the plan is being conducted with a serious policy commitment to sustainability, which many hope might finally carry the region beyond merely rhetorical commitments.

Still, Mexico's political transformation cuts both ways. According to federal officials and environmental advocates, the federal government is generally ahead of state and local governments in defining and implementing a sustainable development policy agenda. Compared to citizen groups, developers and other well-financed private interests are more adept at manipulating municipal decision processes to their benefit. According to several observers close to the process, this has made it more difficult to translate federal sustainability policies to the local level. For example, several critics charged that environmental impact assessments (EIAs) are often merely window dressing, lacking controls, mechanisms of oversight, avenues of judicial redress, or sanctions against defective reports.

Additionally, municipal- and state-level officials often lack the power to prioritize environmental and social issues over the economic development concerns that tend to prevail. For instance, several participants worried openly about potential incompatibilities in the current planning process. In the event of a clash of priorities, they fear that the urban plan will subordinate the ecological plan, thereby prioritizing traditional measures of economic profitability over social or environmental goals. For this reason, they believe it is critical to involve the community more broadly, in the hope that people will gain a stake in the outcomes and rally around the preservation of things that they value.

Conclusion: Toward a Sustainable Future for Los Cabos?

Is it "too late" for a sustainable Los Cabos? One conservationist asserted that even with the accumulated negative impacts of three decades of environmental neglect, many ecosystems are still intact, and there is much to be saved. A more sober analysis, voiced in more than one interview, is that the best hope might be a kind of containment strategy. One the one hand, critics see the tourist corridor as the picture of unsustainability: overuse of fresh water and energy; galloping destruction of soils, vegetation, and native species; rapid urban growth with little control or planning; the creation and reproduction of severe socioeconomic inequity; and a political process that favors economic values over all others. On the other hand, that legacy has produced a concentration of wealth and a major economic engine with a potential to provide opportunities beyond the corridor that has scarcely been explored. From a containment perspective, the challenge is to fight against the expansion of that model, while working both to transform its impact in the longer term, and to harvest some share of that wealth with new, ecologically oriented enterprises in surrounding areas.

The people closest to these processes believe firmly that cultural and value changes are taking place in Los Cabos. For the director of the sea turtle campaign, the program's success confirms the importance of community ties, with training, environmental education, and outreach to students, businesses, and citizens. One public official believes that the emerging third generation of entrepreneurs has been raised with an ethic of sustainability and environmental consciousness. They see economic opportunities in terms of higher value added, and are willing to incorporate conservation and social justice principles into economic planning. Several cases discussed earlier support this claim.

One optimistic respondent argued that Mexico's national political transformation is gradually changing the country's political culture and civil society. She sees a new culture of legality emerging: compliance with laws, an expectation of inspections and oversight, an assumption that agreements will be binding, and democratic values like transparency and accountability becoming the norm. She views sustainability as "a plan for negotiation" and an ongoing effort "to meet, in practice, the goals specified in [Mexico's] local and national laws and international agreements." Along similar lines, another respondent said, "Sustainability doesn't exist in practice. But that doesn't mean that we give up. We continue to take the necessary steps and try to come as close as we can."

REFERENCES

Acerenza, Miguel Ángel. 2007. *Desarrollo sostenible y gestión del turismo*. Mexico: Editorial Trillas.

Carruthers, David. 2005. "From Opposition to Orthodoxy: The Remaking of Sustainable Development." Pp. 285–300 in *Debating the Earth: The Environmental Politics Reader,* Second edition, John S. Dryzek and D. Schlosberg, eds. New York: Oxford University Press.

Centro Mexicano de Derecho Ambiental (CEMDA). 2006. *Diagnóstico jurídico-ambiental del Golfo de California y el Pacífico Norte Mexicano*. Mexico, DF: Centro Mexicano de Derecho Ambiental.

Centro Mexicano de Derecho Ambiental (CEMDA). 2007. *Guía ciudadana para la participación pública en la planeación y desarrollo urbano de las ciudades y pueblos del estado de Baja California Sur.* Mexico, DF: Centro Mexicano de Derecho Ambiental.

Czech, Brian. 2000. *Shoveling Fuel for a Runaway Train.* Berkeley, CA: UC Press.

Daly, Herman. 1990. "Sustainable Growth: An Impossibility Theorem." *Development* 3/4: 45–47.

Daly, Herman. 1996. *Beyond Growth: The Economics of Sustainable Development.* Boston: Beacon Press.

Díez, Jordi. 2006. *Political Change and Environmental Policymaking in Mexico.* New York: Routledge.

Dowie, Mark. 1995. *Losing Ground: American Environmentalism at the Close of the Twentieth Century.* Cambridge, MA: MIT Press.

Dryzek, John. 1997. *The Politics of the Earth.* New York: Oxford University Press.

Faucheux, Sylvie, David Pearce, and John Proops, eds. 1996. *Models of Sustainable Development.* Brookfield, VT: Edward Elgar.

Gámez, Alba E., ed. 2008. *Turismo y sustentabilidad en Cabo Pulmo, BCS.* San Diego CA: San Diego State University, Universidad Autónoma de Baja California Sur, and Consejo Nacional de Ciencia y Tecnología.

The President's Council on Sustainable Development. 1999. *Towards a Sustainable America: Advancing Prosperity, Opportunity, and a Healthy Environment for the 21st Century.* Washington, DC: The President's Council on Sustainable Development. http://clinton4.nara.gov/PCSD/Publications/index.html.

Pueblo Bonito. n.d. *Herencia cultural y desarrollo social.* Pueblo Bonito Oceanfront Resorts and Green Globe.

Riedy, William. 2010. "The Economic Links between Local Agriculture and Tourist Restaurants of Los Cabos, Mexico." Master's thesis, Latin American Studies and Business Administration, San Diego State University.

Sachs, Wolfgang. 1993. *Global Ecology: A New Arena of Political Conflict.* London: Zed Books.

Schmidheiny, Steven. 1992. *Changing Course: A Global Business Perspective on Development and The Environment.* Cambridge: MIT Press.

Secretaría de Medio Ambiente y Recursos Naturales (SEMARNAT). 2006. *La gestión ambiental en México.* Mexico, DF: Secretaría de Medio Ambiente y Recursos Naturales.

Sitarz, Daniel. 1993. *Agenda 21: The Earth Summit Strategy to Save Our Planet.* Boulder, CO: Earthpress.

Torgerson, Douglas. 1995. "The Uncertain Quest for Sustainability: Public Discourse and the Politics of Environmentalism." In *Greening Environmental Policy: The Politics of a Sustainable Future.* Frank Fischer and M. Black, eds. New York: St. Martin's.

Urciaga, José, M. A. Hernández, and D. Carruthers. 2008. "La política ambiental mexicana: Una panorámica." Pp. 67–97 in *Del saqueo a la conservación: Historia ambiental contemporánea de Baja California Sur,* Micheline Cariño and M. Monteforte, eds. La Paz, BCS: SEMARNAT, INE, CONACYT, UABCS.

Wheeler, Stephen. 2004. *Planning for Sustainability: Creating Livable, Equitable, and Ecological Communities.* New York: Routledge.

World Commission on Environment and Development. 1987. *Our Common Future.* Oxford: Oxford University Press.

Part VI.
Conclusions

26

Conclusions

Oscar Arizpe C. and Paul Ganster

Throughout the 25 chapters of this book, the authors have delved into the environmental, social, economic, and cultural-historical components of what we call an environmental and tourism paradise: the region of Los Cabos, Baja California Sur. It has been said that although it has great prospects, this region is vulnerable precisely because of the strong development pressure generated mainly by the tourism sector. This has, in turn, brought about chaotic growth with negative environmental effects, some that are irreversible. Given the circumstances, the authors focused on analyzing the problem as an opportunity with a prospective approach that would contribute to this much talked about and longed for sustainable development of the region.

The analysis of the natural environment—considered a key component for this development—evidences the vocation for tourism development in the region. The contrasts of mountains, deserts, and beaches give shape to a unique landscape, like no other, thus generating a great wealth of terrestrial and marine flora and fauna. However, this wealth is threatened by high population growth, excessive coastal and real estate development, and tourism activities that go beyond the beach.

With population growth, the demand for water resources increases. Due to the region's desert conditions, this resource comes primarily from aquifers. Heavy demand for water and its limited availability limit development in Los Cabos. There are no permanent surface water flows in the region and, although the municipality has 32% of the population of the state of BCS, it only contributes 10% of the water that recharges its aquifers. As a result of the rapid increase in the region's water demand, it has been necessary to decrease the supply to the two main tourism destinations: San Lucas and San José, including the tourist corridor.

In view of the rapid growth in demand—which is expected to continue—decision makers have focused actions on the desalination of seawater. However, due to limited information on the dispersion of hypersaline discharges and their effects on the ecosystem, it is recommended that the precautionary principle be applied and not to view desalination as a panacea. More research is needed on the capture of surface water and the reuse of treated water, as well as alternatives for more efficient use of resources that are now available.

The current flora and fauna of Los Cabos are the result of geological and evolutionary processes of millions of years and, more recently, of the effects of human actions. The geographic and ecological isolation has been important in the evolution of animal life, producing a large number of endemic or unique species. The current challenge is to prevent the disappearance of the richness in species. Measures to address this challenge include urban planning and careful modification of habitats that allow for natural vegetation areas, intact rocky zones between housing developments, and no construction on sand dunes. In addition, it is critical to control introduced species. It is also necessary to make people aware of the value of the region's natural resources and the importance of their conservation through environmental education programs at all levels.

Natural resources make up a fundamental basis for national sovereignty and the integral development of Mexico. Cetaceans and sea turtles, recognized worldwide as important ecotourism components, are particularly abundant in Los Cabos. The growing tourism in whale watching, though not lethal, has brought problems of management; if not carried out properly, it can become a threat.

In view of these scenarios of deterioration, the importance of Natural Protected Areas (NPAs) has grown in the world in an unusual way. The creation, consolidation, and management strategy of NPAs is a key element in preserving the environment. The state of BCS is a model of modern conservation policies in Mexico. It is a leader in the protection of its territory because more than 40% is under some classification of NPA. The Los Cabos region has four NPAs, including

Conclusions

the only coral reef of the so-called aquarium of the world, the Gulf of California.

The description of the natural environment culminates with the analysis of climate change in the region of Los Cabos, which is highly vunerable due to its location and physiographic configuration. For this reason, it becomes gradually more important to assess this vulnerability at the microregional level and then design the strategy for adaptation measures to the irreversible climate change.

Human presence is extremely old in the peninsula. There have been 111 relevant archaeological sites recorded in the municipality, including middens, lithic workshops, and pictographic sites; standing out among them are El Médano and Cabo Pulmo. Evidence of pre-Hispanic times dates back more than seven thousand years. It is noteworthy that, notwithstanding this antiquity and semidesert climate, the indigenous groups of this region were hunters-gatherers-fishers and lived in balance with nature. Due to lifestyle changes and diseases that resulted from the Spanish occupation, the indigenous population decreased from 50,000 who inhabited the peninsula of Baja California in the late sixteenth century, to only 8,000 remaining in the seventeenth century. In 1847, there were 7,500 settlers reported, including emigrants to the region. Officially, the municipality was created in 1981. In a span of two decades, the population of Los Cabos grew from 10,000 inhabitants in 1970 to almost 240,000 in 2010.

Recently, there has been a decline in tourism and a lack of adequate planning of this sector in the municipality. Nonetheless, the model of tourism development in Los Cabos is currently being promoted in other areas of the state, without addressing its consequences for the environment and society. As cited in this work, there are elements of concern—such as those expressed in the *National Geographic Traveler* magazine in 2009, which rated Los Cabos as one of the worst tourist destinations in the world—that make it necessary to review the scope and social costs of applying the model of traditional tourism in the region. The lack of a rational regulation of the use of natural resources, such as water, is having negative impacts that in the long run will be devastating for the region and the tourism sector itself.

Excessive dependence of the state of BCS and the Los Cabos region on traditional tourism of sun and sand and, at the same time, on basing their development on this sector, have produced land speculation, environmental deterioration, and labor exploitation. Tourism is globally known as a tool for economic growth. However, this sector not only has a huge impact on the economy, but also on society and on the use of natural resources.

It is asserted in different forums that the planning of the tourism sector in Los Cabos is inadequate because it does not include non-tourism population settlements. The development of the housing sector for workers has been neglected due to the almost exclusive focus on traditional tourism and urban infrastructure planning (roads; housing; provision of energy, transportation, and communications for local residents). This situation, in turn, has created social, health, and quality-of-life problems. The municipality's rapid population growth has generated a demand for public services that goes beyond the capacity of local governments to meet it. There is a permanent deficit in quantity and quality of paved roads, potable water, sewerage, green areas, and sports and cultural centers. Also characteristic of this area are the inequality in different segments of the population, increase in criminality, and inadequate police and justice administration, coupled with the uncontrolled growth in the poverty belt.

An excellent alternative to supplement the energy supply shortfall is solar energy. Los Cabos has between 5.81 and 6.48 $kWh/(m^2d)$ of solar potential, which is on average twice the potential of the United States and one of the largest in the world. The solar thermal energy program could be expanded in the short term, since it is considered cost effective for the region. Also, there is good potential in Los Cabos for the generation of wind and geothermal energy, which do not cause negative environmental impacts, as do fossil fuels. The growth of the region means a good opportunity to enact building codes in the new tourism developments with the use of renewable energy.

The model of high-density sun and beach tourism cannot be maintained in the long term. Therefore, other development alternatives, such as sustainable tourism, are proposed in each of the municipality's regions assessed in this book. This work can help guide the planning and sustainable development of the municipality with objective criteria and a formal quantitative methodology. It is also important to link tourism development with the primary sectors. Accordingly,

Conclusions

proposals are made and analyzed in this book for their integration into the agriculture and fishing sector. Rural tourism is mentioned as important because local families can offer tourist services. In addition, the ranch culture has turned out to be an attraction for tourism. So, this integration is an area of opportunity with a potential to reduce imports, create jobs, and to thus increase the multiplier effect of tourism.

According to the national tourism program, sportfishing is also an important option for the diversification of tourism attractions and adding value to Mexico's tourist destinations. Although considered a complementary activity, sportfishing is relevant to the region because Cabo San Lucas has become the so-called "marlin capital of the world." The income from this activity has increased markedly in the last decade, and sportfishing is an economic engine for the region.

It is urgent that the local people have a larger share of the economic benefits generated by tourism. This must be reflected, first, in a better quality of life for the region's inhabitants and, second, in the participation of society in government actions through permanent communication schemes and citizen complaints. It is also necessary to enforce appropriate regulatory and urban development policies in order to maintain the tourism competitiveness of Los Cabos, avoid the vulnerability associated with foreign tourism, and prevent overcrowding of the destination.

Currently, in countries that aim to achieve sustainability, environomental planning is essential in land-use planning and in developing productive activities. This is because environmental planning includes approaches and procedures that translate public policies into concrete actions of integral sustainable development. The municipality has an environmental land use plan that was proposed in 1992 and decreed in 1995, which has been overwhelmed by the high population growth. Its update was prepared, discussed, and adjusted in 2007 with the involvement of different population sectors and levels of government. In 2008, it was submitted to the municipal council, undergoing public consultation as part of the decree process. However, to date this official decree has not been enforced. It is urgent that the *ordenamiento* model be adjusted and implemented in order to transform Los Cabos into a truly integrated development pole with an important multiplier effect on the regional and state economy.

All this makes it necessary that a reform process be undertaken in BCS, and particularly in the municipality of Los Cabos, with regard to the growth model followed to date, which tends to benefit the few, generates a growing inequality, and damages the environment. It is important to thoroughly assess environmental impacts of tourism activities. It is also essential to ensure a long-term economic and social development on the solid bases of sustainability. If regions such as the municipality of Los Cabos aspire to reach superior levels of sustainable development, then their society and government need to achieve equity, justice, public safety, public administration efficiency, and respect for private property and the natural environment. Only then will we come close to the sustainable development of this natural paradise that can also be a tourism paradise.

Index

Acacia peninsularis, 42
Acantophora spicifera, 81
Acapulco, 88, 210, 401, 425, 434, 476
Acetabularia calyculus, 74
Adopt a Sea Turtle (*Adopta una Tortuga Marina*), 183
Agrícola Cabeña, 299
agriculture, iv, 40, 44, 57, 147, 150–1, 160, 161, 199, 211–213, 297–301, 305–8, 398, 407, 412, 438, 452, 471, 475, 478, 491
Agroproductos del Cabo, 299
Agua Caliente, 298, 318, 406
Agua Escondida, 19
Airapí, 172
Albizia occidentalis, 42, 45
Allenrolfea occidentalis, 43
Alopias, 69
Ambrosia ambrosioides, 41
amphibians, 48–9, 53, 57
Anadara multicostata, 68
Anadara tuberculosa, 68
Antigonon leptopus, 45
Antigua California, 208
Añuití, 172, 207, 315
aquaculture, 128, 307, 477
aquifers, 4, 17, 23–4, 27–31, 33, 47–8, 132, 148–50, 331, 397, 446, 473, 487–8, *see also* water, ground
Aquila chrysaetos, 51, 53, 55
Arbutus peninsularis, 47
Área de Importancia para la Conservación de las Aves, 51, 70, 149
Aristida adsencionis, 41
Aristida ternipes, 41
Arizona, 258–9
Arroyo Candelaria, 134

Arroyo La Calera, 12
Asia, 57, 253, 258, 300, 427
Asociación Sudcaliforniana de Protección al Medio Ambiente y la Tortuga Marina (ASUPMATOMA), 86–7, 176, 183
Aspidoscelis hyperythra, 50
Aspidoscelis maxima, 50, 56
Atrina maura, 68
Atrina tuberculosa, 68
Auriparus flaviceps, 51
avocado, 135, 212, 300
Azonal, 18

Baccharis glutinosa, 41
Bahamas, 453
Bajo de la Gorda, 63
Balaenidae, 102
Balaenoptera acutorostrata, 101
Balaenoptera borealis, 70
Balaenoptera edeni, 70, 102, 104–6, 109, 111–2, 140
Balaenoptera musculus, 70, 102, 104, 106–7, 109, 111, 114, 118
Balaenoptera novaeangliae, 140, *see also* Megaptera novaeangliae
Balaenoptera physalus, 102, 104–6, 109, 111, 140
Balaenopteridae, 102,
Balandra, 128
Banco Gorda, 118
Bank of Mexico, 305, 401
basil, 300–1
basin, 5, 7–8, 10, 13–4, 24, 26–7, 35, 134, 148–51, 206, 387, 397, *see also* watersheds
Bassariscus astutus, 51–2
Batis maritima, 43

Bahía Concepción, 9
bays, 16–17, 70, 74, 104, 118–9, 128, 131, 137–40, 145, 174, 178–9, 195, 262, 278–9, 446
beaches, iv, 4, 40, 50, 53, 61, 79–80, 83, 85–6, 88, 91–2, 131, 140, 142–3, 147, 155, 171, 173–6, 178–84, 197, 216, 235, 250, 255, 264, 271–3, 276–9, 283, 307, 328, 332, 341, 355, 409–11, 427, 434, 437–8, 446–7, 463–4, 477, 487
benthic fauna, 67–8, *see also* zoobenthos
Berardius bairdii, 102
biodiversity, 40, 42, 48, 53, 57, 61, 65, 101, 115, 126–7, 130, 133–4, 137, 146, 161, 231, 235, 239, 242–4, 271, 432
biota, 39–40, 63, 133, 147
Bipes biporus, 49, 54, 77, 150
birds, 43, 48, 50–3, 55-57, 69–70, 78, 131, 136, 149–51, 183, 354, 427, 477
black oak, 47
boats, 15, 83, 116, 119–20, 131, 140, 142–3, 183, 289, 291, 303, 427, 477
Boca de la Sierra, 52, 150–1, 298, 318, 406–7
Boca del Barranco, 16
border, international, 205, 254, 260, 404
Brazil, 44, 296
Buena Vista, 16, 139–40, 215, 274–6, 288, 291, 318, 349, 372, 409–11
Bufo punctatus, 48
burials, 140, 192, 278
Bursera microphylla, 43
businesses, 88, 142, 213, 228–9, 251, 254–5, 274, 290, 296, 324, 327, 430, 438, 475, 477, 479, 481
Buteo jamaicensis, 78, 136
Buteo swainsoni, 55

*C*abo Cortés, 263, 446–7

Cabo del Este, 290, 409, 433
Cabo Pulmo, 19, 27, 29, 63–6, 68–9, 74, 80, 84–5, 107, 113, 115, 119–20, 128–9, 137–41, 143, 163, 172, 178–179, 192, 196–7, 200, 274–5, 277–8, 282, 288, 291, 318, 387, 409–10, 446, 474–6, 478, 489
Cabo San Lázaro, 8
Cabo San Lucas, 4, 16, 21, 27, 29, 33, 64, 70, 82, 85, 87, 101, 104, 107, 118–20, 128–9, 131, 134, 140, 144–8, 172–3, 178–9, 181, 191–3, 195, 197, 199, 211–5, 231, 236, 238, 249, 265, 272–8, 280, 287–90, 292, 298, 302, 315–6, 318, 327–34, 336, 342, 349, 369, 372–4, 390, 401–3, 412–5, 417, 433, 444–5, 447, 458–61, 463–4, 473, 479, 491
Cabo San Lucas Arch Natural Monument, 129, 144
cactus, 43–4, 49, 146
Caduaño, 10, 150, 298, 318, 406–8
calcium carbonate, 162
Calidris alba, 52, 70
Calidris mauri, 52, 70
Calidris minutilla, 52, 70
California Academy of Sciences, 62, 243
Callisaurus draconoides, 53–4, 150
Calmex (factory ship), 212
Canada, 164, 258, 427
Cañada de La Zorra, 277
Cancún, 88, 257, 336, 346, 401, 425, 434, 464, 476
Canis latrans, 136
Cañón de la Zorra, 49
Caracara cheriway, 51
Caranx caballus, 68
Carcharhinus, 69
Carcharodon megalodon, 13
Cardinalis cardinalis, 51
Caretta caretta, 53, 55, 69, 77, 80, 171
Caribbean, 160, 296, 401–2
Carranco, Lorenzo, 207
Casa Blanca, 332

Index

Catholic University, 230
cattle, 44, 46, 57, 211–2, 330, 407, 409
Caulerpa sp., 65, 67, 74
Caulerpales, 65
Centro Turísticos Integralmente Planificados (CIPs), 205, 213, 254, 260, 264, 272, 336, 401–2, 414, 444
Ceramiales, 65
Cercidium floridum, 42, 146
Cerithea sp. (fossil), 13
Cerralvo Island, 172, 193,
Cerritos Domingo, 19
Cerro Cuevoso, 196
Cerro El Vigía, 144, 146–7
Cerro Garambillo, 19
Cerro Los Tesos, 19
Cetaceans, iv, 70, 101–3, 105, 107–11, 113, 115–20, 488, *see also* whales
Chairina trivirgata, 56
Chelonia agassizii, 53, 55, 69, 137, 171, 178
Chelonia mydas, 69, 80, 171
Chiapas, 451, 460
Chile (snail), 198, 200
Chile (country), 96
Chilomeniscus stramineus, 50, 54, 77, 150
Chione spp., 68
Chlorophyta, 65
Chloroscombrus orqueta, 68
Choeronycteris mexicana, 150
cilantro, 301
city council, 177, 180–1, 223, 276, 319–21, 323, 326, 329, 374–5, 377–8, 384–5, 393, 403,
Ciudad Constitución, 316–7, 459
climate change, iv, 8, 157–60, 163–5, 351, 489
coastal areas, iv, 8–9, 15–6, 18–9, 24, 40, 42–5, 48, 51–2, 61, 66, 69–70, 79, 82, 127, 139, 142, 159, 161–2, 171–4, 183–4, 191, 196, 199, 215, 278–81, 282, 303–4, 307, 353, 398, 405, 409–1, 414–5, 473–4, 477, 487,
coastline, 5, 18, 43, 89, 139, 145, 161–2, 165, 176–7, 179, 262, 356, 369, 382, 435, 464, 476–7
Coleonyx variaegatus, 54, 77, 150
Colinas del Puerto, 447
Colombia, 296
Colonia del Sol, 372, 414, 417, 458–60, 465
Colonia Los Cangrejos, 372, 414, 417
colonias, 372, 407, 414–5, 417, 458–60, 465
Colorado, 258–9
Colorado River, 7
Columba fasciata vioscae, 55
columnar cactus, 44
Comisión Federal de Electricidad (CFE), 343–4, 347–50, 356
Comisión Nacional de Áreas Naturales Protegidas (CONANP), 125–9, 133, 138, 144, 151, 177–8
Comisión Nacional del Agua (CONAGUA), 27–9, 151, 330–1
Comisión Reguladora de Energía (CRE), 345
commerce, 210, 428, 443–4, 448, 458
communications, 211, 213, 251, 258, 272, 365, 444, 490
Comondú, 212–3, 254, 257, 260, 262, 297, 315–7, 339, 349–50, 371, 445, 453, 454, 456, 457–9
companies, *see* businesses
Comunidad y Biodiversidad (COBI), 65
Condalia globosa, 42
Consejo Nacional de Poblacion (CONAPO), 35, 222, 443, 453, 455
conservation, 29, 40, 47, 52–3, 58, 79–80, 82–85, 89–90, 92, 103, 120, 125–9, 133, 136, 141, 143–4, 147, 152, 177–8, 182, 184–5, 216,

242–3, 252, 276, 289–91, 303–4, 335, 342, 385–6, 388–90, 397, 435–6, 471, 473, 477–9, 481, 488
Conus (fossil), 13
Conus brunneus, 139
Conus princeps, 139
Convention on International Trade in Endangered Species of Wild Fauna and Flora (CITES), 102–4
copper, 210
coral, 45, 50, 63, 65, 68–9, 131, 137–9, 141–2, 163, 263, 307, 446, 474, 476, 489
Coral de los Frailes, 196
corn, 211–2, 300
corruption, 327, 337
Coryphaena hippurus, 69
Crassostrea iridescens, 68
Crotalus enyo, 50, 54, 77, 136, 150
Crotalus mitchellii, 50, 55, 77, 136, 150
Crotalus ruber, 50, 55, 77, 136, 150,
cruise ships, 82, 131
Cryptostegia grandiflora, 151
Ctenosaura hemilopha, 49, 54, 77, 150
cucumber, 301
Cultural Pavilion of the Republic (Pabellón Cultural de la República-PCR), 235–43
culture, iv, 126–7, 130, 133–4, 144, 146, 192, 197, 203, 207–8, 216, 231, 236–9, 241–2, 244, 261, 306, 335, 359, 367, 407, 414, 434–5, 437, 481
cyclone, 14–7, 24, 148, 155, 160–1, *see also* hurricane
Cyrtocarpa edulis, 44
Czech Republic, 453

D*asyatis brevis*, 69
Defenders of Wildlife, 177
del Barco, Miguel, 195
delegations, 212, 315, 317–318, 328–30, 403
Delphinidae, 102–3

Delphinus capensis, 103
Delphinus delphis, 103
Dermochelys coriacea, 53, 55, 69, 77, 80, 137, 171, 178
desalination, 23, 33–4, 36, 331–2, 342–3, 355, 473–4, 488
Desarrollo Integral de la Familia (DIF), 319, 321, 326, 364, 375
development, iii–v, 10, 23, 35, 40, 43, 47–8, 57–8, 61–2, 119–20, 125–7, 129, 132–5, 142, 144, 150–2, 162, 165, 171, 179, 183–4, 206, 213, 215, 222, 225–6, 229, 231–2, 237, 239, 241–2, 244, 249–50, 252, 258, 262, 264–5, 272, 276–7, 280, 282, 284, 290, 295–9, 302, 305, 308, 316, 326, 329, 332–7, 341, 344, 346, 352, 356, 363–70, 374–5, 376–9, 381–3, 385, 387–9, 398, 401, 403, 405, 408–14, 423–5, 427, 432–9, 443, 447, 450–1, 453, 455, 458, 460–1, 466, 469–2, 474–6, 478, 480, 487–8, 490–2
development plan, 144, 162, 184, 223, 229, 265, 282, 295, 298, 305, 321–2, 326, 329–30, 332–4, 363–4, 368, 374, 378, 381–2, 425, 437, 477, 479,
development pole, 370, 423–5, 433–4, 436, 491
development, regional, 204, 250, 252–4, 272, 410–1, 424
development, underdevelopment, 451
development, urban, 53, 118, 213, 321–2, 336, 432, 433, 435, 437, 475, 491
Dictyotales, 65
dill, 301
Dipodomys merriami, 52
Dipsosaurus dorsalis, 49, 51
Distichlis spicata var. *stolonifera*, 42
diversity, 51, 53, 66, 70, 101, 103, 108, 111, 125, 127, 130, 137, 163, 172, 206, 237, 239, 240–1, 244, 374, 375, 471

Index

diving, scuba, 84, 87–9, 91, 131, 140–3, 272, 274, 279, 307, 409, 411, 427, *see also* snorkling
Dodonaea viscosa, 47
domestic species, *see* livestock
Dominicans, 207
dorado, 87, 288–9, 291, 302–3, 474
drought, 45, 47, 49, 161, 211, 213
dunes, 16, 42, 58, 138, 140, 175, 184, 387, 488

East Cape, 35, 66, 177, 179, 182, 282, 290–1, 349, 387, 409–10, 476
Eastern Pacific, 14, 62, 130, 137, 157, 174, *see also* Pacific Ocean
echinoderms, 67–8
ecological diversity, 243–4, *see also* biodiversity
economic development, 133, 161, 221, 232, 322, 326, 344, 365–6, 374, 376, 379, 433, 480
economic growth, 144, 212, 222, 252–3, 265, 336, 365, 368, 424–5, 446, 450, 464, 469, 472, 478, 490
economy, 205, 210, 212, 221–2, 233, 253–5, 257, 261, 265, 276, 284, 290, 295–6, 306, 326, 344, 365, 407, 410, 425, 431, 434, 436, 443, 448, 450, 463, 475, 477, 490–1
ecosystems, 15, 24, 29, 61, 126–8, 130, 132, 142, 146, 163, 185, 242, 276, 283, 391, 480
ecotourism, 70, 87–8, 91, 116, 118, 151, 274, 276, 307, 409, 435, 437, 476–7, 488, *see also* tourism
education, iv, 90, 145, 152, 211, 215, 221–2, 225–6, 229–33, 236, 261, 322, 365, 371, 375, 402, 411, 417, 427, 435, 437, 451–3, 455–6, 459, 464–5, 478
ejidos, 40, 151, 213, 298, 385, 403–4, 407, 410, 416, 447, 471, 477–9
El Arco, 277
El Boleo, 210
El Cardón, 178

El Cardoncito, 178
El Estero, 178
El Faro, 176, 178–9
El Médano, 172, 181, 191–3, 197, 199–200, 489
El Mogote, 262
El Niño/Southern Oscillation, 14, 24, 155, 157, 161
El Ranchito, 298, 318, 406–7
El Suspiro, 178, 181
El Zacatal, 298, 318, 406
El Zorrillo, 192, 406
electricity, 140, 243, 342–3, 346, 352, 355–6, 358, 415–6, 432, 456, 459, 478
elephant tree, 42–3
Elgaria paucicarinata, 52, 54, 150
employment, iii, 87, 163, 211–2, 221–2, 225, 228–9, 232–3, 250, 253–5, 258, 261–3, 272, 287, 290–1, 295, 297, 306–7, 324, 359, 367, 368, 371, 376–8, 408, 411, 424–5, 428, 431–2, 435–6, 444, 447–8, 455, 461, 463, 474, 478, 491
endangered species, 86, 102, 140, 181
Endangered Species List (DOF), 104
energy, iv, 13, 341–8, 351–9, 473, 480, 490
energy conservation, 358, 473
energy demand, iv, 341, 345, 349
Ensenada, 174
environment, 10, 13, 42–3, 45, 52, 57, 67, 81, 85, 111, 118, 125, 128, 132, 142, 144, 146–7, 150, 165, 203, 207–8, 222, 241–3, 252, 257, 262–4, 272, 277, 291, 305, 329, 335, 337, 345, 359, 381–3, 389, 391, 405, 423, 425, 432–3, 439, 446, 450, 461, 465–6, 469–70, 472, 474, 478–9, 487–9, 492
environmental education, 58, 144, 231, 239, 427, 481, 488
environmental impacts, 242, 264–5, 436, 445, 452, 473, 480, 490, 492
environmental planning, 382, 491, *see also* land use planning

Epinephelus labriformis, 69
Epinephelus panamensis, 69
epiphytes, 41
Eretmochelys imbricata, 69, 77, 80, 137, 171
Eridiphas slevini, 77, 150
Erythea brandegee, 147
Eschrichtiidae, 102,
Eschrichtius robustus, 70, 102, 104, 106, 109, 111, 114, 118
Estonia, 453
estuary, San José del Cabo, 4, 19, 47–8, 51–2, 70, 85, 128–9, 147–51, 176, 206, 277, 335, 476, *see also* San José watershed basin
Etrumeus teres, 68
Eumeces lagunensis, 52, 54, 77, 150
Euphorbia leucophylla, 42
Europe, 62, 135, 173, 191, 199, 205–9, 215, 241, 250, 253, 258, 300, 427
European Union, 300
Euthynnus lineatus, 69
eutric regosol, 18, 133, 138
expenditures (public), 211, 324, 326

F aro Viejo, 85
fault (geological), 6–10, 13–4, 26
fauna, iv, 39, 40, 47–8, 53, 57, 61, 67, 128–9, 131, 133–4, 137–40, 147, 149, 172, 191, 198–9, 271, 274, 277–9, 382, 427, 487–8
Felis concolor, 136
feral animals, 48, 57
ferry, 413
Fideicomiso de Riesgo Campartido (FIRCO), 305
Fideicomisos Instituidos en Relacion con la Agricultura (FIRA), 305
fish, 64, 66–9, 79, 82, 111, 131, 141, 173–4, 194–8, 288–9, 291–2, 303–4, 307, 410, 476
fishing, 68, 79, 81, 83, 85–8, 90–1, 103, 118, 130–1, 138, 141, 147, 163, 174–5, 183, 194–6, 214, 255, 287–92, 296–7, 302–8, 403, 405, 409–10, 412–3, 444, 447, 464, 474–5, 477, 491, *see also* sportfishing
flora, iv, 39–50, 52, 57, 60–6, 129, 131, 134, 136, 138–9, 146–7, 149, 157, 191, 198, 243, 271, 277, 382, 427, 487–8
Fluvisols, 19
Fonda Nacional de Fomento al Turismo (FONATUR), 253–4, 258, 264, 336, 401–2, 413, 425–7, 444, 474, 476–7
Fondo para la Promoción de la Infraestructura Turística (INFRATUR), 401
forest, 43, 45–47, 51–2, 134–6, 149, 151, 299, 369, 387
Fouquieria diguetii, 44
fox, 183, *see also* gray fox
Franciscans, 207, 317
Free Zone, 213, 257, 444, 464
Fregata magnificens, 52, 70
Friends for the Conservation of Cabo Pulmo, 177
fruit, 40–2, 45–6, 51, 135, 212, 300, 306, 412, 436, *see also* orchards
fuel, 142, 290, 343–6, 351–2, 354–6, 490
Fulica americana, 52, 70
Fungia curvata, 139

g allery vegetation, 134
gardens, 321, 438
gender, 335, 369, 371, 374, 376–9, 402, 404–6, 408, 410–11, 416, 437
gente de razón, 208
geomorphology, 15
global climate change, *see* climate change
globalization, 221, 236, 238, 250, 365
Globicephala macrorhynchus, 103, 111
Globorotalia lenguaensi, 13
Globorotalia mayeri, 13
gneiss, 3, 12

goats, 48, 57, 306
gold, 210
golden eagle (*Aquila chrysaetos*), 51, 53, 55
golf, 34, 82, 255, 258, 262–3, 275, 277, 287, 302, 408, 411, 434, 446–7, 464, 478
government, iii–iv, 127, 130, 143, 151, 177–8, 183–4, 203–5, 209, 211, 215, 223, 228–9, 236–8, 250–1, 253–5, 261–2, 264–5, 272, 282, 284, 296, 317, 320, 322–3, 326, 328, 333–4, 336–7, 353–4, 363, 365–8, 374, 382, 384–5, 388, 401, 425, 434, 436–7, 443, 445–8, 450, 458, 464, 469, 471, 473, 477–80, 490–2
Gracilaria vermicullphyla, 81
graminoids, 41
Grampus griseus, 103, 105–6, 109, 111–2
granite, 3, 9, 12, 138, 194, 198
granodiorite, 3, 12, 198
grass, 41–3, 408
gray fox, 51, 136
Great Depression, 212
grouper, 69, 138, 290
Guadalajara, 240, 425
Guadalupe Island Biosphere Reserve, 131
Guerrero, 88, 214, 224, 401, 460
Guerrero Negro, 348, 353
Gulf of California, 3-10, 16, 24, 27, 61–4, 69, 85–6, 101–3, 105, 107, 109, 111, 113, 115, 117–9, 128, 134, 137–8, 141, 149, 157, 160, 162–3, 165, 172, 176, 178, 206, 271, 287, 404, 409–10, 412, 489, *see also* Sea of Cortez

Habitat Agenda (Programa Habitat), 378
Haematoxylon brassiletto, 44
Haemulon sexfasciatum, 69
Halophila/Halodule, 81

Harengula thrissina, 68
health, iii, 61, 83–4, 211, 242, 251, 272, 300, 322–3, 336, 366, 371, 402, 411, 415, 437, 446, 452, 454–5, 460–1, 465, 473–4, 478, 490
herbaceous plants, 41–2, 44, 46, 149
Heteromeles arbutifolia, 148
Hexaplex brassica, 68
Hexaplex nigritus, 68
highways, 10, 213, *see also* transpenisular highway
Hoffmeisteria fasciculata, 43
Holocene, 12, 172
horticulture, 405, 408, 410, *see also* agriculture
hospitals, 330, 462–3
Hotel Pueblo Bonito, 476
hotels, 31–3, 40, 82, 88, 140, 164, 178–9, 197, 223, 228, 253, 255, 257–61, 263–4, 273–4, 280, 287, 302, 306–7, 331–2, 336, 346, 350–3, 356–8, 401, 409–11, 413–4, 425–8, 430, 435–6, 444, 446, 449, 455, 458, 460, 464–5, 474, 476–9
housing, 15, 58, 135, 191, 206, 263, 272, 327, 334, 337, 341, 366, 371, 401, 410, 414–6, 432, 437, 446, 455–6, 458, 459, 474, 476, 478, 488, 490
Huatulco, 401–2, 425
human capital, 221–2, 264
Human Development Index (HDI), 225–7, 434, 450, 454
human resources, iii, 221, 225, 366
hunting, 40, 51, 53, 57, 80–1, 136, 173, 196, 277–8, 296
hurricane, 14–5, 17, 24–5, 27, 159–61, 164, 257, 369, 397, 426, 458, *see also* cyclone
Hylocharis xantusii, 51, 55
Hymenoclea monogyra, 41
Hypsiglena torquata, 54, 77, 150

Ibervillea sonorae, 45

identity, 144, 146, 177, 204, 215, 231, 235–7, 239–40, 242, 365, 368, 413, 436, 449, 474, 479
igneous (volcanic) rocks, 3–9, 138, 145, 158, 196
illiteracy, 226, 456, 459
immigration, 209, 214, 223–4, 374–5, 452, 455
imports, 257, 296, 306–7, 491
income, iii, v, 120, 135–6, 214, 228, 250, 254, 258–9, 264, 271, 287, 290, 296, 306–7, 323, 330, 336, 354, 376, 378–9, 414–7, 427, 443, 448–55, 458, 461, 465, 478, 491
income, per capita, 225–6, 259, 451–2, 454, 455, 465
indigenous population, 97, 206, 209, 215, 241, 489
Indopacetus pacificus, 102–3
Indo-Pacific region, 131
industry, 87, 147, 164, 174, 177, 214, 228, 260, 263–4, 290–1, 298, 304, 306–7, 323, 348, 353–4, 401, 412, 424, 428, 431, 474–6, 479
inequality, 329, 336–7, 415, 431, 449, 451–3, 465–6, 490, 492
infant mortality, 453, 454
infrastructure, 34, 82, 140, 142, 211–3, 250, 257–60, 262, 271–9, 281, 299–300, 306, 330, 336, 341, 343, 370, 373, 379, 401, 413–4, 424, 427, 432, 434–5, 444, 446, 455, 458, 476
Instituto Mexicano del Seguro Social (IMSS), 461
Instituto Nacional de Antropología e Historia (INAH), 191–2, 197
Instituto Nacional de Estadística Geografía e Informática (INEGI), 403
Instituto Tecnológico de Estudios Superiores de Los Cabos (ITESLC), 231
Intergovernmental Panel on Climate Change (IPCC), 161–2,
International Union for the Conservation of Nature (IUCN), 80, 102–4,
intertidal zone, 63, 67
investment, iii, 144, 221–2, 252–4, 259–64, 273, 290, 305, 324, 337, 344–5, 352–3, 356–8, 376, 379, 424–5, 427, 432, 434–5, 445–8, 450
investment, foreign, 250, 255, 261, 430, 434
investors, 224, 250, 261–2, 423, 434, 438, 447, 449
irrigation, 34, 299, 398, 478
Isla Espíritu Santo, 62, 101, 172, 193
islands, 4, 7–8, 57, 59, 62, 73, 101, 127–8, 132, 172, 193, 206, 296, 307–8, 453, 476
Isostichopus fuscus, 77
Istiophorus platypterus, 69
Ixtapa, 336, 401, 425

Jalisco, 5, 407
Jatropha sp, 42–5
Jatropha cinerea, 43, 45
Jatropha cuneata, 43
Jatropha vernicose, 45
Jesuits, 317
Jouvea pilosa, 42
Justificatory Technical Study (JTS), 129, 144

Katsuwonus pelamis, 69
Kogia breviceps, 102
Kogia sima, 102, 104
Kogiidae, 102
Kuwait, 453

L. candida, 46
La Candelaria, 298, 318, 406, 407
La Fortuna, 179
La Paz, 8–10, 17, 39, 62, 84, 104, 118–9, 128, 132–4, 140, 148, 164–5, 172, 176, 179, 181–2, 193,

Index

209–10, 212, 214, 222–3, 226–7, 236, 256–8, 260–2, 265, 271, 291, 297, 316–7, 326, 331,341–3, 349–50, 371–2, 384, 402–4, 409, 412–4, 443, 445–6, 453–9, 464–5, 470
La Paz Bay, 119, 262
La Playa, 318, 414, 417
La Playita, 85
La Ribera, 44, 140, 215, 263, 291, 298, 318, 330, 332, 372, 378, 403, 409–11, 447, 475
La Trinidad, 10, 13–4, 19, 26, 147–8, 277
labor, 136, 223, 261, 263, 265, 306, 370, 378, 402, 431–2, 455, 461, 490
lagoon, 48, 118, 128, 174, 197, 278–9
Lampropeltis getula, 54, 77, 150
land invasions, 334, 337
land reserves, 321, 326, 334
land use, iv, 40, 43, 57, 151, 299, 321–2, 381–3, 385, 387–9, 392–3, 398, 403–4, 407, 446, 491
land use planning, iii–iv, 277–8, 282, 381–6, 390, 393, 398, 432, 438, 469, 471, 476, 489–91
landfills, 328, 355–6, 435, *see also* trash
Larus heermanni, 56
Larus livens, 56
Las Casitas, 298, 318
Las Cuevas, 24–5, 298, 318
Las Margaritas, 85, 334
Las Palmas, 192–3, 197, 200, 332, 372, 415
Las Veredas, 318, 414–5, 417
Law on Economic Development of the State of Baja California Sur, 324
Law, Treasury (Ley de Hacienda), 324
Law, Fisheries (Ley de Pesca), 90
Law, Sea (Ley Federal del Mar), 90
Law, Wildlife, (Ley General de Vida Silvestre), 90
legumes, 41, 212
León Portilla, Miguel, 204–6, 209

Leptotyphlops humilis, 50
Lepus californicus, 51, 57, 78
Ley General del Equilibrio Ecológico y la Protección al Ambiente (LGEEPA), 137, 152,
life expectancy, 225, 450–1, 453
lighthouse, 63
lighting, 184, 321, 329, 347, 353, 358, 415
lithic tool workshops, 140, 191–2, 196–8, 489
Lithosols, 133
Lithuania, 453
livestock, 31, 40, 44, 46, 57, 135–6, 147–8, 150–1, 160–1, 183, 208, 210–1, 213, 296, 298, 386, 388–9, 398, 405, 407–8, 410, 412, 436, 464, *see also* cattle
Local Economic Development (LED), 364, 367
localities, 32, 63, 66, 272, 403–4, 409–10, 415–7, 453, 457–8, 465
Loreto, 9, 118, 128, 207, 209–10, 213, 254–8, 260, 262, 265, 271, 317, 339, 342–3, 349–50, 371, 401, 434, 445–7, 453–4, 456–60
Los Angeles, 72, 243, 413
Los Barriles, 12, 14, 140, 164, 291
Los Cangrejos, 332, 414
Los Chiles, 196
Los Frailes, 19, 63, 68, 70, 74, 138, 140, 318, 409, 410
Los Naranjos, 10
lowland deciduous forest, 43, 45, 51–2, 59, 149
Lutjanus argentiventris, 69
Lynx rufus, 136
Lysiloma divaricatum, 46

macroalgae, 73
Madracis pharensis, 139
Magdalena Bay, 87, 94, 99, 118
Makaira indica, 69
Makaira mazara, 69
mammals, 48, 50–3, 70, 131, 140, 150

management (natural resources), 52, 57, 118, 120, 125–30, 133, 136, 143–5, 147, 152, 177, 182, 184–5, 291, 303, 307, 321–2, 335, 337, 382–3, 387, 390–1, 397, 469, 471–2, 488
mango, 135, 212
mangroves, 19, 42, 277, 435
mano, 197
manufacturing, 199, 228
marginalization, 376, 435–6, 443, 452–3, 455, 458–60, 465, 478
marina, 75, 81, 85, 151, 263, 275, 411–2, 445
Márquez Almanza, Pedro, 174
marine ecosystem, 36
marjoram, 301
markets, 81, 89, 133, 164, 174, 204, 210–3, 221, 249–1, 254, 258, 264, 271, 273, 291, 296, 300–2, 304–7, 323, 356, 365, 371, 378, 410, 412, 415, 431, 455, 466, 471, 478
marlin, 69, 87, 287–92, 302–3, 474, 491
Masticophis aurigulus, 54, 77
Masticophis fuliginosus, 50
Maytenus phyllanthoides, 42
Mazatlán, 162, 258, 404
meat, 51, 81, 173–4, 292, 329, 436
medicinal plants [Check], 135, 212, 278, 301
Megapitaria aurantiaca, 68
Megapitaria squalida, 68
Megaptera novaeangliae, 70, 104, 106–7, 109, 111, 114, 118, 140 118, see also Balaenoptera novaeangliae
Melongena, 13
Mérida, 165
Merremia aurea, 45
Merychippus-Pliohippus, 13
Mesa Colorada, 332, 334
Mesoplodon peruvianus, 102, 105
Mesoplodon sp. A, 102
Mesozoic, 3, 7, 9, 145
mesquite, 42, 47, 134, 146, 149, 243
metamorphic rocks, 3, 4, 7, 9, 26, 145

metate, 196, 198
Mexico City, 99, 330, 425, 451, 465
Michoacán, 85, 88, 407
Micrathene whitneyi, 55
migration, 16, 19, 27, 29, 46, 85, 179, 204, 210, 213–4, 224, 228, 230, 240–3, 298, 402, 409, 411, 417, 432, 455, 479
Mijares, José Antonio, 316, 317
Mimus poliglotto, 51
mining, 40, 135–6, 147, 204, 210–1, 475, 477
mint, 301
Miocene, 6, 10, 12–3, 20, 39, 61, 133
Miraflores, 10, 151, 298, 318, 329–30, 332, 372, 403, 405–6, 408
missions, iii, 127, 130, 151, 207, 315, 408, 412
Modiolus capax, 198
mollusks, 67–8, 79, 82, 138–9, 191–2, 197, 199
Monterrey, 355
mother-of-pearl, 68, 140, 174, 192–3, 196–7, 200
Mulegé, 9, 212, 254, 257, 260, 262, 297, 316–7, 339, 349–50, 371, 445, 453–4, 456–9
Murex (genus), 13, 139
Murex elenensis, 139
Muricanthus princeps, 139
Museum of Natural History of Paris, 62
music, 323
mussels, 198
Mustelus, 69
Myliobatis californica, 69
mysticetes, 101, 104, 107–8, 111

National Fisheries Chart (Carta Nacional Pesquera), 288
national marine park, 84, 141
National System of Natural Protected Areas, see Comisión Nacional de Áreas Naturales Protegidas (CONANP)

Index

national tourism program, 163, 491
native species, 44, 48, 57, 475, 480
natural protected areas, iv, 48, 132, 144, 206, 263, 277–9
natural resources, iv, 58, 128, 132–3, 136, 144, 152, 165, 183, 185, 216, 250, 252–3, 265, 282, 291, 302, 365, 367, 382–3, 388, 389, 391, 465, 488–90
navigation, 173, 404
Nayarit, 118, 402
neighborhood, 238, 261, 323, 327–30, 336, 375–6, 378, 416, 425, 432, 461
neoliberal, 221
neophytes, 208
nests, sea turtles 50, 53, 69, 79–80, 83–6, 91–2, 142–3, 171–85, 477
Nevada, 258–9
New Mexico, 258–9
New York, 258
nongovernmental organization (NGO), 469, 471
Nopoló, 213, 401
Norma Oficial Mexicana (NOM), 53–4, 68–70, 77, 78, 102–4, 131, 137, 139–40, 150, 171, 288, 292, 345, 476
North America (continent), 5, 7, 139
North American Free Trade Agreement (NAFTA), 257, 444, 464
Nuevo Mundo Orgánico, 299

Oak, 46, 51, 134, 149
oasis, 49, 51–2, 60, 151
Oaxaca, 88, 224, 240, 353, 401–2, 407, 460
observatories, 165
occupation, 140, 199, 206, 353, 385, 416, 432, 489
Octopus spp., 68
Odocoileus hemionus, 51, 136
odontocetes, 101–2, 104–5, 107–8, 111, 113, 140
Oliva sp. (fossil), 13
Opisthonema libertate, 68
Opuntia sp., 146
orange, 50, 135, 296
Orantes Murillo, Manuel, 176–7, 179–81
orchards, 46, 210, 408, 410, 412
Orcinus orca, 70, 103, 105–6, 109, 111–2
organic crops, 300–1, 305, 398
Organismo Operador Municipal del Sistema de Agua Potable, Alcantarillado y Saneamiento de los Cabos (OOMSAPAS), 32, 35–6, 331–2
organpipe cactus, 44

Pachycereus pringlei, 44
Pachycereus sp., 146
Pacific coast, 14–6, 24, 44, 61–4, 85–6, 89, 134, 160, 176, 178–9, 181, 258, 402, 409
Pacific Ocean, 8–9, 14–7, 24, 44, 57, 103, 116, 130–1, 134, 137–9, 145, 157, 160–2, 174, 203, 206, 287, 288, 412, 446, 474
Pacific plate (geology), 5–7
packing plant, 413
Padina-Dictyota, 67
Palo Escopeta, 194–5, 318, 328, 406
Palo Verde, 194
Pandion haliaetus, 51
Pando, Elías, 212, 413
Panulirus inflatus, 68
papaya, 135, 300
Parabuteo unicinctus, 55
parasitic plants, 41
parks, 84, 120, 128–9, 137–42, 178, 277–8, 282, 294, 321, 438, 446
Partido Centro, 209
Partido de Fronteras, 209
Partido Sur, 209, 211
Pavona clivosa, 139
Pavona gigantea, 139
pearls, 62, 139, 173, 210, 307
Pecten aletes, 13

Pelecanus occidentalis, 52, 70
Pennisetum ciliare, 45
Pericú, 134, 138, 140, 172–3, 191–2, 199–200, 206–7, 241, 315–6
petroleum, 344
Petrosaurus thalassinus, 52, 54, 77, 150
Phaeophyta, 65
Phaeozem, 19
Phalacrocorax auritus, 52, 70
Phrynosoma coronatum, 50
Phyllodactylus unctus, 54, 77, 150
Phyllodactylus xanti, 77, 150
Physeter macrocephalus, 70, 102, 104–7, 109, 114
Physeteridae, 102
Piedras Bolas, 178
pigs, 48, 57, *see also* livestock
Pinal, René, 176
Pinctada mazatlanica, 68, 77, 139
pine-oak forest, 47, 51–2, 134
Pinna rugosa, 68
Pinus lagunae, 47
pirates, 173, 204
Pithecellobium dulce, 149
Plan de Desarrollo Urbano de San José del Cabo-San Lucas, 390
Plan Estatal de Desarrollo (PED), 229, 305,
Playa del Amor, 131
Playa El Tule, 19, 179
Playa Migriño, 16, 19, 27, 29, 85, 179, 298, 409
Pleistocene, 10, 12, 39, 139, 172
Pleuroncodes planipes, 87
Pliocene, 6, 12, 13
Pocillopora capitata, 139
Pocillopora damicornis, 139
Pocillopora meandrina, 139
Pocillopora verrucosa, 139
population, 23, 29, 33–4, 40, 44, 46, 48, 61, 129, 141, 148, 161–2, 172, 184, 199, 203–6, 208–11, 214–5, 221–3, 226–30, 238, 240, 243, 254, 258, 261, 263, 272, 282–3, 326–31, 336, 341–2, 344, 365–6, 369–77, 382, 388–9, 401–6, 409–12, 414–7, 428, 433, 436–7, 446–7, 452–9, 461, 464–5, 473, 474, 479, 487, 489–91
Populus brandegeei, 47, 147
Porites panamensis, 139
poverty, 336–7, 431, 436, 451, 478, 490
precipitation, 24, 148, 159–60
primary sector, 296–7, 308, 490
private investment, 250, 414, 435, 447
Procuraduría Federal de Protección al Ambiente (PROFEPA), 81, 90, 177
Procyon lotor, 51
producers, 133, 298, 305–7
productivity, 101, 222, 232, 306
Programa de la Mujer en el Sector Agrario (PROMUSAG), 377
Programa de Manejo de Cabo Pulmo (PMCP), 141, 143
Programa de Ordenamiento Ecológico Local del Municipio de Los Cabos (POEL-MLC), 382–5, 388
Program for the Protection of Sea Turtles (Programa de Protección de Tortugas Marinas), 53, 86, 179–81
Program on Tourism in Protected Areas, 126
progress, 130, 222, 225, 241, 322
projectile points, 196–9
Prosopis articulata, 149
Prosopis sp., 146
prostitution, 251, 261, 434
Psammocora stellata, 139
Pseudacris hypochondriaca, 48
Pseudorca crassidens, 103, 105
public administration, iv, 321, 326, 333, 337, 366–7, 492
Public Registry of Property and Commerce in the municipality of Los Cabos (Registro Público de la Propiedad y del Comercio en el municipio de Los Cabos), 135, 324, 333
public safety, 321–2, 326–8, 337, 415, 433, 492

public services, 261, 282, 319–21, 326–8, 336, 341, 398, 411, 415–6, 431, 437, 490
public works, 142, 152, 211, 319–20, 324, 330, 397, 413
Puerto Escondido, 401
Puerto Los Cabos, 151, 447
Puerto Vallarta, 258, 413, 425
Punta Arenas, 16, 179
Punta Colorada, 16, 179
Punta Conejo, 176
Punta Gorda, 74, 113, 119, 179, 181, 409
Punta Los Anegados, 16
Punta Los Arcos, 16
Punta Palmilla, 16, 63, 74, 413
Punta San Cristóbal, 176

Qatar, 453
quality of life, iii, 126, 143, 222, 225, 261, 265, 272, 277, 295, 365–6, 369, 374, 376–7, 408, 437, 447, 450, 461–3, 465, 490-1
Quercus devia, 47
Quercus tuberculata, 46
Querétaro, 240, 407
Quintana Roo, 88, 213, 316, 318, 346, 401

Ramsar Convention on Wetlands of International Importance, 147, 151–2
Rana catesbeiana, 49, 57
Ranchería La Trinidad, 298
ranching, 46, 135, 211, 213, 216, 241–2, 244, 306, 403–9, 414, 437, 477
ranching culture, 208, 216, 306, 491
Rancho El Chorro, 12, 14, 406
Rancho La Trinidad, 12
real estate, 40, 43, 61, 130, 144–5, 164, 231, 261–2, 282, 323–4, 334, 405, 409–10, 435, 443, 445, 448–9, 452, 471, 474, 487

recreation, 48, 50, 128, 130–3, 141, 145–6, 214, 236, 243, 271, 273, 276, 287–8, 290, 292, 323, 330, 402, 434, 437, 446, 449, 461–4
recreational vehicles (RVs), 274
Red Sea, 4–5
renewable resources, 130, 344–6, 348–9, 351–2, 354, 356–7, 359, 472–3, 490
reptiles, 48–50, 52–4, 57, 69, 77, 150
restaurants, 40, 140, 174, 228, 307, 428–30, 432, 448–9, 478
Revillagigedo Archipelago Biosphere Reserve, 131
Rhodophyta, 65
rhyolite, 12, 198
Río de Janeiro, 469
Rodhymenia sp., 65
Rodríguez, Abeldardo L., 413
rooms, 257–60, 263, 273–4, 280, 350–2, 356, 427–8, 444–6, 455, 464, 474, 476, *see also* hotels
rooster fish, 194, 303
rosemary, 301
rural, 32, 127, 130, 208, 210, 215, 252, 272, 276, 300, 302, 305–6, 344, 348, 352, 356, 377–8, 402–5, 407–11, 427, 437, 478
rural tourism, *see* tourism, rural
Russia, 204, 453

Sage, 301
salaries, 255, 430–1, 449, 461–2, *see also* wages
Salix lasiolepis, 47, 148
salt water intrusion, 149
Salto Seco, 19
San Antonio, 210, 412, 477
San Bernabé, 195, 315, 318, 372, 414, 417
San Carlos, 413, 476
San Cristóbal, 80, 85, 176, 179
San Diego, 174, 244, 413, 427
San Dionisio, 19, 191–2, 282, 318, 396–8

San Francisco (City), 174
San Ignacio, 6, 118, 476
San Jorge, 298, 318, 406–8
San José del Cabo, 10, 13–4, 19, 23, 26–7, 29, 33, 44, 64, 74, 80, 139–40, 144, 147–8, 151, 172, 175–6, 178–9, 207, 209–15, 231, 249, 272–7, 280, 288, 298, 315–8, 327–32, 335, 342, 349, 352, 369, 372, 390, 401–4, 412–5, 417, 432–3, 444–5, 447, 458–60, 464, 479, 488
San José islands, 62, 172,
San José mission, 151, 207–8, 317,
San José Viejo, 318, 372, 414, 417
San José watershed basin, 4, 8, 10, 13, 18, 26–7, 29–30, 35, 48, 148–51, *see also* estuary, San José del Cabo
San Juan Londó, 9
San Lázaro mountains, 8, 10, 14, 17, 19, 23, 27, 194
San Lorenzo, 8, 10, 17, 19, 104, 107, 114–9, 277
San Lorenzo Canal, 104, 107, 115–9
San Luis Gonzaga mission, 4
San Pedro Mártir, 148, 209
sandstone, 12
Santa Anita, 4, 18, 317–8
Santa Anna, Antonio López de, 209
Santa Cruz, 298, 318
Santa Gertrudis, 209
Santa María Bay, 16
Santa Rosalía, 210–1, 316–7, 412, 459
Santiago, 8, 10, 13, 18, 24, 26–7, 29–30, 35, 44, 49, 52, 207–8, 210–2, 275, 298, 316–8, 330, 332, 349, 372, 378, 396–7, 403, 405–6, 408, 471
Santo Domingo, 213, 436
saprophytes, 41
Sarda chilensis, 69
Sarda orientalis, 69
Sargassum horridum, 76
Sargassum liebmanii, 76
Sargassum sinicola, 76
Sargassum sp., 65

Sauromalus obesus, 150
Scaphiopus couchi, 48
scarcity, 342, 446, 473
Scarus ghobban, 69
Sceloporus hunsakeri, 52, 54
Sceloporus licki, 54
Sceloporus liki, 52
Scelopurus hunsaker, 150
schist, 3, 12
scholarship, 470
Scomber japonicus, 68
scrub (vegetation), 42–5, 49, 51–2, 56, 134, 146, 149
scrub, sarcocaulescent, 42–5, 51–2, 134, 146, 149
scrub, sarcocrassicaulescent, 44, 134, 146, 149
scuba diving, *see* diving
sea bass, 138, 303
sea lions, 131, 304
Sea of Cortez, 402, 435, 445
sea turtle eggs, 50, 53, 67–8, 83, 86, 173–4, 179, 182–3, 477
sea turtle, green, 69, 82, 85, 92, 95, 99, 188
sea turtle, hawksbill, 69, 80, 82
sea turtle, leatherback, 97, 176, 179, 181, 188
sea turtle, loggerhead, 50, 53, 69, 82, 171
sea turtle, olive ridley, 53, 69, 80–3, 86–7, 89, 91, 99, 143, 171, 176, 178–9, 182
sea turtles, 49–50, 53, 55, 69, 79–92, 94–5, 131, 137, 142, 143, 171–9, 182–5, 198, 474, 476–7, 479, 481
sea urchin, 197
Secretaría de Agricultura, Ganadería, Desarrollo Rural, Pesca y Alimentación (SAGARPA), 297–9, 302–3, 305
Secretaría de Desarrollo Social (SEDESOL), 132, 356, 382–3
Secretaría de Desarrollo Urbano y Ecología (SEDUE), 132, 176

Index

Secretaría de Educación Pública (SEP), 230–1
Secretaría de Medio Ambiente y Recursos Naturales (SEMARNAT), 53–4, 68, 77–8, 80, 88, 90, 104, 131, 137, 139, 140–1, 144, 150, 177, 273, 289, 303, 310, 386, 390–1, 393, 470, 474, 476
Secretaría de Turismo (SECTUR), 88, 98, 235, 274–5, 278, 287–8, 310, 426
sedimentary rocks, 3–4, 7, 9, 26, 139, 145
sediments, 6, 8, 10, 14, 27, 47
Selene peruvianus, 68
service sector, 272, 405, 443
settlements, 40, 44, 135, 391, 397–8, 414
sewage, 32, 277, 319, 321, 323–4, 331, 335–6, 415, 459, 474, 478, 490, *see also* wastewater
sharks, 69, 198, 288, 292
shell middens, 191–2, 196, 200, 278, 489,
shells, 13, 81, 140, 175, 191–2, 196–200, 278
Shelvocke, George, 195
ships, 143, 210, 212, 257, 258, 404, 412
shrubs, 41–3, 45–6, 49–50, 146
Sierra La Giganta, 8, 133
Sierra La Laguna, 3, 8, 10, 14, 17–19, 23–4, 26–7, 45–7, 51–4, 70, 128–9, 132–6, 147–8, 151, 179, 181, 192, 206, 277–8, 280, 282, 396, 408–9, 473
Sierra La Trinidad, 8, 10, 12, 18–9, 26, 45, 148, 280
Sierra La Victoria, 8, 12–3
silver, 210
Sinaloa, 86, 207, 214, 224
Sistema para Desarrollo Integral de la Familia (SDIF), 364, 374–8
slate, 3
slaughterhouse, 321, 329
snorkeling, 89, 91, *see also* diving

social equity, iii, 229, 337, 368, 375, 425, 436, 446–7, 469, 470, 472, 478, 492
social impacts, 272, 445
Social Promotion Program (Programa de Promoción Social), 376
social security, 437
social services, 370, 374, 432
social welfare, 318, 366, 424
society, iv, 126–7, 130, 165, 177, 215, 221, 231, 233, 235, 239, 244, 262, 264–5, 272, 284, 332, 337, 367–8, 375, 384, 402, 414, 415, 417, 423, 425, 433, 434, 436–7, 439, 450, 460, 465, 481, 489, 490–2
solar energy, 344–5, 351–2, 490, *see also* energy
solid waste, 142, 147, 326, 328–9, 355, *see also* trash
Solonchak, 19
Sonora, 5, 41, 150, 209, 353
Sonoran Desert (ecosystem), 45
sorghum, 300
Spain (country), 134, 151, 184, 203–4, 207, 210, 215, 236, 242, 263, 297, 332, 352, 413, 446, 476, 489
Sphyrna, 69
Spilogale gracilis, 51
Spondylus calcifer, 77
sport fishing, iv, 67, 69, 87–8, 90–1, 140–2, 147, 163–4, 255, 272–3, 275, 279, 287–92, 297, 302–4, 306–7, 405, 409–11, 427, 434, 444, 474, 477, 491, *see also* fishing
sports, 57, 131, 140, 236, 276, 287–9, 321, 326, 335–6, 474, 490
Squatia, 69
State Ecological Reserve, 151–2
Stenella attenuata, 102
Stenella longirostris, 103, 140
Steno bredanensis, 102, 140
Stenocereus gummosus, 44
Sterna antillarum, 52, 56, 70
Sterna hirundo, 52, 70
streets, 82, 145, 225, 328–30, 332, 335, 374, 415–6, 434, 437, 438

Strombus (fossil), 13
Strombus galeatus, 68
Strombus gracilior, 68
Strombus obliteratus, 13
students, 211, 230–2, 411, 461, 479, 481
subsistence, 135, 197–8, 375, 407, 410
succulent plants, 42–5, 51–2, 134, 146, 149
sugar cane, 211–3, 354, 412
sustainable development, iii–v, 127, 130, 132, 229, 242–4, 252, 262, 277, 282, 291–2, 308, 326, 337, 343, 363, 365, 369, 381, 384–5, 391, 423–5, 436, 439, 446, 469–76, 478–81, 487, 490–2
Sylvilagus auduboni, 57
Sylvilagus bachmani, 51

Tabor, 9
Tamaral, Nicolás, 207, 315, 412
Tantilla planiceps, 50
taxes, 209, 290, 296, 323, 324
Taxidea taxus, 53, 56
technology, 207, 221, 231, 299, 332, 343, 473
Tecoma stans, 45, 146
tectonic plates, 9
tertiary sector, 297, 402, 410, 438
Tetrapturus audax, 69
Texas, 258–9, 427
Thais kiosquiformi, 139
Thamnophis valida, 53–4
Thunnus albacares, 69
tidal zone, 42, 63, 67, 84, 138, 183, 356, *see also* coastal zone
Tierra y Libertad, 332
Todos Santos, 118, 176, 182, 206, 208, 316
tomato, 135, 212, 300–1, 412
tonalite, 3, 12
Topolobampo, 404
Torre Iglesias, Juan Manuel, 210

tourism, iii–v, 29, 33, 36, 40, 43, 48, 53, 57–8, 61, 68–70, 81–2, 87–9, 103, 116, 118, 126, 128, 131–2, 135, 140–8, 150–2, 155, 161–4, 177, 185, 213–7, 228, 231–2, 235, 238–9, 249, 250–65, 271–84, 287–8, 290–1, 295–8, 302, 304–8, 316, 320–1, 326, 329–30, 332–3, 336, 341, 349, 353, 369–70, 373–4, 382, 385–6, 388–9, 396, 401–3, 405, 409–13, 415, 417–8, 423, 425–8, 430–9, 443–9, 452, 455, 458, 460–1, 463, 464–5, 471, 473–9, 487–92
tourism (development), v, 23, 36, 45, 53, 57 132, 135, 142, 147–8, 151–2, 177, 191, 251–3, 261, 263, 265, 271, 276–7, 284, 295–7, 306, 332, 329, 359, 369–70, 374, 382, 401–2, 408–9, 412, 418, 423, 425, 427–8, 430, 433–4, 436–7, 439, 444, 447, 452, 458, 464–5, 475, 487, 489–90
tourism centers, 30, 33, 162, 205, 213, 223, 254, 271–2, 276, 282, 296, 444, 460, 464, *see also* Centro Turísticos Integralmente Planificados (CIPs)
tourism sector, iii, 33, 91, 163, 177, 228, 252–3, 255, 257–8, 277–80, 282, 296–7, 306, 333, 342, 349, 373, 389, 401, 426, 448–9, 458, 465, 473, 487, 489–90
tourism, adventure, 276, 409, 437
tourism, alternative, iv, 68, 251–2, 260, 276–7, 280–3, 434, 438, 445, 461, *see also* ecotourism,
tourism, international, 68, 223, 236–8, 250, 253, 256, 258, 260, 264, 273, 349, 401, 425–7, 438, 491
tourism, national, 68, 213, 256, 413, 426, 491
tourism, rural, 276, 306, 405, 477, 491

Index

tourism, traditional, iv, 213, 251, 255, 272, 276, 278, 281–2, 443–4, 452, 466, 489–90
tourist corridor, 18, 29, 33, 144, 148, 179, 263, 275, 280, 331, 369, 402, 404, 408, 412–7, 425, 464, 475–6, 478, 480, 488
tourists, 88–9, 91, 119, 136, 164, 216, 223, 236–8, 243, 250, 253, 255–8, 260, 264, 272–4, 283, 290, 296, 326–7, 332–3, 369, 415, 425–7, 432, 445, 447, 458, 460, 464, 476, *see also* visitors
tournaments, *see* sport fishing
Trachemys sp., 49, 55
trade, iii, 102, 104, 136, 174, 200, 207, 209–10, 228–9, 250, 254, 257, 296–7, 302, 333, 405, 408, 444, 452, 461, 464,
traffic, 103, 131, 142, 183, 265, 283, 321, 327, 330
transpeninsular highway, 9, 403, 415, *see also* highway
transportation, 57, 131, 163, 213, 228–9, 240, 250–1, 254, 257–8, 272, 274, 290, 297, 299–300, 326, 331–4, 346, 404, 412–3, 415–6, 433–4, 437, 448–9, 463, 490
trash, 91, 329, 435, *see also* solid waste
Tropic of Cancer, 147
tuna, 69, 87, 212, 288, 291, 303, 412–3
turbogas, 343–4, *see also* electricity
Turnera diffusa, 146
Turritela abrupta fredea (fossil), 13
Tursiops truncatus, 70, 102, 140
turtles, *see* sea turtles
144

U.S. Department of Agriculture (USDA), 306
Unidades de Manejo (UMAS), 57
United Nations Conference on the Environment and Development (UNCED), 469

United Nations Development Program (UNDP), 225, 450, 452–3
United Nations Educational, Scientific and Cultural Organization (UNESCO), 233, 238, 241, 244
United States, 87–8, 118, 164, 198, 204–5, 209–10, 212, 240, 249–50, 254–5, 257–60, 262–4, 290, 296, 300, 306, 316–7, 352, 358, 369, 410, 412–3, 427, 445, 454, 478, 490
Universidad Autónoma de Baja California Sur (UABCS), 231, 277, 363, 385, 461,
Universidad Mundial (World University), 231
Universidad Pedagógica Nacional (National Pedagogic University), 231
University of California, Berkeley, Herbarium, 62–3,
University of Tijuana, 230
University of Veracruz (UNIVER), 231
urban development, 31, 53, 118, 213, 321–2, 336, 432–3, 435, 437, 475, 491
urban society, 405
urbanization, 23, 58, 82, 211, 261, 272, 282, 341, 402, 411–2, 414–5, 473–4, 488, 490
Urocyon cinereoargenteus, 51, 136
Urosaurus nigricaudus, 54, 78, 150

Vegetables, 34, 135, 300–1, 306, 408, 412, 436, *see also* agriculture
vegetation, 19, 41–8, 51–2, 58, 132, 134, 146, 149, 278–9, 299, 382, 387, 397, 438, 480, 488, *see also* flora
vendors, 225, 434, 437
Veracruz, 224
Viguiera deltoidea, 41
violence, 258, 260, 327

visitors, 135, 143, 164, 214, 216, 224, 239–40, 250–60, 264–5, 271–3, 276–7, 282, 290, 292, 304, 317, 327, 414, 426–7, 443–4, 450, *see also* tourists
volcanic rocks, *see* igneous rocks

Wages, 227–9, 255, 258, 261, 290, 417, 424, 430, 448–9, 461, 463, *see also* salaries
wahoo, 87, 288, 303
Washington (state), 258–9,
Washingtonia robusta, 47, 147, 149
wastewater, 33–4, 36, 82, 147, 330–2, 349–50, 415, 432, 490, *see also* sewage
water quality, 142, 148, 151, 382
water sports, 278, 307, 427, *see also* diving and snorking
water (ground), 3–4, 24–5, 27–31, 33–5, 47, 139, 148–50, 206, 298, 331, 342, 349–50, 352, 355, 397, 473, 487, *see also* aquifers
water (potable and supply), 23, 28–36, 140, 148, 196, 206, 210, 254, 261–2, 265, 277, 297, 299, 305, 319, 321, 323–4, 326, 330–2, 336, 342–3, 352, 407, 415, 446, 456–60, 462–5, 473, 476, 478, 480, 487–90
water (surface), 4, 24, 26, 31, 33–4, 36, 43, 48–9, 51–2, 69, 137–8, 149, 150–1, 197, 206, 292, 298, 355, 351–2, 369, 397–8, 407, 435, 473, 487–8
waterfall, San Miguelito, 151
waterfall, El Cajón, 151
watermelon, 300
watersheds, 24, 26, 28–9, 35, 134, 147–8, 150–1, *see also* basin
wave energy, 197, 352
wetlands, 19, 52, 147, 149, 277–8, 435
whale watching, iv, 87–8, 91, 116, 118–20, 476, 488

whales, iv, 70, 87–8, 91, 101–5, 107–8, 111, 113, 115–6, 118–20, 131, 133, 140, 172, 174, 476, 488, *see also* cetaceans
whales, baleen, *see* mysticetes
whales, toothed, *see* odontocetis
Wildcoast, 177
wildlife, threats, 48, 57, 79–81, 90, 116, 118, 136, 160, 182–3, 243–4, 423, 433, 474
wind energy, 141, 344–5, 348, 351, 353–4, 356–8, 473, 490, *see also* electricity
Woodes Rogers (ship), 195
World Tourism Organization, 253
World War II, 62, 213, 252
Wurdemannia miniata, 62

X*antusia vigilis vigilis*, 52
Xiphias gladius, 69

Yaqui, 210
yellow trumpetbush, 45, 146
Yenecamú, 172
yermosols, 18

Z*alophus californianus*, 70, 78
Zapteryx exasperata, 69
Zenaida sp., 55, 57
Ziphiidae, 102
Ziphius cavirostris, 102, 107
Zona Sujeta a Conservación Ecológica (Area Subject to Ecological Conservation), 152
zoobenthos, 68
zooplankton, 67
Zumaya Adargas, Juan, 175

www.ingramcontent.com/pod-product-compliance
Lightning Source LLC
Chambersburg PA
CBHW021812300426
44114CB00009BA/146